Cultural Anthropology

Barbara D. Miller
The George Washington University

Allyn and Bacon
Boston London Toronto Sydney Tokyo Singapore

Series Editor: Sarah L. Kelbaugh
Editor-in-Chief, Social Sciences: Karen Hanson
Development Editor: Sylvia Shepard
Editorial Assistant: Heather Ahlstrom
Sr. Editorial Production Administrator: Susan McIntyre
Editorial Production Service and Photo Research: Kathy Smith
Composition Buyer: Linda Cox
Manufacturing Buyer: Megan Cochran
Cover Administrator: Linda Knowles
Text Design and Illustrations: Glenna Collett

A Viacom Company
160 Gould Street
Needham Heights, MA 02494

Internet: www.abacon.com

Library of Congress Cataloging-in-Publication Data

Miller, Barbara D., 1948–
Cultural anthropology / Barbara D. Miller.
p. cm.
Includes bibliographical references and index.
ISBN 0-205-16396-3
1. Ethnology. I. Title.
GN316.M49 1998 98-22358
306—dc21 CIP

Photo credits are listed on page 476, which constitutes a continuation of the copyright page.

Printed in the United States of America
10 9 8 7 6 5 4 3 2 1 VHP 04 03 02 01 00 99 98

Contents

Preface *xi*

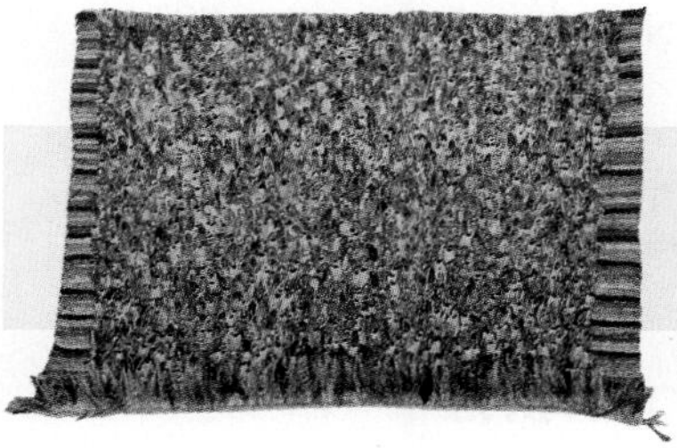

PART I: INTRODUCTION TO CULTURAL ANTHROPOLOGY

Maori feather cloak, New Zealand.

1 Anthropology and the Study of Culture ***3***

THE FIELDS OF GENERAL ANTHROPOLOGY *5*
- Archaeology *5*
- Physical or Biological Anthropology *6*
- *Multiple Cultural Worlds:* Birutė Galdikas and the Orphaned Orangutans *7*
- Linguistic Anthropology *7*
- Cultural Anthropology *8*
- Applied Anthropology: Separate Field or Cross-Cutting Focus? *8*

CULTURAL ANTHROPOLOGY'S DISTINCTIVE FEATURES *8*
- Ethnography and Ethnology *8*
- *Critical Thinking:* Is Samoa Really Different? *11*
- Cultural Relativism *11*
- Valuing and Sustaining Diversity *13*
- Contemporary Debates in Cultural Anthropology *13*

THE CONCEPT OF CULTURE *14*
- Definitions of Culture *14*
- Characteristics of Culture *15*
- *Multiple Cultural Worlds:* Tejano Women and Tamales *17*

MULTIPLE CULTURAL WORLDS *20*
- Class *20*
- *Multiple Cultural Worlds:* A Feast for the "Lords of Poverty" *21*
- Race *22*
- Ethnicity *22*
- Gender *23*
- Age *23*
- Region *24*
- Institutions *25*

ANTHROPOLOGY: A DYNAMIC DISCIPLINE FOR A CHANGING WORLD *25*

SUMMARY *25*

CRITICAL THINKING QUESTIONS *26*

KEY CONCEPTS *26*

SUGGESTED READINGS *26*

2 Methods in Cultural Anthropology ***29***

FIELDWORK IN CULTURAL ANTHROPOLOGY *31*
- The Origin of Participant Observation *31*

BEGINNING THE FIELDWORK PROCESS *31*
- Project Selection *31*
- *Critical Thinking:* "Shells and Skirts in the Trobriand Islands" *33*
- Funding the Project *33*
- Preparing for the Field *34*

IN THE FIELD *34*
- Entering the Field and Site Selection *34*
- Gaining Rapport *35*

Exchanges and Gift Giving 35
Voices: "The Art of Fitting In," by Philippe Bourgois 36
Microcultures and Fieldwork 37
Culture Shock 39
FIELDWORK TECHNIQUES 40
Participant Observation 40
Asking: Interviews and Questionnaires 41
Combining Watching and Asking 42
Other Data-Gathering Techniques 42
RECORDING CULTURE 44
Field Notes 44
Tape Recording, Photography, Videos, and Films 44
DATA ANALYSIS 45
Analyzing Qualitative Data 45
Analyzing Quantitative Data 46
Writing about Culture 47
ETHICS AND RESPONSIBILITY IN CULTURAL ANTHROPOLOGY 47
Ethical Concerns in Perspective 47
Sensitive Issues 48
DANGER IN THE FIELD 49
NEW DIRECTIONS: TOWARD PARTICIPATORY FIELDWORK 50
SUMMARY 50
CRITICAL THINKING QUESTIONS 51
KEY CONCEPTS 51
SUGGESTED READINGS 51

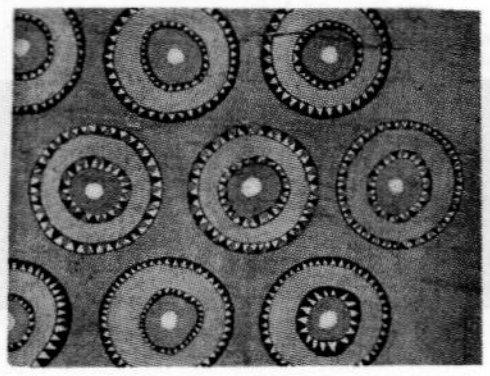

Tapa from Rurutu.

PART II: ECONOMIC AND DEMOGRAPHIC FOUNDATIONS

3 Economies and Their Modes of Production 53

CULTURAL ANTHROPOLOGY AND ECONOMIC SYSTEMS 54
Modes of Production as Types 54
Culture, Nature, and Modes of Production 54
Today's World-Economy 56
FORAGING 56
Labor 57
Multiple Cultural Worlds: The Inuit of Colville Lake 58
Property Relations 59
Foraging as a Sustainable System 59
Changing Cultural Worlds of Foragers: The Tiwi 60
HORTICULTURE 61
Labor 62
Property Relations 63
Horticulture as a Sustainable System 63
Changing Cultural Worlds of Horticulturalists: The Mundurucu 63
PASTORALISM 64
Labor 65
Property Relations 65
Pastoralism as a Sustainable System 66
Changing Cultural Worlds of Pastoralists: Mongolian Nomads 66
Current Event: "Will the Nenets Survive?" 66
Voices: Puravdorj Speaks about Privatization 67
AGRICULTURE 68
Family Farming 68
Multiple Cultural Worlds: Malay Women Farmers Lose Rights to Land 70
Plantation Agriculture 71
Industrial Agriculture 72
Critical Thinking: Was the Invention of Agriculture a Terrible Mistake? 75
The Sustainability of Agriculture 75
INDUSTRIALISM 75
The Formal Sector 76
The Informal Sector 76
Multiple Cultural Worlds: Scavenging in Belmar 77
Changing Cultural Worlds of Industrial Workers: Barberton 78
SUMMARY 78
CRITICAL THINKING QUESTIONS 79
KEY CONCEPTS 79
SUGGESTED READINGS 79

4 Consumption and Exchange 81

CULTURE AND CONSUMPTION 83
What Is Consumption? 83

Modes of Consumption *84*
Consumption Funds *85*
CONSUMPTION INEQUALITIES *86*
- *Critical Thinking:* Assessing One's Own Entitlement Bundle *86*
Entitlements at Three Levels *87*
Famine as Entitlement Failure *87*
CONSUMPTION MICROCULTURES *89*
Class *89*
Gender *89*
Race *89*
Age *90*
CULTURE AND HOUSEHOLD BUDGETING *90*
Patterns of Budgetary Decision Making *91*
FORBIDDEN CONSUMPTION: FOOD TABOOS *92*
Cultural Materialism and Food Taboos *92*
Food Taboos as Systems of Meaning *92*
CULTURE AND EXCHANGE *93*
What Is Exchanged? *93*
- *Multiple Cultural Worlds:* Favors, Gifts, and Banquets in China *94*
- *Multiple Cultural Worlds:* The Rules of Hospitality in Oman *95*
Modes of Exchange *97*
- *Multiple Cultural Worlds:* Sustained Unbalanced Exchange in the Ituri Rainforest *101*
ANALYZING EXCHANGE SYSTEMS *102*
Exchange and Risk Aversion *102*
Exchange and Social Inequality *102*
CHANGING PATTERNS OF CONSUMPTION AND EXCHANGE *103*
The Lure of Western Goods *103*
Cash-Cropping and Declining Nutrition: You Can't Eat Sisal *104*
Privatization's Effects: The New Rich and the New Poor of Russia and Eastern Europe *105*
- *Current Event:* "Could This Be Russia?" *105*
- *Current Event:* "Credit Card Regulation in South Korea" *106*
A New Way of Buying: The Credit Card *106*
Continuities and Resistance: The Potlatch *107*
SUMMARY *107*
CRITICAL THINKING QUESTIONS *108*
KEY CONCEPTS *108*
SUGGESTED READINGS *108*

5 Birth and Death *111*

WORLD POPULATION GROWTH *112*
Modes of Reproduction *112*
- *Current Event:* "Test-Tube Babies Cost $60,000 to $110,000 Each" *116*
CULTURE AND BIRTH *116*
Sexual Intercourse *116*
- *Multiple Cultural Worlds:* The Dani Low-Energy Sexual System in Perspective *117*
The Politics of Fertility *118*
- *Critical Thinking:* Reproductive Rights or Wrongs *120*
Techniques of Fertility Control *122*
- *Current Event:* "Contraception the Natural Way" *122*
- *Multiple Cultural Worlds:* Amniocentesis and the Poor of New York City *124*
CULTURE AND DEATH *124*
Infanticide *125*
Suicide *127*
- *Multiple Cultural Worlds:* Female Infanticide in India *127*
Violence *129*
- *Current Event:* "Consumerism Fuels Dowry Death Wave in India" *129*
Public Violence *129*
SUMMARY *130*
CRITICAL THINKING QUESTIONS *131*
KEY CONCEPTS *131*
SUGGESTED READINGS *131*

6 Personality and Human Development *133*

CULTURE AND PERSONALITY *134*
The "Culture and Personality School" *134*
Class Position and Personality *136*
New Directions *136*
- *Multiple Cultural Worlds:* Corporate Personality Formation: The Making of Salarymen in Japan *136*
BIRTH AND INFANCY *137*
Birth *137*
Sleeping Patterns *138*
Gender and Infancy *138*
CHILDHOOD *139*
Mode of Production and Child Personality *139*
The Preschool Child *140*
Informal Learning *141*
- *Voices:* "Play Potlatches," by Charles James Nowell *141*
Formal Schooling *141*
- *Current Event:* "Desperate Fainting" *142*
- *Multiple Cultural Worlds:* Learning to Be an Orthodox Jewish Woman *143*
ADOLESCENCE *144*

Is Adolescence a Universal Life-Cycle Stage? *144*
Coming of Age and Gender Identity *145*
- *Voices:* "The Initiation of a Maasai Warrior," by Tepilit Ole Saitoti *146*
- *Critical Thinking:* Cultural Relativism, Human Rights, and "Female Genital Mutilation" *147*

Sexual Identity *148*
- *Multiple Cultural Worlds:* Homosexuality and Economic Discrimination in the United States *148*

ADULTHOOD AND MIDDLE AGE *150*
Becoming a Parent *150*
Middle Age *151*
THE SENIOR YEARS *152*
THE FINAL PASSAGE: DEATH AND DYING *153*
SUMMARY *153*
CRITICAL THINKING QUESTIONS *154*
KEY CONCEPTS *154*
SUGGESTED READINGS *154*

7 Illness and Healing *157*

THE ECOLOGICAL/EPIDEMIOLOGICAL APPROACH *158*
Infectious Diseases *158*
ETHNOMEDICINE *160*
Perceptions of the Body *160*
Defining Disease Emically *161*
Preventive Practices *163*
- *Multiple Cultural Worlds:* Anorexia Nervosa as a Culture-Bound Syndrome *163*

Diagnosis *164*
Healing Modalities *165*
- *Critical Thinking:* Why Do People Eat Dirt? *169*

THE INTERPRETIVE APPROACH *170*
- *Voices:* An Ayurvedic Doctor and His Client *171*

CRITICAL MEDICAL ANTHROPOLOGY *172*
The Role of Poverty *173*
Western Medical Training Examined *173*
CLINICAL MEDICAL ANTHROPOLOGY *175*
GLOBALIZATION AND CHANGE *176*
Plural Medical Systems *176*
Applied Medical Pluralism *179*
SUMMARY *179*
CRITICAL THINKING QUESTIONS *180*
KEY CONCEPTS *180*
SUGGESTED READINGS *180*

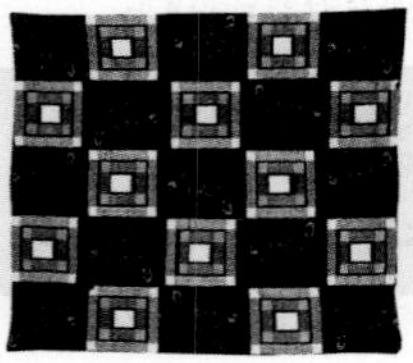

PART III: SOCIAL ORGANIZATION

Quilt cover in *Kasuri* technique, Japan

8 Kinship Dynamics *183*

THE STUDY OF KINSHIP *184*
Kinship Theory *186*
Doing Research on Human Kinship *186*
DESCENT *190*
Unilineal Descent *191*
- *Multiple Cultural Worlds:* The Named and the Nameless in a Cantonese Village *193*
- *Current Event:* "Matrilineal Group Dumps Patriarchal Rite" *194*

Double Descent *195*
Bilineal Descent *195*
- *Critical Thinking:* How Bilineal Is American Kinship? *196*

SHARING *196*
Food Sharing *196*
Adoption and Fostering *197*
Ritually Established Sharing Bonds *199*
MARRIAGE *199*
Toward a Definition *199*
- *Viewpoint:* "I Always Cry at Weddings" *200*

Selecting a Spouse *201*
Marriage Gifts *205*
Weddings *205*
- *Voices:* Nisa's Third Marriage *206*

Forms of Marriage *207*
- *Multiple Cultural Worlds:* Weddings American Style *207*

Change in Marriage *208*
SUMMARY *209*
KEY CONCEPTS *210*
CRITICAL THINKING QUESTIONS *210*
SUGGESTED READINGS *210*

9 Domestic Groups *213*

THE HOUSEHOLD *214*

Household Forms *214*
Household Headship *215*
● *Critical Thinking:* Is Father-in-the-Household Best? *218*
THE HOUSEHOLD AS AN ECONOMIC UNIT *219*
The Gender Division of Labor in Two Household Types *219*
Family Businesses *220*
● *Multiple Cultural Worlds:* Succession Problems in the Japanese Business Elite *221*
Remittances *222*
INTRAHOUSEHOLD DYNAMICS *223*
Spouse/Partner Relationships *223*
Sibling Relationships *224*
● *Multiple Cultural Worlds:* "Love Hotels in Japan" *225*
Domestic Violence *225*
DIVORCE, DEATH, AND REMARRIAGE *226*
Kinship Systems and Divorce *226*
● *Current Event:* "Princess Diana's Divorce Settlement" *227*
Gender and Divorce *227*
Widow(er)hood *228*
Remarriage *229*
KIN NETWORKS BEYOND THE HOUSEHOLD *229*
Marital Roles and Social Networks *230*
● *Multiple Cultural Worlds:* The Importance of a Woman's Natal Kin in Working-Class London *230*
Networks and Poverty *231*
SOCIAL CHANGE AND DOMESTIC LIFE *231*
International Forces of Change *231*
Changing Patterns of Domestic Life in the United States *231*
SUMMARY *232*
KEY CONCEPTS *233*
CRITICAL THINKING QUESTIONS *233*
SUGGESTED READINGS *233*

10 Social Groups and Social Stratification *235*

SOCIAL GROUPS *236*
Friends *237*
● *Multiple Cultural Worlds:* Male and Female Friendship in Rural Spain *238*
● *Voices:* "Memoirs from the Women's Prison," by Nawal El Saadawi *240*
Clubs and Fraternities *241*
● *Current Event:* "Alfalfa Club's Old Boys Bring in the Girls" *242*
Non-Mainstream Groups *242*
Work Groups *245*
Cooperatives *246*
Women's Rights and Human Rights Groups *247*
SOCIAL STRATIFICATION *248*
The Concept of Status Groups *248*
Class: Achieved Status *248*
Race, Ethnicity, and Caste: Ascribed Status *249*
● *Critical Thinking:* What's Missing from This Picture? *251*
● *Voices:* "Growing Up Under Apartheid," by Mark Mathabane *252*
● *Multiple Cultural Worlds:* The Chinese Takeover of Tibetan Medicine *253*
CIVIL SOCIETY: BETWEEN GROUPS AND GOVERNMENT *257*
● *Current Event:* "Fragile Civil Society Takes Root in Chinese Reform" *258*
SUMMARY *258*
CRITICAL THINKING QUESTIONS *259*
KEY CONCEPTS *259*
SUGGESTED READINGS *259*

11 Politics and Leadership *261*

POLITICAL ANTHROPOLOGY *262*
Politics: The Use of Power, Authority, and Influence *263*
Politics: Species Universal, Human Universal? *263*
● *Multiple Cultural Worlds:* Socialization of Women Politicians in Korea *264*
Symbols of Power *265*
POLITICAL ORGANIZATION AND LEADERSHIP *265*
Bands *265*
Tribes *266*
Chiefdoms *270*
States *271*
● *Multiple Cultural Worlds:* The Benefits of Citizenship in Kuwait *272*
● *Current Event:* "Who's Buried in Margarita's Tomb?" *274*
● *Critical Thinking:* How "Open" are Democratic Electoral Politics? *277*
CHANGE IN POLITICAL SYSTEMS *277*
Emergent Nations and Fractured States *277*
Democratization *280*
Women in Politics: New Directions? *280*
Fluctuating World-System Politics *281*
● *Viewpoint:* "The Hope for Europe," by Václav Havel *282*
SUMMARY *282*

CRITICAL THINKING QUESTIONS 283
KEY CONCEPTS 283
SUGGESTED READINGS 283

12 Social Order and Social Conflict *285*

THE ANTHROPOLOGY OF ORDER AND CONFLICT 286
SYSTEMS OF SOCIAL CONTROL 286
- Norms and Laws 287
- Social Control in Small-Scale Societies 287
  - *Voices:* "Letter from the Birmingham Jail," by Martin Luther King, Jr. 288
- Social Control in States 288
- Social Inequality and the Law 290
  - *Viewpoint:* "Something Nasty in the Tea Leaves," by Simon Courtald 291
- Change in Legal Systems 292

SOCIAL CONFLICT AND VIOLENCE 294
- Theoretical Issues 294
- Studying Conflict and Violence 294
- Types of Social Conflict 294
  - *Multiple Cultural Worlds:* Patriarchy, the Police, and Wife Abuse in Rural Kentucky 296
  - *Multiple Cultural Worlds:* "The Bandit Queen of India" 298
  - *Current Event:* "Burundi's Three-Year Campaign of Terror Leaves a Bloody Trail on University Campuses" 300
  - *Critical Thinking:* Yanomami, "The Fierce People"? 302
  - *Current Event:* "Chinese Protest Finds a Path on the Internet" 304

MAINTAINING WORLD ORDER 305
SUMMARY 305
CRITICAL THINKING QUESTIONS 306
KEY CONCEPTS 306
SUGGESTED READINGS 306

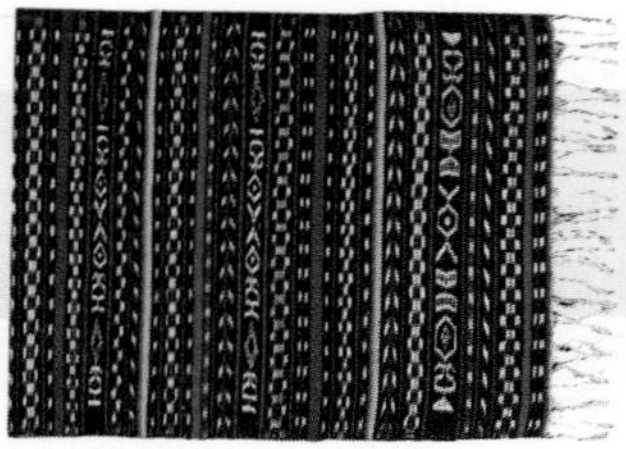

Ikat-dyed cotton shawl, Guatelmala (Totonicpán), early 20th century.

PART IV: SYMBOLIC SYSTEMS

13 Religion *309*

WHAT IS RELIGION? 310
- Magic versus Religion 310
- Theories of the Origin of Religion 311

VARIETIES OF RELIGIOUS BELIEFS 312
- How Beliefs Are Expressed: Myth and Doctrine 312
- Beliefs about Supernatural Forces and Beings 313

BELIEFS IN ACTION: RITUAL PRACTICES 314
- Life-Cycle Rituals 315
- Pilgrimage 316
- Rituals of Reversal 316
- Sacrifice 317

RELIGIOUS SPECIALISTS 317
- Shamans and Priests 317
  - *Critical Thinking:* Why Did the Aztecs Practice Human Sacrifice . . . and Cannibalism? 318
- Other Specialists 319

WORLD RELIGIONS 319
- Hinduism 319
- Buddhism 321
- Judaism 322
  - *Current Event:* Women Raise Their Voices for the Right to Pray Aloud at Wall 324
- Christianity 324
- Islam 326

AFRICAN RELIGIONS 327
- Features of African Religions 327
- Ras Tafari 327

DIRECTIONS AND CHALLENGES OF CHANGE 328
- Revitalization Movements 328
- Contested Sacred Sites 329
- Socialism and Religion 329
  - *Multiple Cultural Worlds:* Aboriginal Beliefs versus Mining at Guratba 329
- Religious Freedom as a Human Right 330

SUMMARY 330
CRITICAL THINKING QUESTIONS 330
KEY CONCEPTS 331
SUGGESTED READINGS 331

14 Communication *333*

INTRODUCING LINGUISTIC ANTHROPOLOGY 334
- Connections with the Other Fields 334
  - *Current Event:* "Easter Island Decipherment" 335
- Fieldwork Challenges 335

HUMAN VERBAL LANGUAGE *336*
Key Characteristics: Productivity and Displacement *336*
Formal Properties of Language *337*
Multiple Levels of Language *338*
Language Origins and Change *340*
LANGUAGE, THOUGHT, AND BEHAVIOR *343*
Opposing Models: Sapir-Whorf versus Sociolinguistics *343*
Multiple Cultural Worlds: Indexing Motherhood in Western Samoa and the United States *345*
DISCOURSE, IDENTITY, AND POWER *346*
Children's Disputes *346*
Adolescent Girls' "Fat Talk" *347*
Cultural Cuing in the Medical Interview *347*
HUMAN PARALANGUAGE *348*
Silence as Communication *348*
Kinesics *348*
Dress and Looks *349*
MASS MEDIA *349*
The Media Process: Studying War Correspondents *350*
Television Studies *350*
Critical Thinking: A Tale of Two Stories: Assessing Institutional Influence on News Reporting *351*
Orientalism in American Popular Culture *353*
LANGUAGE AND SOCIAL CHANGE *354*
Voices: On Decolonising the Mind, by Ngũgĩ wa Thiong'o *355*
SUMMARY *355*
CRITICAL THINKING QUESTIONS *356*
KEY CONCEPTS *356*
SUGGESTED READINGS *356*

15 Expressive Culture *359*

WHAT IS ART? *360*
Viewpoint: Seeing Fine Art in Vietnam, by Susan Brownmiller *361*
STUDYING ART IN SOCIETY *362*
Critical Thinking: Probing the Categories of Art *363*
Focus on the Artist *364*
Ethnicity, Gender, and Power *365*
Multiple Cultural Worlds: Invisible Hands Crafting Israeli Souvenirs *366*
PERFORMANCE ARTS *367*
Music and Gender: Balance among the Temiar *367*
Theater and Myth: Ritual Dance-Drama in India *368*
ARCHITECTURE AND DECORATIVE ARTS *368*
Architecture and Mode of Production *369*
Interior Decoration *369*
Gardens and Flowers *370*
THE ANTHROPOLOGY OF MUSEUMS *371*
Multiple Cultural Worlds: Art Museums and Society in France and the United States *372*
Current Event: "Bilbao to Bid for Guernica" *373*
PLAY AND LEISURE *373*
Games and Sports as Cultural Microcosm *374*
Voices: "Childhood Tales of the Hammam," by Fatima Mernissi *376*
Leisure Travel *376*
CHANGE IN ART AND PLAY *377*
Effects of Westernization *378*
Effects of Tourism *378*
Post-Communist Transitions *379*
SUMMARY *380*
CRITICAL THINKING QUESTIONS *381*
KEY CONCEPTS *381*
SUGGESTED READINGS *381*

PART V: CONTEMPORARY CULTURAL CHANGE

Batik Sarong, Java, north coast, 1900–1920.

16 People on the Move *383*

ANTHROPOLOGY AND MIGRATION *384*
WHAT IS MIGRATION? *385*
Internal Migration *385*
Multiple Cultural Worlds: Urban Migration of Girls in Ghana *386*
International Migration *386*
Current Event: "Free Trade Leads to Bolivians Seeking Jobs in Argentina" *387*
CATEGORIES OF MIGRANTS *387*

Labor Migrants *387*
Displaced Persons *388*
Critical Thinking: Haitian Cane-Cutters in the Dominican Republic—Two Views on Human Rights *389*
Multiple Cultural Worlds: Palestinian Refugees in Lebanon—Uncounted and Unwanted *391*
Institutional Migrants *391*
Soldiers on Assignment *392*
Spouse/Partner Migration *392*
THE NEW IMMIGRANTS *393*
Multiple Cultural Worlds: The New Immigrants and FGM in the United States *393*
The New Immigrants from Latin America and the Caribbean *394*
The New Immigrants from East Asia *396*
Voices: "Saying Goodbye," by Marie G. Lee *398*
The New Immigrants from Southeast Asia *398*
The New Immigrants from South Asia: Asian Indians in New York City Maintain Their Culture *400*
The New Immigrants from Eastern Europe *401*
Multiple Cultural Worlds: Bosnian Trauma Testimonies and Recovery *402*
THE POLITICS AND POLICIES OF INCLUSION AND EXCLUSION *402*
Viewpoint: "The Immigration Wars," by Bart Laws *403*
SUMMARY *404*
CRITICAL THINKING QUESTIONS *404*
KEY CONCEPTS *405*
SUGGESTED READINGS *405*

17 Development Anthropology *407*

ANTHROPOLOGY AND THE STUDY OF CHANGE *408*
Invention *408*
Critical Thinking: Social Impacts of the Green Revolution *409*
Diffusion *409*
Theories of Cultural Change *410*
Multiple Cultural Worlds: Snowmobiles and Sami Reindeer Herding *411*
Multiple Cultural Worlds: The Effectiveness of Redistribution as a Development Strategy in Nadur *414*
Multiple Cultural Worlds: The Shan-Dany Museum and the Construction of Community in Mexico *415*
ORGANIZATIONAL APPROACHES TO DEVELOPMENT *415*
Large-Scale Institutions *415*
Current Event: "Largest-Ever World Bank Loan Mistrusted in India" *417*
The "Development Apparatus" *418*
Grassroots Approaches *418*
THE DEVELOPMENT PROJECT *419*
Anthropologists and the Project Cycle *419*
Comparative Studies *420*
The Anthropological Critique of Development Projects *421*
METHODS IN DEVELOPMENT ANTHROPOLOGY *422*
Rapid Research Methods *422*
Participatory Appraisal *423*
INDIGENOUS PEOPLE'S DEVELOPMENT *424*
Indigenous People as Victims of Development *424*
Voices: "They Told Us That Indian Ways Were Bad" by Tulto *425*
From Victimization to Indigenous People's Development *427*
Current Event: "Online in the Outback" *429*
WOMEN AND DEVELOPMENT *430*
The Male Bias *430*
Women's Organizations for Change *431*
HUMAN RIGHTS AND DEVELOPMENT *432*
SUMMARY *433*
KEY CONCEPTS *434*
CRITICAL THINKING QUESTIONS *434*
SUGGESTED READINGS *434*

References *436*

Index *462*

Preface

Why would anybody want to write an introductory cultural anthropology textbook? Such a project requires years of research, writing, and rewriting, and is a humbling task, considering the amount of material there is to read and the time that must be spent rethinking categories and questions. One reason for my involvement with this book is the fact that over the three years of my teaching large classes in introductory cultural anthropology at the University of Pittsburgh, my enrollments went from 100 in 1991 to 200 in 1992 to 300 in 1993. I figured that I must be doing something right. At the same time, it became clearer to me how my teaching differed from the various texts I had used: My dissatisfaction with the available books centered on their relegation of the topic of social inequality to a separate chapter (usually on "social stratification"). Standard material such as economy, kinship, politics, religion, and language paid little attention to how these topics relate to social inequality.

I was also well aware of how "dead" many of the longstanding subjects had become, including kinship, our traditional core, and how painful it was to teach some topics—especially language—because the material seemed irrelevant to cultural anthropology's goal of understanding why people do what they do and think the way they do. Finally, the available books did not integrate attention to cultural change throughout, but instead resorted to a few standard cases such as "cargo cults" in the chapter on religion and perhaps a separate chapter on international development or urbanization.

I wanted to write a textbook that would reshape and enliven the teaching of cultural anthropology along these lines, with the major emphasis being on social inequality. Why is this theme so important? Whether a person is involved in environmental studies, peace studies, or international business, knowing about the world's cultures is crucial for shaping a vision of what is both possible and appropriate in terms of goals and actions. To this end, *Cultural Anthropology* presents interesting and informative material about "exotic" and distant cultures. More than this, though, it follows a new direction in cultural anthropology by including substantial attention to "Western" cultures (primarily European and European American) and insisting that they require attention and study just as much as non-Western cultures. In this way, it proceeds to "make the strange familiar and the familiar strange" (Spiro 1990).

HOW THIS BOOK IS ORGANIZED

Cultural Anthropology pursues its goal of promoting learning about the world's cultures in two ways, one that will be familiar and comforting (the delivery of information) and the other that may be unsettling and disturbing (asking questions about the information at hand that will make readers realize they don't really know what they thought they knew).

In the first place, readers will encounter abundant, up-to-date *information* about what is known about cross-cultural lifeways: How do people in different parts of the world obtain food, conceive of their place in the universe, and deal with rapid cultural change? This "substantive" material of cultural anthropology begins with two chapters that establish a foundation for understanding what the discipline of anthropology in general is about, how cultural anthropology fits with it, and what the concept of culture means.

All aspects of life are interrelated, and it is often difficult, in "real life" as well as in scholarly analysis, to separate them. The theoretical framework of cultural materialism offers one option for the sense of logical ordering of areas of life, from infrastructure to structure to superstructure. Other theoretical perspectives offer alternative ways of looking at culture.

Chapter 1 ("Anthropology and the Study of Culture") establishes the importance of the themes of social diversity and inequality addressed throughout the book, especially class, race, ethnicity, gender, and age. Chapter 2 ("Methods in Cultural Anthropology") explores how research is conducted in cultural anthropology and how findings are analyzed and presented. Students will be able to link what they already know about general research concepts (for example, inductive versus deductive approaches, qualitative versus quantitative data) with what they learn here about how cultural anthropologists have used such concepts in their research and have come up with distinct approaches to data collection, analysis, and presentation.

Fifteen topical chapters follow, all of which address the two big questions of cultural anthropology: "What do people do?" and "What do people think?" concerning the topic at hand, whether it is work, marriage, or religion. My theoretical grounding in cultural materialism guides the ordering of the chapters. Cultural materialists look first to what can be called the "material" aspects of human life—especially economic systems and how people make a living—in trying to understand why people do what they do and why they think the way they do. Thus, Chapter 3 ("Economies and Their Modes of Production") and Chapter 4 ("Consumption and Exchange") appear at the beginning of the topical chapters as the foundation of the basic infrastructure of culture. The image of a multistoried house might help in understanding this ordering. Economic systems can be said to be the major "rooms" on the ground floor, where one first enters the house. Reproduction, or "making people," can be usefully paired with the topic of production, "making a living." Therefore, treatment of reproduction, "Birth and Death," is placed in Chapter 5, which immediately follows the two chapters on economics.

The book proceeds to the subject of the human life cycle in cross-cultural perspective (Chapter 6, "Personality and Human Development"), presenting material from the exciting subfield of psychological anthropology. This chapter connects with introductory psychology courses that many students will have taken. The next chapter in this cluster about "making people" is Chapter 7 on "Illness and Healing." A rare chapter in introductory cultural anthropology textbooks, this one will be particularly interesting to the many students who are considering careers in health-related fields.

Next are a series of chapters dealing with various aspects of "people in groups," the "structure," or second floor, beginning with Chapter 8 on "Kinship Dynamics."

This chapter incorporates up-to-date research that has enlivened the traditional core area of cultural anthropology. Although traditional categories and definitions are presented, the emphasis is on "kinship in action," and on bringing kinship into a more relevant place in cultural anthropology. Chapter 9, "Domestic Groups," looks at how people are arranged into groups for everyday living. Chapter 10 ("Social Groups and Social Stratification") widens the lens to examine social groups beyond the domestic situation, including clubs and cooperatives. It also addresses how, in different societies, groups may be arranged hierarchically in relation to one another, for example, in India's caste system. Chapter 11 ("Politics and Leadership") presents some standard material on the various forms of political organization cross-culturally but includes more than the usual amount of material on contemporary state-level societies. Chapter 12, "Social Order and Social Conflict," enters the subfield of legal anthropology, an area of interest to preprofessional students considering careers in law and law enforcement.

The next chapters move the reader toward the third floor ("superstructure"), where the topics of ideology, belief systems, and values reside. All the previous chapters have related to belief systems and values in one way or another. But here, the focus becomes explicit, addressing three areas of "mental culture": Chapter 13 on "Religion"; Chapter 14 on "Communication," including verbal language, nonverbal language, and mass media; and Chapter 15 on "Expressive Culture," which includes the arts, the representation of culture in museums, play, and leisure.

The final two chapters bring together many of the topics addressed in Chapters 3–15 in their examination of two of the most important aspects of contemporary change: migration and international development. Each chapter is based on the growing body of anthropological data on the infrastructural, structural, and superstructural aspects of these two topics. Chapter 16, "People on the Move," provides insights about categories of migrants and detailed information on the "new immigrants" in North America, especially the United States. Chapter 17, "Development Anthropology" shows how cultural anthropologists have contributed to making international development projects and processes more culturally appropriate and less harmful to local people, especially marginalized indigenous peoples and minorities. Both Chapters 16 and 17 highlight the "action" aspect of cultural anthropology and underline how it can be relevant to policy issues in the contemporary world.

DISTINCTIVE FEATURES

Several features of this book make it unique and special. First, much attention is given to **social inequality** and **social diversity** (including class, race, ethnicity, gender, and age) throughout the book, not just in one chapter, but in each chapter in the general text and in the "Multiple Cultural Worlds" boxes. In addition to consistent attention to social inequality and social diversity throughout the book, these issues receive more in-depth attention in particular places. The major social categories of class, race, ethnicity, age, and gender are introduced in Chapter 1 as analytical categories, examined in Chapter 2 in terms of how they affect research methods and strategies, and receive more in-depth attention in Chapter 10 ("Social Groups and Social Stratification").

Second, **more material on contemporary change** is included throughout the entire book. This innovation offers the opportunity for understanding how cultural processes actually work, especially in complex "multicultural" societies, and it avoids treating cultures as if they were "frozen in time," thus providing more relevance to students' career interests.

Third, extensive coverage of **cultures of the contemporary United States** (and the "West") is an integrated part of the text. Examples include discussions of the informal sector in "Belmar," Pennsylvania, and the changing industrial culture in "Barberton," Ohio (Chapter 3); theft and looting during the Los Angeles riots as a form of exchange (Chapter 4); amniocentesis and the poor of New York City (Chapter 5); economic discrimination against homosexuals in the United States (Chapter 6); Western biomedicine (Chapter 7); American kinship and weddings American style (Chapter 8); matrifocality and changing domestic patterns (Chapter 9); fraternities and body modification groups (Chapter 10); neighborhood conflicts over dogs (Chapter 12); Protestantism in Appalachia (Chapter 13); mothers' use of language to infants in the United States compared to Samoa and children's dispute talk (Chapter 14); a comparison of social patterns of attendance at art museums in the United States and France (Chapter 15); extensive treatment of the United States' "new immigrants" (Chapter 16) and the role of U.S.-based development institutions such as the World Bank (Chapter 17).

Fourth, an **up-to-date and lively chapter on "language"** (Chapter 14) is innovative in that it deemphasizes more "formal" aspects of linguistic anthropology such as phonetics and phonemics and gives more material on everyday language in use: children's disputes, adolescent girls' "fat talk," and dress and looks as forms of communication. It also includes the latest anthropological research on mass media and how it is culturally shaped, for example, in its consideration of news reporting and television studies. This enhanced treatment will make teaching the subject of language much more pleasant for instructors and much more exciting for students. This discussion also offers more relevance to students who are interested in careers in the many areas of communication.

Fifth, a unique **chapter on medical anthropology** (Chapter 7) is included. I know of no other introductory cultural anthropology book that includes a chapter on this topic. Students in general and especially the large numbers of pre-med students or students pursuing some sort of health career are very interested in this topic.

Sixth, a **chapter on migration** (Chapter 16), unique to this textbook, addresses one of the key issues of contemporary times. It incorporates the leading-edge research in cultural anthropology and addresses issues of personal and professional importance to many students who are themselves from migrant families or intend to work in areas related to migration.

Finally, the **critical thinking approach** prompts readers to question what they think they know. Instead of simply accepting what we hear or read, a critical thinking approach prompts us to ask questions. It establishes a dynamic relationship between the material and the reader, rather than merely allowing for a passive form of information transferral. This approach provides a sense of engagement and is also "good science" and therefore promises to advance student thinking as the material is absorbed. While many other textbooks provide "thought questions" at the end of their chapters, none integrates substantial material focused around questions through the use of boxes.

BOX FEATURES

The pedagogical goals of this book are advanced through the use of five distinctive and original boxes:

Multiple Cultural Worlds

124 Part II Economic and Demographic Foundations

Multiple Cultural Worlds

Amniocentesis and the Poor of New York City

Culture and Death

Given the book's underlying and pervasive theme of cultural variation and social inequality within and between cultures, Multiple Cultural Worlds boxes are used to present material that demonstrates cultural variation and, often, but not always, inequalities by class, race, ethnicity, gender, and age. For example:

Crazy Quilt by E. T. Willis

- "Invisible Hands Crafting Israeli Souvenirs"
- "Amniocentesis and the Poor of New York City"
- "Bosnian Trauma Testimonies and Recovery"

Critical Thinking

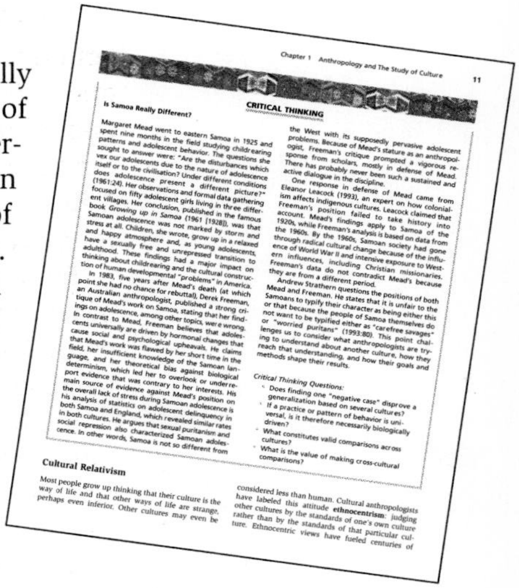
Chapter 1 Anthropology and The Study of Culture 11

Critical Thinking

Is Samoa Really Different?

Cultural Relativism

The book's commitment to giving students practice in how to think critically is carried out in each chapter through a Critical Thinking box. In most of these boxes, students will read about an issue and how it has been interpreted from two different, conflicting perspectives. The students are then asked to consider how the researchers approached the issue, what kind of data they used, and how their conclusions are influenced by their approach. Many of the boxes carry through on the three theoretical issues presented in Chapter 1 as characterizing contemporary cultural anthropology (biological determinism versus cultural constructionism, emics versus etics, and individual agency versus structurism). For example:

Kilim Rug, E. Anatolia. Turkey

- "Reproductive Rights or Wrongs"
- "Why Do People Eat Dirt?"
- "A Tale of Two Stories: Assessing Institutional Influence on New Reporting"
- "Haitian Cane-Cutters in the Dominican Republic—Two Views"

In other boxes, students are asked to reflect on "received wisdom" from a new angle:

- "Was the Invention of Agriculture a Terrible Mistake?"

New categories of analysis are introduced and old ones are reassessed:

- "Assessing One's Own Entitlement Bundle"
- "Probing the Categories of Art"

Current Event

These brief boxes demonstrate how anthropology connects to everyday events in the world. They help "de-exoticize" cultural anthropology by bringing it to issues such as:

- "Credit Card Regulation in Korea"
- "Consumerism Fuels Dowry Death in India"
- "Bilbao to Bid for Guernica"

Some boxes highlight recent discoveries in anthropology:

- "Easter Island Decipherment"
- "Who's Buried in Margarita's Tomb?"

Voices

Fiji tapa

The inclusion of "first-person" voices, especially those of minorities, women, and indigenous people emphasizes that the people anthropologists study, even the most marginalized, have their own active "voices" in which they describe their experiences and express their views. These boxes help make the material come alive and add to its relevance. Examples include:

- "Puravdorj Speaks of Privatization"
- "Play Potlatches"
- "Memoirs from the Women's Prison"

Viewpoint

Silk with multicolored embroidered threads, Laos

Viewpoint boxes present editorial-type views on a particular issue by an expert, who is not always an anthropologist. These boxes are aimed at showing students how to develop and express an argument about a particular topic. For example,

- "Something Nasty in the Tea Leaves"
- "Seeing Fine Art in Vietnam"
- "The Hope for Europe"

SUPPLEMENTS FOR INSTRUCTORS

Along with this textbook come an array of supplements that will assist instructors in using the book and enriching the students' learning experience.

Instructor's Manual and Test Bank

An unusual feature of the Instructor's Manual and Test Bank is that it is written by the textbook author herself. In this manual, I include teaching tips and classroom exercises that I have used in many years of teaching cultural anthropology within a general cultural materialist framework and in teaching the many cases and examples included in the book.

Computerized Test Bank Computerized versions of the test bank from the Instructor's Manual and Test Bank are available in DOS, Windows, or Macintosh formats.

Allyn & Bacon Interactive Video and User's Guide This custom video covers a variety of topics, both national and global. The up-to-the-minute video segments are great to launch lectures, spark classroom discussion, and encourage critical thinking. The user's guide provides detailed descriptions of each video segment, specific tie-ins to the text, and suggested discussion questions and projects.

Allyn & Bacon Video Library Qualified adopters may select from a wide variety of high-quality videos from such sources as Films for the Humanities and Sciences and Annenberg/CPB.

PowerPoint Presentation and User's Guide This PowerPoint presentation for *Cultural Anthropology* combines approximately 150 graphic and text images into fifteen modules. Using either Macintosh or DOS/ Windows, a professor can easily create customized graphic presentations for lectures. PowerPoint software is not required to use this program; a PowerPoint viewer is included to access the images.

Pretested multiple-choice questions are provided for each chapter, along with hints about how to steer post-test concerns about particular questions into positive directions.

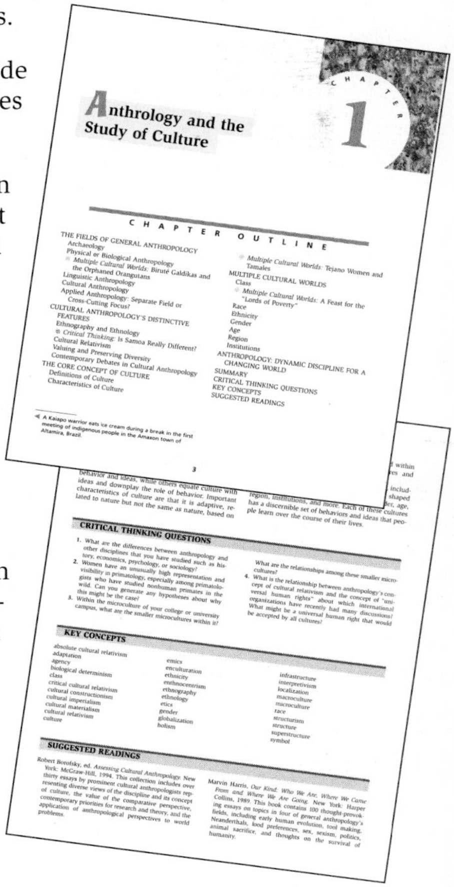

In-Text Pedagogy

I have included many pedagogical tools in the book to help students learn and to help teachers teach. In addition to the box features already mentioned, each chapter opens with a chapter outline. The box features in each chapter are outlined here, as well as the main topics to be covered. Also, in addition to the Critical Thinking boxes throughout the book, each chapter ends with **critical thinking questions** for the students. Another feature is the list of **key terms** at the end of each chapter. Each key term is listed along with the page number on which it appears. Key terms also appear in boldfaced text throughout the chapter. Finally, each chapter ends with a list of **suggested readings.**

ACKNOWLEDGMENTS

This book has evolved out of my long relationship with cultural anthropology which began with my first anthropology course in 1967 when I was an undergraduate at Syracuse University. Agehananda Bharati was an important figure in my undergraduate training as were Michael Freedman and cultural geographer David Sopher. Since then, and especially beginning with the writing of my dissertation, my theoretical perspectives have been most deeply influenced by the work of anthropologists Marvin Harris, Jack Goody, G. William Skinner, and economist Ester Boserup. My research in India has been enriched especially by the work of Pauline Kolenda, Stanley Tambiah, Gerry Berreman, and Sylvia Vatuk. The list of my many other favorite writers within and beyond anthropology is too long to include here, but much of their work is woven into the book.

Four reviewers carefully and insightfully labored their way through an early draft: Elliot Fratkin (Smith College), Maxine Margolis (University of Florida), Russell Reid (University of Louisville), and Robert Trotter II (University of Arizona). Each reviewer offered me richly detailed comments about what to fix and how to do it. I cannot overemphasize the importance of their contribution in catching me up, time and again, preventing me from making many errors and overstatements and indicating areas that just didn't work. Their words of praise were equally welcome.

During the several years of research and writing for this book, I received invaluable advice, information, and encouragement from many anthropologists, including Lila Abu-Lughod, Vincanne Adams, Catherine Allen, Joseph Alter, Donald Attwood, Diane Bell, Nancy Benco, Marc Bermann, Alexia Bloch, Lynne Bolles, John R. Bowen, Don Brenneis, Alison Brooks, D. Glynn Cochrane, Liza Dalby, Timothy Earle, David Gow, Curt Grimm, Richard Grinker, Daniel Gross, Marvin Harris, Michael Herzfeld, Barry Hewlett, Michael Horowitz, Robert Humphrey, Anstice Justin, Ian Keen, Laurel Kendall, Dorinne Kondo, Conrad Kottak, Ruth Krulfeld, Joel Kuipers, Takie Lebra, David Lempert, Samuel Martínez, Catherine McCoid, Leroy McDermott, Kirin Narayan, Sarah Nelson, Gananath Obeyesekere, Hanna Papanek, Deborah Pellow, Gregory Possehl, Joanne Rappaport, Jennifer Robertson, Nicole Sault, Joel Savishinsky, Richard Shweder, Chunghee Soh, Martha Ward, James (Woody) Watson, Rubie Watson, Van Yasek, and Bernard Wood. Robert Humphrey, the book's cartoonist, read the entire draft manuscript in order to generate the artwork.

My research and writing were also encouraged and aided by many nonanthropologists, who were colleagues or friends or often both: Avery Andrews, Nathan Brown, Cynthia Deitch, Frances Gouda, Cynthia Harrison, Christopher Heaton, Alf Hiltebeitel, Jonathan Higman, James Hoag, Lester Lefton, Craig Linebaugh, John Logsdon, Neal Oxenhandler, Gary Price, Jon Rohde, Carol Sigelman, Samuel Skogstad, Stanley Stevens, and Jeff Weinstein. These people, and no doubt many more whom I have failed to name, were helpful in a variety of ways, from offering periodic supportive comments to providing critiques of certain sections and sending material or photographs to include in the book.

Harry Harding, Dean of the Elliott School of International Affairs at the George Washington University, helped the project move forward by counting it as a valid research activity for a faculty member in his school, and by allocating research assistance to me each year. My four assistants, who helped track down library material and check references, were Joseph Mineiro, Han Quyen Thi Tran, Hena Khan, and Omar McDoom. Marilyn Millstone of George Washington University's Publication Specialist Summer Internship Program came to my rescue in 1997 by providing me with a summer intern, Lisa Chappelear, who moved production along substantially by working on the permissions.

Ever since I first became interested in writing a textbook in cultural anthropology, my students have been a source of strength and inspiration. Students in my introductory cultural anthropology classes have provided helpful comments about aspects of the book that worked more or less well. They have seemed to enjoy looking at cultural anthropology from a "critical thinking" perspective, thus giving me hope that this approach does indeed work. I thank them and all my students, both undergraduate and graduate in anthropology, international affairs, and women's studies, for their patience and support. Two former George Washington University graduate students, Ed Keller III and Roshani Kothari, contributed many of the book's photographs, as well as cheer and encouragement.

Sylvia Shepard, my development editor, first caught sight of this project in 1993. I cannot speak strongly enough to the importance of having Sylvia work on this book. She knows so much about anthropology and about how to write an excellent textbook. Her advice extended from deep content analysis to heading changes and line-by-line suggestions about word choice. My praise of Sylvia's contribution is made on the basis of her hundreds of hours of careful, thorough, and relentless work on my manuscript in its several stages. I can say with surety that without Sylvia, this book would not exist.

At Allyn and Bacon, series editor in advanced sociology and anthropology, Sarah Kelbaugh, was a helpful presence during the production stages of the book. Other people at Allyn and Bacon who provided support during the production process are Susan McIntyre, Heather Ahlstrom, and Jennifer Miller. The book's copy editor and project manager, Kathy Smith, had a good eye for editorial improvement of the text and a knack for discovering photographs to fit my sometimes bizarre specifications.

Closer to home, I thank "the Millers"—my parents, siblings, aunts and uncles, and nieces and nephews—for their interest and support throughout the four years of writing. The same applies to "the Heatons"—my former in-laws, including parents-in-law, brothers- and sisters-in-law, and nieces and nephews. Most of all, I thank my son Jack Heaton, for being an inspiration to my writing, a superb traveling companion on our trip around the world with the Semester at Sea Program, and a delicately effective critic of my (occasional) excesses in thinking. This book is dedicated to him.

Barbara D. Miller
Washington, DC

Cultural Anthropology

CHAPTER 1

Anthropology and the Study of Culture

CHAPTER OUTLINE

THE FIELDS OF GENERAL ANTHROPOLOGY
- Archaeology
- Physical or Biological Anthropology
  - *Multiple Cultural Worlds:* Birutė Galdikas and the Orphaned Orangutans
- Linguistic Anthropology
- Cultural Anthropology
- Applied Anthropology: Separate Field or Cross-Cutting Focus?

CULTURAL ANTHROPOLOGY'S DISTINCTIVE FEATURES
- Ethnography and Ethnology
  - *Critical Thinking:* Is Samoa Really Different?
- Cultural Relativism
- Valuing and Sustaining Diversity
- Contemporary Debates in Cultural Anthropology

THE CORE CONCEPT OF CULTURE
- Definitions of Culture
- Characteristics of Culture
  - *Multiple Cultural Worlds:* Tejano Women and Tamales

MULTIPLE CULTURAL WORLDS
- Class
  - *Multiple Cultural Worlds:* A Feast for the "Lords of Poverty"
- Race
- Ethnicity
- Gender
- Age
- Region
- Institutions

ANTHROPOLOGY: DYNAMIC DISCIPLINE FOR A CHANGING WORLD

SUMMARY

CRITICAL THINKING QUESTIONS

KEY CONCEPTS

SUGGESTED READINGS

◀ A Kayapó warrior eats ice cream during a break in the first meeting of indigenous peoples in the Amazon town of Altamira, Brazil.

Old bones, *Jurassic Park,* cannibalism, hidden treasure, *Indiana Jones and The Temple of Doom.* In America, the popular impression of anthropology is based mainly on movies and television shows that depict anthropologists as adventurers and heroes. Many anthropologists do have adventures, and some discover treasures such as ancient pottery, medicinal plants, and jade carvings. But most of their research is less than glorious, involving repetitive and tedious activities. What do anthropologists do, and why do people study anthropology?

This chapter offers an overview of general anthropology, an academic discipline devoted to the study of human life throughout history and in all its variations. General anthropology encompasses several subareas, or fields. The field that is the subject of this book, cultural anthropology, is devoted to the study of **culture,** learned and shared human behaviors and ideas. Learning about how one culture differs from or resembles another, and why, and how different cultures influence each other, is cultural anthropology's major goal. In pursuing this goal, cultural anthropology offers insights about different cultures and world events that in one way or another affect us all. For example, the media presents disasters such as famine in Sudan as the problem of helpless people in a faraway land. Cultural anthropologists have provided insights about how people in famine situations attempt to cope with disaster, not as passive victims, but as creative people struggling to maintain their cultures and lives. With its interests in the relationships among cultures, cultural anthropology adds another dimension of complexity by exposing how North Americans are a part of the world hunger problem. High levels of food consumption by many people in North America are related to low levels of food consumption elsewhere, as well as within North America itself. Ultimately, cultural anthropology decenters us from our own cultures, teaching us to look at ourselves from the "outside" as somewhat "strange." Melford Spiro (1990) aptly asserts that the work of anthropology is to "make the strange familiar and the familiar strange." A good example of "making the familiar strange" is the case of the Nacirema, who were first described in 1956:

> They are a North American group living in the territory between the Canadian Cree, the Yaqui and the Tarahumare of Mexico, and the Carib and the Arawak of the Antilles. Little is known of their origin, though tradition states that they came from the east. According to Nacirema mythology, their nation was originated by a culture hero, Notgnihsaw, who is otherwise known for two great feats of strength—the throwing of a piece of wampum across the river Pa-To-Mac and the chopping down of a cherry tree in which the Spirit of Truth resided. (Miner 1965 [1956]: 415)

Primatologist Dian Fossey interacts with a gorilla during fieldwork in Rwanda.

The anthropologist goes on to describe the unusually intense focus of Nacirema culture on the human body and its beauty and its wide variety of private and personal rituals. He gives a detailed account of one ritual that is performed daily within the homes at a specially constructed shrine area:

> The focal point of the shrine is a box or chest which is built into the wall. In this chest are kept the many charms and magical potions without which no native believes he could live. These preparations are secured from a variety of specialized practitioners. The most powerful of these are the medicine men, whose assistance must be rewarded with substantial gifts. . . . Beneath the charm box is a small font. Each day every member of the family, in succession, enters the shrine room, bows his head before the charm-box, mingles different sorts of holy water in the font, and proceeds with a brief rite of ablution. (415–416)

If you don't know this tribe, try spelling its name backwards. (One note: Please forgive Miner for his use of the masculine pronoun in describing Nacirema society in general; his writings are now nearly a half-century old.)

THE FIELDS OF GENERAL ANTHROPOLOGY

Most anthropologists agree that the discipline of anthropology, or general anthropology, is divided into four fields:

- archaeology (sometimes called prehistory),
- physical anthropology (sometimes called biological anthropology),
- linguistic anthropology, and
- cultural anthropology (sometimes called social anthropology).

Most anthropologists say that training in anthropology ideally should involve knowledge in all four fields and awareness of the linkages between them because of anthropology's broad goal of understanding all human behavior and changes in it. In much of Europe and in countries whose educational systems were influenced by European colonialism, the term "anthropology" usually includes only the subject matter of cultural anthropology.

Other anthropologists contend that the four-field approach is no longer relevant and should be abandoned. The sheer amount of knowledge in the various fields has increased over time, and apparently greater differences in theory, methods, and subject matter have emerged, making interchange across fields less frequent or useful. Clifford Geertz (1991), an opponent of the four-field approach, says that it has become "a little unreal" because even when all four fields exist in one department, they do not interact and cross-fertilize each other in the true spirit of the four-field approach. A few universities have divided their department of anthropology into two or more separate units. Most, however, remain committed in some way to the principle of four-field interchange and feel that anthropology cannot really exist without it. The following section provides a brief description of each field.

Archaeology

This field is devoted to studying the life-ways of past cultures by examining material remains. Data include stone and bone tools, skeletal material, remains of buildings, and refuse such as pot shards (broken pieces of pottery) and coprolites (fossilized fecal matter). Since its beginnings in the mid-eighteenth century, archaeology has contributed knowledge about the emergence of the great early states of Egypt, Phoenicia, the Indus Valley, and Mexico (Bahn 1996). New research is questioning some previous conclusions about "kingdoms." For example, excavations at a royal burial site of the Old Silla Kingdom of Korea, which extended from 57 BCE to AD 668, reveal that queens were often the rulers (Nelson 1993). This finding challenges the earlier generalization that centralized state systems always involve male political dominance.

While archaeological research continues to discover grand sites and artifacts of gold and jade, a new area of research looks at the role of smaller towns and villages. This pursuit takes archaeologists to less grand and glamorous sites, although the findings are equally important. Marc Bermann encapsulates the effects of what he calls "capital-centric" archaeological research in the Andes: "Because of this, we know far more about urban sites than we do about villages, far more about temples than about houses, and far more about regional administration than about day-to-day life" (1994:3). His research at a site in Bolivia called Lukurmata investigates how state formation, expansion, and decline were experienced by people living away from the urban capitals in peripheral areas. Bermann's findings demonstrate the importance of "studying down" in archaeology to the level of the household and even individuals within it, showing that "important" social changes existed at these levels as well as in the power centers, a fact often overlooked by archaeologists.

The archaeology of the recent past is another new research direction; an example is the "Garbage Project," which is being conducted by archaeologists at the University of Arizona at Tucson (Rathje and Murphy 1992). The "Garbage Archaeologists" are excavating the Fresh Kills landfill on Staten Island, near New York City. Its mass is estimated at 100 million tons and its volume at 2.9 billion cubic feet. Thus, it is one of the largest human-made structures in North America. Through excavation of artifacts such as poptop can tabs, disposable diapers, cosmetic containers, and telephone books, the Garbage Archaeologists are learning about recent consumption patterns. These findings also provide lessons for the future. They reveal how long it takes for contemporary goods to decompose. Urban planners and other people interested in recycling may be surprised to learn that the kinds of garbage that people often blame for filling up landfills, such as fast-food packaging, polystyrene foam, and disposable diapers, are less serious problems than paper. Paper, especially newspaper, is the major culprit because of sheer quantity. This kind of information can help improve recycling efforts in the United States.

Physical or Biological Anthropology

One description of the field states that the broad field of biological (or physical) anthropology deals with everything from evolutionary theory to the human fossil record and the identification of human skeletal remains from crime scenes and accidents (Park 1996: vii). Genetics, anatomy, animal and human behavior, ecology, nutrition, and forensics are subject areas included in this field. In seeking to understand human variation, adaptation, and change, physical anthropologists study many forms of life, human and nonhuman, past and present. Many physical anthropologists do research on animals other than humans in order to understand human origins or to use them as models for understanding contemporary human behavior.

Within physical anthropology, the subfield of primatology is focused on studies of nonhuman primates and how their behavior compares with that of human primates. Primatologists are well known for their pioneering work in studying nonhuman primates in their natural habitats (see the Multiple Cultural Worlds box). Jane Goodall's (1971, 1986) research on Tanzanian chimpanzees revealed rich details about their social relationships. Barbara Smuts (1985) has studied friendships and coalitions between baboons and has shown how females especially rely on solidarity with other females.

An ongoing debate in physical anthropology concerns which nonhuman primate is the closest to humans. Most evidence points to the chimpanzee. Chimpanzees and humans have about 99 percent of their DNA in common. In contrast, Jeffrey Schwartz (1987) argues for the role of orangutans as the most recent nonhuman primate ancestor and therefore the one bearing the closest resemblance to humans. His argument relies on a key difference between humans and chimpanzees: Human females do not experience estrus (a periodic phase of sexual interest). The chimpanzee model puts anthropologists in the difficult position of having to explain why, how, and when estrus disappeared in the evolutionary line from chimpanzees to humans. The orangutan model avoids this problem. Schwartz's orangutan hypothesis is controversial, but he is encouraged by growing support from other physical anthropologists. At the end of his latest book, he comments that "[T]here's lots more research, reanalysis, and debate over the alternative hypothesis still to be done. But I'm not dead yet" (1993:268).

Physical anthropologists share many research interests with archaeologists, given their study of evidence from the past. One such area is the question of when human beings first emerged as *homo sapiens.* An early population named the Neanderthals, dated about 130,000–30,000 years ago, are at center of this question. Some experts consider them the earliest humans ever discovered. Others say that they should not be considered *homo sapiens.* The fossil in question is a skull cap found in 1856 in Germany's Neander Valley (Park 1996:233). Key features that support the "humanness" of Neanderthals include large cranial capacity (skull size); evidence of tool making and tool use; and the ability to think symbolically, as suggested by burial of the dead, sometimes with offerings such as animal bones, tools, and maybe flowers. But differences are also notable. The Neanderthals' foreheads are sloped, the back of the skull is bulging, and brow ridges are large. Arguments about "humanness" rest on which features are more important and should carry more weight. One conclusion is that it is impossible to draw a hard-and-fast line between humans and prehumans because humans evolved gradually over millions of years: There was no "moment in time" when "modern humans" sprang forth from our primate ancestors.

Another area linking physical anthropology with archaeology is paleopathology, the study of diseases in prehistoric times. Analysis of trace elements in bones, such as strontium, provides surprisingly detailed information about the diets, activities, and health of prehistoric people, including whether they were primarily meat eaters or vegetarians and how their diets affected their health. Stress marks on bones provide information on changing work patterns; for example, who threw spears, who carried heavy loads, and how these activities affected health. We can also learn age at death, age at birth of first child for a woman, and birth rate per woman. Data from several time periods provide clues about how the transition to agriculture altered people's health and longevity (Cohen 1989; Cohen and Armelagos

Multiple Cultural Worlds

Biruté Galdikas and the Orphaned Orangutans

Primatologist Biruté Galdikas first went to Indonesia to study orangutans in 1971 (Montgomery 1991). Soon after arriving, she and her husband began to use their camp as a rehabilitation center for orphaned orangutans. The orphans were originally separated from their mothers by poachers who intended to sell them. Sometimes these kidnapped orangutans were confiscated by government officials who returned them to the jungle. The transition was not easy. Biruté and her camp began to serve as a way-station for these dislocated orangs.

> Few wild orphans are as pathetically vulnerable as a baby orangutan. In the wild an infant clings constantly to its mother's coarse orange fur for most of its first two years. It nurses until age eight. You cannot put an orangutan baby down as you would a human infant. A healthy infant orangutan hangs on so tight with its four-fisted grip that it leaves bruises on your flesh; any attempt to dislodge the infant from your body, even for a moment, brings high-pitched, pathetic screams. . . .
>
> Biruté's first infant was not her own Binti; it was Sugito. The year-old male orangutan arrived only days after she and Rod had set up camp. Sugito had been taken from his mother in the wild and had lived in a tiny crate until he was found and confiscated by Indonesian government officials. Determined to mother him as a female orangutan would care for her baby, Biruté slept, ate, and bathed with the wide-eyed infant clinging to her side, legs, arms, or head. Only three times in the first year did she force him off her body.
>
> Shortly thereafter followed Sinagae, Akmad, Siswoyo, Sobiarso, Gundul. . . . Biruté has mothered more than eighty ex-captives. Most arrive worm-infested, stunted, diseased. Many have died in her arms. But those who survive their infancy are then free, like Supinah, to roam through camp and its outlying forests until they voluntarily leave for life in the wild. (11–13)

Biruté Galdikas' personal life has been much affected by her long-term and intense involvement with the orangutans and with Indonesia. She and her husband raised their son, Binti, with orangs for friends instead of humans. Her husband Rod fell in love with Binti's Indonesian babysitter, and eventually he, she, and Binti left for Canada (Biruté visits Binti annually when she returns to teach at Simon Fraser University in Vancouver). Biruté subsequently fell in love with, and married, an Indonesian man of the Dayak tribe. She, her husband, and children live in Camp Leakey, which employs and houses thirty Indonesian helpers and their families. In order to try to gain some distance from the orangutans and find some privacy, she now discourages orangutans from coming into the house and dining hall. But orangutans are still prominent features of life in Camp Leakey: "As you walk the neat dirt paths connecting the visitors' dormitory with the dock and dining hall, at any moment an orangutan may leap onto your back, grab for your camera, or gently take your hand in a hairy hand or foot and stroll beside you as casually as a lover." (15)

Biruté Galdikas (wearing glasses) converses with Chris Schurmann at Camp Leakey, Indonesia.

1984; Cohen and Bennett 1993). In Peru, expansions in size and power of the Incan empire brought marked improvements in the health and longevity of males, but less for females (Costin 1993). This discovery reveals how changes in political organization affected social inequality.

Linguistic Anthropology

Linguistic anthropology emerged in the United States in the later nineteenth century when researchers began to document disappearing Native American languages. Early cultural anthropologists studied linguistic anthropology to learn how to document unwritten languages because they often researched cultures with no writing system. Both purposes have declined in importance since most "disappearing" languages have either been recorded or lost, and most previously unwritten languages have been transferred into written form. Thus, some anthropologists say that linguistic anthropology is no longer needed as a separate field and should be merged with the field of cultural anthropology or the discipline of linguistics. Others offer reasons for maintaining it as a separate field. First, language change goes on all the time, and anthropologists should document and analyze what kinds of changes are occurring and why. Many changes are related to politics and conflict worldwide. For example, in Moldova, a former Soviet republic, speakers of Russian and Ukrainian in eastern Moldova have been in conflict since 1992 over the official language policy of Moldova. Second, instead of having a shrinking area of study, linguistic anthropology is broadening its scope to include many aspects of communication such as the media, electronic mail, popular music, and advertising. These new research directions connect linguistic anthropology with psychology, journalism, television and radio, education, and marketing.

Cultural Anthropology

Cultural anthropology encompasses all aspects of human behavior and ideas including making a living and distributing goods and services, reproduction and group formation, political patterns, religious systems, forms of communication, and expressive aspects of culture such as art, dance, and music. In addition, cultural anthropologists consider how change occurs in all of these areas.

Applied Anthropology: Separate Field or Cross-Cutting Focus?

Applied anthropology, or practicing anthropology, involves the use or application of anthropological knowledge to help solve social problems. Applied anthropology emerged in the United States during and after World War II. Its first concern was with living peoples and their needs, thus initially placing applied anthropology within the field of cultural anthropology. The number of anthropologists working in applied anthropology grew substantially in the later twentieth century. One reason for this growth was the decline in college and university teaching positions in anthropology since the late 1970s. This unfavorable fact prompted anthropologists to explore jobs outside academia and led to positive change in the discipline by promoting practical use of anthropological skills and knowledge. Given this expanded role of applied anthropology, many anthropologists feel that applied anthropology should be considered a fifth field.

An alternate position is that application of knowledge to help solve particular social problems is, and should be, part of all four fields. Just like theory, application is a valid aspect of every branch of the discipline and should not be pulled out from the individual fields. Many archaeologists in the United States are employed, for example, in Cultural Resource Management (CRM), undertaking professional assessments of possible archaeological remains before construction projects such as roads and buildings can proceed. Physical anthropology has many applied aspects. For example, forensic anthropologists participate in criminal investigations through labwork identifying bodily remains. Others work in the area of primate conservation. Applied linguistic anthropologists consult with educational institutions about how to improve standardized tests for bilingual populations, or they may do policy research for governments. Development anthropology refers to an aspect of applied anthropology concerned with how so-called developing countries change and how knowledge in anthropology can play a role in formulating and implementing more appropriate kinds of change.

CULTURAL ANTHROPOLOGY'S DISTINCTIVE FEATURES

Several features of cultural anthropology have traditionally distinguished it from other disciplines. However, scholars in other disciplines have been adopting anthropological approaches, so disciplinary overlaps have emerged. Cultural anthropology's traditional characteristic features may thus no longer be unique to anthropology, but they are still part of its general identity and character.

Ethnography and Ethnology

Cultural anthropologists approach the study of contemporary human life in two basic ways: deep study and description of one culture, and comparative study of a particular topic in more than one culture. The first approach, **ethnography,** meaning "culture writing," is a firsthand, detailed description of a living culture based on personal observation. Ethnography is usually presented in the form of a full-length book; it is based on experiences gained by going to the place of study and living there for an extended period. As cultural anthropologist Richard Shweder says:

> An ethnography begins with an ethnographic experience: with your eyes open you have to go somewhere. . . . The first thing that strikes an anthropologist in the field are details that seem alien. It is April 5, 6 A.M., 90 degrees Fahrenheit, and I'm in a remote region of India on a tennis court fashioned out of the earth of termite mounds. Music, cacophonous to a foreign ear, is blaring over a loudspeaker. In India, the gods and ancestral spirits, who are not hard of hearing but are sometimes a long way off, not only like to eat food offerings, they also like to be entertained. To a foreigner for whom the gods don't exist, in the midst of a tennis match at six in the morning on a very hot day, the magnified blare is a nuisance. After two sets my Indian doubles partner finally takes off his heavy wool sweater. (1986:1, 38)

In the first part of the twentieth century, early ethnographers wrote about "exotic" cultures located far from the homes of European and North American

Anthropologist Rick Shweder (left) having an ethnographic experience.

anthropologists. Classics of this phase of ethnography include A. R. Radcliffe-Brown's *The Andaman Islanders* (1964 [1922]), a study of people living on a group of small islands off the coast of Burma; Bronislaw Malinowski's *Argonauts of the Western Pacific* (1961 [1922]), concerning a complex trade network linking several islands in the South Pacific; and Reo Fortune's *Sorcerers of Dobu* (1959 [1932]), which describes a culture in the Western Pacific islands, with a focus on its social and religious characteristics.

For several decades, ethnographers tended to treat a particular tribal group or village as a bounded unit. The era of village studies in the ethnography of India, extending from the 1950s through the 1960s, is an example of this trend. Dozens of anthropologists went to India for fieldwork, and each typically studied in one village and then wrote an ethnography describing that village. Their goal was to provide a holistic understanding of the connections between different aspects of culture within one context. Examples of such studies include Adrian Mayer's *Caste and Kinship in Central India* (1960), S. C. Dube's *Indian Village* (1967), and Gerald Berreman's *Hindus of the Himalayas* (1963). The topics of concern were caste, agricultural practices, kinship, and religion. Little attention was given to exploring links between villages, or to determining the effects of world forces such as nineteenth-century colonialism or twentieth-century neocolonialism on the villagers' lives. Berreman's book is an exception; it includes a detailed chapter on "The Outside World: Urban Contact and Government Programs."

More recent ethnographies, especially from 1980 onward, differ from earlier ethnographies in several ways. First, they are more likely to treat local cultures as embedded within regional and global forces. Conrad Kottak's *Assault on Paradise: Social Change in a Brazilian Village* (1992) draws attention to how this fishing village changed with the introduction of motorboats, the presence of international hippies in the area, the pervasiveness of television, and the rise of alcoholism. Second, many contemporary ethnographies are focused on one topic of interest and avoid a more holistic approach. Cultural anthropologists in this category feel that holism is an impossible goal, since no one can perceive cultures from all their complex angles. For example, Gananath Obeyesekere's book, *Medusa's Hair: An Essay on Personal Symbols and Religious Experience* (1981), presents the life histories of four Sri Lankan people, three women and

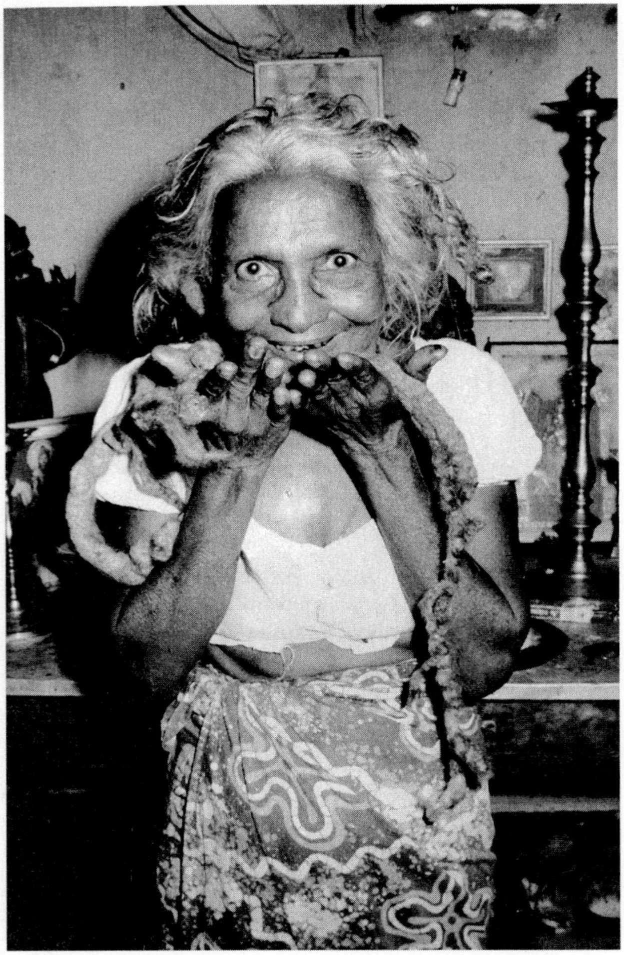

One of the Sri Lankan women whose life story Gananath Obeyesekere analyzed, a priestess to the deity Kataragama, stands in the shrine room of her house holding her long matted hair.

one man. In comparison to a village study, this kind of ethnography provides little background material on Sri Lankan culture. The emphasis instead is on the four life histories and Obeyesekere's analysis of the content of the stories. We learn that each individual became a religious devotee and that each had mysteriously matted hair, which became twisted in a snakelike fashion and could not be combed out. The devotees say that the god's presence is in their hair. Obeyesekere's interpretation suggests that these people have suffered deep psychological afflictions, including sexual anxieties, and that their matted hair symbolizes this suffering and provides them with a special status as holy. A third trend is expanded interest in incorporating attention to history. Gillian Feeley-Harnick's book, *A Green Estate: Restoring Independence in Madagascar* (1991), traces the history and effects of French colonial domination on this island located off the coast of East Africa and the emergence of Madagascar as an independent country after 1960. This research required a combination of archival data and fieldwork data. A fourth trend is for an increasing number of ethnographic studies to be situated in Western, industrialized cultures. Philippe Bourgois's research in East Harlem in New York City for his book *In Search of Respect: Selling Crack in El Barrio* (1995) explores how people in one neighborhood cope with poverty and dangerous living conditions. While this topic may superficially resemble something that a sociologist might study, with its focus on the urban United States, the approach of a cultural anthropologist provides a unique perspective that is more richly detailed from the everyday perspective of the people.

Many factors explain these new trends in ethnography, including the expanded number of anthropologists seeking research topics and areas of theoretical importance; social changes in the world that provide new topics for study; varying strengths and interests of anthropology doctoral programs that shape the theoretical and regional focus of their students; and trends in funding institutions' interests and budgetary priorities. Answering the question of why ethnographies have changed in the ways they have would require a separate book.

In contrast to ethnography, **ethnology** is cross-cultural analysis, or the study of a particular topic in more than one culture using ethnographic material. Ethnologists have compared such topics as marriage forms, economic practices, religious beliefs, and childrearing practices in order to discover patterns of similarity and variation and possible causes for them. One of the earliest and most famous examples of a comparative approach to a particular topic is Margaret Mead's study of adolescence in Samoa (1961 [1928]), an island in the South Pacific and in the United States (see the Critical Thinking box).

Obviously ethnography and ethnology are closely linked endeavors. Ethnographic studies provide indepth information that can be compared with other ethnographic reports to reveal more general theoretical issues. These questions in turn demand further ethnographic research.

CRITICAL THINKING

Is Samoa Really Different?

Margaret Mead went to eastern Samoa in 1925 and spent nine months in the field studying childrearing patterns and adolescent behavior. The questions she sought to answer were: "Are the disturbances which vex our adolescents due to the nature of adolescence itself or to the civilisation? Under different conditions does adolescence present a different picture?" (1961: 24). Her observations and formal data gathering focused on fifty adolescent girls living in three different villages. Her conclusion, published in the famous book *Growing up in Samoa* (1961 [1928]), was that Samoan adolescence was not marked by storm and stress at all. Children, she wrote, grow up in a relaxed and happy atmosphere and, as young adolescents, have a sexually free and unrepressed transition to adulthood. These findings had a major impact on thinking about childrearing and the cultural construction of human developmental "problems" in America.

In 1983, five years after Mead's death (at which point she had no chance for rebuttal), Derek Freeman, an Australian anthropologist, published a strong critique of Mead's work on Samoa, stating that her findings on adolescence, among other topics, were wrong. In contrast to Mead, Freeman believes that adolescents universally are driven by hormonal changes that cause social and psychological upheavals. He claims that Mead's work was flawed by her short time in the field, her insufficient knowledge of the Samoan language, and her theoretical bias against biological determinism, which led her to overlook or underreport evidence that was contrary to her interests. His main source of evidence against Mead's position on the overall lack of stress during Samoan adolescence is his analysis of statistics on adolescent delinquency in both Samoa and England, which revealed similar rates in both cultures. He argues that sexual puritanism and social repression also characterized Samoan adolescence. In other words, Samoa is not so different from the West with its supposedly pervasive adolescent problems. Because of Mead's stature as an anthropologist, Freeman's critique prompted a vigorous response from scholars, mostly in defense of Mead. There has probably never been such a sustained and active dialogue in the discipline.

One response in defense of Mead came from Eleanor Leacock (1993), an expert on how colonialism affects indigenous cultures. Leacock claimed that Freeman's position failed to take history into account. Mead's findings apply to Samoa of the 1920s, while Freeman's analysis is based on data from the 1960s. By the 1960s, Samoan society had gone through radical cultural change because of the influence of World War II and intensive exposure to Western influences, including Christian missionaries. Freeman's data do not contradict Mead's because they are from a different period.

Andrew Strathern questions the positions of both Mead and Freeman. He states that it is unfair to the Samoans to typify their character as being either this or that because the people of Samoa themselves do not want to be typified either as "carefree savages" or "worried puritans" (1993:80). This point challenges us to consider what anthropologists are trying to understand about another culture, how they reach that understanding, and how their goals and methods shape their results.

Critical Thinking Questions:

- Does finding one "negative case" disprove a generalization based on several cultures?
- If a practice or pattern of behavior is universal, is it therefore necessarily biologically driven?
- What constitutes valid comparisons across cultures?
- What is the value of making cross-cultural comparisons?

Cultural Relativism

Most people grow up thinking that their culture is *the* way of life and that other ways of life are strange, perhaps even inferior. Other cultures may even be considered less than human. Cultural anthropologists have labeled this attitude **ethnocentrism**: judging other cultures by the standards of one's own culture rather than by the standards of that particular culture. Ethnocentric views have fueled centuries of efforts at changing "other" people in the world, sometimes in the guise of religious missionizing and sometimes in the form of secular colonial domination. Looking back to the era of European colonial expansion beginning in the fifteenth century, it is clear that exploration and conquest were intended to extract wealth from the colonies. In addition to plundering their colonies, the Europeans also imposed their culture on indigenous groups. The British poet Rudyard Kipling reflected the dominant view when he said that it was "the white man's burden" to spread British culture throughout the world. Christian missionaries played a major role in European attempts to transform non-Christian cultures into a European model. Many contemporary Western powers hold similar attitudes, making foreign policy decisions that encourage the adoption of capitalism.

The opposite of ethnocentrism is **cultural relativism,** the idea that each culture must be understood in terms of the values and beliefs of that culture and should not be judged by the standards of another culture. Cultural relativism assumes that no culture is better than any other. How does a person gain a sense of cultural relativism? Besides living with other people, ways to develop a sense of cultural relativism include traveling, especially extended periods of study abroad, taking a course such as this, eating different foods, listening to music from Appalachia or Brazil, reading novels by authors from other cultures, making friends who are "different" from you, and exploring the multicultural world on your campus. In sum, exposure to "other" ways, with a sympathetic eye and ear to appreciating differences, is the key.

Can a person ever completely avoid being ethnocentric? The answer is probably no, because we start learning about other cultures from the position of the one we know first. Even the most sensitive person who has spent a long time living within another culture still carries an original imprint of her or his native culture. As much as we might say that we think we are viewing Culture B from the inside (as if we were natives of Culture B), that is a logical impossibility because everything about Culture B—the language, dress, food habits, social organization, work habits, leadership patterns, and religion—was learned in relation to or in comparison with what we already knew about Culture A.

One way that many anthropologists have interpreted cultural relativism is what I call **absolute cultural relativism,** which says that whatever goes on in a particular culture must not be questioned or changed because no one has the right to question any behavior or idea anywhere—it would be ethnocentric to do so. The position of absolute cultural relativism can lead, however, in dangerous directions. Consider the example of the Holocaust during World War II in which millions of Jews and other minorities in much of Eastern and Western Europe were killed as part of the German Nazis' Aryan supremacy campaign. The absolute cultural relativist position becomes boxed in, logically, to saying that since the Holocaust was undertaken according to the values of the culture, outsiders have no business questioning it. Can anyone feel truly comfortable with such a position?

Critical cultural relativism offers an alternative view that poses questions about cultural practices and ideas in terms of who accepts them and why, and who they might be harming or helping. In terms of the Nazi Holocaust, a critical cultural relativist would ask, "Whose culture supported the values that killed millions of people on the grounds of racial purity?" Not the cultures of the Jews, Gypsies, and other victims. It was the culture of Aryan supremacists, who were one subgroup among many. The situation was far more complex than a simple absolute cultural relativist statement takes into account because there was not "one" culture and its values involved. Rather, it was a case of **cultural imperialism,** in which one dominant group claims supremacy over minority cultures and proceeds to change the situation in its own interests and at the expense of the minority cultures. By taking a close look at a practice or value attributed to a "culture," critical cultural relativism recognizes oppressors and victims, winners and losers, and struggles over practices and values within particular cases. Critical cultural relativism is situated within the general framework of cultural relativism in which we try to view all cultures empathetically from the inside. A growing number of cultural anthropologists seek to critique (meaning to probe underlying power interests, not just to come up with negative comments as in the general usage of the term "criticism") the behavior and values of groups from the standpoint of some set of more or less generally agreed on human rights. As prominent French anthropologist Claude Lévi-Strauss commented, "No society is perfect" (1968:385), even when considered from what that society claims as moral values. While considering the "imperfections" of any and all cultures, cultural anthropologists should examine and discuss their own biases, and then try to treat all cultures equally. This means looking equally critically at all cultures—their own and those of "others."

Valuing and Sustaining Diversity

As a whole, anthropologists value and are committed to cultural diversity just as environmentalists value and are committed to biological diversity. Cultural anthropologists regret the decline and extinction of different cultures. Anthropologists contribute to the preservation of cultural diversity by describing cultures as they have existed, as they now exist, and as they change. Many have become activists in the area of cultural survival. Since 1972, an organization named Cultural Survival has been working with indigenous people and ethnic minorities to deal as equals in their interactions with industrial society. As printed on the inside cover of their publication, *Cultural Survival Quarterly* (1998), Cultural Survival's guiding principle is:

> We insist that cultural differences are inherent in humanity; protecting this human diversity enriches our common earth. Yet in the name of development and progress, native peoples lose their land, their natural resources, and control over their lives. The consequences often are disease, destitution, and despair—and war and environmental damage for us all. The destruction is not inevitable.

To that end, Cultural Survival sponsors programs to assist indigenous peoples and ethnic minorities to help themselves in protecting and managing natural resources, claiming and reclaiming land rights, and diversifying their means of livelihood.

Contemporary Debates in Cultural Anthropology

Within the rich variety of cultural anthropology, enduring theoretical debates both divide the discipline and provide threads that give it coherence. In spite of disagreements, cultural anthropologists form a loosely united group because, at least, they tend to agree about the issues worth arguing about. Three important contemporary debates are explained briefly here and will resurface throughout the book. Each is concerned with cultural anthropology's basic interest in understanding the reasons why people behave and think the way they do.

Biological Determinism versus Cultural Constructionism

Biological determinism gives priority to such biological features as people's genes and hormones in explaining human behavior and ideas. Thus, biological determinists search for the gene or hormone that might lead to certain forms of behavior such as homicide or alcoholism. They also examine cultural practices in terms of how they contribute to the "reproductive success of the species," or how they contribute to the gene pool of subsequent generations through promoting the numbers of surviving offspring produced in a particular population. Behaviors and ideas that have reproductive advantages logically are more likely than others to be passed on to future generations. Biological determinists, for example, have provided an explanation for why human males apparently have "better" spatial skills than females. They say that these differences are the result of evolutionary selection because males with "better" spatial skills would have an advantage in securing both food and mates. Males with "better" spatial skills impregnate more females and have more offspring with "better" spatial skills. **Cultural constructionism,** in contrast, is a position that says that human behavior and ideas are best explained as products of culturally shaped learning. In terms of the example of "better" male spatial skills, cultural constructionists would provide evidence that such skills are passed on culturally through learning, not genes. They would say that parents socialize their sons and daughters differently in spatial skills and that boys are more likely to gain greater spatial skills through learning than girls, in general. Anthropologists who favor cultural construction and learning as an explanation for behaviors such as homicide and alcoholism also point to the role of childhood experiences and family roles as being more important than genes or hormones.

Emics versus Etics

This distinction is a philosophical issue that is unique to cultural anthropology. The term **emic** (pronounced like the last two syllables of "phonemic") refers to what insiders do and perceive about their culture. It includes their perceptions of reality and their explanations for why they do what they do. One goal of cultural anthropology fieldwork is to gain as much knowledge of emics as possible. **Etics** (pronounced like the last two syllables of "phonetics") refers to the analytical framework and tools used by outsiders in searching for patterns and regularities of the insider's culture.

A philosophically interesting question arises about whether a truly emic ethnographic representation of a culture can be provided by anyone—either insider or outsider—because the very concept of ethnography is etic. Ethnography, even of the most descriptive kind, necessarily involves the abstraction of selected aspects of a culture. Even when an insider (or native) of a culture writes an ethnography about it, etic categories are likely to appear, such as "kinship" or "social inequality." No pure etic exists, either. A cultural anthropologist's etic framework logically is part of that particular person's emic world. Nevertheless, these two terms stand as distinct approaches to understanding what people do and think, and why.

Interpretivism is the leading school of thought in cultural anthropology that favors an emic approach. Interpretivism explicitly rejects etic theorizing as too externalist and controlling. Interpretivism focuses on representing people's own interpretations of their lives, their own sets of meaning about the world and themselves. For example, if Hindus in India say that they don't eat cows because cows are sacred, that is what the interpretivist writes about.

Cultural materialism, on the other hand, is the most prominent theoretical school in cultural anthropology that emphasizes the importance of etics in studying and explaining human behaviors and ideas. Cultural materialists take as basic the material features of life, such as the environment, natural resources, and ways of making a living. Infrastructure is the term that refers to these crucial material factors. **Infrastructure** largely shapes the other two domains of culture: **structure** (social organization, kinship, and political organization) and **superstructure** (ideas, values, and beliefs). Cultural materialists seek explanations for behavior and ideas by looking first and primarily at infrastructural factors. For example, a materialist explanation for a taboo restricting the eating of a particular animal first considers the possibility that such an animal plays a more important role alive, such as cows' utility in agricultural work in India.

Individual Agency versus Structurism

This debate concerns the question of how much individual will, or **agency,** has to do with why people behave and think the way they do versus the power of forces, or "structures" that are beyond individual control. Western philosophical thought gives much emphasis to the role of agency. The individual is supposed to be able to choose how to behave and think. In contrast, **structurism** emphasizes that "free choice" is an illusion since choices are structured by larger forces such as the economy, social and political organization, and ideological systems. Explaining why people are poor, unemployed, or on welfare in the United States has been approached from both positions by cultural anthropologists and others. Those who emphasize the power of individual agency in explaining behavior and ideas say that people are poor, unemployed, or on welfare because of their own choices. If they wished, they could choose to be otherwise. Structurists would say that the poor and unemployed are trapped by larger forces and are unable to escape these traps. Furthermore, they would argue that the people at the bottom of the economic ladder have, in reality, little opportunity to exercise choice.

THE CONCEPT OF CULTURE

Definitions of Culture

Culture is the core concept in cultural anthropology, so it seems likely that cultural anthropologists agree about what it is. This may have been the case in the early days of the discipline when there were far fewer anthropologists. In the 1950s, two anthropologists, Alfred Kroeber and Clyde Kluckhohn (1952), gathered 164 definitions of culture that had appeared in anthropological writings since the 1700s. Over the past two hundred years, there has been continuing tension in the use of the terms between culture as a means for attaining certain ends or goals or culture as ideas, a division that persists to the present.

The first definition was proposed by British anthropologist Edward Tylor in 1871. He said that "Culture, or civilization . . . is that complex whole which includes knowledge, belief, art, law, morals, custom, and any other capabilities and habits acquired by man as a member of society" (Kroeber and Kluckhohn 1952:81). The phrase "that complex whole" is the most longstanding feature of this proposition. It has contributed to commitment to the perspective of **holism,** which emphasizes the importance of looking at cultures as complex systems that cannot be fully understood without attention to their different components—including economics, social organization, and ideology. Two other features of Tylor's definition have not stood the test of time. First, most anthropologists now avoid use of "man" to refer generically to all humans and instead use generic words such as "humans" and "people." While you may argue that the word "man" can be used generically according to its linguistic roots, many studies indicate that this usage can be confusing. Second, most anthropologists no longer equate culture with civilization. The term "civilization" implies a sense of "highness" versus noncivilized "lowness" and sets up an invidious distinction placing "us" (the so-called civilized nations of Europe and North America) in a superior position to "them"—the other societies.

In contemporary cultural anthropology, the theoretical positions of the interpretivists and the cultural materialists correspond to two different definitions used by leaders of each school of thought. Clifford Geertz, speaking for the interpretivists, states that culture consists of symbols, motivations, moods, and thoughts. This definition focuses on people's perceptions, thoughts, and ideas, and does not include behavior as a part of culture. Cultural materialist Marvin Harris states that "A culture is the total socially acquired life-way or life-style of a group of people. It consists of the patterned repetitive ways of thinking, feeling, and acting that are characteristic of the members of a particular society or segment of society" (1975:144). Like Tylor's definition of over one hundred years ago, Harris's definition pays attention to both behavior and ideas (beliefs). The definition of culture usde in this book follows Harris's more comprehensive approach.

Culture, as all learned and shared behavior and ideas, is found universally among human beings. Thus, it exists in a general way as something everyone has. Some anthropologists have referred to this universal concept of culture as Culture with a capital "C." Culture also exists in a more specific way because all cultures are not the same. The term **microculture,** or local culture, refers to distinct patterns of learned and shared behavior and ideas found in localized regions and among particular groups. Microcultures include ethnic groups, racial groups, genders, and age categories. **Macroculture** refers to learned and shared ways of behaving and thinking that cross local boundaries, such as a sense of national culture that some governments seek to promote to enhance unity, or the global consumer culture that pervades upper-middle and upper-class groups transnationally from Brazil to China.

Characteristics of Culture

Culture Is Adaptive

The concept of **adaptation,** which derives from the Darwinian biological evolutionary model, refers to a process of adjustment that plants and animals make to their environments that enhances their survival and their reproduction. According to Darwinian theory, the process of evolution proceeds through the selective survival of plants and organisms with the most successful patterns of adaptation, leading over time to improvements in the population. This occurs through changes, often interrelated, in human biological characteristics and human culture.

Fossil and archaeological evidence have revealed some of the changes in human physical and cultural characteristics that have occurred over the millions of years of human evolution. For instance, cranial capacity has increased, allowing for enhanced symbolic thought and communication abilities. Bipedalism, or two-footed movement, replaced walking on all fours and freed the upper arms for other activities. Such physical changes are related to cultural changes such as the evolution of verbal language that depends on certain physical formations in the larynx and certain forms of tool use that depend on having an "opposable thumb" (meaning that the thumb can touch the little finger).

Human economic systems (ways of making a living) are a primary form of cultural adaptation. The earliest forms of subsistence were most directly dependent on the physical environment. Hunting certain animals could be done only where those animals existed, for example. Many economic strategies now are independent of context. For example, a computer software specialist is able to work in a wide variety of geographical settings. However, other occupations are still environmentally limited; being a ski instructor requires the presence of snow. Besides ways of making a living and providing food and shelter, human cultures that promote certain forms of social organization, intergroup communication, and even leisure behavior are adaptive within their contexts. In many ways, culture can be viewed as humanity's most powerful strategy for survival.

Culture Is Not the Same as Nature

The relationship between nature and culture is of basic interest to cultural anthropologists in their quest to understand people's behavior and thinking. This book emphasizes the importance of culture over nature, while recognizing that in some instances, nature shapes culture. For example, biological traits that affect peoples' behavior and lifestyles are aspects of physiology, including certain diseases such as sickle-cell anemia or hemophilia, or physical disabilities such as blindness. But even in these instances, it is not easy to predict how a person possessing them in Culture A will resemble or differ from a person possessing them in Culture B.

Another way of seeing how culture diverges from nature, even though related to it, is to see how basic "natural" demands of human life are met in different ways because of culturally defined variations. The universal human functions that everyone must perform to stay alive are eating, drinking, sleeping, and eliminating. (Requirements for shelter and clothing vary, depending on the climate. Procreation is not necessary for individual survival, although it is for group survival, so it is not included in this discussion.) The natural demands mean that, if they are not met in a certain time period, a person will die. Thus, nature allows us to predict that in all cultures, people will eat, drink, sleep, and eliminate. But beyond this, we cannot predict how, when, or where these functions will be fulfilled. Nor can we say much about the meanings that they all have in various cultures without in-depth study.

Eating. Culture shapes what one eats, how one eats, and when one eats, and influences ideas about eating. The human body requires certain nutrients for survival, but they can be provided in many ways. For example, eating meat is not a necessity for survival. Many vegetarian cultures have avoided meat eating of any sort for centuries. Some cultures have taboos against eating certain kinds of meat; for example, Muslims and Jews avoid eating pork.

Preferences about what tastes good vary markedly, and many examples exist of foods that are acceptable in one culture and not in another. In China, most people think that cheese is disgusting, but in France, most people love cheese. One distinction exists between eating animals that are alive and animals that are dead. In a few cultures, consumption of live, or nearly live, creatures is considered a gourmet specialty; for example, a Philippine dish includes ready-to-be-born chicks. In many cultures where hunting and fishing are dominant ways of procuring food, people believe that the freshness of the catch is important. They consider canned meat or fish highly undesirable. Although some scientists and anthropologists have attempted to delineate universal taste categories into four basic types (sweet, sour, bitter, and salty), cross-cultural research disproves these as universals. Among the Weyéwa people of the highlands of Sumba, an island in Eastern Indonesia, categories of flavors are sour, sweet, salty, bitter, tart, bland, and pungent (Kuipers 1991).

How to eat is also an important area of food behavior. Rules about eating are one of the first things you will confront when entering another culture. Proper dining manners in India require that a person eats using only the right hand because the left hand is reserved for elimination purposes. A clean right hand (one that has been rinsed in water, preferably) is believed to be the cleanest dining implement, since silverware, plates, and glassware that have been touched by others, even though washed, are never truly pure.

Food has culturally endowed meaning. Everyday food patterns and ceremonial food use may express ethnic and religious identity, promoting in-group cohesion and setting boundaries in relation to other groups. Adhering to cultural rules about food preparation and consumption can be a defining feature of who is a "good" member of a particular group (see the Multiple Cultural Worlds box).

Drinking. The cultural elaboration of drinking is as complex as for eating. Every culture defines the appropriate substances to drink, when to drink, and with whom. French culture allows for consumption of relatively large amounts of table wine with meals. In the United States, water is commonly consumed during meals, but in India one takes water only after the meal is finished. Different categories of people drink different beverages. In cultures where alcoholic beverages are consumed, males tend to consume more than women. Coffee is the liquid of choice among "house-

Multiple Cultural Worlds

Tejano Women and Tamales

The preparation of tamales is a strong symbol of women's commitment to their families and thus of the "good wife" among Tejano migrant farm workers in the United States. The Tejanos are people of Mexican descent who live in Texas during the winter and work in Illinois during the summer (Williams 1984). Among Tejanos, tamales are the most important cultural identity marker. Wrapped in corn husks that contain a soft outer paste of flour and a rich inner mash of pig's head meat, tamales are extremely time consuming to prepare. Only women make tamales. Many women cooperate over several days in the required tasks: buying the pigs' heads, stripping the meat, cooking the mash, preparing the paste, and stuffing, wrapping, and baking or boiling the tamale itself.

Tamales symbolize and emphasize women's routine nurturance of men. Such immersion in domestic tasks might be considered oppressive by middle-class people in the United States, but most Tejano women value their role in food preparation. One elderly migrant woman, at home in Texas for Christmas, made 200 tamales with her daughters-in-law, nieces, and goddaughter. They were distributed to friends, relatives, and local taverns. The effort and expense involved were enormous, but it was worth it as a way for her to commemorate the holiday, obligate people she might need to call on later, and befriend the tavern owners so that they would watch over her male kin who drink there.

Tamales can also become statements of rebellion on the part of women. One way for a woman to express dissatisfaction with her marriage is to refuse to make tamales. Because the link between being a good wife and making tamales is so strong, such a refusal could be taken by a husband as grounds for divorce. In fact, a young migrant male sued his wife for divorce in Illinois on the grounds that she refused to cook tamales for him (in addition to the fact that she danced with other men at fiestas). The judge refused to grant a divorce on such grounds. The migrant community was outraged. The Tejano women claimed that a proper wife should cook tamales for her husband.

wives" in the United States, while martinis might be the choice for male corporate executives. The meaning of particular drinks and the style of drinking and serving them are heavily influenced by culture. If you were a guest and the host offered you water, you might think it odd. If your host then explained that it was "sparkling water from France," you might be more impressed. Social drinking, whether the beverage is coffee, beer, or vodka, creates and reinforces bonds. Beer drinking "rituals" of American college fraternities are a dramatic example. In a brief ethnographic film entitled "Salamanders" made at a university in the northeastern United States, the brothers run to various "stations" in the fraternity house, downing a beer at each (Hornbein and Hornbein 1992). One brother chugs a beer, turns with a stagger toward the next station, and then falls flat on his face and passes out (most viewers laugh when he falls). The movie also documents a drinking ritual in which both young men and women at fraternity parties swallowed live salamanders, sometimes two or three at a time, with large gulps of beer.

Sleeping. Going without sleep for an extended period would eventually lead to insanity and even death. Common sense might say that sleep is the one natural function that is not shaped by culture, because people tend to do it every twenty-four hours, everyone shuts their eyes to do it, everyone lies down to do it, and most everyone sleeps at night. But there are many cultural aspects to sleep, including the question of who sleeps with whom. Cross-cultural research reveals varying rules about where infants and children should sleep: with the mother, with both parents, or by themselves in a separate room. Among indigenous cultures of the Amazon, mothers and babies share the same hammock for many months, and breastfeeding occurs whenever the baby is hungry, not on a schedule. Culture also shapes the amount of time a person sleeps. In rural India, women sleep fewer hours than men since they have to get up earlier to start the fire for the morning meal. In fast-track, corporate America, "A-type" males sleep relatively few hours and are proud of that fact—to have slept too much is to be a wimp.

Elimination. This subject takes the discussion into more private territory, but it cannot be overlooked as it is one of the major biological functions of humans. How does culture affect the elimination process? Anyone who has traveled internationally knows that there is much to learn about elimination when you leave familiar territory. The first question is: Where to eliminate? Differences emerge in the degree to which elimination is a private act or can be done in more or less public areas. Public options include street urinals for males but not for females, as in Paris. Cultures tend to allow males to urinate in public, but not females. In most villages in India, houses do not have interior bathrooms. Instead, early in the morning, groups of women and girls leave the house and head for a certain field where they squat and chat. Men go to a different area. No one uses toilet paper; instead everyone carries in their left hand a small brass pot full of water with which they splash themselves clean. This practice has ecological advantages because it adds fertilizer to the fields and leaves no paper litter. Westerners may consider the village practice unclean, but village Indians would think that the Western system is unsanitary because paper does not clean one as well as water.

In many cultures, the products of elimination (urine and feces) are considered dirty, polluting, and disgusting. People do not try to keep such things, nor do they in any way revere them. In Papua New Guinea, in the South Pacific, people take great care to bury or otherwise hide their fecal matter. They fear that someone will find it and use it for magic against them. A negative assessment of the products of elimination is not universal, however. In some cultures, these substances are believed to have positive effects. Among Native American cultures of the Pacific Northwest, urine, especially women's urine, was believed to have medicinal and cleansing properties and was considered the "water of life" (Furst 1989). In certain death rituals, it was sprinkled over the corpse in the hope that it might rejuvenate the deceased. People stored urine in special wooden boxes for ritual use, including the first bath that a baby was given (the urine was mixed with water for this purpose).

Culture Is Based on Symbols

The making of money, creating art, or practicing religion are all based on symbols. A **symbol** represents something else. Symbols are arbitrary (bearing no necessary relationship with that which is symbolized), unpredictable, and diverse. Because symbols are arbitrary, we cannot predict how a particular culture will symbolize any particular thing. Although we might predict that people who are hungry would have an expression for hunger involving their stomach, no one could predict that in Hindi, the language of much

In India, a white sari (women's garment) symbolizes widowhood. To these women, the Western custom of a bride wearing white would seem inauspicious.

of northern India, a colloquial expression for being hungry says that "rats are jumping in my stomach." The linguistic history of this book's author—Barbara—reveals that originally, in the Greek, it referred to people who were outsiders, "barbarians," and, by extension, uncivilized and savage. On top of that, it referred to such people as "bearded." The symbolic content of the American name, Barbara, does not immediately convey a sense of beardedness in its current context because symbolic content can change over time. Through symbols, culture is shared, stored, and transmitted over time.

Culture Is Learned

Because culture is based on arbitrary symbols, it cannot be predicted or intuited, but must be learned. Cultural learning, or **enculturation,** begins from the moment of birth, if not before (some people think that an unborn baby takes in and stores information through sounds heard from the outside world). It can be unconscious or conscious. A large but unknown amount of people's cultural learning is unconscious, occurring as a normal part of life through observation. Schools, in contrast, are a formal way to learn culture. Not all cultures throughout history have had formal schooling. Instead, children learned appropriate cultural patterns through guidance from elders and observation and practice. Hearing stories and seeing performances of rituals and dramas are other longstanding forms of enculturation.

Cultures Are Integrated

To state that cultures are internally integrated is to assert the principle of holism, which says that the many domains of human life—economy, reproduction, life cycle changes, health and illness, kinship relationships and household organization, larger groups and political systems, conflict and conflict resolution, religious beliefs, communication, and expressive culture such as art, music, and dance—are all linked with each other. Thus, studying only one or two aspects of culture provides understanding so limited that it is more likely to be misleading or wrong than more comprehensively grounded approaches. Consider what would happen if a researcher were to study intertribal warfare in Papua New Guinea and focused only on the actual practice of warfare without examining other aspects of culture. A key feature of highland New Guinea culture is the exchange of pigs at political feasts. To become a political leader, a man must acquire many pigs. Pigs eat yams, which men grow, but pigs are cared for by women. This division of labor means that a man with more than one wife will be able to produce more pigs and rise politically by giving more feasts. Such feasting enhances an aspiring leader's status and makes his guests indebted to him. With more followers attracted through feasting, a leader can gather forces and wage war on neighboring villages. Success in war brings gains in territory. So far, this example pays attention mainly to economics, politics, and marriage systems. But other aspects of culture are involved, too. Supernatural powers affect the success of warfare. Painting spears and shields with particular designs helps increase their power. At feasts and marriages, body decoration, including paint, shell ornaments, and elaborate feather headdresses, is an important expression of identity and status. It should be obvious that looking at just warfare itself will yield a severely limited view of its wider cultural dimensions.

The fact of cultural integration is also relevant to applied anthropologists who are involved in suggesting certain kinds of cultural change. Attempting to introduce change in one aspect of culture without giving attention to what its effects will be in other areas is irresponsible and may even be detrimental to the survival of a culture. For example, Western missionaries and colonialists in parts of Southeast Asia banned the practice of head-hunting. This practice was embedded in many other aspects of culture, including politics, religion, and psychology (a man's sense of identity as a man sometimes depended on the taking of a head). Although stopping head-hunting might seem like a good thing to readers of this book, it had disastrous consequences for the cultures in which it had been a practice. This book will consider such controversial issues and examples.

Cultures Interact and Change

Cultures interact with and affect each other in many ways, through trade networks, telecommunications, education, migration, and tourism. Interaction and change can occur from the local level to the global, a process called **globalization.** Or, global trends can be transformed within the local context to something new, a process called **localization.** When Jamaican reggae singer Bob Marley started singing in Jamaica, he was first popular locally, in Kingston, and then on the entire island. Subsequently, his popularity expanded to the regional (Caribbean) level, and finally he gained international fame. From the international level, reggae and Bob Marley have filtered down into localities where they have been subject to reinterpretation.

The culture of dominant groups often serves as the "index culture" for other groups. Index cultures are found at all levels: a village elite, a city compared to a rural area, and global capitals, which influence cultures in the periphery. In Bolivia, many indigenous Aymara women migrate from the rural highlands to the capital city of La Paz, where they work as domestic servants for the wealthy (Gill 1993). In the city, they stop wearing their traditional dress and adopt the urban styles of skirts, hats, and haircuts. In Kathmandu, Nepal, the index culture for hairstyles among some upper-class women is Parisian (Thompson 1998). "Western culture" is an important index culture, but it is not the only one. As exported around the world, Western culture is a multicultural mix. This cultural melange is documented by travel writer Pico Iyer in his book, *Video Night in Kathmandu* (1989). He went to Bali, a "tourist paradise" tropical island in Indonesia, and reported on what he saw:

> I had come into town the previous afternoon watching video reruns of Dance Fever on the local bus. As I wandered around, looking for a place to stay, I had noted down the names of a few of the stores: the Hey Shop. The Hello Shop. Easy Rider Travel Service. T.G.I. Friday restaurant. And after checking into a modest guesthouse, where Vivaldi was pumping out of an enormous ghetto blaster, I had gone in search of a meal. I ran across a pizzeria, a sushi bar, a steak house, a Swiss restaurant, and a slew of stylish Mexican cafés. Eventually, however, I wound up at T.J., a hyper-chic fern bar, where long-legged young blondes in tropical T-shirts were sitting on wicker chairs and sipping tall cocktails. Reggae music floated through the place as a pretty waitress brought me my corn chips and salsa. (29)

Global cultural dominance, or hegemony, as a driving force of international change is influenced by the material and political interests of the powerful nations and international business corporations. The spread of American merchandise, including well-known items such as Coca Cola and Marlboro cigarettes and less well-known but economically important items such as pharmaceuticals, is part of conscious marketing. Many cultural anthropologists question the value of much of this marketing since it often does more to enhance the profits of Western businesses than to improve human health and welfare. The promotion of American cigarettes to adolescents in the United States and in developing countries, as a compensation for the declining adult market in America, is an alarming case of cultural hegemony and inhumane mercantilism. Defenders of the practice, who emphasize the power of human agency, argue that global marketing simply increases people's choices and stress that ultimately it's up to individuals to decide whether to purchase a particular item.

MULTIPLE CULTURAL WORLDS

As mentioned earlier in this chapter, numerous microcultures exist within every macroculture, and microcultures exist even within microcultures. Much of this internal cultural differentiation is structured by the factors of class, race, ethnicity, gender, age, region, and institutions. A particular individual is likely to be a member of several microcultures and may identify more or less strongly with a particular microculture. Macrocultures and microcultures are not necessarily positioned next to each other, like different pieces in a mosaic (Hannerz 1992:72–74). They may overlap or they may be related to each other hierarchically. The contrast between difference and hierarchy is important. People and groups can be considered different from each other on a particular criterion, but not unequal. For example, in the United States, people with blue or brown eyes might be recognized as different, but this difference does not entail unequal treatment or status. In other instances, such differences do become the basis for inequality.

Class

Class refers to a category based on people's economic position in society usually measured in terms of income or wealth and exhibited in terms of lifestyle. Class societies may be divided into upper, middle, and lower classes. An earlier definition of class associated with Karl Marx and Frederick Engels says that class membership is determined by people's relationship to the "mode of production," or how people make a

A view into the yard of a house of a low-income neighborhood of Kingston, Jamaica. People in these neighborhoods prefer the term "low-income" to "poor."

living. Separate classes are, for example, the working class (people who trade their labor for wages) and the landowning class (people who own land on which they or others labor). In either sense, classes are related in a hierarchical system, with certain classes dominating others (see the Multiple Cultural Worlds box). According to Marx and Engels, class struggle is inevitable as those at the top seek to maintain their position while those at the bottom seek to improve theirs. People at the bottom of the class structure may attempt to improve their class position by gaining access to resources and by adopting aspects of upper-class symbolic behavior such as speech and dress, leisure and recreation.

Class is a key basis of cultural differentiation and stratification in most contemporary states, but it is a relatively recent social development in human history. For example, in precontact tribal groups in the Amazonian region, all members had roughly equal wealth. In complex and large capitalist states, however, classes are prominent forms of cultural differentiation. Some scholars say that global systems of

Multiple Cultural Worlds

A Feast for the "Lords of Poverty"

A glaring, and ironic, class difference is apparent in the high-level consumption styles of some of the very people who are supposedly involved in helping the world's poor. Graham Hancock (1989), an investigative journalist, wrote an exposé of the inner workings of large-scale development organizations such as the World Bank, the United Nations, and the United States Agency for International Development. His point is that these agencies often do more good for themselves and their employees than they do for the world's poor. He describes activities at the annual meeting of the International Monetary Fund and the World Bank, held in Washington, DC:

Barber Conable, the former US Congressman who became President of the World Bank in 1986, was in full oratorical flow at the meeting I attended . . . he took the podium to say this:

> Our institution is mighty in resources and in experience but its labours will count for nothing if it cannot look at our world through the eyes of the most underprivileged, if we cannot share their hopes and their fears. We are here to serve their needs, to help them realise their strength, their potential, their aspirations.

The 10,000 men and women attending the conference looked extraordinarily unlikely to achieve this noble objective; when not yawning or asleep at the plenary sessions they were to be found enjoying a series of cocktail parties, lunches, afternoon teas, dinners and midnight snacks lavish enough to surfeit the greediest gourmand. The total cost of the 700 social events laid on for the delegates during that single week was estimated at $10 million. . . . Ridgewells, a well-known Washington catering company, prepared twenty-nine parties in one day alone, according to executive Jeff Ellis who added: "This year the hosts want more expensive menus, and they're inviting 30 percent more people. No one is stinting—but, then, they never have." A single formal dinner catered by Ridgewells cost $200 per person. (38–39) cultural integration now mean that indigenous tribal groups, which themselves have little internal class differentiation, have become part of a global class structure, with their position being at the bottom.

Race

Race is a pervasive, though not universal, basis for social differentiation. The term refers to bounded groups of people distinguished by selected biological traits. In South Africa, race is mainly defined on the basis of skin color, as it is in the United States. In pre-twentieth-century China, however, the basis of racial classification was body hair (Dikötter 1998). Greater amounts of body hair were associated with "barbarian" races and the lack of "civilization." Chinese writers typified male missionaries from Europe, with their beards, as "hairy barbarians." Even in the twentieth century, some Chinese anthropologists and sociologists divided humans into evolutionary stages on the basis of their body hair. One survey of humankind provided a detailed classification on the basis of types of beards, whiskers, and moustaches.

Physical features do not explain or account for behavior or ideas. Instead, the fact of being placed in a particular racial category and the status of that category in society are what explain "racial" behaviors and ideas. Rather than being a biological category, race in the anthropological view is a cultural or social category just like class. Racial differentiation has been the basis for some of the most invidious oppression and cruelty throughout history. A concept of racial purity inspired Hitler to pursue his program of exterminating Jews and others who were not of the Aryan "race." Racial apartheid in South Africa denied citizenship, security, and a decent life to all those labeled "Black." Political scientist Andrew Hacker states that race is the most important criterion of social difference in the United States. In his book, *Two Nations: Black and White, Separate, Hostile, Unequal* (1992), he writes that no one who is White in America can truly understand what it is like to be Black. He offers the following parable, asking that the White reader assume that what follows might actually happen:

The Visit

You will be visited tonight by an official you have never met. He begins by telling you that he is extremely embarrassed. The organization he represents has made a mistake, something that hardly ever happens.

According to their records, he goes on, you were to have been born black: to another set of parents, far from where you were raised.

However, the rules being what they are, this error must be rectified, and as soon as possible. So at midnight tonight, you will become black. And this will mean not simply a darker skin, but the bodily and facial features associated with African ancestry. However, inside you will be the person you always were. Your knowledge and ideas will remain intact. But outwardly you will not be recognizable to anyone you now know.

Your visitor emphasizes that being born to the wrong parents was in no way your fault. Consequently, his organization is prepared to offer you some reasonable recompense. Would you, he asks, care to name a sum of money you might consider appropriate? He adds that his group is by no means poor. It can be quite generous when the circumstances warrant, as they seem to be in your case. He finishes by saying that their records show that you are scheduled to live another fifty years—as a black man or woman in America.

How much financial recompense would you request? (31–32).

Hacker goes on to discuss the racial income gap, inequities in schooling, and crime. In all these areas, the Black population of America in general participates in a different cultural world than the better-off White population.

Ethnicity

Ethnicity refers to a sense of group affiliation based on a distinct heritage or worldview as a "people," for example, African Americans or Italian Americans of the United States, the Croats of Eastern Europe, and the Han peoples of China. This sense of identity can be vigorously expressed through political movements or more quietly stated. It can be a basis for social ranking, claimed entitlements to resources such as land or artifacts, and a perceived basis for defending or retrieving those resources. Compared to the term "race," "ethnicity" is often used as a more neutral or even positive term. But ethnicity has often been a basis for discrimination, segregation, and oppression. The "ethnic cleansing" campaigns conducted in the

Native American dancers perform at the annual Gateway Pow Wow in Brooklyn, New York.

early 1990s by the Serbs against Muslims in former Yugoslavia is an extreme case of ethnic discrimination. Expression of ethnic identity has been politically suppressed in many cultures, such as the Tibetans in China. Tibetan refugees living outside Tibet are struggling to keep their ethnic heritage alive. Among many Native American groups in the contemporary United States, a shared ethnicity is an important basis of tribal revival.

Gender

Gender refers to patterns of culturally constructed and learned behaviors and ideas attributed to males, females, or sometimes a blended or "third gender." Gender thus can be contrasted to *sex,* which uses biological markers to define categories of male and female. Sex determination relies on genital, chromosomal, and hormonal distributions and thus depends on Western science to determine who is male or female. Cultural anthropology shows that a person's biological makeup does not necessarily correspond to gender. A simple example is that in the West, people tend to associate the activity of sewing with women, but in many other areas of the world, sewing (or tailoring) is mainly men's work. The task, in other words, has nothing to do with biology. Only a few tasks are more related to biology, such as nursing babies. Cross-culturally, gender differences vary from societies in which male and female roles and worlds are largely shared, with few differences, to those in which genders are sharply differentiated. In much of rural Thailand, males and females are about the same size, their clothing is quite similar, and their agricultural tasks are complementary and often interchangeable (Potter 1977). Among the Hua of the New Guinea Highlands, extreme gender segregation exists in almost all aspects of life (Meigs 1984). The *rafuri,* or men's house, physically and symbolically separates the worlds of men and women. The men live in strict separation from the women, and they engage in rituals seeking to purge themselves of female influences and substances: nose or penis bleeding, vomiting, tongue scraping, sweating, and eye washing. Men possess the sacred flutes, which they parade though the village from time to time. If women dare to look at the flutes, however, men have the right to kill them for that transgression. Strict rules also govern the kinds of food that men and women may eat. In many cultures, the lives of gay and lesbian people are adversely affected by discrimination based on gender identity and sexual preferences. In general, Southeast Asian cultures, such as Thailand and Indonesia, are less repressive about homosexuality than Western cultures.

Age

The human life cycle, from birth to old age, takes a person through a range of cultural stages that change dramatically and for which appropriate behavior and thinking must be learned anew. Special rituals marking physical maturation, marriage, or the end of a period of learning are found in all societies, with varying degrees of elaboration. Depending on the cultural context, each life stage places a person in a new position within the culture. Age categories intersect with other categories, such as class and gender, to define a person's status in relation to other people and groups. In many African herding societies, elaborate age categories for males define their roles and status as they move from being boys with few responsibilities and little status, to young men who are warriors and live apart from the rest of the group, to finally becoming adult men who are allowed to marry, have children, and become respected elders. "The Hill," or the collective members of the United States Senate and the House of Representatives, is a highly age-graded microculture (Weatherford 1981). The Hill can be considered a gerontocracy (a group ruled by senior members) in which the older politicians dominate younger politicians in terms of amount of time for speaking and how much attention a person's words receive. It may take a junior member between ten and twenty years to be as effective and powerful as a senior member. In many cultures, adolescents are in a particularly powerless category since they are neither children, who have certain well-defined rights, nor adults. Given this "threshold" position, many adolescents behave in ways of which the larger society disapproves and defines as deviance, crime, or even psychopathology (Fabrega and Miller 1995). Youth gangs in the United States are an example of a situation in which adolescents have a marginal social position associated with signs of psychological deviance. Concerning women, cross-cultural research shows that in many preindustrial societies, middle-aged women have the highest status in their life cycle if they are married and have children (Brown 1992).

Region

Region refers to a distinct spatial area with a name and cultural characteristics that separate it from other areas. These characteristics may include the more obvious ones such as speech, dress, and food, as well as deeper patterns of social interaction, political behavior, and religious values. Environmental features often play an important role in defining the boundaries of a region, such as the Tibetan plateau of inner Asia or the Andean region of Latin America. Cultural geographer Joel Garreau (1981) divides North America into nine major regions that cross state and national boundaries. These regions are, beginning in the northeast and swinging south, then west and northwest: "Quebec" (most of northeastern Canada), "New England" (the standard area), "The Foundry" (from and including New Jersey and New York to Illinois), "Dixie" (from south of the Mason-Dixon line into part of Texas), "The Islands" (the Caribbean islands and southern Florida), "Mexamerica" (northern Mexico and the southern parts of the southwestern United States), "Breadbasket" (much of Texas and the central states of the United States), "Ecotopia" (a slim strip of the West Coast from San Francisco to southern Alaska), and "The Empty Quarter" (most of the western United States and Canada). Each of these regions, according to Garreau, is distinguished by certain microcultural features—their own "capitals," their particular economy, their social webs of power and influence, their own dialects and mannerisms, their own music, and even their own poets. Garreau points out, for example, that each regional culture has a distinct attitude toward energy, given their different endowments. "New England," he says, appropriately favors austerity and conservation because it has limited resources, a compact geography, and good public transportation. "Quebec's" hydroelectric potential is vast, and it is actively pursuing industries with heavy energy demands such as manufacturing aluminum products. The "Empty Quarter," with its relatively rich endowment of resources and vast areas to traverse, views energy conservation as supported in "Ecotopia" as a crazy idea. As with all generalizations, there are exceptions and large regional cultures contain within them alternative patterns. Their borders, furthermore, are permeable.

The study of regional cultures has been somewhat neglected by cultural anthropologists in their pursuit of holistic understanding of small, bounded communities. Two pioneers in this endeavor are William Skinner and Jack Goody. Skinner (1964) did work on how the role of markets and trade shaped regional integration in China. His work showed that people who live in seemingly isolated rural villages in fact may have far-reaching contacts. Jack Goody formulated generalizations about regional cultures of Europe, Asia, and Africa and how they compare to each other in terms of economic systems, marriage, food culture, and even the cultivation and use of flowers. His work, for example, revealed the more prominent role of women in crop production in Africa than in Europe and Asia. Regional studies may have to sacrifice local depth for comparative breadth (although they are based on in-depth local studies in generating their wider pictures), but their findings provide meaning to localized studies by placing them in a wider context.

Institutions

Institutions, or enduring group settings formed for a particular purpose, have their own characteristic microcultures. Institutions include hospitals, boarding schools and universities, and prisons. Anyone who has entered such an institution has experienced that feeling of strangeness, of not "knowing the ropes." Until you gain familiarity with the often unwritten cultural rules, you are likely to make mistakes that offend or perplex people, that fail to get you what you want and make you feel marginal, just as if you went to a land where people are speaking a language that you don't know and are doing things that you don't understand. Consider the microculture of a large urban hospital in the United States. Melvin Konner, an anthropologist who had studied among a group of indigenous hunting-gathering people of southern Africa and had taught anthropology for many years, decided to become a doctor. In his book *Becoming a Doctor* (1987), he reports on his experience in medical school, providing an anthropologist's insights about the hospital as a particular kind of cultural institution. One of his most striking conclusions is that medical students undergo training that in many ways functions to dehumanize them, numbing them to the pain and suffering that they will confront each day. Medical training involves, for example, the need to memorize massive amounts of material, sleep deprivation, and the learning of a special form of humor and vocabulary that seems crude and even cruel. Some special vocabulary items are: *boogie*—a verb meaning to move patients along quickly in a clinic or emergency room (as in "Let's boogie!"); a *dud*—a patient with no interesting findings; and a *gomer*—an acronym for Get Out of My Emergency Room, referring to an old, decrepit, hopeless patient whose care is guaranteed to be a thankless task, usually admitted from a nursing home.

Relationships of power and inequality exist within institutions and between different institutions. These relationships cross cut those of other microcultures, such as gender. Recent claims by women prisoners in the United States of rape and abuse by prison guards are an example of intrainstitutional inequality linked with gender inequality. Within and between universities, rivalries are played out in the area of competition for large research grants as well as in athletics. Within the classroom, studies document that many professors are not egalitarian in the way they call on and respond to students, depending on their gender, race, or "looks."

ANTHROPOLOGY: A DYNAMIC DISCIPLINE FOR A CHANGING WORLD

Anthropology, and its four fields, has to be a discipline that is itself adaptive and changing, because its subject matter—human life—is constantly adapting and changing. Lying somewhere between "pure" science and "pure" art, anthropology studies and seeks to understand why we all do what we do and think what we do. There is no other discipline with this goal.

SUMMARY

The discipline of anthropology comprises four interrelated fields in its attempt to understand all facets of human life from its very beginnings until the present: archaeology, physical or biological anthropology, linguistic anthropology, and cultural anthropology. Each field contributes a unique but related perspective. Each has a capability of making both theoretical and applied contributions. Cultural anthropology is mainly concerned with describing and analyzing contemporary people's learned and shared behaviors and beliefs.

Cultural anthropology has several distinctive features that set it off from the other fields of general anthropology and from other academic endeavors. It uses ethnographical and ethnological approaches, supports the view of cultural relativism, and values cultural diversity. Contemporary debates are those between biological determinism and cultural constructionism, between emics and etics, and between individual agency and structurism.

Culture is the foundational concept of the field. Some anthropologists define culture as both shared behavior and ideas, while others equate culture with ideas and downplay the role of behavior. Important characteristics of culture are that it is adaptive, related to nature but not the same as nature, based on symbols, and learned. Cultures are integrated within themselves, but interact with other cultures and thereby change.

People participate in many cultural worlds, including global macrocultures and microcultures shaped by such factors as class, race, ethnicity, gender, age, region, institutions, and more. Each of these cultures has a discernible set of behaviors and ideas that people learn over the course of their lives.

CRITICAL THINKING QUESTIONS

1. What are the differences between anthropology and other disciplines that you have studied such as history, economics, psychology, or sociology?
2. Women have an unusually high representation and visibility in primatology, especially among primatologists who have studied nonhuman primates in the wild. Can you generate any hypotheses about why this might be the case?
3. Within the microculture of your college or university campus, what are the smaller microcultures within it? What are the relationships among these smaller microcultures?
4. What is the relationship between anthropology's concept of cultural relativism and the concept of "universal human rights" about which international organizations have recently had many discussions? What might be a universal human right that would be accepted by all cultures?

KEY CONCEPTS

absolute cultural relativism, p. 12
adaptation, p. 15
agency, p. 14
biological determinism, p. 13
class, p. 20
critical cultural relativism, p. 12
cultural constructionism, p. 13
cultural imperialism, p. 12
cultural materialism, p. 14
cultural relativism, p. 12
culture, p. 4
emics, p. 13
enculturation, p. 19
ethnicity, p. 22
ethnocentrism, p. 11
ethnography, p. 9
ethnology, p. 10
etics, p. 14
gender, p. 23
globalization, p. 19
holism, p. 15
infrastructure, p. 14
institutions, p. 25
interpretivism, p. 14
localization, p. 19
macroculture, p. 15
microculture, p. 15
race, p. 22
region, p. 24
structure, p. 14
structurism, p. 14
superstructure, p. 14
symbol, p. 18

SUGGESTED READINGS

Robert Borofsky, ed. *Assessing Cultural Anthropology.* New York: McGraw-Hill, 1994. This collection includes over thirty essays by prominent cultural anthropologists representing diverse views of the discipline and its concept of culture, the value of the comparative perspective, contemporary priorities for research and theory, and the application of anthropological perspectives to world problems.

Marvin Harris, *Our Kind: Who We Are, Where We Came From and Where We Are Going.* New York: Harper Collins, 1989. This book contains 100 thought-provoking essays on topics in general anthropology's four fields, including early human evolution, tool making, Neanderthals, food preferences, sex, sexism, politics, animal sacrifice, and thoughts on the survival of humanity.

Pearl T. Robinson and Elliott P. Skinner, eds., *Transformation and Resiliency in Africa: As Seen by Afro-American Scholars.* Washington, DC: Howard University Press, 1983. Framed by an introductory essay on Black scholarship on Africa and a conclusion that looks toward the future, nine chapters explore different areas of African culture, including labor migration in Kenya, politics and government in Nigeria, religion in the Ivory Coast, religion and popular art in urban Africa, and the transformation of African music.

George W. Stocking, Jr., *The Ethnographer's Magic and Other Essays in the History of Anthropology.* Madison: University of Wisconsin Press, 1992. This book provides a detailed examination of the emergence of cultural anthropology from Tylor through Boas and Mead, with a summary chapter on major paradigms in the history of general anthropology.

Eric R. Wolf, *Europe and the People without History.* Berkeley: University of California Press, 1982. This book examines the impact since 1492 of European colonial expansion on the indigenous cultures with which they came into contact. It also traces various phases of trade relationships, including the slave trade and goods such as fur and tobacco, and the emergence of capitalism and its effects on the movement of people and goods between cultures.

CHAPTER 2

Methods in Cultural Anthropology

CHAPTER OUTLINE

FIELDWORK IN CULTURAL ANTHROPOLOGY
- The Origin of Participant Observation

BEGINNING THE FIELDWORK PROCESS
- Project Selection
- *Critical Thinking:* "Shells and Skirts in the Trobriand Islands"
- Funding the Project
- Preparing for the Field

IN THE FIELD
- Entering the Field and Site Selection
- Gaining Rapport
- *Voices:* "The Art of Fitting In"
- Exchanges and Gift Giving
- Microcultures and Fieldwork
- Culture Shock

FIELDWORK TECHNIQUES
- Participant Observation
- Asking: Interviews and Questionnaires
- Combining Watching and Asking
- Other Data-Gathering Techniques

RECORDING CULTURE
- Field Notes
- Tape Recording, Photography, Videos, and Films

DATA ANALYSIS
- Analyzing Qualitative Data
- Analyzing Quantitative Data
- Writing about Culture

ETHICS AND RESPONSIBILITY IN CULTURAL ANTHROPOLOGY
- Ethical Concerns in Perspective
- Sensitive Issues

DANGER IN THE FIELD

NEW DIRECTIONS: TOWARD PARTICIPATORY FIELDWORK

SUMMARY

CRITICAL THINKING QUESTIONS

KEY CONCEPTS

SUGGESTED READINGS

◀ During the course of winter travels with the Hare Indians, anthropologist Joel Shavishinsky holds a 25-pound lake trout. His dog team is resting behind him.

Tau, Manu'a

March 24, 1926

This will be my last bulletin from Manu'a and very probably the last from Samoa. I'll probably leave Manu'a in about three weeks. . . .

At dawn on March 8th, a boat arrived from Ofu and lured by thoughts of ethnological gain I decided to go back with the boat—a 15-foot rowboat . . . I decided it would be expensive but pleasant. So we set out in the broiling sun with a crew of some nine Samoans. The girls were desperately seasick but I rested my head on a burlap bag of canned goods, and . . . enjoyed the three-hour pull in the open sea. The swell is impressive when viewed from such a cockleshell of a boat. The Samoans chanted and shouted. . . .

The whole conduct of the *malaga* [ceremonial visiting party] was charming. My two companions were my talking chiefs, functionally speaking. They made all the speeches, accepted and dispersed gifts, prepared my meals, etc. . . . And these were merry companions. Even when they went to wash my clothes, one carried the clothes but the other carried the ukelele. . . . There were some slight difficulties. Once I killed 35 mosquitoes *inside* my net *in the morning*, and all had dined liberally. (Mead 1977:55–57)

There are many important differences between being a tourist and doing research in cultural anthropology, as this excerpt from one of Margaret Mead's letters from Samoa demonstrates. Most cultural anthropologists gather data by doing **fieldwork,** that is, going to "the field," which includes any place where people and culture are found (Robson 1993). A cornerstone method of fieldwork in cultural anthropology is **participant observation,** in which an anthropologist simultaneously lives in and studies a culture for a long period of time. Cultural anthropologists believe that learning about another culture from a distance provides a more limited and distorted understanding than participant observation offers. Researchers in many disciplines such as geology and botany also do fieldwork, but the particular fieldwork method of participant observation is a distinguishing feature of research in cultural anthropology.

Compared to the other three fields of general anthropology, cultural anthropology is most associated with participant observation as its primary technique for gathering data. Because archaeologists work mainly with artifacts from bygone cultures, they cannot truly participate in the cultures they study. Many physical anthropologists, especially primatologists, live in primate habitats for long periods of time, but the limited degree to which humans and nonhuman primates can communicate with each other constrains true participation. Linguistic anthropologists who work with contemporary populations most resemble cultural anthropologists in their use of fieldwork and participant observation. They are able to both observe and participate in the same ways that cultural anthropologists do.

In contrast to the current emphasis on participation, research in cultural anthropology one hundred years ago was not based on fieldwork and participant observation. Referred to as the "armchair approach," it involved reading reports from travelers, missionaries, and explorers and then providing an analysis. Edward Tylor (1871), who proposed the first definition of culture, was an armchair anthropologist. So was James Frazer, another famous founding figure of anthropology, who wrote *The Golden Bough* (1978 [1890]), a multivolume collection of myths, rituals, and symbols from around the world compiled from reading other people's reports. In the second stage of the late nineteenth and early twentieth centuries, some anthropologists moved out from their homes and libraries and traveled to foreign countries, where they spent time living near, but not with, the people they were studying. This pattern is nicknamed the "verandah approach" because typically the anthropologist would send out for "native" informants to come to the verandah for interviewing. Verandah anthropology was practiced by many anthropologists who worked for colonial governments. They lived within colonial settlements, not with the indigenous people. The third stage is the current one of fieldwork and participant observation. The field can be practically anywhere: a school, a rural community, a corporation, a clinic, an urban neighborhood, in any part of the world. In some ways, the field is equivalent to a scientist's lab. A cultural anthropologist, however, does not perform experiments, but follows a less obtrusive approach.

Once in the field, cultural anthropologists use particular **research methods** or strategies and techniques to learn about culture. Within the overall approach of participant observation, many different methods are available. The choice of methods for data gathering and the subsequent interpretation and analysis of the data depend on the anthropologist's theoretical perspective. For example, cultural materialist Marvin

Harris and interpretivist Clifford Geertz approach the study of culture differently. According to Marvin Harris, "The ultimate goal of cultural anthropology is to describe the cultures of all human societies and to explain why they differ in some respects and are similar in others" (1975:144). Harris supports the use of a **deductive research** method, which involves posing a research question or hypothesis, gathering data related to the question, and then assessing the findings in relation to the original hypothesis. Thus, fieldwork should be devoted to the collection of detailed observational and interview data in order to learn what people do as well as how people explain what they do and why they do it. Data analysis often involves interpreting the disjuncture between what people say and their actions. Because Harris is a theorizer and a seeker of explanation, he also pursues deeper causes for certain forms of behavior and ideas through cross-cultural comparison.

In contrast, for Clifford Geertz, the goal of anthropological research lies in "constructing an account of the imaginative make-up of a society" through the pursuit of detailed information on insiders' views, or cultural emics (1983:5). His primary source of information is **discourse**—people's talk, stories, and myths. People's discourse, he believes, reveals their perceptions of important themes and concepts. For Geertz, cross-cultural comparison is a waste of time, since each system of local knowledge makes sense only in itself. Attempts to find causal connections between, say, a people's economic system and their religious beliefs, is a foolish—even "megalomaniac" path. Geertz claims that those who, like Harris, attempt to formulate and test theories are erroneously following what they assume is a straight path to truth but which is only an illusion of truth. Instead, "understanding" of other people's subjective meanings comes from meandering on "detours" and "sideroads." Thus, Geertz favors a more **inductive research** approach, which avoids hypothesis formation in advance of the research and instead takes its lead from the culture being studied.

Whether an anthropologist values a more etic or emic approach or uses more deductive or inductive methods during fieldwork, all cultural anthropologists seek to know about a culture from more angles than most individuals in that culture would be likely to do. A cultural anthropologist circles around a culture, moving from person to person and context to context. The researcher sees the culture from multiple viewpoints and has the privilege, later, of sitting back from the data and analyzing how it all fits together. Most individuals, in their normal lives, do not have the opportunity of doing such intensive research and analysis of their own lives and cultures.

FIELDWORK IN CULTURAL ANTHROPOLOGY

The Origin of Participant Observation

The first lesson about the values of participant observation as a fieldwork method came from Lewis Henry Morgan, a nineteenth-century lawyer who lived in upstate New York near the Iroquois. Morgan did not do participant observation in the sense of living for a long time, say a year or two, with the people, but he did make several two-week field trips to Iroquois settlements (Tooker 1992). This experience, though brief, provided him with important insights into the lives of the Iroquois and formed the basis for his book, *The League of the Iroquois* (1851). This book helped dismantle the prevailing Euro-American perception of the Iroquois as "dangerous savages."

Bronislaw Malinowski is generally considered the "father" of participant observation because he first placed it in the center of cultural anthropology methods. Malinowski's discovery of the value of participant observation came about accidentally. An Austrian in Australia at the outbreak of World War II, he was considered an enemy of the Allied forces and was prevented from returning to Europe. With time on his hands, Malinowski decided to study the people of the Trobriand Islands in the Pacific. "For two years, he set his tent in their midst, learned their language, participated as much as he could in their daily life, expeditions, and festivals, and took everything down in his notebooks" (Sperber 1985:4). Malinowski made the crucial step of learning the local language, and therefore was able to able to dispense with interpreters. Direct communication brings the researcher much closer to the lived reality of the people being studied, as is evident in his ethnography about the Trobrianders, *Argonauts of the Western Pacific* (1961 [1922]).

In the early days of cultural anthropology (the late 1800s and early 1900s), a primary goal was to record as much as possible of a people's language, songs, rituals, and social life because many cultures were disappearing. Given the belief that small, localized cultures could be studied in their totality, early cultural anthropologists focused on gaining a holistic view of a single group. Today, few isolated cultures remain to be studied. The integration of most cultures into wider economic and political spheres has prompted new research topics and revised methods of study. Most cultural anthropologists retain some commitment to holism, but they are casting their research projects in ways that are both more locally selective—focusing on a topic such as marriage or health—and more globally expansive to take into account the effects of wider systems on local culture.

Three examples of contemporary ethnographies demonstrate the simultaneous attention to local patterns and wider cultural links. Dan Rabinowitz conducted fieldwork in Galilee on Israeli–Palestinian relations for his book, *Overlooking Nazareth: The Ethnography of Exclusion in Galilee* (1997). His research encompassed topics such as political leaders' views on Israeli nationalism, popular perceptions of ethnic tension, and the real estate market. Carolyn Sargent studied medical care and childbirth among the Bariba people of Benin, West Africa. She gathered interview data on people's traditional medical beliefs and practices and their experiences with an urban hospital's obstetrics ward that employed more Westernized medical care. In her book, *Maternity, Medicine, and Power* (1989), she interweaves attention to the clinical setting, women's beliefs about how to be a proper Bariba woman, they must not express pain during delivery, and power relationships between Westernized medicine and indigenous medicine. Jennifer Robertson focused on the local neighborhood impact of thousands of new immigrants from rural areas to a Japanese city where she did her fieldwork. Her book, *Native and Newcomer* (1991), involves attention to the long-term residents' perceptions of the city and their role in it, and how they reacted to the many newcomers. She studied contemporary changes in popular religious festivals as expressions of identity of both longstanding residents and newcomers and the city's leaders' attempts to create a sense of civic unity.

Jennifer Robertson celebrates the publication of *Native and Newcomer* with several administrators from Kodaira city hall. This informal gathering at a local restaurant followed a formal ceremony at the city hall where Robertson presented her book to the mayor of Kodaira, an event covered by city and regional newspapers.

BEGINNING THE FIELDWORK PROCESS

Project Selection

The first step in all cultural anthropology research is deciding on the research topic, since no one goes to the field without any idea of what they want to learn, not even researchers of the most inductive persuasion. Cultural anthropologists often find a topic to research by reviewing reports on what has been done already. Through library research, also called *secondary research,* they may find a gap that needs to be filled. For example, in the 1970s, many cultural anthropologists began to focus on women because they realized that little previous research had addressed women's lives (Miller 1993). Other topics have emerged because of historical events. The discovery of the AIDS virus and its social dimensions stimulated interest from cultural anthropologists, many working within the subfield of medical anthropology. The recent rise in the numbers of immigrants and refugees in the United States prompted studies of the adaptation of these groups of people. The fall of state socialism in

CRITICAL THINKING

Shells and Skirts in the Trobriand Islands

A lasting contribution of Malinowski's ethnography, *Argonauts of the Western Pacific* (1961 [1922]), is its detailed examination of the *kula,* a trading network linking many islands in the region in which men have longstanding partnerships with other men for the exchange of both goods such as food and highly valued necklaces and armlets. More than half a century later, Annette Weiner (1976) traveled to the Trobriand Islands to study wood carving. She settled in a village less than a mile from where Malinowski had done much of his research and began making startling observations: "On my first day in the village, I saw women performing a mortuary [death] ceremony in which they distributed thousands of bundles of strips of dried banana leaves and hundreds of beautifully decorated fibrous skirts. Bundles of banana leaves and skirts are objects of female wealth with explicit economic value" (xvii).

She decided to investigate women's activities and exchange patterns. Weiner discovered a world of production, exchange, social networks, and influence that existed among women, but that Malinowski and other earlier (male) observers had overlooked. Men, as Malinowski described, exchange shells, yams, and pigs. Women, as Weiner discovered, exchange bundles of leaves and intricately made skirts. Power and prestige derive from both. Reading Malinowski alone informs us about the dramatic and exciting world of men's status systems. But that is only half the picture. Reading *Women of Value, Men of Renown* (1976) provides an account of the linkages between domains of male and female power and value. Weiner shows how understanding of one domain requires understanding of the other.

Critical Thinking Questions

- How did Malinowski miss the importance of women's exchange patterns?
- Do the findings of Annette Weiner simply provide another one-sided view?
- What unexplored areas of Trobriand life might still exist to be studied by the next anthropologist who goes there?

Russia and Eastern Europe shifted attention to that region. Conflicts in Ireland, Rwanda, former Yugoslavia, and other places have spurred cultural anthropologists to ask what keeps states together and what makes them fall apart (Harris 1992). Even serendipity can lead to a research topic. Spanish anthropologist María Cátedra (1992) stumbled on an important issue during exploratory fieldwork in rural northern Spain. A suicide occurred in a hamlet in the mountains near where she was staying. She learned that the local people did not consider suicide strange. In fact, the area was characterized by a high rate of suicide. Later she went back and did long-term research on the social dynamics of suicide in this area.

"Restudies" are another way to design a research project. Decades of previous anthropological field studies provide us with a base of information. It makes sense for contemporary anthropologists to go back to a place that had been studied earlier to examine the changes that have occurred, or to look at the culture from a new angle. For her dissertation research, Annette Weiner (1976) decided to go to the Trobriand Islands, following in the footsteps of Malinowski. She was surprised at what she discovered about Trobriand women's lives, a subject Malinowski had almost entirely overlooked (see the Critical Thinking box).

Funding the Project

Private or government foundations provide research funding on a competitive basis. A research proposal is usually required for consideration by the funding source. It describes the project; explains why it is important; and provides information about how the research will be conducted, how much it will cost, and what the results will be—a book, scholarly papers, a film, or a detailed report. Several government and private funding sources exist in the United States for cultural anthropology research.

Preparing for the Field

Once the project is defined and funding secured, it is time to begin preparing for going to the field. Visas, or formal research permission from the host government, may be required and may take a long time to obtain. On the other hand, they may not be needed if the research is conducted in one's native country. The government of India, for example, is highly restrictive about research by foreigners, with "sensitive" topics such as "tribal people" or family planning being off limits. Some nations have been completely closed to anthropological research for decades and are only now relaxing their restrictions. China's restrictions against allowing American anthropologists to do research there have been lifted only in the past ten years or so, and Russia's restrictive policies have changed even more recently.

Preparation often involves buying equipment, such as a tent or special clothing. For example, Alexia Bloch had to purchase a special sleeping bag that could keep its occupant warm at temperatures below 20° Fahrenheit during her fieldwork in Siberia (1993, personal communication). Health preparations may involve having a series of shots to protect the researcher from contagious diseases such as yellow fever. For research in malaria-endemic areas, researchers are advised to start taking anti-malaria pills weeks before arrival to build up immunity. If the project is to take place in a remote area far from adequate medical care, a well-stocked medical kit is essential. Research equipment and supplies are another important aspect of preparation. Cameras, video recorders, tape recorders, and laptop computers are becoming basic field equipment, reflecting technological changes in doing fieldwork from the days of the simple notebook and pen.

If a researcher is unfamiliar with the local language, intensive language training before going into the field is a necessity. If a particular language is not taught anywhere in the anthropologist's home country, intensive language study should be started on arrival in the country where the research will be done. Even with language training in advance, cultural anthropologists often find that they need to learn the local version of the more standardized language they studied in a classroom. Many cultural anthropologists have worked with the assistance of a local interpreter.

IN THE FIELD

According to one definition, fieldwork is "The method that throws the researcher directly into the life-worlds under investigation and requires careful recording (through fieldnotes) of the problematic and routine features of the world" (Denzin 1981, quoted in Van Maanen 1988:117). Fieldwork is a lengthy social process that involves the researcher's coming to terms with an unfamiliar culture. The anthropologist attempts to learn the language of the people, live as they do, understand their lives, and be a friend. In daily life, we are continually learning culture, but fieldwork is different because it is conscious, purposive, intense, and focused.

Entering the Field and Site Selection

Once "in country," it may be necessary to secure permission to work in a particular area. Depending on the bureaucracy, this process can be more or less difficult. Nigel Barley (1983), a British anthropologist who worked among the Dowayos of Cameroon, West Africa, provides an account of his attempts to get local research clearance:

> It was broken to me gently by my hosts, with a form of bemused tolerance reserved for the innocent or dull-witted, that I could not leave town in my Peugeot 404 without sorting out the papers. At various points there would be gendarmes with nothing on their minds but the inspection of documents.... I trooped off to the *préfecture* with the required documents in my hand. Then began the most convoluted and bizarre paper-chase. I was told I would be charged a £120 registration fee.... I secured a piece of paper to take to the Finance Ministry who rejected it on the grounds that it did not have 200 francs' worth of fiscal stamps on it to pay administration costs.... Fiscal stamps, under rules spontaneously invented for that day alone, could only be purchased at the post office at the counter marked "parcels." The post office had no fiscal stamps for any sum less than 250 francs, so I attached one of these. At the Finance Ministry this was held to be improper and contrary to good administrative order. The Inspector would have to decide what to do. Alas, it was to be regretted that the Inspector was 'detained at lunch on business' but he would surely return. He did not return that day. (31)

After another day of dealing with the bureaucracy, Nigel Barley achieved his goal and drove out of town in search of the Dowayos.

The researcher may have a basic idea of the area where the fieldwork will occur—for example, a *favela* (shanty town) in Rio de Janeiro or a village in Scotland—but it is difficult to know exactly where the project will be located until after arriving. Selecting a research site depends on many factors. For example, it may be necessary to find a large village if the project involves looking at social class differences in work patterns and food consumption, or a clinic if the study concerns health care behavior. Locating a place where the people welcome the researcher and the project, which offers adequate housing, and which fits the requirements of the project may not be easy. Jennifer Robertson's (1991) selection of Kodaira as a research site in Japan for her study of urban residents and immigrants was based on a combination of good advice from a Japanese colleague, available housing, a match with her research interests, and the happy coincidence that she already knew the area:

> I spent my childhood and early teens in Kodaira [but] my personal past did not directly influence my selection of Kodaira as a fieldsite and home.... A colleague, Matsumura Mitsuo of the Institute for Areal Studies in Tokyo, suggested that the Mutashine region in central Tokyo prefecture would be an ideal locus for a historical anthropological study of village-making (*mura-zakuri*), the substance of my initial research proposal. That I wound up living in my old neighborhood in Kodaira was determined more by the availability of a suitable apartment than by a nostalgic curiosity about my childhood haunts. As it turned out, I could not have landed at a better place at a better time. (6)

Gaining Rapport

Rapport refers to the relationship between the researcher and the study population. In the early stages of research, the primary goal is to establish rapport, probably first with key leaders or decision makers in the community who may serve as gatekeepers (people who formally or informally control access to human or material resources to the group or community). Gaining rapport involves trust on the part of the study population, and their trust depends on how the researcher presents herself or himself. In many cultures, local people will have difficulty understanding why a person would come to "study" them, since they do not know about universities and research and cultural anthropology. In their attempt to understand this puzzle, they may provide their own often inaccurate explanations, based on previous experience with outsiders whose goals differed from those of cultural anthropologists, such as tax collectors, family planning promoters, and law enforcement officials.

Much has been written about the problem of how the anthropologist presents herself or himself in the field and how the local people interpret "who" the anthropologist is and why the anthropologist is there at all (see the Voices box on page 36). Stories about such role assignments can be humorous. Richard Kurin (1980) reports that in the earliest stage of his research among the Karan in the Punjab region of northwest Pakistan, the villagers thought he was a spy—from America, Russia, India, or China. After he convinced them that he was not a spy, the villagers came up with several other acceptable roles for him—first as a "teacher" of English because he was tutoring one of the village boys, then as a "doctor" because he was known to dispense aspirin, then as a "lawyer" who could help villagers in negotiating local disputes because he could read court orders, and, finally, as a descendant of a local clan through the similarity between his last name and that of an ancestral king! He gained acceptance in the village in all these roles, but the crowning touch, for him, was being considered a true "Karan."

Exchanges and Gift Giving

Giving gifts to local people can help the project proceed, and they are sometimes an expected part of exchange relationships in the culture. Gifts should be culturally and ethically appropriate. Many cultural anthropologists working in developing countries have provided basic medical care, such as wound dressing, as a regular part of their interactions. Some have offered to teach in a local school part time. Others have helped support individuals in obtaining a higher education degree outside their homelands.

Learning the local rules of exchange is important, including what constitutes an appropriate or inappropriate gift, how to deliver the gift (timing, in private or public, wrapped or unwrapped), and how to behave as a gift giver (for example, should one be

VOICES

"The Art of Fitting In" by Philippe Bourgois

In my first months on the block, though, I was not debating complex theoretical points.... I was primarily concerned with how to persuade Primo, the manager of the crack house on my block—known as the Game Room—that I was not an undercover police officer. I remember vividly the night I first went to the Game Room. My neighbor Carmen—a thirty-nine-year-old grandmother who I had watched over the past three months become addicted to crack and transform herself into a ninety-nine pound harpie... —brought me over to the manager of the Game Room and told him in Spanish, "Primo, let me introduce you to my neighbor, Felipe...." Staring out into the street, he asked Carmen in English, loud enough for me to hear, "What precinct did you pick him up at?" I hurriedly mumbled an embarrassed protest about not being "an undercover" and about wanting to write a book.... I had the good sense not to impose myself, however, and instead slunk into the background after buying a round of beers. Even in my largesse, I managed to prolong the awkwardness by purchasing the wrong kind of beer—an unstreetwise brand whose taste Primo did not like....

Despite my inauspicious first evening, it took less than two weeks for Primo to warm up to my presence.... It was not until two years later at 2 a.m. in the stairwell of Primo's mother's high-rise project... that they told me what their first impressions of me at the Game Room had been:

> When I first met you, Felipe, I was wondering who the hell you were, but you sounded interesting so, of course ... *te recibi como amigo, con respeto* [I welcomed you as a friend, with respect].

Source: Bourgois 1995:39–43.

modest and emphasize the smallness of the gift?). Matthews Hamabata (1990) reports on his experiences with the complex forms of gift giving in Japan during his study of Japanese business families. One of his primary contacts in the field was Mrs. Itoo:

> My first serious encounter with gift exchanges involved Mrs. Itoo.
>
> By February 1980, I had developed a close relationship with Mrs. Itoo and her only daughter, Sanae. We had been meeting frequently to discuss the prospect of an American college education for Sanae, and in fact, I had helped Sanae with her applications to Princeton, Columbia, Stanford, and other universities. By mid-February all of the applications had been completed, and the three of us gathered to celebrate and talk about what college life in the United States would be like for Sanae. Mrs. Itoo's extravagant tastes dictated that we meet at one of the small but very expensive bistros that dot Roppongi.... This particular evening was not different from the others: interesting food and conversation. Just as we were about to part company, Mrs. Itoo handed me a small, carefully wrapped box and a card, saying that she was embarrassed at presenting me with something so inadequate in return for all the help I had given Sanae. "It's nothing," she claimed in English.
>
> On the subway ride home, I discovered that I had received a Valentine's Day card and a box of chocolates. It was a small present, but I was touched.... I opened the box at home with the intention of sharing the chocolates with my roommate, and out fell 50,000 yen (then about $250).... I was, at once, shocked, insulted, and hurt. "Who do the Itoos think they are? They can't buy me or my services!" (21–22)

After his anger subsided, he consulted another American anthropologist working in Japan and his Japanese informants. The anthropologist suggested he simply return the money. The Japanese asked him very specific questions about his relationship with the Itoos and how the presentation had been made. Their final judgment was that returning the money would be an insult to the Itoos. Their gift implied the wish to have a longstanding relationship. In order to maintain the relationship, but in a less dependent position, Hamabata carefully calculated, with advice, that an appropriate return gift would be one that would leave him ahead by 25,000 yen. The culturally appropriate goal was for him not to balance the relationship but to modify it.

Microcultures and Fieldwork

An anthropologist's class, race, gender, and age all affect how he or she will be interpreted by local people. It is clear from Bourgois's commentary in the Voices box on page 36 that race was a dominant factor in people's initial response to him. An anthropologist who is a young, unmarried female studying childrearing practices may not be taken seriously because since she is not herself a mother, how could she possibly understand? Or, bearded males who look like "hippies" may alienate local people whose experiences with true hippies have not been positive.

Class

In most fieldwork situations, the anthropologist is generally more wealthy and powerful than the people studied. This difference is obvious to the people. They know that the anthropologist must have spent hundreds or thousands of dollars to travel to the research site. They see the expensive equipment (camera, tape recorder, video recorder, even a vehicle) and valuable trade items (stainless steel knives, cigarettes, flashlights, canned food, medicines). This class difference affects how people in the field relate to the researcher. When Ernestine Friedl (1986) and her husband did fieldwork in a Greek village, their status as "professors" influenced people's behavior. Village men would refrain from telling sexual jokes or swearing when the professor was present (213).

This pattern—of the anthropologist having more wealth and status than the people being studied—has typified cultural anthropology throughout its history. Laura Nader (1969) has urged a departure from this typical pattern. She says that some anthropologists should also "study up" by doing research among powerful people such as business elites, political leaders, and government officials. Cultural anthropologists who "study up" find themselves in research situations in which they are less wealthy and less powerful than their informants. Dorinne Kondo's (1998, in press) research on the high fashion industry of Japan placed her in touch with many members of the Japanese elite, influential people capable of taking her to court if they felt she wrote something defamatory about them. The people being studied are able to read the book or articles that the anthropologist writes. The effects of a "studying up" situation on an anthropologist's research may be that the anthropologist has to be extremely careful about what goes into the ethnography. But all anthropologists, regardless of the research context, should be respectful of their informants.

Race

For most of its history, cultural anthropology has been dominated by Euro-American White researchers who have studied "other" cultures, most often non-White and non-Euro-American. The effects of "Whiteness" on role assignments range from the anthropologist being labeled as a god or ancestor spirit to his or her being reviled as a representative of a colonialist past. While doing research in Jamaica, Tony Whitehead (1986) learned how race and status interact. For Whitehead, an African American, being essentially the same "race"—of African descent—did not automatically create solidarity between him and the African-descent residents of Haversham. The people of Haversham have a complex status system that relegated Whitehead to a position that he did not predict:

> I am a black American who grew up in the rural South to impoverished sharecropper parents. Regardless of the upward mobility I experienced when I went to Jamaica, I still perceived of myself as one of the little people.... (i.e., lower status) because of my experience as an ethnic minority in the United States.... With such a self-image in tow, I was shocked when the people of Haversham began talking to me and referring to me as a "big," "brown," "pretty-talking" man. "Big" was not a reference to my weight but to my higher social status as they perceived it, and "brown" referred not only to my skin color but also to my higher social status.... More embarrassing than bothersome were the references to how "pretty" I talked, a comment on my Standard English speech pattern.... Frequently mothers told me that their children were going to school so that they could learn to talk as pretty as I did. (214–215)

Whitehead's fieldwork was not impeded by the Jamaicans' assignment of him to a higher status role than he expected, but it did prompt him to rethink the complexities of race and status cross-culturally.

Gender

The literature on the impact of gender on fieldwork is large and growing (for example, Golde 1986; Whitehead and Conway 1986). Generally, if a female researcher is young and unmarried, she is likely to face more difficulties than a young unmarried male or

Crossing gender boundaries in anthropological fieldwork can be tricky if not impossible.

an older female, married or single, because a young, unmarried female who is on her own is often an anomaly (Warren 1988:13–15). Rules of gender segregation may dictate that a young unmarried woman should not move about freely without a male escort and her status may prevent her from attending certain events or being in some places. Gender boundaries exist cross-culturally to varying degrees, and a researcher probably can never fully overcome them. A woman researcher who studied a secretive male gay community in the United States comments:

> I was able to do fieldwork in those parts of the setting dedicated to sociability and leisure—bars, parties, family gatherings. I was not, however, able to observe in those parts of the setting dedicated to sexuality—even quasi-public settings such as homosexual bath houses. . . . Thus my portrait of the gay community is only a partial one, bounded by the social roles assigned to females within the male homosexual world. (Warren 1988:18)

Gender segregation limits male researchers from gaining access to a full a range of activities as well, especially in the domestic domain. In an unusual study, Liza Dalby (1983) lived with the geishas of Kyoto, Japan and trained to be a geisha. Through this, she learned more about the inner workings of this microculture than a man ever could.

Age

Typically, adult anthropologists are responsible for studying people in all age categories. Although some children and adolescents readily welcome the particIpation of a friendly adult in their daily lives and respond to questions openly, others are much more tentative. Margaret Mead (1986) commented that "Ideally, a three-generation family, including children highly trained to understand what they experience, would be the best way to study a culture" (321). She recognized that this ideal would not be possible or practical, and that the best a fieldworker could do was to be imaginative and flexible in order to gain rapport with members of special age categories, each of which belongs to its own microculture and each of which must be studied on its own terms. This may involve learning and using age-specific language, for the same reason that an anthropologist's rapport is improved by learning the language of a foreign culture. A team of anthropologists studying sexuality among American adolescents discovered that establishing rapport required attention to age-appropriate language:

Liza Dalby in full geisha formal dress in the person of Ichigiku.

> Rapport is destroyed if the interviewer speaks over the head of the interviewee or if the interviewer is constantly asking the child to explain his or her response. In addition, questions that use outdated slang are sometimes the focus of ridicule rather than serious thought. . . . In some cases, scientifically accurate terminology must yield to more common wording, even though the latter may be ambiguous. For example, when attempting to assess the adolescent's level of sexual activity, the precise term to use is sexual intercourse. In our experience, when asking an adolescent, especially a younger adolescent, a sensitive question such as "Have you ever had sexual intercourse?" the child spends far too much time in awe of the word "intercourse," investigating its meaning, and giggling at this clinical term. It is better for the researcher to ask simply, "Have you ever had sex?" (Weber, Miracle, and Skehan 1994:44)

Other Factors

The fieldworker's role is affected by many more factors than the characteristics listed above, including language, dress, and religion. Being the same religion as the elderly Jewish people at the Aliyah Center in California helped Barbara Myerhoff (1978) in establishing rapport in her first meeting with members of the Center. This is evident in her conversation with one old woman named Basha:

> "So, what brings you here?"
>
> "I'm from the University of Southern California. I'm looking for a place to study how older Jews live in the city."
>
> At the word *university,* she moved closer and nodded approvingly. "Are you Jewish?" she asked.
>
> "Yes, I am."
>
> "Are you married?" she persisted.
>
> "Yes."
>
> "You got children?"
>
> "Yes, two boys, four and eight," I answered.
>
> "Are you teaching them to be Jews?" (14)

Myerhoff was warmly accepted into the lives of people at the Center, and her plan for one year of research grew into a longstanding relationship. In contrast, being Jewish posed a potential problem for Diane Freedman (1986). She conducted research in Romania, a country where anti-semitism is strong. She was hesitant about telling the villagers that she was Jewish, but she was also reluctant to lie about her identity. Early in her stay, she attended the village church. The priest asked what her religion was. Upon revealing that she was Jewish, she found to her relief that this did not result in her being alienated from the community.

Culture Shock

Culture shock refers to persistent feelings of uneasiness, loneliness, and anxiety that often occur when a person has shifted from one culture to a different one. Perhaps the more "different" the two cultures are, the more severe the shock is likely to be. Culture shock happens to many cultural anthropologists, no matter how much they have tried to prepare themselves for the field. Culture shock can happen to students who study abroad, Peace Corps volunteers, or anyone who spends a significant amount of time living and participating in another culture. It can range from problems with food to the language barrier. Food differences were a major problem in adjustment for a Chinese anthropologist who came to the United States (Shu-Min 1993). American food never gave him a "full" feeling. For Martha Ward (1989), who went to an island in the Pacific named Pohnpei to study the interactions between social modernization and high blood pressure, language caused the most serious adjustment problems. She spent much time in the early stages of her research learning basic phrases and vocabulary, and she reports on the frustration she felt:

> . . . when even dogs understood more than I did. . . . The subtleties and innuendo I wanted to express (and could in English) were impossible. For months, I sweated profusely when I had to carry on a full conversation in Pohnpeian. It was no gentle perspiration, either; it was the sweat of hard, dirty work.
>
> Nonetheless, I will never forget the elation of deciphering and using relative clauses and personal pronouns. Nor will I forget the agony of stepping on a woman's toes. Instead of asking for forgiveness, I blurted out, "His canoe is blue." (14)

A psychological aspect of culture shock is the feelings of reduced "competence" as a cultural actor. At home, the anthropologist is highly competent. Everyday tasks like shopping, talking with other people, mailing a letter, or sending a fax can be done without thinking. In a new culture, the most simple task becomes difficult and one's sense of self-efficacy is undermined. In extreme cases, an anthropologist may have to abandon a project because of an inability to adapt to the fieldwork situation. For most, however, culture shock is a temporary affliction that subsides as the person becomes more familiar with the new culture.

"Reverse culture shock" can occur on returning home. Alan Beals (1980) describes his feelings on returning to San Francisco after a year of fieldwork in a village in India:

> We could not understand why people were so distant and hard to reach, or why they talked and moved so quickly. We were a little frightened at the sight of so many white faces and we could not understand why no one stared at us, brushed against us, or admired our baby.
>
> We could not understand the gabble of voices on the television set. When we could understand people, they seemed to be telling lies. The trust and warmth seemed to have gone out of life to be replaced by coldness and inhumanity. People seemed to have no contact with reality. All of the natural human processes—eating, sleeping together, quarreling, even playing—seemed to be divorced from earth and flesh. Nowhere could we hear the soft lowing of cattle or the distant piping of the shepherd boy. (119)

FIELDWORK TECHNIQUES

Fieldwork is devoted to collecting data for subsequent analysis. The main approaches to data collection, **quantitative research** and **qualitative research,** provide different kinds of data and follow different analytical routes (Bernard 1995; Hammersley 1992). Quantitative data and analysis include numerical information, counting, and the use of tables and charts in presenting results. Qualitative methods rely more on generating detailed descriptions, and they generally avoid counting or quantifying. Some researchers concentrate on quantitative data, some rely on qualitative data, and others use a blend of both. Regardless of these variations, participant observation is the basic research method through which the data are collected.

Participant Observation

Participating

Being a participant means that the researcher tries to adopt the same lifestyle as the people being studied as much as possible, living in the same kind of housing, eating similar food, wearing similar clothing, learning the language, and participating in the daily round of activities and in special events. Participation over a long period yields many benefits, and it gives the researcher time to establish rapport. The importance of long-term participation in a culture is particularly evident in Chagnon's (1992) work with the Yanomamo of the Brazilian Amazon. A second trip to the Yanomamo revealed that the people had given him wrong kinship information during his first visit. Further probing revealed that uttering the name of someone who has died is taboo and could lead to the death of the Yanomamo person who violates the taboo. Therefore, they made up silly and sometimes obscene names for dead relatives—all of which Chagnon had unwittingly recorded. Without long-term participation in several villages, Chagnon might never have learned that the early kinship data he gathered were invented. Additionally, the more time the researcher spends living a "normal" life in the field area, the more likely it is that the people being studied will also live "normal" lives. In this way, the researcher is able to overcome the **Hawthorne effect,** a phenomenon first discovered in the 1930s during a study of an industrial plant in the United States in which informants altered their behavior in ways that they thought would please the researcher.

Observing

While participating in everyday life, the researcher carefully and thoroughly observes everything that is going on: who lives with whom, who interacts with whom in public, who are leaders and followers, what work people do, how people organize themselves for different activities, and far more. The range of topics that a participant observer must pay attention to is vast. Obviously, not everything can be covered. Unstructured observations form the basis for a daily fieldnote diary in which the researcher attempts to record as much detail as possible about what has been observed. This process generates masses of qualitative data.

More formal methods of gathering quantitative observational data involve planned observations of a particular activity. One type of quantitative observational research is time allocation study, which can be an important tool for understanding people's behavior: work and leisure patterns, social interactions and group boundaries, and religious activities. This method relies on using Western time units as the basic matrix and then labeling or coding the activities that occur within certain time segments (Gross 1984). Each coding system responds to its particular context. For example, activity codes for types of "garden labor" designed for a horticultural society—burning, cutting, fencing, planting, soil preparation, weeding, and harvesting—would not be useful in a time allocation study in a retirement home. Observation may be continual, at fixed intervals (for instance, every forty-eight hours), or on a random basis.

Compared to other techniques for finding out about how people spend their time, observational methods are very time-consuming. Continuous observation limits the number of people that can be observed because it is so time-consuming. Spot observations may inadvertently miss important activities. In order to increase coverage, time allocation data can be collected by asking people to keep daily logs or diaries. Of course, self-reporting may include intentional or unintentional biases, but observations can help correct some of these.

Asking: Interviews and Questionnaires

In contrast to observing and recording events as they happen, an **interview,** or the gathering of verbal data through questions or guided conversation, is a more purposeful approach. An interview involves at least two people, the interviewer and the interviewee, and more during "group" interviews. Cultural anthropologists use varying interview styles and formats, depending on the kinds of information they seek, the amount of time they have, and their language skills. The least structured type of interview is called "open-ended." In an open-ended interview, the respondent (interviewee) takes the lead in setting the direction of the conversation, the topics to be covered, and the amount of time to be spent on a particular topic. The interviewer does not interrupt or provide prompting questions. In this way, the researcher discovers what themes are important to the respondent.

Surveys and questionnaires administered during an interview session, in contrast, are more formal since they involve structured questions. Structured questions limit the range of possible responses, for example, by asking informants to rate their positions on a particular issue as very positive, positive, negative, very negative, or "no opinion." Ideally, the researcher should have enough familiarity with the study population to be able to design a formal questionnaire or survey that makes cultural sense (Fitchen 1990). Yewoubdar Beyene (1989) dedicated time to an exploratory research phase in order to obtain background information before beginning formal interviews in her comparative study of women's reproductive experiences in Mexico and Greece:

> During this initial phase of participant observation, I obtained data on women and their roles and activities, conducting unstructured and informal interviews with persons in the communities. Unstructured interviews were conducted with key informants such as older women, traditional healers, midwives, and medical personnel in the health services and clinics that served the villagers. As the process of participant observation and informal interviewing unfolded, a series of culturally relevant categories and information was developed around the issues of the menopausal experiences of women in the villages, which became the topics for the formal interviews. (6)

Researchers who take ready-made questionnaires to the field with them should, at the minimum, ask another researcher who knows the field area to review the instrument to see if it makes cultural sense. Additional revisions of the questionnaire may be required in the field to make it more appropriate to local conditions. A pilot survey, or trial run, before proceeding with a formal survey will reveal areas that need to be changed before the final version is used and should be considered an essential step.

Psychologists and other social scientists have designed many standardized tests for use in the United States, and some cultural anthropologists have used these tests. Anthropological research on educational practices of the Old Order Amish of Pennsylvania, Ohio, and Indiana, involved a combination of methods including participant observation in the schools, unstructured interviews with teachers and students, and formal questionnaires and tests (Hostetler and Huntington 1992). The formal methods, including the "Draw-a-Man Test" and the "Myers-Briggs Type Indicator Test," were directed at learning about possible personality types. The latter test asks questions such as: "Would you rather work under someone who is (a) always kind or (b) always fair?" The answers to such questions are analyzed to reveal personality types along four dimensions: extroversion/introversion, sensing/intuition, thinking/feeling, and judgment/perception. Cultural anthropologists disagree about the relevance of such formalized tests for cross-cultural or even intracultural research.

Combining Watching and Asking

Many cultural anthropologists agree that some formal methods are useful for amassing enough data on a topic so that generalizations can be constructed. Likewise, many agree that the use of formal interviews and questionnaires should be complemented by observational data on what people actually do. The ideal is to have both self-reported and observed information. Consider this example of a study that relied on formal questionnaire data alone to examine the relationship between personal characteristics of fisher people and participation in a fishing cooperative in Newfoundland, Canada (Jentoft and Davis 1993). The researchers conducted formal interviews with a questionnaire among fifty-one members of the fishing cooperative. Questions probed such issues as whether members were willing to donate their time to cooperative projects, and what they valued most about the cooperative. On the basis of their responses, the researchers categorized the members into two basic groups: "rugged individualists" and "utilitarians." The people in the first group tended to be older and less educated than those in the latter group. According to the questionnaire responses, the rugged individualists were more willing to donate time to cooperative activities compared to the utilitarians. Since observational studies were not conducted, however, there is no way to know whether the respondents' self-reported participation in the cooperative corresponded to their actual involvement. Further research should be done to discover what these Newfoundlanders do in relation to what they say they do.

Other Data-Gathering Techniques

Besides participating, observing, and asking questions of various types, cultural anthropologists use an array of other more specific methods to gather data to fit their project goals. This section provides a sample of some of these methods. These techniques, and others, will be discussed throughout this book as they relate to particular topics.

Kinship Data

One of the oldest field methods in cultural anthropology involves collecting data on kinship, or people's beliefs about who is related to whom and how. In most cases, dependable and straightforward kinship information can be obtained through interviews. But, as Chagnon found, cultural taboos may make it difficult to obtain accurate information. Judith Okely (1993 [1984]) had a similar experience doing research on gypsies in England. A Gypsy friend warned her during her research that she "could be burned" for writing down a family history (4).

Life History

A **life history** is a qualitative, in-depth portrait of a single life experience as narrated by that person to the researcher. A life history provides the most "micro" perspective on culture possible. In the early days of life history research, the anthropologist tried to choose someone who was somehow typical or average or representative. Anthropologists differ in their views about the value of the life history as a method in cultural anthropology, however. Early in the twentieth century, Franz Boas rejected this method as too unreliable since informants might lie or exaggerate (Peacock and Holland 1993). One of his students, Paul Radin, disagreed, however. He believed that "personal reminiscences and impressions" would throw light on the "workings of the mind" (1963, orig. 1920:2). Radin's publication of the autobiography of a Winnebago Indian of Wisconsin, referred to only by his initials S.B., reveals much about how his life course was affected by involvement in the Peyote Cult that was active in Nebraska. He provides vivid descriptions of the visions and feelings he had while under the influence of the drug, peyote: "Now this is what I felt and saw. The one Earthmaker (god) is a spirit and that is what I felt and saw. All of us sitting there, we had all together one spirit or soul; at least that is what I learned. I instantly became the spirit and I was their spirit or soul. Whatever they thought of, I (immediately) knew it." (59)

Current understanding of microcultural variation throws into question the possibility of ever finding people who are representative of an entire culture. Thus, some anthropologists seek informants who occupy a particularly interesting social niche; for example, James Freeman's book, *Untouchable* (1979), provides a lengthy life history of a man belonging to India's most marginal social category. Alternatively, life histories of several people within one social category can be collected to provide a picture of both shared experiences and individual differences. James Freeman's book, *Hearts of Sorrow* (1989), is an example of this approach. It presents "cuts" from several life stories of Vietnamese refugees living in southern

California. Together, the story cuts portray both a shared sadness of the refugees about the loss of their homeland and a range of adaptive experiences of the different individuals.

The ability of informants to "present" a story of their lives varies, depending on the cultural context. An attempt to gather life histories from women on Goodenough Island of Papua New Guinea was difficult because telling one's life story is a masculine style of presentation and the women were reluctant to adopt it (Young 1983). Marjorie Shostak (1981), in contrast, found a willing and extremely expressive informant for a life story in Nisa, an indigenous woman of the Ju/wasi of the Kalahari Desert in southern Africa. Nisa's book-length story, presented in her voice, includes rich details about her childhood and several marriages.

Texts

Many cultural anthropologists, especially interpretive anthropologists, emphasize the value of collecting and analyzing texts. The category of "text" includes written or oral stories, myths, plays, sayings, speeches, jokes, and transcriptions of people's everyday conversations. In the early twentieth century, Franz Boas collected thousands of pages of texts from Native American groups of the Northwest Coast of Canada, including myths, songs, speeches, and accounts of how to perform rituals. These texts are useful records of cultures that have changed since the time of his fieldwork. Surviving tribal members have even referred to the texts to recover forgotten aspects of their culture. Texts also provide data with which linguistic and symbolic analyses can be undertaken.

Historical Sources

History is culture of the past, and it therefore has much relevance to understanding contemporary cultures. Ann Stoler (1985, 1989) is a pioneer in the anthropological use of archival resources in her study of Dutch colonialism in Java. Her research has exposed rich details about colonial strategies, the culture of the colonizers themselves, and their impact on indigenous Javanese culture. Most countries have libraries and historical archives in which written records of the past are maintained. Local official archives are rich sources of information about land ownership, agricultural production, religious practices, and political activities. National archives in London, Paris, and Amsterdam contain records of colonial contact and relations. Parish churches throughout Europe have detailed family histories. Land-holding records and family registers are a rich source of historical data in Japan and China.

Fieldwork among living people can also yield rich historical information. Several methods exist to help the anthropologist delve into the cultural past. When investigating the recent past of Native American culture in New England, William Simmons (1986) knocked on doors of houses where the mailboxes had names that seemed of possible Native American heritage. He sometimes discovered long-forgotten diaries and family memorabilia tucked away in the closets and attics of these homes. Interviewing older informants about what they remember can often reveal not only events about their earlier lives but also history that they were told by their parents and grandparents. The "anthropology of memory" is a current research topic. Anthropologists study patterns of what people remember and what they don't, how culture shapes their memories and how their memories shape their culture. Jennifer Robertson's (1991) study of people's memories of life in Kodaira before the influx of immigrants is an example of this kind of research. She relied on interview data to reconstruct people's remembered past in addition to archival data. Other sources of information on how memory is shaped exist in collections of letters, diaries, and family photograph albums.

Multiple Research Methods and Team Projects

Most cultural anthropologists use several different methods for their research, since just one would not provide all the kinds of data necessary to understand a given problem. For example, a small survey of forty households provides some breadth of coverage, but adding some life histories (of five men and five women, perhaps) provides depth. **Triangulation** is a technique that involves obtaining information on a particular topic from more than one angle or perspective (Robson 1993:290). Asking only one person something provides information from only that person's viewpoint. Asking two people about the same thing doubles the information and often reveals that perspectives differ. The researcher may then want to check other sources on the same topic, such as written records or newspaper reports for additional perspectives.

A multidisciplinary team comprising anthropologists, engineers, and agricultural experts from the United States and Sudan meet to discuss a resettlement project.

Another way of gaining a more complex and complete view is through team projects that involve cultural anthropologists and researchers from other disciplines to provide additional skills. A research project designed to assess the effects of constructing a dam on the agricultural and fishing practices of people in the Senegal River Valley, West Africa, included cultural anthropologists, hydrologists, and agronomists (Horowitz and Salem-Murdock 1993). In another project, a cultural anthropologist and a nutritionist worked together to study the effects of adopting new agricultural practices in the Amazon (Gross and Underwood 1971).

RECORDING CULTURE

Field Notes

The classic impression of anthropological research is that of the cultural anthropologist observing a ritual, with notebook and pen in hand. From the beginning of cultural anthropology, field notes have been the basic way to record observations. Field notes include daily logs, personal journals, descriptions of events, and notes about those notes. Ideally, researchers should "write up" their field notes each day. Otherwise, a backlog piles up of daily "scratch notes," or rough jottings made on a small pad or note card carried in the pocket (Sanjek 1990a:95–99). Trying to capture, in the fullest way possible, the events of a single day is a monumental task and can result in dozens of pages of handwritten or typed field notes each day. The bulk of an anthropologist's time in the field is probably spent taking scratch notes by hand. The invention of the laptop computer now allows anthropologists to enter many of these notes directly into the computer.

Tape Recording, Photography, Videos, and Films

Tape recorders are an obvious aid to fieldwork because they allow the accurate recording of much more information than taking notes by hand. However, tape recording may raise problems such as informants' suspicions about a machine that can capture their voices, and the ethical issue of maintaining anonymity of informants whose actual voices are preserved on tape. María Cátedra (1992) reports on her use of tape recording during research in rural Spain in the 1970s:

> At first the existence of the "apparatus," as they called it, was part wonder and part suspect. Many had never seen one before and were fascinated to hear their own voice, but all were worried about what I would do with the tapes. . . . I tried to solve the problem by explaining what I would do with the tapes: I would use them to record correctly what people told me, since my memory was not good enough and I could not take notes quickly enough. . . . One event helped people to accept my integrity in regard to the "apparatus." In the second *braña* [small settlement] I visited, people asked me to play back what the people of the first *braña* had told me, especially some songs sung by a group of men. At first I was going to do it, but then I instinctively refused because I did not have the first people's permission. . . . My stand was quickly known in the first *braña* and commented on with approval. (21–22)

A problem with tape recordings is that they have to be transcribed (typed up), either partially or completely.

Each hour of recorded talk takes between five to eight hours to transcribe, on average. Even more time is needed if the recording is garbled, many voices are heard at once, or complications in translation arise.

Like tape recordings, photographs, films, or videos may catch and retain more detail than scratch notes. Any researcher who has watched people doing a ritual, taken scratch notes, and then tried to reconstruct the details of the ritual later on in field notes will know how much of the sequencing and related activity is lost to memory within just a few hours. Reviewing photographs or a video recording of the ritual provides a surprising amount of forgotten, or missed, material. But there is a trade-off. Using a camera or video recorder precludes taking notes simultaneously. Since field notes are invaluable, even if the video is also available, it is best to use a team approach. Kirsten Hastrup (1992) provides an insightful description of her use of photography—and its limitations—in recording the annual ram exhibition in Iceland that celebrates the successful herding in of the sheep from mountain pastures. This event is exclusively for males, but Hastrup was allowed to attend:

> There were no women present but plenty of men and a mass of huge rams. The smell was intense, the light somewhat dim and the room full of indiscernible sounds from some 120 rams and about 40 men. A committee went from one ram to the next noting their impressions of the animal, in terms of its general beauty, the size of the horns and so forth. Measurements were made all over but the decisive measure (made by hand) was the size and weight of the ram's testicles. The air was loaded with sex and I realized that the exhibition was literally and metaphorically a competition of sexual potence. . . . I heard endless sexual jokes and very private remarks. The bursts of laughter followed by side-glances at me conveyed an implicit question of whether I understood what was going on. I did. (9)

Hastrup took many photographs. After they were developed, she was struck by how flat they were and how little of the totality of the event they conveyed. Photographs and films, just like field notes and other forms of recorded culture, provide only partial images of a cultural event. Furthermore, photographs and videos are no more objective than any other form of recorded culture since it is the researcher who selects what the camera will capture.

DATA ANALYSIS

During the research process, a vast amount of data in many forms is collected. The question is how to put these data into some presentable form. In data analysis, as with research, two basic varieties exist: qualitative (prose-based description) and quantitative (numeric) data. Often, researchers analyze qualitative data in qualitative terms, as described below. Similarly, quantitative data lends itself to quantitative analysis. But matters are never this straightforward. Qualitative data are often rendered in quantitative terms, and reporting on quantitative results necessarily requires descriptive prose to accompany graphs, charts, and computations.

Analyzing Qualitative Data

Qualitative data include descriptive field notes, informants' narratives, myths and stories, and songs and sagas. Relatively few set guidelines exist for undertaking a qualitative analysis of qualitative data. One general procedure of qualitative analysis is to search for themes, or regularities, in the data. This approach involves exploring the data, or "playing" with the data, either "by hand" or with the use of computer. Jennifer Robertson's analysis of her Kodaira data was inspired by writer Gertrude Stein's approach to writing "portraits" of individuals, such as Picasso (1951). Robertson says that Stein was a superb ethnographer who was able to illuminate the "bottom nature" of her subjects and their worlds through a process that Stein referred to as "condensation." To do this, "she scrutinized her subjects until, over time, there emerged for her a repeating pattern of their words and actions. Her literary portraits . . . were condensations of her subjects' repeatings" (Robertson 1991:1). Like Stein, Robertson reflected on all that she had experienced and learned in Kodaira, beginning with the years when she lived there as a child. Emerging from all this was the dominant theme, *furusato,* which literally means "old village." References to *furusato* appear frequently in people's accounts of the past, conveying a sense of nostalgia for a more "real" past. Many qualitative anthropologists use computers to help sort for tropes (key themes). Computer scanning of data offers the ability to search vast quantities of data more quickly and perhaps accurately than the human eye. The range of software available for such data management, for example ETHNO and The Ethnograph, is expanding. Of course, the quality of the results depends on, first, careful and complete inputting of the data and, second, an intelligent coding scheme that will tell the computer what it should be scanning for in the data.

The ethnographic presentation of qualitative data relies heavily on the use of quotations of informants—their stories, explanations, and conversations. Although most ethnographies also include analytical commentary, some provide just the informants' words. Lila Abu-Lughod followed this approach in her book, *Writing Women's Worlds* (1993). She presents Bedouin women's stories and conversations within a light authorial framework that organizes the stories into thematic clusters such as marriage, production, and honor. Although she provides a rather traditional, scholarly introduction to the narratives, she offers no conclusion. In her view, a conclusion would give a false sense of authorial control over the narratives. She prefers to prompt readers to think for themselves about the meanings of the stories and what they say about Bedouin life.

Some anthropologists question the value of interpretive analyses on the ground that they lack verifiability or reliability: Too much depends on the individual selection process of the anthropologist, and too much is built around too few cases. Qualitative anthropologists would respond that verifiability in the scientific sense is not their goal and it is not a worthwhile goal for cultural anthropology in general. Instead, they seek to provide a plausibly attractive interpretation, an evocation, or new understanding that has detail and richness as its strengths rather than representativeness or replicability. They would criticize purely quantitative research for its lack of richness and depth of understanding even though it has the appearance of validity.

Analyzing Quantitative Data

Analysis of quantitative, or numeric data, can proceed in several directions. Some of the more sophisticated methods require knowledge of statistics, and many require the use of a computer and a software package that can perform statistical computations. In my research on low-income household budgeting patterns in Jamaica, I used computer analysis first to divide the sample households into three income groups (higher, medium, lower). I then used the computer to calculate percentages of expenditures in the three categories on individual goods and groups of goods such as food, housing, and transportation (see Table 2.1). Because the number of households I was working

Table 2.1
Mean Weekly Expenditure Shares (Percentage) in Eleven Categories by Urban and Rural Expenditure Groups, Jamaica, 1983–1984

	Urban				*Rural*			
Item	*Group 1*	*Group 2*	*Group 3*	*Total*	*Group 1*	*Group 2*	*Group 3*	*Total*
Number of Households	26	25	16	67	32	30	16	78
Food	60.5	51.6	50.1	54.7	74.1	62.3	55.7	65.8
Alcohol	0.2	0.4	1.5	0.6	0.5	1.1	1.0	0.8
Tobacco	0.8	0.9	0.9	0.9	1.1	1.7	1.2	1.4
Dry Goods	9.7	8.1	8.3	8.7	8.8	10.2	14.3	10.5
Housing	7.3	11.7	10.3	9.7	3.4	5.7	3.9	4.4
Fuel	5.4	6.0	5.0	5.6	3.7	3.9	4.1	3.9
Transportation	7.4	8.2	12.4	8.9	3.0	5.3	7.6	4.9
Health	0.3	0.6	0.7	0.5	1.5	1.4	1.7	1.5
Education	3.5	2.8	3.1	3.2	1.2	2.1	3.0	1.9
Entertainment	0.1	0.9	1.1	0.6	0.0	0.1	0.3	0.2
Other	5.2	8.3	6.9	6.8	2.1	6.0	6.9	4.6
Total*	100.4	99.5	100.3	100.2	99.4	99.8	99.7	99.9

*Totals may not add up to 100 due to rounding.

Source: Miller 1987a.

with was relatively small (120), the analysis could have been done "by hand." However, using the computer helped the analysis proceed more quickly and more accurately.

Writing about Culture

Ethnography, or writing about culture, is one of the main projects of cultural anthropology. Ethnographies have been categorized into several different types; two of the most distinct categories can be called "realist" ethnographies and "reflexive" ethnographies (Van Maanen 1988). Both types of ethnographic writing involve truths or insights about culture, and both are valid presentations of something about culture by someone from another culture who is participating in the culture being described. In realist ethnographies, authors include less material about themselves directly in the text. In a realist ethnography, a single author typically narrates the findings in a dispassionate, third-person voice. The ethnography includes attention to the behavior of members of the culture, theoretical coverage of certain features of the culture, and usually a brief account of why the work was undertaken. The result is a description and explanation of certain cultural practices. Realist ethnographies appear to be a more scientific approach and attempt to present findings that more than one person would be able to discover about another culture. Most early works by such anthropologists as Malinowski, Mead, and Radcliffe-Brown are in the category of realist ethnographies, and realist ethnographies are still the predominant form of ethnography. For example, Katherine Verdery's study of economic and political change in Romania, *What Was Socialism, and What Comes Next?* (1996), is a realist ethnography. In this book she presents both description and analysis about how Romanian socialism operated politically and economically and how its effects are now being felt in terms of Romanian nationalism and nationalist sentiments in the post-socialist era. A clear argument threads through the descriptive material: Verdery says that socialism did not cause the current conflicts and sentiments about Romanian nationhood, but it did contribute to them by perpetuating and intensifying them.

In contrast, the goal of reflexive ethnographies is to explore the research experience itself, a goal that outweighs interest in generating or presenting wider theoretical arguments and analysis: "The story itself ... is a representational means of cracking open the culture and the fieldworker's way of knowing it" (Van Maanen 1988:103). Reflexive ethnographies are distinguished by the degree to which the authors include their fieldwork experience as an important part of the ethnography. They "attempt to explicitly demystify fieldwork or participant-observation by showing how the technique is practiced in the field.... Stories of infiltration, fables of fieldwork rapport, minimelodramas of hardships endured (and overcome), and accounts of what fieldwork did to the fieldworker are prominent features" (Van Maanen 1988:73). They are thus characterized by highly personalized styles and findings. In contrast to realist ethnographies, reflexive ethnographers frequently use the word "I" in their writings. Reflexive ethnographers offer more poetically insightful perspectives that might not be perceived or grasped by anyone except the particular anthropologist involved. An example in this category is Vincent Crapanzano's (1980) classic study, *Tuhami* (1980), which explores the life history of a Moroccan man who believed he was possessed by spirits. Crapanzano interweaves the effects of his own presence and perspectives into an understanding of how ethnography is an iterative process. Crapanzano explains, "As Tuhami's interlocutor, I became an active participant in his life history.... Not only did my presence, and my questions, prepare him for the text he was to produce, but they produced what I read as a change of consciousness in him. They produced a change of consciousness in me, too" (11).

ETHICS AND RESPONSIBILITY IN CULTURAL ANTHROPOLOGY

Ethical Concerns in Perspective

Anthropology was one of the first disciplines to devise and adopt a code of ethics. Two major events in the 1950s and 1960s led cultural anthropologists to reconsider their role in research in relation to both the sponsors (or funders) of their research and the people whom they were studying. The first was the infamous "Project Camelot" of the 1950s. Project Camelot was a plan of the United States government to influence political leadership and stability in South America (I. Horowitz 1967). To further this goal, the United States government employed several anthropologists, who were to gather detailed information on political events and leaders in particular countries without revealing their purpose, and then report back to their sponsor (the United States government) about their findings. It is still unclear whether the anthropologists involved were completely informed about the purposes to which their data would be put.

The second major event was the Vietnam War (or the American War, as it is called in Vietnam). This brought to the forefront conflicts about government interests in ethnographic information, the role of the anthropologist, and the protection of the people studied. Two bitterly opposed positions emerged within anthropology. On one side was the view that all Americans as citizens should support the American military effort in Vietnam and that anthropologists possessing information that could help subvert communism should provide that information to the United States government. The conflicting position stated that the anthropologist's responsibility is first and always to protect the people being studied, and this responsibility takes priority over politics. Anthropologists in this position tended to oppose the United States's participation in the war and to see the people of South Vietnam as victims of Western neocolonialist interests. They revealed cases in which anthropological research about local leadership patterns and political affiliations had been turned over to the United States government and resulted in military actions against those people. This period was the most divisive in the history of anthropology.

In 1970, a standard code of ethics was adopted by the American Anthropological Association (AAA). This code states that the anthropologist's primary responsibility is to ensure the safety of the people being studied. It implies that individuals wishing to help their government during wartime by providing sensitive information on people that could result in the people's deaths should not work in the role of an anthropologist. A related principle is that cultural anthropology does not condone covert or "undercover" research. The people being studied should be informed that they are being studied and the purposes for which they are being studied. Long a practice in biomedical research, the principle of **informed consent** requires that the researcher fully inform the research participants of the intent, scope, and possible effects of the study and seek their consent to be in the study. Anthropology is beginning to pay attention to the issue of informed consent and how it can be made applicable to the varied contexts in which cultural anthropologists work (Fluehr-Lobban 1994). Many anthropologists say that the nature of anthropological research often makes it difficult to apply the strict standards of informed consent that are used in medical settings. For example, people in nonliterate societies may be frightened by being asked to sign a typed document of consent that they cannot read. Given that the intent of informed consent is a good one—people should be aware of the purpose and scope and possible effects of a study involving them—each anthropologist should consider some way to achieve this goal. Holding a "town meeting" with all community members present and explaining the research project is one approach.

In presenting the results of one's research, whether in a book or a film, all efforts should be made to protect the anonymity of the people in the study unless they give permission for their identities to be revealed. The usual practice in writing ethnographies has been to change the name of the specific group, area, or village, blur the location, and use made-up names for individuals mentioned.

Sensitive Issues

Some topics are more sensitive than others, and some topics are sensitive to some groups and not others (Lee and Renzetti 1993). Governments may decree that certain subjects are simply off limits for research by foreigners. Strictly speaking, an anthropologist should abide by the AAA code of ethics guideline stating that rulings of host governments are to be respected. Sometimes, such rules can be highly restrictive. For example, the Indian government allows no foreigners to visit the Nicobar Islands, and it has strict regulations that limit how long foreigners—tourists or anthropologists—can spend in the Andamans (only thirty days as of 1997). Foreigners arriving in Port Blair, capital city of the Andamans, have to register with the police. If they attempt to stay longer than thirty days, a member of the police department will track them down and make sure they get on a boat or plane immediately. Foreigners can visit only a small number of areas outside Port Blair, and they have to fill out special registration forms when entering these areas. Major factors influencing the extreme sensitivity of the Indian government about foreigners in the Andaman and Nicobar Islands include the islands' strategic location near Burma and Indonesia and the need to protect the indigenous peoples from unwanted contact.

Sexual behavior is another important example of a potentially sensitive research issue, more from the point of view of informants than host governments. Sexual practices and ideas cannot be researched in depth without excellent rapport. In most cultures, homosexuality is even more difficult to research than heterosexuality because it is likely to be more taboo in terms of mainstream norms or even laws. Richard Parker (1991) gained access to the culture of both homosexuals and heterosexuals in Brazil, although that was not the original intention of his research (it was to look at historical and political aspects of Carnival). His research on Carnival led him straight to its pervasive sexual symbolism, and his contacts and interviews about Carnival set him on the wider path of researching Brazil's sexual culture in general. Parker found that once he had gained people's trust, "informants often seemed to take a certain pleasure in being part of a project which seemed to break the rules of proper decorum . . . that while they often resisted, understandably, speaking too directly about their own sexual lives, they seemed to enjoy (and, at times, to take a positive delight in) the opportunity to speak freely about the question of sex more generally" (177). His interviewing skills and rapport with his informants are evident in the rich data that he collected on such taboo topics as masturbation, oral sex, and anal sex. Beyond such ethnographic details, however, Parker's conversations with informants involved him in engaging them in interpreting and analyzing their behavior in terms of key symbols and deeper meanings. The sheer sensitivity of a topic does not always imply that it is beyond the scope of a sensitive researcher!

DANGER IN THE FIELD

Fieldwork can involve serious physical and psychological risks to the researcher and to members of his or her family if they are also in the field. A pervasive value on "the anthropologist as hero" has muffled, to a large degree, both the physical dangers and psychological risks of fieldwork. Dangers from the physical environment can be fatal. The slippery paths of the highlands of the Philippines caused the death in the early 1980s of Michelle Zimbalist Rosaldo, one of the major figures in contemporary cultural anthropology. Disease is another major risk factor. Many anthropologists have contracted contagious diseases, such as malaria and typhoid, which stay with them throughout their lives. Bernard Deacon (Gardener 1984), a young British anthropologist who went to Malekula, a South Pacific island, was a victim of tropical disease. His memoir, composed of letters he wrote from the field and published after his death by the woman he would have married on his return, records his observations of the prevalence of disease among the Malekulans:

> I am terribly overstrained, my work here seems all to be going to bits. There seems nothing here but Death—a man was dead in the village this morning of dysentery. . . . In one village of 20, 9 died in one week. . . . It's not like death in war or crisis—it is the final death, the death of a people, a race, and they know it more clearly than we do. . . . Spanish influenza has wiped out whole villages in Santo, Pentecost & Malekula, one might say districts. As for work, I despair & despair again. (34–35)

A few days before he was to leave the field, Deacon caught blackwater fever, which caused his death at the age of twenty-four.

Social violence in the field figures prominently in some recent ethnographic research experiences. During the five years that Philippe Bourgois lived in East Harlem, he witnessed a shooting outside his window, a bombing and machine-gunning of a numbers joint, a shoot-out and police car chase in front the pizza parlor where he was eating, the aftermath of a firebombing of a heroin house, a dozen serious fights, and "almost daily exposure to broken-down human beings, some of them in fits of crack-induced paranoia, some suffering from delirium tremens, and others in unidentifiable pathological fits of screaming and shouting insults to all around them" (1991:32). He was rough-handled by the police several times because they could not believe that he was "just a professor" doing research, and he was mugged for the sum of $8. Bourgois's research placed in him in physical danger as well as psychological risk. Nevertheless, it also enabled him to gain understanding of oppression from the inside.

Nancy Howell conducted the first and only comprehensive study of health and hazards involved in anthropological fieldwork. She explains her motivation at the beginning of her book, *Surviving Fieldwork* (1990):

> My interest in the questions of this report started to develop more than twenty years ago, when I was a sociology student in graduate school at Harvard working with anthropologists. . . . I finished my Ph.D. in sociology and married an anthropologist, ethnographer Richard Lee, and went to the Kalahari desert as the demographer on an anthropological expedition, living for two years in one of the most remote locations in the world, working with the !Kung Bushmen [Ju/wasi].
>
> Typically of new fieldworkers, I had no training or preparation for prevention of illness or accidents. . . . Over the years, as I taught students preparing to go into the field and heard stories from anthropologists about adventures and scrapes with disaster, it had crossed my mind that someone should make a systematic study of health and safety in anthropological fieldwork. I thought of the project as learning "the costs of anthropology to anthropologists" but that project never came, naturally and gradually, to the top of my own research agenda.
>
> Instead, it came horribly into focus for me in June 1985 when my 14-year-old son, Alex Lee, was suddenly killed and my other son, David, was injured, in a truck accident in Botswana. In the months that followed that accident, many anthropological friends and acquaintances offered information on similar and different fieldwork accidents. (ix)

She pointed out to the American Anthropological Association the lack of attention to fieldwork safety. The AAA responded with financial and moral support for her to undertake a detailed inquiry into regional variations, hazard types, and variations by field within anthropology. She devised a way to draw a sample of 311 anthropologists listed as employed in the AAA's Guide to Departments. She sent them a questionnaire asking about their gender, age, work status, health status, and work habits in the field, and asked them to give reports of health and other hazards they had experienced in the field. Of the 311 people in the sample, 236 completed the questionnaire. From this, she learned much about this unknown area, including such rarely discussed topics as mental health problems while in the field. One discovery, for example, is that anthropologists in all four fields have equal patterns of hazard frequency, and the same applies for men and women. Regional variations did appear, however, with Africa being the area of highest hazard rates, followed by India, Asia and the Pacific, and Latin America. She ends her study with some specific recommendations about how fieldworkers can prepare themselves more effectively for risks they may face.

NEW DIRECTIONS: TOWARD PARTICIPATORY FIELDWORK

The freedom of a cultural anthropologist to represent a culture as she or he perceives it is a power issue that is increasingly being brought into question, especially by indigenous peoples who read about themselves in Western ethnographies. The people that anthropologists have traditionally studied—the nonelites of rural India, Ireland, and Papua New Guinea—are now able to read English, French, and German. They can therefore critique what has been written about their culture. Annette Weiner (1976) learned from people in the Trobriand Islands that some Trobrianders who had read sections of *Argonauts of the Western Pacific* thought that Malinowski had not gotten things right (xvi).

One of the newest directions in cultural anthropology fieldwork is the attempt to involve the study population in actively shaping the data collection and presentation. This change reflects an interest on the part of anthropologists to refrain from treating people as "subjects" and to consider them more as collaborators in writing culture. Anthropologists also are taking more responsibility for the effects that their work may have on the cultures they study.

SUMMARY

Cultural anthropologists conduct research by doing fieldwork and using its characteristic method called participant observation. Depending on one's theoretical perspective, specific research techniques may emphasize quantitative or qualitative data gathering. Cultural materialists tend to focus on quantitative data, while interpretivists gather qualitative data.

Fieldwork and participant observation as cornerstones of cultural anthropology methods became generally accepted only after Malinowski's work in the Trobriand Islands during World War I. Since then, some basic steps in doing fieldwork have been established. They include selecting a site, gaining rapport, and dealing with culture shock. The mechanical aspects of participant observation have been improved through new recording technologies such as audio and video recorders.

Data collection, analysis and presentation are guided by the anthropologist's theoretical orientation and goals. Emphasis on quantitative or qualitative techniques of data collection shape the way the data are organized and presented; for example, they determine whether statistics and tables are used or avoided. Interpretivist anthropologists attempt to present accounts that are as emic as possible, with little presence of an outside analyst.

Anthropology developed a set of ethical guidelines for research in 1970, following two decades of concern about what role, if any, anthropologists should play in research that could conceivably harm the population being studied. The first rule of the code of ethics states that the anthropologist's primary responsibility is to maintain the safety of the people involved. Thus, anthropologists should never engage in covert research and should always endeavor to explain their purpose to the people in the study and maintain anonymity of the location and individuals.

CRITICAL THINKING QUESTIONS

1. Choose one other discipline that you have studied and sketch out its research goals and methods. How do they differ from or resemble those of cultural anthropology?
2. How honest should an anthropologist be when he or she is attempting to establish rapport in the early stages of fieldwork?
3. Does it seem more effective for a cultural anthropologist to decide to do research among people whom they are "like" or people whom they are very "different" from? Why?
4. Why is it important to have a code of ethics in anthropology?

KEY CONCEPTS

culture shock, p. 39
deductive research, p. 31
discourse, p. 31
fieldwork, p. 30
Hawthorne effect, p. 40
inductive research, p. 31
informed consent, p. 48
interview, p. 41
kinship, p. 42
life history, p. 42
participant observation, p. 30
qualitative research, p. 40
quantitative research, p. 40
rapport, p. 35
research methods, p. 30
triangulation, p. 43

SUGGESTED READINGS

H. Russell Bernard, *Research Methods in Cultural Anthropology: Qualitative and Quantitative Approaches.* 2nd edition. Newbury Park, CA: Sage Publications, 1995. This is a sourcebook of anthropological research methods—from how to design a research project to data analysis and presentation.

Peggy Golde, ed. *Women in the Field: Anthropological Experiences.* 2nd edition. Berkeley: University of California Press, 1986. This text provides fifteen chapters on fieldwork by women anthropologists including Margaret Mead's fieldwork in the Pacific, Laura Nader's fieldwork in Mexico and Lebanon, Ernestine Friedl's fieldwork in Greece, and Jean Briggs's fieldwork among the Inuit of the Canadian Arctic.

Bruce Grindal and Frank Salamone, eds. *Bridges to Humanity: Narratives on Anthropology and Friendship.* Prospect Heights, IL: Waveland Press, 1995. The fourteen chapters of this text explore the "humanistic" dimension of fieldwork, in which the anthropologist reflects on the friendships established in the field, how they contributed to the fieldwork, and how or if they can be continued once the anthropologist leaves the field.

Hortense Powdermaker, *Stranger and Friend: The Way of An Anthropologist.* London: Secker & Warburg, 1966. This is a classic report by an esteemed ethnographer about her fieldwork experiences in Mississippi, Hollywood, and Rhodesia. Powdermaker holds the view that cultural anthropology is both a science and an art.

Roger Sanjek, ed. *Fieldnotes: The Makings of Anthropology.* Ithaca: Cornell University Press. This text includes sixteen chapters by cultural anthropologists on various aspects of taking and using field notes in ethnographic research in diverse settings.

CHAPTER 3

Economies and Their Modes of Production

CHAPTER OUTLINE

CULTURAL ANTHROPOLOGY AND ECONOMIC SYSTEMS
- Modes of Production as Types
- Culture, Nature, and Modes of Production
- Today's World-Economy

FORAGING
- *Multiple Cultural Worlds:* The Inuit of Lake Colville
- Labor
- Property Relations
- Foraging as a Sustainable System
- Changing Cultural Worlds of Foragers: The Tiwi

HORTICULTURE
- Labor
- Property Relations
- Horticulture as a Sustainable System
- Changing Cultural Worlds of Horticulturalists: The Mundurucu

PASTORALISM
- Labor
- Property Relations
- Pastoralism as a Sustainable System
- *Current Event:* "Will the Nenets Survive?"
- Changing Cultural Worlds of Pastoralists: Mongolian Nomads
- *Voices:* Puravdorj Speaks about Privatization

AGRICULTURE
- Family Farming
- *Multiple Cultural Worlds:* Malay Peasant Women Lose Rights to Land
- Plantation Agriculture
- Industrial Agriculture
- The Sustainability of Agriculture
- *Critical Thinking:* Was the Invention of Agriculture a Terrible Mistake?

INDUSTRIALIZATION
- The Formal Sector
- The Informal Sector
- *Multiple Cultural Worlds:* Scavenging in Belmar
- Changing Cultural Worlds of Industrial Workers: Barberton

SUMMARY

CRITICAL THINKING QUESTIONS

KEY CONCEPTS

SUGGESTED READINGS

◀ On the island of Tonga in the South Pacific, women have the important role of basket weaving.

Everyone has to satisfy certain basic needs in order to survive. The world's cultures offer diverse opportunities for making a living: farmer, film star, shaman, scientist, geisha, herder, salesclerk, beggar, and hundreds more. How people make their living, or how they manage to survive if they are unemployed is the most basic feature of existence, according to a cultural materialist perspective. It affects a person's social position, relationships, values, and aspirations—in short, his or her overall lifestyle. The oldest way of providing food is through hunting and gathering edible substances available in nature such as berries, nuts, fish, and animals. This system is now endangered as other forms of livelihood encroach on the older patterns. Thus, different kinds of economies may conflict with each other for resources, as in Congo today where Bantu farmers look down on the pygmy forest dwellers and at the same time seek to take land from them (*The New York Times*, June 16, 1997).

CULTURAL ANTHROPOLOGY AND ECONOMIC SYSTEMS

Economics is the study of the material welfare of humankind. It comprises three major subject areas: **production** (making goods or money), **consumption** (using up goods or expending funds), and **exchange** (transferring goods or money between people or institutions). Economic anthropology, the subject of both this chapter and Chapter 4, is the subfield of cultural anthropology that deals with these topics. These three concepts are tightly interrelated; for example, a given system of production is usually associated with characteristic consumption and exchange patterns.

The term **economic system** refers to a particular way of organizing production, distribution, and consumption. The economic system of **feudalism** in medieval Europe was based on extraction of labor from the landless through the institution of the manor (Prestwich 1996). **Capitalism** emerged first in Europe in the sixteenth and seventeenth centuries, and reached its full development during the Industrial Revolution of the eighteenth century (Deane 1996). It is a mode of production oriented toward sale of goods with the goal of profit-making. Another term for capitalism is *market economics*. **Socialism** as an economic system is centered on the belief that the means of production (such as land) should be collectively owned and that market exchange should be replaced by collectively controlled distribution based on social needs (Hirst 1996).

Modes of Production as Types

Within each economic system, the **mode of production** refers to the dominant way of providing for people's material needs, such as an agricultural mode of production or an industrial mode of production. Categorizing a certain society as having a particular mode of production implies an emphasis on that type of production and does not mean that it is the only kind of production undertaken. In a given society, not everyone will necessarily be involved in the dominant mode of production. Also, a particular individual may be involved in more than one strategy; for example, a person could be both a farmer and a herder. In most cultures, however, a dominant mode of production exists that analysts use as a basis for classification. The categories sometimes blend with and overlap each other, but they are useful as broad generalizations. The modes of production are discussed in order of their historical appearance in the human record (see Figure 3.1). This continuum does not mean that a particular mode of production evolves into the one following it—for example, foragers do not necessarily transform into horticulturalists—and so on, across the continuum. Nor does this ordering imply any kind of judgment about level of sophistication or superiority of the more recent modes of production. Even the oldest system involves complex and detailed knowledge about the environment that a contemporary North American city dweller, if transported to a rain forest, would find difficult to learn as a basis for survival. Each system involves particular social arrangements in terms of tasks and sharing of goods, and each has detailed ideological structures that explain and justify why people do what they do economically. Furthermore, none of these systems of production is "frozen in time," for they have all undergone change. Archaeological research helps reveal some of these changes from the distant past, while social historians provide information on more recent changes such as the rise of industrialism in Britain in the eighteenth century.

Culture, Nature, and Modes of Production

In its most basic sense, human economic adaptation must deal with what nature has to offer in terms of

300,000 years ago ← 12,000 years ago 10,000 years ago present →

FORAGING **HORTICULTURE** **PASTORALISM** **AGRICULTURE** **INDUSTRIALISM (capitalist)**

FORAGING	INDUSTRIALISM (capitalist)
Reason for Production Production for use Consumption level: low Exchange: sharing-based	**Reason for Production** Production for profit Consumption level: high Exchange: market-based
Division of Labor Family-based Overlapping gender roles	**Division of Labor** Class-based High degree of occupational specialization
Property Relations Egalitarian and collective	**Property Relations** Stratified and private
Resource Use Extensive and temporary	**Resource Use** Intensive and expanding
Sustainability High degree	**Sustainability** Low degree

FIGURE 3.1
Modes of Production

resources and the constraints it places on satisfying human material needs. A general finding about Western society is that it has a **dualist** view that separates nature from culture and places culture in a dominant position over nature. This ideology has been said to fit with a capitalist economic strategy that requires domination and exploitation of nature by people. A major question in cultural anthropology concerns whether such dualism is a cultural universal. Do all cultures follow a clear differentiation between "culture" and "nature," as most Westerners do?

Sherry Ortner (1974) made a now-classic statement many years ago that a nature/culture distinction is universal and that culture is always more highly valued than nature. She pairs that distinction with another that is universal: male and female, with a similar higher valuation on the male than the female. The simple formula she generated says that "nature:culture:female:male" or, "nature is to culture as female is to male." Ortner asserts that females in all cultures are thought to be closer to nature because of their reproductive physiology involving childbirth and related domestic roles. Men, in contrast, are thought to be involved in "the projects of culture." Ortner explains that "in reality," women are not any closer to nature than men, but that is the model that all cultures have constructed. This is all theory, however, since she does not provide ethnographic data with which to examine her assertion.

Since the time of Ortner's theoretical proposition, many cultural anthropologists have considered the question of the universality of the nature/culture duality. Cross-cultural data indicate that many cultures do not have a binary distinction between nature and culture, they do not liken culture and nature to gender categories, and they do not place nature in a subdominant position. For example, the Hagen people of highland New Guinea divide the world into three categories: humans and human activity, spirits, and the wild (M. Strathern 1980). None of these categories match the English terms "nature" and "culture." There is no strict gender match-up with these categories since males and females can be found in all three. And there is no hierarchical relationship among the three. In another example, the Nayaka, a South Indian tribal group, conceive of the natural environment with metaphors that involve relatedness and not separateness, as in the Western model (Bird-David 1993). The Nayaka's image of relatedness is based on the intrahousehold caring relationship between an adult and a child in which nature, like a parent, gives generously to its children. In ritual and everyday discourse, these people frequently describe and address the forest as a parent, and thank it for affection, food, and other provisions. They often say that the forest gives them food and other necessities. Other tribal cultures also have relatedness metaphors concerning the natural environment, including the Cree of North America, the Western Desert Aborigines of Australia, and the Ju/wasi of southern Africa. The evidence strongly suggests that relatedness metaphors, compared to binary/hierarchical metaphors, are widely found in preindustrial cultures.

These nondualistic ideologies relate to particular ways of making a living that are precapitalist. They also seem correlated with different environmental outcomes. The Western binary distinction between culture and nature supports resource exploitation in the global competition for economic growth. The nondualistic conceptualizations of nature relatedness correspond to economies and lifestyles that demand less from the environment in terms of resources and contribute to sustainability in the long term.

Today's World-Economy

The emergence and evolution of capitalism has had far-reaching effects on all modes of production. According to social theorist Immanuel Wallerstein (1979), capitalism involves world trade in goods and global transfers of labor and resources; capitalism is a "world-economy." Competition among capitalist nations—and, since the 1950s, socialist nations as well—for markets, resources, and labor has led to ever-increasing incorporation of "peripheral" societies by the "core" societies. A third category is "semiperipheral" societies, which are either declining core societies or rising peripheral societies (Hall 1996). Core societies specialize in manufacturing, while periphery nations provide raw materials. Core societies also have strong governments and play a prominent role in the affairs of noncore societies. Periphery societies have weak governments and are heavily influenced by core societies. According to Wallerstein, this system works to the advantage of core nations and the disadvantage of periphery nations. Thus, core nations experience economic growth and become wealthy and developed, while periphery nations are trapped in poverty and dependency. This chapter will examine several modes of production that over time have been increasingly affected by the power and influence of the world-economy.

FORAGING

Foraging means searching for and collecting food that is available in nature (fruits, vegetables, nuts, animals, fish), either by gathering, fishing, or hunting. It is the oldest economic system, having existed since the appearance of *homo sapiens* at least 300,000 years ago, perhaps earlier. Other systems, discussed below, did not emerge until about 10,000 years ago. While foraging stood the test of time for millennia, it is now in danger of extinction as a "pure" form. Very few people—roughly only a quarter of a million people—support themselves predominantly from foraging. European colonialism and contemporary industrial development have drastically changed their life-ways. Foragers now are mostly located in what are considered marginal areas, such as deserts, the circumpolar region, and some dense tropical forest regions. Many people living in other types of economies use foraging as a supplement to their main strategy for obtaining food. Foraging survived as the predominant mode of production for 90 percent (or more) of human existence because it maintains a general balance between resources and lifestyle.

Foraging is no simple matter, since doing it successfully requires substantial and sophisticated knowledge of the natural environment: how to find particular roots buried deep in the ground, how to follow animal tracks and other signs, and how to judge the weather and water supply. It also relies on the use and maintenance of tools to aid in the processing of wild foods, including nutcrackers, seed-grinders, and cooking containers. Depending on the environment in which foragers live, the main activities include gathering such food as nuts, berries, roots, honey, insects, and eggs; trapping or hunting birds and animals; and fishing. Foragers do not grow food in gardens or keep domesticated animals. Their tools include digging sticks for removing roots from the ground and for penetrating the holes dug by animals in order to get the animals out, bows and arrows, spears, nets, and knives. Baskets of many types are important for carrying foodstuffs. For processing raw materials into edible food, foragers use stones to mash, grind, and pound. Meat can be dried in the sun or over fire, and fire is used for cooking either by boiling or by roasting. In sum, for foragers, obtaining and processing food requires few nonrenewable fuel sources beyond wood or other combustible substances for cooking.

Shelters require little in the way of materials. They tend to be temporary because the foraging subsistence mode necessitates that people move frequently in their search for food. Foraging is an **extensive strategy**, a mode of production involving temporary use of large areas of land and much spatial mobility. It makes little sense for people to construct elaborate and durable shelters in one place. Before they were contained in reservations and settled into agricultural contexts, the Ju/wasi of southern Africa moved several times during a year, depending on the seasonal availability of water sources. Each cluster of families would return to "their" territory, reconstructing or completely rebuilding their shelters with sticks for frames and leaf or thatch coverings. Sometimes the shelters were attached to two or three small trees or bushes for support. Among the Ju/wasi, the amount of investment of time, labor, and material in constructing shelters is modest.

In contrast to foragers of temperate climates, those of the circumpolar regions of North America, Europe, and Asia had to devote more time and energy to food procurement and providing shelter. The specialized technology of circumpolar peoples includes making spears, nets, and knives as well as building sleds and using domesticated animals to pull them. Inuit sled dogs or other animals that are used to pull sleds are an important aspect of circumpolar peoples' economic technology, just as tractors are for contemporary farmers (see the Multiple Cultural Worlds box on page 58). Considerable amounts of labor are needed to construct durable igloos or permanent log houses, which are necessary adaptations to the cold temperatures. Protective clothing, including warm coats and boots, is another feature of circumpolar economic adaptation.

Hare Indian children use their family's sled and dogs to haul drinking water to their village from Colville Lake, Northwest Territories, Canada.

Labor

Among foraging peoples, occupational specialization (assigning particular tasks to particular people) exists to varying degrees and depends mainly on gender and age. Among foraging cultures located in temperate climates, a minimal gender-based division of labor exists. Most people get the majority of their food by gathering roots, berries, grubs, small birds and animals, and fish. One difference is that, when hunting is done, men are more likely to be involved in long-range expeditions to hunt large animals. However, hunting large animals provides only a small portion of the diets of temperate-climate foragers. In contrast, hunting large animals, including seals, whales, and

Multiple Cultural Worlds

The Inuit of Colville Lake

The Colville Lake community consists of seventy-five members of the Hare Indians, a small group of Canadian Inuit (Savishinsky 1974). They survive by hunting, trapping, and fishing in one of the harshest environments in the world. Joel Savishinsky's major research interest was to analyze the experience of stress, tension, and anxiety among this isolated group and observe how they cope with it. Ecological stress factors include "extreme temperatures, long and severe winters, prolonged periods of isolation, hazardous weather and travel conditions, an often precarious food supply, and the constant need for mobility during the harshest seasons of the year" (xiv). Social and psychological stress factors also exist, including contact with White people: fur traders and missionaries.

During his research, Savishinsky made an important discovery about the importance of dogs in relation to the economy and psychological well-being:

> [L]ater in the year when I obtained my own dogteam, I enjoyed much greater freedom of movement, and was able to camp with many people whom I had previously not been able to keep up with. Altogether I travelled close to 600 miles by dogsled between mid-October and early June. This constant contact with dogs, and the necessity of learning how to drive, train and handle them, led to my recognition of the social and psychological, as well as the ecological significance of these animals in the lives of the people. (xx)

Among the fourteen households, there are a total of 224 dogs. Some households have as many as 4 teams, with an average of 6.2 dogs per team, corresponding to people's estimation that 6 dogs are required for travel. More than being only economically useful, dogs play a significant role in people's emotional lives. They are a frequent topic of conversation: "Members of the community constantly compare and comment on the care, condition, and growth of one another's animals, noting special qualities of size, strength, color, speed, and alertness" (169). Emotional displays, not generally common among the Hare, are significant between people and their dogs:

> The affectionate and concerned treatment of young animals is participated in by people of all ages, and the nature of the relationship bears a striking resemblance to the way in which people treat young children. Pups and infants are, in essence, the only recipients of unreserved positive affect in the band's social life, all other relationships being tinged with varying degrees of restraint and/or negativism. (169–170)

bears, and capturing large fish is an important part of food provision in circumpolar groups, and gender-based specialization is therefore more marked.

In the past, many anthropologists have emphasized a "Man the Hunter" model for prehistoric humans and contemporary foragers in general (for example, Lee 1979). This view takes men's hunting roles in some foraging groups and uses them as the model for all foraging groups, both now and in the past. These roles were also used as the basis for theories about social patterns of male dominance in the past and the present. Comparative studies of foragers around the world indicate that greater male involvement in hunting is found in more depleted and resource-limited environments (Hiatt 1970). The implication is that men's hunting of large game is an adaptation to increasing resource scarcity in recent times and thus was not necessarily a predominant practice throughout the long history of foraging. In contrast to the "Man the Hunter" model, some cultural anthropologists have proposed a "Woman the Gatherer" model (Slocum 1975). This model seems to make more sense, since the bulk of everyday food in most foraging systems came from gathering, the primary work of women. Among the Ju/wasi, for example, women's gathering provides 75 to 80 percent of the diet, while large game provided by men accounted for the rest. In some cultures, women have roles in hunting game similar to those of men, as among the Agta of the Philippines (Estioko-Griffin 1986; Estioko-Griffin, Goodman, and Griffin 1985). The Agta pattern is that some of the women go out hunting while other women stay at the camp caring for the small children, thus disproving the proposition that women's maternal roles universally prevent them from hunting. Most cultural anthropologists would now agree that the "Man the

The gender division of labor among foragers.

Hunter" model is an example of male bias in interpretation. However, the "Man the Hunter" model is still strong in much popular thinking and is perpetuated through textbook images and museum displays (Gifford-Gonzalez 1993).

Age is a basis for task allocation in all societies since children and the aged generally spend less time in food provision. In foraging societies, both boys and girls perform various tasks that North Americans would label as "work," particularly gathering food. Among the Ju/wasi, young boys begin practicing hunting skills through the games they play with small bows and arrows. They gradually take on more adult skills as they mature. Among the Agta of the Philippines in which women hunt, both girls and boys learn to hunt along with their mothers.

Property Relations

The concept of private property in the sense of owning something that can be sold to someone else is not found in foraging societies. Instead, it is more appropriate to use the term **use rights,** which means that a person or group has socially recognized priority in access to particular resources such as gathering regions, hunting and fishing areas, and water holes. This access, however, is willingly shared with others by permission. Among the Ju/wasi, certain family groups are known to control access to particular water holes and the territory surrounding them (Lee 1979:58–60). Visiting groups are welcome and will be given food and water. In turn, the host group, at another time, will visit other camps and be given hospitality there. In the Andaman Islands, family groups each control known offshore areas for fishing. Again, sharing is a common practice if permission has been given. Encroaching on someone else's area without permission is a serious misdemeanor that could result in violence. While some instances of conflict between foraging groups over territory and other resources have been documented by anthropologists, the level of conflict is less intense and less likely to be lethal than in settled groups with rules of private property. In foraging groups, use rights are generally invested in the collective group and passed down equally to all children who are members of the group.

Foraging as a Sustainable System

When untouched by outside influences and with abundant land available, foraging systems are sustainable, meaning that crucial resources are regenerated over time in balance with the demand that the population makes on them. Evidence of the sustainability of foraging systems comes from many places, but the Andaman Islands provide the clearest case because their island habitats have been "closed" systems with little, if any, outmigration from specific areas of habitation in recent centuries. The few hundred Andamanese living on Sentinel Island, which has never been entered by outsiders, seem to have been able to maintain their lifestyle within a fairly limited area since earliest observations of them (from a distance) by the British over a century ago. Foraging breaks down as a sustainable system when outsiders enter the system and place restrictions on land use. As with other extensive systems described below, such restrictions destroy sustainability by intensifying resource use within areas decreasing in size.

One reason for the sustainability of foraging is that foragers' needs are modest. Some anthropologists have typified the foraging lifestyle as the "original affluent society" because needs are satisfied with minimal labor efforts. This term is used metaphorically to signal the fact that foraging economies should not be dismissed as poor and inadequate attempts at making a living. That is an ethnocentric judgment made from the perspective of a consumer culture with different economic and social values. Highly industrialized societies may be maladaptive in the long run because they promote overconsumption of nonrenewable resources. In the 1960s, when the Ju/wasi of the Kalahari desert were still a foraging system, the major food source was the mongongo nut, which was so abundant that there was never a shortage (Howell 1986). In addition, hundreds of species of plants and animals were considered edible. Yet the people were very thin and often complained of hunger, year round. Their thinness may be an adaptation to seasonal fluctuations in food supply. Rather than maximizing food intake during times of plenty, they minimize it. Mealtime is not an occasion for stuffing oneself with treats until there is no room for anything more. Ju/wasi culture taught that one should have a hungry stomach, even in the midst of plentiful food.

Since foragers' needs for goods are not great, minimal labor efforts are required to satisfy them. They would typically work fewer hours a week than the average employed North American. In traditional (undisturbed) foraging societies, people spend as few as five hours a week "working," so they have more leisure time that they spend in activities like storytelling, playing games, and resting. Foraging populations also traditionally enjoyed good health records. During the 1960s, the age structure and health status of the Ju/wasi compared to that of the United States of around 1900—without any modern medical facilities (Lee 1979:47–48). They were described as a "healthy and vigorous population with a low incidence of infections and degenerative diseases." The high level of needs satisfaction and general health and well-being of foragers is the basis of their being called the "original affluent societies."

Changing Cultural Worlds of Foragers: The Tiwi

The Tiwi live on two islands off the north coast of Australia (Hart, Pilling, and Goodale 1988). As foragers, the Tiwi survived through gathering food, especially vegetables (such as yams) and nuts, grubs, small lizards, and fish. Women provided the bulk of the daily diet with their gathered vegetables and nuts that were ground and cooked into a kind of porridge. Occasionally men would hunt kangaroos, wildfowl, and other game such as *goanna,* larger lizards. Vegetables, nuts, and fish were abundant the year around. The Tiwi lived a more comfortable life than aboriginal groups of the mainland where the environment was less hospitable.

The Tiwi have long been in contact with different foreign influences, beginning in the 1600s with the arrival of the Portuguese, who were attracted to the islands as a source of iron. Later, in 1897, an Australian buffalo hunter named Joe Cooper came to the islands and kidnapped two native women to train as mainland guides in the Tiwi language. Cooper and his entourage greatly changed the Tiwi by introducing a desire for Western goods, especially tobacco. Later, Japanese traders arrived, offering manufactured goods in return for Tiwi women. In the early 1900s, the French established a Catholic mission on Bathurst Island. The mission disapproved of the traditional Tiwi marriage pattern of polygamy (multiple spouses, in this case a man having more than one wife) and promoted monogamy in its place. The year 1942 brought World War II to the Tiwi as the Japanese bombed and strafed an American airstrip in nearby Darwin in what is called the "Australian Pearl Harbor." Military bases were prominent on the islands. Tiwi dependency on Western manufactured goods increased. Today, they are incorporated in the modern world as a part of the Australian nation. Over these many decades of contact, Tiwi residence patterns changed substantially. From mobile hunter-gatherers, the Tiwi changed into settled villagers living in houses built of corrugated iron sheets. Tiwi men now participate on football (soccer) teams, competitive javelin throwing, and water polo. Tiwi art, especially carving and painting, is highly recognized in Australia and, increasingly, internationally. Tiwi are active in public affairs and politics, including the aboriginal rights movement. Jane Goodale, an anthropologist who has studied among the Tiwi for many years, comments that the

> 1990s should be an extremely interesting period for the Tiwi as they regain individual and collective control over their life and lands in full. . . . After almost 80 years of control and "development" by representatives from foreign and dominating cultures, the Tiwi of the early 1980s were faced once again with the responsibility of self-development. They viewed this challenge of deciding their own future with both anxiety and

Aboriginal artist Eymard Tungatalum retouches a traditional Tiwi carving in an art gallery in Australia's northern territory. Tungatalum's carvings, along with songs and poems, are an important part of the aboriginal people's efforts to revive their culture.

courage, while they continued to train their children to survive in their land, and at the same time aspired that they would one day be recognized as fully equal by other citizens in the larger Australian society. With increasing numbers of non-Tiwi as tourists coming to know the people and county of Melville and Bathurst islands, it is also possible, as one Tiwi told me in 1986, "that white people too will learn to live with and survive in the country." (Hart, Pilling, and Goodale 1988:144–145)

HORTICULTURE

Both horticulture and pastoralism emerged only within the last several thousand years of human existence. They both involve an emerging dependence on the **domestication** of plants and animals, or their control by humans in terms of both their location and reproduction. No one is sure as to when and where domestication first occurred, and whether the domestication of plants and animals occurred at the same time or sequentially. At this point, some evidence seems to favor plant domestication coming first.

Horticulture is the growing of domesticated crops in gardens with simple hand tools. It emerged first around 12,000 BCE in the Middle East. A horticultural economy is based mainly on food crops that people plant and harvest. The food grown in gardens is often supplemented by foraging for wild foods and trading with pastoralists for animal products. Horticulture is still practiced by many thousands of people mainly in sub-Saharan Africa; South and Southeast Asia, including the Pacific island of Papua New Guinea; Central and South America; and some parts of the Caribbean islands. Prominent horticultural crops include yams, corn, beans, grains such as millet and sorghum, and several types of roots, all of which are rich in proteins, minerals, and vitamins.

Horticulture involves the use of hand-held tools, such as digging sticks, hoes, and carrying baskets. Rain is the sole source of moisture, and there are no artificial sources. Horticulture requires rotation of garden plots in order to allow used areas to regenerate and thus is also termed "shifting cultivation." Crop yields from horticulture can be great and can support denser population levels than foraging. Surpluses in food supply emerge as a new element of this mode of production. These surpluses enable trade relationships to increase and cause greater affluence for some people. In some cases, horticulture was the foundation for complex civilizations, for example in Central Africa and in the Mayan civilization of Central America. Average plot sizes are less than one acre, and 2.5 acres can support a family of five to eight members for a year. Yields are sufficient to support semipermanent village settlements of 200 to 250 people. Overall population density per square mile is low because horticulture, like foraging, is a land-extensive strategy. But horticulture is more labor-intensive than foraging because of the energy required for plot preparation and food processing. Horticulturalists supplement their diets by fishing or hunting, or both, or perhaps trade with nearby foragers.

Anthropologists distinguish five phases in the horticultural cycle:

- *Clearing:* To start the garden area, a section of the forest is cleared, either partially or completely. Common techniques are cutting trees and brush down, then setting the area on fire to burn off other growth. This burning creates a layer of ash that is rich fertilizer. Sometimes people refer to horticulture as "slash and burn cultivation" because of the importance of the two stages of cutting and burning.
- *Planting:* This is accomplished either with a digging stick to loosen the soil into which seeds or slips of plants are placed or through the broadcasting method of simply scattering the seeds by hand over the surface of the ground.
- *Weeding:* Weeds are a relatively minor problem because of the ash cover and somewhat shady growing conditions.
- *Harvesting:* This phase requires labor mainly to cut or dig crops and carry them to the residential area.
- *Fallowing:* After cultivating the same garden plot for a certain number of years (which varies depending on the environment and the type of crop grown), the land has to be left unused, or fallow, for a period of time before it can be gardened again with any success.

Labor

As with foraging groups, no class differences exist in terms of work in horticultural societies. A family of husband, wife, and children form the core work group for cultivation, but groups of men form for hunting and fishing expeditions, and women often work in collective groups for food processing. Gender is the key factor structuring the organization of labor, with male and female work roles often being clearly differentiated. Male and female roles fall into three general patterns (Martin and Voorhies 1975). Most commonly, men do the clearing, and men and women plant and tend the staple crops that are the basis of the people's everyday diets. This pattern exists in Papua New Guinea, much of Southeast Asia, and parts of West and East Africa. In the second pattern, men do the clearing and women cultivate the staple crops; men cultivate prestige crops (used in ceremonies and for exchange) and may also hunt. Many horticultural societies of East Africa fit this pattern. This pattern is, however, reversed in some cultures, notably the precontact Iroquois of upstate New York. Iroquois women were in charge of cultivating maize, the most important crop, and their economic importance was reflected in the overall social and political importance accorded to women (Brown 1975). In the third pattern, which is the least common, men do both the clearing and the cultivating. The Yanomami of the Amazon (Chagnon 1992) are an example of this male-dominated horticultural production system. Yanomami men clear the fields, plant and maintain the gardens, and harvest the crops. Yanomami women are not idle, however. They work, on average, more hours than men because they are responsible for performing the arduous and time-consuming tasks involved in processing manioc. Manioc, the main food source, is a starchy root poisonous to humans unless put through a lengthy process of soaking in water, which is carried from the river by teams of women. Once soaked, the manioc is grated by hand and cooked before it is ready for consumption.

While no simple explanation exists for why these three patterns developed in particular areas, each one does have implications for female status in society. Peggy Sanday (1973) examined the relationship between women's roles in horticulture and their social status as indicated in terms of women's economic and political rights: female control over produce, the value placed on female produce, female participation in political activities, and female organizations devoted to female economic or political interests. She found evidence to support a correlation between women's contribution to horticulture and their social status. For example, both are high among the (precontact) Iroquois, among the Yoruba of West Africa, and in Samoa in the South Pacific. Where women's contribution was low, their status was also low, as in South America. A complication in the correlations appeared, however: Women's status was not always high in societies in which women's horticultural roles were significant. The conclusion is that female contribution to subsistence is a "necessary but insufficient" cause of high female status. A major role in production does not necessarily bring high status if one does not have control over the goods that are produced, as in systems of slavery (Friedl 1975).

Children do much productive work in horticultural societies, perhaps more than in any other type of economy. A famous comparative research project, the "Children of Six Cultures" study (Whiting and Whiting 1975), examined children's roles in different modes of production. The Gusii of Kenya were the most dependent on horticulture. Compared to children in the other five cultures, Gusii children were assigned more tasks at younger ages. Both young boys and girls were responsible for caring for siblings, fetching fuel, and hauling water. The reason horticultural societies involve children in "responsible" adult-like tasks more than other societies has to do with the fact that in most horticultural societies, adult women's time allocation to work is very high and children's labor in the domestic domain serves as a replacement.

Property Relations

As in foraging societies, the concept of private property as something that an individual can own and sell is not operable in horticultural societies. Use rights are paramount and become even more definitively demarcated on the basis of cultivation activity. By clearing and planting an area of land, an individual puts an indisputable claim on it and its produce. As horticultural societies produce surplus goods, the possibility of social inequality in access to goods and resources emerges. Rules of group sharing, as found among foraging groups, may decline or even disappear as some groups gain access to higher status.

Horticulture as a Sustainable System

Crop rotation and fallowing are crucial factors in the sustainability of horticulture. Crop rotation varies the demands made on the soil. Fallowing allows the plot to rest completely and recover its nutrients. It also promotes soil quality and helps prevent compaction by allowing the growth of weeds, whose root systems help keep the soil loose. Once the fallow period is over, the weeds are burned off, providing a layer of ash that serves as a rich source of natural fertilizer. The benefits of a well-managed system of shifting cultivation are clear.

A major constraint in horticulture is the time required for fallowing in situations of pressure on the land. In general, seven years or more of fallow time are required for a year of cultivation. If the fallowing time is reduced, negative consequences quickly arise, including soil nutrient depletion and soil erosion through insufficient tree and brush coverage on slopes. Several factors may contribute to reusing plots that should be left fallow (Blaikie 1985):

- pressures on land access from ranchers, miners, farmers, tourists;
- government pressure on horticulturalists to intensify production for cash in order to pay taxes and other fees;
- interest of horticulturalists in boosting production for cash in order to buy manufactured commodities; and
- pressure from population growth when outmigration is not an option.

The last factor, population growth, is often blamed as the sole culprit, but often, it is not involved at all. For example, in one case in eastern India, the major causes of land degradation were heavy government taxes and fees and growing indebtedness to merchants in the plains: "Up to thirty years ago, the hill area occupied by the Sora was covered by dense jungle, while today the hillsides are near-deserts of raw red soil. Shifting agriculture is practised with only three to four year fallow periods, as opposed to over ten years some generations ago. The population has grown only slowly, and certainly at a much slower rate than the rapidly increased destruction of the environment might suggest." (128)

Changing Cultural Worlds of Horticulturalists: The Mundurucu

Outside economic and political factors have made major impacts on horticultural societies. The rubber industry's impact on indigenous peoples of the Amazon ranges from the complete loss of traditional life-ways to comparatively moderate change. The Mundurucu illustrate two patterns of change (Murphy and Murphy 1985). After the arrival of rubber planters in the Brazilian Amazon in the late nineteenth century, many Indians began to work for the Brazilian planters as latex tappers. For over a century, Mundurucu men combined their traditional horticultural life with seasonal work in the rubber area collecting latex. Cultural retention survived over a century of this kind of interaction. Marked cultural change occurred later when many Mundurucu opted to leave their traditional villages, migrating to live in the rubber area year-round.

In the traditional villages, men live in a separate house at one side of the village, with husbands visiting wives and children in their group houses. In the rubber settlement, husbands and wives live in their own houses and there is no separate men's house. In the traditional villages, women's communal work groups shared water-carrying. Such groups do not exist in the rubber settlement villages. So, the husbands have taken over the task of carrying the water and thus, men work harder than in the traditional village. Women continue to work more hours per day than men, however, but they believe that life is better in the rubber settlement area because they like living in the same house with their husbands.

PASTORALISM

Pastoralism is a mode of production based on the domestication of animal herds and the use of their products such as meat and milk for 50 percent or more of the pastoral society's diet. Pastoralism has long existed in the "old world"—Europe, Africa, and Asia, especially in regions where rainfall is limited and unpredictable. In the Western hemisphere, pastoralism did not exist until the Spanish colonialists introduced it during the fifteenth century. Some Native American groups, especially in the southwestern United States, still rely on herding animals. Pastoralism may be based on a wide variety of animals, including cows, sheep, goats, horses, camels, and reindeer, but most pastoralists specialize in one main type of animal. Pastoralism can succeed in a variety of environments, depending on the animal involved. For example, reindeer herding is popular in the circumpolar regions of Europe and Asia, and cattle and goat herding is common in India and Africa.

Pastoralism is geared to providing daily food, primarily milk. Thus, this mode of production is limited in what it can provide, so pastoralist groups forge trade links with settled groups. In this way, they can secure food and other goods they cannot produce themselves, particularly grains and manufactured items like cooking pots in return for their animals, hides, and other animal products. Pastoralism may seem to resemble contemporary large-scale ranching operations, but in fact, ranches resemble modern industry more than traditional pastoralism (Fratkin, Galvin, and Roth 1994; Loker 1993). The primary purpose of ranching is to provide meat for sale, whereas pastoralism provides many animal products. Also, pastoralism involves the movement of animals to pasture, while ranching moves the fodder to the animals.

A common problem for all pastoralists is the continued need for fresh pasture for their animals. This need makes pastoralism, like foraging and horticulture, an extensive form of economic adaptation. Herds must move or else the pasture area will become depleted. A useful distinction is made between pastoralists depending on whether they move their herds for short or long distances (Fratkin, Galvin, and Roth 1994). The Nuer are an example of short-distance herders. E. E. Evans-Pritchard's (1965 [1947]) classic study describes the Nuer, cattle herders of Sudan in the late 1930s. Depending on the availability of water, the Nuer would spend part of the year in settled villages and part in temporary camps. Cows provided food for the Nuer from their milk, meat, and blood (the Nuer, and other pastoralists, extract blood from the cow's neck, which they then drink). They provided hides, horn, and other materials for everyday use and were the medium of exchange for marriage and payment of fines. The economic and social importance of cattle is reflected in the Nuer's detailed vocabulary for naming types of cattle on the basis of their colors and markings, just as Americans have many different words for money.

Pastoralist systems vary greatly in terms of their level of wealth and the degree of political organization among groups. Environmental setting seems to explain much of this variation. The Qashqai of Iran are long-distance sheep herders and camel drivers (Beck 1986). This area of the Middle East is relatively lush, with a rich and varied natural resource base that supports agriculture and urban centers, including the important city of Shiraz. The nomadic pastoralism of the Qashqai involves seasonal migration to remote pastures, separated by about three hundred miles. Long-distance herding makes the Qashqai vulnerable to raids and requires negotiation with settlements along the way for permission to cross their land. This vulnerability prompted them to develop a confederacy of tribes into a centralized political organization for protection. The Qashqai thus show how ecology, economy, and political organizations are linked within an environment well-endowed with resources and with many settled communities. In areas with fewer resources and sparser settlements, such as Mongolia in Central Asia or the circumpolar region, pastoralist groups are less politically organized and less wealthy than the Qashqai.

Among the Ariaal, herders of Kenya, men are in charge of herding camels. Here, an Ariaal herder watches over two baby camels.

Labor

As with horticulturalists, the pastoralist division of labor is not structured by class differences. Families and clusters of related families are the basic unit of production. Gender is an important factor in the allocation of work. In many pastoralist cultures, little overlap exists between male and female tasks. Men are often in charge of the herding activities—moving the animals from place to place. Women tend to be responsible for processing the herd's products, especially the milk. A cultural emphasis on masculinity characterizes many herding populations. Traditional reindeer herding among the Sami of Finland was connected to male identity (Pelto 1973). The definition of being a man was to be a reindeer herder. As traditional herding practices declined and many men no longer made their living from herding, they had to redefine their sense of identity. In contrast, women are the predominant herders among the Navajo of the American Southwest. Navajo men traditionally had little to do with herding the sheep. Instead, their major role is crafting silver jewelry.

The size of the animal involved appears to be a factor in the gender division of labor. Women are often the herders of smaller animals, perhaps since smaller animals need to graze less widely and can be kept penned near the house. Men tend the animals that are pastured at longer distances. This difference suggests the emergence of a distinction between men's wider spatial range than women's, something that becomes further accentuated in many agricultural systems.

Children often play important roles in tending herds. Among the cattle-herding Maasai of Kenya and Tanzania, parents prefer to have many children so that they can help with the herds. Before boys in these pastoralist societies advance to the "warrior" stage, beginning around adolescence, their main task is herding. Once they become warriors, this task is left to the younger boys, girls, and women.

Property Relations

The most important forms of property among pastoralists include animals, housing (such as tents or

Girls are in charge of herding water buffaloes to the Ganges River, at Banaras, India, for watering.

yerts), and use rights to pasture land and migratory routes. Some sense of private property exists with the animals since they may be traded by the family head for other goods. A family's tent or yert is also theirs. However, no private rights in land or travel routes exist; instead, these are generally accepted informal agreements. Many pastoral societies emphasize male ownership of the herds, and sons inherit herds from their fathers. In other societies, such as the sheep-herding Navajo of the southwestern United States, women are the primary herders and they pass the herds from mother to daughter.

Pastoralism as a Sustainable System

Pastoralism is a highly extensive system, requiring the ability of groups to range widely with their herds in search of grass and water. Pastoralists have been able to develop successful and complex cultures in extremely limited environments; an example is the Mongolian herders, who created a vast and powerful empire. As such, pastoralism can be a highly successful and sustainable economic adaptation that functions complementarily with other economic systems. As with horticulture, however, when outside forces begin to squeeze the space available for migration, overexploitation of the environment results and pastoralism then becomes accused of depleting the environment. Many forms of outside pressure, including national interests to "sedentarize" (settle down) pastoralists so that they will be easier to tax, and commercial interests in pastoralists' land threaten the sustainability of pastoralism (see the Current Event box).

Current Event

Will the Nenets Survive?

- Archaeologists recently came upon a group of about 1,000 Nenet reindeer herders who have had almost no contact with Western culture.
- The Nenets have preserved and extended a cultural heritage that may be 10,000 years old. The Nenets appear to be living proof that humans not only can adapt to the harshest conditions, but they may prefer them.
- The Nenets are pastoralists who depend very little on outside sources for their food. They live on reindeer, fish, and other items they forage from the Arctic soil. Ceramic teacups, obtained from the outside, are common, but most of what they use is made by hand.
- After thousands of years of existence, the Nenets now face a great challenge. Outsiders are interested in exploiting the gas and oil fields in their area. Previous gas and oil operations have already damaged reindeer grazing sites. Pollution in rivers is bringing an end to fishing.
- Igor Krupnick, an anthropologist with the Russian Academy of Sciences and the Smithsonian Museum of the United States, is an optimist. He says: "They'll survive. . . . In this region local fishermen have been saying the Nenets are doomed for at least a hundred years. But their nomadic life has made them flexible. They're not going to disappear now. . . . No Arctic people that we know of have persisted for so long and so defiantly."

Source: The New York Times, November 22, 1994.

Changing Cultural Worlds of Pastoralists: Mongolian Nomads

In the early 1990s, cultural anthropologist Melvyn Goldstein and physical anthropologist Cynthia Beall (1994) were allowed to do fieldwork among herders in Mongolia, a landlocked and mountainous country located between Russia and China. Mongolia has the highest ratio of livestock to people of any country in the world. Currently, 70 percent of its agricultural production comes from cattle raising, although goat, sheep, and horse herding are also important—they had traditionally been the most important herd animals. Goldstein and Beall wanted to study how the transformation from a socialist, collectivized economy to a capitalist, market system was affecting the people.

> As our truck crossed a ridge and descended the rough dirt road onto a broad plain, two herders on horses not much bigger than American ponies emerged from a ravine, driving hundreds of sheep across our path. They rode grandly, integral extensions of their horses, as they fluidly darted back and forth constraining stragglers and urging the herd forward. Their effortless skill reminded us that we had come to this remote place because these were the descendants of the

> brilliant Mongol nomad cavalry who had terrorized much of Eurasia 750 years earlier, conquering a vast empire that stretched from the Pacific Ocean to the Danube River. (15)

Since the 1950s, the communist party of the USSR ruled Mongolia and sought to transform it from a herding system into an agricultural and industrial state. They established several urban centers. The population changed from being 78 percent rural in 1956 to 42 percent rural in 1989. In addition, given USSR policies against private property, ownership of herds was socialized. The state provided all social services such as health and education. There was no homelessness or unemployment. The transition was not smooth or easy: Collectivization first resulted in a 30 percent reduction of livestock and produced a revolt in the western part of the country (Barfield 1993:169). Subsequently, policy was altered and the people were allowed to control some of their own animals. Nevertheless, the predominant organization of pastoralism was collectivized and labor was organized along the lines of a factory system.

Starting in the late 1980s, the transition away from socialist economic policies spread throughout Russia, including Mongolia. By the early 1990s, **privatization,** a process of transferring the collective ownership and provision of goods and services under socialism to a capitalist system of private ownership, was the government's policy guideline. In Mongolia, this took the form of ending collective ownership of herds and reinstating family-organized production. At the same time, the government cut back on state-provided services. Goldstein and Beall wanted to learn about the reactions to these changes among more traditional Mongols, herders who still lived in *ger,* tents made of felt. They headed for Moost district in the Altai Mountain area in the southeastern part of the country. The district includes over 10,000 square miles of mountain and valley land, of which 99.9 percent is pasture. The area contains about 4,000 people and about 115,000 head of livestock. Goldstein and Beall set up their *ger* and were immediately welcomed by an invitation to have milk-tea, a hot drink made of tea, water, milk, butter, and salt. During their stay, they spoke with many of the nomads, participated in their festivals, and learned about perceptions of economic change. One of their informants, Puravdorj, became a democratically elected district head, and thus an important rural leader and administrator (see the Voices box).

Changes in the wider Mongolian economy during privatization created serious problems for the herders. Their standard of living declined markedly in the early 1990s. Goods such as flour, sugar, candy, and cooking oil were no longer available. Prices for meat fluctuated widely, and the nomads had to learn to adjust to the vagaries of the market versus the security of state-controlled prices. Lower meat prices resulted in fewer herd animals being slaughtered. Larger herd sizes increased the potential for exceed-

VOICES

Puravdorj Speaks about Privatization

The anthropologists asked Puravdorj what the nomads thought about the collective system versus privatization. He answered, shaking his head:

> It varies, but in general they don't understand market economics very well and are afraid it will harm their income and threaten their welfare benefits. All they know is the *negdel* (the herding collective). It will take time to educate them about managing and marketing on a household basis. But it must happen. The Soviet Union can't help us anymore, and a free-market economy and trade with democracies like the U.S. and Japan is our only hope for security and prosperity.... I think the *negdel* has been good for us.... We have plenty of food, free health care for our children, and free education. Two of my sons are in school at the district and my oldest daughter is in teacher's college in another province. But I am a Mongol, so if the government now says we need to change to have a better life, perhaps we do. At first we nomads vehemently hated the collectives and opposed their creation, but it turned out all right, so maybe going back to privatization and a market economy will also be good. (Goldstein and Beall 1994:52–53)

ing the carrying capacity of the grasslands. Beall and Goldstein close their book with this statement: "As we said our final good-byes to the herders in August of 1992, we had mixed emotions—sadness mingled with respect and hope. It was sad to have witnessed such a sudden and dramatic decline in the nomads' standard of living. The feasts of 1990 were no more and no one thought they would return soon. An era had ended" (164). On a somewhat brighter note, another expert on pastoralism in central and inner Asia comments that the cultural identity of the descendants of Genghis Khan "is so closely tied to the history of great deeds by men on horseback that even as their number declines, their role as symbols of a proud way of life will grow" (Barfield 1993:176).

AGRICULTURE

Both horticulture and **agriculture** emphasize food growing over food gathering. A major difference between the two is that agriculture is an **intensive strategy** of production. Intensification involves new techniques that allow the same land to be used repeatedly without losing its fertility. Key inputs include more labor power for weeding, conscientious use of fertilizers, and control of water supply. The earliest agricultural systems are documented from the time of the neolithic period, beginning around 10,000 BCE in the Tigris-Euphrates valley, India, and China. Agricultural systems now exist on all continents except for Antarctica.

Agriculture involves the use of domesticated animals for plowing, transportation, and organic fertilizer—manure or composted materials. It also relies on irrigation as a source of water and the construction of elaborate terraces and other ways of increasing the amount of land available for cultivation. Settlements are permanent and houses are not movable. Permanent homes, investment in private property, and increased yields all promote larger family size as a way of further increasing production through the use of household labor. Population density increases substantially in agricultural societies, and urban centers of thousands of people develop. Occupational specialization increases. Instead of people repairing their own tools and weapons, some people take on this work as a full-time job and no longer grow their own food but become dependent on trading their skills for food with farmers. Other specializations that emerge as full-time occupations are political leaders, religious leaders or priests, healers, artisans, potters, musicians, and traders. Four major types of agriculture are described here.

Family Farming

Over one billion people, or about one-fourth of the world's population, belong to households involved in family farming (what cultural anthropologists formerly termed "peasant agriculture"). In family farming, farmers "produce much of their own subsistence as well as some food or fiber to sell, supplying labor largely from their own households, and possessing continuing, heritable rights to their own resources" (Netting 1989:221). Family farming is always part of a larger market economic system (Wolf 1966a:8). It is found throughout the world, but is more prevalent in primarily agrarian countries such as Mexico, India, Poland, and Italy than in more industrialized countries. Family farmers exhibit much cross-cultural variety: They may be full-time or part-time farmers, they may be more or less closely linked to urban markets, and they may or may not grow cash crops such as coffee or sugar cane. Major tasks include plowing, planting seeds and cuttings, weeding, caring for terraces and irrigation systems, harvesting, and processing.

Labor

The family (or household) is the basic unit of production. Gender and age are important factors around which productive roles are organized. A gender-based division of labor tends to be marked in most family farm economies. Cross-cultural analysis of gender roles in forty-six family farm societies revealed that men perform the "bulk" of the labor in thiry-eight, or more than three-fourths of the sample (Michaelson and Goldschmidt 1971). The few societies in which females predominate in agriculture were located in Southeast Asia. In general, men work more hours in agricultural production than in the previous systems considered, and women's work tends to be more devoted to activities near the home, such as processing food and child care (Ember 1983). This division of labor has been typified as the basis of the **public/private dichotomy** in family farm societies, in which men are more involved with the nondomestic world and women are increasingly involved in activities in or near the home.

Analysis of time allocation data for men and women in horticultural and agricultural societies reveals that both men's and women's work hours are substantially higher in agricultural economies, but in differing proportions to inside and outside work (Ember 1983). The data indicate that women's contribution to production is not less in agriculture. Instead, the shares of time devoted to particular activities shift. Women's inside work hours increase absolutely and relatively (compared to men's), and their outside work hours increase absolutely, but decline relative to those of men. Why do many family farm agricultural systems increase men's workloads and increase women's involvement in the domestic domain? One hypothesis is based on the importance of plowing fields in preparation for planting, and the fact that plowing is almost exclusively a male task (Goody 1976). This fact has led some anthropologists to argue that men plow simply because they are stronger than women or have the advantage of greater "aerobic capacity" (the ability of the circulatory system to nourish the blood through processing air). In south-central India, weather patterns require that plowing be accomplished in a very narrow time band (Maclachlan 1983). Assigning the task to the physically stronger gender ensures that it can be done more quickly and is thus an adaptive strategy because it optimizes chances for a good crop. Another hypothesis says that women are not involved with plowing and other field work because such tasks are incompatible with child care (J.K. Brown 1970). Yet another view emphasizes that agriculture increases the demand for labor within and near the house (Ember 1983). Winnowing, husking, grinding, and cooking of agricultural products such as rice are extremely labor-intensive. The high demand for family labor in agriculture prompts people to want many children, so child care becomes a more demanding task that is relegated to women. As women become isolated from other women within their households, they are less able to depend on labor contributions from other women than in modes of production where women live and work collectively. In family farms in the United States, the gender division of labor is clear. The husband is usually primarily responsible for daily farm operations while wives' participation ranges from equal to that of husbands to minimal (Barlett 1989:271–273). Women do run farms in the United States, but generally only when they are divorced or widowed. Wives are generally responsible for managing the domestic domain. On average, women's daily work hours are 25 percent more than those of men. A new trend is for family farm women to take salaried jobs off the farm to help support the farm. Children in the United States are not formally employed in farm work, but many family farms rely on children's contributions on weekends and during summer vacations. Amish farm families rely to a significant extent on contributions from all family members (Hostetler and Huntington 1992).

In some farming systems, females play an equal or even more important role in agricultural production and distribution than males. In terms of cross-cultural distribution, such "female farming systems" are numerically fewer than male farming systems. They are especially found in Southeast Asia, a region where **wet rice agriculture** is practiced. This is a highly labor-intensive way of growing rice that involves starting the seedlings in nurseries and transplanting them to flooded fields. Males play a role in the initial plowing of the fields, but this work is less arduous than in dry-field agriculture, since the earth is wet. Women's labor and decision making are the backbone of the operations. Why women predominate in wet rice agriculture is a question that has intrigued anthropologists and economists (Bardhan 1974; Goody 1976; Winzeler 1974), but no one has provided a solid explanation for this pattern yet. Its consequences are clearer than its causes: Where female farming systems exist, women are more likely to have access to rights to land ownership, a greater role in household decision making, more autonomy, and higher status in general (Dyson and Moore 1983; Stivens et al. 1994).

A third variation in the gender division of labor in family farming involves complementary and balanced task allocations between males and females, with males involved in agricultural work and females involved in food processing and marketing. This form of gender division of labor is common among highland communities of Central and South America. For example, among the Zapotec Indians of southern Mexico's state of Oaxaca (pronounced Wah-haka), men grow maize, the staple crop, and cash crops—bananas, mangoes, coconuts, and sesame (Chiñas 1992). Zapotec women contribute substantially to household income by selling produce in the town markets and by making tortillas and selling them from their houses. The farming household thus derives its income from the labor of both genders working interdependently on different aspects of the production process. Male and female status is also relatively balanced.

Children's roles in agricultural societies range from being prominent to rather minor, depending on the context (Whiting and Whiting 1975). The "Children of Six Cultures" study found lower rates of child work in the North Indian and Mexican agricultural villages, compared to the horticultural village in Kenya. But in some agricultural societies, children's work rates are very high, as shown through detailed observations of children's activities in two Asian villages, one in Java and the other in Nepal. In these villages, an important task of children, even as young as six to eight years old, is tending the farm animals (Nag, White, and Peet 1978), and children spent more time caring for animals than adults did. In both villages, girls aged six to eight spend more time than adults in child care. Some of the Javanese children in the six- to eight-year-old group worked for wages. In general, girls did more hours of work daily than boys at all ages.

Property Relations

The investments in land such as clearing, terracing, and fencing that agriculture requires are linked to the development of firmly delineated and protected property rights. Rights to land, the most important resource, can be acquired and sold. Clear guidelines exist about inheritance and transfer of rights to land through marriage. Social institutions such as law and police emerge to protect private rights to resources. The more marked gender division of labor in many family farming systems often means that men have access to the more highly valued tasks and to goods that have value in the outside world. The women are more involved with food processing, childbearing and childrearing, and family maintenance, tasks that generate no income and have no exchange value. This division of labor is related to gender-differentiated inheritance systems. In family farming systems where male labor and decision making predominate, women and girls tend to be excluded from land rights and other forms of property control. Conversely, in female farming systems, inheritance rules tend to regulate the transmission of property rights more often through females (see the Multiple Cultural Worlds box). Class distinctions become more rigid, and there are greater gaps between those who have access to resources and those who do not.

Changing Cultural Worlds of Family Farmers: Zinacantan and Locorotondo

Some applied anthropologists and other development specialists have said that peasants in closed communities are "risk averse" because they avoid adopting innovations such as new techniques for cultivation, new seed varieties, or new forms of fertilizer. Economic anthropologists have shown, in contrast, that such conservatism may be adaptive. Family farmers have intimate knowledge of the systems within which they work, and they are capable of assessing costs and benefits of innovations. These contrasting perspectives both emphasize the farmers' agency as decision makers, determining whether they should change in certain directions. On the other hand, development projects such as the construction of roads, global patterns in demand for certain products, and labor opportunities shape the choices that farmers have to consider, as the following two examples demonstrate. The two examples share some features, which are characteristic of such change in all parts of the world. Each example has unique features as well.

Several outside influences have led to major changes in family farming as Frank Cancian's (1989) study of economic change in rural Mexico shows. In 1960, Cancian first went to the village of Zinacantan to study the economy of the Maya Indians in the southern state of Chiapas. The Zinacantecos mostly earned their living by growing corn and selling part of their crops in a nearby city. When Cancian returned in the 1980s, significant economic change had occurred because of government road building that linked rural communities with urban market centers. The number of households that relied solely on growing corn had declined substantially. Many farmers had been displaced from the land they had rented by the landowners, who put the land into cattle production, and by the construction of a dam. These farmers began to take up wage work in the area that was created by these changes. Others began to participate in labor migration to nearby cities for wage work for up to a year or two at a time.

Anthony Galt's (1992) study of Locorotondo village in southern Italy also reveals how external economic changes and opportunities affected a family farm system. Until the early twentieth century, agriculture in Locorotondo was based on the intensive cultivation of grapes. Vineyard land had been created through a complex and arduous process of clearing and terrac-

MULTIPLE CULTURAL WORLDS

Malay Women Farmers Lose Rights to Land

Interventions by Western development experts have promoted changes in family farming systems worldwide. One feature of this change is toward increasing male economic roles. Many projects ignore women's traditional agricultural roles, assuming that men are always the farmers (Rogers 1979). Projects have targeted men for receiving new tools and techniques regardless of the actual division of labor. This bias leads to failed projects since the men may have no interest in or knowledge of farming and thus the true farmers were bypassed.

Economist Ester Boserup (1970) pointed out decades ago that colonial governments often undermined women's status by denying them formal rights to land. Access to land is a major determinant of wealth and social status, especially in developing countries where most sources of income are related to the land. Women's access to land is even more crucial than men's because women have less access to other forms of income such as wage labor (Stivens et al. 1994). In Malaysia, gender inequality is less severe than in many parts of the world. Daughters traditionally inherited land equally with sons, and in the southern Rembau district, land is inherited through women predominantly. In terms of labor force participation, women again ranked high. Women's economic rights produced a significant degree of autonomy for rural women.

But this has changed. Both colonialism and international development programs have brought disadvantages to Malay women that did not exist before. Beginning with the British colonial regime, women's land rights have eroded. British officials registered land in the name of men only, regardless of whether the property was owned by a woman, or jointly owned by a husband and wife. Agricultural development programs, as elsewhere, have been aimed at males, bypassing the women. The Green Revolution promoted mechanized rice farming and displaced thousands of female workers from their jobs. In one hundred years, the gender division of labor and women's economic rights and status have been steadily transformed from one in which women had high status to one in which men now have dominant roles.

ing the rocky and uneven slopes. Both men and women were involved in cultivating and harvesting the grapes. Early in the twentieth century, two processes began leading to significant economic changes in Locorotondo. First was the opportunity to migrate to the United States to earn capital. Several people left Locorotondo to work in a coal mine in West Virginia. Second, the world market penetrated Locorotondo. In 1991, major vermouth producers established wineries in the area. Construction of a new railroad line facilitated the marketing of grapes. By selling their grapes to the vermouth producers, Locorotondo's grape growers became dependent on the world market and its fluctuations. Yet, many succeeded in making economic gains, and a middle class emerged. Many families have now become dual-income families, with both husband and wife taking up wage work in the public or private sectors. Family farming is declining, as many young people have no interest in agriculture.

Plantation Agriculture

Plantation agriculture involves concentrated ownership of land, with the means of production in the hands of one family or corporation, the use of hired labor, and mono-crop production for sale. As a form of production, the plantation system exhibits some of the most severe inequalities between owners and workers of any production system. Plantation workers worldwide endure some of the most deplorable working conditions. Many have started to organize in order to improve these conditions. Anthropological studies of plantation agriculture have tended to take a historical view and have focused on slavery (forced and unpaid labor) and the slave trade that developed as means to provide labor to support this system as well as an economic end in itself (E. Wolf 1982). Archaeological research in the United States and the Caribbean has revealed much about how plantations worked in the past (D.V. Armstrong 1990). However, participant observation studies of contemporary plantation systems are difficult to conduct because plantations do not welcome close study.

The plantation mode of production is still prominent in some of Europe's former colonies. Plantations exist, for example, in Sri Lanka, the small island off the southern coast of India, where plantations still produce tea, coffee, rubber, and coconuts. British colonialists first developed coffee plantations there in the late 1880s and brought in laborers from South India. Sri Lanka is now well known as having an excellent human welfare record, by far the best in South Asia. Social programs since World War II led to admirable national health and literacy achievements. A survey study of the plantation sector reveals significant disparities between it and the nonplantation sector (Jayawardena 1984). Sri Lanka's plantation sector is the largest contributor to the Gross National Product (GNP) and the largest source of employment. As tea and rubber cultivation developed, women laborers were especially brought in to pick tea leaves and to tap rubber. The plantation labor force in Sri Lanka is now over half female. Children aged fourteen to sixteen years are a legal part of the labor force, while younger children often help their mothers on an unpaid basis. The plantation workers' health status is far worse than the national level, however. Among the plantation population, infant malnutrition rates and mortality rates are higher than in the general population. Housing is crowded, and most households occupy only one or two rooms. Child care facilities for working mothers are nonexistent, poorly run, or located at a distance too far from the place of work. Illiteracy is high among plantation workers, while the general population in Sri Lanka has the highest literacy rate in the region.

Industrial Agriculture

Industrial agriculture produces crops through means that are "capital-intensive, substituting machinery and purchased inputs such as processed fertilizers for human and animal labor" (Barlett 1989:253). It is practiced in the capitalist countries of the United States, Canada, Germany, Russia, and Japan; it is increasingly being exported to developing nations such as India and Brazil; and it is also found in socialist countries such as China. Thus far, few cultural anthropologists have studied this form of production, and of the studies that have been done, most have focused on the United States.

Corporate Farming in the United States

In the United States, the rural population continues to dwindle. In 1988, fewer than 5 million Americans lived on farms (Sazbo 1988). Industrial agriculture has brought the advent of a new subcategory of **corporate farms,** huge enterprises that produce goods solely for sale and that are owned and operated by companies who rely entirely on hired labor. Studies reveal four aspects of the evolution of industrial agriculture over the past 150 years:

- The increased use of complex technology, including machinery, chemicals, and genetic research on new plant and animal varieties. This new technology has social impacts. Replacing mules and horses with tractors for plowing in the South during the 1930s led to the eviction of small-scale sharecroppers from the land as the landowners were able to cultivate larger units.

In Japan, farming now often combines elements of industrial mechanization and intensive labor. This farmer works near a highly urbanized area of Kyoto.

The invention of mechanical cotton pickers prompted research on varieties of cotton that were more easily picked by machine. These innovations combined to displace field laborers.

- The increased use of **capital** (wealth used in the production of more wealth—either in the form of money or property). Industrial agriculture uses the most capital per unit of production of any farming system (Barlett 1989:260). The high ratio of capital to labor has enabled farmers to increase production, but it reduces flexibility. If a farmer invests in an expensive machine to harvest soybeans and then the price of soybeans drops, the farmer cannot quickly change from growing soybeans to potatoes.
- The increased use of energy—primarily gasoline to run the machinery and provide nitrates for fertilizer—to grow crops, often exceeds the calories of food energy yielded in the harvest. Calculations of how many calories of energy are used to produce a calorie of food in industrial agricultural systems reveal a very high ratio of perhaps 2.5 calories of fossil fuel to harvest one calorie of food, and more than 6 when processing, packaging, and transport are counted (Barlett 1989:261). In this sense, industrial agriculture is a less efficient mode of production than foraging, horticulture, and pastoralism.
- The decline of the family farm. In the United States, family farms were the predominant pattern until a few decades ago. Now, experts speak of "the death of the family farm." Increasing numbers of family farms have fallen into debt and cannot compete with industrial farms. In Canada, foreclosure notices to family farms tripled between 1984 and 1990 (Young and Van Beers 1991).

A key difference between corporate farms and family farms is that corporate farms depend completely on hired labor rather than on family members. Much of the labor demand in industrial agriculture is seasonal, creating an ebb and flow of workers, depending on the task and time of year. Large ranches hire seasonal cowboys for round-ups and fence mending. Crop harvesting is another high demand point. Leo Chavez (1992) studied the lives of undocumented (illegal) migrant laborers from Central America who work in the huge tomato, strawberry, and avocado fields owned by corporate farms in southern California. Many of these migrants are Indians from Oaxaca, Mexico. They sneak across the border to work in the United States as a way of making ends meet. In the San Diego area, they live temporarily in shantytowns, or camps that Chavez describes as resembling Third World living conditions (63). Here is what a camp, where all male workers live, is like on Sunday when the men do not go out to work in the fields:

> On Sundays, the campsites take on a community-like appearance. Men bathe, and wash their clothes, hanging them on trees and bushes, or on lines strung between the trees. Some men play soccer and basketball, using a hoop someone has rigged up. Others sit on old crates or tree-stumps as they relax, talk, and drink beer. Sometimes the men talk about fights from the night before. With little else to do, nowhere to go, and few outsiders to talk to, the men often drink beer to pass the time on Saturday nights and Sundays. Loneliness and boredom plague them during nonworking hours. (65)

Collectivized Agriculture in Romania

Collectivized agriculture is a form of industrialized agriculture that involves nonprivate control of land, technology, and goods produced. Collectivism is inspired by the work of social theorists Marx and Engels (1964 [1848]), whose call: "Workers of the world unite," in *The Communist Manifesto* inspired many social movements. In China, Mao Tse-tung undertook what is indisputably the most massive effort to engineer collective production in China. Collectivism's basic goal was to provide for greater economic equality and a greater sense of group welfare than is possible under competitive capitalism. A variety of collective agriculture arrangements have been used in places such as Russia and Eastern Europe, China, Tanzania, Ethiopia, and Nicaragua. Cultural anthropology studies of collectivized agriculture are rare. This section presents some of the findings from one study conducted in Romania, specifically its Olt Land region, which comprises about sixty-five villages and a high degree of social homogeneity (Kideckel 1993). David Kideckel conducted fieldwork in two periods: first, in 1974 during a period of optimism for socialism, and later in 1990, after the revolution that brought socialism's end.

Romanian socialism was brought in through Soviet support. Thus, its model was Stalinist and it involved highly centralized state planning. Romania had the most comprehensive and centralized system of Eastern Europe. The state oversaw nearly every aspect of society, from university enrollments to the production of steel and tractors. Romanian agriculture was organized into state farms and collective farms. With the completion of collectivization in the early 1960s, about 30 percent of the land was in state farms, 60 percent in collectives, and 10 percent privately held. Workers on state farms were employees and were paid wages. They received a small garden for their own use. Organized like a rural factory, the state farm provided services such as child care facilities and shopping centers. Collective farms, in contrast, were "ostensibly" owned and controlled by their members, who pooled land, labor, and resources. Their earnings were determined by total farm production, and their wages tended to be lower than state farm worker wages. Collective farm workers were entitled to a "use plot" of the collective land. These plots could provide up to three-fourths of subsistence needs. Most of the private land existed in mountain zones where ecology limited the feasibility of collectivization. Private herders who lived in the mountains were able to evade many state demands through their mobility, and many of them became quite wealthy.

Labor was separated into tasks according to whether it was manual or mental labor. Although manual laborers were elevated in state rhetoric and they were more highly paid than intellectuals, in fact, intellectual work was more highly valued than manual work. In spite of the socialist rhetoric proclaiming equality between all workers, it did not erase economic distinctions between males and females. Women were relegated to agricultural and reproductive labor while rural men moved into industry. While women were the mainstay of collective farm labor, they were underrepresented among the leadership. Nevertheless, women's increased involvement in wage-earning and their roles in cultivating household use plots strengthened their influence in the household and the community. Overall, the gender division of labor involves substantial overlap between male and female roles in the rural sector.

The 1980s brought serious economic decline to Romania, and in December 1989, the Romanian revolution began. Conflict continued through 1990, when the opposition party won the national election. By 1991, about 80 percent of the farm land had reverted to private ownership. The revolution had mixed results throughout Romania and Olt Land: "At first it improved people's daily lives and brightened their outlook. . . . Ultimately, however, the persistent uncertainties intensified the competitive and divisive forces that had so long been at work in Olt Land society" (216). The transition to private land was not easy. State farms gave up land reluctantly, and many collective farmers had second thoughts about private agriculture:

> One couple in their early forties . . . were horrified when they heard a rumor that people were to be required to take back the land. . . . They had no desire to work in agriculture, and to them the half hectare to which they were entitled was a burden. Many people who were close to retirement or recently pensioned and some younger unmarried people also saw private agriculture as not worth the effort. They had grown accustomed to the shared risk and shorter workdays

This Romanian collective farm work team is sorting potatoes. Note the feminization of agricultural labor. Teams were composed of close friends, relations, and neighbors so that farms could take advantage of local social relations to satisfy their labor needs.

CRITICAL THINKING

Was the Invention of Agriculture a Terrible Mistake?

Most Euro-Americans have a "progressivist" view that agriculture is a major advance in cultural evolution because it brought with it so many things that Westerners admire: cities, centers of learning and art, powerful state governments, and monumental architecture:

> Just count our advantages. We enjoy the most abundant and varied foods, the best tools, and material goods, some of the longest and healthiest lives, in history.... From the progressivist perspective on which I was brought up, to ask "Why did almost all our hunter-gatherer ancestors adopt agriculture?" is silly. Of course they adopted it because agriculture is an efficient way to get more food for less work (Diamond 1987:106).

Another claim about the advantage of agriculture is that it allows more leisure time, so art could flourish. Why would one rather be a hunter-gatherer, struggling every day to make ends meet?

On the other hand, many scholars raise serious questions about the advantages of agriculture. These "revisionists" argue that agriculture may be "the worst mistake in the history of the human race," "a catastrophe from which we have never recovered" (Diamond: 105–106). Some of the "costs" of agriculture include social inequality; disease; despotism; and destruction of the environment from soil exhaustion and chemical poisoning, water pollution, dams and river diversions, and air pollution from tractors, transportation, and processing plants. With agriculture, life did improve for many people, but not all. Elites emerged with distinct advantages, but the gap between the haves and the have-nots increased. Health improved for the elites, but not the landless poor and laboring classes. With the vast surpluses of food created by agricultural production, elaborate state systems developed with new forms of power exercised over the common people.

Critical Thinking Questions

- What is your definition of the "good life"?
- Given your definition, how does life in pre-agricultural societies compare to life in contemporary agricultural and industrial societies?
- What are the benefits and costs of achieving the good life among the Ju/wasi compared to contemporary agricultural and industrial societies?
- Who gets the good life in each type of economy?

> of collective farming.... Some young people liked the idea of private agriculture but doubted that they knew enough to be successful at it. (221–222)

The Sustainability of Agriculture

Agriculture, as we have seen, requires more in the way of labor inputs, technology, and the use of nonrenewable natural resources than the other systems discussed earlier. The ever-increasing spread of corporate agriculture is displacing other longstanding economic systems, including foraging, horticulture, and pastoralism. It is resulting in the destruction of important habitats, notably rain forests, in its search for agricultural land (along with commercial ranching and other aspects of industrialism, discussed next), and for water and other energy sources to support its enterprises. Intensive agriculture itself is nonsustainable, and it is also undermining the sustainability of other systems. Anthropologists have pointed to some of the social costs of agriculture as well (see the Critical Thinking box).

INDUSTRIALISM

Industrialism refers to the production of goods through mass employment in business and commercial operations. In industrial capitalism, the form of capitalism found in most industrialized nations, the bulk of goods produced are not for basic needs, but to satisfy consumer demands for nonessential goods. Employment in agriculture decreases while jobs in manufacturing and the service sector increase. In some industrialized countries, the number of manufacturing jobs are declining, with more people being employed in service occupations and in the growing area of "information processing" (such as computer programming, data processing, communications, and teaching). Some experts feel that the United States, for example, is moving out of the industrial age and into the "information age."

An important distinction emerges within industrial capitalism between the **formal sector,** which is salaried or wage-based work registered in official statistics, and the **informal sector,** which includes work that is outside the formal sector, not officially registered, and sometimes illegal. If you have done babysitting and were paid cash that was not formally recorded by your employer (for tax deduction purposes) or by you (for income tax purposes), then you have participated in the informal sector. Informal sector activities that are illegal are referred to as being part of the "underground economy."

The Formal Sector

The formal sector comprises a wide array of occupations, ranging from stable and lucrative jobs in what has been labeled the "primary labor market" to unstable or part-time and less lucrative jobs in the "secondary labor market" (Calhoun, Light, and Keller 1994). Cultural anthropologists could conduct research in any number of domains ranging from huge multinational corporations to neighborhood beauty parlors. Some anthropologists have pursued the former direction, but the tendency has been to focus on small-scale organizations, especially factories. Factory studies are an important genre in cultural anthropology. They apply the tools and insights of anthropology into the micro-domain of a work-focused institution. Typical fieldwork techniques in factory studies include conducting interviews with workers and managers in the plant and in their homes, and observing plant operations. Their findings shed light on how people adapt to this environment, the stresses that arise, and the role of culture.

One study used a team approach of cultural anthropologists and graduate students and focused on the role of ethnicity in shaping social relationships in a Miami clothing factory (Grenier et al. 1992). The clothing plant, a subsidiary of the largest U.S. clothing manufacturer, employs about 250 operators, mainly women. The majority of employees are Cuban women who immigrated to Miami many years ago. As these employees are aging and beginning to retire, they are being replaced by new immigrants from Central America, some Haitians, and some African Americans. The workers are organized into a union, but members of the different ethnic groups have more solidarity with each other than with the union. Interethnic rivalry exists around the issue of management's treatment of members of different groups. Many non-Cuban workers claim that there is favoritism toward Cuban employees. Some supervisors and managers expressed ethnic stereotypes, but not always consistent ones: "Depending on whom one listens to, Haitians are either too slow or too fast; Cubans may talk too much or be extraordinarily dedicated workers" (75). The management sees ethnic-based competition and lack of cooperation as a key problem that they attempt to deal with by enforcing an environment that downplays ethnicity. For example, management banned workers from playing personal radios and installed a system of piped-in music supposedly by a radio station that alternates between "American" and "Latin" songs.

The Informal Sector

In contrast to conducting research in the formal sector, studying the informal sector presents several challenges. People who work in the informal sector may not be "organized" in one location, like a factory (see the Multiple Cultural Worlds box). Often, workers are involved in illegal activities, which means they are even less willing than other people to be "studied." In general, it is easier to do research on aspects of people's lives of which they are proud. Informal economy work may yield a sense of pride less often than formal economy work. On the other hand, some research advantages also arise. People involved in the informal economy, compared to a CEO of a multinational corporation, may have more time to share with the anthropologist. This is not always the case, however, since many informal sector workers are involved in more than one enterprise in an attempt to make ends meet, as well as being responsible for child care.

The illegal drug industry is an important part of the informal economy in many nations, including the United States. Neither international drug dealers nor street sellers pay income tax on their profits, and their earnings are not part of the official GNP of any nation. In the United States, many young males, especially

MULTIPLE CULTURAL WORLDS

Scavenging in Belmar

Melvin Williams's (1992) research in Belmar, a poor African American neighborhood in Pittsburgh, Pennsylvania, illuminates one aspect of the informal sector: scavenging, a legal way to earn money. In discussing what he calls a "marginal enterprise" undertaken by aged people, he says:

> In a society that emphasizes achievement, competition, success, status, fame, money, wealth, recognition, possessions, property, prestige, and power, the poor and old are especially left in abandon. . . . But these expectations have a by-product . . . relaxation in social control. A category with such altered attitudinal flexibility allows its members to participate in marginal activities that would be considered inappropriate for younger members of the society. (112–113)

One such activity is collecting pop bottles. A common sight on the streets of Belmar is an aged man or woman, with a pushcart, wagon, shopping cart or in an old truck, collecting soft drink or beer bottles. John Collier, for instance, who is seventy-four years old, leaves home every day at about seven in the morning. Taking a toy wagon that was broken and discarded, he proceeds in a different direction each day. Large bottles bring in ten cents each and the small ones are worth five cents. His weekly earnings average between $25 and $30, which constitutes a substantial increment to the small amounts he receives through welfare and Social Security. Young people in the neighborhood look down on scavenging; as one said, "Man! I wouldn't be caught dead pulling a wagon with pop bottles in it. People would laugh me outa town. I need money, but not that bad, and I damn sure don't need that kind of money. I'd go hungry first" (113). Says John Collier, "You know, when you get old, things ain't what they used to be. I woulda been too proud to do this when I was a young buck, but now the old man do what he can and he don't worry about what people say. Money is money. It don't matter how you make it as long as it's honest work. At least I ain't stealing" (114).

African Americans, are drawn into the drug economy as sellers. Their lives are fractured with danger and violence. Some anthropologists have undertaken research in such settings, including Philippe Bourgois (1994), who reports on his findings in Harlem (recall his Voices box, "The Art of Fitting In" in Chapter 2):

> Regular displays of violence are necessary for success in the underground economy—especially at the street-level drug-dealing world. Violence is essential for maintaining credibility and for preventing rip-off by colleagues, customers, and hold-up artists. Indeed, upward mobility in the underground economy requires a systematic and effective use of violence. . . . Behaviour that appears irrationally violent and self-destructive to the middle class (or the working class) outside observer, can be reinterpreted according to the logic of the underground economy, as a judicious case of public relations, advertising, rapport building, and long-term investment in one's "human capital development." (29)

In many parts of the world, prostitution is illegal, but exists as part of the informal sector, both locally and globally. In the United States, prostitution is legal only in the state of Nevada, where incomes from prostitution are taxable just like any other occupation. In other states, it is illegal and part of the informal economy. Prostitution, like topless or nude dancing, is technically illegal but largely tolerated.

In Thailand, the sex industry is the leading sector of the economy (Petras and Wongchaisuwan 1993). In 1990, Thailand's sex industry accounted for about 10 percent of Thailand's GNP, following closely behind income from all agricultural imports. Much of the income derives from Thailand's international popularity as a place for "sex tourism," which is travel that includes a "sex package." Thai prostitutes are also part of the international "export" sex industry. Over 200,000 Thai prostitutes live in Europe, while many others live in Japan, Hong Kong, Taiwan, Singapore, the United States, Saudi Arabia, and Kuwait.

Child prostitution in Thailand is an increasingly important part of this informal economy. The number of child prostitutes under sixteen years old is estimated to be about 800,000, or 40 percent of the total prostitute labor force. Recent changes, especially the fear of AIDS, have stepped up the demand for ever younger prostitutes, since people associate child sex with safe sex. "During the 1980s most child prostitutes were over 10 years old; in the 1990s recruitment of children began as young as 6 years old" (Petras and Wongchaisuwan 1993:441). Declining rural incomes in the northern areas of Thailand prompt more parents to sell their daughters into prostitution, with the price of a child ranging between $280 and $1200 depending on her looks. Health risks are high for prostitutes. In Thailand, statistics show that AIDS is increasing rapidly among child prostitutes. Many international organizations have become involved in focusing attention on the issue of child prostitution in Thailand. Thai authorities have responded by making a few arrests of foreign customers, who are sentenced to long jail terms.

Changing Cultural Worlds of Industrial Workers: Barberton

Increased mechanization is a major aspect of change in industry worldwide, and it has marked impacts on labor. Unemployment and manufacturing declines in America's Rust Belt are well-known trends in industrial life-ways. Gregory Pappas (1989) studied unemployment in Barberton, a working-class Ohio town. A tire company that had been the town's major employer closed in 1980, eliminating 1,200 jobs. Pappas lived in Barberton for a year, interviewing many people and sending a questionnaire to over 600 displaced workers for further information. His work sheds light on how unemployed workers cope either by migrating or by finding new ways to spend their time in Barberton. These people are faced with having to construct a new identity for themselves: "For factory workers the place of employment is crucial; their identities are bound up in a particular place, and plant shutdowns compromise their ability to understand themselves" (83). As one unemployed man commented, "I don't know who I am anymore." In this context of decline, levels of stress and mental disorder have increased for many people.

The Future of Industrialism

Many experts question the current and future sustainabiity of a mode of production that relies so heavily on the use of nonrenewable resources and that is also polluting the very planet that thus far has provided those resources. Others suggest that new forms of energy will be discovered and many planets besides earth will be able to provide both resources and places of human habitation. Given the global interconnections of industrialism—its demand for raw materials, markets, and labor, and its social and environmental effects—cultural anthropologists are now being challenged to devise new theories and methods to study such complexity.

SUMMARY

The dominant ways of providing for people's needs, or modes of production, include foraging, horticulture, pastoralism, agriculture, and industrialism. These modes of production can be arranged historically in a production continuum, with contrasting features emerging between foraging, the oldest mode of production, and industrialism.

In foraging societies, production is geared toward use and is family-based, with the only division of labor being based on gender and age. Sharing of food is common, and no people or groups are excluded from access to food. All people have roughly equal access to resources such as land and water holes, which are held collectively by family groups and shared with others as needed. Foraging is regionally extensive, with groups migrating periodically. Most evidence indicates that foraging, with its strategy of limited exploitation of local resources in combination with seasonal migration within bounded areas, has long-term sustainability when not affected by encroachments from other economic systems.

Industrial systems, particularly industrial capitalism, are geared toward production for profit, with the goal being to satisfy ever-increasing consumer demands through market sales. Sharing networks still exist among close family groups, but society is socially stratified, with some classes of people having more access to goods and resources while others are excluded. Work is socially differentiated by class as well as by gender and age, with a division between primary and secondary labor markets and the existence of widespread unemployment. Given its intensive and ever-expanding exploitation of nonrenewable resources, industrialism lacks long-term sustainability.

In between foraging and industrialism, the modes of production of horticulture, pastoralism, and agriculture exhibit some characteristics of foraging societies and, with increasing integration into the world-economy, more of the traits of industrial societies. Because horticulture and pastoralism are extensive strategies, requiring the sequential fallowing of plots in horticulture and the seasonal migration of animals to fresh pastures in pastoralism, these systems frequently come in conflict with agricultural and industrial systems that seek to claim their territories for more intensive use.

CRITICAL THINKING QUESTIONS

1. Which are the leading countries in today's world-economy and why? Were these the same leading countries two hundred years ago? One hundred years ago? What accounts for your answer?
2. Are there examples of foraging being practiced in the contemporary United States or Canada?
3. How does one measure the efficiency of a mode of production? Given your definition, how does foraging compare to agriculture as a way of producing food and goods?

KEY CONCEPTS

agriculture, p. 68
capital, p. 73
capitalism, p. 54
collectivized agriculture, p. 73
consumption, p. 54
corporate farm, p. 72
domestication, p. 61
dualism, p. 55
economic system, p. 54
exchange, p. 54
extensive strategy, p. 57
feudalism, p. 54
foraging, p. 56
formal sector, p. 76
horticulture, p. 61
industrial agriculture, p. 72
industrialism, p. 75
informal sector, p. 76
intensive strategy, p. 68
mode of production, p. 54
pastoralism, p. 64
plantation agriculture, p. 71
privatization, p. 67
production, p. 54
public/private dichotomy, p. 68
socialism, p. 54
use rights, p. 59
wet rice agriculture, p. 69

SUGGESTED READINGS

Anne Allison, *Nightwork: Sexuality, Pleasure and Corporate Masculinity in a Tokyo Hostess Club.* Chicago: University of Chicago Press, 1994. Based on the author's participant observation, this book explores what it is like to work as a hostess in a club that caters to corporate male employees and discusses how that microculture is linked to men's corporate work culture.

Frances Dahlberg, ed. *Woman the Gatherer.* New Haven: Yale University Press, 1981. These path-breaking essays examine the role of women in four different foraging societies, provide insights on human evolution from studies of female chimpanzees, and give an overview of women's role in human cultural adaptation.

Elliot Fratkin, *Ariaal Pastoralists of Kenya: Surviving Drought and Development in Africa's Arid Lands.* Boston: Allyn and Bacon, 1998. Based on several phases of ethnographic research among the Ariaal beginning in the 1970s, this book provides insights about pastoralism in general and the particular cultural strategies of the Ariaal, including attention to social organization and family life.

David Uru Iyam, *The Broken Hoe: Cultural Reconfiguration in Biase Southeast Nigeria.* Chicago: The University of Chicago Press, 1995. Based on fieldwork among the Biase people by an anthropologist who is a member of a Biase group, this book examines changes since the 1970s in the traditional forms of subsistence—agriculture, fishing, and trade—and related issues such as environmental deterioration and population growth.

Katherine S. Newman, *Falling from Grace: The Experience of Downward Mobility in the American Middle Class.* New York: The Free Press, 1988. This book provides ethnographic research on the downwardly mobile of New Jersey as a "special tribe," with attention to loss of employment by corporate managers and blue-collar workers, and the effects of downward mobility on middle-class family life, particularly women.

CHAPTER 4

Consumption and Exchange

CHAPTER OUTLINE

CULTURE AND CONSUMPTION
- What Is Consumption?
- Modes of Consumption
- Consumption Funds

CONSUMPTION INEQUALITIES
- *Critical Thinking:* Assessing One's Own Entitlement Bundle
- Entitlements at Three Levels
- Famine as Entitlement Failure

CONSUMPTION MICROCULTURES
- Class
- Gender
- Race
- Age

CULTURE AND HOUSEHOLD BUDGETING
- Patterns of Budgetary Decision Making

FORBIDDEN CONSUMPTION: FOOD TABOOS
- Cultural Materialism and Food Taboos
- Food Taboos as Systems of Meaning

CULTURE AND EXCHANGE
- *Multiple Cultural Worlds:* Favors, Gifts, and Banquets in China
- What is Exchanged?
- *Multiple Cultural Worlds:* The Rules of Hospitality in Oman
- Modes of Exchange
- *Multiple Cultural Worlds:* Sustained Unbalanced Exchange in the Ituri Rainforest

ANALYZING EXCHANGE SYSTEMS
- Exchange and Risk Aversion
- Exchange and Social Inequality

CHANGING PATTERNS OF CONSUMPTION AND EXCHANGE
- The Lure of Western Goods
- Cash-Cropping and Declining Nutrition: You Can't Eat Sisal
- Privatization's Effects: The New Rich and the New Poor of Russia and Eastern Europe
- *Current Event:* "Could This Be Russia?"
- A New Way of Buying: The Credit Card
- *Current Event:* "Credit Card Regulation in the Republic of Korea"
- Continuities and Resistance: The Enduring Potlatch

SUMMARY

CRITICAL THINKING QUESTIONS

KEY CONCEPTS

SUGGESTED READINGS

◀ An itinerant cloth peddler, rural Ghana.

Imagine that it is the late eighteenth century and you are a member of the Kwakwaka'wakw tribe of British Columbia in Canada's Pacific Northwest region. Along with the rest of your local tribal group, you have been invited to a **potlatch,** a grand feast in which guests are invited to eat and to receive gifts from the hosts (Suttles 1991). Be prepared to eat a lot because potlatch guests are given abundant helpings of the most honorable foods: eulachon oil (oil from the eulachon fish, which has high fat content), high-bush cranberries, and seal meat, all served in ceremonial wooden bowls. The chief will present the guests with many gifts: hand-embroidered blankets, canoes, and carefully crafted household articles such as carved wooden boxes and woven mats, and food to be taken back home. The more the chief gives, the higher his status will rise, and the more his guests will be indebted to him. Later, when it is the guests' turn to hold a potlatch, they will try to give away as much as—or more than—their host did, thus shaming him into giving the next potlatch. Before the arrival of the Europeans, tribes throughout the Pacific Northwest were linked with each other through a network of potlatching relationships. The Europeans tried to stop potlatching because they thought it was "wasteful," and because it contained elements that offended Christian principles they were trying to promote. In spite of the fact that the colonialists even made potlatching illegal, it survived to the present among some groups and is being revived by others.

A granary in West Africa allows for the saving of food crops for several months. The fact that it is raised above ground protects it from being eaten by animals and from moisture damage.

One of many anthropological theories about the potlatch is a **functional theory,** which looks at a given practice or belief in terms of its contribution to cultural continuity. This theory says that potlatch networks provided a food safety net for people in the region (Piddocke 1969). Because of local annual fluctuations in food supply, a particular group might have a substantial surplus of fish, berries, and nuts during one year, but a deficit in the next year. Food stuffs could not be saved for long enough to deal with this unevenness. Instead of saving food, people "banked" food through potlatching: A group experiencing an abundant season would be inspired to potlatch its neighbors and distribute its surplus to others. In the future, a former host group would be the guests at a neighboring group's potlatch when they had a surplus.

This brief sketch of potlatching demonstrates how closely linked production, consumption, and exchange are. Potlatches relate to levels of production; they are opportunities for consumption; and they involve exchange of goods among groups. This chapter follows Chapter 3 closely in taking up the cultural anthropology of consumption and exchange as the two remaining parts of economic systems. As in Chapter 3, we use the results of cross-cultural research in delineating differences between dominant modes of consumption and exchange, moving across the production continuum from foraging to industrialism (see Figure 4.1).

300,000 years ago ← FORAGING · HORTICULTURE · 12,000 years ago · PASTORALISM	10,000 years ago · AGRICULTURE · present → INDUSTRIALISM (capitalist)
Mode of Consumption Minimalism Finite needs	**Mode of Consumption** Consumerism Infinite needs
Social Organization of Consumption Equality/sharing	**Social Organization of Consumption** Class-based inequality
Primary Budgetary Fund Basic needs	**Primary Budgetary Fund** Rent/taxes, luxuries
Mode of Exchange Balanced exchange	**Mode of Exchange** Market exchange
Social Organization of Exchange Small groups, face-to-face	**Social Organization of Exchange** Anonymous market transactions
Primary Category of Exchange The gift	**Primary Category of Exchange** The sale

FIGURE 4.1
Modes of Consumption and Exchange

CULTURE AND CONSUMPTION

What Is Consumption?

Consumption has two general senses: First, it is a person's "intake" in terms of eating or other ways of using things; second, it is a person's "output" in terms of spending or using resources. Thus, consumption includes eating habits and household budgeting practices. People consume many things: Food, drink, clothing, and shelter are the most basic consumption needs. Beyond that, they may acquire and use tools, weapons, means of transportation, computers, books and other items of communication, art and other luxury goods, and energy for heating and cooling one's residence.

In order to consume, one must have something to consume or to trade for something consumable. In a market economy, most consumption depends on having cash. A person's ability to consume would thus be measured in terms of cash income. Economists who study consumption in cash-based market economies often use data on people's cash income or expenditures as measures of consumption. However, cultural anthropologists are interested in all economic systems, not just market economies, so the categories they use for analysis of economic processes must be more broadly applicable. In all economies, people expend something to satisfy their needs. In premarket economies, instead of expending cash, people "spend" time, labor, or trade goods in order to provide for their needs. While it may seem odd to consider time or labor as equivalent to cash, this conceptual framework allows for cross-cultural comparison of people's access to resources and how it influences their consumption patterns.

The relationship between the processes of consumption and exchange also differs between nonmarket and market systems. In nonmarket economies, many consumption needs are satisfied without any exchange at all, or only to a limited degree. In market economies, most consumption items are not self-produced and must be purchased. Thus, aspects of consumption and exchange overlap substantially. For example, when a horticulturalist grows food for home consumption using seeds saved from the previous year, no exchange is involved in providing for consumption. If a farmer purchases seeds and fertilizer to grow food, then exchange has become an essential part of providing for consumption needs. In nonmarket economies, relatively few goods must be obtained through exchange, while in market economies most goods are obtained this way.

Modes of Consumption

On the basis of cross-cultural evidence on consumption, we can construct a general picture of **modes of consumption** (dominant patterns of using things up or spending one's resources in order to satisfy demands) that corresponds generally with the production continuum (see Figure 4.1 on page 83). At the opposite ends of the continuum, two contrasting modes of consumption exist, defined on the relationship between demand (what people want) and supply (the resources available to satisfy demand) (Sahlins 1972). **Minimalism** is a mode of consumption that emphasizes simplicity and is characterized by few and finite (limited) consumer demands and an adequate and sustainable means to achieve them. At the other end of the continuum is **consumerism,** in which people's demands are many and infinite and the means of satisfying them are, therefore, insufficient and become depleted in the effort to meet demands. Minimalism is most clearly exemplified in (free-ranging) foraging societies, while consumerism is the distinguishing feature of industrial cultures (of the capitalist variety). In between these two extremes are blended patterns, with a decreasing trend toward minimalism and an increasing trend toward consumerism as one moves from left to right. Changes in the mode of production influence the transformation in consumption. Notably, the increase of surpluses and the ability to store wealth for long periods of time allow for a more consumerist lifestyle to emerge.

The social organization of consumption also changes as one moves across the continuum. As noted in Chapter 3, social inequality in access to resources increases as one moves from foraging to agricultural and industrial (especially capitalist) societies. In foraging societies, everyone has equal access to all resources. Food, land, water, and materials for shelter are communally shared as among the traditional Ju/wasi:

> Food is never consumed alone by a family; it is always (actually or potentially) shared out with members of a living group or band of up to 30 (or more) members. Even though only a fraction of the able-bodied foragers go out each day, the day's return of meat and gathered foods are divided in such a way that every member of the camp receives an equitable share. The hunting band or camp is a unit of sharing, and if sharing breaks down it ceases to be a camp. (Lee 1979:118)

The distribution of personal goods, such as clothing or "leisure" items such as musical instruments or smoking pipes, is also equal. In horticultural and pastoral societies, group sharing is still a prevalent ethic, and it is the duty of leaders to make sure that everyone has food and shelter.

At the other end of the continuum, we find the United States, the leading consumerist culture of the world (Durning 1993). Consumption levels in the United States, since the 1970s, have been the highest of any society in human history. Consumerism is widely promoted as a good thing, a path to happiness. Increasing one's consumption level and quality of life is a primary personal goal of most people, and of the government, too. Many other nations around the world have growing economies that allow some of the population to demand consumer goods and have the energy capabilities to support a westernized lifestyle (cars, air conditioning, and other appliances). These countries include the rapidly developing nations of Southeast Asia, such as Thailand and Vietnam, and many countries in Africa and Latin America. For example, Ghana's economy has grown at about 5 percent a year for the past decade. At the same time, electricity consumption increased almost 11 percent a year in the nation and in Accra, the capital, at over 13 percent a year. At this rate, national consumption of electricity will double in five years. The increase is the result of both industrial growth and increased consumer demand. Once unattainable luxuries—electrical appliances and other gadgets such as fans, refrigerators, televisions, stereos, air conditioners, VCRs, computers, and fax machines—are increasingly common in Ghanaian homes (*The Economist* November 26, 1994:45).

In all, the amount of goods that the world's population consumed in the past fifty years equals what was consumed by all previous generations in human history. Minimalism was sustainable over hundreds of thousands of years. In contrast, many experts have provided data documenting the nonsustainability of consumerism. Some nations, such as Sweden, have taken steps to control consumerism and its negative environmental effects:

> Stockholm is attempting to reduce the dependence on cars. The city is laid out to encourage walking, bicycling, and, in the long winter, cross-country skiing. Continuous paths through parklands encircle many of the islands on which the city is built, and Stockholm's commercial district is laced with bicycle routes, wide sidewalks, and pedestrian zones. Buses move swiftly through the metropolis, and the national bus and railway depot is in the heart of the city. People commute not only by foot and cycle, but also by kayak through the city's dozens of channels and waterways. (Durning 1993:23)

Consumption Funds

A **consumption fund** is a category of a person's or household's budget used to provide for their demands. Cross-cultural analysis of expenditures (including time or labor and cash) reveal the existence of a set of categories that are universal, although the amount of the budget allocated to each category varies according to the mode of production and the amount of surplus goods available in the society. In looking at a typical set of consumption funds, it is important to remember that foragers in nonmonetized contexts "spend" time or labor, not cash.

In a forager's "budget," the largest share of expenditures goes into the **basic needs fund,** which includes food, beverages, shelter, fuel, clothing, and the tools needed to obtain these items. In other words, foragers "spend" the largest proportion of their "budget" on providing basic needs. The next most important category for foragers is the **recurrent costs fund,** which supports repair and maintenance of tools and baskets, weapons, and shelter. Smaller amounts of expenditure are made to the **entertainment fund,** for personal leisure, and the **ceremonial fund,** for public events beyond the immediate group such as a potlatch. No funds go to the **tax/rent fund** (payments to a government or landowner for civic responsibilities or use of land or housing).

Consumption budgets in consumerist cultures differ in the overall size of the budget and in the proportions allocated to particular funds. First, the budget size is larger. People in agricultural and industrial societies work longer hours (unless they are unemployed); thus, they "spend" more time and labor than foragers. They also have cash budgets that may be substantial, depending on class position. In terms of budget shares, the basic needs fund shrinks to being the smallest fund. This change follows a well-known economic principle that says: budgetary shares for food and housing decline as income rises. The word "shares" is important. People with higher incomes may spend more on food and housing in an absolute sense than people with lower incomes, but the proportion of their total budget devoted to food and housing is less. For example, someone who earns a total of $1,000 a month and spends $800 on food and housing, expends 80 percent of his budget in that category. Someone who makes $10,000 a month and spends $2,000 a month on food and housing, expends only 20 percent of her budget in this category, even though she spends more than twice as much as the first person, in an absolute sense. Another marked change is that people living in agricultural and industrial cultures devote the largest proportion of their budget to the tax/rent fund. In some agricultural contexts, tenant farmers and sharecroppers provide one-third or one-half of their crops to the landlord as rent. Income taxes constitute over 50 percent of income in countries such as Japan, Sweden, the Netherlands, and Italy (Pechman 1987). Another change is the increased importance of the entertainment fund, which is used for recreation such as attending movies and sports events, travel, and buying "home entertainment" appliances.

CONSUMPTION INEQUALITIES

Amartya Sen (1981), an economist and a philosopher, came up with the concept of **entitlements,** which are socially defined rights to life-sustaining resources, in order to explain why some groups suffer more than others during a famine. In this book, we will extend the use of the concept of entitlements to nonfamine situations as well, as a way of looking at consumption inequalities in everyday life. Also, Sen's original use of the entitlement concept was in terms of intrasocietal patterns, but we will use it at three levels: global, national, and household. The concept of entitlements is an important tool for understanding how social inequality works. So far, it has been underutilized by cultural anthropologists. This section, and other areas in this book, should make clear its value.

According to Sen, a person possesses a set or "bundle" of entitlements. A person may own land, earn cash from a job, be on welfare, or live off an inheritance, for example. Through these entitlements, people provide for their consumption. A crucial factor in entitlement theory is that some kinds of entitlements are more secure and more lucrative than others, and thus they provide more secure and luxurious levels of consumption (see the Critical Thinking box). **Direct entitlements** are the most secure form of entitlement; in an agricultural society, for example, owning land that produces food is a direct entitlement. **Indirect entitlements** are ways of gaining subsistence that depend on exchanging something in order to obtain consumer needs—for example, labor, animal hides, welfare checks, or food stamps. Indirect entitlements entail dependency on other people and institutions, and they are thus riskier bases of support than direct entitlements. For example, labor or animal hides may drop in value or no longer be wanted, and food stamps may cease to be awarded. People who have no direct entitlements and only one or two forms of indirect entitlements in their bundle are in the most vulnerable position during economic recession, famine, or other times when access to resources becomes squeezed. In foraging societies, everyone has the same entitlement bundles and, except for infants and the very aged, the bundles are direct (infants and the aged are dependent on sharing from members of the group for their food and shelter and so could be said

CRITICAL THINKING

Assessing One's Own Entitlement Bundle

- Do you own land on which you grow your own food? If yes, then a basic part of your entitlement bundle consists of direct entitlements to food.
- Or, do you buy your food? If so, where do you get the money to buy food? If parents or other relatives give you money to buy food, then your entitlement bundle consists of indirect entitlements of two sorts: cash transfers from other people and then exchange of cash for food. Maybe you work for someone who pays you cash in return for your labor. That's an indirect entitlement, too.
- What would you do if every cafeteria, restaurant, and grocery store declared that they no longer would accept money in exchange for food?
- Do you have any other entitlements in your bundle that you could use to get food? You might take some of your personal goods, such as your bicycle or computer, to trade for food. You might see if some of your friends or relatives have some stored-up supplies that they would give you or lend you. If you own land, you might start planting food crops, but that would not help in the short run. In an extreme situation in which none of these options worked, you might be driven to stealing food, but theft is not considered an entitlement because it is illegal.
- If none of these strategies succeeds, you have experienced "entitlement failure" and the end result could be starvation.

to have indirect entitlements). In industrial capitalist societies, entitlement bundles, in terms of access to food and resources, are preponderantly indirect. The few people who still grow their own food are a small proportion of the total population, and even they are dependent on indirect entitlements for electricity and other aspects of maintaining their lifestyle. In the highly monetized cash economies of industrialized societies, the most powerful entitlements are those that provide a high and steady cash income such as having a good job, savings, and a retirement fund.

Entitlements at Three Levels

Applied globally, entitlement theory allows us to differentiate between nations that have more secure and direct access to life-supporting resources than others. Nations with strong rates of food production have a stronger entitlement to food than nations that are dependent on imports, for example. Growing cash crops rather than food crops puts a nation in a situation of indirect entitlement to food. The same applies to access to energy sources that may be important for transportation to work or for heating homes. Direct access to energy resources is preferable to indirect access. The current structure of the world-economy, as noted in Chapter 3, places some countries in far more secure positions than others.

In a parallel way, the entitlement concept can be applied at the micro level of the household to examine within-household entitlement structures. In contemporary industrial societies, having a job, owning a business or farm land, owning a home, or having savings and investments puts a person in a more secure position. This means that often adult members, and males more than females in most industrial societies, have more secure entitlements than other household members. Depending on the cultural context, inheritance practices may ensure that certain children receive entitlements to certain assets (the family business, for example) while others are left out, thus passing on entitlement bundles over time.

Famine as Entitlement Failure

Famine is massive death resulting from food deprivation in a geographically widespread area. It tends to reach a crisis point and then subside. Famines have been recorded throughout history for all parts of the world, including Europe (Dando 1980:113). Between

Homeless children rest by a storefront grate in Ho Chi Minh City, Vietnam. The transition from socialism to capitalism has brought with it social inequalities and a growing class of people with no direct entitlements to food. These children and their families depend on begging to survive.

the year 10 AD and 1850, 187 famines were recorded in what is now the United Kingdom. India, Russia, and China experienced major famines in the twentieth century. Most recently, famines have occurred mainly in the Sahel: the Sahelian famine of 1969–1971, the Ethiopian famine of 1982–1984, the Sudan and Somalian famines of 1988–1992, and the North Korean famine (or near-famine) of 1996–1997.

Most people think that famines are caused by "too many people to feed," or natural disasters such as droughts and floods. Neither overpopulation nor natural disasters are sufficient explanations for famine. First, calculations of world food supply in relation to population indicate that there is enough food produced every year to feed the world's population. Second, natural factors are often catalysts of famines, but natural disasters happen in many parts of the world and are not necessarily followed by famine. For example, Florida's devastating Hurricane Andrew did not cause a statewide famine. The answer to what causes famine lies in entitlement failures at three levels: global, national, and household.

Global Entitlements

World-economy theory, sometimes called political

economy theory, provides an improved understanding of famine causation (Chen 1991; Lappé and Collins 1986). First, it shows that throughout history, many countries that were colonized by external powers are now more resource-depleted than before and more dependent on food imports. Colonization changed local production from that of food crops for the farmers themselves to cash crops for sale. Thus, massive replacement of direct entitlements to food to indirect entitlements occurred. International relations in contemporary times often involve the "politics of food." As a journalist reported on the Sudan in 1988: "There is, cruelly, food to be had. The land is fertile, the rains were good, and this year's harvest will be the best in a decade. But 4 million people are starving because of a civil war. . . . On both sides the terrible weapon is increasingly food, not bullets" (Wilde 1988:43). The northern army blocked the delivery of food aid to the south, and the food that did get through was often diverted by the southern rebel troops. Norway donated substantial amounts of maize, but the United States was slow to get involved because it did not want to upset its diplomatic relationship with the Sudanese government. Global politics were a key causal factor in the Bengal famine of 1943–44. This massive famine was related to British efforts during World War II to stop the Japanese forces from advancing into India from Burma. The region of Bengal at that time included what is now a state of India (named West Bengal) and the nation of Bangladesh (called East Bengal when it was part of British India). Bengal was a lush food-producing region located, unfortunately, adjacent to Burma. As the Japanese moved closer to India, the British devised and implemented a plan to destroy food supplies in Bengal that could be used by the advancing enemy. The British burned standing crops and seeds that were being stored, and destroyed fishing boats as well (Greenough 1982; Sen 1981). This policy succeeded in stopping the Japanese, but at a terrible cost to thousands of Bengalis.

National Entitlements

Within nations, entitlement inequalities lead to particular patterns of suffering. In no famine, ever, has everyone in the affected area starved. Instead, many people grow wealthy by hoarding food and selling it at inflated prices. During the Bengal famine, the people who were most affected were those lacking direct entitlements to food: the landless poor who normally worked as laborers for the landowners and were paid in cash food shares, and fishing people who could not fish without boats (Sen 1981). In the meantime, rich landowners and merchants bought up the rice that existed and secretly stored it. As food prices rose astronomically during the famine, they grew even richer by selling hoarded rice.

Intrahousehold Entitlements

Within households, famine conditions force decisions about how to allocate scarce resources or deal with the absence of any resources at all. No cultural anthropologist was on the scene during the Bengal famine, studying intrahousehold decision making. However, indirect historical evidence of how decisions were made can be found in records kept by the Bengal Relief Committee about people who came to their centers for relief, mainly in the form of food, but also medicine and clothing (Greenough 1982). These records contain information about the households of those who appeared at the centers for help. One of the clearest findings is that the famine caused the break-up of households. In Bengali culture, males are valued over females and adults are valued over children. In the household, the senior male is the head of household and has the highest authority and responsibility. These values are reflected in resource allocation choices during times of scarcity: Adults are valued over children and males over females. During the famine, spouses frequently separated, with the husband either leaving the wife behind or sending her away. The relief records show a high number of abandoned married women. Women who were interviewed said that "their husbands were unable to maintain them at the present moment and asked them to go elsewhere to search for food" (quoted in Greenough 1992:220). Many of these women migrated to cities, such as Calcutta, where their options for survival were limited to dependency on relief hand-outs, begging, or prostitution. Some women and girls were sold by their families into prostitution. Children of both genders were sold by desperate families either in hope that someone else could give them food or for the immediate purpose of obtaining cash. Many children were simply abandoned by the roadside. The preeminence and importance of the male head of household and the emphasis on preservation of the family line through males in Bengal shaped this pattern of decision making that differentially deprived women and children from household support.

CONSUMPTION MICROCULTURES

This section provides some examples of consumption microcultures, in the basic categories of class, gender, race, and age. People's consumption patterns are rarely the consequences of just one microculture, but are shaped by affiliation with multiple and intersecting microcultures that determine entitlement bundles and ways of consuming resources.

Class

Class differences, which are defined in terms of levels of income and wealth, are reflected in class-specific consumption patterns. In cultures with class structures, upper-class people spend more on consumption than the poor. The poor, however, spend a higher percentage of their total income on consumption than the rich, especially on basic needs such as food, clothing, and shelter. Class differences in consumption in contemporary industrial societies may seem so obvious that they are scarcely worth studying. A team of French researchers, however, undertook a national sample survey with over 1,000 responses to study class differences in consumer preferences and tastes (Bourdieu 1984). The results revealed strong class patterns in, for example, choice of favorite painters or pieces of music, most closely associated with people's level of education and their father's occupation. An overall pattern of "distance from necessity" in tastes and preferences characterized members of the educated upper classes, who were more likely to prefer abstract art. Their goal was to keep "necessity" at a distance. In comparison, the working classes, given their economic position, were closer to "necessity" and their preference was for realist art. Bourdieu provides the concept of the "game of distinction," in which people of various classes take on the preferences of others in order to enhance their own standing. Education provides the means for learning how to play the game of distinction.

Gender

In many cultures, especially those where males and females have more highly demarcated roles and status, consumption patterns are clearly gender-marked as well. Specific foods may be thought to be "male foods" or "female foods." In cultures where alcoholic beverages are consumed, the overwhelming pattern is that males drink more than females. Following is a vivid example of differences in food consumption that are unequal between males and females in a cultural context in which males generally have higher status than females—Papua New Guinea. This example begins with the eruption of a mysterious disease, with the local name of *kuru,* among the Fore (pronounced FOR-AY), a highland foraging group (Lindenbaum 1979). Between 1957 and 1977, about 2,500 people died of *kuru,* but the victims were mostly women. Shirley Lindenbaum tells us about the onset and development of the disease:

> An initial shivering tremor usually progresses to complete motor incapacity and death in about a year. Women, the prime victims of the disease, may withdraw from the community at the shock of recognizing the first symptoms—pain in the head and limbs, and a slight unsteadiness of gait. They resume their usual gardening activities a few weeks later, struggling to control their involuntary body movements until forced by gross physical incoordination to remain at home, sedentarily awaiting death. (9–10)

The Fore believed that *kuru* was caused by sorcery, but a team of medical researchers and a cultural anthropologist (Lindenbaum) showed that *kuru* was a neurological disease caused by the consumption of the flesh of deceased people who were themselves *kuru* victims. Who was eating human flesh, and why? Among the Fore, it was considered acceptable to cook and eat the meat of a deceased person, although it was not considered a preferred form of food. Some Fore women were turning to eating human flesh because of the increased scarcity of the usual sources of animal protein in the region. Population density had increased, areas under cultivation had increased, forest areas had decreased, and wild animals as a protein source were scarce in the Fore region. This scarcity acted in combination with the Fore's strongly male-preferential system of consumption: Preferred protein sources go to men. Some women, therefore, turned to consumption of less-preferred foods and thereby contracted *kuru.*

Race

The racial apartheid that was a matter of national policy in South Africa until recently is one of the world's clearest examples of explicit definition of racial inequalities in consumption. Whites owned property, had wealth, and lived prosperous lives that included good food, housing, and educational opportunities for their children. Blacks were denied all of these things. It remains to be seen how the current government in South Africa will be able to redress decades of deprivation linked to racial categories.

In the United States, political scientist Andrew Hacker (1992) has pointed to the continuing and extreme racial differences in consumption and welfare. One area in which racial discrimination affects consumption is housing, a subject that has been studied by both economists and cultural anthropologists (B. Williams 1988; Yinger 1995). Access by Blacks to housing in integrated neighborhoods is limited by the tendency of Whites to move out as more Black families move in. A 1992 survey conducted in Detroit found that most Blacks prefer to live in an integrated neighborhood, but nearly half of the Whites surveyed said they would move out if the neighborhood were one-third Black (Farley 1993, cited in Yinger 1995:7).

The other side of racial deprivation is racial privilege, a topic that few cultural anthropologists have explicitly addressed. Scholar and essayist Peggy McIntosh (1988) listed a total of twenty-six areas in which she could identify the daily effects of White privilege in her life. Of these, the ones that relate most directly to consumption are:

> If I should need to move, I can be pretty sure of renting or purchasing housing in an area which I can afford and in which I would want to live.
>
> Whether I use checks, credit cards, or cash, I can count on my skin color not to work against the appearance of financial reliability.
>
> I can swear, or dress in second hand clothes . . . without having people attribute these choices to the bad morals, the poverty, or the illiteracy of my race.
>
> I can easily buy posters, postcards, picture books, greeting cards, dolls, toys, and children's magazines featuring people of my race.
>
> I can choose blemish color or bandages in "flesh" color and have them more or less match my skin.
>
> I can be sure that if I need legal or medical help, my race will not work against me. (210–211)

Age

Different age categories also have characteristic consumption patterns that are culturally shaped. In different contexts, certain foods are believed appropriate for infants, young children, adolescents, adults, and the aged. Consider the category of "the aged." Biologically, the elderly have "more critical and unique nutritional needs" than other age groups (Shifflett and McIntosh 1986–1987). In spite of these special needs, in many cultures, the very old fall into a category with declining entitlements and declining quality of consumption. In the United States, the elderly tend to decrease their physical activities, and they tend to omit important food groups, especially fruits and vegetables. Little exercise and inadequate diet lead to increased obesity and reduced resistance to disease. Among elderly Virginians, several factors related to dietary change were discovered, including lack of social support and loneliness. One respondent reported that she had been widowed for ten years and that she had undergone a negative change in her food habits soon after her husband died. For several years she felt she "had nothing to live for." She reported she ate only junk foods and meals she could prepare with the least effort, resulting in a rapid weight gain up to 200 pounds, but "One day I realized what I was doing to my health and I went on a diet. I tried to eat a balanced diet and am still trying to eat better now" (10).

Aging affects everyone, regardless of class level, but wealth can protect the elderly from certain kinds of marginalization and deprivation. Money can often buy better health care, and studies show that income level is positively related to longevity (lifespan) around the world (Sen 1994:30). Wealthier people can afford home care when they become infirm and unable to care for themselves. Middle-class people may spend their last years in a nursing home, and the poor fare even worse. Park benches and shelters provided by local governments and voluntary organizations may be their only option (Vesperi 1985).

CULTURE AND HOUSEHOLD BUDGETING

As some of the previous examples demonstrate, intrahousehold decisions about resource allocations respond to wider cultural rules and thus vary, depending on the cultural context. This statement contrasts with a model prevalent in economics until only recently that sees the household as an egalitarian unit that treated all members equally in the overall interest of the unit as a whole (Becker 1964). This model assumed egalitarian intrahousehold relationships as a given, without considering the possibility that viewing the household as an unexamined "black box" (Folbre 1986) might be inaccurate in many cases. A more appropriate hypothesis is that in particular cultural contexts, household decision makers may or may not differentially treat various members in order to maximize socially constructed individual and collective goals. Cultural anthropologists who have studied the internal dynamics of households look first at the decision makers, and then at the results of their decisions in terms of resource allocations.

Patterns of Budgetary Decision Making

Four major categories of decision making about household budgeting have been found cross-culturally, based on studies of husband-wife units (Pahl 1980, 1983):

- *Male budgetary control:* This form of budgetary management is found in cultures where the husband is sole or main earner and he retains financial control of his income, giving his wife a set amount for household purchases. It is common in Western societies, the Middle East, and India, and in urban, elite cultures around the world that have been influenced by westernization. About one-fourth of all households in the United Kingdom follow this system. In Lusaka, Zambia, this model is termed "doling out":

  > Husbands tend to argue that this arrangement is necessary because their wives are careless with their money. For instance, one husband, a university graduate and senior civil servant explained, "I keep all the money myself and give [sic] my wife when necessary. If you entrust money to a wife, you invite trouble." . . . Many wives appear to be unhappy about their husbands' strict control of the finances. One unemployed wife who had a primary school education complained, "He keeps all the money and makes the budget every month." Wives appear to be unable to alter the arrangement . . . husbands who were particularly authoritarian not only stopped their wives from going out to work, but also exercised strict control of the family income. (Munachonga 1988:187–188)

- *Female budgetary control:* This form of budgetary management is found in cultures where both the wife and the husband are earners, but all earnings are placed under the management of the wife, who gives the husband an allowance for personal expenses. This pattern is common throughout Southeast Asia, including the Philippines, Indonesia, and the mainland. A common belief in Indonesia is that women are more practically minded than men and thus are better money managers. A study in an Indonesian city found that the majority of households were under female budgetary control (Papanek and Schwede 1988). In most of these households, a wife would consult her husband about big expenses, but in one of every four, the wife would make all decisions without consultation.
- *Pooling system:* Both partners place whatever earnings they make into a common fund, both are responsible for managing the common pool, and both may take personal spending money out of the pool. This system is found mainly in dual-income households in Europe and North America.
- *Nonpooling system:* Partners keep their earnings separate and they do not have access to each other's funds; each is responsible for certain expenditures, although there may be transfers between husband and wife (Guyer 1988). The nonpooling system is common in African cultures south of the Sahara.

How do these different organizational models affect intrahousehold decisions about consumption spending? Not enough data are available to answer this question conclusively, but some evidence suggests that women as budgetary managers tend to favor allocations to basic needs and child welfare more than men, who are more likely to shift expenditure shares away from basic needs to personal expenditures (Bruce and Dwyer 1988:5–6). My data on household budgets in Jamaica support this generalization. I found that within a sample of low-income households, budgetary shares for food and housing were larger in households headed by women than in households headed jointly by a man and woman (Miller 1987a). In male-dominated budgetary systems, women have to bargain with the male budget controller for an adequate allowance for domestic needs. In a nonpooling system, the wife is often the one who provides for most of the household's food needs, while the husband is responsible for costs of lodging and children's schooling expenses.

A few anthropologists have begun studying intrahousehold distribution of resources. Biased distribution of food, money, and even affection, may be based on the child's gender, birth order, "looks," or a combination of these things. Inequality of some sort tends to be the norm, even when parents say that their intention is to treat all children equally. Gender is a major distinguishing factor, with son preference a common phenomenon worldwide. Evidence from a few cultures—the United States, Peru, and Malaysia—reveals a sort of "gender alliance," with mothers favoring daughters and fathers favoring sons (Thomas 1991).

Biases regarding particular adult family members have also been documented. In Ghana, West Africa, a bias in expenditures in favor of adult males occurs in both urban and rural areas, and in different regions and religious groups (Deaton 1987). A study in western Nepal reveals that mothers there have the most limited food shares within the household (Gittelsohn 1991).

FORBIDDEN CONSUMPTION: FOOD TABOOS

Anthropologists have a longstanding interest in trying to explain culturally specific food **taboos,** or rules of prohibition. This interest has generated several conflicting theories, with the strongest difference between the cultural materialists, led by Marvin Harris, and those who favor symbolic or meaning-centered theories.

Cultural Materialism and Food Taboos

Marvin Harris (1974) asks why there are Jewish and Muslim taboos on eating pig when pig meat is so enthusiastically consumed in many other parts of the world. He says, "Why should gods so exalted as Jahweh and Allah have bothered to condemn a harmless and even laughable beast whose flesh is relished by the greater part of mankind?" (36). Harris proposes that we consider the role of environmental factors during early Hebrew times and the function of this prohibition in terms of its fit to the local ecology:

> Within the overall pattern of this mixed farming and pastoral complex, the divine prohibition of pork constituted a sound ecological strategy. The nomadic Israelites could not raise pigs in their arid habitats, while for the semi-sedentary and village farming populations, pigs were more of a threat than an asset.... The pig has a further disadvantage of not being a practical source of milk, and of being notoriously difficult to herd over long distances.... Above all, the pig is thermodynamically ill-adapted to the hot, dry climate of the Negev, the Jordan Valley, and the other lands of the Bible and the Koran. Compared to cattle, goats, and sheep, the pig has an inefficient system for regulating its body temperature. Despite the expression "To sweat like a pig," it has recently been proved that pigs can't sweat at all. (41–42)

Raising pigs in this context would be a luxury. On the other hand, in "pig-loving" cultures of Southeast Asia and the Pacific, climatic factors including temperature, humidity, and the presence of forest cover (good for pigs) promote pig raising. There, pigs offer an important protein source in people's diets that complements yams, sweet potatoes, and taro. In conclusion, Harris acknowledges that not all religiously sanctioned food practices can be explained ecologically, and he allows that food practices do have a social function in promoting social identity. But first and foremost, analysis of food consumption should consider ecological and material factors of production.

Food Taboos as Systems of Meaning

Mary Douglas (1966) claims that what people eat has less to do with the material conditions of life (hunger) than with the value of food as a way of communicating meaning about the world. For Douglas, people's mental categories provide a psychological ordering of the world. Anomalies, or things that don't fit into the categories, become reminders to people of moral problems or things to avoid. She uses this approach of ordered categories and disordered anomalies in her analysis of food prohibitions in the Old Testament book of Leviticus. One rule is that people may eat animals with cloven hoofs and that chew a cud. Several tabooed animals are said to be unclean, such as the camel, the pig, the hare, and the rock badger. Among a pastoral people, she says, it is logical that the model food animal would be a ruminant (a cloven-hoofed, cud-chewing, four-footed animal such as cattle, bison, goats, and sheep). In contrast, a pig is a four-footed animal with cloven hoofs, but it does not chew a cud, thus the pig is an anomaly and taboo as food. In this way, Leviticus sets up a system that contrasts sacred completeness and purity (the animals one can eat) with impurity and sinfulness (the animals one cannot eat) to remind people of God's holiness and perfectness and people's responsibility toward God.

Stanley Tambiah (1985) provides a similar meaning-centered theory about food taboos, using data from Thailand. In rural Thailand, he says, animals are classified in terms of their nearness to people. There are animals of the house, the village, and the forest. Animals of the village include the dog, cat, ox, buffalo, pig, chicken, and duck, but only dogs and cats will live inside houses with people. The categories of animals parallel categories of people with whom one may have sex and marry. At the extreme ends of each series—the nearest and farthest categories—taboos prohibit interaction either through consumption (animals) or sex and marriage (humans). This coding, in Tambiah's view, works to bind individuals and groups to moral rules of conduct. Thus, rules about food are important as guides to proper behavior among humans.

People who favor either a cultural materialist or meaning-centered approach to food taboos all acknowledge that there is more to food than just eating. But those on each side object to their position being ignored by the other side. For example, Douglas chooses to emphasize the importance of food rules as forms of communication, downplaying the "practical" aspects of food, which she says "sidetrack" analysts from studying the meaning of food (Douglas and Isherwood 1979:59). Harris would concur that food rules serve such purposes, but that focusing only on meaning gives a partial view because it overlooks material aspects of food practices and rules.

CULTURE AND EXCHANGE

Cultural anthropologists have been fascinated with gifts and other forms of exchange since the early twentieth century studies by Malinowski of the kula of the Trobriand Islands (described below) and Boas's research on the potlatch of the Pacific Northwest. We know that in all economic systems, individuals and groups exchange goods and services with others, so exchange is a cultural universal. But variation arises in several areas. What is exchanged; how are goods exchanged; when does exchange take place; and with what effects does exchange vary from culture to culture? (See the Multiple Cultural Worlds box on page 94.)

What Is Exchanged?

Exchange involves the transfer of something that may be material or immaterial between at least two persons, groups, or institutions. The items exchanged may be purely utilitarian or they may carry meanings and have a history, or "social life," of their own (Appadurai 1986). In contemporary industrial societies, money is a key item of exchange. In less market-oriented cultures, it is purely utilitarian: No dollar bill has more meaning or significance than any other. In many other economies, money plays a less important role and valued items such as time, labor, and goods are prominent exchange items. But nonmonetary exchange exists in contemporary industrial societies, too. Hosting dinner parties, exchanging gifts at holiday times, and sharing a bag of potato chips with a friend are examples of common forms of nonmonetary exchange. Some people would even include giving caresses, kisses, loyalty, and glances (Blau 1964).

Material Goods

Food is one of the most common exchange goods, both in everyday life and on ritual occasions. Marriage arrangements often involve complex stages of gifts and countergifts exchanged between the groom's family and the bride's family. As Lévi-Strauss commented many years ago, "[M]arriage is regarded everywhere as a particularly favourable occasion for the initiation or development of a cycle of exchanges" (1969:63). Wedding exchanges among the Nias of northern Sumatra, Indonesia, provide a good illustration. From the betrothal onward to the actual marriage, there is a scheduled sequence of events at which gifts are exchanged between the families of the bride and groom (Beatty 1992). At the first meeting, the prospective groom expresses his interest in a betrothal. He and his party visit the bride's house and are fed: "The guests are given the pig's lower jaw (the portion of honour) and take away with them raw and cooked portions for the suitor's father" (121). Within the next week or two, the groom brings a gift of three to twelve pigs to confirm the betrothal. He also returns the container used for the pig meat given to him on the previous visit, filled with a certain kind of nut. The groom gives pigs and gold as the major gift that seals the marriage.

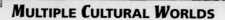

Multiple Cultural Worlds

Favors, Gifts, and Banquets in China

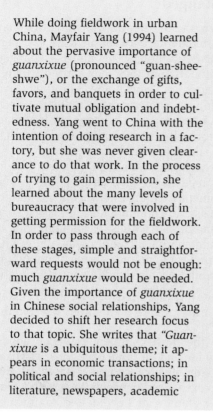

While doing fieldwork in urban China, Mayfair Yang (1994) learned about the pervasive importance of *guanxixue* (pronounced "guan-shee-shwe"), or the exchange of gifts, favors, and banquets in order to cultivate mutual obligation and indebtedness. Yang went to China with the intention of doing research in a factory, but she was never given clearance to do that work. In the process of trying to gain permission, she learned about the many levels of bureaucracy that were involved in getting permission for the fieldwork. In order to pass through each of these stages, simple and straightforward requests would not be enough: much *guanxixue* would be needed. Given the importance of *guanxixue* in Chinese social relationships, Yang decided to shift her research focus to that topic. She writes that "*Guanxixue* is a ubiquitous theme; it appears in economic transactions; in political and social relationships; in literature, newspapers, academic journals, theater, and film. . . . Compared with other social practices, there also seems to be a greater cultural elaboration of vocabulary, jokes, proverbs, and etiquette surrounding *guanxixue.*" (1994:6).

Guanxixue involves getting what one wants through giving. If you give someone a gift and they accept it, or if you invite someone to dinner, then—later—you can ask a favor of the person and the rules of *guanxixue* prescribe that your favor will be granted. *Guanxixue* is not the same as bribery because it is indirect and usually handled discretely. Yang describes one interaction that is less discrete since the first, discrete attempt failed:

> A worker wanted to get a few authorized days off from work to attend to some personal business. He first tried to give presents in private to the factory manager, but the latter declined. So he cunningly worked out a way to make the manager accept. He waited for an opportunity when the manager was in the presence of many other workers to give the gift to him. . . . He said to the manager, "Here is the gift which my father, your old comrade-in-arms . . . asked me to deliver to you. Please accept it so his feelings are not hurt." Both the worker and the manager knew that the story about his father being an old friend of his was made up, so the real aim of the gift was apparent to the manager. In front of so many people, however, the manager was in danger of losing face if he refused to accept the gift unless he could come up with a good reason." (133–134)

The manager did not want to say in public that he would not accept the gift because that would appear to be ungenerous. And he did not want to call the worker a liar because the worker would lose too much face. The manager was forced to accept the gift. Later, when the inevitable request for authorized days off work arrived, he would have to say yes or else the factory people would talk about his lack of generosity.

Gifts will continue to be exchanged between the two families over many years.

Exchanging alcoholic beverages is an important feature of many communal, ritual events in Latin America. In an Ecuadorian village called Agato, the San Juan fiesta is the high point of the year (Barlett 1980). The fiesta consists of four or five days during which small groups of celebrants move from house to house, dancing and drinking. The anthropologist reports on the event:

> I joined the groups consisting of the president of the community and the elected *alcaldes* (councilmen and police), who were accompanied by their wives, a few friends, and some children. We met each morning for a hearty breakfast at one house, began drinking there, and then continued eating and drinking in other homes throughout the day and into the evening. . . . Some people drink for only one or two days, others prefer to make visits mainly at night, while some people drink day and night for four days. . . . The host or hostess greets the group with a bucket of *chicha* (home-made corn beer) and a dipper or bottle of *trago* (purchased cane liquor) and a shotglass. One member of the group, often the oldest man, accepts the liquor and distributes drinks to the entire party. Participants are urged to "do their share" to consume the liquor, but refusals are also accepted easily. After several rounds of drink, the server returns the empty bottle or bucket to the host, the group choruses goodbyes and hurries into the street. (118–119)

Guests who drink at someone's house will later serve their former hosts alcohol in return. In this way, social ties are reinforced. (See the Multiple Cultural Worlds box below for another example.)

Symbolic Goods

Intangible valuables such as myths (sacred stories) and rituals (sacred practices) are sometimes exchanged in ways similar to material goods. In lowland areas of Papua New Guinea, men trade myths, rituals, dances, flutes, costumes, and styles of body decoration for the pigs of highland men (Harrison 1993). Certain secret spells were some of the most prestigious trade items. In the Balgo Hills region of Australia, longstanding exchange networks transfer myths and rituals among groups of women (Poirier 1992). Throughout the region, the women may keep important narratives and rituals only for a certain time and then must pass them on to other groups. One such ritual is the *Tjarada*, a love-magic ritual with an accompanying narrative. The *Tjarada* came to the women of Balgo Hills from the north. They kept it for about fifteen years and then passed it on to another group in a ceremony that lasted for three days. During the time that the Balgo Hills women were custodians of the *Tjarada*, they incorporated some new elements into it. These elements are retained even after its transfer to the next group. Thus, the *Tjarada* contains bits of local identity of each group that has had it. A sense of linked community and mutual responsibility thereby develops and is sustained among the different groups that have held the *Tjarada*.

Labor

In labor-sharing groups, people contribute labor to other people on a regular basis (for seasonal agricultural work such as harvesting) or on an irregular basis (in the event of a crisis such as the need to rebuild a barn damaged by fire). Labor sharing groups are part of what has been called a "moral economy" since no one keeps formal records on how much any family puts in or takes out. Instead, accounting is socially regulated. The group has a sense of moral community based on years of trust and sharing. In Amish communities of North America, labor sharing is a major factor of production, infrastructure maintenance, and social cohesion. When a family needs a new barn or faces repair work that requires group labor, a barn-raising party is called. Many families show up to help. Adult men provide manual labor, and adult women provide food for the event. Later, when another family needs help, they call on the same people.

MULTIPLE CULTURAL WORLDS

The Rules of Hospitality in Oman

In much of the Middle East, where women spend little time in the public domain, social visits among women are much anticipated and carefully planned events with complex rules about what should be served (Wikan 1982). In the town of Sohar, in Oman, men go out to work, while women spend most of their time at home. When women do venture outside, they wear head veils, face masks, and full-length gowns. Their main social activity outside the home involves visits to other women in their homes. A typical visit involves sitting, chatting, and eating snacks. Social etiquette dictates what should be served and how:

> Dates and coffee compose the traditional food of entertainment between close neighbors. Nowadays, biscuits, inexpensive caramels, and popcorn tend to be favored substitutes. Between neighbors who interact on a daily basis, or nearly so, a single dish will do. But all other visitors, even solitary ones, should be offered at least two plates, with different contents, or the hostess is thought stingy. If the guests are more numerous, the amounts or variety must be increased, up to a minimum of four plates. Three or four plates may also be offered to one or two guests when the hostess wishes to honor them.
>
> The rules of etiquette require that approximately half of the food served be left for the hostess' household. (130–132)

Cooked food, such as meat and sweets, is served when entertaining more important guests, or for weddings, seasonal feasts, and burials. With cooked food, though, the hosts may never eat with their guests: "Even if the consequence is that the guest must eat all alone, in a separate room, it would be disrespectful to arrange it otherwise." (133)

A Guatemalan woman works at her hand loom. Mayan weaving is closely linked with identity and ethnicity. This association is especially evident in women's embroidered blouses, huipiles (hu-wee-PEEL-es), which convey messages about the wearer's wealth, age, and home region. Three decades of civil war have threatened Mayan culture in Guatemala, but many Mayan groups are now revitalizing their traditions, including weaving.

Money

Money, or currency, refers to things that can be exchanged for many different kinds of items (Godelier 1971:53). Besides being a medium of exchange, money can be a standard of value and a store of value or wealth (Neale 1976). Anthropologists have labeled as money or currency such diverse items as shells, salt, cattle, furs, and iron hoes. Compared to other exchange items, money or currency is a relatively recent innovation. Although no one knows when money first appeared, one of the earliest forms of coined money was in use by the Greeks in Asia Minor (Turkey) in the seventh century BCE. Pre-coin money undoubtedly existed well before that time.

Items that can be exchanged for only a few other items are called **limited-purpose money.** Raffia cloth serves as limited-purpose money among the Lele of central Africa (Douglas 1962). Raffia cloth, made from the fibers of a certain kind of palm, is a medium of payment for certain ritual and ceremonial events, such as a marriage, and as a payment of compensation for wrongdoing. It is not used for commercial transactions such as buying food or houses or for renting or buying land. Modern money is **multipurpose money,** or a medium of exchange that can be used for all goods and services available.

Rights in People

Throughout history, some people have been able to gain control of other people and treat them as objects of exchange, as in systems of institutionalized slavery and in underground, criminal activities even today. The particular topic of women as "items" of exchange in marriage is a puzzling one in anthropology and has attracted much debate. Lévi-Strauss proposed many years ago that the exchange of women between men is one of the most basic forms of exchange in human culture. His argument about exchange is based on the universality of some sort of "incest taboo," which he defines as a rule preventing a man from marrying or cohabiting with his mother or sister (1969 [1949]). Such a rule, he says, is a logical motivation for equal exchange: "the fact that I can obtain a wife is, in the final analysis, the consequence of the fact that a brother or father has given her up" (62). According to this theory, men are thus impelled to develop exchange networks with other men. This process leads to the beneficial emergence of social solidarity between groups. For Lévi-Strauss, the incest taboo is the basis of the original form of exchange and thereby the emergence of an important aspect of culture.

This theory, while intriguing, has appeared as completely male-centered and denies agency to the females involved. In an influential essay called "The Traffic in Women," Gayle Rubin (1975) partially agrees with the theory, but goes on to say that it is incomplete since it disregards the many foraging societies in which men do not have rights in women that they exchange with other men. Evidence from horticultural and agricultural societies of Southeast Asia has been put forward as further refutation of a universal model of men exchanging women (Peletz 1987). In these systems, the focus of marriage arrangements is on the exchange of men and control of their labor power and productivity. Adult women arranged their daughters' marriages, selecting the groom themselves. In the case of divorce, the man had no right to his wife's property, including a house that he may have built for her, or to the marriage gold.

Modes of Exchange

Like the two contrasting modes of consumption described earlier, two distinct modes of exchange can be delineated. They are **balanced exchange,** or a system of transfer in which the goal is either immediate or eventual balance in value, and **market exchange,** a system of transfers in which one party attempts to make a profit. In balanced exchange, the dominant form of transfer is the gift, while in market exchange, it is the sale. While balanced exchange can be found among people with close social ties in any form of economy, it is the dominant mode of exchange within foraging, horticultural, and pastoral societies. Market exchange becomes increasingly important in agricultural societies where production is geared for sale and in industrial economies where production for sale is the primary goal.

Balanced Exchange

The category of balanced exchange contains two subcategories based on the social relationship of the two parties involved in the exchange and the degree to which a "return" is expected. **Generalized reciprocity** is a transaction that involves the least conscious sense of interest in material gain or thought of what might be received in return. When, or if, a possible return might be made is not calculated. Such exchanges often involve goods and services of an "everyday" or mundane nature, such as a cup of coffee. Generalized reciprocity is the predominant form of exchange between people who know each other well and have a high degree of trust in each other. It is the predominant form of exchange in foraging societies and it is also found among close kin and friends cross-culturally. **Balanced reciprocity** is the exchange of approximately equally valued goods or services, usually between people of roughly equal social status; the exchange may occur simultaneously from both parties, or an agreement or understanding may exist that stipulates the time period within which the exchange will be completed. This aspect of the timing contrasts with generalized reciprocity, in which there is no fixed time limit for the return. In balanced reciprocity, if the second party fails to complete the exchange, the relationship will break down. Balanced reciprocity is less personal than generalized reciprocity and, according to Western definitions, more "economic."

The *kula* is an example of balanced reciprocity. Men of many different Trobriand groups participate in the exchange of necklaces and armlets, giving them to their partners after keeping them for awhile. The trading includes local trading partners who are neighbors and people in far-away islands who are visited via long canoe voyages on high seas. Men are distinguished by the particular armlets and necklaces that they trade,

Shell ornaments are still important items to be worn at ceremonial events, as shown on this man of the Sepik River area of Papua New Guinea.

since certain armlets and necklaces are more prestigious than others. However, the *kula* social code dictates that "to possess is great, but to possess is to give." Generosity is the essence of goodness and stinginess is the most despised vice. The higher the man's social rank, the more he must give. *Kula* exchanges should involve items of equivalent value. If a man trades a very valuable necklace with his partner, he expects to receive in return a very valuable armlet as a *yotile* (equivalent gift). At the time, if one's partner does not possess an equivalent item, he may have to give a *basi* (intermediary gift). The *basi* stands as a token of good faith until a proper return gift can be given. The *kudu* ("clinching gift") will come later and balance the original gift. The equality of exchange ensures a tight social bond between the trading partners and a statement of social equality and mutual trust. When a man sails to an area in which there may be danger because of previous raids or warfare, he can count on having a friend to receive him and give him hospitality.

Redistribution

Redistribution is a form of exchange that involves one person collecting goods or money from many members of a group; then, at a public event at a later time, he "returns" the pooled goods to everyone who contributed. In comparison to the two-way pattern of reciprocity, redistribution involves some sort of "centricity." It contains the possibility of institutionalized inequality since what is returned may not always equal what was contributed. The pooling group may continue to exist in spite of inequality because of the leadership skills of the person who mobilizes contributions. Highland New Guinea political leadership involves redistribution in a system of contributions and ritual feasts called *moka* that may take several years to organize. Formal taxation systems of industrial societies can be considered a form of redistribution. People pay taxes to a central institution, and they receive services from the government in return. Depending on the context, the return may or may not appear to be satisfactory to the contributors. Unfair taxation practices have led to a breakdown in the "pooling group," as among the English settlers in Boston at the onset of the American Revolution. The degree of personal contact in different redistributive systems varies just as with forms of reciprocity. Similarly, the contexts in which greater personal interaction is involved tend to be more egalitarian and less exploitative than the impersonal forms.

Market Exchange

Marketing is the buying and selling of commodities under competitive conditions in which the forces of supply and demand determine value (Dannhaeuser 1989:222). In a market transaction, the people involved may not be related to or know each other at all. They may not be social equals, and their exchange is not likely to generate social bonding. Many market transactions take place in a marketplace, a physical location in which buying and selling occur. Markets evolved from other, less formal contexts of **trade,** formalized exchange of one thing for another according to set standards of value. In order for trade to develop, someone must have something that someone else wants. Specialization in producing a particular good promotes trade between regions. Particular products are often identified with a town or region. In Oaxaca, Mexico,

Moroccan pottery is for sale here in a regular market in Marrakech.

different villages are known for blankets, pottery, stone grinders, rope, and chili peppers (Plattner 1989:180–181). In Morocco, the interior city of Fez is famous for its blue-glazed pottery, while the Berber people of the southern mountain region are known for their fine blankets, rugs, and other woven goods. Specialization develops with illegal commodities, too, for example, Jamaican marijuana is well known for its high quality in the United States, and many tourists focus their trip around the Negril beach area especially. Market exchange may be based on the exchange of goods or money.

The periodic market, a site for market transactions that is not permanently set up but takes place regularly, emerged with the development of agriculture and urban settlements. As Stuart Plattner (1989) points out, however, a periodic market (or what Plattner calls a "peasant market") is more than just a place for buying and selling, it is also a place of social activity:

> [C]rowds come from the countryside to sell their farm products and buy manufactured goods and foodstuffs from other areas. Government officials often visit on market days, and local places of worship hold services so that farm families can combine economic, political, and religious activities at one time and place. Peasant market arenas ... have much of the excitement of a fair, with friendships made, love affairs begun, and marriages arranged. In many societies, the end of market day is often marked by drinking, dancing, and fighting. (171)

Worldwide, permanent markets situated in fixed locations have long served the everyday needs of villages and neighborhoods. Permanent markets throughout China, for example, have long provided for the everyday needs of local people (Skinner 1964). The persistence of the role of such localized markets can be seen in the number of neighborhood shops in the city of Shanghai (Lu 1995). Shanghai is the most westernized city in China, but in the back streets and neighborhoods, small-scale and personalized marketing still prevails with the same shops selling sesame-cakes, hot water, wine, traditional Chinese medicine, coal, tobacco paper, soy sauce, and locally produced groceries. More contemporary, less personalized forms of permanent marketplaces in the United States include shopping malls and the New York Stock Exchange.

Other Forms of Unbalanced Exchange

Several forms of unbalanced exchange other than market transactions exist that involve the transfer of goods from one person or institution to another without an equivalent return. In extreme instances, no social relationship is involved; in others, sustained unequal relationships are maintained over time between people. These forms range from the extreme example of giving something with no expectation of return to taking something with no expectation of return. These forms of unbalanced exchange can occur anywhere along the continuum of economic systems, but they are more likely to be found in large-scale or culturally complex societies where more options for other than face-to-face, balanced exchange exist.

In China, many marketers are women. These two women display their wares in a regular neighborhood food market in a city about an hour from Shanghai.

The pure gift. A **pure gift** is something given with no expectation or thought of a return.

The pure gift could be considered an extreme form of generalized reciprocity. Examples of a pure gift may include donating money for a food drive, in which the giver never knows or sees the receiver, or donations to famine relief, blood banks, and religious organizations. Some people say that a truly pure gift does not exist since one always gains something, no matter how difficult to measure, in giving—even if it is just the good feeling of generosity. Parental care of children is said to be a pure gift by some but not by others. Those who say that parental care is a pure gift argue that most parents do not consciously calculate how "much" they have spent on their children with the intention of "getting it back" later on. Those who do not consider parental care a pure gift say that even if the "costs" are not consciously calculated, parents have unconscious expectations about what their children will "return" to them, whether the return is material (care in old age) or immaterial (making the parent feel proud).

Theft. Theft is taking something with no expectation or thought of returning anything to the original owner for it. It is the logical opposite of a pure gift. The study of theft has been neglected by anthropologists, perhaps because it might involve danger. One insightful analysis considers food stealing by children in Africa (Bledsoe 1983). During fieldwork among the Mende of Sierra Leone, Caroline Bledsoe's research focus was on child fostering (placing a child in the care of friends or relatives, usually so they can receive apprenticeship training or education in a city school). She learned that children who are fostered out, especially older ones, receive less food at meal times than children living with a biological parent, specifically less meat and leafy green sauces. The nutritional status of fostered children, however, was not as low as their limited food shares would indicate. Further investigation revealed a widespread pattern of children foraging for wild food and a "clandestine economy" of food stealing. Children frequently foraged for wild fruits and greens growing near the outskirts of town and in the nearby forest. In town, a common target for theft are fruits such as mangoes, guavas, and oranges. Bledsoe at first dismissed cases of food stealing as rare exceptions, "But I began to realize that I rarely walked through town without hearing shouts of anger from an adult and cries of pain from a child being whipped for stealing food" (2). Since her goal was to assess children's nutritional status, she needed to know about how much food children were gaining from foraging and stealing. Her discussion of methods for this kind of research is illuminating:

> An important technique I relied on to learn about stealing was open-ended interviewing of both children and adults, and by sending my assistant out to interview children he encountered. I focused on eliciting information primarily from children themselves. This required careful effort, because children wanted to avoid getting in trouble. Most were reluctant at first to divulge their strategies. However, as children saw that I regarded their efforts as they themselves did—as almost an art—they disclosed some of their more creative techniques of "tiefing," ("TEEF-ing") as petty stealing is referred to in Sierra Leone Creole.
>
> Another technique I tried was meal simulations in which people showed me how children "tiefed" even at meal time, both when the food was being prepared as well as while groups of children were seated together, eating rice and sauce with their hands out of a communal bowl, as most people eat. Since this was simulation, people greatly enjoyed demonstrating the subtleties of "tiefing" and bad etiquette.
>
> Finally, I asked school children to keep diaries for me to elicit information on "tiefing." At first, children wrote about more legitimate ways they acquired food, such as doing errands for small tips, playing soccer games for stakes, soliciting relatives for "munching" money, asking friends to share snacks with them, and visiting friends at meal times. As they grew to trust that I would not show their diaries to their teachers, they hesitantly alluded to "tiefing." And by the time we had finished the diary projects, food "tiefing" dominated their themes. (p. 2)

Thus, fostered children participate more in food stealing than children living with their natal families. Food stealing can be seen as children's attempts to compensate for their less-than-adequate food shares at home. They do this by claiming food that is not part of their rightful entitlement, by "tiefing."

Stealing as a conscious attempt to alter an unfair entitlement system underlies an analysis of the "looting" that occurred in Los Angeles in 1992 following the Rodney King verdict (Fiske 1994). This looting can be seen to be rooted in the economic inequities faced by the African American community of South Central Los Angeles at the time of the Rodney King decision.

> Between 1982 and 1989, 131 factories closed in LA with the loss of 124,000 jobs.... The jobs that were

> lost were ones that disproportionately employed African Americans . . . in the four years before 1982, South Central, the traditional industrial core of LA, lost 70,000 blue-collar jobs. In Black eyes, this pattern is produced not by a raceless free market, but by racism encoded into economics: To them the 50 percent Black male unemployment in South central does not look like the result of neutral, let alone natural, economic laws. (469–470)

A particular feature of consumption inequality is the presumed assumption of equality: that, in America, everyone's dollar has the same purchasing power. In South Central Los Angeles, this is not the case: "For the deprived, shopping is not, as it is for the wealthy, where success in the sphere of production is materially rewarded: it is an experience of exclusion and disempowerment. Shopping is painful" (481). How does all of this relate to exchange? The "looting" during the Los Angeles uprising can be seen as an expression of deep-seated resentment about economic discrimination. "Looting" could instead be termed "radical shopping" in the sense that it was political protest, just as consumer boycotts are protests of a different sort. The politics of language emerge: The media's use of the word "looting" linked the uprising to the domain of crime, leaving prison as the only solution. By constructing the uprising as a law-and-order issue only, the public's interpretation was diverted from seeing its roots in severe economic discrimination.

Obviously, much theft that occurs in the world is motivated by greed, not economic deprivation or oppression. The world of theft in expensive commodities such as gems, drugs, and art has not been researched by cultural anthropologists.

Exploitation. Exploitation (getting something of greater value for less in return) is extreme and persistent unbalanced exchange. Slavery is a form of exploitation in which people's labor power is appropriated without their consent and with no recompense for its value. Slavery is rare among foraging, horticultural, and pastoral societies. Social relationships that involve sustained unequal exchange do exist between members of different social groups that, unlike pure slavery, involve no overt coercion and a certain degree of return by the dominant member to the subdominant member (see the Multiple Cultural Worlds box). Some degree of covert com-

MULTIPLE CULTURAL WORLDS

Sustained Unbalanced Exchange in the Ituri Rainforest

Relationships between the Efe, who are "pygmy" foragers, and the Lese, who are farmers, in Congo (formerly Zaire) is an example of sustained unequal exchange (Grinker 1994). The Lese live in small villages located along a dirt road. The Efe are seminomadic, and they live in temporary camps near Lese villages. Men of each group maintain exchange partnerships with each other: "These partnerships are complex, long-term, hereditary relationships in which a Lese man and the son of his father's Efe partner inherit one another as partners. Members of the two groups describe their relationship simply: the Lese give cultivated foods and iron to the Efe and the Efe give meat, honey, and other forest goods to the Lese" (42).

Each Efe partner is considered a member of the "house" of his Lese partner, although he lives separately. Their main link is the exchange of food items, a system conceptualized by the Lese not as trade, per se, but as sharing of coproduced goods, as if the two partners were a single unit with a division of labor and a subsequent division or cosharing of the goods produced. Richard Grinker, who studied relationships between the Efe and the Lese, describes this system as "interlocking," with the implication of a "joint utility function" in which both parties benefit. Yet there is evidence of inequality in these trading relationships, with the Lese having the advantage. The Efe provide much-wanted meat to the Lese, but this role gives them no status, for it is the giving of cultivated foods by the Lese to the Efe that conveys status. In fact, the Lese claim that the Efe are *their* dependents, denying that their interest in Efe meat supplies actually makes them dependent. Another area of inequality is in marital and sexual relationships. Lese men may marry Efe women, and sometimes do, and the children are considered Lese. Efe men cannot marry or have sexual intercourse with Lese women.

pulsion or dependence is likely to be present, however, in order for relationships of unequal exchange to endure.

ANALYZING EXCHANGE SYSTEMS

Exchange and Risk Aversion

At the beginning of this chapter the potlatch system was presented as an exchange network with an economic security function. By linking together with other groups, the unevenness of a particular local economy could be "smoothed" out to a certain extent. Many more such examples can be found cross-culturally. Carol Stack (1974) was perhaps the first cultural anthropologist to study how exchange patterns among kin and friends in urban America serves as a social safety net. She did research in "The Flats," the poorest section of a Black community in a midwestern city that she calls Jackson Harbor. Jackson Harbor is marked by racial inequality with, for example, a much higher proportion of Blacks than Whites living in deteriorating or severely dilapidated housing. Stack's approach differed from earlier studies of the Black family in America by avoiding negative comparisons with middle-class White lifestyles. She instead looked at the Black family members' strategies for dealing with poverty and uncertainty.

> I found extensive networks of kin and friends supporting, reinforcing each other—devising schemes for self-help, strategies for survival in a community of severe economic deprivation.... Their social and economic lives were so entwined that not to repay an exchange meant that someone else's child would not eat. People would tell me, "You have to have help from everybody and anybody," and "The poorer you are, the more likely you are to pay back." (28)

Stack spent nearly three years in The Flats, studying the complex exchange system. She also became involved in the system: "If someone asked a favor of me, later I asked a favor of him. If I gave a scarf, a skirt, or a cooking utensil to a woman who admired it, later on when she had something I liked she would usually give it to me. Little by little as I learned the rules of giving and reciprocity, I tried them out" (28). Timing is important in the "swapping system." The purpose is to obligate the receiver over a period of time; thus, swapping rarely involves simultaneous exchange. The swapping system of The Flats lies between the categories of generalized and balanced reciprocity, both of which are related to the maintenance of social bonds.

Exchange and Social Inequality

Exchange may also support and perpetuate social hierarchies. Paul Bohannan (1955), an early economic anthropologist, studied the economy of the Tiv, horticulturalists of Nigeria, before European monetary systems entered their economy. He learned that, besides gift exchange, three spheres of market exchange existed in which items of equivalent value are traded for each other. Each of the three spheres carried different levels of prestige. The lowest ranking sphere is the arena of women's trade. It includes chickens, hoes, baskets, pots, and grain. "For a woman to sell yams to buy a pot, for her to make a pot and sell to buy yams—these are considered to be normal buying and selling (*yamen a yam*)." This domestic sphere has the most frequent activity, but no prestige. The second ranking category included brass rods, special white cloth, guns, cattle, and slaves. While slavery had been abolished at the time of Bohannan's research and the brass rods were increasingly rare, the Tiv still talked about the relative value of these items. For example, one brass rod was equivalent to one large piece of white cloth, and five rods or pieces of cloth were equal to a bull, while ten equalled a cow. Young men seeking marriage would accumulate such goods in order to enhance their prestige and to impress elder males. The top-ranking exchange sphere contains only one item: rights in women. This category ranks highest in the Tiv moral sphere since a male's highest goal is to gain and maintain family dependents (wife and children). As Bohannan says, "The drive toward success leads most Tiv, to the greatest possible extent, to convert food into prestige items; to convert prestige items into dependents—wives and children," a process of up-trading he terms conversion. Subsequent analyses have pointed out that the Tiv spheres of exchange, like those of many other African cultures, support the power structure of elder males (Douglas and Isherwood 1979). They maintained dominance over the entire social system by keeping tight control over marriageable women. This forces younger males into competition for marriage and for eventual entry into the ranks of the elders.

CHANGING PATTERNS OF CONSUMPTION AND EXCHANGE

In recent times, several trends are notable in the transformation of change in consumption and exchange. The concepts of globalization and localization capture well many of these changes. The powerful market forces of the first world are the predominant shapers of global change. At the same time, local cultures variously adopt and adapt to global patterns of consumption and exchange, and sometimes resist them outright.

The Lure of Western Goods

Steel Machetes and Sugar in the Amazon

There is now scarcely any human settlement that does not engage in exchanges beyond its boundaries to acquire new consumer goods (Gross et al. 1979). Katherine Milton, a biological anthropologist who has studied recently contacted foraging groups in the Brazilian Amazon, comments: "Despite the way their culture traditionally eschews possessions, forest-living people embrace manufactured goods with amazing enthusiasm. They seem to appreciate instantly the efficacy of a steel machete, ax, or cooking pot. It is love at first sight. . . . There are accounts of Indian groups or individuals who have turned their backs on manufactured goods, but such people are the exception" (1992:40). Their love for these goods has brought significant economic, political, and social changes to their lives. In the early decades of the twentieth century, when the Brazilian government sought to "pacify" Amazonian groups, they used manufactured goods. They placed pots, machetes, axes, and steel knives along Indian trails or hung them from trees. These techniques proved so successful that they are still used. Milton describes the process:

> Once a group has been drawn into the pacification area, all its members are presented with various trade goods—standard gifts include metal cooking pots, salt, matches, machetes, knives, axes, cloth hammocks, T-shirts, and shorts. Not all members of the group get all of these items, but most get at least two or three of them, and in a family, the cumulative mass of new goods can be considerable.
>
> The Indians initially are overwhelmed with delight—this is the honeymoon period when suddenly, from a position in which one or two old metal implements were shared by the entire group, a new situation prevails in which almost every adult individual has some of these wonderful new items. The honeymoon is short-lived, however. Once the Indians have grown accustomed to these new items, the next step is to teach them that these gifts will not be repeated. The Indians are now told that they must work to earn money or must manufacture goods for trade so that they can purchase new items.
>
> Unable to contemplate returning to life without steel axes, the Indians begin to produce extra arrows or

Cases of locally produced beer, "333," are unloaded near the port of Ho Chi Minh City, Vietnam, where logos of many Western products are familiar sights in the growing capitalist economy.

> blowguns or hunt additional game or weave baskets beyond what they normally need so that this new surplus can be traded. Time that might, in the past, have been used for other tasks—subsistence activities, ceremonial events, or whatever—is now devoted to production of barter goods. (40)

Adoption of Western foods has negatively affected the nutrition and health of indigenous Amazonian peoples. In the Amazon, "The moment manufactured foods begin to intrude on the indigenous diet, health takes a downward turn" (Milton 1992:41). The Indians have begun to use table salt, which they have been given by outsiders, and refined sugar. Previously, they consumed small quantities of salt made by burning certain leaves and collecting the ash. The sugar they consumed came from wild fruits, in the form of fructose. Sucrose tastes "exceptionally sweet" in comparison, and the Indians get hooked on it. As a result, tooth decay, obesity, and diabetes become new health risks.

In some places in the Amazon rain forest, a few communities are still largely outside the market system, but market exchange takes place in most communities. Simple exposure to Western goods has often been suggested as the reason for widepread market participation. Daniel Gross and his colleagues (1979) question this assumption. They did research on the amount of exposure to western goods in four different villages in Brazil and found no correlation between exposure to the West and market involvement. They found, instead, that the degree of difficulty in making a living from horticulture accounted for the differences. The village where people had to invest the most time and labor in horticultural activities was most involved in market relationships.

The White Bread Takeover in Ecuador

A cross-cultural analysis of food cultures, with attention to contemporary change, revealed an enduring and growing distinction between bread and porridge worldwide (Goody 1977). Bread is associated with dominant, colonizing cultures, and porridge is associated with dominated and colonized cultures. An illustration of this dichotomy in contemporary times comes from a study of consumption in rural Ecuador (Weismantel 1989). In the village of Zumbagua, bread has been a high status, special-occasion food for many years. Recently, children have begun pressuring parents to serve bread regularly to replace the usual barley gruel for breakfast. Children prefer bread. The anthropologist reports, "Many of the early morning quarrels I witnessed in Zumbagua homes erupted over the question of bread. This conflict arises between young children and their parents. Pre-school children, especially, demand bread as their right" (93). But "Zumbagua adults do not feel that bread is appropriate for everyday meals because it is a part of a class of food defined as *wanlla*. *Wanlla* is anything that is not part of a meal . . . bread is the *wanlla* par excellence. It is the universally appropriate gift" (95). Importantly, bread consumption requires cash income. The husband (more frequently than the wife) works for wages in the city. He often returns with a gift of bread for the family, while the wife provides the traditional boiled grain soups or gruels. Children's demands for bread increase the role of purchased foods. This in turn leads to increased dependence on the cash economy and on male wages rather than on traditional female provisioning.

Cash Cropping and Declining Nutrition: You Can't Eat *Sisal*

Increasing numbers of horticultural and agricultural groups have been persuaded to change over from growing crops for their own use to cash crop production. Intuition might tell you that cash cropping should lead to a rising standard of living. Some studies show, to the contrary, that often people's nutritional status declines with the introduction of cash cropping. A carefully documented analysis of how people's nutritional status was affected by introducing *sisal* (a plant that has leaves used for making rope) as a cash crop in Brazil is one such case (Gross and Underwood 1971). Around 1950, *sisal* was widely adopted in arid parts of northeastern Brazil. The traditional economy was based on some cattle raising and subsistence farming. Many poor subsistence farmers gave up farming and took up work in the *sisal* processing plants. They thought that steady work would be preferable to being dependent on the unpredictable rains in this dry region.

Processing *sisal* leaves for rope is an extremely labor-consuming process. One of the most demanding jobs is being a "residue man," whose tasks include shoveling soggy masses of fiber, bundling fiber, and lifting bundles for weighing. In families that contained a "residue man," the amount of money required for food was as much as what the *sisal* worker earned. In one case study household, the weekly budget was completely spent on food. The greatest share of the food goes to the *sisal* worker himself because of his increased energy output in *sisal* work. Analysis of data on the nutritional status of several hundred children in *sisal*-processing areas showed that: "Some *sisal* workers in northeastern Brazil appear to be forced systematically to deprive their dependents of an adequate diet . . . if they did not they could not function as wage earners. In those cases where the workers' dependents are growing children, the deprivation manifests itself in attenuated growth rates" (736).

Privatization's Effects: The New Rich and the New Poor of Russia and Eastern Europe

As the countries of the former Soviet Union dismantle socialism and enter the market economy, income inequality is rising. The new rich are enjoying unprecedented levels of comfortable living (see the Current Event box). The influx of Western goods, including sugared soft drinks and junk food, nicknamed "pepsistroika" by an anthropologist who did fieldwork in Moscow (Lempert 1996), allows people to change their traditional diets in ways that nutritional guidelines in the United States would advise against.

At the same time, consumption levels have fallen among the newly created poor. Historically, average reported levels of food intake in what is now Russia and Eastern Europe have exceeded those of most middle-income countries (Cornia 1994). Between 1961 and 1988, consumption of average calories, proteins, and fats rose and were generally higher than those recommended by the World Health Organization. These countries were also characterized by full employment and low income inequality, so the high consumption levels were shared by everyone. This is not to say that diets were perfect. Characteristic weaknesses, especially in urban areas and among low-income groups were low consumption of good-quality meat, fruits, vegetables, and vegetable oils, while people tended to overconsume cholesterol-heavy products (eggs and animal fats), sugar, salt, bread, and alcohol.

> **Current Event**
>
> **Could This Be Russia?**
>
> - At opening night in Moscow, women in low-cut dresses accompanied by men wearing bright pink sports jackets, strode through the glare of television cameras to enter the showroom. There, as a jazz band blared Dixieland, guests sipped cocktails and admired several shiny sedans whose sticker price was $200,000. This is Russia's first Rolls-Royce showroom.
> - In 1988, Mercedes Benz was selling only 70 new cars a year in Russia, mainly to foreign diplomats. In 1992, sales jumped to 3,500, mostly to Russian citizens.
> - The company now has more than 15 dealerships in Russia, with three in Moscow. While sales are small compared with those in the United States, Russia is still the fastest-growing market in the world for Mercedes.
>
> *Source: Business Week,* August 2, 1993, p. 40.

Since 1988, poverty has emerged and increased sharply. There are two categories of poor people: "the ultra-poor" (those whose incomes are below the subsistence minimum, or between 25 and 35 percent of the average wage) and "the poor" (those whose incomes are above the subsistence minimum but below the social minimum, or between 35 and 50 percent of the average wage). The largest increases in the number of ultra-poor occurred in Bulgaria, Poland, Romania, and Russia where, in 1992, between 20 to 30 percent of the population could be classified as ultra-poor and another 20 to 40 percent as poor. Overall calorie and protein intake diminished significantly. People in the ultra-poor category are substituting less expensive sources of nutrients, so now they consume more animal fats and starch, and less milk, animal proteins, vegetable oils, minerals, and vitamins. These changes are affecting the growth rates of children. In Bulgaria, the prevalence of growth stunting among infants rose from under 2 percent in 1989–1990 to 17 percent in 1991. Rates of low-birthweight babies rose in Bulgaria and Romania, reflecting the deterioration in maternal diets. The rate of childhood anemia has also risen dramatically in Russia.

Current Event

Credit Card Regulation in the Republic of Korea

- Conspicuous consumption is still frowned upon in the Republic of Korea. Newspapers criticize the "orange tribe" of well-to-do youngsters in Seoul who live it up with their parents' money when they should be studying.
- In 1993, the government relaxed limits on credit-card spending. Koreans responded with heavy spending, and the government restored the limit, hoping to encourage more saving that helps finance industrial development.

Source: The Economist, April 23, 1994.

A New Way of Buying: The Credit Card

Throughout the world, certain markets have long allowed buyers to purchase goods on credit. Such informal credit purchasing was usually based on personal trust and face-to-face interaction. It is only recently, however, that the credit card has made credit purchasing a massive, impersonal phenomenon in the United States and many other countries: "New electronic technology in the 1970s and deregulation in the 1980s offered retail bankers exciting opportunities to experiment with credit as a commodity, and they did experiment, wildly, at 'penetrating the debt capacity' of varied groups of Americans" (B. Williams 1994:351). Among middle-class people in the United States, the use of credit cards is related to their attempts to maintain a middle-class life style:

> The primary users of installment credit appear to be those between ages twenty-five and forty-four whose incomes are stagnant or falling. Many have relied on credit to shape an appropriately classed life course: to attend college, purchase durables and set up households, meet the needs of kin, and launch children. . . . They have served like domestic partners to some who cannot live on one income. Thus, for the last ten years, many normative middle-class people have not been able to support the households they want when they want them, or to organize their lives, without loans and liens. (B. Williams 1994:353)

People's attitudes about their credit card debts vary. Some people express feelings of guilt similar to having a drug dependency. One woman reported, "Last year I had a charge-free Christmas. It was like coming away from drug abuse" (354). Others who are in debt feel grateful: "I wouldn't be able to go to college without my credit card" (355). Williams suggests that, no matter what people's attitudes are, credit cards are sinking many Americans deeply into

The changing/enduring potlatch.

debt. The cards buy a lifestyle that is not actually affordable, and therefore they "mask" actual economic decline in America. The culture of electronic credit is a subject that cultural anthropologists will no doubt be devoting more attention to in the future, in the United States, where credit card use is expanding, and around the world (see the Current Event box).

Continuities and Resistance: The Potlatch

Potlatching among native peoples of the northwest coast of the United States and Canada was subjected to decades of opposition from Europeans and Euro-Americans (Cole 1991). The missionaries opposed potlatching and other un-Christian activities. The government thought it was wasteful and excessive, out of line with their goals for the "economic progress" of the Indians. In 1885, the Canadian government outlawed the potlatch. Among all the northwest coastal tribes, the Kwakwaka'wakw resisted prohibition most strongly and for a longer time. Potlatching among the Haida and Tlingit, in contrast, disappeared with relatively little resistance. Potlatches are no longer illegal, but a long battle was required to remove restrictions.

Contemporary reasons for giving a potlatch are similar to those in traditional times: naming children, mourning the dead, transferring rights and privileges, and marriages and the raising of totem poles (Webster 1991:229). However, the length of time devoted to planning a potlatch has changed. In the past, several years were involved in planning a proper potlatch. Now, about a year is enough. Still, much property must be accumulated to make sure that no guest goes away empty handed, and the guest list may include between 500 and 1000 people. The kinds of goods exchanged are different today: typical potlatch goods now include crocheted items such as cushion covers, afghans, and potholders, glassware, plastic goods, manufactured blankets, pillows, towels, articles of clothing, and sacks of flour and sugar.

SUMMARY

The totality of economic systems includes production, consumption, and exchange. A general contrast can be drawn between the modes of consumption and exchange associated with production for use versus production for profit, or nonmarket versus market-based systems of production. In the former, minimalism is the dominant mode of consumption, with needs being finite. In the latter, consumerism is the dominant mode of consumption, with needs being infinite. Foraging societies typify the minimalist mode of consumption, while industrial capitalist societies typify the consumerist mode of consumption. The modes of production that emerged between foraging and industrialism exhibit varying degrees of minimalism and consumerism.

Cross-cultural research on exchange reveals that many valued items of exchange are culturally specific; items of exchange can be either material or nonmaterial "goods"; and exchanges have both social and symbolic content and meaning.

The mode of exchange corresponds to the modes of production and consumption. In foraging societies, the mode of exchange is balanced exchange, with the goal of keeping the value of the items exchanged roughly equal over time. The balanced mode of exchange, most typical of foraging societies, involves people who know each other and have a social relationship with each other that is reinforced through balanced exchange. At the opposite end of the continuum is market exchange, with its goal of making a profit through exchange. In market exchange, the people involved in the transaction are less likely to know each other or to have a social relationship that is related to their exchanges. In fully marketized economies, most transactions are anonymous; that is, no social relationship is involved at all, as in the growing mail-order business.

Key areas of recent change in consumption and exchange include the increasing attractiveness of Western goods in non-Western cultures, including steel tools and food items such as sugar and white bread, increased involvement in cash-cropping in areas formerly devoted to subsistence food production, and the spread of world capitalism to many formerly socialist states. Along with such pervasive changes, cultural anthropologists have documented cases of resistance to westernization, of which the contemporary revival of the potlatch is a notable example.

CRITICAL THINKING QUESTIONS

1. Think of the events that involve feasting and gift-giving in your experience. Try to apply a functional explanation, like the one described in this chapter for the potlatch, to these events. Does this approach provide any new insights?
2. Native Americans of the northwest coast were predominantly foragers, yet they often accumulated surplus goods and participated in lavish feasts and competitive gift-giving. Where do they fit on the continuums of production, consumption, and exchange?
3. How important are food taboos in contemporary North America? What are prominent food taboos? How would a cultural materialist or meaning-centered theory apply to them?
4. Is there really such a thing as a pure gift?
5. Do recent changes in consumption in the post-Soviet states reflect the exercise of "free choice" in an expanding market of consumer options or are they the result of successful advertising and the power of Western media to transform other cultures?

KEY CONCEPTS

balanced exchange, p. 97
balanced reciprocity, p. 97
basic needs fund, p. 85
ceremonial fund, p. 85
consumerism, p. 84
consumption fund, p. 85
direct entitlement, p. 86
entertainment fund, p. 85
entitlement, p. 86
exploitation, p. 101
famine, p. 87
functional theory, p. 82
generalized reciprocity, p. 97
indirect entitlement, p. 86
limited-purpose money, p. 96
market exchange, p. 97
minimalism, p. 84
mode of consumption, p. 84
money, p. 96
multipurpose money, p. 96
potlatch, p. 82
pure gift, p. 99
recurrent costs fund, p. 85
redistribution, p. 98
tax/rent fund, p. 85
trade, p. 98

SUGGESTED READINGS

Elizabeth Cashdan, ed., *Risk and Uncertainty in Tribal and Peasant Economies*. Boulder, CO: Westview Press, 1990. Twelve chapters explore links between environment and diet, food-sharing networks, and risk-management strategies among different foraging, horticultural, and agricultural societies.

Daisy Dwyer and Judith Bruce, eds., *A Home Divided: Women and Income in the Third World*. Stanford: Stanford University Press. The introductory chapter links women's budgetary control to fertility patterns; then, ten case studies present variations in women's budgeting roles cross-culturally, with the final chapter offering theoretical perspectives on the "new household economics."

Betsy Hartmann and James Boyce, *Needless Hunger: Voices from a Bangladesh Village*. San Francisco: Institute for Food and Development Policy, 1982. Evidence from fieldwork in rural Bangladesh shows that poverty and hunger in Bangladesh are primarily caused by severe class inequalities in economic entitlements. The text includes a critique of the role of foreign aid in perpetuating inequalities, as well as suggestions for change.

Sidney W. Mintz, *Sweetness and Power: The Place of Sugar in Modern History*. New York: Penguin Books, 1985. Combining historical and anthropological techniques, this book traces an important part of the story of world capitalism—the transformation of sugar from a luxury item to an omnipresent item of consumption worldwide.

Henry J. Rutz and Benjamin S. Orlove, eds., *The Social Economy of Consumption*. Monographs in Economic Anthropology No. 6. New York: University Press of America, 1989. This text includes an introductory chapter by the editors, followed by fourteen chapters on various aspects of the politics of consumption, the relationship between consumption and class, and household production and consumption linkages.

Joseph J. Tobin, ed., *Re-Made in Japan: Everyday Life and Consumer Taste in a Changing Society.* New Haven: Yale University Press, 1992. After an introduction by the editor, twelve essays address different aspects of Japanese consumption trends, including drinking patterns, interior decoration, Tokyo's Disneyland, department stores, and a Japanese-French restaurant in Hawaii.

CHAPTER 5

Birth and Death

CHAPTER OUTLINE

WORLD POPULATION GROWTH
- Modes of Reproduction
  - *Current Event:* "Test-Tube Babies Cost $60,000 to $110,000 Each"

CULTURE AND BIRTH
- Sexual Intercourse
  - *Multiple Cultural Worlds:* The Dani Low-Energy Sexual System in Perspective
- The Politics of Fertility
  - *Critical Thinking:* Reproductive Rights or Wrongs
- Techniques of Fertility Control
- Current Event: "Contraception the Natural Way"
  - *Multiple Cultural Worlds:* Amniocentesis and the Poor of New York City

CULTURE AND DEATH
- Infanticide
  - *Multiple Cultural Worlds:* Female Infanticide in India
- Suicide
- Violence
  - *Current Event:* "Consumerism Fuels Dowry Death Wave in India"
- Public Violence

SUMMARY

CRITICAL THINKING QUESTIONS

KEY CONCEPTS

SUGGESTED READING

◀ A mother and her infant, South Africa.

- A common belief among Hindus in India is that men are weakened by sexual intercourse because semen is a source of strength, and it takes a long time to replace even a drop. Yet India has a high rate of population growth.
- The Chinese government policy of urging parents to have only one child significantly decreased the population growth rate. It also increased the death rate of female infants to the extent that there is now an emerging shortage of future brides.
- The highest birth rates in the world are found among the Mennonites and Hutterites in the United States and Canada. In these Christian groups, women on average bear nine children.

Such "population puzzles" can be understood using anthropological theories and methods. These population dynamics, along with many other examples of human variation in births and deaths, are an important area of life that is culturally shaped and that changes over time in response to changing conditions. This chapter provides a glimpse into some aspects of **demography,** or the study of population dynamics, and how it is culturally regulated. Demography, along with economics, fits within the category of infrastructure (M. Harris 1995:61; and see Chapter 1). It is hard to say whether economics influences demography or vice versa because they interact so strongly. Economic factors may have the edge in shaping demography, however, which is why it was covered first in this book. This chapter starts by discussing aspects of demography in relation to the modes of production (Chapter 3). It then proceeds to show how and to what effect culture shapes the important natural processes of birth and death in different contexts.

Demography includes three areas: **fertility** (births, or rate of population increase from reproduction), **mortality** (deaths, or rate of population decline in general or from particular causes), and **migration** (movement of people from one place to another). Many cultural anthropologists examine these processes, focusing on small populations and samples and examining the relationships between population dynamics and other aspects of culture such as gender roles, sexual beliefs and behavior, marriage, household structure, child care, and health and illness. While demographers compile statistical reports, cultural anthropologists contribute understanding of what goes on behind the numbers and provide insights about the causes of demographic trends. For example, demographers may find that fertility rates are falling more rapidly in one nation than in another. They may be able to correlate certain factors with it such as changing literacy rates or economic growth. A cultural anthropologist involved in studying these issues would take a closer look at the causes and processes involved in the declining birth rates, including some that might not be included in official censuses or other statistical sources. They would gather information on household-level, and also individual-level behavior and attitudes.

WORLD POPULATION GROWTH

Over the hundreds of thousands of years of human evolution, the world's population has grown and is now found residing on all of the earth's land surfaces except Antarctica. People also have lived for lengthy periods of time in space, and faraway planets may be "home" for humans in the future. The rate of population growth has not been even, however. While population growth rates were stable throughout Africa for thousands of years, they are now the highest in the world. European populations are currently experiencing "negative population growth," that is, declining numbers. Anthropological research on population dynamics shows that the stereotypic view of our ancient ancestors or "other" cultures as having "natural fertility" (no means to control the number of births) is wrong: Every human population has had culturally constructed ways to either promote or limit population growth. Anthropologists are interested in the cultural factors that influence birth and death rates. Cultural materialists examine the relationship between **reproduction,** or the "making of people," and production, or the "making of things."

Modes of Reproduction

Archaeologists and cultural anthropologists have provided enough data to allow the construction of general models of reproduction corresponding with modes of reproduction from the earliest human times to the present (see Table 5.1). Three general modes of reproduction are proposed. The foraging mode of

Table 5.1
Modes of Reproduction

Foraging	*Agricultural*	*Industrial*

Population growth: level
  Moderate birth rates
  Moderate death rates
	Population growth: high
	  High birth rates
	  Declining death rates
		Population growth: mixed
		  Industrialized nations—negative population growth
		  Developing nations—high

Value of children: moderate	Value of children: high	Value of children: mixed

Fertility control
  Indirect means
    Low fat diet of women
    Women's work and exercise
    Prolonged breastfeeding
    Spontaneous abortion
  Direct means
    Induced abortion
    Infanticide
	Fertility control
	  Increased reliance on direct means
	    Pronatalist techniques
	      Herbs
	    Antinatalist techniques
	      Induced abortion
	      Infanticide
		Fertility control
		  Direct methods grounded in science and medicine
		    Chemical forms of contraception
		    In vitro fertilization
		    Abortion

Social aspects
  Homogeneous demography
  Few specialists
	Social aspects
	  Emerging class differences
	  Increasing specialization
	    Midwifery
	    Herbalists
		Social aspects
		  Highly stratified demography
		    Globally, nationally and locally
		  Highly developed specialization

reproduction, which existed for most of human history, had low population growth rates because of a combination of moderate birth rates and moderate death rates. The agricultural mode of reproduction emerged with sedentarization. As increased food surpluses became available to support more people, birth rates increased over death rates and high population densities were reached in agricultural societies such as India and China. In the industrialized mode of reproduction, exemplified in Europe, Japan, and the United States, population growth rates declined because of falling birth rates and declining death rates. Horticulturalists and pastoralists possess some features of the foraging mode of reproduction and the agricultural mode of reproduction, depending on specific conditions. Thus far, anthropologists have done far less research on reproduction compared to production, so it is impossible to provide as much detail for modes of reproduction as for modes of production.

The Foraging Mode of Reproduction

Archaeological evidence about prehistoric populations, from about six million years ago to the Neolithic era of agricultural development around 10,000 years ago, indicates that population growth rates among foragers remained low over millions of years (Harris and Ross 1987). Foraging societies' need for daily and seasonal spatial mobility would call for a relatively small number of children to facilitate movement. The low population growth rates over thousands of years were likely the result of several factors, of more or less importance in different contexts, that would suppress fertility: high rates of spontaneous abortion because of heavy workloads of women, the seasonality of diets that created reproductive stress on women, long breastfeeding of infants, induced abortion, and **infanticide** (deliberate killing of offspring). Low birth rates appear to be more important in leading to population stability than mortality. In relatively undisturbed contemporary foraging societies, low population growth rates are still typical.

Nancy Howell (1979) conducted research on the demography of the Ju/wasi that sheds light on how population homeostasis is achieved. Howell's data show that birth intervals (the time between one birth and a subsequent birth) among the Ju/wasi are often several years in duration. What accounts for the long birth intervals? Two factors emerge as most important among the Ju/wasi:

- *Breastfeeding:* Frequent and long periods of breastfeeding inhibit progesterone production and thus suppress ovulation.
- *Women's low level of body fat:* A certain level of body fat is required for ovulation (Frisch 1978). Ju/wasi women's diets contain little fat. Their body fat level is also kept low through the physical exercise their work entails. The combination of diet and exercise maintained Ju/wasi women's body fat at low levels, suppressing ovulation.

Thus, ecological factors (food supply and diet) and economic factors (women's workloads) are basic determinants of Ju/wasi demography. This mode of reproduction can be interpreted as highly adaptive to the Ju/wasi environment and sustainable over time. Among the Ju/wasi who have given up foraging and become sedentarized farmers or laborers, fertility levels have increased, perhaps because of higher consumption levels of grains and dairy products (Howell 1979).

The Agricultural Mode of Reproduction

Settled agriculture promotes and supports the highest fertility rates of any mode of production. **Pronatalism,** an ideology promoting many children, emerges as a key value of farm families. It is prompted by the need for a large labor force to work the land, care for animals, process food, and do marketing. In this context, having many children is a rational reproductive strategy related to the mode of production. Thus, people living in family farming systems cross-culturally have their own "family planning"—which is to have many children—including the Mennonites and Hutterites of the United States and Canada.

In rural North India, sons are especially important, given the gender division of labor. Men provide the crucial work of plowing the fields and protecting the family in the case of village quarrels over land rights and other matters. When Western family planning agents came to the village of Manupur in North India in the late 1950s to promote small families, the villagers did not see the value of their ideas (Mamdani 1972). To them, a large family equals wealth and success, not poverty and failure. Mahmoud Mamdani describes the villagers' responses to the family planning agents:

Throughout much of Asia, sons are preferred to daughters. A complex system of cultural factors including economics, kinship, and religion promotes and sustains this view.

> One group displayed an air of amused tolerance which was typified by the weaver who told me he thought the "outsiders" were just plain "ignorant." Then there were those who were genuinely puzzled about the motives of the study. Consider the following inquiry, one that I encountered several times during my stay in Manupur: "It's strange they offered to give free medicine to stop women from bearing children, but had nothing to help those who could not bear children. That's where medicine could be of use to us."
>
> The final response represented a rather serious charge. . . [one] farmer, gently stroking his young son's hair, told me: "These Americans are enemies of the smile on this child's face. All they are interested in is war or family planning." (147)

Western family planning agents, with their antinatalist agenda, made the mistake of thinking that non-Western people had no thoughts of their own about what constitutes the desired family size and that they could simply provide modern contraceptive techniques to an interested market. The key point is that having many children in a family farming system "makes sense." When mechanization is introduced, cheap hired labor becomes widely available, or socialized agriculture is established, then farm families change their mode of reproduction and opt for smaller numbers of children because it makes less sense to have many children.

The Industrial Mode of Reproduction

In industrial societies, either capitalist or socialist, reproduction tends to decline to the point of **replacement-level fertility** (the number of births equals the number of deaths, leading to maintenance of current population size) or **below-replacement-level fertility** (the number of births is fewer than the number of deaths, leading to population decline). Children are less useful in production because of the changing labor demands of industrialism. Furthermore, children are required to attend school and cannot work for their families as much. Parents respond to these changes by having fewer children and by "investing" more resources in the fewer children they have. Below-replacement-level societies include Canada; Japan; several European countries such as Austria, Belgium, Hungary, Denmark, and Norway; and some countries that the United Nations categorizes as "developing," including Barbados, Cuba, Hong Kong, the Republic of Korea, and Singapore (United Nations 1994: 174, 201).

Changes during the industrial mode of reproduction correspond to what demographers call the **demographic transition,** which refers to a change from the high fertility and high mortality of the agricultural mode of reproduction to the low fertility and low mortality of industrialized societies. This model proposes two phases. First, mortality declines due to improved nutrition and health, leading to high rates of population growth. The second phase is reached when fertility also declines, resulting in low rates of population growth. Cultural anthropologists have critiqued the demographic transition model as being too narrowly focused on the role of industrialism and not allowing for alternate models (Ginsberg and Rapp 1991). They claim that industrialism, with its reduced need for labor, is not the only factor that reduces pronatalism. China, for example, began to reduce its population growth rate before widespread industrialism (Xizhe 1991). Instead, strong government policies and a massive family planning program were key factors: "China's transition has been, by and large, not a natural process, but rather an induced one" (281) because its motivation came mainly from the government rather than from couples themselves. Nevertheless, reduced population growth in China is consistent with the government's program of stepping up the level of industrialization and thereby reducing the demand for labor in comparison to agrarianism.

One prominent characteristic of capitalist industrial states is their socially stratified demographies. Middle- and upper-class people tend to have few children, with high survival rates. Among the poor, both fertility and mortality rates are high. Brazil, a newly industrializing state with the most extreme inequality of income distribution in the world, also has extreme differences in demographic patterns between the rich and the poor. Another characteristic feature of population change in industrial countries is population aging. In Japan, for example, the total fertility rate declined to replacement level in the 1950s, and subsequently reached the below-replacement level (Hodge and Ogawa 1991:vii). If 1990s trends continue, Japan will experience a decline in population growth of about 15 percent per generation. At the same time, Japan is experiencing a rapid aging of the population (Sen 1994). Many people are moving into the senior category, creating a population bulge not matched by population increases in younger age groups. A third major distinguishing feature of industrial demographies is the high level of involvement of scientific (especially medical) technology in all aspects of pregnancy: preventing it, achieving it, and even terminating it (Browner and Press 1995, 1996). The growing importance of "new reproductive technologies" such as *in vitro* fertilization are a major part of a growing market in scientific reproduction (see the Current Event box on page 116). This technologization of reproduction is accompanied by increasing levels of specialization in providing the new services.

Current Event

Test-Tube Babies Cost $60,000 to $110,000 Each

- Test-tube babies cost the nation's health care system an average of $60,000 to $110,000 for each successful pregnancy. A single attempt at *in vitro* fertilization typically costs $8,000, but most attempts do not produce children. The average cost of having a baby this way is over $70,000. Some cases range as high as $800,000.
- Those with the most severe fertility problems have to try many times, greatly affecting costs. The age of the mother and the father's low sperm counts are two key factors affecting success.
- Some insurance companies pay for *in vitro* fertilization, but many do not. Several states in the United States require insurance companies to cover the costs.

Source: The Washington Post, July 28, 1994a.

CULTURE AND BIRTH

Cultures shape human reproduction from its very beginning, if that can be said to be sexual intercourse itself. Cultural practices and beliefs about pregnancy and birth affect the viability of the fetus during its gestation as well as the infant's fate after birth.

Sexual Intercourse

Anthropological research on sexuality and sexual practices is particularly difficult to undertake. Sexuality involves private, sometimes secret, beliefs and behaviors. The ethics of participant observation disallow intimate observation or participation, so data can be obtained only indirectly. Biases in people's reports to an anthropologist about their sexual beliefs and behavior are likely for several reasons. They may be too shy to talk about sex in the first place, too boastful to give accurate information, or simply unable to remember the answers to questions such as "How many times did you have intercourse last year?" If people do provide detailed information, it might be inappropriate for an anthropologist to publish it because of the need to protect confidentiality. Malinowski (1929) wrote the first anthropological study of sexuality, based on his fieldwork in the Trobriands. He discusses the sexual lives of children; sexual techniques; love magic; erotic dreams; husband-wife jealousy; and a range of topics related to kinship, marriage, exchange, and morals. Since the late 1980s, cultural anthropologists have paid more attention to the study of sexuality, given the increase in cases of sexually transmitted diseases (STDs), including HIV/AIDS.

When to Begin Having Intercourse?

Biologically speaking, sexual intercourse between a fertile female and fertile male is normally required for human reproduction, although artificial insemination is an option in some contexts. Biology also defines the time span within which a female is fertile: from menarche (the onset of menstruation) to menopause (the cessation of menstruation). Globally, average age at menarche is between twelve and fourteen years, with earlier ages found in the industrial nations and later ages in developing nations, presumably because of different diets and activity patterns. Average age at menopause varies more widely, from the forties to the fifties, with later ages characteristic in industrialized societies (the higher fat content of diets in industrialized nations may be related to this difference).

Cultures socialize children about the appropriate time to begin sexual intercourse. Guidelines for initiating sexual intercourse may differ by gender, class, race, and ethnicity. In many cultures, menarche marks the beginning of adulthood for a girl. She should marry soon after menarche, and she should become pregnant as soon as possible in order to demonstrate her fertility. Rules more strictly forbid premarital sexual activity of girls than boys. In Zawiya, a traditional Muslim town of northern Morocco, as in much of the Middle East, the virginity of the bride—but not the groom—is highly valued (Davis and Davis 1987). The majority of brides conform to the ideal. Some unmarried young women do engage in premarital sex, however, and if they choose to have a traditional wedding, then they must somehow deal with the requirement of producing blood-stained wedding sheets. How do they do this? If the bride and the groom have been having premarital sexual relations, the groom may assist in the deception by nicking a finger with a knife and bloodying the sheets himself. Another option is to buy fake hymeneal blood in the drugstore.

In many cultures, a high value is placed on a woman becoming pregnant soon after she reaches menarche, making "teenage pregnancy" a desired condition instead of a "social problem," as perceived by many experts in the United States (Ginsberg and Rapp 1991:320). The concept of a thirty-year-old *prima para* (first-time mother) would shock villagers in Bangladesh, for example, as to both its physical possibility and its social advisability. Commonly in South Asia, Africa, and elsewhere, a married woman's status depends on her having children. The longer she delays, the more her spouse and in-laws might suspect her of being infertile. In that case, they might send her back to her parents or bring in a second wife.

How Often Should One Have Intercourse?

Cross-cultural studies indicate a wide range in frequency of sexual intercourse, confirming the role of culture in shaping sexual desire (see the Multiple Cultural Worlds box). However, the relationship between sexual intercourse frequency and fertility, the subject of this section, is not simple. A common assumption is that people in cultures with high rates of population growth must have sexual intercourse frequently. Without "modern" birth control, such as condoms, coitus interruptus, or the "rhythm method," intercourse frequency would seem to lead to high rates of fertility.

A comparison of reported intercourse frequency for Euro-Americans in the United States and Hindus in India reveals that Indians had intercourse far less frequently (less than twice a week) than the Euro-Americans did (two to three times a week) in all age groups (Nag 1972). Several features of Indian culture limit sexual intercourse. The Hindu religion teaches the value of sexual abstinence, thus providing ideological support for limiting sexual intercourse. Hinduism also suggests that one should abstain from intercourse on many sacred days: the first night of the new moon, the first night of the full moon, and the eighth day of each half of the month (the light half and the dark half), and sometimes not on Fridays. As many as one hundred days each year could be observed as non-sex days. A more subtle psychological factor is Hindu men's belief in what anthropologists have termed the "lost semen complex." Morris Carstairs (1967) learned about this complex during fieldwork in the Indian

Multiple Cultural Worlds

The Dani Low-Energy Sexual System in Perspective

The Dani are horticulturalists of Irian Jaya, the Indonesian-controlled part of the island shared with Papua New Guinea in the South Pacific. Karl Heider (1976) studied among the Dani in the 1970s, and offered his interpretation that the Dani have "low" rates of sexual intercourse and relatively little interest in sex. He reports that Dani men express little frustration over the cultural rule against having sex with one's wife for four to six years after she has given birth: "Most people have no alternative sexual outlets." No one, according to Heider, shows signs of unhappiness or stress during the period of abstinence (1976: 188). The Dani, like many other horticultural groups, probably have the longest **post-partum taboos,** or rules stating how long a couple should abstain from having sexual intercourse after the woman has given birth.

Heider's assessment of low sexual interest implies a comparison with some "norm" of, say, an "average-energy sexual system," although what that might be is unstated. The comparatively short post-partum taboo in the United States of six weeks, and the apparent high interest in sex in North American popular culture (as evidenced, at least, in the content of many television shows) would suggest, in contrast to the Dani, a high-energy sexual system.

Because of the scarcity of anthropological studies of sexuality, we cannot say much about whether the Dani's low-energy sexual system is characteristic of other horticulturalist societies of New Guinea or elsewhere. One explanation for the existence of this system is its contribution to suppressing population growth. Cross-cultural analysis of the relationship between the length of the post-partum taboo and fertility rates does indicate a relationship, although a weak one, between longer periods of post-partum abstinence and lower fertility rates (Nag 1968). This would be a logical conclusion: no sex, no conceptions. So we might wonder why the relationship is not stronger. One reason may be that the analysis depends on reported norms about sexual abstinence rather than data on whether people actually adhere to the norm.

state of Gujarat: "Everyone knew that semen was not easily formed; it takes forty days and forty drops of blood to make one drop of semen.... Semen of good quality is rich and viscous, like the cream of unadulterated milk. A man who possesses a store of such good semen becomes a super-man.... Celibacy was the first requirement of true fitness, because every sexual orgasm meant the loss of a quantity of semen, laboriously formed" (83–86, quoted in Nag 1972:235). The architecture of rural Indian houses does not allow much privacy for sexual intercourse. In better-off households, a separate sleeping room may be available for a newly married couple.

The fact remains, however, that fertility is higher in India than in many other parts of the world where such restrictions on sexual intercourse do not exist. Obviously, sheer frequency of intercourse is not the explanation. It takes only one act of sexual intercourse at the right time of the month to create a pregnancy. The point of this discussion is to show that "reverse reasoning" from high fertility to assuming that people have nothing better to do than have sex is wrong. In fact, the cultural dynamics of sexuality in India function to restrain sexual activities and thus may keep fertility lower than it otherwise would be.

The Politics of Fertility

This section explores power issues related to decision making about birth at three levels: the family level, the national level, and the global level. Within the context of the family unit, decision makers weigh factors influencing why and when to have a child. What choices do they have for manipulating their own reproduction? At the national level, governments seek to plan their overall population level on the basis of particular goals that are sometimes pronatalist and sometimes antinatalist. What strategies do they employ and how successfully are they enacted? At the global level, we can see that powerful economic and political interests are at work influencing the reproductive policies of individual nations and, in turn, families and individuals within them.

Family-Level Decision Making

At the family level, parental and other family members' perceptions about the value and costs of children influence their reproductive decision making (Nag 1983). Assessing the value and costs of children is a complex matter, involving many factors. It is difficult to know how much any of these factors affect reproductive decision making in any particular society. Four variables are most important in affecting the "demand" for children in different cultural contexts:

- children's labor value
- children's value as old-age support for parents
- infant and child mortality rates
- economic costs of children

In the first three, the relationship is positive: When children's value is high in terms of labor or old-age support, fertility is likely to be higher. When infant and child mortality rates are high, fertility rates also tend to be high in order to "replace" offspring who do not survive. Costs—including direct costs (for food, education, clothing) and indirect costs (employment opportunities that the mother gives up)—have a negative relationship. Higher costs promote the desire for fewer children. Industrial society alters the value of children in several ways: "Industrialization, improvement in income, urbanization, and schooling are likely to reduce the labour value of children" (Nag 1983:58) and greatly increase their costs. Provision of old-age security and pension plans by the state may reduce that fertility incentive, although few developing countries have instituted such policies thus far. A reduction in infant and child mortality rates is correlated with subsequent declines in overall fertility as parents gain confidence that their children will survive.

Depending on the gender division of labor and other social features related to gender, sons or daughters may be relatively more valued. Son preference is widespread, especially in Asia and the Middle East, but it is not a cultural universal (Williamson 1976). In some cultures, people prefer a balanced sex ratio in their offspring, while in others daughters are preferred. Daughter preference is found in some Caribbean populations, in Venezuela, and some parts of Africa south of the Sahara. Longitudinal research from 1956 to 1991 among the Tonga of Gwembe District, Congo, documents a female-biased population system that has persisted for at least the second half of the twentieth century (Clark, Colson, Lee, and Scudder 1995). This study finds that "at most ages, men's death rates in Gwembe are higher than those of women" (104). Differences in mortality are especially great for the very young and the elderly, among whom males die at twice the rate of females the same age. The authors link this female-survival advantage to both the **matrilineal** kinship system of the Tonga, through which property is passed down from mother to daughter and the payment of bridewealth from the groom to the bride's father:

> Gwembe women must have daughters to perpetuate their *basimukoa,* or matrilineage. When a daughter is born, women customarily give two cries of joy as opposed to one for the birth of a boy. Women who have given birth to a disproportionate number of boys . . . are criticized by their kin for their failure to provide for the continuity of their matrilineage. Men also prefer daughters whose marriages will bring them wealth in the form of marriage payments. The birth of a girl, unlike that of a boy, is called *lubono,* or wealth. . . . A man with a large number of sons and few or no daughters sees himself as disadvantaged. A preference for daughters is a fact of Gwembe life. (105)

In Tokugawa, Japan, during the period between 1702 and 1872, husbands and wives had different fertility preferences based on the different value to them of sons versus daughters (Skinner 1993). Tokugawa wives, as is still common in Japan, preferred to have "first a girl, then a boy." This preference is related to the benefit in having a girl to help the mother in her work and to care for subsequent children, especially the boy it was hoped would come next. Husbands prefer a son-first strategy since a son helps them with their work. William Skinner hypothesized that husbands and wives would each try to achieve their goals with the one method available: **sex-selective infanticide,** or the killing of offspring on the basis of sex. Depending on their relative power position, either the husband or wife would be able to dominate the decision making about whether a child born would be kept. In order to test this hypothesis, Skinner needed information on the relative power of husbands and wives. He was lucky to have data on the ages of spouses at the time of marriage. Age differences in Japan are a key status index: Seniority requires deference, respect, and obedience. Working with this principle, Skinner devised three categories of marital power based on age differences at the time of marriage: low husband power (when the wife is older than the husband), intermediate husband power (when ages are about equal), and high husband power (when the husband is older than the wife). Over one-third of the marriages involved men who were at least ten years older than their wives, about 60 percent were in the intermediate category, and less than 6 percent were in the low husband-power category. Was the gender of children related to marital power relations? The analysis indicated a strong positive association. Without intervention, births should be about 50 percent male and 50 percent female. In the Tokugawa population, the following percentages were found among first-born children according to marital power type:

- *high husband-power households:* 84 percent of first-born children were male
- *intermediate husband-power households:* 53 percent of first-born children were male
- *low husband-power households:* 34 percent of first-born children were male

It seems clear that parental preferences about whether a girl or boy would be more valuable to them did exist and were acted on, depending on the balance of power within the family that would determine whose values would win out.

In a highland village in the Oaxacan region of southern Mexico, men and women have different preferences about the number of children (Browner 1986). Men are more pronatalist than women. Among women with only one child, 80 percent were content with their present family size. Most men (60 percent) who were satisfied with their present family size had four or more children. Carole Browner, the anthropologist who studied husband-wife differences in fertility preferences, offers further insights:

> Women with large families said they resented the demands of child care and the limitations it placed on them. Many saw children as a burden. They considered them too much work, too hard to raise, a source of problems. . . . They viewed children as pesky disturbances who kept them tied to the house. One woman told me, "[The people of the community] want us to have many children. That's fine for them to say. They don't have to take care of them and keep them clean. My husband sleeps peacefully through the night, but I have to get up when the children need something. I'm the one the baby urinates on; sometimes I have to get out of bed in the cold and change both our clothes. They wake me when they're sick or thirsty, my husband sleeps through it all" (714).

At the National Level

National governments play key roles in decreasing or increasing rates of population growth within their boundaries, shaped by their concerns about providing employment and public services, maintaining the tax base, filling the ranks of the military, maintaining ethnic and regional proportions, and dealing with population aging. The former Soviet Union faced significant planning challenges created by the contrasts between the below-replacement fertility of the "European" areas and high fertility rates in the Central Asian and Muslim regions such as Tajikistan and Kyrghizstan. Some governments, including Japan and France, which are concerned about declining population growth rates, have urged women to have more babies. Israel is openly pronatalist, given its interest in boosting its national population level as a political statement of strength and supporting its expansionist economic policies.

Romania, from the mid-1960s until the end of Nicole Ceausescu's regime in 1989, was an example of extreme state pronatalism. Romania openly pursued the nationalist goal of a growing population in order to provide a strong labor force and ensure "the triumph of socialism" (Kligman 1995:236). According to Gail Kligman, women's bodies were thus turned into instruments to be used for the service of the state. Most notably, a previously liberal abortion law was replaced by a strict one, permitting abortion only in cases in which the mother's life was endangered. Along with policies to promote increased reproduction, women were urged to take greater part in production. The state was to assist by providing ample maternity leave, child care facilities, and job security. Mothers who had many children were honored as "heroes of socialist labor" and were given awards and privileges with the highest award of Heroine Mother for women who delivered and reared ten or more children (Kligman notes that the high rate of infant mortality, especially in rural areas, meant that even women who had given birth to ten or more children might not earn this highest honor). Throughout this period, contraceptives were available only through the black market, an option open mainly to urban, educated, and upper-class women. Increasing rates of illegal abortion emerged as the ironic result of state attempts to tightly control women's fertility choices.

At the Global Level

The broadest, most far-reaching layer that affects decision making about fertility occurs at the international level, where power structures such as the World Bank, pharmaceutical companies, and religions influence national, and ultimately individual, priorities about fertility. For example, religious positions in the global politics of family planning were visible at the 1994 Cairo Population conference. Roman Catholic and Islamic leaders opposed promoting birth control technology in developing countries. Many European and North American groups support selected aspects of modern family planning. Population policies of the governments of donor countries affect the welfare of people in developing countries since funding for particular programs may wax or wane depending on political currents. Following the initial wave of enthusiasm in the 1950s for promoting family planning programs of many types, the United States has adopted a more restricted policy of limited support for family planning and withdrawal of support for specific features such as abortion (see the Critical Thinking box).

Another important aspect of international forces that affects reproduction is what Shellee Colen (1995) refers to as "globally stratified reproduction," in which lower-class people from poor countries migrate to other countries as marginally employed child care providers of the well-off. Colen's ethnographic study of West Indian women who work in this capacity in New York City provides personal-level data on this trans-

CRITICAL THINKING

Reproductive Rights or Wrongs

Beginning in the 1980s, serious criticism of Western family planning programs in relation to reproductive rights emerged from several directions. In the United States, the conservative Reagan administration opposed support of abortion and other forms of population control at home and abroad. At the same time, critics on the left claimed that the Western-supported and Western-styled family planning programs in the Third World were a form of neocolonialism. Areas of debate include sterilization of women and the use of incentives such as cash payments, radios, or clothing to attract people into being sterilized.

Betsy Hartmann, an early critic of Western family planning promotion in developing countries, wrote an influential book called *Reproductive Rights and Wrongs* (1987). In the mid-1970s, she did fieldwork in a village in Bangladesh. Two key lessons about women's reproductive freedom emerged. First, in one area, there were women who were satisfied with the number of children they had, and they wanted to adopt some form of "modern" contraception, but none was available. Second,

> in other areas of Bangladesh, population control programs were in full force, indiscriminately putting women on the pill, injecting Depo-Provera, or inserting IUDs without offering adequate medical screening, supervision, or follow-up. As a result, many women experienced negative side-effects and became disillusioned with contraception. The government's response was not to reform the program to meet women's needs, but instead to further intensify its population control efforts by pushing sterilization. (x–xi)

In both instances, women were denied control over their own reproduction. Hartmann pursued the topic of reproductive freedom by reading the available literature, corresponding with many experts involved in family planning and health, and contacting reproductive rights activists. By the mid-1980s she was involved in exposing the United States's involvement in sterilization abuse in Bangladesh. She argued that sterilization was being heavily targeted at the poorest women and involved "coercive" incentives. The incentive given to a man or woman for sterilization was Taka 175, equivalent to several weeks' wages. Women also received a *sari* (women's clothing worth about Taka 100), and men received a *lungee* (men's clothing worth about Taka 50). In some cases, food incentives were given: Poor women who approached local government officials for wheat as part of a special food aid program were told that they would get wheat if they had the "operation." Food aid was found to be withheld from women who refused. The number of sterilizations increased during the autumn months when food was scarcest. Doctors and clinic staff received a bonus for each sterilization. Some family planning workers who failed to meet the sterilization quota for the month suffered pay cuts.

Barbara Pillsbury (1990) examined numerous reports on female sterilization in Bangladesh, which began in 1966, to assess to what degree the criticisms raised above might be valid. She reports:

> Sterilization services are easily the most closely monitored and thoroughly studied component in the Bangladesh health and family planning program. The government of Bangladesh, donors, and various non-governmental organizations have invested a great amount of time and several millions of dollars on sterilization-related monitoring, research and evaluation efforts that focused solely or partly on issues of voluntarism. The U.S. government alone (through A.I.D.) has since 1983 funded approximately 20 quarterly sterilization surveys. As international attention focused on sterilization in Bangladesh, the number of studies and evaluations increased. Methodologies were developed and refined to measure the degree to which people chose sterilization voluntarily, their satisfaction with the procedure, and the effects of compensation payments on the sterilization decision-making process. Hundreds of other research studies and evaluations have focused on related aspects of family planning. In short, the Bangladesh family planning program is among the best studied in the world. (169)

The critics' charges, she concludes from all these studies, are not borne out. Specifically, the "compensation payment does not appear to be an important influence on the decision as to whether or not to get sterilized" (181). In most cases, the women "gained" nothing economically. Pillsbury explains that choice, not incentives, prompt Bangladeshis to seek sterilization:

> Why do so many Bangladeshis voluntarily choose sterilization? The basic reason is the same as in other countries—they do not want any more children. Why? Mostly to avoid the economic burden of a child that they can ill afford. Many Bangladeshi women also say that they choose sterilization because another pregnancy would be hard on their health, which in many cases is poor already. *No one,* of all the people who were interviewed in all of the studies cited above, said that he or she was compelled or deceived into getting sterilized. (183)

Critical Thinking Questions

- On what data do these experts base their opinions? Are the data adequate?
- From the information available, does individual agency or structurism appear to be more important in shaping people's decision making about sterilization?
- How might anthropological fieldwork provide more information on the role of agency and individual decision making concerning family planning choices?
- How might an anthropological approach provide more specific information on the role of structural influences on individual decision making concerning family planning choices?
- If you were a population policy maker for the United States, would you support family planning programs in Bangladesh and the use of incentives such as cash payments? How would you justify your position?

national process that involves uncounted numbers of women who are "like mothers" to the children they care for, while at the same time having greatly reduced time to care for their own children.

Techniques of Fertility Control

All cultures throughout history have had ways of influencing their fertility, including ways to increase it, reduce it, and regulate its spacing. Some of these are direct, such as using certain herbs or medicines that induce abortion. Others are indirect, such as long periods of breastfeeding, which reduce chances of conception. Hundreds of indigenous fertility control methods are available cross-culturally, many of which were in existence long before modern science came on the scene (Newman 1972, 1985). One study conducted in Afghanistan, for example, found about five hundred fertility-regulating techniques in just one region of the country (Hunte 1985). In Afghanistan, as in most preindustrial cultures, the women are mainly the holders of this information. Certain specialists, such as midwives or herbalists, provide further guidance and expertise. Of the total number of methods in the Afghanistan study, 72 percent were aimed at increasing fertility, 22 percent were contraceptives (preventing fertilization of the ovum by the sperm), and 6 percent were used to induce abortion. These methods predominantly involve plant and animal substances prepared in different ways. Herbs are made into tea and taken orally, some substances are formed into pills, some steamed and inhaled as vapors, some vaginally inserted, and others rubbed on the woman's stomach. Contemporary medical research reveals the efficacy of many indigenous fertility regulating methods (see the Current Event box).

Induced Abortion

Direct intervention in a pregnancy may be resorted to in order to prevent fetal development and lead to abortion (expulsion of the fetus from the womb). Induced abortion, in its many forms, is probably a cultural universal. A review of ethnographic literature on about four hundred societies indicates that it was practiced in virtually all societies (Devereaux 1976). It is usually done either by the woman herself or with assistance from another woman, perhaps a midwife. Social attitudes toward abortion include:

- *Absolute approval:* Abortion under any condition is acceptable.
- *Conditional approval:* Abortion is acceptable under specified conditions.
- *Tolerance:* Abortion is regarded with neither approval nor disapproval.
- *Opposition:* Abortion is sometimes deemed to deserve punishment of different types.

Methods of inducing abortion include hitting the abdomen, starving oneself, taking drugs (such as *kava*), jumping from high places, jumping up and down, lifting heavy objects, and doing hard work. In Afghanistan, the midwife inserts into the pregnant woman objects such as a wooden spoon or stick treated with copper sulphate that cause bleeding and abortion (Hunte 1985).

Motivation for inducing abortion. Economic and social factors largely explain why people induce abor-

Current Event

Contraception the Natural Way

- After having sex, some women of the Appalachian region in Virginia and North Carolina take a teaspoonful of seeds from the common weed called Queen Anne's lace. They crush the seeds, stir them into a glass of water, and drink the mixture. They believe that it keeps them from getting pregnant.
- In rural areas of northern India, women chew and swallow the same kind of seeds dry as a form of contraception.
- Women in both regions possess knowledge that can be traced back at least 2,500 years—to ancient Greek physicians who prescribed seeds of Queen Anne's lace as a contraceptive and as an herbal "morning-after pill."
- Experiments on animals show that some 450 plant species worldwide contain natural substances that prevent ovulation, block fertilization, stop implantation, or reduce fertility in some other way.
- What about peas? In the history of Tibet, the population was stable for long periods of time. The Tibetans subsisted mainly on barley and peas. When mice were fed a diet of 20 percent peas, litter sizes dropped by half. At 30 percent peas, the mice failed to reproduce at all.

Source: The Washington Post, July 25, 1994b.

tion (Devereaux 1976: 13–21). Nomadic women, for example, work very hard and have to carry heavy loads, sometimes for long distances. This lifestyle does not allow women to care for many small children at one time. Poverty is another motivating factor: When faced with another birth in the context of limited resources, abortion may appear to be the most rational choice. Culturally defined "legitimacy" of a pregnancy, along with possible social penalties for bearing an illegitimate child, has been a prominent reason for abortion in Western societies. At a more macro level, some governments have intervened in family decisions to regulate access to abortion in varying ways, sometimes promoting it, and other times forbidding it. Since the late 1980s, China has pursued one of the most rigorous campaigns to limit population growth (Greenhalgh 1994). Its One-Child Policy, announced in 1978, allowed most families to have only one child. It involved strict surveillance of pregnancies, strong group pressure toward women pregnant for the second time or more, and forced abortions and sterilizations. Inadvertently, this policy simultaneously led to an increase in female infanticide as parents, in their desire for a son and with only one child allowed to them, opted to kill any daughters born to them.

People regularly visit and decorate statues in memory of their aborted or "returned" fetuses in Japan.

Religion and abortion. There is no simple relationship between what a particular religion teaches about abortion and what people actually do. Catholicism forbids abortion, but thousands of Catholic women have sought illegal abortions throughout the world. Islamic teachings forbid abortion and female infanticide, yet sex-selective abortion of female fetuses is known to be practiced covertly in Pakistan and by Muslims in India. Hinduism teaches *ahimsa*, or nonviolence toward other living beings, including a fetus whose movements have been felt by the mother ("quickening"). Yet, thousands of Hindus seek abortions every year, and many of them are specifically to abort a female. In contrast, Buddhism provides little in the way of overt rulings against abortion. In fact, Japanese Buddhism teaches that all life is fluid and that an aborted fetus is simply "returned" to a watery world of unshaped life and may, some time later, come back to live with humans (LaFleur 1992). This belief fits well with the fact that abortion has, in recent years at least, been the most commonly used form of birth control in Japan as it passed through its demographic transition.

The new reproductive technology. Women's reproductive rights are an important contemporary issue facing all cultures (Corrêa 1994). In one context, these rights may involve the choice of seeking abortion, while in another, the right to bear a child. They include the difficult issue of the right to decide the gender or other characteristics of one's unborn child. Since the early 1980s, new forms of reproductive technology have been developed and been made available in many places around the world. One important new development is the ability to gain genetic information about the fetus, which can be used by parents in decision making about whether to keep or abort it. In the United States and some European countries, amniocentesis is a legal test used to reveal certain genetic problems in the fetus such as Down's syndrome or spina bifida. Experts have begun to question the social equity involved in this testing and the ethical issues related to the ever-growing role of technology in birth

Multiple Cultural Worlds

Amniocentesis and the Poor of New York City

Rayna Rapp (1993) did research on the cultural context of genetic testing among poor women in New York City. Nationally, amniocentesis has become a "ritual of pregnancy," mainly among the more educated, urbanized sectors of the White middle classes. In New York City, where Rapp did participant observation in the Prenatal Diagnosis Laboratory (PDL), the situation is different. The PDL of the City of New York was established in 1978 to offer amniocentesis to low-income women who are mainly African American or Hispanic. Some of the clients, however, are economically better-off, and most of them are White. Rapp discovered differences in the behavior and attitudes of the clients who are poor and on Medicare and the better-off clients. About 50 percent of the poor clients don't keep their initial appointment for genetic counseling, while only 10 percent of the better-off clients break their appointment. Upon having an amniocentesis procedure recommended by a counselor, more of the poor refuse to follow through with having the test done. Rapp witnessed many counseling sessions. She also interviewed several "refusers" in their homes about their attitudes toward the testing:

> The commentary of refusers provides clues to the cultural contradictions involved in the technological transformation of pregnancy.... When a woman had birthed four other children, comes from a family of eight, and all her sisters and neighbors have had similar histories, she has seen scores of babies born without recognizable defects. It requires a leap of faith ... to contrast these experiences with a number produced by a lady in a white coat proclaiming that the risk of a baby with a birth defect is steadily rising with each pregnancy. (392)

Awareness of societal discrimination figures into some accounts as well:

> One Haitian father, firmly rejecting prenatal testing on his wife's behalf, said, "The counselor says the baby could be born retarded. They always say Haitian children are retarded. What is this retarded? Many Haitian children are said to be retarded in the public schools. If we send them to the Haitian Academy (a community-based private school) they learn just fine." (392)

While medical innovations such as amniocentesis are promoted as "advances for women," Rapp finds that poor women who are advised to seek genetic testing during their pregnancy are not fully aware of all that is involved. The new technology and its option for more "choice," in fact, Rapp argues, does not empower them. Instead, it overpowers them.

and reproduction (see the Multiple Cultural Worlds box).

CULTURE AND DEATH

Cultural anthropologists have done many studies of fertility, but their research on mortality is relatively scant (Bledsoe and Hirschman 1989). This difference is partly because mortality is more difficult to research in a typical fieldwork period in the traditional fieldwork setting of a village or urban neighborhood. In a year, several births might occur in a village of 1,000 people, while fewer infant deaths will occur and perhaps no murders or suicides. (Of course, if one did fieldwork in a home for the aged in the United States, then death would be far easier to study than birth.) Another reason for the difference in research emphasis between fertility and mortality is the greater availability of funding for fertility studies, given the worldwide concern with population growth and family planning.

Death may occur randomly and from biological causes that impair the body's functioning. However, cultural factors often put certain people more at risk of dying from a certain cause and at a particular age than others. Consider statistics on deaths from car accidents. According to many studies, the rate of severe accidents is higher among men, and men exhibit more high-risk driving behavior such as driving at high speeds and driving under the influence of alcohol (Hakamies-Blomqvist 1994). A study of fatal accidents in older male and female drivers in Finland finds a clear increase among older female drivers. The analysis found that older women drivers had substantially less driving experience in terms of mileage and conditions, compared to older men drivers. The lower experience level of women drivers, in turn, was related to more men having held jobs to which they commuted. This lack of experience may place women at a disadvantage when it comes to coping with the effects of aging on driving. If the division of labor were to change and more women had jobs to which they commuted, the accident pattern of older drivers might also change.

Causes of death can be analyzed on several levels. For example, if an infant living in a poor, tropical country dies of dehydration, what might be the cause? Levels of causality considered in population studies are proximate, intermediate, and ultimate causes. A proximate cause is the one that is closest to the actual outcome. In the case of the infant death, dehydration was the proximate cause of death and one that might be written on the death certificate. Why was the baby dehydrated? A closer look into the situation might show that the baby was malnourished. Malnutrition leads to diarrhea and subsequent dehydration. Malnutrition could be considered the intermediate cause of death. Why was the baby malnourished? This question takes us down a complex pathway of inquiry—perhaps the family was very poor and could not afford adequate food for the baby; perhaps the baby died during a period of extreme food scarcity in the area; or maybe the baby was an unwanted third daughter and was fed less than she needed in order to thrive. The question of ultimate causation takes the inquiry out of the realm of medical and nutritional experts and into an analysis of the ultimate, or deeper economic, political, and social factors that put a particular individual at increased risk of dying.

Infanticide

Deliberate killing of offspring has been widely documented, although it is not usually a frequent or common practice in any particular society (Dickemann 1975, 1979; Divale and Harris 1976; Scrimshaw 1984). Infanticide takes different forms. Marvin Harris (1977) distinguished **direct infanticide** from **indirect infanticide.** Direct infanticide is the death of an infant or child resulting from actions such as beating, smothering, poisoning, or drowning. Indirect infanticide, a more subtle process, may involve prolonged practices such as food deprivation, failure to take a sick infant to a clinic, or failure to provide warm clothing in winter, that bring about the death of an infant. The most frequent motive for direct infanticide reported in the cross-cultural record is that the infant was "deformed" or very ill (Scrimshaw 1984:490– 491). Other motives for infanticide include sex of the infant, an adulterous conception, an unwed mother, the birth of twins, too many children in the family already, and poverty. A study of 148 cases of infanticide in contemporary Canada found that the mothers convicted of killing their offspring were likely to have given birth at a younger age and may thus have had fewer supportive resources to help them (Daly and Wilson 1984).

Family Resource Constraints and Child "Fitness"

In all cultures, parents have expectations for their children—what roles they will play as children, their future marital status, and their roles as adults. If an infant appears to be unable to meet these expectations, parental disappointment and detachment may occur. When family resources are extremely limited, parents may opt for infanticide. As yet, no general theory has been formulated to explain precisely the relationship between resource constraints and perceived child "fitness." Not all people living in poverty practice infanticide, nor do all people practice infanticide when a child is born with certain disabilities. The most likely association that can be drawn at this point is that the extremeness of resource constraints may be a key causal factor, especially when found in conjunction with a perception of child unfitness.

Culturally accepted infanticide has long existed among the Tarahumara, a large group of indigenous peoples of northern Mexico (Mull and Mull 1987). The approximately 50,000 Tarahumara live in a rugged mountainous area about the size of three New England states. Thus, they have been able to retain more of their cultural identity than many other indigenous groups in Mexico. Most live in log houses with dirt floors and no running water and electricity. They make their living by growing corn and beans and raising sheep and goats, mainly for their own use. Human strength is valued in adults as well as in children, since children begin helping with herding and child care early in their lives. Dorothy and Dennis Mull first learned of the possible existence of culturally sanctioned infanticide when Dennis was working as a volunteer physician in a hospital. A twelve-month-old girl who had been admitted several months earlier had developed a complication necessitating the amputation of half her foot. During the course of her recovery in the hospital, her mother's visits became less frequent, to the point of being only a few minutes long while she was in town on other errands. In conversations with the medical staff, the mother expressed a restrained but deep anger about the fact that her daughter had lost half her foot. The Mulls returned to the United States and learned later that the child had been dismissed from the hospital. A few weeks later she reportedly "failed" and died. When the Mulls returned to the area the next year, they discussed the case with several people:

> One said immediately, "Oh, her family killed her—probably by hitting her. Or they gave her a poisoned drink." Another agreed, adding, "Well, after all, with only half a foot she'd never be able to walk right or work hard. She might never find a husband." . . . We next asked several health care providers in the Tarahumara region whether they had ever treated or nurtured a child over a long period of time only to have it die at home soon after discharge. Most had had such an experience. (116–117)

In order to learn more, they interviewed twenty Tarahumara women about their knowledge of infanticide. All of the women had heard of at least one case of infanticide in the area, 95 percent of the women knew of at least one case of infanticide when the mother had no husband or had "too many children," 55 percent knew of at least one case of infanticide of a "damaged" child, and 10 percent knew of at least one case in which a sickly infant had been killed.

Among the poor of urban Brazil, a similar pattern of indirect infanticide exists that is driven by poverty (Scheper-Hughes 1993). Life is hard for the poor residents of the shantytown called Bom Jesus. Life expectancy is low, although precise information on mortality is not available for these shantytown dwellers. Nancy Scheper-Hughes used a variety of research methods to assess infant and child mortality rates. Some official records were available in the town registry office, but they did not cover all births and deaths. Scheper-Hughes found another source of data by going through the records of the local coffin-maker, since everyone who dies is buried in a coffin. Adult coffins and children's coffins are built along similar styles, with cardboard tops and plywood bottoms. Adult coffins are painted brown, and children's coffins are "sky blue, the favorite color of the Virgin [Mary]" (289). The coffin maker showed his current records of coffin requisitions to Scheper-Hughes and told her that earlier ledgers were kept at the town hall. Her analysis reveals that infant and child mortality rates were extremely high in 1965, about 493/1,000 live births, declining to a still-high rate of 174/1,000 in 1985, with some indication in 1989 of a "significant upward turn in child, and especially infant, deaths" (296).

These statistics on infant and child mortality in Bom Jesus since the 1960s led Scheper-Hughes to coin the ironic phrase, the "modernization of mortality." The modernization of mortality in Brazil refers to a deep division between mortality patterns of the rich and the poor. Recent economic growth in Brazil has brought rising standards of living for many. The national **infant mortality rate** (deaths of children under the age of one year per 1,000 births) has declined substantially in recent decades. However, such developments have been unevenly distributed. Instead, there has been a concentration of high death rates among the poorest classes of society and a concentration of infant deaths (under one year of age) as a proportion of all child deaths, with infant death almost replacing child death. Poverty and class differentiation are at the base of these trends. Poverty forces mothers to selectively (and unconsciously) neglect babies that seem sickly or weak, sending them to heaven as "angel babies" rather than trying to keep them alive with the inadequate resources available. The people's religious beliefs, a form of Catholicism, provide ideological support for this practice of indirect infanticide since it allows mothers to believe that their dead babies are now safe in heaven. According to Scheper-Hughes, the mothers also believe that they should not weep over the death of their angel baby since their tears will fall on the baby's angel wings and prevent the baby from flying to heaven.

Female Infanticide

When the infant's sex is the basis for infanticide, females tend to be the target (Miller 1997 [1981]: 42–44). Among foraging groups, sex-selective infanticide is rare, being found mainly among some Inuit groups. Presumably, this practice relates to the greater importance of raising males who will provide food through large-game hunting. Among horticultural societies, a correlation exists between the level of intergroup warfare and the practice of female infanticide (Divale and Harris 1976). Warfare puts a premium on raising males, to the detriment of investing care and resources in females. Indirect female infanticide exists in contemporary times in much of China, the Republic of Korea, Hong Kong, India, Pakistan, and parts of the Middle East (see the Multiple Cultural Worlds box). In these countries, female infanticide is related to a com-

Unbalanced sex ratio.

plex set of factors, including the gender division of labor and marriage practices and costs.

Suicide

Suicide, or the taking of one's own life, is known in all societies, but the degree to which it is viewed as a positive or negative act varies. In some cultures, suicide is legally or religiously defined as a crime. Catholicism defines suicide as a sin, and suicide rates tend to be lower in Catholic countries than in Protestant countries (Durkheim 1951:152). Buddhism does not condone suicide, nor does it consider it a punishable crime. Indeed, Buddhists have sometimes resorted to suicide as a political statement. Several suicides of Buddhist priests and nuns by self-immolation during the Vietnam War were protests of the Catholic president's persecution of Buddhism.

Multiple Cultural Worlds

Female Infanticide in India

In North India in the eighteenth century, direct female infanticide was fairly widespread, with upper-caste Hindu groups such as Rajputs, Jats, and Brahmans in the North often keeping none or few of the daughters born to them. Entire villages were reported with no daughters at all. Census data for 1871 revealed that there were between 115 and 120 boys per 100 girls among the Hindu population in a large region of northern India. Over one hundred years later, similar juvenile sex ratios persist in this region in spite of increased economic development literacy and communication (Miller 1987b). Today, the Indian population has 55 million fewer females than males. Much of this gap, although precisely how much is not known, is caused by indirect female infanticide and sex-selective abortion. Baby girls are breastfed less often and for a shorter period of time than baby boys, and they are taken to clinics for treatment of illnesses less frequently. Hospital admissions in the North are 2:1 boys to girls, and that is not because more boys are sick than girls, but because parents and grandparents are more willing to allocate time and money for the health of boys than girls (Miller 1997 [1981]). Discrimination against daughters and in favor of sons in terms of household allocations of food, health care, and even attention are more marked in northern India than in its southern and eastern regions. This pattern corresponds with two features of the economy: production and marriage exchanges. The northern plains are characterized by dry-field wheat cultivation, which requires intensive labor inputs for plowing and field preparation and then moderate amounts of field labor for sowing, weeding, and harvesting, with women assisting in the latter tasks as unpaid family labor. Production in southern and eastern India relies more on wet rice cultivation, in which women form the bulk of the paid agricultural labor force. In much of southern India, women of the household may even participate on an equal footing with men in terms of agricultural planning and decision making.

Paralleling this regional difference in labor patterns is a contrast in costs related to marriage. In the North, marriage typically requires, especially among the propertied groups, **groomprice** or **dowry**—the transfer

(continued)

of large amounts of cash and goods from the bride's family to the groom's family (Miller 1997 [1981]). Marriage costs in the South among both propertied and unpropertied groups were more likely to emphasize **brideprice**—the transfer of cash and goods from the groom's side to the bride's father, along with a tradition of passing gold jewelry through the female line from mother to daughter. From a parent's perspective, the birth of several daughters in the northern system is a financial drain. In the South, a daughter is considered a valuable laborer and source of wealth. Importantly, much of northern dowry and southern bridewealth circulates: An incoming dowry can be used to finance the marriage of the groom's sister, and bridewealth received in the South at the marriage of a daughter can be used for the marriage of her brother. Logically, in the North, the more sons per daughter in the household the better, since more incoming dowries will allow for a "better" marriage of a daughter.

The economic costs and benefits to a household of having sons versus daughters in India also varies by class. This variation relates to both work patterns and marriage patterns. Middle- and upper-class families, especially in the North, tend to keep girls and women out of the paid labor force more than the poor. Thus, daughters are a greater economic liability among the better-off than among the poor where girls, as well as boys, may earn money in the informal sector, for example, doing piece-work at home. This class difference is mirrored in marriage costs. Among the poor, marriage costs are less expensive than among the middle and upper classes, and sometimes involve more balanced exchange between the bride's and groom's families. Thus, marital costs of daughters are lower and the benefits of having sons are not that much greater than having daughters.

Poverty is therefore not the major driving factor of female infanticide or female-selective abortion in India. It is more related to a drive to maximize family status and wealth by having sons and avoiding having daughters: If one has two sons and one daughter in the North Indian marriage system of huge dowries, then two dowries will come in with the brides of the sons and only one dowry will be expended. Incoming dowries can be used to finance the dowry of one's own daughter, so one can provide a huge outgoing dowry that will attract a "high quality" husband. If, on the other hand, one has two daughters and one son, the ratio of incoming to outgoing wealth changes significantly. This situation would impoverish a family rather than enrich it.

Throughout much of Asia and the South Pacific, suicide is considered a noble and honorable act. When Cheyenne Brando, daughter of Marlon Brando and Tahitian actress Tarita, committed suicide in Tahiti, the local mayor called her suicide "a beautiful gesture" (Gliotto 1995:70). Aged twenty-five years old at the time of her death, she had been depressed for many years, especially after the death of her fiancé, who was killed by Cheyenne's brother, Christian, in what he claims was an accidental shooting. Honorable suicide is also found in Japan, where it seems to result from a strong commitment to group goals and a feeling of failure to live up to those goals (Lebra 1976). In this way, suicide is a way of "saving face."

Sati (pronounced SUT-TEE), or the suicide of a wife upon the death of her husband, has been practiced in parts of India for several hundred years and, on occasion, into the present. According to Hindu scriptures, a woman whose husband dies does an act of great personal and group honor if she voluntarily joins his corpse on the funeral pyre and thus burns to death. No one knows for sure how common this was in the past, but its ideal is still upheld by conservative Hindus. The most recent reported sati occurred in the northern state of Rajasthan in 1987 by a young widow named Roop Kanwar. Historians and social scientists have debated the degree of voluntarism involved in such suicides, as there is evidence of direct coercion in some cases—the widow was drugged, or physically forced onto the pyre. Indirect coercion is also culturally embedded in the belief that a woman whose husband dies is to blame for his death. Perhaps she didn't serve him with enough devotion, pray or fast for him enough, or she ate too much and didn't give him enough food. The life of surviving widows is difficult, involving loss of status, shame, and material deprivation. Knowing this, a new widow may decide she would be better off dead.

In terms of sheer numbers, suicide is more prevalent in the industrialized, urbanized societies of Europe than elsewhere. However, in several developing nations, such as Sri Lanka and Samoa, suicide rates have risen steeply in recent decades. The general explanation proposed for the cross-cultural variation in suicide rates is that the rapid social changes brought about by industrialism, the spread of education, and global change in consumer values are often not matched by people's ability to attain new goals and satisfy new aspirations. French sociologist Emile

Durkheim (1951 [1897]) used the term *anomie* to refer to the feelings of dislocation and dissatisfaction caused by rapid social change and thwarted ambitions. The concept of anomic suicide seems to apply well to the rising trend of youth suicide worldwide.

Violence

Violent death can be the result of private, interpersonal conflict or it can occur in a public arena, either through informal conflict between individuals or groups such as gang fights, or formal conflict such as war. Throughout history, millions of people have died from private and public violence. Often their deaths have culturally defined patterns.

Private Violence: Spousal Abuse

Throughout the world, private violence resulting in death is all too common. One example, infanticide, was discussed above. Murder of spouses is a frequent occurrence, with far more women killed by husbands or male partners than vice versa. Lethal spousal violence is known to exist throughout most of the world in varying degrees, although it is difficult to pinpoint cross-cultural rates because statistics are undependable or unavailable. Anecdotal, case-by-case evidence suggests that in much of the Middle East, a husband may kill his wife or daughter with a fair amount of impunity, as if it is within his rights in terms of protecting family honor. The United States has high rates of lethal spousal violence, with Kentucky holding the highest reported rates of wife killing (anthropological studies of the dynamics of domestic violence cross-culturally are discussed elsewhere in this book, see pages 225–226).

In India, beginning in the 1980s, many cases of an apparently new form of femicide were reported in the media. Called *dowry death,* such murders were characteristically committed by a husband, often in collusion with his mother, and carried out by throwing a flammable substance over the victim and then lighting her on fire. These murders are especially prevalent in northern cities, among the middle and upper classes (see the Current Event box). They are spurred by an obsessive material interest in extracting wealth from the wife's family through first her dowry and later, a continuing stream of demanded gifts. If the bride's family cannot comply with these demands, the bride's life is endangered. This form of **femicide,** or murder of a person based on the fact of being female, is related to the overall low value of women in India, especially in the North and among the status-aspiring middle and upper classes. Dowry deaths are prompted by the greed of a bride's in-laws for more and more gifts from her family, even after the marriage has occurred.

> **Current Event**
>
> **Consumerism Fuels Dowry Death Wave in India**
>
> - In the northern city of New Delhi, twenty-year-old Asha endured three years of a hellish marriage until she was murdered. She wrote letters to her father, reporting beatings and once being given milk spiked with pesticide, an attempt to poison her.
> - According to her father, Asha was killed by her husband's family. They gagged her, beat her and electrocuted her with a live wire. They bundled her body in a quilt and called her father to say that she had had an accident. "I knew instantly she had been killed," said the father. "It was a case of dowry death."
> - Police say reported dowry deaths increased 170 percent in India in the last decade. Reported numbers in 1994 were 6,200—an average of seventeen women burned, poisoned, strangled, or otherwise killed each day because of their marital family's continued pressure on the natal families to provide more dowry gifts. These statistics do not include the tens of thousands of incidents of nonfatal dowry harassment and physical and mental abuse inflicted on wives by husbands and in-laws.
>
> *Source: The Washington Post,* March 17, 1995.

Public Violence

Warfare is a common form of public violence (political aspects of warfare are discussed in Chapter 11). The few studies that have addressed mortality from warfare cross-culturally reveal that among horticultural societies, warfare accounts for the highest proportion of male deaths and can thus be seen to function as a major mechanism of population control in such societies (Divale and Harris 1976). Horticulture's requirement for large territories puts many groups in conflict with one another. In recent decades, conflicts with outsiders have increased; for example, the Yanomami of the Brazilian and Venezuelan Amazon region are squeezed by outsiders such as cattle ranch developers and miners (Ferguson 1990). This external pressure impels them to engage in intergroup raids that often result in the deaths of male fighters, but also sometimes women, who may be captured and then killed. In some especially vulnerable groups of Yanomami, it has been reported that up to one-third of all adult males die as a result of intergroup raids and warfare (Yanomami warfare is discussed in greater detail in Chapter 12).

In contrast, in industrialized societies, the death rates of males actively involved in warfare constitute a much smaller proportion of total death rates, being replaced by such causes as automobile accidents or heart disease. The Vietnam War (American War) of the 1960s and 1970s resulted in the death of about 60,000 Americans in Vietnam (mostly males), and many times that number of Vietnamese.

Some scholars distinguish **ethnocide,** destruction of a culture without physically killing its people, from **genocide,** the destruction of a culture and its people through physical extermination (Chalk and Jonassohn 1986:180). The Chinese occupation of Tibet, the Khmer Rouge's massacres in Cambodia, the Serbian-Bosnian conflict, the Hutu-Tutsi conflict in Rwanda, and the Indonesian government's actions in East Timor are other examples of politically motivated genocide (Maybury-Lewis 1997b). The history of Native American demography can also be interpreted as one of genocidal destruction and has been called "the American holocaust." Although there is disagreement among scholars about the numbers involved, it is likely that well over 50 million Amerindians died as a result of contact with the Europeans from 1492 through the seventeenth century (Stannard 1992). For example, the conquest of Mexico by Hernando Cortés had the following demographic results:

> Tenochtitlán, with its 350,000 residents, had been the jewel of an empire that contained numerous exquisite cities. All were destroyed. Before the coming of the Europeans, central Mexico, radiating out from the metropolitan centers over many tens of thousands of square miles, had contained about 25 million people—almost ten times the population of England at that time. Seventy-five years later hardly more than one million were left. And central Mexico, where 60 out of a hundred people perished, was typical. . . . In western and central Honduras 95 percent of the native people were exterminated in half a century. In western Nicaragua the rate of extermination was 99 percent—from more than one million people to less than 10,000 in just sixty years. (430)

The native population of the Caribbean islands was completely killed off. Only archaeological evidence and Spanish archival documents recording fragments of the original peoples' culture remain. And this is only the Western hemisphere; European colonialism's effects were felt globally.

SUMMARY

Far from being purely "natural" functions of biology, the demographic processes of fertility and mortality are everywhere shaped by culture. The various modes of production can be viewed as basic structures to which demography responds. For thousands of years, foragers maintained a balanced level of population through direct and indirect means of fertility regulation. As sedentarization increased and food surpluses became more available and storable, population growth increased as well, culminating in the highest rates of population growth in human history among settled agriculturalists.

Cultures have developed many techniques for increasing fertility, reducing it, and regulating its timing. Anthropological studies of indigenous fertility-regulating mechanisms reveal hundreds of different methods, including the use of herbs and other natural sources for inhibiting or enhancing fertilization, and for inducing abortion if an undesired pregnancy occurs. In preindustrial societies, the knowledge and practice of fertility regulation was largely unspecialized and available to all women. Early specializations included midwives and herbalists. In the industrial mode of reproduction, scientific and medical specialization abounds, and most knowledge and expertise is no longer in the hands of women themselves. Class-stratified access to fertility-regulating methods exists globally and within nations.

Population growth and change are also shaped through the cultural manipulation of death. The practice of infanticide is probably of ancient origin, and it still exists today. Infanticide may be done in response to familial resource limitations, perceptions of "fitness" of the child, or preferences about the gender of offspring. Deaths from suicide and public and private violence also reflect particular cultural patterns that "target" certain people or groups.

CRITICAL THINKING QUESTIONS

1. How would a cultural anthropologist explore the concept of "recreational sex" cross-culturally? Would this be a useful research project?
2. Besides the United States, are there other countries where violence has erupted over the issue of pregnancy termination through abortion? If so, what are the key issues involved? If not, why would the United States be so special in this area?
3. How do the theories of free choice versus structurism (see Chapter 1) apply to the cases of parents living in deep poverty who kill a child they consider "deformed" or weak?
4. Is the fact that Black males in the United States have such high mortality rates a case of indirect genocide? How could anthropological analysis contribute to a better understanding of this situation?

KEY CONCEPTS

below-replacement-level fertility, p. 115
brideprice, p. 128
demographic transition, p. 115
demography, p. 112
direct infanticide, p. 125
dowry, p. 127
ethnocide, p. 130
femicide, p. 129
fertility, p. 112
genocide, p. 130
groomprice, p. 127
indirect infanticide, p. 125
infant mortality rate, p. 126
infanticide, p. 113
matriliny, p. 118
migration, p. 112
mortality, p. 112
post-partum taboo, p. 117
pronatalism, p. 114
replacement-level fertility, p. 115
reproduction, p. 112
sex-selective infanticide, p. 119

SUGGESTED READINGS

Caroline Bledsoe and Barney Cohen, eds., *Social Dynamics of Adolescent Fertility in Sub-Saharan Africa.* Washington, DC: National Academy Press, 1993. An anthropologist and a demographer examine national survey data on cultural factors related to high fertility rates among adolescents in sub-Saharan Africa. Attention is given to patterns of adolescent sexuality, attitudes toward marriage, women's status, knowledge and practice of contraception, and the role of education in change.

Thomas E. Fricke, *Himalayan Households: Tamang Demography and Domestic Processes.* New York, Columbia University Press, 1994. An example of demographic anthropology, this is a local study of population patterns and change in one region of Nepal. The book includes chapters on the subsistence economy, fertility and mortality, the life course, household dynamics, and recent changes.

W. Penn Handwerker, ed., *Births and Power: Social Change and the Politics of Reproduction.* Boulder,CO: Westview Press, 1990. An overview chapter by the editor is followed by eleven case studies, including studies of the Inuit of Canada, the Bariba of West Africa, the Mende of Sierra Leone, Hungary, Bangladesh, studies from the United States addressing teen pregnancy, and an essay on AIDS in Africa.

Marvin Harris and Eric B. Ross, *Death, Sex and Fertility: Population Regulation in Preindustrial and Developing Societies.* New York: Columbia University Press, 1987. This text provides a wide-ranging overview of key factors affecting fertility under different modes of production.

Nancy Howell, *Demography of the Dobe !Kung.* New York: Academic Press, 1979. This classic book describes the demography of a group of South African foragers before they were sedentarized. The text considers how anthropological methods contribute to demographic analysis of small-scale societies, causes of illness and death, fertility and sterility, and population growth rates.

Nancy Scheper-Hughes, *Death without Weeping: The Violence of Everyday Life in Brazil.* Berkeley: University of California Press, 1993. This book is a landmark "ethnography of death," based on fieldwork in a Brazilian shantytown over several periods of time. The author argues that poverty drives a demographic system of very high infant mortality rates and high fertility.

中央
中央

CHAPTER 6

Personality and Human Development

CHAPTER OUTLINE

CULTURE AND PERSONALITY
- The "Culture and Personality School"
- Class Position and Personality
- New Directions
- *Multiple Cultural Worlds:* Corporate Personality Formation: The Making of Salarymen in Japan

BIRTH AND INFANCY
- Birth
- Sleeping Patterns
- Gender and Infancy

CHILDHOOD
- Mode of Production and Child Personality
- The Preschool Child
- Informal Learning
- *Voices:* Charles James Nowell, "Play Potlatches"
- Formal Schooling
- *Current Event:* "Desperate Fainting"
- *Multiple Cultural Worlds:* Learning to Be an Orthodox Jewish Woman

ADOLESCENCE
- Is Adolescence a Universal Life-Cycle Stage?
- Coming of Age and Gender Identity
- *Voices:* Tepilit Ole Saitoti, "The Initiation of a Maasai Warrior"
- *Critical Thinking:* Cultural Relativism, Human Rights, and "Female Genital Mutilation"
- Sexual Identity
- *Multiple Cultural Worlds:* Homosexuality and Economic Discrimination in the United States

ADULTHOOD AND MIDDLE AGE
- Becoming a Parent
- Middle Age

THE SENIOR YEARS

THE FINAL PASSAGE: DEATH AND DYING

SUMMARY

CRITICAL THINKING QUESTIONS

KEY CONCEPTS

SUGGESTED READINGS

◀ Schoolchildren in Japan exhibit an eagerness to participate in class.

The Mehinaku are peaceful horticulturalists of the Brazilian Amazon whose society, thus far, is mainly intact (Gregor 1981). Nonetheless, the Mehinaku are aware of the presence and power of Brazilians (non-Indians). An analysis of 385 dreams of the Mehinaku indicates that they have deep anxieties about the outsiders. Of the total set of dreams, over half contained indications of some level of anxiety. In 31 of the dreams, Brazilians were central characters, and of these, 90 percent of the dreams were tinged with fear, evidencing a clear focus of anxiety on the outsiders. Recurrent themes in the dreams with outsiders as key characters were fire, assault, and disorientation. While the Mehinaku's land and culture are so far intact, their inner tranquility is gone.

Psychological anthropologists consider many of the topics of contemporary Western psychology: learning, perception, cognition, memory, intelligence, the emotions, sexuality and gender, personality, and mental health problems. Psychological anthropologists study these topics cross-culturally and have revealed the ethnocentrism involved in applying Western psychological concepts universally, including definitions of what is "normal." An enduring question in psychological anthropology is whether and how much human psychology is the same cross-culturally or whether variation overrides universals.

This chapter provides a general background on how cultural anthropology has approached the study of the individual within culture, particularly how cultures shape **personality,** an individual's patterned and characteristic way of behaving, thinking, and feeling. We then proceed through major life cycle stages, noting key anthropological findings about the role of culture in human development. The focus in this chapter is largely on "normal" human development, however that is defined culturally. Problematic aspects of human development, including what Western psychology defines as mental illness, are discussed in Chapter 7.

CULTURE AND PERSONALITY

Cultural anthropologists have mainly pursued the line of argument that personality is formed through enculturation, or socialization, the process of cultural transmission to infants and other new members. They seek answers to the questions: Do different cultures try to enculturate their members into different personalities? If so, why?

The "Culture and Personality School"

The American-based culture and personality school began in the 1930s and persisted through the 1970s. Cultural anthropologists who were part of this group adopted some aspects of Freudian theories, especially the concept of the unconscious; the importance of childhood experiences in shaping personality; and the symbolic analysis of people's dreams, words, and stories. They differed from Freud in rejecting universalism in favor of particularism. The culture and personality movement believed that each culture has a unique history that affects its values, behavior, and personality types.

Personality Plasticity and Child Rearing

In the early 1930s, Margaret Mead went with another anthropologist, Reo Fortune, to the Sepik River area of northern New Guinea. Her subsequent publication, *Sex and Temperament in Three Primitive Societies* (1963 [1935]), revealed striking differences in how male and female roles and personalities were defined and acted out. Once again, Mead's findings seemed to provide clear proof that nature is subservient to culture, in this case with nature not dictating what is male and what is female. Among the Arapesh, the first group she studied, both men and women had nurturant and gentle personalities. Both valued parental roles and both participated equally in child care. Thus, Arapesh males and females all behave according to what is stereotypically defined as "female" in Western cultures. Among the Mundugumor, in contrast, both males and females corresponded to the Western stereotype of "male" behavior. Adults in general were assertive, aggressive, loud, and even fierce. Children were treated indifferently by their parents, with neither mothers nor fathers expressing nurturance. The situation among the Tchambuli was equally surprising to Mead and her readers: The men fussed about their looks, gossiped with each other most of the day, and did little in the way of productive work. The women were competent and responsible, providing most of the food through fishing and gardening, and managing the household. Among the Tchambuli, women played a dominant role in the culture and their

Margaret Mead, during some of her later years of fieldwork, observes children's interactions in Sicily.

personalities reflected this importance. In all, these findings show that gender is a very arbitrary matter, defined culturally and shaped through childrearing patterns. Mead's detailed analysis of variations in child care, including even differences in degrees of tenderness or neglect during breastfeeding, provide ample evidence of how children in different contexts begin to learn patterns of personality formation from an early age.

Cultural Patterns and National Character

Ruth Benedict, a leading figure of the culture and personality school, argued that personality types characterize whole cultures or even nations. In her first book, *Patterns of Culture* (1959 [1934]), she proposed that cultures are formed through the unconscious selection of a few cultural traits from the "vast arc" of potential traits. For example, one culture may emphasize monetary values while another overlooks them. The selected traits "interweave" to form a cohesive pattern, a **cultural configuration,** characteristic of everyone's thoughts and behaviors in the culture. Benedict first formulated her theories while doing research on Native American cultures. In her view, the Pueblo Indians of the American Southwest had personalities that exemplified a "middle road," involving moderation in all things and avoiding excess and violence. She termed the Pueblo an "Apollonian" culture, after the greek deity Apollo. In contrast, she labeled the Kwakwaka'wakw Indians of the Pacific Northwest, "Dionysian," after the Greek god of revelry and excess (and drinking wine), mainly because of their potlatches and high levels of expressive emotionality. Looking back on this approach, one is struck by the odd choice of classical Greek labels in the first place and the tendency to label an entire culture with one term.

Later, Benedict was commissioned by the United States Office of War Information during World War II to analyze Japanese personality structure and submit reports to the government to help defeat the Japanese. During the war, she could not do fieldwork, so she did "anthropology at a distance." This research strategy, while not ideal, was the best she could do. She consulted secondary sources (newspapers, magazines, movies) and she interviewed Japanese Americans. Her book, *The Chrysanthemum and the Sword* (1969 [1946]), presents a set of essential features of Japanese character: importance of *on* (obligation, the necessity to repay gifts and favors), the concept of virtue, the value on self-discipline, keeping one's name "clear" or honorable, and rules of etiquette. Following Benedict's work on Japan, **national character studies** that defined basic personality types and core values of nations became a prominent pursuit of psychological anthropologists. Contemporary anthropological standards, however, find three major faults with national character studies:

- They are ethnocentric: They classify cultures according to Western psychological values and features.
- They are reductionist: They emphasize only one or two features.
- They are totalizing: They obscure intranational variation in their construction of a single national character: *the* French, *the* English, *the* Japanese.

Class Position and Personality

Two cultural anthropologists of the mid-twentieth century came up with similar theories: that poverty produces passive personalities, which in turn lead to the perpetuation of marginal conditions. George Foster (1965), who did research among small-scale farmers in Mexico, proposed his model of a world view called the **image of the limited good.** People who have this world view believe that the resources or wealth available within a particular social group are finite. If someone increases his or her wealth, other people will necessarily lose out. The pie analogy illustrates how the image of the limited good works. If a group of eight people equally divides a pie into eight pieces, everyone gets the same share. But if one person takes two pieces, only six pieces remain for everyone else. One person's gain is another's loss. The image of the limited good, according to Foster, is found along with a "status quo" mentality that prevents people from trying to improve their economic condition. Major personality traits associated with the image of the limited good are jealousy, suspiciousness, and passivity. Oscar Lewis (1966a, 1966b) proposed a related concept, the **culture of poverty,** to explain personality and behavior among the poor and why poverty persists. He typified poor Mexican people as, among other things, "improvident," lacking a future time-orientation, and sexually promiscuous. Because of these personality characteristics, poor people are trapped in poverty and cannot change their situation.

The models proposed by Foster and Lewis are discredited by contemporary anthropologists on similar grounds to those applied to national character studies. Foster and Lewis are products of their capitalistic culture, which places a highly positive value on aggressive self-assertion, competitiveness, and a belief that resources are infinite. Their marital values are based in a Euro-American puritan tradition. The personality traits they attributed to the poor and the negative valence they attached to them, can be seen as ethnocentric, self-serving, and a form of "blaming the victim."

New Directions

More recent studies of personality formation in particular economic niches have tried to be less ethnocentric in their interpretations. For example, one ethnography of a poor Black neighborhood in a city in the midwestern United States uses words such as "resourceful" and "resilient" in describing how people adapt to difficult circumstances (Stack 1974). Other work in cultural anthropology more broadly considers the many cases of revolution and resistance among the poor and marginalized of the world, providing a complete reversal of the models proposed by Foster and Lewis about passivity. At the opposite end of the class spectrum, psychological anthropologists are beginning to "study up" the class structure. An examination of how corporate culture shapes personality in Japan is a landmark in this new direction in showing how child care patterns and demands of the business world fit together to create compliant male workers (see the Multiple Cultural Worlds box).

MULTIPLE CULTURAL WORLDS

Corporate Personality Formation: The Making of Salarymen in Japan

Research in Japan on the personality of "salarymen," males employed in the fast-paced corporate world, links male personality with the demands of the business world (Allison 1994). Salarymen work long hours for the company. They leave home early in the morning and return late at night and thus are nicknamed "7–11 men." Many Tokyo salarymen eat dinner with their family only a few times a year. After work, they typically spend many hours with fellow workers at expensive nightclubs. Groups of about five to ten men go out together after work. A few drinks and light snacks can result in a tab in the hundreds of dollars for one hour. The corporation picks up the bill. At the club, men relax and have fun after a long day at work. This is ensured by having a trained hostess sit at the table, keeping the conversation moving along in a lightly playful tone. Her job is to flatter and flirt with the men and to make them feel good.

In order to learn about this night world, Anne Allison did participant observation while working as a hostess. She found that conversations are full of teasing and banter, with much of it directed at the hostess and most of it derogatory: The hostess's breasts are too small, her hair is not right, and so on. The hostess must take all of this with a smile, and even joke along with it: "Yes, I have no breasts at all." Allison calls this type of banter "breast talk." How should this focus on the female breast be interpreted? Salarymen's night club behavior appears to be linked with their upbringing. Given the near total absence of the father from the home scene, children are raised mainly by the mother. The concentration of maternal attention is especially strong toward sons and their school achievements. The goal is that the boy will do well in school, get into a top university, and then gain employment with a large corporation. These corporations pay well, guarantee lifelong employment, and provide substantial benefits after retirement. In the corporation, hierarchies are clear, total loyalty is required, work hours are long, and the pressure to perform is high. Regular socializing at the club solidifies bonds between salarymen and strengthens their loyalty to the corporation.

Salarymen's behavior in night clubs can also be viewed as a reaction to their upbringing, with its total control by the mother. Club culture puts the man in control, reversing the power differential of his childhood. At the club, he has guaranteed control over a desirable woman who flatters him and flirts with him. She will never control him because after an hour or so of fun, he leaves and there is no enduring relationship. Club culture provides only temporary ego gratification for a salaryman: He needs to return again and again for reinforcement. This fact keeps salarymen away from their homes, leaving their own sons in the isolated care of the mother.

BIRTH AND INFANCY

In the United States, commonly accepted life stages include infancy, childhood, adolescence, middle age, and old age (psychologists and other experts concerned with human development construct even finer substages). Western life-cycle stages are based on biological features such as the ability to walk, puberty, and parenthood (Bogin 1988). These stages are not cultural universals, however, nor are the associated features that the Western scheme accepts as largely natural.

Birth

Cultural anthropologists have asked whether the style and ambience of the event of birth itself have psychological effects on the infant. Through their cross-cultural research, they have discovered variations in the birth experience that may affect an infant's psychological development. Brigitte Jordan (1983), a pioneer in the cross-cultural study of birth, conducted research on birth practices in Mexico, Sweden, Holland, and the United States. She studied the birth setting, including its location and who is present, the types of attendants and their roles, the birth event, and the post-partum period. Among Mayan women in Mexico, the midwife is called in the early stages of labor. One of her tasks is to give a *sobada* (massage) to the mother-to-be. She also provides psychological support by telling stories, often about other women's birthing experiences. The husband is expected to be present during the labor, so that he can see "how a woman suffers." The woman's mother should be present, along with other female kin such as mother-in-law, godmother, sisters, and friends. Compared to many other birthing contexts, the Mayan mother is surrounded by a large group of supportive people.

In the United States, hospital births are the norm. The newborn infant is generally taken to the nursery where it is wrapped in cloth, placed in a plastic crate under bright lights, and often fed with sugar water rather than always being taken to the mother when it seems hungry. Some critics argue that the Western hospital-based system of highly regulated birth is

The life cycle.

extremely technocratic and "too managed," alienating the mother—and the father as well as other members of the family and the wider community—from the birthing process and the infant (Davis-Floyd 1992). Such criticism of the birth process and the subsequent physical separation of the infant from the mother has led to consideration of how to improve the way birth is conducted and the context it sets (or doesn't set) for maternal support and infant bonding. Many contemporary Western psychological theorists say that immediate contact and bonding at the time of birth are crucial for forming parent–infant relationships throughout life. This early "skin-to-skin" contact is said to be crucial for setting in motion parental feelings of bonding. If this bonding is not established at the time of the infant's birth, Western specialists say that it will not develop later (oddly enough, given these theories, many Western hospital-based births result in separation of the infant from the mother). Explanations for juvenile delinquency or other unfavorable child development problems often include reference to lack of proper infant bonding at birth.

Nancy Scheper-Hughes (1993), whose research in a Brazilian shantytown was discussed earlier, questions Western bonding theory. She argues that bonding does not necessarily have to occur at birth to be successful. Her observations in Bom Jesus show that many mothers do not exhibit bonding with their infants at birth. Bonding occurs later, if the child survives infancy, when it is several years old. She proposes that this pattern of later bonding is related to the high rate of infant mortality among the poor of Brazil. If women were to develop strong bonds with their infants, they would suffer untold amounts of grief. Western bonding is adaptive in low-mortality/low-fertility societies in which strong maternal attachment is reasonable because infants are likely to survive.

Sleeping Patterns

Related to bonding theory is the question of where and with whom the infant sleeps. In Japan, co-sleeping is the norm, including a long period of mother–child co-sleeping. One survey found that Japanese people rarely sleep alone at any time during their lives (Caudill and Plath 1966). Co-sleeping has been hypothesized to promote "interconnected" personalities and weak ego formation, while independent sleeping leads to more "autonomous" personalities and stronger ego formation. While these patterns may apply to some cultures, they are not universal, given the results of a study of the Basque people of southern Spain (Crawford 1994). Basque culture is characterized by long periods of co-sleeping. Interviews with 217 Basque mothers probed topics such as their attitudes about parenting, religious beliefs, dreams, personality characteristics, and the mother's childhood sleeping patterns. Of these women, 167 had slept in their parents' room for two to three years. The women who had been co-sleepers were found to have greater ego strength, greater sense of connectedness, a more relaxed personality, and a higher index of health. Thus, co-sleeping does not necessarily prevent the development of a strong ego.

Gender and Infancy

As noted in Chapter 1, cultural anthropologists distinguish between sex and gender. Sex is something that everyone is born with. In the view of Western science, it has three biological markers: genitals, hormones, and chromosomes. Males are defined as people who have a penis, more androgens than estrogens, and the XY chromosome. Females have a vagina, more estrogens than androgens, and the XX chromosome. Increasingly, however, scientists know that these two categories are not air-tight. In all populations, some people are born with indeterminate genitals, similar proportions of androgens and estrogens, and chromosomes with more complex distributions than simply XX and XY. Thus, a continuum model of gender might be more accurate than a strict binary model.

Gender refers to the learned behavior and beliefs associated with maleness and femaleness, and thus varies culturally (Miller 1993). Individuals acquire their gender identity, roles, and status through learning, much of which is unconscious. From the moment of birth, an infant's life course is shaped by whether it is labeled male or female and what the defined roles and status of "male" and "female" are in a particular culture. Most cultural anthropologists believe in the high degree of human "plasticity," as demonstrated by Mead's early work on gender roles and personality in New Guinea, and that gender socialization can to a large extent "override" sex-linked features such as hormones.

Many other researchers continue to insist on a wide range of supposedly sex-linked personality characteristics as being innate. A major problem arises in how to test for innate characteristics. First, one needs data on infants before they are subject to cultural treatment. But culture starts shaping the infant from the moment of its birth through handling and treatment by others (some scholars say that socialization could begin even in the womb through exposure to sound and motion). Second, studying and interpreting the behavior of infants is fraught with potential bias. Studies of infants have focused on assessing the potential innateness of three major Euro-American personality stereotypes: whether infant males are more aggressive than infant females, whether infant females are more social than infant males, and whether males are more independent (Frieze et al. 1978: 73–78). Boy babies do tend to cry more than girl babies, and some people believe this is evidence of higher levels of inborn aggression in males. An alternate interpretation is that baby boys on average tend to weigh more than girls. They therefore are more likely to have a difficult delivery from which it takes time to recover, so they cry more, but not out of aggressiveness. In terms of socialness, baby girls smile more often than boys. Does this mean girls are born to be people pleasers? Evidence of caretakers smiling more at baby girls shows that the more frequent smiling of girls is a learned, not innate response. In terms of independence or dependence, studies thus far reveal no clear gender differences in how upset babies are when separated from their caretakers. Taken as a whole, studies seeking to document innate gender differences through the behavior of infants are not convincing. Two questions continue to be important: If gender differences are innate, why do cultures go to so much trouble to instill them? Second, if gender differences are innate, then they should be similar throughout history and cross-culturally which, of course they aren't. Throughout the rest of this chapter, cultural constructions of gender at various stages of the life cycle are explored.

CHILDHOOD

The concept of "the child" as a special age category may have emerged first in Europe in the last few centuries (Ariès 1962). In art, portraits of children became commonplace only in the seventeenth century. Other changes occurred at the same time: new interests in children's habits, more elaborate terminology about children and childhood, and special clothing for children instead of small-sized versions of adult clothing. The special focus on "the child" is associated with the emergence of industrial capitalism's need for an ever-expanding market. "The child" becomes a new niche for sales, which allowed for the production and sale of clothes, books, and toys specifically for that niche. In less industrialized cultures, "the child" is not regarded as having such specialized needs. In these societies, children are expected to take on adult tasks at an earlier age. These different expectations about what a child should do and be have implications for personality formation.

Mode of Production and Child Personality

This book takes the cultural materialist perspective that uses the mode of production to provide the basic framework for thinking about the deeper causes of how gender is defined, how it is socialized into children, and what the psychological outcomes are. The "Six Cultures Study" is a renowned cross-cultural study designed to provide comparative data on children's personalities in relation to their activities and tasks (Whiting and Whiting 1975). Researchers observed a total of sixty-seven children between the ages of three to eleven years. They recorded many forms of behavior, such as being supportive of other children; hitting other children; and performing tasks such as child care, cooking, and errands. These behaviors were analyzed in the following personality dimensions: "nurturant-responsible" or "independent-dominant." Nurturant-responsible personalities are characterized by more caring and sharing acts toward other children. The independent-dominant personality involves fewer acts of caring and sharing toward other children, and more acts that asserted dominance over other children. Six teams of researchers were trained in the methodology and conducted intensive research in six contexts:

- The Gusii, a Bantu group living in a horticultural village in Kenya;
- A horticultural/agricultural village in Oaxaca, Mexico;
- Tarong, a small-scale agricultural village in the Philippines;
- Taira, a rice-growing intensive-agricultural village in Okinawa, Japan;
- The Rajputs, a land-owning group of an intensive-agricultural village in North India; and
- Orchard Town, a small town in New England.

Results showed that the Gusii children of Kenya have the highest prevalence of a nurturant-responsible personality type, while the children in Orchard Town had the lowest. Orchard Town children had the highest prevalence of the independent-dominant personality type. The range of variation in the prevalence of these dimensions followed a general pattern correlating with the economy. The six cultures fit into two general groups, economically and in terms of child tasks and personality development. "Group A" cultures (Kenya, Mexico, Philippines) all had more nurturant-responsible children. Their economies are similar: They are more reliant on horticulture and other forms of less intensive production. The economies of "Group B" cultures (Okinawa, North India, New England) were based on either intensive agriculture or industry. Investigation into how the mode of production would influence child tasks and personality revealed that the key underlying factor is differences in women's work roles. In Category A cultures, women are an important part of the labor force and spend much time working outside the home. In these cultures, children take on more family-supportive tasks and thereby develop personalities that are nurturant/responsible.

Sibling caretaking, as shown here in Ghana, is a common task of older children cross-culturally, but especially so in preindustrial societies.

When women are mainly occupied in the home, as in Category B cultures, children have fewer tasks and less responsibility. They develop personalities that are more independent/dominant. Gusii children were responsible for the widest range of tasks and at earlier ages than in any other culture in the study, often performing tasks that an Orchard Town mother does. While some children in all six cultures took care of other children, Gusii children (both boys and girls) spent the most time doing so. They also began taking on this responsibility at a very young age, between five and eight years old.

This study has implications for Western child development experts. In one direction, we can consider what happens when the independent-dominant personality develops to an extreme level—into a **narcissistic** personality. A narcissist is someone who constantly seeks self-attention and self-affirmation, with no concern for other people's needs. The Western consumer-oriented economy supports the development of narcissism through its inculcation of identity formation through ownership of self-defining goods (clothing, electronics, cars) and access to self-defining services (vacations, therapists, fitness salons). The Six Cultures Study's findings suggest that involving children in more household responsibilities might result in less self-focused personality formation.

The Preschool Child

The category of the "preschool child" emerged in the industrialized countries as a by-product of widespread, compulsory elementary schooling that first created the "school child" category. This age group includes children from infancy to about age five years. Many of the world's children in this age group spend these years within the family, cared for by family members. In recent years, institutionalized care in day care centers and preschools has increased. Parents send their child to preschool as a substitute for family care while they are working, for social enrichment, or as a way to "fast-track" the child intellectually. A comparative study conducted in Japan, China, and the United States reports on parents' goals and expectations about preschooling (Tobin, Wu, and Davidson 1989:189–191). Parents in all three contexts emphasized the importance of learning cooperation and how to be a member of a group. In all three cultures, the fertility rate is low, reducing the possibility of learning cooperative behavior in the home. In Japan and the United States, many middle- and upper-class families have one child. In China, the One-Child Policy has created a generation of spoiled only-children, called "little emperors," who become the total focus of attention from their parents and grandparents. And, in contrast to the usual pattern in preindustrial societies, children in Japan, China, and the United States are less free to form community play groups since most are raised in isolated nuclear families. Parents have a second reason for sending children to preschool in China and the United States: "to give children a good start academically." This was not a concern of Japanese parents since most Japanese children are taught to read and write at home by their mothers.

Informal Learning

Play, toys, and the media constitute another important area for child socialization and personality acquisition. One study considered children's cartoon shows aired on American television in the 1980s (Williams 1991). Content analysis reveals two types of shows, one featuring interpersonal relationships and one featuring battles:

> One was aimed at little girls and included groups of characters joined by relational values. "Rainbow Brite" had a set of multicolored friends; both friends and kin surrounded "My Little Pony...." "Strawberry Shortcake" presided over a group, mostly little girls.... At the other extreme are programs that toy companies intended for boys.... All presented heroes on teams.... Teammates had no common ties or work other than those involving fighting. Each good team faced an evil team that chased, attacked, captured, and deceived them. (114–115)

Boy-focused cartoons emphasized the importance of group identity in the face of "the enemy." Enemy teams look different from the heroes: the Thundercats (heroes) battle the Mutants (enemies), and He-Man (hero) takes on Skeletor (enemy).

Toys and games also shape personality. Cross-cultural evidence indicates that childhood games are serious socialization for adult roles (see the Voices box), and learning certain personality traits is a key part of the process. Among hunting peoples such as the Yanomami, young boys learn to be future hunters by shooting small arrows from small bows at small targets such as beetles. They learn to kill animals without sentimentality. In contrast, caring for animals as pets is a prominent part of child socialization in the West, where many animals are taboo as food. Some games, such as chess, teach strategic thinking that appears to be correlated with social-political patterns of hierarchy and obedience.

Formal Schooling

Universal primary education exists in most nations, but not all. For example, in Mali, one of the world's poorest countries, only 25 percent of children attend primary school (United Nations 1994). Poorer children

VOICES

"Play Potlatches" by Charles James Nowell

Charles James Nowell is a Kwakwaka'wakw man born in 1870 at Fort Rupert, in what is now British Columbia. He was interviewed in English in 1940.

> When I was a boy we used to give potlatches of small canoes to imitate the potlatches of older people. I had small canoes made for me just the shape of the big ones. My second brother made some of them, and I paid other older people tobacco and things to make some others for me. When I have enough to give my potlatch, I go around to all the boys of the other tribes at Fort Rupert. I call my own tribe boys to come in front of my house and to count these small canoes and put them in rows according to the rank of the fathers of the boys....
>
> Our fathers and brothers teach us to give these potlatches, and help us do it, telling us all about what we should do to do it right. That is just like teaching what we should do when we get grown up and give real potlatches. My older brothers were the ones who taught me, but they didn't come and watch us while we gave them. They only heard about it and how we did afterwards. When I come home, they tell me that is fine. They are the ones that started it—I wouldn't have done it if they hadn't started it—and they helped me all the time with my play potlatches.

Source: Hirschfelder 1995:103–104

Yanomami boys acquire skills necessary for hunting and warfare at an early age.

cross-culturally face more problems enrolling and remaining in school. In some countries, the school system is inadequate, with too few local schools available. In poor families, children are needed to work. The schooling experience is also diminished for the poor because malnourished and exhausted children have more difficulty concentrating during class. Their level of achievement is likely to be lower than better-off children because of economic factors. Teachers, however, may interpret their performance as a sign of "bad attitude," apathy, and laziness.

In Malawi, a poor nation of southern Africa, all children face obstacles in completing primary education, but it is especially difficult for girls (Davison and Kanyuka 1992). An ethnographic study of this situation included eighty students (forty boys and forty girls) at two grade levels. It was conducted in four poor rural districts where girls' school participation rates were among the lowest and their drop-out rates the highest. Most of the children came from agricultural families. Both boys and girls face the same constraints in terms of the quality of the schools and teachers. Girls also had to contend with negative attitudes from male teachers about the value of schooling for them. This discouragement of their academic achievement in the schools is mirrored by their home situation, where parents indirectly discourage girls from valuing schooling and instead instill in them the values of domesticity. Girls are supposed to learn to assume the traditional roles of wife and mother. The combination of school systems that offer little in the way of creative learning experiences, home situations that are unsupportive of girls' achievement, and conservative political elements in the wider society combine powerfully to constrain both cognitive achievements and the attainment of independent, autonomous personalities among women (see the Current Event box).

In school, children and youths learn much about how they should behave and think, both formally through the curriculum and informally through clubs, peer pressure, and sports. Illustrations in textbooks may informally socialize children into particular roles and personality patterns. In socially stratified societies, "tracking" or sorting of students takes place. In this process, students are consciously or uncon-

Current Event

"Desperate Fainting"

- A mysterious outbreak of fainting among high-school girls in Egypt occurred in 1993. Egyptian feminist Eqbal Baraka agreed with the government's assessment that it was a kind of mass hysteria, but she disagreed with the official view that dismissed the matter, attributing it to the "spoiled nature of girls."
- Baraka interprets the fainting as a cry for help from a generation of girls who come from crowded homes filled with problems and desperation. Their schools provide no outlet for artistic expression, and classrooms are so overcrowded that some students have to stand.
- Baraka contrasts girls of this generation with her own, more idealistic post-revolutionary generation. She and her classmates believed they could create a more egalitarian society. "But today," she writes, "the boy next door is a fundamentalist who looks contemptuously upon his neighbor and her ambitions."

Source: World Press Review, August 1993, p. 35.

sciously separated into groups according to race, class, gender, and physical abilities. Stereotypic presentations of "active males" and "inactive females" or males as physicians and females as mothers are common in children's books the world over, and only recently have attempts been made to change such images. Tracking female students into domestic roles still characterizes formal education throughout much of the world, especially in conservative cultures. The students in these situations may experience conflicts about such tracking and resist it to varying degrees (see the Multiple Cultural Worlds box).

MULTIPLE CULTURAL WORLDS

Learning to Be an Orthodox Jewish Woman

An illuminating study of school-based socialization of girls for domesticity takes into account the interplay of religion, gender, and adolescent education in a Zionist-Orthodox school in Israel (Rapoport, Garb, and Penso 1995). Judaism, like other religions, shapes the socialization of its adherents directly and indirectly. Religious schools are one direct method of socialization. A dilemma faced by religious-Zionist education is how to reproduce classical Jewish womanhood in the modern context.

Research was conducted in an *ulpana* (an all-girls religious boarding high school corresponding to the Yeshiva high schools for boys) of which there were a total of nine in Israel at the time, attended by a total of about 2,000 girls. These schools are explicitly aimed at strengthening the religiosity of girls and preparing them for family life in the modern world, but it also emphasizes academic excellence, and the girls are highly motivated to achieve. In terms of curriculum, the school offers lectures, lessons, religious activities, and volunteer community work. Religious study excludes the canonic texts, promoting instead everyday religious practice and emphasis on morality, wifehood, childrearing, and purity.

Close supervision of the girls is maintained by teachers, peers, and older girls who serve as "big sisters." Even during "free time," the girls are supposed to discuss religion in *sicha,* free talk or conversation. Two themes emerged: the girls' daily experience of modesty and their anticipation of family life. According to the school teachings, a woman's modesty is part of her essence. The ideal of selfhood involves invisibility, with no suggestion of an affirmative self-presence. A woman is to be mute in the outside, public world.

The ulpana girls are taught that their sexuality should be treated as a secret, hidden treasure, with self-restraint a key virtue in contrast to how girls behave in the secular world. One student commented: "For example, I walk by some [secular] girl with exposed legs, so she has no value, she simply presents herself as an object, she doesn't say, first look for my character.... And I feel so proud, so I look at her to show her that I don't think much of her, and I feel very proud that I am modest" (54). However, some girls expressed highly ambivalent feelings about the value on modesty and self-restraint.

The most serious conflicts occur in relation to career aspirations, especially in the arts, since Judaism discourages women's participation as it would negate the values of motherhood and family: "Ronit is anguished by the command to keep her musical gift from the public as part of the erection of boundaries between the interior and the exterior.... "I write songs and I compose and play, and I can't do anything with it.... So what did God give it to me for? Why did I get it? If it is to test me, then I can't bear it.... I really feel I am simply choking with it" (55). She talked to the rabbi and his wife about it. He said there was nothing wrong with singing onto a cassette, but that sitting on a stage would mean that some man might look at her, fall in love with her and seduce her—"A woman's voice is to be regarded like her genitals" (55).

Ulpana schooling places strong emphasis on family roles. It causes conflicts with the simultaneous pressure for academic achievement. One girl commented that the teachers told them that the main thing was to find a good husband and establish a home in Israel, but when their grades were low, they questioned them about it. The girls resolve the dilemma of career aspirations and achievement versus the domestic role by opting for certain career paths that will accommodate their family role, or by giving up further studies. Even the most rebellious girl eventually became channeled into conformity through, she said, her own choice. The school thus successfully achieves its goals of constructing women's subjectivity into the service of "divine law and the male world" by training girls into a perception of themselves as controlled, spiritual, and pure.

ADOLESCENCE

Is Adolescence a Universal Life-Cycle Stage?

Puberty is a time in the human life cycle that occurs universally and involves a set of biological markers. In males, the voice deepens and facial and body hair appear; in females, menarche and breast development occur; in both males and females, pubic and underarm hair appear and sexual maturation is achieved. **Adolescence,** in contrast, is a culturally defined period of maturation from around the time of puberty until adulthood is attained, usually marked by becoming a parent, getting married, or becoming economically self-sufficient. Some scholars have argued that a prolonged period of adolescence is a product of industrialized society. Others say that all cultures define a period of adolescence. One study using data from the Human Relations Area File on 186 societies indicated the "ubiquity" of a culturally defined phase of adolescence (Schlegel 1995; Schlegel and Barry 1991). Cultures as diverse as the Navajo and the Trobriand Islanders, among others, have special terms comparable to the American term "adolescent" for a person between puberty and marriage. This apparent ubiquity has been taken by some sociobiologists as grounds for generating a theory that adolescence is a response to the biological phase of the "growth of human reproductive capacity" that is biologically adaptive because it provides a period of "training" for parental readiness (Schlegel 1995:16). Thus, adolescence is seen to be a function of reproductive roles.

Psychiatrist Horacio Fabrega and I (1995) reviewed historical and anthropological studies of the life cycle and found substantial evidence that questions the universality of adolescence and its function as reproductive training or preparation. Along with many examples of elaborate recognition and marking of adolescence, such as costly rituals, years of specialized training (including "higher education" such as college), and separate residence and lifestyle, we also found many examples of no recognized period of adolescence. Moroccan anthropologist Fatima Mernissi (1987) comments unequivocally that adolescence was not a recognized life cycle phase for females in Morocco until recently. Upon menarche, girls were married and transformed directly into adult women: "The idea of an adolescent unmarried woman is a completely new idea in the Muslim world, where previously you had only a female child and a menstruating woman who had to be married off immediately so as to prevent dishonorable engagement in premarital sex" (xxiv). Within cultures, the length of the period of adolescence, or whether it exists at all, can be related to gender. In many horticultural or pastoral societies where men are valued as warriors, as among the Maasai, a lengthy period between childhood and adulthood is devoted to training in warfare and developing solidarity among males. Females, on the other hand, move directly from being a girl to being a wife. For example, a Maasai girl learns her adult roles while she is a child, assisting in the care of cattle and doing other tasks. In many cultures, females have long periods of separation between girlhood and womanhood, marked by seclusion from general society, during which they learn special skills and lore, and then reemerge into society as marriageable (J. Brown 1978). Such evidence of variation seems to speak against any theory that depends on "ubiquity" for its basic assumption.

The fact that adolescence is found in many preindustrial societies also contradicts the simple association between adolescence and industrial economies. A cultural materialist approach can provide a more informed explanation that takes into account the variable distribution of adolescence cross-culturally. First, it looks to the relationship between adolescence and the mode of production, suggesting that a prolonged period of adolescence is likely to be preparation for culturally valued adult roles as either workers, warriors, or reproducers. For example, the definition of adolescence for females in many preindustrial societies, accompanied by years of training and seclusion, is found where adult females have high rates of participation in food production (Brown 1978). This correlation can be explained by the need to train young women for their adult roles. Likewise, certain areas of employment in industrialized societies, especially in most of the professions such as medicine and law and the upper echelons of the corporate world, require a university education. The many years of study in a context outside mainstream society can be considered a key part of the adolescent period preceding the assumption of adult roles. A comparison of adolescence in pre-war Japan and post-war Japan demonstrates the emergence of a clearly defined period of adolescence in the latter period, a change related to economic transformations of that time (Hogan and Mochizuki 1988). Adolescence for most Japanese youth in contemporary Japan, especially for males, corresponds with a period of formal education in high school and college. This new pattern is consistent with the rapid development of a powerful corporate economy requiring university-trained employees. In Japan, female employment is less often full-time or as highly professionalized as that of males (Brinton 1993). They spend fewer years in formal schooling than males and get married at a younger age than males, meaning that they have a shorter period of adolescence.

During the latter half of the twentieth century, industrialization worldwide has been accompanied by the emergence and elongation of adolescence. Access to higher education has increased, delaying the time when a full-time job is obtained. The age at marriage has risen as young people attempt to finish their educations and find employment before starting a family (Xenos 1991). At the same time, clear class differences exist. Those who are poor tend to have shorter adolescent phases: They spend less time in formal education, and they are likely to become parents at younger ages.

Coming of Age and Gender Identity

Margaret Mead made famous the phrase "coming of age" in her book, *Coming of Age in Samoa* (1961 [1928]). It can refer generally to the period of adolescence or specifically to a ceremony or set of ceremonies that marks the boundaries of a period of adolescence (starting college and graduation from college, for many people in the West), or the more direct transition from childhood to adulthood. What are the psychological aspects of this phase of life? While sexuality and sexual feelings are said to exist in all life cycle phases, many cultures choose the time around puberty to transform children into either males or females.

Among the Sambia, a highland New Guinea group, people do not believe that a young boy will "naturally" grow into a man (Herdt 1987). Instead, a boy's healthy maturation requires that he join an all-male initiation group. In this group, he becomes a partner of a senior male, who regularly transfers his semen to the youth orally. Ingesting semen nourishes the youth and provides for his healthy growth. After a period in this initiation group, the youth will rejoin society and take up a heterosexual relationship and raise children.

Ceremonies that provide the transition from youth to adulthood often involve marking of the body in some way as if, through this, to impress the person undergoing it with a clear sense of gender identity as well as group identity. Such marking includes scarification, tattooing, and genital surgery. (A discussion of ritual and symbolic aspects of puberty rituals appears in Chapter 13.) In many societies, adolescent males undergo genital surgery that involves removal of part of the skin around the tip of the penis (see the Voices box on page 146). Without this operation, the boy would not become a full-fledged male (many Westerners assert that male circumcision has proven health benefits, but recent studies do not support this claim).

For girls, the physical fact of menstruation is marked by rituals in some cultures; in others it is not noted publicly at all. In Turkey, and elsewhere in the Middle East, menstruation is not even mentioned to young girls, who are thus surprised and shocked at menarche (Delaney 1988:79). Turkish girls generally feel ashamed and embarrassed by menstruation. Their Islamic culture teaches them that menstruation is the result of Eve's disobedience against Allah. Eve allowed herself to be persuaded by Satan to eat a forbidden fruit, and so was punished by being made to bleed monthly. In contrast, elaborate feasts and celebrations for girls are held upon their first menstruation in South India, although not in the North (Miller 1997 [1981]). In the absence of studies on the psychological impact of these differences, one can only speculate at this point that being made the person of honor at a celebration would have positive effects on a girl's sense of self-esteem, whereas ignoring or linking menstruation with shamefulness would have the opposite effect.

The Western term **"female genital mutilation" (FGM)** refers to a range of genital cutting practiced on females, including the excision of part or all of the clitoris, perhaps also part or all of the labia, and sometimes also "infibulation," the stitching together of the vaginal entry with only a small aperture left for drainage of menstrual blood. These procedures are usually performed when the girl is between seven to fifteen years of age. Some form of genital cutting is

VOICES

"The Initiation of a Maasai Warrior" by Tepilit Ole Saitoti

Three days before the ceremony my head was shaved and I discarded all my belongings, such as my necklaces, garments, spear, and sword. I even had to shave my pubic hair. . . .

I was summoned to the main cattle gate, in my hand a ritual cowhide from a cow that had been properly slaughtered during my naming ceremony. . . . I laid the hide down and a boy was ordered to pour ice-cold water, known as *engare entolu* (ax water), over my head. It dripped all over my naked body and I shook furiously. In a matter of seconds, I was summoned to sit down. A large crowd of boys and men formed a semicircle in front of me; women are not allowed to watch male circumcisions and vice-versa. That was the last thing I saw clearly. As soon as I sat down, the circumciser appeared, his knives at the ready. He spread my legs and said, "One cut," a pronouncement necessary to prevent the initiate from claiming that he had been taken by surprise. He splashed a white liquid, a ceremonial paint called *enturoto,* across my face. Almost immediately, I felt a spark of pain under my belly as the knife cut through my penis' foreskin. I happened to choose to look in the direction of the operation. I continued to observe the circumciser's fingers working mechanically. The pain became numbness and my lower body felt heavy, as if I were weighed down by a heavy burden. After fifteen minutes or so, a man who had been supporting me from behind pointed at something, as if to assist the circumciser. I came to learn later that the circumciser's eyesight had been failing him and that my brothers had been mad at him because the operation had taken longer than was usually necessary. All the same, I remained pinned down until the operation was over. I heard a call for milk to wash the knives, which signaled the end, and soon the ceremony was over. . . .

I was carried inside the house to my own bed to recuperate. . . . I laid on my own bed and bled profusely. The blood must be retained within the bed, for according to Maasai tradition, it must not spill to the ground. . . . I stopped bleeding after about half an hour but soon was in intolerable pain. I was supposed to squeeze my organ and force blood to flow out of the wound, but no one had told me, so the blood coagulated and caused unbearable pain. The circumciser was brought to my aid and showed me what to do, and soon the pain subsided.

The following morning, I was escorted by a small boy to a nearby valley to walk and relax, allowing my wound to drain. This was common for everyone who had been circumcised, as well as for women who had just given birth. . . . In two weeks I was able to walk and was taken to join other newly circumcised boys far away from our settlement. . . . Our heads were shaved, we discarded our black cloaks and bird headdresses and emerged as newly shaven warriors, Irkeleani.

As long as I live, I will never forget the day my head was shaved and I emerged a man, a Maasai warrior. I felt a sense of control over my destiny so great that no words can accurately describe it.

Source: Saitoti 1986:67–71.

most common in the Sahelian countries of Africa, from the west coast to the east coast. It is also found in Egypt, in some groups of the Middle East (particularly among Bedu tribes), and among some Muslim groups in South and Southeast Asia. The distribution of some form of genital cutting encompasses many groups in which female labor participation is high, but others where it is not. In terms of religion, genital cutting is often associated with people who are Muslim, but not always. In Ethiopia, for example, some Christian groups practice it. As yet, no one has presented a clear explanation for the regional and social distribution of female genital cutting.

Infibulation is still widely practiced, in spite of its having been outlawed in most nations, including Somalia, where it is the most prevalent. In Somalia, senior women, especially those who usually help with births, perform the operations (van der Kwaak 1992). Here is a brief description of a Somalian infibulation operation:

> Infibulation always takes place in the morning. Several female relatives hold the girl, while the circumciser, who sits between her legs, performs the operation. She closes the wound with a couple of acacia thorns held in place by a piece of string. She puts *mal-mal*, a substance taken from a local tree, with egg-yolk and sugar on the wound and the girl's legs are tied together. . . . During the first 48 hours the passage of urine is anxiously awaited, and after some 7 days the thorns are removed and the result of the operation is inspected. If the results of the operation are satisfactory, the upper legs will be tied together for another fortnight. (779)

Indigenous views supporting female genital cutting say that, like male circumcision, it is a necessary step toward full womanhood. It is required for a woman to be considered marriageable in societies in which marriage is the normal path for women. Fathers say that an uncircumcised daughter is unmarriageable and will bring no brideprice. Aesthetically, supporters claim that removal of the labia makes a woman beautiful and, removing "male" parts, makes her a complete woman. Many young girls have been reported to look forward to the ceremony so that they will then be freed of having to do childhood tasks and can take on the more respected roles of an adult woman. In other cases, anthropologists have reported hearing statements of resistance. Among the Ariaal, pastoralists of northern Kenya, a new bride undergoes FGM on the day of her wedding (Fratkin 1998:60). The Ariaal practice involves removal of the clitoris and part or all of the labia majora. At one wedding, a bride-to-be was heard to say: "I don't want to do this, I don't even know this man, please don't make me do this." The older women told her to be strong and that it would soon be over. The bride-to-be is expected to emerge in a few hours to greet the guests and join the wedding ceremony. Fewer issues have forced the questioning of cultural relativism more clearly than female genital mutilation (see the Critical Thinking box).

CRITICAL THINKING

Cultural Relativism, Human Rights, and "Female Genital Mutilation"

The Western view, which is increasingly shared by many people who traditionally practiced what many Western health experts and feminists term female genital mutilation (FGM), is that FGM is both a sign of low female status and an unnecessary cause of women's suffering. Feminists claim that cutting of the female genitals constitutes a violation of basic human rights and is a patriarchal "sado-ritual" that should be banned everywhere (Daly 1978). Female genital mutilation has been linked with a range of health risks, including those related to the surgery itself (shock, infection), and future genito-urinary complications. Infibulation causes scarring and malformation of the vaginal canal that obstruct delivery and cause lacerations to the mother and even death of the infant and mother. The practice of having a new bride's husband "open" her, using a stick or knife to loosen the aperture, is both painful and an opportunity for infection. After giving birth, a woman is usually reinfibulated, and the process begins again. Health experts have suggested that the repeated trauma to the woman's vaginal area could increase the risk of contracting HIV/AIDS. The effects on a woman's sexual enjoyment of both clitoridectomy and infibulation can only be assumed to be highly negative. Clitoral orgasm, for one thing, is no longer possible.

Critical Thinking Questions

- Why would female genital mutilation be considered a violation of human rights?
- Social pressures in the West prompt many young women to undergo expensive and painful plastic surgery such as "nose jobs," implants to increase breast size, and eyelid lifting among Asian Americans. Are these practices a violation of human rights?
- Are there any similarities between adolescent rites of passage involving body cutting and fraternity hazing rituals?
- Direct and indirect hazards seem especially to face adolescents in many cultures. What reasons might exist to explain this?

Sexual Identity

Puberty is the time when sexual maturity is achieved and sexual orientation becomes more apparent. Scholars have long debated whether sexual preferences are biologically determined (somehow mandated by genetic or hormonal factors) or culturally constructed and learned. Biological anthropologist Melvin Konner (1989) takes a middle position, saying that both factors play a part, but simultaneously warning us that no one has a simple answer to the question of "who becomes gay":

> Neither science nor art has yet produced a single answer. Yet perhaps that in itself is the answer: that anything so complicated and various and interesting could have a single origin seems wrongheaded. Socrates and Tennessee Williams, Sappho and Adrienne Rich, to take only four people, representing only two cultures, seem so certain to have come to their homosexuality in four such different ways as to make generalizations useless. In the further reaches of the anthropological universe, we find variations that knock most folk theories for a loop. (60)

Lesbian feminist poet Adrienne Rich's (1980) approach combines attention to both biology and culture in her view that all people are biologically bisexual, but that patriarchal cultures try to mold them into being heterosexual. This "compulsory heterosexual project," she says, will never be completely successful in overcoming innate bisexuality, and so some people will always opt out of the heterosexual mold and become either homosexual or bisexual.

The cultural constructionist position emphasizes socialization and childhood experiences as the most powerful factors shaping sexual orientation. Potential support for this position comes from a recent study in the United States that high parity (later-born) children are more likely to be homosexual than earlier-born children (Blanchard et al. 1995). This result applies more strongly for gay men, about whom more studies have been conducted. For lesbians, fewer studies are available, but they do indicate that lesbians tend to be later-born and to have more sisters than heterosexual women. In terms of birth order and socialization of sexual orientation in the United States, a hypothesis worth investigating is whether parents unconsciously promote "girl"-like behavior in the last-born when they have a string of sons in order to have a child to fulfill female roles, and the same for a late-born girl who follows several sisters. Another indication of the relatively weak role of biology is that many people change their sexual orientation more than once during their lifetime. In the Gulf state of Oman, the *xanith* is a male who becomes more like a female, wearing female clothing and having sex with other men, often for several years and then reverts to a standard male

Multiple Cultural Worlds

Homosexuality and Economic Discrimination in the United States

Studies confirm that a "lavender ceiling," or barrier against economic achievement of gay people, exists in the United States (Folbre 1995). Records of 1,680 full-time employees drawn from a nationally representative sample found that male workers who have had at least one same-sex partner earn between 11 percent and 27 percent less than heterosexual men with the same education, job experience, occupation, marital status, and geographic location. Female workers who have had same-sex encounters earn less than their heterosexual counterparts, although the differences were not statistically significant. One finding concerning lesbian workers is that they are concentrated in the lowest-paying occupations, earning on average 18 percent less than heterosexual women. While about 15 percent of straight women held managerial positions, fewer than 9 percent of lesbian and bisexual women did. Lesbians face the double jeopardy of discrimination based on gender and sexual orientation. The key difference is that gay men experience direct discrimination; they are paid less than straight men with the same qualifications in the same jobs. Lesbians suffer more from indirect discrimination; they are concentrated in lower-paying jobs, have limited access to benefits, and have lower household incomes than heterosexual women.

role, marries a woman and has children (Wikan 1977). Similar fluidity during the life cycle between homosexuality and heterosexuality occurs among Sambia males (Herdt 1987). These examples indicate that, given the same biological material, a person can assume different gender identities over time.

No matter what theoretical perspective one takes on the causes of sexual preferences, it is clear that homosexuals are discriminated against in many cultural contexts where heterosexuality is the norm of mainstream society. Homosexuals in the United States have been the frequent victims of violence, legal biases, housing discrimination, and problems in the work place. They also experience economic discrimination (see the Multiple Cultural Worlds box). They suffer from being stigmatized by parents, other students, and the wider society. The psychological damage done to their self-esteem is related to the fact that homosexual youths in the United States have substantially higher suicide rates than heterosexual youths.

Many cultures explicitly allow for more than two strictly defined genders and permit the expression of varied forms of sexual orientation without societal condemnation. Most "third genders" are neither purely "male" nor "female," according to a particular culture's definition of male and female. But they are typically ways for "males" to cross gender lines and assume more "female" behaviors, personality characteristics, and dress. Parallel institutionalized third gender roles that allow "females" to cross over into "male" territory have been less documented in the anthropological literature.

The **berdache** (this term derives from a French word, which itself is derived from a Persian word; Native American tribes have their own, varied terms) of many Native American cultures is someone who is biologically male, but conforms to cultural definitions of the female role (Williams 1992). A berdache is a male (in terms of genital configuration) who opts to wear female clothing, may engage in intercourse with a man, and is involved with female tasks such as basket-weaving and pottery-making. The berdache constitutes an accepted and admired third gender role. Evidence is not completely clear about how a particular person becomes a berdache. Some people say that parents, especially if they have several sons, choose one to become a berdache. Others say that a boy who shows interest in typically female activities or who likes to wear female clothing is then allowed to become a berdache. Such a child is a focus of pride for the family, never disappointment or stigma. The impact of Euro-American culture on the institution of the berdache was negative, however. Native Americans became aware of Euro-American disapproval and derision of the berdache (Roscoe 1991), and they began to suppress it as a cultural pattern. In the 1980s, as Native American cultural pride resurged, so has the open presence of the berdache. Native American cultures in general continue to be more tolerant of homosexuality than mainstream Euro-American society.

In India, there is an institutionalized third-gender group called the *hijiras* (*hijira* is their North Indian name; in the South they are termed *alis*). Hijiras dress and act like women, but are neither truly male nor truly female (Nanda 1990). Many hijiras were born

A Zuni berdache, We'wha, wearing the ceremonial costume of Zuni women and holding a pottery bowl with sacred corn meal. *(The National Anthropological Archive, Smithsonian Insitution.)*

with male genitals, or with genitals that were not clearly male or female. Hijiras have the traditional right to visit the home of a newborn, inspect its genitals and claim it for their group if the genitals are neither clearly male nor female. Some evidence exists that hijiras may forcibly claim or steal babies in order to increase their population. Hijiras born with male genitals may opt to go through an initiation ceremony that involves cutting off of the penis and testicles. Hijiras roam large cities of India, earning a living by begging from store to store (and threatening to lift their skirts if not given money). Because women do not sing or dance in public, the hijiras play an important role as performers in public events, especially as dancers or musicians. Given this public role and the hijira's association with prostitution, people in the mainstream do not admire or respect hijiras, and no family would be delighted to hear that their son has decided to become a hijira. The hijiras form a separate group from mainstream society, in contrast to the berdache among Native American groups.

Likewise, in Thailand, three basic gender categories have long existed: *phuuchai* (male), *phuuyung* (female), and *kathoey* (transvestite/transsexual/hermaphrodite) (Morris 1994). Like the berdache and hijira, a kathoey is "originally" a male who crosses into the body, personality, and dress defined as female. Sexual orientation of kathoeys is rather flexible, including either male or female partners. In contemporary Thailand, explicit discussion and recognition of homosexuality exists, usually couched in English terms, conveying a sense of its foreignness. The words for lesbian are *thom* (from the word "tomboy") and *thut* (an ironic usage from the American movie *Tootsie* about a heterosexual male transvestite). As in many parts of the world, reflecting the widespread presence of patriarchal norms, lesbianism is a more suppressed form of homosexuality than male homosexuality, which has long been legitimated as a form of romantic love, even in ancient poetry.

ADULTHOOD AND MIDDLE AGE

Adulthood for most of the world's people means the likelihood of some form of marriage (or long-term domestic relationship) and bearing and raising children (later chapters present material on marriage and domestic organization). This section discusses selected aspects of adulthood related to identity, personality formation, and psychology.

Becoming a Parent

More studies have been done of how cultures shape maternal roles than paternal roles, so that is where this section begins. Biologically, a woman becomes a mother when she gives birth to an infant: She is transformed from a pregnant woman to a mother. Motherhood, the cultural process of becoming a mother, has been termed **matrescence** (Raphael 1975). Like adolescence, the culturally defined and shaped phase of motherhood varies in terms of its beginning, duration, and meaning. In some cultures, a woman is transformed into a mother as soon as she thinks she is pregnant. In others, she becomes a mother and is granted full maternal status only when she delivers an infant of the "right" sex, as in much of northern India.

In preindustrial cultures, matrescence starts at birth and occurs in the context of supportive family members. Some cultures promote prenatal practices, abiding by particular food taboos, which can be regarded as part of matrescence. Such rules make the pregnant woman feel that she has some role in helping to make the pregnancy turn out right. In the West, medical experts during the twentieth century have increasingly defined the prenatal period as an important phase of matrescence, and they have issued many scientific and medical rules for potential parents (Browner and Press 1995, 1996). Pregnant women are urged to seek prenatal examinations; be under the regular supervision of a doctor who monitors the growth and development of the fetus; follow particular dietary and exercise guidelines; and undergo a range of tests such as ultrasound scanning. More research is needed to study and compare the psychological implications for mothers in highly "medicalized" settings versus mothers in nonmedicalized contexts. One emerging contrast is the greater likelihood of post-partum depression among mothers in medicalized settings, which may be a result of their feeling a lack of control in the birthing process.

Patrescence, or becoming a father, usually is less socially noted than matrescence. The practice of **couvade** is an interesting exception to this generalization. Couvade refers to "a variety of customs applying to the behavior of fathers during the pregnancies of their wives and during and shortly after the births of their children" (Broude 1988:902). In the "classical" form of couvade, the father takes to his bed before, during, or after the delivery. He may also experience pain and exhaustion during and after the delivery. More common is a pattern of couvade that involves a set of prohibitions and prescriptions for male behavior. For example, an expectant father may not hunt a certain animal, eat certain foods, cut objects, or engage in extramarital sex. Early theories of why the couvade exists relied on Freudian interpretations that men were seeking cross-sex identification (with the female role) in contexts where the father role was weak or fathers were absent. Cross-cultural examination of the existence of couvade shows quite the opposite: Couvade occurs in societies where paternal roles in child care are prominent. This interpretation views couvade as one phase of men's participation in parenting: Their good behavior as expectant fathers helps ensure a good delivery for the baby. Another interpretation of couvade is that it offers support for the mother. In Estonia, a folk belief is that a woman's birth pains will be less if her husband helps by taking some of them on himself (Oinas 1993).

Is there something psychologically innate about females and males dictating that females are universally primary child caretakers? Most cultural anthropologists would agree that child care is predominantly the responsibility of females worldwide but not universally, pointing to differences in the degree of involvement and other possible caretakers besides the biological mother. In many cultures of the South Pacific, child care is shared across families, and women breastfeed other women's babies. Paternal involvement varies as well. Among the Aka pygmy hunter-gatherers of Central Africa, paternal child care is prominent (Hewlett 1991). The Aka are an exceptional case, perhaps even unique, in comparison to other societies because of the high involvement of fathers in child care. Aka fathers are intimate, affectionate, and helpful, spending about half of their time each day holding or within arm's reach of their infants. While holding their infants, they are more likely to hug and kiss them than mothers are. Good fatherhood among the Aka means being affectionate toward children and assisting the mother when her workload is heavy. Among the Aka, a prevailing ideology of gender equality exists and violence against women is unknown; the high level of paternal involvement in child care probably helps explain this pattern.

An Aka father and his son. Aka fathers are affectionate caretakers of infants and small children. Compared to mothers, they are more likely to kiss and hug children.

Cultural definitions of what "motherhood" constitutes change over time, providing an argument against fixed, innate features of the role. Maxine Margolis (1984) traced changes in how the maternal role was defined in the United States from the late 1700s to the present. The amplification or constriction of women's maternal and domestic roles was a clear function of the wider economic demands for female labor. During World War II, when many men were away in the armed forces, women's motherhood roles were downplayed as they replaced men in the factories. When the war ended and the men returned, public rhetoric exhorted women to return to the home and to child care duties. The 1950s brought the creation of a highly intensified domestic role for mothers in the United States, involving time-consuming devotion to housekeeping and childrearing.

Middle Age

Perceptions of the boundaries of "middle age" have changed in industrial countries as the life span has increased. A generation ago, people in their thirties were considered middle aged, while now a turning point is more likely to be the fortieth birthday. Stanley Brandes explores the meanings of turning forty to American middle-class men in a book entitled *Forty: The Age and the Symbol* (1985). The "forty syndrome" comprises feelings of restlessness, rebelliousness, and unhappiness that often lead to family break-ups. The syndrome is so well known in popular American culture that it even appears in a *Peanuts* cartoon strip: Charlie Brown confides to Lucy, in her psychiatrist role, that he is concerned about his father, who sits every night in the kitchen eating cold cereal and looking at pictures in his high school yearbook. Lucy asks how old the father is. Charlie Brown says he thinks he just turned forty. "Nothing to worry about," advises Lucy. "He's right on schedule!" (25). One possible reason behind this relatively new emphasis on forty as a turning point for males is that it reflects the current midpoint of a "typical" life span for a middle-class American man.

Menopause is a significant event of middle age for women in some, but not all, cultures. A comparative study examined differences in perception and experience of menopause among Mayan women of Mexico and rural Greek women (Beyene 1989). Among the Mayan women, menopause is not a time of stress or crisis. They associate menstruation with illness and look forward to the time when they no longer have menses. Menopause among these women is not associated with physical or emotional symptoms. In fact, none of the women reported hot flashes or cold sweats. Among the Mayan women, menopause brought no associated role changes. In contrast, Greek women in the village of Stira recognized menopause as a natural phenomenon that all women experience and one that causes temporary discomfort, *exapi,* which is a phase of hot flashes especially at night, that may last about a year. The women did not think exapi was terribly serious, certainly nothing worthy of medical attention. Postmenopausal women emphasized the relief and freedom they felt. Postmenopausal women can go into cafes by themselves, something they would never do otherwise, and they can participate more fully in church ceremonies. In Japan, also, menopause is a minimally stressful experience and rarely considered something deserving medical attention (Lock 1993). These variable findings raise the question of how much perceived suffering from menopause in the United States is **iatrogenic,** that is, an affliction caused by medical definition or intervention.

THE SENIOR YEARS

The "senior" life cycle stage may be a particular development of contemporary human society because, like most other mammals, our early ancestors rarely lived beyond their reproductive years (Brooks and Draper 199b [1991]). The category of the aged, like several other life cycle stages discussed, is variably recognized, defined, and valued. In many cultures, elders are highly revered and their life experiences are valued as the greatest wisdom. In others, aged people become burdens to their families and to society. In general, the status and well-being of the elderly cross-culturally is higher where they continue to live with their families (Lee and Kezis 1979). This pattern is more likely to be found in preindustrial societies than in highly industrialized ones, where the elderly are increasingly experiencing a shift to "retirement homes." In such age-segregated settings, people have to create new social roles and ties and find new ways of gaining self-esteem and personal satisfaction. Anthropological research in a rural central New York retirement home shows that being allowed to have pets has a positive effect on people's adjustment (Savishinsky 1991).

Much research indicates that people living in retirement homes benefit psychologically from having animal companions.

THE FINAL PASSAGE: DEATH AND DYING

It may be that no one in any culture welcomes death, unless he or she is in very poor health and suffering greatly. The contemporary United States, with its dependence on medical technology, appears to have a leading position in resistance to death, often at very high cost. In many other cultures, a greater degree of acceptance is common. A study of attitudes toward death and dying among Alaskan Inuits revealed a pervasive feeling that people are active participants in their death rather than passive victims (Trelease 1975). The usual pattern for a person near death is that the person calls friends and neighbors together, is given a Christian sacrament, and then, within a few hours, dies. The author comments, "I do not suggest that everyone waited for the priest to come and then died right away. But the majority who did not die suddenly did some degree of planning, had some kind of formal service or celebration of prayers and hymns and farewells" (35).

In any culture, loss of a loved one is accompanied by some form of sadness, grief, and mourning. The ways of expressing such emotions vary from extended and public grieving that is expressively emotional to no visible sign of grief being presented. The latter pattern is the norm in Bali, Indonesia, where people's faces remain impassive at funerals and no vocal lamenting occurs (Rosenblatt, Walsh, and Jackson 1976). No one knows how these different modes of expression of a universal experience of loss might affect the actual experience of loss itself (Brison and Leavitt 1995). Does highly expressive public mourning contribute to a "faster" healing process, or does a quietly repressed sense of grief play an adaptive role, as Scheper-Hughes (1993) argues for the poor of Brazil? The domain of emotional suffering surrounding death is a relatively new area of study for psychological anthropologists, one that promises to provide intriguing insights. The expression of grief surrounding death is also of interest to anthropologists who study religion (Bowen 1998). Research shows that beliefs about the dead, and how the dead may affect the living, shape people's experience of death and mourning.

SUMMARY

Cultural anthropologists studying aspects of psychology cross-culturally have provided substantial evidence that enculturation is able to create a variety of personality types that are more related to the cultural context than to a person's biological heritage. Preagricultural and preindustrial modes of production emphasize the formation, generally, of nurturant/responsible personalities, while a dominant/independent personality is more characteristic of agricultural and industrial societies.

Human development and the shaping of a person's psychology begins from the moment of birth, because that is when enculturation commences. Margaret Mead was a pioneer in showing how infant care practices such as breastfeeding, the way the baby is held, and the amount of contact the infant has with others can affect personality formation, including gender identity. Her study of the Arapesh, Mundugumor, and Tchambuli peoples of New Guinea indicates that gender is a largely "plastic" aspect of human enculturation.

In many cultures, informal and formal learning continue to mold young people into their future adult roles and thereby shapes their sense of identity in various ways, including gender. Adolescence, a cultural time around puberty and before adulthood (however that is defined in a particular culture), varies cross-culturally from being nonexistent to being long in duration, involving detailed and rigorous training and elaborate ceremonies. "Coming of age" ceremonies sometimes involve bodily cutting. These seem most clearly to denote membership of the initiate in a particular gender and, according to some emic reports, are essential in providing the sense of being a "man" or a "woman." In contrast to the sharp binary distinction between "male" and "female" laid out in Western science and folk belief, many cultures have longstanding traditions of third gender identities, most prominently for males, or people of indeterminate biological sex markers, to become more like females in those cultures. The berdache was never looked down on in Native American society until

Euro-American culture arrived and projected its negative view.

Following the fact that women tend to be more involved in child care than males, cultures generally provide more in the way of enculturation of females for this role. In preindustrial societies, learning about motherhood is largely embedded in other aspects of life, and knowledge about birthing and child care is shared mainly among women. In industrialized cultures, the scientific and medical establishments have assumed a large role in defining the maternal role. This change reduces the autonomy of women and creates a dependency on external, non–kin-based structures.

The senior years in preindustrialized societies are typically shorter than in industrialized societies with their longer life span. Often, elder men and women in preindustrialized societies are treated with respect, are considered to be the most knowledgeable, and retain a strong sense of their place in the culture. Increasingly in industrialized societies, elderly people are removed from their families and spend many years in age-segregated institutions. This transition tends to have negative implications for their psychological well-being; these trends have been studied, to some extent, by cultural anthropologists who are able to offer recommendations for ways to combat their sense of loss and loneliness.

CRITICAL THINKING QUESTIONS

1. Why do industrialized cultures socialize their members into being more "self-centered" than preindustrialized cultures?
2. During colonial New England's Salem witch trials, many young girls reportedly were subject to fainting spells. Are there any similarities between the Salem fainting epidemic and that of the Egyptian school girls reported in the Current Event box?
3. After his circumcision, Tepilit Ole Saitoti felt a great sense of "self-control" of his destiny. Why do you think he felt this way? Would you? If yes, why; if no, why not?
4. Why is female genital mutilation, in the eyes of much the world, a more controversial practice than male circumcision?

KEY CONCEPTS

adolescence, p. 144
berdache, p. 149
couvade, p. 150
cultural configuration, p. 135
culture of poverty, p. 136
enculturation, p. 134
female genital mutilation (FGM), p. 145
iatrogenic, p. 152
image of the limited good, p. 136
matrescence, p. 150
narcissism, p. 140
national character study, p. 135
patrescence, p. 150
personality, p. 134
puberty, p. 144

SUGGESTED READINGS

Evalyn Blackwood, ed. *The Many Faces of Homosexuality: Anthropological Approaches to Homosexual Behavior.* New York: Harrington Park Press, 1986. This text contains chapters on how anthropological writings have treated lesbianism, and case studies of ritualized male homosexuality in Irian Jaya, the berdache in North America, hijiras of India, lesbian relationships in Lesotho, and Mexican male homosexual interaction patterns in public.

Michael Moffatt, *Coming of Age in New Jersey: College and American Culture.* New Brunswick: Rutgers University Press. Based on a year's participant observation in a college dormitory in a university in the eastern United States, this study presents insights on sexuality, race relations, and individualism.

Richard Parker, *Bodies, Pleasures and Passions: Sexual Culture in Contemporary Brazil.* Boston: Beacon Press, 1991. This ethnographic study of contemporary sexual culture in Brazil addresses such topics as sexual socialization, bisexuality, sadomasochism, AIDS, prostitution, samba, the symbolism of breasts, courting, and carnival.

Joel Savishinsky, *The Ends of Time: Life and Work in a Nursing Home.* New York: Bergin & Garvey, 1991. Fieldwork in a nursing home in upstate New York provides insights about the psychology of the residents, especially how they cope with being institutionalized and what kinds of support were helpful in combatting loneliness, lack of privacy, and inactivity.

James W. Stigler, Richard A. Shweder, and Gilbert Herdt, eds. *Cultural Psychology: Essays on Comparative Human Development.* New York: Cambridge University Press, 1990. The introductory chapter provides a definition of cultural psychology, and twenty other chapters explore cross-cultural patterns of cognition, moral development, mathematics learning, adolescent rituals, the self, male dominance and sexual anxiety, and language development in children.

RASA AYAM
40

CHAPTER 7

Illness and Healing

CHAPTER OUTLINE

THE ECOLOGICAL/EPIDEMIOLOGICAL APPROACH
- Infectious Diseases

ETHNOMEDICINE
- Perceptions of the Body
- Defining Illness Emically
- *Multiple Cultural Worlds:* Anorexia Nervosa as a Culture-Bound Syndrome of the Industrialized World
- Preventive Practices
- Diagnosis
- Healing Modalities
- *Critical Thinking:* Why Do People Eat Dirt?

THE INTERPRETIVE APPROACH
- *Voices:* An Ayurvedic Doctor and His Client

CRITICAL MEDICAL ANTHROPOLOGY
- The Role of Poverty
- Western Medical Training Examined

CLINICAL MEDICAL ANTHROPOLOGY

GLOBALIZATION AND CHANGE
- Plural Medical Systems
- Applied Medical Pluralism

SUMMARY

CRITICAL THINKING QUESTIONS

KEY CONCEPTS

SUGGESTED READINGS

◀ Mentawai healers treat a woman suffering from a toothache on Siberut Island, Indonesia.

Primatologist Jane Goodall witnessed a polio epidemic among the chimpanzees she was studying in Tanzania (Foster and Anderson 1978: 33–34). A group of healthy animals watched a stricken member try to reach the feeding area, but did not help him. Another badly paralyzed chimpanzee was simply left behind when the group moved on. Humans also sometimes resort to isolation and abandonment, as seen in the Inuit practice of leaving aged and infirm people behind in the cold; the stigmatization of HIV/AIDS victims; and the ignoring of the homeless mentally ill in the United States. Compared to our nonhuman primate relatives, however, humans have created more complex and variable ways of interpreting health problems and highly creative methods of preventing and curing them.

Since the 1970s, medical anthropology has been one of the fastest growing areas of inquiry in all of anthropology's four fields. As carried out within the perspective of cultural anthropology, medical anthropology encompasses five major research foci: (1) the interaction of natural and social factors in disease causation; (2) the health systems of non-Western cultures; (3) the analysis of illness and healing as systems of meaning; (4) the way health systems are structured by economic and political factors; and (5) the application of anthropological knowledge to improving health care (Joralemon 1999; Lieban 1977). These five foci can be brought to bear on the study of changing medical systems as a result of contemporary globalization. This chapter addresses each of these areas in turn.

THE ECOLOGICAL/EPIDEMIOLOGICAL APPROACH

The **ecological/epidemiological approach** examines how aspects of the natural environment and social environment interact to cause illness. This approach considers multiple causes for illness, including the possible role of social "risk factors" such as age, gender, class, and ethnicity, and thus differs from a purely biological approach, which seeks to show how biological factors, such as genetics and hormones, affect disease patterns regardless of context. For example, in learning about an infestation of hookworm in a village in China, researchers discovered that only rice cultivators had the disease because they worked the in fields where night soil (human waste) was used as a fertilizer. Thus, environment and occupation were related causes.

Infectious Diseases

The 1950s brought hope that infectious diseases were being controlled through Western scientific advances such as antibiotic drugs, vaccines against childhood diseases, and improved technology for sanitation. In the United States, deaths from infections common in the late nineteenth and early twentieth centuries were no longer major threats in the 1970s. In tropical countries, pesticides lowered rates of malaria by controlling the mosquito populations. The 1980s, however, marked an era of shaken confidence. New concern with infectious diseases is expressed, for example, in a 1995 report of the U.S. government's Committee on International Science, Engineering, and Technology (CISET) on "Global Microbial Threats in the 1990s." While the HIV/AIDS epidemic was a top concern noted in the report, another key challenge is presented by the fact that many infectious microbes have reappeared in forms that are resistant to known methods of prevention and treatment. In addition, new contexts for exposure and contagion are being created through increased international travel and migration, expansion of populations into previously uninhabited forest areas, changing sexual behavior, and overcrowding in cities. Several new and re-emerging diseases are caused by unsafe technological developments. For example, the introduction of soft contact lenses has caused eye infections from the virus *acanthamebiasis*. In the early 1980s, many women in the United States were diagnosed with a new disease, toxic shock syndrome, caused by toxic-producing strains of bacteria and precipitated by tampon use.

Many medical anthropologists have studied how infectious diseases spread, in the past and the present, within a broad ecological/epidemiological model. They are contributing their expertise through studying social patterns and cultural practices that are related to the spread of these new diseases. Research about HIV/AIDS has addressed how factors such as intravenous drug use, sexual behavior, and condom use vary among different groups and how, based on this knowledge, intervention programs could be better designed and targeted. For example, one study assessed attitudes toward condom use among White, African American, and Hispanic respondents in the United States (Bowen

In Vietnam, the government has taken an active role in promoting awareness of HIV/AIDS risk. In Vietnam, HIV/AIDS is known as SIDA, from the French acronym for "syndrome immuno-déficitaine acquis." This poster emphasizes contagion through needles and unsafe sex.

and Trotter 1995). Whites were more likely to use condoms, followed by Hispanics, with lowest use among African Americans. Across all groups, people with "main partners" compared to "casual partners" were more likely to use condoms, as were older people and people classified as having a higher level of personal assertiveness. Recommendations for increasing condom usage include targeted self-awareness programs and assertiveness training, especially for younger people in casual relationships.

Colonial Contact, Disease, and Death

Anthropologists have applied the ecological/epidemiological approach to the study of the impaired health and survival of indigenous peoples as a result of colonial contact. Some key questions involve how the introduction of European pathogens (disease-producing organisms) and their effect vary on the basis of size of the populations involved, and the indigenous people's ecological and economic base, technology, organizational complexity, and prior disease experience (Larsen and Milner 1994). Basic methodological issues involve trying to find and analyze data that would provide assessments of the precontact cultures' population levels and disease experience. Available skeletal evidence provides spotty information on comparatively few sites and what does exist is difficult to generalize from. Relatively more data are available for postcontact transitions, such as archival material provided by the colonizers documenting their use of indigenous people as laborers. Colonial records, however, must be carefully examined for biases in presentation (Joralemon 1982). Overall, findings about the effects of Western colonial contact are negative, from the worst examples being quick and outright extermination of indigenous peoples, to other groups showing resilience within drastically changed conditions.

Considering only the "New World" situation, it is generally agreed that European colonialism brought a dramatic decline in the indigenous populations they contacted, although disagreement exists about the numbers involved (Joralemon 1982). It is impossible to know how many indigenous peoples inhabited the New World prior to 1492, so some scholars say it is more fruitful to look at the causes involved in depopulation rather than trying to determine numerical change. One area of inquiry is to assess the role of disease in depopulation as compared to other factors such as warfare, harsh labor practices, and general cultural disruption, and to discover which diseases were most important. Research along these lines indicates that the precontact New World was largely free of the major European infectious diseases of smallpox, measles, and typhus, and perhaps also syphilis, leprosy, and malaria. The exposure of indigenous peoples to these infectious diseases, therefore, was likely to have a massive impact, given the people's complete lack of resistance. One analyst compared contact to a "biological war":

> Smallpox was the captain of the men of death in that war, typhus fever the first lieutenant, and measles the second lieutenant. More terrible than the conquistadores on horseback, more deadly than sword and gunpowder, they made the conquest by the whites a walkover as compared to what it would have been without their aid. They were the forerunners of civilization, the companions of Christianity, the friends of the invader (Ashburn 1947:98, quoted in Joralemon 1982:112).

This quotation emphasizes the importance of the three major diseases in Latin American colonial history: smallpox, measles, and malaria. A later arrival, cholera, also had severe effects since its transmission through contaminated water and food finds an ideal context in areas of poor sanitation.

Diseases of Development

Another area of research that traces the spread of illnesses with attention to the links between ecological factors and social factors is the study of **diseases of development,** diseases that are caused or increased by economic development activities that affect the environment and people's relationship with it (Hughes and Hunter 1970). Examples of diseases in this category are schistosomiasis, river blindness, malaria, and tuberculosis (Foster and Anderson 1978:27).

In many developing countries, dramatically increased rates of schistosomiasis (a disease caused by the presence of a parasitic worm in the blood system) have been traced to the construction of dams and irrigation systems. It is estimated that over 200 million people suffer from this debilitating disease (Foster and Anderson 1978). The larvae of this particular form of worm hatch from eggs and mature in slow-moving water such as lakes and rivers. Upon maturity, they can penetrate human (or other animal) skin with which they come into contact. People who wade or swim in infected waters are highly likely to become infected. Once inside the human body, the adult schistosomes breed in the veins around the human bladder and bowel. They send fertilized eggs through urine and feces into the environment, which then continue to contaminate water in which the eggs hatch into larvae. Anthropologists' research has documented dramatic increases in the rates of schistosomiasis that have occurred at many high dam sites (Scudder 1973). This heightened risk is caused by the dams slowing the rate of water flow. In stagnant water systems, as opposed to the undisturbed rapid flow, an ideal environment emerges for the development of the larvae. Many anthropologists have used this information to speak out against the construction of large dam projects, especially those that do not give attention to the potential health hazards involved for people who live near the project area.

Formerly unidentified diseases of development continue to appear. One of these, which has been studied by a medical anthropologist, is Kyasanur forest disease, or KFD (Nichter 1992). This viral disease was first identified in 1957 in southern India:

> Resembling influenza, at onset KFD is marked by sudden chills, fever, frontal headaches, stiffness of the neck, and body pain. Diarrhea and vomiting often follow on the third day. High fever is continuous for five to fifteen days, during which time a variety of additional symptoms may manifest themselves, including gastrointestinal bleeding, persistent cough with blood-tinged sputum, and bleeding gums. In more serious cases, the infection progresses to bronchial pneumonia, meningitis, paralysis, encephalitis, and hemorrhage. (224)

Between 1982 and 1984, an epidemic of KFD swept through over thirty villages in a part of Karnataka state near the Kyasanur forest. During this time, mortality rates in hospitals ranged between 12 and 18 percent of those admitted. Investigation of the social distribution and causes of the epidemic revealed that KFD especially affects agricultural workers and cattle-tenders who were most exposed to newly cleared areas near the forest. In the cleared areas, international companies established plantations and initiated cattle-raising. Ticks, which had long existed in the local ecosystem, increased in number in the cleared area and found inviting hosts in the cattle and their tenders. Thus, human modification of the ecosystem through deforestation and introduction of cattle-raising caused the epidemic and shaped its social distribution.

ETHNOMEDICINE

Medical anthropologists have a longstanding interest in studying **ethnomedicine,** or the medical systems of particular (usually non-Western) cultural groups. They investigate how different cultures perceive of the body as a locus of health and illness; classify and interpret illnesses; practice preventive measures; offer therapeutic approaches (including magical-religious techniques, use of medical substances, and mechanical techniques such as dentistry and surgery); and involve specialists in treating illness.

Perceptions of the Body

Anthropological research documents how cultures define the body and its parts in relation to illness and treatment. The highland Maya of Chiapas, southern Mexico, have a detailed vision of the exterior body, but do not focus much attention on internal organs, a fact related to the nonexistence of surgery as a healing technique among them (Berlin and Berlin 1996). In the West, separation of the mind from the body has long pervaded popular and scientific thinking about health and illness. Thus, Western medicine has a special category called "mental illness," which addresses certain health problems as if they were located only in the mind. In many cultures where such a mind-body distinction does not exist, the category of "mental illness" does not either. Cross-cultural variation exists in perceptions of which bodily organs are most critically involved in the definition of life versus death. In the West, a person may be declared dead while the heart is still beating if the brain is judged "dead." In many other cultures, this definition of brain death is not accepted, perhaps an indication of the relatively great value accorded to the brain in Western culture (Ohnuki-Tierney 1994).

In Japan, negative attitudes about cutting the body help explain the much lower rates of surgery there than in the United States. The Japanese concept of *gotai* refers to the value of maintaining bodily intactness in life and death. "Even today ear piercing is uncommon.... Newspapers reported that one of the qualifications of a bride for Crown Prince Naruhitao was that she not have pierced ears" (Ohnuki-Tierney 1994:235). Confucian doctrine states that an intact body insures rebirth. Historically, the warrior's practice of beheading the victim was the ultimate form of killing because it violated the integrity of the body and prevented the enemy's rebirth. Gotai is also an important reason for the widespread popular resistance to organ transplantation in Japan (although recently some Japanese people, including many physicians, have begun to reject gotai in favor of promoting transplant surgery).

A second area of study related to the body is the assessment of whether the body is considered to be a bounded physical unit, with disease treatment thus focused on just the body, or whether the body is considered to be connected to a wider social context, in which case treatment addresses a wider social sphere (Fabrega and Silver 1973). Western biomedicine typically addresses a clearly defined, individual physical body (or mind). In contrast, many non-Western healing systems encompass the social context within which an individual's physical body is situated. Diagnoses that address the "social body" in preindustrial, non-Western medical systems may include the family or community members as responsible, or they may look to the supernaturals as being in some way unhappy. A cure is brought about by holding a family or community ritual that seeks to regain correct social relations or that will appease the deities.

Defining Disease Emically

Western biomedicine defines and labels diseases according to its diagnostic criteria, and sets them down in written manuals and guides used by physicians in treating patients. Other systems emphasize different symptoms or attribute disease to different causes. In the late 1980s, when HIV/AIDS was first recognized in Haiti, may Haitians thought it was a "disease of the city," contracted through sexual intercourse, or a "jealousy sickness" brought on one poor person by another through magic (Farmer 1990). In the first instance, condoms were believed to be a form of prevention, while in the second, only certain charms would help. It should not be thought that non-Western perceptions of illness are "wrong." Like Western perceptions, they are embedded in their social context and "make sense" within the cultural system.

Cross-culturally, many locally specific, noninfectious disorders have been labeled and their treatments outlined. Anthropologists refer to such afflictions as **culture-bound syndromes** or "folk illnesses" (see Table 7.1 on page 162). A culture-bound syndrome is a collection of signs and symptoms that is restricted to a particular culture or a limited number of cultures (Prince 1985:201). While Western psychiatrists would label these afflictions psychiatric disorders, in fact, they do not match that category well. Culture-bound syndromes are caused by psychosocial factors such as stress or shock, but they may have biophysical symptoms. For example, *susto,* or "fright disease," is a widely distributed culture-bound syndrome of Latino cultures. People afflicted with susto attribute it to shock, such as loss of a loved one or experiencing a frightening accident (Rubel, O'Nell, and Collado-Ardón 1984). In the Chiapas area of Mexico, one woman reported that her susto was brought on by an accident in which a lot of pottery she had made got broken on its way to market, while a man said that

Table 7.1
Selected Culture-Bound Syndromes

Syndrome	*Cultural/Geographic Location*	*Symptoms*
aiyiperi	Yoruba (Nigeria)	hysterical convulsive disorders, posturing and tics, psychomotor seizures
amok	Malaysia and Indonesia	dissociative episodes, outbursts of violent and aggressive or homicidal behavior directed at people and objects, persecutory ideas, amnesia, exhaustion
anfechtung	Hutterites (Manitoba, Canada)	withdrawal from social contact, feeling of having sinned, rumination of religious unworthiness, temptation to commit suicide
brain fag	Nigerian and East African students	pain, heat or burning sensations, pressure or tightness around head, blurring of vision, inability to assimilate what is read, inability to concentrate when studying, anxiety and depression, fatigue and sleepiness despite adequate rest
cholera	Guatemala	nausea, vomiting, diarrhea, fever, severe temper tantrums, unconsciousness and dissociative behavior
ghost sickness	Navajo of the southwestern United States	varied symptoms attributed to witchcraft, including weakness, bad dreams, feelings of danger, confusion, feelings of futility, loss of appetite, feelings of suffocation, fainting, dizziness, sometimes hallucinations and loss of consciousness
koro	South China, Chinese and Malaysian populations in southeast Asia, Hindus of Assam	anxiety in males that the penis will recede into the body and for females that the vulva and breasts will recede into the body. Among males the penis is held by the victim or someone else or devices are attached to prevent its receding.
latah	Malaysia and Indonesia	the "startle" illness—a response to a startling stimulus through which the afflicted person becomes flustered and may say and do things that appear amusing, such as mimicking people's words and movements
mal ojo (evil eye)	Mediterranean and Latin American Hispanic populations	fitful sleep, crying without apparent cause, diarrhea, vomiting, fever in a child or infant explained as caused by a fixed stare from an adult
pibloktoq (Arctic hysteria)	Inuit of the Arctic, Siberian groups	brooding, depressive silences, loss or disturbance of consciousness during seizure, tearing off of clothing, fleeing or wandering, rolling in snow, speaking in tongues or echoing other people's words
windigo	Cree, Ojibwa, and related Native American groups of central and northeastern Canada	depression, nausea, distaste for usual foods, feelings of being possessed by a cannibalistic monster, homicidal (sometimes suicidal) impulses
shinkeishitsu	Japan	fear of meeting people, feelings of inadequacy, anxiety, obsessive-compulsive symptoms, hypochondriasis

Source: Adapted from Simons and Hughes 1980:91–110.

Multiple Cultural Worlds

Anorexia Nervosa as a Culture-Bound Syndrome

Anorexia nervosa and a related condition called *bulimia* are examples of recently emerging culture-bound syndromes found predominantly found among Euro-American adolescent girls of the United States (Brumberg 1988), although some cases have also been documented among African American girls in the United States, as well as a small number of cases in Japan, Hong Kong, and urban India (Fabrega and Miller 1995). Anorexia nervosa's cluster of symptoms include self-perceptions of fatness, aversion to food, hyperactivity, and, as it progresses, continuous wasting of the body and often death. The association between anorexia with industrial culture suggests that as industrialism and westernization spread throughout the world, it is likely that the associated culture-bound syndromes will, too.

No one has found a biological cause for anorexia nervosa, and thus, it stands as a clear example of a culturally constructed affliction. It is very difficult to cure with either medical or psychiatric treatment (Gremillon 1992), which is a logical result of its cultural foundations. Pinpointing what the cultural causes are, however, has also not proved easy. Many experts point to the societal pressures on young girls in the United States toward excessive concern with their looks, especially body weight. Others feel that anorexia is related to girls' unconscious resistance to overcontrolling parents. To such girls, food intake may appear to be the one thing they control. This need for self-control through food deprivation becomes addictive and entrapping. Although the primary cause may be rooted in culture, the affliction becomes intertwined with the body's biological functions. Extreme fasting leads to the body's inability to deal with ingested food. A starving anorexic literally may no longer be able to eat and derive nourishment from food, which is why some medical treatments involve intravenous feeding to override the biological block.

his susto came on after he saw a dangerous snake. Susto symptoms include appetite loss, loss of motivation, breathing problems, generalized pain, and nightmares. Analysis of many cases of susto in three villages showed that the people most likely to be afflicted were those who were in some way socially marginal or experiencing a sense of role failure. The woman whose pottery had broken, for example, had also suffered two spontaneous abortions and was worried that she would never have children. People who fall ill with susto have higher mortality rates than the unafflicted population, a finding that suggests that a deep sense of social failure (culturally diagnosed as a discrete event such as broken pottery) places the afflicted person at a higher risk of dying. Thus, some culture-bound syndromes are not only "psychological" problems.

Medical anthropologists first studied culture-bound syndromes in non-Western cultures, and this focus has led to a bias in thinking that all culture-bound syndromes are found in "other" cultures. Now, it is recognized that some afflictions of the West are also culture-bound syndromes, such as *agoraphobia*, or an obsessive fear of leaving one's home and going to public places, or eating disorders such as anorexia nervosa and bulimia (see the Multiple Cultural Worlds box).

Preventive Practices

Numerous practices based in either religious or secular beliefs exist cross-culturally for preventing misfortune, suffering, and illness. Among the Maya of Guatemala, one of the major illnesses is called *awas* (Wilson 1995). This illness is especially likely to occur among infants. Difficult labor may be a sign of awas in the infant, and stillbirths and infant deaths are attributed to this disease. Children born with awas show symptoms such as lumps under the skin, marks on the skin, or albinism. Causes of awas are related to events that happen to the mother during her pregnancy: She may have been denied food that she desired or pressured to eat food she didn't want, or she may have encountered a rude, drunk, or angry person (usually a male). In order to help prevent awas in babies, the Mayans go out of their way to be careful around pregnant women. A pregnant woman, like land before the planting, is considered sacred and treated in special ways: She is always given the food she wants, and people behave with respect in her presence. In general, the ideal is to keep a pregnant woman in a state of *kalkab'il,* or peace, contentment, and optimism.

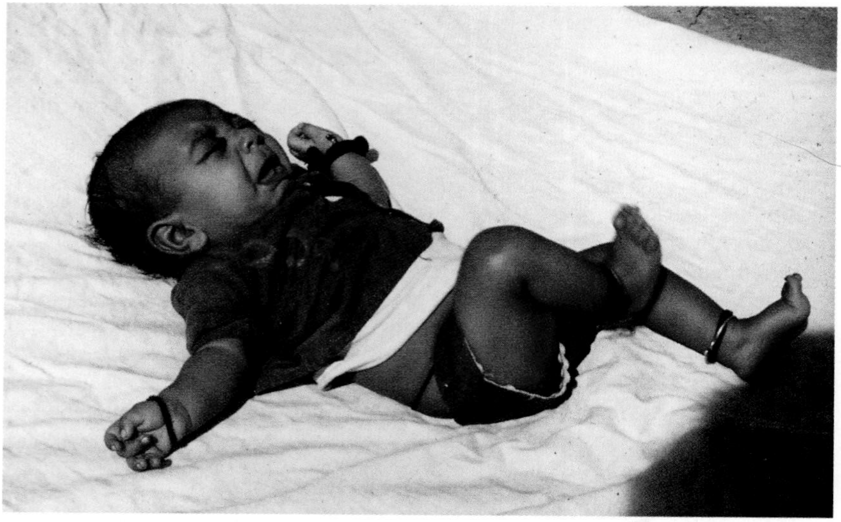

Throughout northern India, people believe that the tying on of strings provides protection from malevolent spirits and forces. This baby has five protective strings.

Common forms of ritual health protection include charms, spells, and strings tied around parts of the body. After visiting a Buddhist temple in Japan, for example, one might purchase a small band to tie around the wrist to prevent future problems related to good health and fertility. Wrist ties are commonly placed on infants in rural areas in India, especially by Hindus. Tying strings onto a tree or part of a shrine when undertaking a pilgrimage is another way that people attempt to secure their wishes for the future. An anthropologist working in Thailand learned of the display of carved wooden phalluses throughout a village as protection against a certain form of sudden death among men (Mills 1995). In 1990, fear of a widow ghost attack spread throughout a wide area of northern Thailand. The fear was based on several radio reports of unexplained deaths of Thai migrant men working in Singapore. Local people interpreted these sudden deaths as caused by widow ghosts. Widow ghosts are known to roam about, searching for men whom they take as their "husbands." Mary Beth Mills was conducting research in Baan Naa Sakae village at the time of the fear:

> I returned to Baan Naa Sakae village after a few days' absence to find the entire community of two hundred households festooned with wooden phalluses in all shapes and sizes. Ranging from the crudest wooden shafts to carefully carved images complete with coconut shell testicles and fishnet pubic hair, they adorned virtually every house and residential compound. The phalluses, I was told, were to protect residents, especially boys and men, from the "nightmare deaths" (*lai tai*) at the hands of malevolent "widow ghosts" (*phii mae maai*). (249)

In Isan culture, and wider Thai culture too, spirits (*phii*) are a recognized source of illness, death, and other misfortunes. One variety of phii, a widow ghost is the sexually voracious spirit of a woman who has met an untimely and perhaps violent death. When a seemingly healthy man dies in his sleep, a widow ghost is blamed. The wooden phalluses hung on the houses were protection against a possible attack. Mills reports:

> [I]nformants described these giant penises as decoys that would attract the interest of any *phii mae maai* which might come looking for a husband. The greedy ghosts would take their pleasure with the wooden penises and be satisfied, leaving the men of that household asleep, safe in their beds. (251)

As the radio reports ceased, the villagers' concerns about the widow ghosts died down, and the phalluses were removed.

Diagnosis

If an affliction has been experienced and the person with the condition decides to seek help for it, diagnosis is the first stage in treatment. Diagnosis attempts to find out what is wrong and to label the affliction in order to determine the proper form of treatment. It includes magical-religious techniques such as **divination,** in which a specialist uses techniques to gain supernatural insights, and secular techniques such as asking the ill person to supply detailed descriptions of symptoms. Among the Navajo, three types of diagnostic techniques exist: hand trembling, star gazing, and listening (W. Morgan 1977). The hand trembling diagnosis works this way: The specialist enters the hogan of the afflicted person and, with friends and relatives present, discusses the problem. The specialist sits facing the patient, closes his eyes, and thinks of all the possible causes. When the correct one comes to mind, the specialist's arm involuntarily shakes, revealing the diagnosis. In all three forms of Navajo diagnosis, the specialist goes into a trance-like state that lends authority to the outcome since people believe that the diagnosis has been given by the supernaturals.

Among the urban poor of Bahia in Brazil, a flexible approach exists to ascertaining the cause of disease (Ngokwey 1988). In Feira de Santana, the second largest city in the state of Bahia, with a population of about a quarter of a million people, traditional etiological (causal) systems include both supernatural and secular models. In the poorer neighborhoods, unemployment is high. Those who work are bricklayers, plumbers, seamstresses, vendors, and laborers. Health problems are typical of northeastern Brazil, the poorest region in the nation, including nutritional deficiencies; infectious diseases such as diarrhea, tuberculosis, measles, ascaridiasis, and schistosomiasis; and chronic diseases. Illness causation theories in Feira de Santana can be divided into the following domains: natural, socioeconomic, psychological, and supernatural.

Natural domain causes include exposure to the environment. Thus, "too much cold can provoke gripe; humidity and rain cause rheumatism; excessive heat can result in dehydration. . . . Some types of winds are known to provoke *ar do vento* or *ar do tempo,* a condition characterized by migraines, hemiplegia, and 'cerebral congestion'" (795). Other natural domain explanations for illness take into account the effects of aging, heredity, personal nature (*natureza*), and gender. Heredity is a common explanation for mental retardation. Contagion is another "natural" explanation, as are the effects of certain foods and eating habits. In the socioeconomic domain, popular knowledge connects the lack of economic resources, proper sanitation, and health services with illnesses. "One informant said, 'There are many illnesses because there are many poor'" (796).

In the psychosocial domain, certain emotions are attributed to illness: "Anger and hostile feelings (*raiva*), anxiety and worry are possible causes of various illnesses ranging from *nervoso,* a folk illness characterized by 'nervousness,' to heart problems and *derrame* (cerebral hemorrhage)" (796). In the supernatural domain, illness is caused by spirits and magical acts. The African-Brazilian religious systems of the Bahia region encompass a range of spirits who can inflict illness, including spirits of the dead and devil-like spirits. Some spirits cause specific illnesses, while others bring general misfortune. Spells cast by envious people with the evil eye (*ohlo grosso*) are a well-known cause of illness. People also recognize multiple levels of causality. In the case of a stomach ache, for example: a quarrel (the ultimate cause), which prompted the aggrieved party to seek the intervention of a sorcerer, who cast a spell (the instrumental cause), which led to the illness. This multiple etiology then calls for a range of possible treatments.

Healing Modalities

This section considers two different cultural ways of conceptualizing and dealing with the healing process. They include the very public and participatory group healing of the Ju/wasi and the "humoral" system of bodily balance through food intake in Malaysia.

Community Healing Systems

A general distinction can be drawn between private and public healing, with the former addressing bodily ailments more in isolation and the latter taking social context more into account. Compared to Western biomedicine, many non-Western systems involve greater use of public healing and community involvement. An example of public or community healing comes from the Ju/wasi foragers of the Kalahari desert in southern Africa. Ju/wasi healing emphasizes the mobilization of community "energy" as a key element in the cure:

> For the Kung [Ju/Wasi], healing is more than curing, more than the application of medicine. Healing seeks to establish health and growth on physical, psychological, social, and spiritual levels. It involves work on the individual, the group, and the surrounding environment and cosmos. . . . The culture's emphasis on sharing and egalitarianism, its vital life of the spirit and strong community, are expressed in and supported by the healing tradition. The central event in this tradition is the all-night healing dance.

A Ju/wasi healer in a trance, in the Kalahari desert, southern Africa. Most healers are men, but some are women.

> Four times a month on the average, night signals the start of a healing dance. The women sit around the fire, singing and rhythmically clapping. The men, sometimes joined by the women, dance around the singers. As the dance intensifies, *num* or spiritual energy is activated by the healers, both men and women, but mostly among the dancing men. As num is activated in them, they begin to *kia* or experience an enhancement of their consciousness. While experiencing kia, they heal all those at the dance. Before the sun rises fully the next morning, the dance usually ends....
>
> The dance is a community event at which the entire camp participates. The people's belief in the healing power of num brings substance to the dance. All who come are given healing. In the dance, the people confront the uncertainties and contradictions of their experience, attempting to resolve issues dividing the group, reaffirming the group's spiritual cohesion....
>
> A broad range of fundamental activities are focused in the dance. Healing in the most generic sense is provided. It may take the form of curing an ill body or mind, as the healer pulls out the sickness; or of mending the social fabric as the dance provides for a manageable release of hostility and an increased sense of social solidarity; or of protecting the village from misfortune, as the healer pleads with the gods for relief from the Kalahari's harshness (Katz 1982: 34–36).

An important aspect of the Ju/wasi healing system is its openness—everyone has access to it. The role of healer is also open: There is no special class of healers with special privileges. In fact, more than half of all adult men and about 10 percent of adult women are healers.

Humoral Healing Systems

Humoral healing systems are based on a philosophy of balance among certain natural elements within the body (McElroy and Townsend 1996). Food and drugs have different effects on the body and are classified as either "heating" or "cooling" (the quotation marks indicate that these properties are not the same as thermal measurements per se). Diseases are classified as being the result of bodily imbalances—too much heat or coolness, which must then be counteracted through dietary changes or medicines that will bring back the desired balance. Humoral healing systems have been practiced for thousands of years in the Middle East, the Mediterranean, and much of Asia and were diffused to the New World through Spanish colonization. They have shown substantial resilience in the face of Western biomedicine, often incorporating it into their own framework, for example, in the classification of biomedical treatments as either heating or cooling.

In contemporary Malaysia, several different humoral traditions coexist, reflecting the region's history of contact with outside cultures. Malaysia has been influenced by trade and contact between its indigenous culture and that of India, China, and the Arab-Islamic world for around two thousand years. Indian, Chinese, and Arabic medical systems are similar in that all define health as the balance of opposing elements within the body, although each has its own variations (Laderman 1992:272). Indigenous belief systems may have been especially compatible with these imported models because they also were based on concepts of heat and coolness.

Insights about what the indigenous systems were like comes from ethnographic accounts about the Orang Asli, aboriginal peoples of the interior who are relatively less affected by contact. A conceptual system of hot–cold opposition dominates Orang Asli cosmological, medical, and social theories. The properties and meanings of heat and coolness differ from those of Islamic, Indian, or Chinese humoralism in several ways. In the Islamic, Indian, and Chinese systems, for example, death is the ultimate result of too much coolness. Among the Orang Asli, excessive heat is the primary cause of mortality. Heat emanates from the sun, and it is associated with excrement, blood, misfortune, disease, and death. Humanity's hot blood makes people mortal, and their consumption of meat speeds the process. Heat causes menstruation, violent emotions, aggression, and drunkenness. Coolness, in contrast, is vital for health. Health is protected by avoiding the harmful effects of the sun by staying in the forest shade. This belief justifies the rejection of agriculture by some groups because it exposes people to the sun. Treatment of illness is designed to reduce or remove heat. If someone were to fall ill in a clearing, the entire group would relocate to the coolness of the forest. The forest is also a source of cooling leaves and herbs. Healers are cool:

> [H]ealers' bodies are superhumanly cool, and they take steps to retain their coolness by bathing in cold water and sleeping far from the fire. Their eyes are especially cool, enabling them to see the true nature of things, hidden to ordinary people. After removing their patients from the hot clearing to the cool jungle, they blow their cooling breath upon their patients' backs, treat them with cooling medications, call upon beneficent spirits to assist them in magically infusing the sick body with refreshing (sometimes invisible) liquid, which they draw from a bowl placed under hanging leaf ornaments. (275)

Extreme cold, however, can be harmful. Dangerous levels of coolness are associated with the time right after birth since the mother is believed to have lost substantial heat: "She must avoid decreasing her heat further by refraining from drinking or bathing in cold water. She adds to her heat by tying sashes containing warmed leaves or ashes around her waist, bathing herself and her newborn child in warm water, and lying near a fire" (275–276).

Healers

In an informal sense, everyone is a "healer" since self-treatment is always the first consideration in dealing with a perceived health problem. Yet, in all

A Korean mansin performs the Tale of Princess Pari, a female hero who braves the perils of the underworld in quest of an herb that will restore her dying parents. Twenty years ago, this segment of the kut for the dead would have been performed outside the house gate. In urban Korea, it is performed inside to avoid complaints about noise and traffic obstruction.

cultures some people become recognized as having special abilities to diagnose and treat health problems. Notable forms of specialists include: midwife, bonesetter (someone who resets broken bones), **shaman** (a healer who mediates between humans and the spirit world), herbalist, general practitioner, psychiatrist, acupuncturist, chiropractor, and dentist. Cross-cultural evidence indicates some common features of healers (Foster and Anderson 1978:104–115):

- *Selection:* Certain individuals may show more ability for entry into healing roles. In Western medical schools, selection for entry rests on apparently objective standards such as pre-entry exams and college grades. An interesting argument exists about whether persons who have certain forms of "neurosis-like" affliction are more likely to become healers. Shamanic healing systems often select persons with unusual abilities to go into trances, or who exhibit other special behavior. Among the Ainu of northern Japan, shamans were men who had a special ability to go into a sort of seizure called *imu:* (Ohnuki-Tierney 1980).
- *Training:* This often involves years of observation and practice, and the period of training may be extremely arduous, even dangerous. In some non-Western traditions, a shaman must make dangerous journeys, through trance or use of drugs, to the spirit world. In Western biomedicine, medical school involves immense amounts of memorization, separation from family and normal social life, and long periods of work without sleep.
- *Certification:* This may be either legal certification as in the United States or ritual certification as when a shaman goes through a formal initiation ritual announcing his or her competence.
- *Professional image:* The healer role is demarcated from ordinary people through behavior, dress, and other markers such as the white coat in the West or the Siberian shaman's tambourine for calling the spirits.
- *Expectation of payment:* Compensation in some form is expected for all formal healers, whether in kind or cash. Payment level may vary depending on the status of the healer, but other factors are also reported. In North India, the strong preference for sons is reflected in payments to the midwife for helping with the delivery; in rural areas, the payment is twice as great if a son is born. In the United States, medical professionals in different specializations receive markedly different salaries.

Healing Substances

Around the world, thousands of different natural or manufactured substances are used as medicines for preventing or curing health problems. Anthropologists have spent more time studying the use of medicines in non-Western cultures than in the West, although a more truly cross-cultural approach is emerging that examines the use of Western pharmaceuticals as well (van der Geest, Whyte, and Hardon

Ingredients for traditional medicines available in a shop in Singapore include deer and antelope horns, monkey gall bladders, amber, fresh water pearls, and ginseng.

1996). **Ethnobotany** is an area of inquiry exploring in different settings the cultural knowledge of local plants and their use for a variety of purposes. As linked with medical anthropology, ethnobotany contributes understanding of the use of plants as medicines. The increasing awareness of the range of potentially useful plants worldwide has provided a strong reason for protecting the world's cultural diversity since people are the ones with the knowledge of different botanical resources (Posey 1990). Leaves of the coca plant, for example, have for centuries been a key part of the medicinal systems of the Andean region, although it has broader uses in ritual, in covering hunger pains, and in combatting the cold (Carter, Mamani, and Morales 1981). Coca is used most commonly for gastrointestinal problems, and next most commonly for sprains, swellings, and colds. A survey of coca use in Bolivia showed a high prevalence rate: Of the 3,501 people asked if they use coca medicinally, about 85 percent answered yes. The leaf may be ingested alone (chewed), and it is frequently combined with other substances in a *maté,* or drink composed of any of a variety of herbs in a water base. Specialized knowledge about preparing some of the matés is reserved for trained herbalists. One maté, for example, is for treating asthma. Made of a certain root and coca leaves, it should be taken three to four times a day until the patient is cured.

Minerals are also widely used for prevention and healing. For example, bathing in sulphurous waters or water that contains high levels of other minerals has wide popularity for promoting health and curing several ailments, including arthritis and rheumatism. About 40,000 people a year go to the Dead Sea, which lies beneath sea level between Israel and Jordan, for treating skin diseases (Lew 1994). The adjacent sulfur springs and mud from the shore are believed to be helpful for people with skin ailments such as psoriasis. In fact, expenses for a therapeutic trip to the Dead Sea are tax deductible in the United States. German studies conclude that it is more cost-effective to pay for a trip to the Dead Sea than to hospitalize a psoriasis patient. While these practices seem clearly to show therapeutic value, instances of people's eating dirt appear to be less understandable within the framework of therapy (see the Critical Thinking box).

CRITICAL THINKING

Why Do People Eat Dirt?

Geophagia, the eating of earth, is a special form of "pica," or the "habitual consumption of items not commonly considered to be food or the compulsive consumption of otherwise normal food items" (Reid 1992). It presents a fascinating puzzle that has been studied by medical anthropologists, cultural geographers, historians, and medical experts. Geophagia has been documented in several Native American groups of South America and the American Southwest, in the Mediterranean region, among women and children in India, among pregnant African American women and children, and in some African cultures. There is typically a preference for certain kinds of earth or clay, and the clay is often baked before consumption, or formed into tablets, or mixed with other substances such as honey.

Medical experts offer explanations based on pathology; in other words, they feel people eat earth or clay because there is something wrong with them. Some pathologies implicated in geophagia are colon perforation, fecal impaction, severe tooth abrasion, and, especially, anemia. According to this view, anemic persons consume earth as an unconscious way of increasing iron levels. Therefore, geophagia can be "cured" through iron therapy. Other experts argue that the arrow of causation in the opposite direction: Clay consumption reduces the body's ability to absorb iron, so it causes anemia. The anemia arguments are complex and the data often inconclusive because of small samples or lack

(continued)

of good control groups. Thus, while an association between geophagia and anemia seems to often (but not always) exist, the direction of causation is undetermined.

Some medical anthropologists propose that geophagia may have a positive adaptive value. Eating clay, they say, may function as a supplement to dietary minerals. Clay from markets in Ghana, for example, have been found to contain phosphorus, potassium, calcium, magnesium, copper, zinc, manganese, and iron. Another adaptive role of geophagia is in traditional antidiarrheal preparations. Many clays of Africa have similar compositions to that of Kaopectate, a Western commercial antidiarrheal medicine. A third hypothesis is that consumption of clay along with plant materials that contain certain toxins (poisons) serves as a detoxicant. Nausea or indigestion from eating such foods is thus avoided. This hypothesis receives support from the common practice of clay eating during famines. This would help people digest leaves, bark, and other uncommonly eaten and hard-to-digest foods. In addition, laboratory rats react to exposure to chemical toxins or new flavors by eating clay.

Critical Thinking Questions

- Is it likely that only one of the above explanations for geophagia is correct in all cases? Why or why not?
- Could all of the above explanations be correct?
- Could none be correct?
- Choose one of the approaches. Formulate a research hypothesis to assess its validity, and design a research project that would prove or disprove it.

Western patent medicines have gained popularity worldwide. There are benefits to the use of these medicines, as well as detriments, including use without prescription and overprescription. Often, sale of patent medicines is unregulated, and they are available for purchase from local markets by self-treating individuals. The popularity of capsules and even injections has led to overuse in many cases. Medical anthropologists are assessing the distribution channels of medicines, the increased commodification of medicine, and cross-cultural perceptions of the efficacy of various types of medicines, among other important topics.

THE INTERPRETIVE APPROACH

The interpretive approach to health systems looks at them primarily as systems of meaning. It examines how people in different cultures label, describe, and experience illness and how healing modalities offer meaningful responses to individual and communal distress. Many interpretive anthropologists have examined aspects of healing, such as ritual trance, as symbolic performances. Claude Lévi-Strauss established this approach in a classic essay called "The Effectiveness of Symbols" (1963). He examined how a song sung during childbirth among the Cuna Indians of Panama lessens the difficulty of childbirth. His main point was that healing systems provide meaning to people who are experiencing seemingly meaningless forms of suffering. The provision of meaning offers psychological support and courage to the afflicted and may enhance healing through what Western science calls the **placebo effect** (a healing effect obtained through the positive power of believing that a particular method is efficacious). Anthropological research suggests that between 10 and 90 percent of the efficacy of medical prescriptions lies in the placebo effect (Moerman 1979, 1983, 1992). Several features may be involved: the power of the person prescribing a particular treatment, the very act of prescription, and concrete details about the medicine such as its color, name, and place of origin (van der Geest, Whyte, and Hardon 1996). For example, many international migrants prefer to obtain medicines from their homelands. In other situations, the prestige of a medicine from Sweden or Switzerland is an important factor.

Margaret Trawick (1987), in her study of Ayurvedic healing in India, follows the "healing is in the meaning" approach in interpreting some aspects of the enduring efficacy and appeal of Ayurvedic treatments. Ayurvedic medicine is a widely used Indian health system based on texts composed from the beginning of the Christian era to about 1000 AD. Based on humoral principles, Ayurvedic diagnoses take into account bodily "channels" controlling the flow of life in the human body as to whether they are blocked or open and clear. A transcribed interview between an eighty-year-old Ayurvedic physician and an old woman of a poor caste group reveals the themes of channels, processes of flow, points of connection (the heart is believed to be the center of all channels), and everyday activities that regulate the flow of life (see the Voices box). After the interview, the doctor offers dietary prescriptions to "quicken" the patient's body—avoidance of tamarind since that causes "dullness," and consumption of light food so that it won't get crowded inside her. Finally, he gently tells her that,

VOICES

An Ayurvedic Doctor and His Client

Doctor: What village?
Patient: Kadalnallur.
D: Let's see your eyes. Let's see your pulse. Is your age over sixty?
P: Probably.
D: You don't know your age exactly, do you? But I think you are sixty, judging from the condition (*amaippu*) of your body. Is there chest pain?
P: A little.
D: Does your heart flutter. . . ?
P: It flutters.
D: At night does sleep come to you?
P: For ten days, good sleep comes, and for ten days good sleep won't come.
D: Does urine pass okay? Is hunger and all good? From time to time does weariness come?
P: Yes.
D: Does weariness come alone or does it come with dizziness? Is there obstruction of the ears, blurring (*mayakkam*) of the eyes? Is there obstruction of the ears?
P: Yes.
D: Do your eyes see well?
P: Somewhat diminished.
D: Is there pain in the joints?
P: Yes.
D: Is this pain always there, or does it come more in the day and less at night?
P: In the day it is felt; at night it is not felt. I sleep well.
D: Are you a woman who is able to work every day?
P: I am idle.
D: You are just in the house eating.
P: Yes.
D: Very good. Do you bathe daily?
P: I don't bathe daily.
D: How often do you bathe?

(continued)

P: I bathe once every two or three days.
D: Have you taken any treatment for this?
P: I have taken no treatment at all.
D: So you have just kept it, letting it be however it wants to be?
P: Whatever.... A person from our village came to you and got well. I came because of that boy. If you make me well many people will come from there.
D: Are your feet and all numb?
P: They feel very numb.... They feel as though they have sandals on.
D: I will give you medicines and all. Your blood is ill ... and your age too is sixty, isn't it? Your body and the skin on your feet has lost its feeling and is in the condition that between it and the flesh there is no connection. Therefore it is as though a thing were stuck on the outside. The blood that it needs is in a turbulence in all places in the body. At night your hands and feet and all become cold; they become very much like sticks. For that I will give an oil to rub on the body and bathe. Rub the oil on and then pour warm water. For the head, all the nerves of the brain, eyes, ears, nose, tongue—all of these are feeling nerves, aren't they? The strength of all these has decreased. I will give an oil to keep it from decreasing even faster. To keep vigorous what hunger you have, for feces to move when you have eaten, for urine to separate properly, for the body to be light, I will give medicine. You take that regularly, and with the medicine it will get better.

What is called food is an important matter ... if you eat whatever you feel like and take medicine it is useless. Therefore I will tell you a diet. If you eat according to that discipline it will become better. Are you in the habit of drinking coffee?
P: I drink coffee.
D: Drink two coffees, in the morning a coffee and in the evening a coffee. Add palm sugar to the coffee, filter it and remove the dirt, add cow's milk and drink it. Buffalo milk will not be digested.... If you want feeling to return to your nerves you should not eat very heavy things ... [several more detailed food prescriptions are given] ... Don't eat very many sweet items.... Eat wheat grain made soft.... At three o'clock drink only one cup of coffee. Eat more food than coffee....

The perceptual power of the nerves of your brain has diminished, eyesight has diminished, your ears don't hear sound, your nose is without good feeling, without smelling well, your tongue is though you had eaten a lot of hot spice. All this will change and your regular body will return. For all this to get better, it will take fifteen days....

I will give you a medicine. In the time of age, at this age of sixty, if the strength of your body has diminished it is difficult for it to return. Therefore you must carry with you your existing strength without its diminishing still more quickly. You must carry it without evils coming and without making room for other diseases. Don't show your head and mix in noisy places and take the air for too long. You must go to mountain places refreshing to the mind, and seeing the plants and trees there be happy. Or else go to the temple and worship God. From that your mind will be pure. A good refuge for your body will be found.

Source: Trawick 1992:138–139. From Charles Leslie and Allan Young, eds., *Paths to Asian Medical Knowledge.* Berkeley: University of California Press.

basically, she is growing old. In this interaction, the meanings conveyed through the interview offer the client a sense that she is being taken seriously by the caregiver and a measure of self-efficacy in that there are things she can do to alleviate her distress, specifically carefully following a dietary regime.

CRITICAL MEDICAL ANTHROPOLOGY

Critical medical anthropology is the analysis of the way economic and political structures shape people's health status, their access to health care, and the prevailing medical systems. Much research of critical medical anthropologists is devoted to revealing how economic and political systems create and perpetuate social inequality in health status. In such analyses, critical medical anthropologists take a cultural constructionist position, arguing that illness is more often a product of one's culturally defined position than something "natural." In another direction, critical medical anthropologists have exposed the power of **medicalization,** or the labeling of a particular issue or problem as medical and requiring medical treatment when, in fact, the particular issue or problem may be economic or political. While critical medical anthropologists tend to look first at how larger structural forces determine the distribution of illness and people's responses to it, some are also concerned to see how individuals may, though personal agency, attempt to resist or reshape such forces. Another important area of research in critical medical anthropology addresses Western biomedicine from an analytical point of view, assessing it as a global power structure, critiquing medical training, and looking at doctor–patient relationships from the perspective of whether they are manifestations of a pattern of social control rather than social liberation.

The Role of Poverty

Broad distinctions exist between the most prevalent afflictions of the richer, more industrial nations and the poorer, less industrial nations. For the former, the United Nations Human Development Report lists these categories of death: circulatory diseases, malignant cancers, AIDS, alcohol consumption, and tobacco consumption (1994:191). For developing countries, a different profile appears: tuberculosis, malaria, and AIDS. Substantial empirical evidence says poverty is a major cause of morbidity and mortality in both industrial and developing countries. It may be manifested in different ways, for example, by causing extreme malnutrition in Chad or Nepal, and high death rates from street violence among the poor of affluent nations.

Throughout the developing world, rates of childhood malnutrition are inversely related to income. As income increases, calorie intake as a percent of recommended daily allowances also increases (Zaidi 1988:122). Thus, increasing the income levels of the poor may be the most direct way to influence health and nutrition. Yet, in contrast to this seemingly logical approach, many health and nutrition programs around the world have been focused on treating the outcomes of poverty rather than its causes.

An early study in critical medical anthropology conducted by Michael Taussig (1978), who was trained as both a medical doctor and an anthropologist, looked at the problem of malnutrition in Colombia. In the 1970s, many United States development organizations were involved in projects devoted to changing people's dietary habits, specifically getting them to eat more soybeans since soybeans were a major new crop being introduced in the area.

Taussig's research delved beyond people's food habits to the basic causes of their malnutrition. The answer lay in the fact that they had lost much of their farm land because of the recent, massive expansion of plantations and large farms devoted to export production. Most the of local farmers now owned plots too small to provide for their own subsistence, and they were thus forced to work for low wages as day laborers on the estate farms. The development of large-scale agriculture in the area has brought wealth to the large landowners, but impoverishment and malnutrition for those who have been squeezed out of their traditional land entitlements. This development-induced problem, as Taussig so clearly points out, is then addressed by "development experts," who provide advice to the poor about how to change their diets, specifically by eating more soybeans, a crop the indigenous people have never produced for their consumption and that they do not consider a fit food for humans.

In fact, the vast majority of the soybean crop is produced for sale as animal fodder in Colombia and internationally. The major point of this study is that a problem (in this case, malnutrition among the poor) is misattributed to the behavior of the poor themselves rather than being attributed to economic interests of the powerful. A solution (a nutrition education program) is devised that fails to address underlying causes. The poor farmers themselves would suggest that the solution lies in land reform, something that the powerful and wealthy do not wish to consider.

The widespread practice of "treating" the health outcomes of poverty and social inequality with pills or other medical options has been documented by many anthropologists. It is a system that obviously serves the interests of pharmaceutical companies in the first place, and, more widely, helps to keep inequitable social systems in place. Similar critical analyses have shown how psychiatry treats symptoms and serves to keep people in their places, rather than addressing the root causes of affliction, which may be powerlessness, unemployment, and thwarted social aspirations in general. High rates of depression among women in Western societies, and their "psychologization," are a notable example in this area.

Western Medical Training Examined

Medical culture is a central feature of Western society. At the level of "popular culture" (mass-consumed culture such as television, magazines, and novels), being a doctor and the hospital as a work place are important themes in the United States. In 1994, a new Barbie doll was introduced by Mattel: She was a pediatrician. Fictionalized representations of the Western doctor's life have been made into popular television shows, beginning with *Dr. Kildare* and *Dr. Ben Casey* of the 1960s. The fascination with medical training is served by many best-selling nonfictional books about medical school. One of the earliest is Michelle Harrison's account of her experiences during her residency in obstetrics and gynecology, called *A Woman in Residence* (1982). She found the training to be so inhumane and inadequate at one medical school she attended that she did not complete her work there. An anthropologist who had done fieldwork among the Ju/wasi for his Ph.D. in anthropology, Melvin Konner, later attended medical school and wrote about this experience in his well-known book, *Becoming a Doctor: A Journey of Initiation in Medical School* (1987). Konner's descriptions of his experiences as a medical student at Harvard provide insight into how medical students are systematically "broken down" through overwork, study pressures, and sleep deprivation. Similar themes emerge in Perri Klass's book, *A Not Entirely Benign Procedure: Four Years as a Medical Student* (1987). She was especially challenged in making it through the "initiation" of medical school because she was pregnant during part it and then a mother. Writer and English professor Lee Gutkind provides an ethnographic account of doctors, staff, patients, and their families in his book called *One Children's Place* (1990) about Children's Hospital in Pittsburgh, Pennsylvania. These books are a small sample of the many "general audience" books on American medical culture.

Since the 1980s, critical medical anthropologists have pursued the study of Western biomedicine as a very powerful cultural system. Much of their work critiques the dehumanization of medical school training and the overriding emphasis on technology. They often advocate for greater recognition of social factors in diagnosis and treatment, reduction of the spread of biomedical technology, and diversification of medical specialists to include alternative healing such as massage, acupuncture, and chiropractry (Scheper-Hughes 1990).

In one example of such work, Robbie Davis-Floyd (1987) examined the culture of obstetric training in the United States. She interviewed twelve obstetricians, ten male and two female. As students, they absorbed the technological model of birth as a core value of Western obstetrics. This model treats the body as a machine. The physician-technician uses the assembly-line approach to birth in order to promote efficient production and quality control. One of the residents in the study explained: "We shave 'em, we prep 'em, we hook 'em up to the IV and administer sedation. We deliver the baby, it goes to the nursery and the mother goes to her room. There's no room for niceties around here. We just move 'em right on through. It's not hard to see it like an assembly line" (292). The goal is the "production" of a healthy baby. The doctor is in charge of achieving this goal, and the mother takes second place. One obstetrician said, "It is what we all were trained to always go after—the perfect baby. That's what we were trained to produce. The quality of the mother's experience—we rarely thought about that. Everything we did was to get that perfect baby" (292). This goal involves the use of sophisticated monitoring machines. One obstetrician said, "I'm totally dependent on fetal monitors, 'cause they're great! They free you to do a lot of other things. . . . I couldn't sit over there with a woman in labor with my hand on her belly, and be in here seeing 20 to 30 patients a day" (291). Use of technology conveys status: "Anybody in obstetrics who shows a human interest in patients is not respected. What *is* respected is interest in machines" (291).

How does obstetrical training socialize medical students into accepting this technological model? First, medical training involves a lengthy process of "cognitive retrogression" in which the students go through an intellectual hazing process. During the first two years of medical school, most courses are "basic sciences"; learning tends to be rote, and vast quantities of material must be memorized. The sheer bulk of the memorization required forces students to adopt an uncritical approach to it. This mental overload socializes students into a uniform pattern, giving them a kind of "tunnel vision" in which the knowledge of medicine assumes supreme importance. One informant said:

> Medical school is not difficult in terms of what you have to learn—there's just so much of it. You go through, in a six-week course, a thousand-page book. The sheer bulk of information is phenomenal. You

> have pop quizzes in two or three courses every day the first year. We'd get up around 6, attend classes till 5, go home and eat, then head back to school and be in anatomy lab working with a cadaver, or something, until 1 or 2 in the morning, and then go home and get a couple of hours of sleep and then go out again. And you did that virtually day in and day out for four years, except for vacations. (298–299)

The second phase, which could be termed *dehumanization,* is one in which medical school training succeeds in overriding humanitarian ideals through its emphasis on technology and objectification of the patient. Another informant explained that "Most of us went into medical school with pretty humanitarian ideals. I know I did. But the whole process of medical education makes you inhuman . . . by the time you get to residency, you end up not caring about anything beyond the latest techniques you can master and how sophisticated the tests are that you can perform" (299). The physical aspect of hazing through exhaustion intensifies during the residency years. The last two years of medical school and the four years of residency are devoted primarily to hands-on experience. The obstetrical specialization involves intensive repetition and learning of technical skills, including surgery. One obstetrician summed up the entire process of transformation: "It doesn't seem to matter—male or female, young or old, wealthy or poor—it is only the most unusual individual who comes through a residency program as anything less than a technological clone" (307).

CLINICAL MEDICAL ANTHROPOLOGY

Clinical medical anthropology refers to the application of anthropological knowledge to further the goals of health care providers, for example, in improving doctor–patient understandings in multicultural settings, making recommendations about culturally appropriate health intervention programs, and providing insights about factors related to disease that medical practitioners do not usually take into account. In their work, different clinical medical anthropologists draw on the ecological/epidemiological approach, the ethnomedical approach, or the interpretive approach. While critical medical anthropology and clinical medical anthropology may seem diametrically opposed to each other (with the first seeking to critique and even limit the power and range of the medical establishment and the second seeking to make it more effective), some medical anthropologists are building bridges between the two perspectives.

An example of a clinical medical anthropologist who combines the first two approaches is Robert Trotter (1987), who conducted research on lead poisoning among children in Mexican American communities. The three most common sources of lead poisoning of children in the United States are eating lead-based paint chips, living near a smelter where the dust has high lead content, and eating or drinking from pottery made with an improperly treated lead glaze. The discovery of an unusual case of lead poisoning by health professionals in Los Angeles in the early 1980s prompted investigations that produced understanding of a fourth cause: the use of a traditional healing remedy, *azarcon,* which contained lead, by people of the Mexican American community. Azarcon is given for the treatment of a culture-bound syndrome named *empacho,* which is a combination of indigestion and constipation, believed to be caused by food sticking to the abdominal wall.

Trotter was called on by the U.S. Public Health Service to investigate the availability and use of azarcon. His research took him to Mexico, where he surveyed the contents of herbal shops and talked with *curanderos* (local healers). He learned about an alternate name for azarcon, *greta,* which helped him trace the distribution of this lead-based substance in the United States. His work led to U.S. government restrictions on azarcon and greta to prevent their further use, recommendations about the need to provide a substitute remedy for the treatment of empacho that would not have harmful side-effects, and ideas about how to advertise this substitute. Throughout his involvement, Trotter combined several roles: researcher, consultant, and program developer, all of which brought anthropological knowledge toward the solution of a health problem.

Like Trotter's work, much clinical medical anthropology involves issues related to health communication (Nichter and Nichter 1996:327–328). Anthropologists can help health educators in the development of more meaningful messages through:

- addressing local images of ethnophysiology and acknowledging popular health concerns;

- taking seriously local illness terms and conventions;
- adopting local styles of communication;
- identifying subgroups within the population that may be responsive to different types of messages and incentives;
- monitoring the response of communities to health messages over time and facilitating corrections in communication when needed; and
- exposing possible victim-blaming in health messages.

Medical anthropologist Mark Nichter (1996) employed these principles in his study of local response to public vaccination programs in several countries of Asia and Africa. Vaccination programs, especially as promoted by UNICEF, are often introduced in countries with much fanfare, but they are sometimes met with little enthusiasm or trust by the target population. In India, for example, some people are suspicious that vaccination programs are clandestine family planning programs. In other instances, fear of foreign vaccines prompts people to reject inoculations. Overall, acceptance rates of vaccination have been lower than expected by Western public health planners, given their assumption that people would quickly realize the benefit. Nichter reviews the factors that have influenced vaccination acceptance and finds that public health planners have not paid enough attention to: broad reasons for why certain innovations are accepted or not; problems in supply (clinics do not always have vaccines on hand); cultural understandings of illness and the role of inoculations; and the vague messages given out by vaccination programs that do not respond to local cultural conditions. Surveys show, for instance, that many mothers have a partial or even inaccurate understanding of what the vaccines protect against. In some cases, people's perceptions and priorities of major diseases did not match with what the vaccines were supposed to address. In others, people did not see the value of multiple vaccinations. In Indonesia, a once-vaccinated and healthy child was not considered to be in need of another inoculation. Another aspect of communication is how to explain side-effects of a vaccination, such as fever, so that family members do not perceive the vaccination as negative. Key features in the overall communication strategy are to promote trust of the public health establishment and to provide locally sensible understandings of what the vaccinations do and do not do.

GLOBALIZATION AND CHANGE

Other than the market system itself, perhaps no other aspect of Western society has so permeated the rest of the world as Western biomedicine. As biomedicine is adopted in other contexts, it undergoes localization and change, given local priorities and meaning systems. A task that faces medical anthropologists of all persuasions is the study of how such change occurs and why, and what the effects are.

Plural Medical Systems

One outcome of the meeting of exogenous and indigenous medical systems is **medical pluralism,** the simultaneous existence of more than one model of prevention, diagnosis, and cure. Given the spread of biomedicine, medical pluralism often involves choices among one or more local medical systems and biomedicine. Another usage of the concept of medical pluralism refers to attempts by governments or health development agencies to create a blended system of health care that selects traits from several systems.

Medical systems operate by naming the problem and then dealing with it. This is complicated enough within a particular culture, but cross-cultural variation adds immensely to the challenges of prevention and treatment. Major conceptual problems may arise in several areas. First, something may be classified as a health problem in some cultures and not in others. For example, spirit possession is sought after and welcomed in some cultures, but might be considered schizophrenia in the West. Second, the same issue may be classified as having a different cause (such as supernatural versus germ theories) and therefore requiring a different treatment. Third, certain treatment modalities may be rejected as violating cultural rules. All of these issues affect how a particular culture will react to exogenous medical practices. In some cases, anthropologists document a seemingly easy relationship of coexistence between many forms of healing that offers clients a range of choices, while in others, conflicting explanatory models of disease and healing result in serious misunderstandings between healers and clients.

Selective Pluralism: The Case of the Sherpas

The Sherpas of Nepal offer an unusual example of a newly capitalizing context in which preference for traditional healing systems remains strong, along with the adoption of certain aspects of biomedicine (V. Adams 1988). Former pastoralist-farmers, the Sherpas are now heavily involved in providing services for international tourism. They work as guides, porters, cooks, and administrators in trekking agencies, and in hotels and restaurants. Thus, many Sherpas are well acquainted with the cosmopolitan cultures of international travelers (506). The wide variety of healing therapies available in the Upper Khumbu region fit into three general categories:

- Orthodox Buddhist practitioners, such as lamas, who are consulted for both prevention and cure through their blessings and *amchis,* who practice Tibetan medicine, a system largely derived from India's Ayurvedic medicine.

Among the many forms of medical treatment available to the Sherpa of Nepal, shamanic healing remains a popular choice.

- Unorthodox religious or shamanic practitioners, who perform divination ceremonies for diagnosis.
- Biomedical practitioners, who used their diagnostic techniques and medicines for tourists, and later established a permanent medical facility in 1967.

The hospital supports seven outpatient health posts, mainly for referral to the hospital; there is a government-supported health post in one town; and another post supported by the Himalayan Trekkers Association serving mainly tourists. Several foreign physicians provide private services. The hospital, however, is the dominant and most-used biomedical facility in the region. There, the fee is one rupee, which is insignificant to the Sherpas. After a session with a physician lasting five to fifteen minutes, the patient leaves, usually with some medication "even if only aspirin" (508). Little explanation is given to the patient.

Given the variety of services available in the region, one wonders how a Sherpa decides where to seek health care. Vincanne Adams explains:

> Sherpas claim they follow an illness-specific pattern of therapy use—following a loose hierarchy of resort for specific illnesses. Most often villagers will say that they use the Kunde hospital for traumatic injuries, superficial wounds, burns, abrasions, etc., but that they consult a *lama* or shamanic healer for less identifiable problems. Urban Sherpas state that they nearly always will go to a biomedical practitioner for care—usually a hospital or private physician if one can be afforded. When questioned about specific illness episodes . . . however, both Kathmandu [urban] and Khumbu Sherpas were observed to use traditional medical practitioners as well as biomedical services. . . . Villagers tend to be less critical of shamanism and *lamaism,* and at the same time less laudatory of biomedicine than urban Sherpas. (509)

In Khumbu, traditional healers are thriving and in no way threatened by wider economic changes brought by the tourist trade and influx of wealth. The reason for this tenacity is that high mountain tourism is a particular form of capitalist development that does not radically change the social relations involved in production. Tourism brings in money, but does not require large-scale capitalist investment from outside. The Sherpas have maintained control of their productive resources, their family structures have remained largely the same, and wider kinship ties have remained important in the organization of tourist business. Thus, participation in this service industry is less disruptive of traditional patterns than other forms of economic change.

When Explanatory Models Don't Fit: A Samoan Case

The disjuncture between biomedicine and particular local cultural patterns has been documented by many anthropologists. In some instances, miscommunication occurs between biomedical doctors and clients in matters as seemingly simple as a prescription that should be taken with every meal. The doctor assumes that this means three times a day, but in some situations people do not eat three meals a day and thus unwittingly do not follow the doctor's prescription.

One anthropological study of a case in which death ultimately resulted from cross-cultural differences shows how complex this issue of communication across medical cultures is. The F family are Samoan immigrants living in Honolulu, Hawaii (Krantzler 1978). Neither parent speaks English. Their children are "moderately literate" in English, but speak a mixture of English and Samoan at home. Mr. F was trained as a traditional Samoan healer. Mary, a daughter, was first stricken with diabetes at the age of sixteen. She was taken to the hospital by ambulance after collapsing, half-conscious, on the sidewalk near her home in a Honolulu housing project. After several months of irregular contact with medical staff, she was again brought to the hospital in an ambulance, unconscious, and she died there. Her father was charged with causing Mary's death through "medical neglect." Nora Krantzler analyzes this case from the perspectives of the Western medical providers and Samoan culture. First, the medical sector view, beginning with her first admission to the hospital:

> At that point, her illness was "discovered" and diagnosed as juvenile onset diabetes mellitus. She was initially placed in the Pediatric Intensive Care Unit for 24 hours, then transferred to a pediatric ward for about a week until her diabetes was "under good control." She, her parents, and her older sister were taught how to give insulin injections, and Mary was shown how to test her urine for glucose and acetone. She was given a 1-month supply of insulin.... She was further "counseled" about her diet.... She was then to be followed up with visits to the outpatient clinic. Following the clinic's (unofficial) policy of linking patients with physicians from their own ethnic group, she was assigned to see the sole Samoan pediatric resident. (326–327)

Over the next few months, she was seen once in the clinic by a different resident (a physician at the stage of training following internship). She missed her next three appointments, came in once without an appointment, and was readmitted to the hospital on the basis of test results from that visit. At that time, she, her parents, and her older sister were once again advised about the importance of compliance with the medical advice they were receiving. Four months later, she returned to the clinic with blindness in one eye and diminished vision in the other. She was diagnosed with cataracts, and Dr A, the Samoan physician, again advised her about the seriousness of her illness and the need for compliance. He wanted her to be admitted to the hospital to have the cataracts removed. Her father initially refused, but then was persuaded. Dr A wrote in Mary's chart:

> Her diabetes seemed to be very much out of control at the time but I was having a very difficult time with the patient and her father.... I consented to the father's wishes to have him supplement the insulin with some potion of his that he had prepared especially to control her sugar.... He did not believe that there was such an illness which would require daily injection for the rest of one's life and thanked me for my efforts but claimed that he would like to have total control of his daughter's illness at this time. (328–329)

The medical experts increasingly judged that "cultural differences" were the basic problem, and that in spite of all their attempts to communicate with the F family, they were basically incapable of caring for Mary. Legal sanctions were used to force her family to bring her to the hospital for surgery.

The family's perspective, in contrast, was grounded in *fa'a Samoa*, the Samoan way. Their first experience in a large hospital occurred after Mary's collapse:

> When Mr. F first arrived at the hospital, he spoke with different hospital staff (using a daughter as a translator) and was concerned that there was no single physician caring for Mary. (Since it was a teaching hospital, she was seen by residents as well as by attending physicians.) He felt that the hospital staff members gave him different interpretations of Mary's illness, including discrepant results, leading him to perceive her care as experimental and inconsistent. The family also observed a child die while Mary was in the Intensive Care Unit, further reinforcing this perception and instilling fear over Mary's chance of surviving in this hospital. Partly due to language difficulties, they

> felt they did not get an adequate explanation of her problem over the course of her treatment. When they asked what was wrong with her, their perception was that "everyone said 'sugar.'" What this meant was not clear to the family; they were confused about whether she was getting too much sugar or too little. Mary's mother interpreted the explanations to mean she was not getting enough sugar, so she tried to give her more when she was returned home. Over time, confusion gave way to anger, and a basic lack of trust of the hospital and the physicians there developed. The family began to draw on their own resources for explaining and caring for Mary's illness, relying heavily on the father's skills as a healer. (330)

From the Samoan perspective, the F family behaved logically and appropriately. The father, as household head and healer in his own right, felt he had authority. Dr A, although Samoan, had been resocialized by the Western medical system and alienated from his Samoan background. He did not offer the personal touch that the F family expected. Samoans believe that children above the age of twelve are no longer children, but can be expected to behave responsibly. Assigning Mary's twelve-year-old sister to assist her with her insulin injections and recording results makes sense to them. Also, appointments are not required at the hospital in American Samoa.

Applied Medical Pluralism

Since 1978, the World Health Organization has endorsed the incorporation of traditional medicine, especially healers, in national health systems (Velimirovic 1990). This policy emerged in response to increasing levels of national pride in their own medical traditions and to the shortage of trained biomedical personnel. Debates continue about the relative efficacy of many traditional medical practices as compared to biomedicine. For instance, opponents of the promotion of traditional medicine claim that it has no effect on such infectious diseases as cholera, malaria, tuberculosis, schistosomiasis, leprosy, and others. They insist that it makes no sense to allow for or encourage ritual practices against malaria, for example, when a child has not been inoculated against it. Supporters of traditional medicine as one aspect of a planned, pluralistic medical system, point out that biomedicine neglects a person's mind and soul while traditional medicine is more holistic. Also, indigenous curers are more likely to know clients and their families, thus facilitating therapy. One area where progress has been made in maintaining positive aspects of traditional health care is in midwifery. Many developing country governments have designed training programs that equip traditional birth attendants (TBAs) with rudimentary training in germ theory and provide them with basic "kits" that include a clean razor blade for cutting the umbilical cord. The many thousands of TBAs working at the grassroots level around the world thus are not squeezed out of their work but continue to perform their important role with some enhanced skills and tools.

SUMMARY

The relatively young subfield of medical anthropology, within cultural anthropology, has pursued five directions of research. In the first, which emphasizes the links between ecological or environmental factors and social factors, medical anthropologists have shown how certain categories of people are at risk of contracting particular diseases, within various contexts in historical times and the present. Change in either ecological/environmental or social factors is often accompanied by heightened risk for some groups, as research on colonialism and international development reveals.

Research on ethnomedicine reveals both differences and similarities across medical systems. Perceptions of the body as holistically linked to the community are related to health and curing frameworks in most preindustrial societies. In industrial societies, emphasis is placed on the body as a discrete unit and the individual (body or mind) is addressed in cases of disease. Community healing systems are more characteristic of preindustrial societies, while industrialized societies emphasize private healing.

The interpretive approach places in the forefront the study of meaning in illness and healing. Medical anthropology research in this area shows how, cross-culturally, the definitions of affliction and suffering are embedded in meaning and so are methods of prevention and healing. This approach places a high value on looking at the placebo effect in different cultural contexts.

Critical medical anthropology, following the inspiration of the political economy perspective, studies health and healing from a cultural constructionist perspective. Their studies have mainly looked at societies in which social inequality exists along a variety of dimensions, including health status and access to health care. Their studies "denaturalize" disease by showing how its apparent inevitability is in fact culturally variable and shaped by deeper economic and political interests. In their examination of Western medicine, critical medical anthropologists have shown how this system, rather than being one of purely humanitarian care, is co-opted into power structures that put the physician in the role of a controlling, detached, technical expert.

In contrast to critical medical anthropology, clinical medical anthropology diverts its attention from questioning the system within which it works, and seeks to make biomedicine more effective by providing cultural information to its practitioners. Clinical anthropologists are at the forefront of helping biomedical clinicians prevent diagnostic and communication errors when dealing with people who have alternate medical models.

Medical cultures everywhere are facing constant change in the face of the spread of Western biomedicine, a process that has prompted reconsideration of "traditional" medicine and its potential. Along with market economics, medicine presents a powerful example of global change, no doubt because of the close connection between the two in industrialized nations.

CRITICAL THINKING QUESTIONS

1. Consider a major disease, such as HIV/AIDS or lung cancer. Look at the five foci explained in this chapter, and discuss what a medical anthropologist would want to contribute to further understanding of the particular disease.
2. In the West, many beliefs about how to manipulate one's diet for better health are said to be based on scientific evidence. Yet this is an area where remarkable variation occurs, as, for example, the contradictory views about whether eating red meat makes people healthy or sick. Such differing views are all supposedly based on science. How can we explain these differences?
3. Given the anthropological critique of Western biomedical training and practice, what could be done to improve it?
4. Should medical pluralism be promoted more widely around the world? Should anthropologists be involved in such an effort? If so, how? If not, why not?

KEY CONCEPTS

clinical medical anthropology, p. 175
critical medical anthropology, p. 172
culture-bound syndrome, p. 161
disease of development, p. 160
divination, p. 164
ecological/epidemiological approach, p. 158
ethnobotany, p. 169
ethnomedicine, p. 160
humoral healing system, p. 166
medicalization, p. 172
medical pluralism, p. 176
placebo effect, p. 171
shaman, p. 168

SUGGESTED READINGS

Berlin, Elois and Brent Berlin. *Medical Ethnobiology of the Highland Maya of Chiapas, Mexico.* Princeton: Princeton University Press, 1996. This detailed report discusses the range of gastrointestinal diseases classified by the highland Maya, including the diarrheas, abdominal pains, and worms, and how the Maya use knowledge of plants to treat them within a humoral system.

Paul Farmer, *AIDS and Accusation: Haiti and the Geography of Blame.* Berkeley: University of California Press, 1992. This text combines attention to the global structures related to the spread of HIV/AIDS with in-depth study in one village in Haiti where HIV/AIDS is locally interpreted as one more phase in people's long-term exposure to afflictions and suffering.

Richard Katz, *Boiling Energy: Community Healing among the Kalahari Kung.* Cambridge: Harvard University Press, 1982. This account of the healing practices of the Ju/wasi [!Kung] of the Dobe area between Namibia and Botswana focuses on several different healers, their training, and styles.

Emily Martin, *The Woman in the Body: A Cultural Analysis of Reproduction.* Boston: Beacon Press, 1987. This text explores how Western medical texts represent women's reproductive experiences and how they compare to a sample of Baltimore women's perceptions and experiences of menstruation, childbirth, and menopause.

Carol Shepherd McClain, ed., *Women as Healers: A Cross-Cultural Perspective.* New Brunswick: Rutgers University Press, 1989. This collection of eleven studies is preceded by a general overview. Case studies include Ecuador, Sri Lanka, Mexico, Jamaica, the United States, Serbia, Korea, Southern Africa, and Benin.

CHAPTER 8

Kinship Dynamics

CHAPTER OUTLINE

THE STUDY OF KINSHIP
- Kinship Theory
- Doing Research on Human Kinship

DESCENT
- Unilineal Descent
  - *Multiple Cultural Worlds:* The Named and the Nameless in a Cantonese Village
  - *Current Event:* "Matrilineal Group Dumps Patriarchal Rite"
- Double Descent
- Bilineal Descent
  - *Critical Thinking:* How Bilineal Is American Kinship?

SHARING
- Food Sharing
- Adoption and Fostering
- Ritually Established Sharing Bonds

MARRIAGE
- Toward a Definition
  - *Viewpoint:* I Always Cry at Weddings
- Selecting a Spouse
- Marriage Gifts
- Weddings
  - *Voices:* Nisa's Third Marriage
  - *Multiple Cultural Worlds:* Weddings American Style
- Forms of Marriage
- Change in Marriage

SUMMARY

KEY CONCEPTS

CRITICAL THINKING QUESTIONS

SUGGESTED READINGS

◀ During part of a contemporary Maasai wedding in Kenya, the bride walks with her friends to the groom's household. The bride is in the center, with her head bowed.

The closest and most intense human relationships often involve people who consider themselves related to each other through kinship. All cultures have ideas about what defines a kinship relationship and rules for appropriate behavior between kin. These rules can be informal or formally defined by law, such as the United States law forbidding marriage between first cousins. Everyone begins learning about their particular culture's **kinship system** (the combination of ideas about who are kin and what kinds of behavior kinship relationships involve) from infancy. Like one's first language, one's kinship system becomes so ingrained that it tends to be taken for granted as something "natural" rather than cultural.

In fact, learning another culture's kinship system is as challenging as learning another language. This was true for Robin Fox (1995 [1978]) during his research among the Tory Islanders of Ireland. Some of the Irish kinship terms and categories he encountered were similar to American English usage, but others were not. For example, the word *muintir* can mean "people" in its widest sense, as in English. It can also refer to people of a particular social category, as in "my people" referring to close relatives. Another similarity is with *gaolta*, the word for "relatives" or "those of my blood." In its adjectival form, gaolta refers to kindness like the English word "kin," which is related to "kindness." Tory Islanders have a phrase meaning "children and grandchildren," also like the English term "descendants." In other cases, no one-to-one match exists. For example, the word for "friend" on Tory Island is the same as for "kin." This difference reflects the particular cultural circumstances on Tory Island with its small population (264 people in 1961), all living in close proximity. Everyone is related by kinship. So, logically, friends are also kin. Another difference is that in Gaelic, no term exists for the concept of the nuclear family as understood in English. This absence also reflects the Tory Islanders' particular conditions. There is an extreme scarcity of housing, so grown "children" tend to remain living with their parents even after marriage because they have no way of setting up their own nuclear household.

Studying diverse kinship systems thus offers surprising discoveries. In some cultures, an uncle has a closer relationship with his sister's children than with his own children. In others, a child considers his or her mother's sisters as mothers and is close to all of them. Cousins, including first cousins (offspring of one's mother's and father's siblings), are preferred as marriage partners in much of the Middle East and in parts of South Asia where cousin marriages are both common and legal. In the United States, in contrast, first cousin marriage is illegal. **Polygyny** (marriage between one man and more than one woman simultaneously) was openly practiced by many people of the Mormon religion in the United States until it was outlawed in the 1800s. On the other hand, in the United States it is legal for a person to have multiple spouses over time (called serial monogamy). Increasing numbers of people in Europe and North America choose to cohabit with a partner and never get married.

In all cultures, kinship links modes of production, reproduction, and ideology. Depending on the type of economy, it accordingly shapes children's physical growth and personality development, influences a person's marriage options, and affects the status and care of the aged. In small-scale pre-industrial cultures, kinship is the primary, and often only, principle that organizes people into coherent and meaningful groups. In such contexts, the kinship group performs the functions of ensuring the continuity of the group through arranging marriages; maintaining social order through setting moral rules and punishing offenders; and providing for the basic needs of members through regulating production, consumption, and distribution. In large-scale industrial societies, kinship ties exist, but many other forms of social affiliation draw people together into groups that have nothing to do with kinship. Many formal institutions such as courts and the police replace kinship groups as moral arbiters and providers of welfare and security.

THE STUDY OF KINSHIP

Of all academic disciplines, anthropology pays the most attention to kinship. The four fields offer insights into why kinship systems exist, how they vary across cultures, and why they change. Physical anthropologists and palaeoarchaeologists attempt to trace the early origins of contemporary human kinship patterns. They ask, for example, if Neanderthals had any kind of institution like marriage, or if their partnerships were more flexible. They also do research on family and group behavior among other animals, especially nonhuman primates. Archaeologists have learned about early human kinship relationships in their studies of the size and structure of ancient dwellings. Linguistic anthropologists have researched, for example, patterns of husband–wife communication and how they relate to power dynamics within the family. The work of cultural anthropologists, the subject of this chapter, includes attention to both the form of kinship relations and their content: how people think about kinship and how they behave as kin to one another.

Links between cultural anthropology's study of kinship extend to other disciplines such as social history and family economics, and professional fields such as family law, social work, and family counseling. The greatest overlap is with sociology. While marriage and the family are core topics of sociology, sociologists have mainly conducted their research among industrial societies of North America and Europe. They have tended to assume that dominant patterns in those societies were the "norm" and that other forms were "deviant." Cultural anthropology's cross-cultural data show that Euro-American patterns such as the nuclear family are neither "typical" nor "normal." Cultural anthropologists do not term any kinship system or family form "deviant." Since the 1960s, however, convergence between sociologists and cultural anthropologists has occurred. Some sociologists now take a more comparative view, and many conduct research in non-Western settings. Martin King Whyte (1993), for example, studies Chinese family patterns. He relies mainly on survey data to address such topics as contemporary patterns of marriage choices and gift exchanges and husbands' and wives' marital satisfaction in arranged marriages versus "love marriages" (Xiaohe and Whyte 1990). Cultural anthropologists also are now more often studying kinship dynamics in Western industrial and urban contexts. Through participant observation, Micaela di Leonardo (1984) learned about the everyday kinship dynamics among Italian Americans in California. She coined the phrase "kinship work" to refer to women's activities that support and maintain kinship links within and beyond their immediate family: visits, playing cards, sending thank-you notes, making phone calls, exchanging gifts and monetary loans, and organizing holiday festivities.

Kinship is said to be the core of cultural anthropology. Early anthropologists documented the importance of kinship in the societies they researched. Lewis Henry Morgan and others argued that kinship was the most important organizing principle in prestate cultures. While taking some form of kinship as a cultural universal, they also discovered that definitions of who counts as kin differed from those of contemporary Europe and the United States. Western cultures emphasize "blood" relations as primary, that is, relations between people linked by birth from a biological mother and father (Sault 1994). Ties through marriage are secondary. This model is expressed in the English-language adage: "blood is thicker than water." Not all cultures define who is a "blood" relative in the same way. In some, males in the family are of one "blood" (or "substance"), while females are of another. This contrasts with the American definition that all biological children of the same parents share the same "blood." In yet others, a more important criterion is through breastfeeding: Babies who were nursed by the same woman are considered related and cannot marry each other. The popular Western view of kinship as based on "blood" relationships and its contemporary grounding in a genetic relationship with the birth mother and "procreative father" (the male who provides the semen that fertilizes the female's ovum) is so widely accepted as real and natural that understanding other kinship theories is difficult for Westerners.

Lewis Henry Morgan (1818–1881) studied Native American culture in central New York state and was adopted as a member by the Seneca.

Kinship Theory

Social Exchange Theory

In his writings of the 1940s, French anthropologist Claude Lévi-Strauss dealt with the question of why human beings have developed kinship systems. In his classic ethnological study, *The Elementary Structures of Kinship* (1969 [1949]), he argues that incest avoidance motivated men to exchange women between families (recall discussion of this topic under "Rights in People" in the discussion of exchange in Chapter 4). This exchange is the foundation for social networks and social solidarity beyond the immediate group. Such networks allow for trade between areas with different resources and the possibility that peaceful relations will exist between bride-exchangers. He took bride exchange as the basis for distinguishing two types of systems: **restricted exchange systems,** in which women are exchanged only between two groups (A and B exchange with each other) and **generalized exchange systems,** in which exchange involves more than two groups and occurs in a more diffuse and delayed way (A gives to B, who gives to C, and then C gives to A). These two types of exchange determine how intensive or extensive a group's social network becomes. Restricted exchange systems build dense and tightly interwoven local networks. Generalized exchange systems create extensive and loose systems. Why should two such different systems exist? One hypothesis is that generalized exchange is an adaptation to risky economic contexts because it offers a wider security net of social relationships, similar to the role of the potlatch feasting system in the Pacific Northwest.

Production, Property, and Kinship

Most contemporary cultural anthropologists are not interested in pursuing the question of why people have kinship systems. They are more concerned with documenting and explaining the differences and similarities in kinship systems and how they link with other cultural domains. The work of British anthropologist Jack Goody (1976), a leading kinship theorist of the later twentieth century, has advanced thinking in these areas. Goody developed a broadly comparative approach that reveals enduring differences between the kinship systems of rural sub-Saharan Africa and Eurasia. His approach is cultural materialist in that it links modes of production to kinship. In sub-Saharan African groups that rely on horticultural production, women are prominent as producers, reproducers, marketers, and decision makers. Their **matrilineal descent** system recognizes and perpetuates the importance of women by tracing **descent** (kinship relationship traced through parent–child links) through the female line, providing for property to be inherited through the female line, and favoring marital residence with or near the bride's family. In rural Eurasia, in contrast, plough agriculture has long been the characteristic mode of production. As discussed in Chapter 3, males are primarily involved with plough agricultural systems, while women play complementary roles in animal care, food processing, weeding, and harvesting. The **patrilineal descent** system often associated with this mode of production does not give women's tasks high value; it highlights the importance of the male line in tracing descent, inheritance of property, and determining marital residence of a couple with or near the groom's family.

Doing Research on Human Kinship

Challenges in the Field

Gathering data on kinship is basic to most anthropological research projects because one of the first fieldwork tasks is to learn "who is who." Areas of questioning include asking informants about who they live with, whether or not they are married, how many children they have, and who in their family may have died. In many cultures, the researcher finds that people openly provide such information. In other situations, gathering accurate kinship data may be difficult. Recall Judith Okely's difficulties gaining the trust of the gypsies in England with whom she worked (Chapter 2). In the United States, an example of potential bias in gathering kinship data relates to rules about the welfare system. Among low-income people on welfare, a woman is eligible for welfare payments only if she is not married (either formally or through common law). In order to protect her eligibility for welfare payments, a married woman may report herself as living alone even if she has a permanent, coresident partner.

Napoleon Chagnon (1992) learned about a taboo against saying the names of certain relatives during his fieldwork among the Yanomami. During his first several months of fieldwork, Chagnon gathered kin-

Anthropologist Napoleon Chagnon has studied among the Yanomami since 1964. During his first year of fieldwork, the Yanomami gave him false information about dead relatives.

ship data from many respondents and carefully recorded it in his notebooks. Once, when visiting a village about ten hours' walk from his research area of Bisassi-teri, he was chatting with the village headman about the headman of Bisassi-teri. Chagnon's mention of the headman's name was greeted by gales of laughter. In this way, he learned that his informants in Bisassi-teri had given him misinformation about their names and those of their relatives. Out of sheer mischief, many had provided people with fake names that were silly and rude such as "asshole" or "fart breath." Eventually, he was able to obtain the "real" names for people. Still, Chagnon had problems getting people to say the names of dead relatives. He discovered that the Yanomami have a taboo against speaking the name of deceased kin, so they would invent a fake name. In order to construct a full picture of kinship relations, Chagnon was determined to learn about these dead relatives. He came up with an idea that worked. He would take a Polaroid photograph of an informant with him to a nearby village, show them the picture, and ask them to provide the names of the photographed person's relatives, dead or alive. This did not break their taboo, and so Chagnon was able to construct a solid data set of many people's kin.

Kinship Diagrams, Genealogies, and Terminology

Early anthropological work on kinship tended to focus, as Chagnon did, on finding out who is related to whom and in what way. Typically, the anthropologist would interview one or two people, asking questions such as: What do you call your brother's daughter? Can you (as a man) marry your father's brother's daughter? or What is the term you use to refer to your mother's sister? In another approach, the anthropologist would interview an individual and ask him or her to name all their relatives, explain how they are related to them, and provide the terms by which they refer to them. From this kind of reported information, the anthropologist would construct a **kinship diagram,** a schematic way of presenting data on the kinship relationships of an individual, called "ego" (see Figure 8.1 on page 188). It depicts all of ego's relatives, as remembered by ego and reported to the anthropologist. Strictly speaking, information gained from the informant for his or her kinship diagram is not supplemented by asking other people to fill in where ego's memory failed (as opposed to a genealogy, see below). In cultures where kinship plays a greater role in social relations, it is likely that an informant will be able to provide information on more relatives than in one where kinship ties are less important in comparison to other networks such as friendships and work groups. When I took a research methods course as an undergraduate, I interviewed my Hindi language teaching assistant about his kin for a class assignment. He was able to remember a total of over sixty relatives in his father's and mother's families, thus providing a much more extensive kinship diagram than I would have been able to for my Euro-American family.

In contrast to a kinship diagram, a **genealogy** is constructed beginning with the earliest ancestors (rather than starting with ego and working outward) that can be traced and working down to the present. The Tory Islanders were not comfortable beginning with ego when Robin Fox was attempting to construct

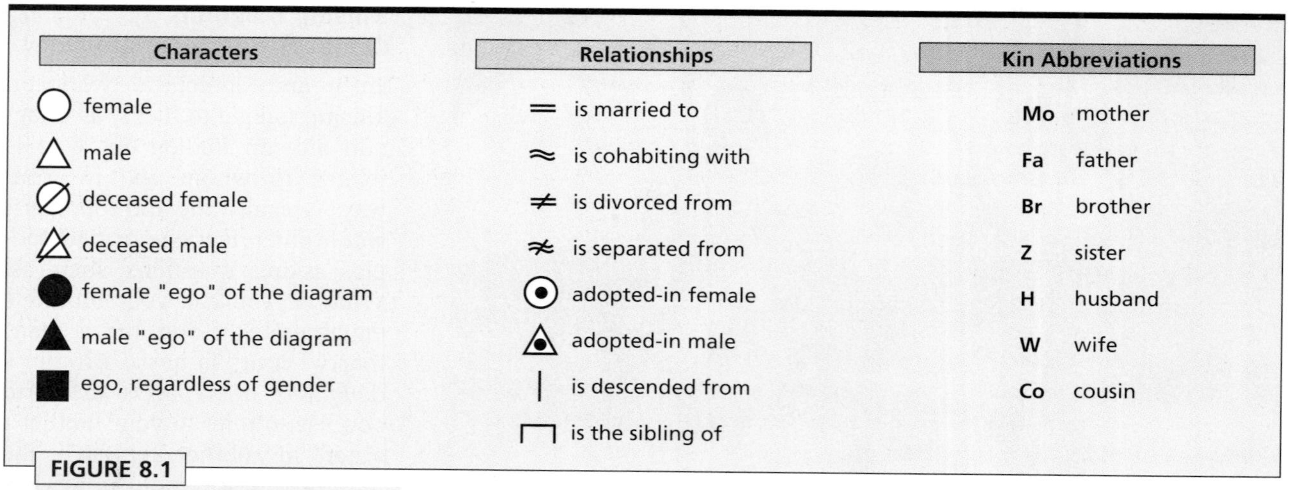

Characters		Relationships		Kin Abbreviations	
○	female	=	is married to	**Mo**	mother
△	male	≈	is cohabiting with	**Fa**	father
⊘	deceased female	≠	is divorced from	**Br**	brother
△̸	deceased male	≉	is separated from	**Z**	sister
●	female "ego" of the diagram	⊙	adopted-in female	**H**	husband
▲	male "ego" of the diagram	△̇	adopted-in male	**W**	wife
■	ego, regardless of gender	|	is descended from	**Co**	cousin
		⊓	is the sibling of		

FIGURE 8.1

Symbols Used in Kinship Diagrams

kinship diagrams. They preferred to proceed genea-logically, so he followed their preference. Tracing a family's complete genealogy may involve archival research in the attempt to construct as full a record as possible. Many cultures have trained genealogists whose task is to help families discover or maintain records of their family lines. In Europe and the United States, Christians often record their "family tree" in the front of the family Bible.

Decades of anthropological research have produced a mass of information on kinship terminology, or the terms that people use to refer to people they consider to be kin of various types. For example, in Euro-American kinship, children of one's father's sister and brother and one's mother's sister and brother are all referred to by the same kinship term: cousins. Likewise, one's father's sister (aunt) and brother (uncle) and your mother's sister and brother have the same terms. And the terms "grandmother" and "grandfather" can refer to the ascending generation on either one's father's or mother's side. In some cultures, different terms are used for kin on one's mother's and father's side. In North India, one's father's brother is called *chacha,* and one's mother's brother *mama;* one's father's father is *baba* and one's mother's father is *nana.* Another type of system emphasizes solidar-

Kinship Diagram

ity along lines of siblings of the same gender so that one's mother and mother's sisters all have the same term, which translates as "mother." This system is found among the Navajo, for example. Anthropologists have classified the cross-cultural variety in kinship terminology into six basic types, named after groups that were first discovered to have that type of system; for example, there is an "Iroquois" type and an "Eskimo" type (see Figure 8.2). Cultures that have similar kinship terminology are then placed into one of the six categories. The Yanomami would, in this way, be identified as having an Iroquois naming system. (My perspective is that a mere presentation of these six types of terminology is not a fruitful way to promote understanding of actual kinship dynamics, the focus of this chapter, so this text avoids going through them all.)

During the 1960s and 1970s, anthropologists' studies of kinship led to a high degree of formal analysis and creation of typologies. George Peter Murdock (1967 [1949]), an American anthropologist, was a major contributor to classifying the cross-cultural findings on kinship. He used ethnographic data for 250 societies in order to analyze the distribution and frequency of different aspects of kinship organization such as the number of spouses allowed cross-culturally and the distribution of family types. Among other discoveries, Murdock learned that about half of the cultures in the sample possessed some form of **extended family** (which comprises more than one parent–child group), while only about one-fourth were characterized by the nuclear family. Murdock's work in compiling a large collection of ethnographies and codifying their contents served as the foundation for many subsequent comparative analyses. Called the Human Relations Area File (HRAF), this collection of case studies has been used by anthropologists to analyze the cross-cultural distribution of marriage patterns, family structure, childrearing, religion, and more, and to measure correlations between these and other variables such as the division of labor, political leadership roles, or frequency of warfare (the HRAF dataset is available in a computerized format in some college libraries).

Getting beyond Diagrams and Terms

The formalism of earlier kinship studies led many students of anthropology—and some of their professors—to think that kinship is a tedious and boring subject. Kinship studies have moved from their early place in the center of the discipline to having a marginal position and dreaded reputation. Fortunately, a renewed interest in kinship is occurring that considers it in relation to other topics such as power relations, reproductive decision making, women's changing work

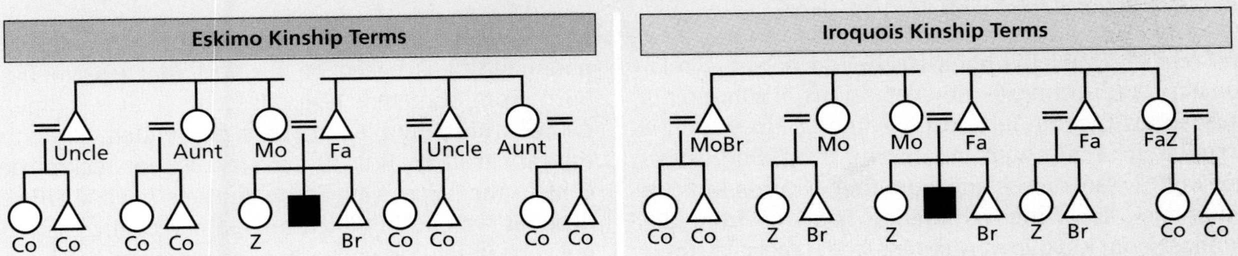

Eskimo kinship terminology, like that of most Euro-Americans, has unique terms for kin within the nuclear family that are not used for any other relatives: mother, father, sister, brother. This fact is related to the freestanding aspect of the nuclear family. Another feature is that the same terms are used for relatives on both the mother's and father's sides, which is related to bilineal descent.

Iroquois kinship terminology operates in unilineal systems. One result is that there are different terms for relatives on the mother's and father's sides and distinctions between cross and parallel cousins. Another feature is the "merging" of one's mother with one's mother's sister (both are referred to as "mother") and one's father with one's father's brother (both are referred to as "father").

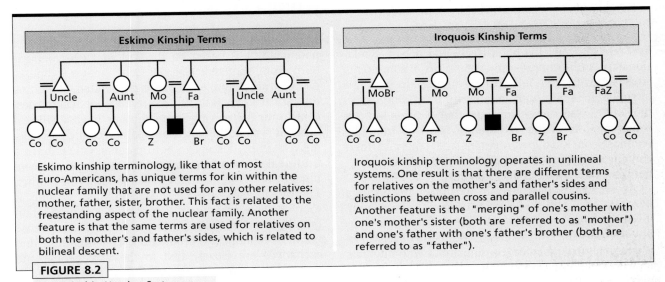

FIGURE 8.2
Two Kinship Naming Systems

roles, and ethnic identity. While much of the jargon and terminology can be left behind in the current approach, some of the complexity of kinship systems cross-culturally must be faced. Margaret Trawick (1992) offers advice in her book on Tamil kinship in South India:

> Getting through this chapter will take some patience. Please have faith. Kinship jargon and diagrams can look forbidding from certain angles, and perhaps some readers, finding them here, may say "Why is she doing this to us? What does this have to do with anything real?" I will try to explain.
>
> Tamils and neighboring peoples have a very elegant set of ways of organizing their families and larger kin groups into patterned systems. Any person trying to understand South Indian culture must eventually come round to examining and trying to comprehend these elegant patterns of kinship organization. They connect with many things that are happening in the South Indian world.... [In addition] these patterns have a kind of real beauty. I would argue that South Indian people create such patterns not only because they "work," not only because they perform some necessary social "function," but also because, in their beauty, they give their creators pleasure.... Kinship patterns can be understood as objects of artistic appreciation, in the same way that mathematical proofs or car engines are, for some people, such objects. Opening the hood of a fancy sports car, some of us will see nothing but a confusing jumble of ugly machinery. Others, who understand such things, will be perfused with bliss. It is the same with kinship patterns. (117–118)

The rest of Trawick's book traces the personal relationships and feelings—the expressions of sentiments such as love, care, and desire—among kin within a large Tamil family with whom she lived. She examines myths and stories and how they express kinship sentiments. This line of thinking takes us from the emphasis on kinship structures and labels to their content and process, especially to the meanings they hold for individuals in everyday life.

As anthropologists attempt to study kinship as a dynamic aspect of life, they are increasingly turning to varied sources of data gathering, rather than simply interviewing informants. Participant observation is extremely valuable for learning about who interacts with whom, how they interact with each other, and why their relationship has the content it has. Observations can provide understanding, for example, of the frequency and intensity of people's kinship interactions and the degree to which they have supportive social networks. Another approach, the life history method (see Chapter 2), reveals changes through an individual's lifetime and the way they are related to other events such as migration, a natural disaster, or political change. Focused life histories are useful in targeting key events related to kinship such as marriage or cohabitation, divorce, or widowhood/widowerhood. Anthropologists interested in population dynamics, for example, use focused life histories, interviews, and questionnaires to gather information on personal demographics to learn at what age a woman commenced sexual relations, how many pregnancies she had, if and when she had an abortion or bore a child, whether the child lived or died, and when she stopped having children.

In approaching the basic question of how a culture defines kinship relations and their content, research shows that, depending on the culture, the closest and most enduring ties are based on one or more of the following principles: descent, sharing, and marriage. The rest of this chapter is devoted to exploring each of these three ways that kinship systems are formed. The following chapter follows up on how these bases for kinship shape people's domestic arrangments and everyday life.

DESCENT

Descent is the tracing of kinship relationships through parentage. It is based on the fact that everybody is born from someone else. Descent creates a line of people from whom someone is descended, stretching through history. But all cultures do not reckon descent in the same way. Some cultures have a **bilineal descent** system, in which a child is recognized as being related by descent to both parents. Others have a **unilineal descent** system, which recognizes descent through only one parent, either the father or mother. The distribution of bilineal and unilineal systems is roughly correlated with different modes of production (see Figure 8.3). This correspondence makes sense because economies—production, consumption, and exchange—are closely tied to the way people and their labor power are organized and how commodities are used and transferred. This section begins with

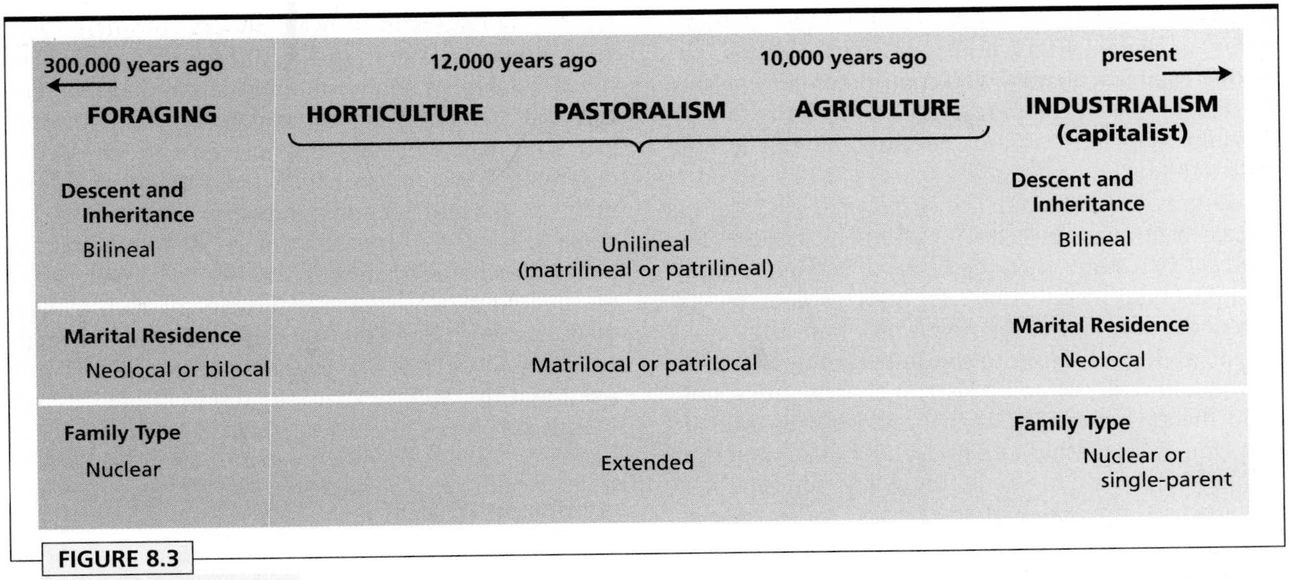
300,000 years ago
12,000 years ago
10,000 years ago
present
FORAGING
HORTICULTURE
PASTORALISM
AGRICULTURE
INDUSTRIALISM (capitalist)
Descent and Inheritance
Bilineal
Unilineal (matrilineal or patrilineal)
Descent and Inheritance
Bilineal
Marital Residence
Neolocal or bilocal
Matrilocal or patrilocal
Marital Residence
Neolocal
Family Type
Nuclear
Extended
Family Type
Nuclear or single-parent

FIGURE 8.3
Economies and Kinship

the descent system that is the most prevalent cross-culturally.

Unilineal Descent

Unilineal descent systems are the basis of kinship in about 60 percent of the world's cultures, making some form of unilineality the most common form of descent. In general, unilineal systems characterize societies with a "fixed" resource base such as crop land or herds over which people have some sense of ownership. Inheritance rules that regulate the transmission of property through only one line help maintain cohesiveness of the resource base. Unilineal systems thus are most associated with pastoralism, horticulture, and agricultural modes of production. Unilineal descent systems have higher frequencies of extended families than bilineal cultures (discussed in Chapter 9).

Two patterns of unilineal descent are: patrilineal descent (kinship is traced through the male line alone) and matrilineal descent (kinship is traced through the female line alone). In a patrilineal system, only male children are considered members of the kinship lineage. Female children "marry out" and become members of the husband's lineage. The same applies in matrilineal descent systems, in which only daughters are considered to carry on the family line. These descent systems also affect the organization of labor through their determination of marital residence. After marriage in a patrilineal descent system, it is likely that the new couple will live with or near the groom's family, and the groom will continue to be a part of his family's work force with the addition of the bride.

The question of why a particular culture is matrilineal or patrilineal has not been resolved, but the implications of patrilineality and matrilineality for the relative status of men and women are more clear. Members of the gender that controls the resources (both productive and reproductive) tend to have higher status. Thus, in general, women have higher status in matrilineal societies and men have higher status in patrilineal societies.

Patrilineal Descent

Patrilineal descent is found among about 44 percent of all cultures. It is prevalent in most pastoral societies, most of India, East Asia, the Middle East, Papua New Guinea, northern Africa, and some horticultural groups of sub-Saharan Africa. Cultures with patrilineal descent tend to have ideologies that are consistent with that concept. For example, theories of how conception occurs and how the fetus is formed give priority to the male role. Among the Kaliai people of Papua New Guinea, people say that an infant is composed entirely of *aitama aisuru,* the "father's water" or semen, which is channeled to the fetus. The mother is an "incubator" who contributes nothing substantial to the developing fetus. The mother's relationship with the infant develops later, through breastfeeding.

Margery Wolf's book, *The House of Lim* (1968), is a classic ethnography of a patrilineal system. She lived for two years with the Lims, a Taiwanese farming household (see Figure 8.4). In her book, she first describes the village setting and then the Lim's house, giving attention to the importance of the ancestral hall with its family altar, where the household head meets guests. She then provides a chapter on Lim Han-ci, the father and household head, and then a chapter on Lim Hue-lieng, the eldest son. She next introduces the females of the family: wives, sisters, and an adopted daughter. The ordering of the chapters reflects the importance of the "patriarch" (senior, most powerful male) and his eldest son who will, if all goes according to plan, assume the leadership position as his father ages and then dies. Daughters marry out into other families. In-marrying females (wives, daughters-in-law) are always considered outsiders, never fully merged into the patrilineage. The Lim's kinship system exemplifies strong patrilineality in that it heavily weights position, power, and property with males. In such systems, girls are raised "for other families" and are thus not fully members of their natal (birth) family; however, they never become fully merged into their marriage family, always being considered somehow "outsiders." Residence of married couples is typically **patrilocal,** with or near the husband's natal family. The world's most strongly patrilineal systems are found in East Asia, South Asia, and the Middle East (see the Multiple Cultural Worlds box).

Matrilineal Descent

Matrilineal descent exists in about 15 percent of all cultures. It traces kinship through the female line exclusively, and children belong to their mother's group. Less common than patrilineal descent, it is found among many Native North American groups, across a large band in central Africa; among many

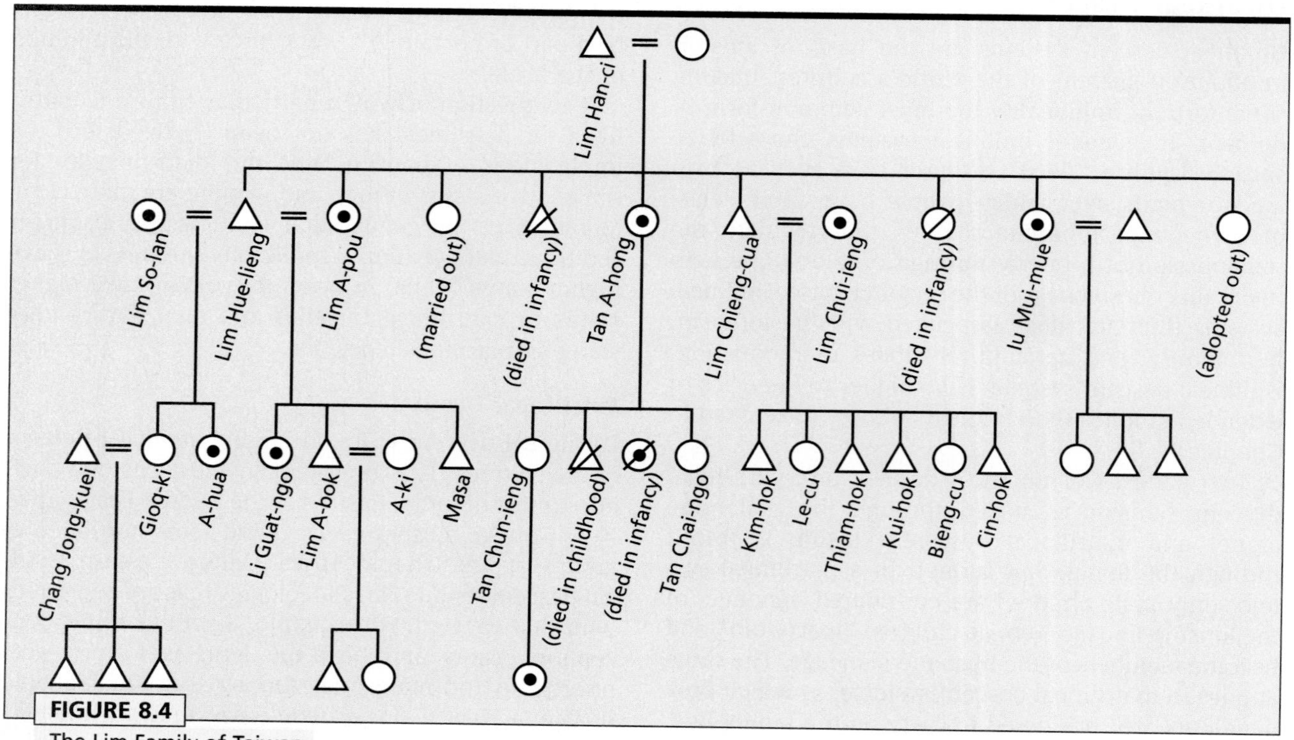

FIGURE 8.4
The Lim Family of Taiwan

MULTIPLE CULTURAL WORLDS

The Named and the Nameless in a Cantonese Village

The village of Ha Tsuen is located in the northwest corner of a rural area of Hong Kong's New Territories (Watson 1988). About 2,500 people live in the village. All the males belong to the same patrilineage and have the same surname of Teng. They are descended from a common ancestor who settled in the region in the twelfth century. In Ha Tsuen, as in its wider region, kinship is reckoned patrilineally. Daughters of Ha Tsuen marry out of the village. Sons of Ha Tsuen marry brides who come in from other villages, and marital residence is **virilocal.** In Ha Tsuen, as in most strongly patrilineal systems, women do not own property, and they have no direct control of the means of production. Few married women are employed in wage labor; rather, they depend on their husbands for financial support. Local politics is a male domain, as is all public decision making. Women's primary role is in reproduction, especially of sons. A woman's status as a new bride is low; indeed, the transition from daughter to bride can be difficult psychologically. As a woman bears children, especially sons, her status in the household increases.

The naming system reflects the greater power, importance, and autonomy of males. A child is first given a name referred to as his or her *ming* when it is thirty days old. Before that time, the mother and infant are secluded to prevent soul loss in the infant. The thirty-day ceremony is as elaborate as the family can afford if the baby is a boy, including a banquet for neighbors and village elders, and the presentation of red eggs to everyone in the community. For a girl, the thirty-day ceremony is likely to involve just a special meal for close family members. Paralleling this bias toward sons in monetary expenditure is the amount of thinking that goes into the selection of the ming and its meaning. A boy's ming is more distinctive and flattering, perhaps having a literary or classical connection. A girl's ming often has negative connotations, such as "Last Child," "Too Many," "Little Mistake," or "Joined to a Brother," which implies hope that this daughter will be a lucky charm to bring the birth of a son next. Uncomplimentary names may be given to a boy, but the goal is for protection: to trick the spirits into thinking he is only a worthless girl so that they won't take him. Thus, a precious son may be given the ming "Little Slave Girl."

Marriage is the next formal naming occasion. When a male marries, he is given or chooses for himself a *tzu* or marriage name. Gaining a tzu is an integral part of the marriage ceremony and a key marker of male adulthood. The tzu is not used in everyday address, but appears mainly on formal documents. A man will have a *wai hao,* "outside name," which is his public nickname. As he enters middle age, he may also take a *hao* or courtesy name, which he chooses and which reflects his self-aspirations and self-perceptions. In the case of a woman, her ming ceases to exist upon marriage. She no longer has a name, but instead her husband refers to her as *nei jen,* "inner person," since now her life is restricted to the domestic world of household, husband's family, and neighborhood. In her new world of kin, she is referred to by **teknonyms** (names for someone based on their relationship to someone else), such as "Wife of So and So," "Mother of So and So." Her personhood and identity are rigidly defined by the kinship system and her names will be derived from her place in that system. In old age, she becomes *ah po,* "Old Woman," like every other aged female in the village.

Throughout their lives, men accumulate more and better quality names than women, and they can choose them themselves. Over the course of their lives, women have fewer names than men. Women's names are standardized rather than personalized, and they have no control over them.

groups of Southeast Asia and the Pacific, and Australia; parts of eastern and southern India; in a small pocket of northern Bangladesh; and in localized areas of the Mediterranean coast of Spain and Portugal. Matrilineal societies vary greatly, from foragers such as the Tiwi of northern Australia to settled ranked societies such as the Nayar of southern India (Lepowsky 1993:296). The majority, however, are found in horticultural systems where women have primacy in production and distribution of food and other goods. Married couples tend to reside **matrilocally,** that is, with or near the wife's natal family. Often, but not always, matrilineal kinship is associated with recognized public leadership positions for women, as among the Iroquois or Hopi. In general, women's status is likely to be higher in matrilineal descent systems than in patrilineal descent systems.

In matrilineal cultures, ideologies about conception give primacy to female contributions to the fetus. Among the Malays of Langkawi island, people say that children are created from the seed of their father and the blood of their mother (Carsten 1995:229). The seed spends forty days inside the body of the father. The first, fifteenth, and thirtieth days of the month are the days on which "the seed falls." Then the seed "descends to the mother." There it mixes with her menstrual blood. It has only to mix with the mother's menstrual blood once in order to conceive. After that, the seed is nourished in the mother's womb from her blood.

The Minangkabau (pronounced mee-NAN-ka-bow, the last syllable rhyming with "now") of Indonesia are the largest matrilineal group in the world (Blackwood 1995). They are primarily rural agriculturalists, producing substantial amounts of surplus rice, but many of them also participate in migratory labor, working for wages in Indonesian cities for a time, then returning home. In their matrilineal kinship system, women hold power through their control of lineage land and its products and of agricultural employment on their land and through their pre-eminent position in business (especially having to do with rice). Inheritance passes from mothers to daughters, making the matrilineal line the enduring controller of property. Each submatrilineage, constituting perhaps four generations, lives together in a lineage house or several closely located houses. The senior woman has the power—her decisions are sought in terms of all economic and ceremonial matters. She is called *Bundo Kanduang,* "womb mother" or "elder woman" or "wise woman." Her advice is respected by all, although group consensus (not dictatorial power of the senior woman) is the guiding principle in group dynamics and is shaped by all senior members. The senior male of the sublineage has the role of representing its interests to other groups, but he is only a representative, not a powerful person in himself.

Matrilineal kinship appears to be declining worldwide in the face of globalized Western/European cultural forces such as colonialism and neocolonialism, which have had a strong effect in establishing patrilineal kinship norms through the spread of Western education, religion, and law. European colonial rule in Africa and Asia contributed to the decline in matrilineal kinship by registering land and other property in the names of assumed male heads of household, even where females were the heads (Boserup 1975). This process effectively eroded women's previous rights and powers. Western missionary influence throughout much of the world also transformed matrilineal cultures into more patrilineal systems (Etienne and Leacock 1980). European influences have led to the decline of matrilineal kinship among Native North Americans which, for long, have constituted one of the largest distributions of matrilineal descent worldwide (although not all Native North American groups were or are matrilineal). A comparative study of kinship among three diverse areas of the Navajo reservation in Arizona shows that matrilineality exists where conditions most resemble the pre-reservation era (Levy, Henderson, and Andrews 1989). In the case of the Minangkabau of Indonesia, matrilineal kinship is being undermined by the combined forces of Dutch colonialism, which promoted the image of male-led nuclear families as an ideal; the Islamic faith, which currently promotes female domesticity and male household dominance; and the modernizing Indonesian state, which insists on naming males as heads of households (see Chapter 9) (Blackwood 1995). Some cultures, however, are managing to maintain matrilineality (see the Current Event box).

Current Event

"Matrilineal Group Dumps Patriarchal Rite"

- The Ghanaian *Times* reported that the matrilineal Gomoa-Assin people have ended an age-old custom through which men extracted wealth from women: immediately upon the birth of her tenth child, a woman was required to buy her husband a ram, an expensive "thank you" for creating more children for her clan.
- As Ama Ata Aidoo, a Ghanaian feminist author commented, "She had to thank him for her fertility!" Further, she noted that "There is no parallel for this in patrilineal societies; not in Ghana or anywhere else have we heard of institutionalized form of thanking *women* for making children for *men's* clans!"

Source: Ms. 3:11, 1992.

Double Descent

A minority of cultures have **double descent** systems (also called double unilineal descent) that combine patrilineal and matrilineal descent. In these systems, offspring are believed to inherit different personal attributes and property from both their father's line and their mother's line. Many early anthropologists mistook this mixed system for a patrilineal system, demonstrating once again the power of ethnocentrism in interpretation. For example, the Bangangté of Cameroon in West Africa have a double descent system, although it was first described by anthropologists as patrilineal (Feldman-Savelsberg 1995). This misrepresentation was probably the result of interviewing only men and focusing on the inheritance of landed property rather than other traits. "While Bangangté, in their conversations with inquisitive anthropologists, first list the property and titles they inherit from their fathers, they present a much more complex picture to those who listen further" (486). Research among married women uncovered double descent. Through the maternal line, one inherits movable property (such as household goods and cattle), personality traits, and a type of witchcraft substance that resides in the intestines. Patrilineal ties determine physical resemblance and rights to land and village residence. Matrilineally related women tend to bond together and visit each other frequently, consulting on marriage partners for their children, advising on child naming choices, and supporting each other in times of trouble.

Bilineal Descent

Bilineal descent traces kinship from both parents, more or less equally, to the child. Family groups tend to be nuclear, with strong bonds between father, mother, and their children. Marital residence is predominantly **neolocal.** Both residence types offer more flexibility than what is usual in unilineal systems. Inheritance of property from the parental generation is allocated equally among all offspring regardless of their gender. In bilineal descent systems, conception theories emphasize an equal biological contribution to the child from the mother and father. For example, contemporary Western science states that the sperm contributed by the male and the ovum contributed by the female are equally important in the formation of a new person.

Bilineal descent is found in less than one-third of the world's cultures (Murdock 1965 [1949]:57). The highest frequency of bilineal descent is found at the opposite ends of the production continuum (refer back to Figure 8.3 on page 191). For example, the Ju/wasi have bilineal descent, and most people think bilineal descent is the prevalent pattern in the United States (see the Critical Thinking box on page 196). A minority pattern of bilineal descent is called **ambilineal descent.** This system recognizes that a person is descended from both parents, but allows for choice in determining which descent group to be more affiliated with and is therefore characterized by **bilocal** residence (a choice is available between living near or with the family of either the groom or the bride). For example, in Tahiti, newly married couples choose to live either with or near either the bride's or groom's family with no particular preference involved (Lockwood 1993).

Given that most of the world's people recognize the biological connection between a baby and both parents, it is puzzling as to why the majority of kinship systems (which are unilineal) emphasize only one parent. Evolutionists of the late 1800s claimed that in early societies, the father was not known. Bilineal kinship, they said, emerged as "higher civilization" and male dominance emerged, granting the male greater recognition in paternity. Thus, unilineal kinship systems are remnants of earlier times. This argument is weak on two grounds. First, it is ethnocentric to claim that contemporary bilineal cultures, especially Euro-American culture, represent the only source of knowledge of the father's biological role. Evidence from many unilineal cultures indicates widespread understanding of this fact. Second, foraging peoples tend to have bilineal kinship, suggesting that the world's earliest peoples may have also had bilineal kinship.

In attempting to explain the relative scarcity of bilineal systems, cultural materialists offer a theory that looks to the mode of production as influencing the type of kinship system. They point out that bilineal kinship systems are associated mainly with two modes of production: foraging and industrialism. Both modes of production rely on a flexible gender division of labor in which both males and females contribute, relatively equally, to production and exchange. Logically, then, a bilineal kinship system recognizes the strengths of both the mother's and father's side. Bilineal kinship is also an adaptive system for members of foraging and industrial populations because it allows for small family units that are spatially mobile. Bilineal kinship offers the most flexibility in terms of residence, keeping open opportuni-

CRITICAL THINKING

How Bilineal Is "American Kinship"?

"American kinship" refers to a general model based on the bilineal system of Euro-Americans of the 1960s (Schneider 1968). According to this model, children are considered to be descended from both mother and father, and general inheritance rules suggest that property would be divided equally between sons and daughters. Given the rich cultural diversity of the United States and Canada, most would now consider the label "American kinship" and its characterization as bilineal to be overgeneralized. Biases are often prominent toward either patrilineality or matrilineality. Indicators of patrilineality include the prevalent practice of a wife dropping her surname at marriage and taking her husband's surname, and the use of the husband's surname for offspring. Although inheritance is supposedly equal between sons and daughters, often it is not. In many business families, the business is passed from father to sons, while daughters are given a different form of inheritance such as a trust fund. On the other hand, a certain degree of **matrifocality** (a domestic system in which the mother is the central figure) arises from another source: high rates of divorce and the resulting trend of young children living with the mother more often than the father. A matrifocal emphasis creates mother-centered residence and child-raising patterns but may not affect inheritance patterns.

Critical Thinking Questions

- Each student in the class should draw his or her kinship chart.
- The students should note their ethnicity at the top of the chart, choosing whatever label with which they feel comfortable.
- Then the students should draw a circle around the relatives who are "closest" to ego, including parents, grandparents, aunts, uncles, cousins—whoever fits in this category.
- How many students drew equal circles around relatives on both parent's sides? How many emphasized the mother's side? How many emphasized the father's side?
- Classify the charts by ethnicity. Do any ethnic patterns emerge in terms of the circled kin?
- From this nonrandom sample, what can be said about "American kinship"?

ties related to making a living. As the world becomes increasingly urbanized and industrialized, and if the gender division of labor and resource entitlements were to become more equal, then bilineal kinship might increase in distribution.

SHARING

A growing number of studies indicate that many cultures give priority to kinship that is not based on biologically defined birth, but through acts of sharing and support. These relationships may be informal or formally certified, as in legalized adoption. Ritually formalized kinship also fits in this category, including godparenthood (kinship based on ritual ties) and blood brotherhood (kinship based on sharing of "blood" or some other substance).

Food Sharing

Cultural anthropologists have devoted relatively little attention to studying food-based kinship, but examples are increasing in the literature. Among the Kaliai, as noted above, fathers are said to be related to their children by descent, while mothers are related to them through breastfeeding. Sharing-based kinship is common throughout much of Southeast Asia, New Guinea, and Australia (Carsten 1995). On an island of Malaysia, the process of developing sharing-based relatedness starts in the womb and continues throughout a person's life. The first food sharing is when the fetus is fed by the mother's blood. After birth, the infant is fed from its mother's breast. Breast milk is believed to derive from the mother's blood and thus "blood becomes milk." This tie is crucial. A child who is not breastfed will not "recognize" its mother. Breastfeeding is the basis of the incest rule:

> [K]in who have drunk milk from the breast of the same woman may not marry. . . . The salience of a prohibition on marriage between milk siblings is rendered greater by the fact that many children spend a considerable part of their childhood in houses other than their maternal ones. The frequency of formal and informal fostering arrangements . . . substantially increases the possibility that a child may drink the milk of a woman who is not its birth mother. . . . It is quite easy to imagine that a child who has been casually put on the breast of a neighbor or distant kinswoman might later marry her child. This ever-present threat looms large in the minds of villagers and runs through their discourse on incest. (227)

After the baby is weaned, its most important food is cooked rice. Sharing cooked rice, like breast milk, becomes another way the kinship ties are created and maintained, especially between mothers and children. Men are often away—on fishing trips, in coffee shops, or at the mosque—and so they are less likely to have these rice-sharing bonds.

Adoption and Fostering

Transferring children from their birth parent to the care of others through adoption and fostering is found in all cultures. Adoption offers a cultural solution to the natural unevenness in human reproduction. Common motivations for adopting a child include infertility and the desire to obtain a particular kind of child (often a son). Motivations for the birth parent to transfer the child to someone else's care include a premarital pregnancy in cultures that do not condone children being born outside a marriage relationship, having "too many" children as defined in that culture, or having "too many" of a particular gender of child. For example, among the Maasai, if a woman had several children, she might "give" one of hers to a friend, neighbor, or aged person who had no children or no one to care for them.

Fostering a child is sometimes similar to a formal adoption in terms of permanence and a developed sense of a close relationship. Or it may involve a temporary placement of a child with someone else for a specific purpose, with little development of a sense of kinship. Such "child transfers" (relocating a child's residence and primary care from one social unit to another) often fall midway between what Westerners would consider formal adoption and fostering. Given these several options for defining relations between adults and children, several questions arise for cultural anthropologists: How do different kinship systems deal with the issue of adoptive (or otherwise "transferred") offspring? Do adopted and fostered children have special problems constructing their personal identity and sense of self? Does this vary by culture? How do adopted offspring gain a sense of belonging if they are raised by people other than their birth parents? For the most part, these questions await in-depth research.

Legalized Adoption in the United States

Currently, about one of every ten couples in the United States is infertile, and many of these couples would like to have children. Some use fertility drugs, *in vitro* fertilization, or surrogate child-bearing. Many

An orphanage in Shanghai, China. Human rights activists have claimed that abuse was widespread in Chinese orphanages, especially of children with physical handicaps. Following this allegation, foreign media were invited to visit the Shanghai Children's Welfare Institute.

people, including those who have biologically recognized children, choose to adopt. Since the mid-1800s, adoption has been a legalized form of child transfer in the United States. It is "a procedure which establishes the relationship of parent and child between persons not so related by nature" (Leavy and Weinberg 1979, v, quoted in Modell 1994:2). Judith Modell, cultural anthropologist and adoptive parent, studied people's experiences of adoptees, birth parents, and adoptive parents. According to Modell, the biological relationship of kinship is so pervasive in the United States that the legal process of adoption attempts to construct the adoptive relationship to be as much like a biological one as possible. The adopted child is given a new birth certificate. After adoption, the birth parent ceases to have any relationship to the child. This pattern is called "closed adoption." A recent trend is toward "open adoption," in which adoptees and birth parents have access to information about each other's identity and have freedom to interact with one another. Of the twenty-eight adoptees Modell talked with, not all were interested in searching for their birthparents:

> A few said they were "mildly curious" about their birthparents while others had requested birth and medical records. Ten had established some kind of relationship with a birth family. . . . No one said they thought searching was bad. Those who did not want to find any more information were convinced that all adoptees had a "right to know." Four told me they would never consider searching. "I would just never go looking for her [birth mother] or my father. It just isn't something I consider important enough for me to do—in the first place, she could have passed away." One admitted that he had a "burning curiosity," but considered it would be "a selfish move on my part" to find out anything further. Another who said she had no "desire to go looking," added, "I wish I could see a photograph of my parents without meeting them." A fourth said, in an uncertain tone of voice, "Maybe I am just not curious enough." (144–145)

For many adoptees, a search for birth parents involves an attempt to discover "who I really am." It is a search for an identity that is believed to lie in genealogical roots. For others, such a search is backward-looking and not a path toward formulating one's identity. Given this diversity of views, it is not possible to formulate firm generalizations. The momentum of the movement for open adoption signifies many people's adherence to the biological model of selfhood and identity. Thus, in the United States, we could interpret the system of legal adoption as one that legalizes sharing-based kinship, but does not completely replace a sense of descent-based kinship for everyone involved. This statement also applies to many birth parents who seek to reconnect with the children they gave up for adoption.

The Adopted Daughter-in-Law in China

During his research in Taiwan, Arthur Wolf (1968, 1995) discovered that about one-third of the wives in the study population were *sim-pua,* or daughters-in-law raised from childhood in their marital family. This practice involves the "adoption" or "fostering" of a young girl from another family with the explicit intention of her becoming the wife of a son of the family when she is old enough. Wolf was fascinated by this practice and its frequency in northern Taiwan, which is inhabited by Hokkien-speaking people who moved there from southern China. He gathered data on marriage patterns in several villages over the course of many years of research. He reported that sim-pua marriage tends to be associated with poorer families, and it carries a certain "second-class" sense. In fact, it is termed "minor marriage," as opposed to a "major marriage" that is carried out with traditional arrangements between a bride and groom who have been raised separately. Marriage costs for the groom's side are much lower in a sim-pua marriage because the groom's parents give little to the bride's family in the form of brideprice. The girl who is adopted is often treated poorly. She is expected to work harder and consume less than the other children. Her relationship with her mother-in-law is one of submission. Given these factors, Wolf hypothesizes that one function of sim-pua marriage is to reduce the potential social friction caused by bringing in someone "from outside the family" as a son's wife. A sim-pua daughter-in-law has spent many years being socialized into a submissive role by the time she marries. Wolf also considered the potential effect of sim-pua marriage in reducing sexual attraction between husband and wife:

> The Chinese ideal of a distant and unemotional relationship between husband and wife recognizes the danger of a mother's jealousy. A man should never display any affection for his wife outside of the privacy of their bedroom, and as far as possible he

> should avoid even speaking to her except to give orders. Unfortunately, for the harmony of those families that choose the major form of marriage, this social device does not prevent the mother's resenting her daughter-in-law's role as a wife. A woman's son is too important in Chinese society for her to accept an intimacy from which she is excluded (Wolf 1968, reprinted in Suggs and Miracle 1993:223–224).

Here, Wolf is inspired by the **Westermarck hypothesis,** proposed in 1891 by Edward Westermarck, which states that early childhood association inhibits sexual attraction between those children raised together and can even lead to sexual aversion. Sim-pua marriages, if the Westermarck hypothesis is correct, would involve less sexual attraction between the partners because they were raised together. Wolf does not have data on sexual intercourse frequency or sexual satisfaction within marriage for major or minor marriages. Instead, he considers fertility rates and divorce rates in both types of marriage as indicators of reduced sexual attraction. The data on several thousand marriages indicate that fertility is consistently higher in major marriages than in minor marriages (A. Wolf 1995). In addition, divorce rates are higher in minor marriages than in major marriages. The Westermarck hypothesis thus seems at least indirectly supported. Critics of Wolf's argument point out that his evidence is just that—indirect. They say that other factors may be responsible for these differences, such as the more dominating role of the mother over her son in sim-pua marriages. These critics point to the substantial evidence worldwide of strong sexual desire between children raised together, including siblings. The argument remains unresolved, and one wonders what kind of data would be convincing.

Ritually Established Sharing Bonds

Godparenthood

Ritually defined "sponsorship" of children descended from other people is common throughout the Christian—especially Catholic—world from South America to Europe and the Philippines. Relationships between godparents and godchildren often involve strong emotional ties and financial flows from the former to the latter. In Arembepe, a village in Bahia state in northeastern Brazil, "Children asked their godparents for a blessing the first time they saw them each day. Godparents occasionally gave cookies, candy, and money, and larger presents on special occasions" (Kottak 1992:61). In wealthier, more urbanized contexts, godparents can provide major financial support, including costs of education. They may be expected to assume the role of "adoptive" parents in the event of death of the child's birth parents (Woodrick 1995: 223). In the village of Santa Catalina in the Oaxaca Valley of southern Mexico, godparenthood is both a sign of the sponsor's status and the means to increased status (Sault 1985). A request to be a sponsor is acknowledgment of a person's ability to care for the child. The prestige of being asked to be a sponsor reflects well on one's entire family. It also gives the godparent influence over the godchild. Because the godparent can call on the godchild for labor, being a godparent of many children increases power through the ability to amass a major labor force when needed. In Santa Catalina, the majority of sponsors are male-female couples, but a notable number of sponsors were women alone, while no male alone was a sponsor. This difference is related to the relatively important role and high status of women in the Mayan culture of the Oaxaca region.

MARRIAGE

The third major basis for forming close interpersonal relationships is through marriage or other forms of "marriage-like" relationships such as long-term cohabitation. This section presents anthropological material mainly on formal marriage (other domestic arrangements are discussed in Chapter 9).

Toward a Definition

Anthropologists recognize that some form of marriage exists in all cultures, with different form and functions. However, what constitutes a cross-culturally valid definition of marriage is open to debate. A standard definition from 1951 is now discredited: "Marriage is a union between a man and a woman such that children born to the woman are the recognized legitimate offspring of both parents" (Barnard and Good 1984:89). This definition says that the partners must be of different genders. It implies that a child born outside a marriage is not socially recognized as legitimate. Exceptions exist to both these features cross-culturally. Same-gender marriages are now legal in Denmark and Sweden. In the United States, same-gender marriages may be legalized in Hawaii in the future, and policy debates are ongoing about whether same-gender "domestic partners" are eligible for "spousal" employment benefits (see the Viewpoint box). Even the question of whether marriage always involves two people is salient, given ethnographic examples of ritual marriages between people and gods and people and trees. Marriage patterns among the matrilineal Nayars and the patrilineal Nambudiri brahmans of Kerala, in South India, have forced anthropologists to stretch their concept of what marriage is. The Nayars are well-known in anthropology for their high levels of female education, female autonomy, and complex marriage patterns (Fuller 1976; Mencher 1965). A young Nayar woman would be married to a Nayar man according to the proper ritual rules, and the marriage would be sexually consummated after the ceremony. From then on, the wife would wear a *tali,* gold wedding necklace. Complexity arises, however, because Nayars are of the kshatriya caste cluster (traditionally a warrior category). Nayar men, in the past, went away for many years, fighting battles in distant regions. The Nayars followed the residence rule of matrilocality (a married Nayar woman continued to live with her mother and her line of relatives including aunts and uncles, nieces and nephews). During the husband's absence, it was considered perfectly appropriate for a married Nayar woman to enter into "side marriages" called *sambandhan* relationships with other men. These relationships were often arranged by a woman's father or brothers. Sambandhan relationships could include Nambudiri brahman men.

The Nambudiri brahmans were the local priestly caste and also rich landowners. In contrast to their

VIEWPOINT

"I Always Cry at Weddings" by Jeff Weinstein

A married woman is her husband's property, and property is theft. There was no question about this twenty years ago, at least among the crowd I ran with. Years later, as property became identity, many of my friends, women and men, told me that they had misgivings about their stand, doubts centered around their children-to-be. And one or two admitted that they sought the "commitment" marriage signified, although they still hated the inequitable institution itself. Need I say that most of these men and women have gotten married, some married and divorced?

Me, I supported any and all of this from the sidelines: I was gay then, and gay now, and a faggot (a very p.c. term at the time) could afford to be ideologically pure. But on March 1, 1993 . . . we have the option, my long-suffering honey and I, to go to City Hall and register as domestic partners. Will we take it? Shall we pretend to tie some kind of knot?

Anyone who's read the papers knows that registered domestic partnership isn't marriage and doesn't confer the legal status, tax privileges, benefits, and general acclaim that marriage does. So is it ritual we want? John and I could have gotten "married" years ago, exchanging religious or secular vows, the way some lesbian and gay male couples have. In fact, I think my former dentist had a rabbi perform an ecumenical service in Central Park for her ceremony. That's fine. If I had attended the wedding, I would have cried: I always cry at weddings, any kind of wedding. But my partner and I mistrust the historical vestments of religion almost as much as we reject the deed-of-ownership certificate of marriage; this is one of the reasons we get along.

Will good things happen when the unmarriageable register at City Hall? If our partners die, we'll have a piece of paper to show we were family, so we won't get thrown out of our rent-stabilized apartments. We'll finally possess the inalienable right to visit our loved ones in those cheerful city hospitals and prisons; gay workers may also count on bereavement leave and unpaid family leave.

Source: The Village Voice 38:16, 1993.

The marriage of two gay men in the United States in 1996. So far, Hawaii is the only state in which gay marriage is legal.

neighboring Nayars, they have patrilineal kinship and they practiced **primogeniture,** whereby only the eldest son could inherit the family property. Another Nambudiri rule was that only the oldest son was allowed to marry a Nambudiri bride. Younger brothers' only option for marriage was through sambandhan relationships with Nayar women. They did not live with their Nayar wives, however, but maintained a visiting relationship with them. Any child born to a Nayar woman was said to be born from a Nayar man.

Thus, high parity (later-born) Nambudiri sons were excluded from contributing reproductively to their lineage. What happened to the "surplus" of marriageable Nambudiri girls? According to Hindu cultural principles, a key parental duty is to see to the proper marriage of daughters. Spinsterhood is not a respectable option. Nambudiris were the highest status group in the area, and it would not have been acceptable for them to marry anyone lower than they. These rules combine to create a serious bind: a Nambudiri girl must marry, she cannot marry beneath her status, and there are not enough first sons among the Nambudiris to go around. The solution was found in ritual marriage. Many Nambudiri girls were married to a tree believed to be a deity. A marriage ceremony, complete with the bride circling the "groom" seven times as in any Hindu marriage ceremony, was performed and she would then wear the marriage tali. This ritual effectively placed Nambudiri females into a position parallel to a Catholic nun who "marries" god and pledges herself to lifelong celibacy. Over time, these relationships between the matrilineal Nayars and the patrilineal Nambudiris have declined, mainly because of the decline of Nayar military service and legal changes made by the national government that restrict matrilineality.

In terms of the legitimacy of children, in many cultures, no distinction is made between legitimate or illegitimate children on the basis of whether they were born within a marriage. Many women in the Caribbean region, for example, do not marry until later in life. Before that, a woman has sequential male partners with whom she bears children. None of her children are considered more or less "legitimate" than any other.

Other definitions of marriage focus on rights over the spouse's sexuality. But not all forms of marriage involve sexual relations; for example, the practice of woman–woman marriage exists among the Nuer of the Sudan and some other African groups (Evans-Pritchard 1951:108–109). In this type of marriage, a woman with economic means provides a brideprice to obtain a "wife," goes through the marriage rituals with her, and brings her into the residential compound just as a man would who married a woman. This wife contributes her productive labor to the household. The two women do not have a sexual relationship. Instead, the in-married woman will have sexual relations with a man. Her children will belong to the compound into which she married, however. Thus, this arrangement provides the adult woman's labor and her children's labor to the household compound.

Given the range of practices that can come under the heading of marriage, some anthropologists have given up trying to find a working definition that will fit all cases. Others have suggested an open checklist of features, some of which may be satisfied in some contexts but not others, such as reproduction, sexual rights, raising children, or a ritual ceremony. One might accept the following as a working definition of **marriage:** a more or less stable union, usually between two people, and who are likely, but not necessarily, to be coresident, sexually involved with each other, and procreative with each other.

Selecting a Spouse

All cultures have preferences about whom one should and should not marry or with whom one should or should not have sexual intercourse. Sometimes these preferences are informal and implicit and other times formal and explicit.

Rules of Exclusion

Some sort of **incest taboo** is one of the most basic and universal rules of excluding certain people as marital or sexual partners. As noted in Chapter 4, one theory for the widespread existence of incest taboos is to ensure that people establish social relationships with people outside their immediate group, thus promoting the formation of larger groups and the evolution of culture itself (Arens 1996). Western genetic research suggests an alternate theory: that larger breeding pools help reduce the frequency of certain genetically transmitted conditions. Both theories are functional, in that they attribute the universal existence of incest taboos to their adaptive contribution, although in two different ways. No one has resolved the question of why incest taboos exist. Another area of debate concerns whether people have a natural tendency toward incestuous relationships that culture needs to make rules against, or whether closely related people are likely to be sexually unattracted to each other (the Westermarck hypothesis).

More fruitful research lies in the direction of comparative studies of the parameters of various cultures' incest rules, whom they apply to, and whether people adhere to them. The most basic and universal prohibition is against marriage or sexual intercourse between fathers and their children, and mothers and their children. In most cultures, brother–sister marriage has also been forbidden. The most well-known example of brother–sister marriage being allowed comes from Egypt at the time of the Roman Empire (Barnard and Good 1984:92). Census data from that era show that between 15 and 20 percent of marriages were between full brothers and sisters, not just within a few royal families, as is popularly believed. In other cultures, such as the Nuer of Sudan, the incest taboo extends to the entire extended lineage, which may include hundreds of people. The question of cousins is dealt with in highly contrasting ways cross-culturally: Notably, incest taboos do not universally rule out marriage or sexual intercourse with cousins.

In addition to incest taboos, many other rules of exclusion exist, such as prohibiting marriage with people of certain religions, races, or ethnic groups. Such exclusionary rules are often stated in the inverse—as rules of preference for marriage within a particular religion, race, or ethnic group.

Preference Rules

A variety of preference rules exist cross-culturally concerning whom one should marry. Rules of **endogamy** (or marriage within a particular group) stipulate that the spouse must be chosen from within a defined pool of people. In kin endogamy, certain relatives are preferred, often cousins. Two major forms of cousin marriage exist: between **parallel cousins** (children of either one's father's brother or one's mother's sister—the term "parallel" indicates that the gender of the linking siblings is the same) or between **cross cousins** (children of either one's father's sister or one's mother's brother—the term "cross" indicates the different genders of the linking siblings). Parallel-cousin marriage is favored by many Islamic groups, especially the subform called *patrilateral parallel-cousin marriage*, which indicates a tendency for cousin marriage in the direction of the father's line rather than the mother's. Hindus of southern India favor cross-cousin marriages, especially matrilateral cross-cousins (through the mother's line). But, while cousin marriage is the preferred form, it nonetheless constitutes a minority of all marriages in the region. A survey of 3,527 couples in the city of Chennai [formerly called Madras] in south India showed that three-fourths of all marriages involved unrelated people, while one-fourth were between first cross-cousins (or uncle–niece, which is considered the same relationship as cross-cousin) (Ramesh, Srikumari, and Sukumar 1989). Westerners who are unfamiliar with cousin marriage systems may find them objectionable on the basis of the potential genetic disabilities from "close inbreeding." A study of thousands of such marriages in South India, however, revealed only a very small difference in rates of certain "birth defects" as compared to cultures in which cousin marriage is not practiced (Sundar Rao 1983). This finding may exist because marriage pools are in fact quite diffuse, offering many options for "cousins," in contrast to kin endogamy in a close pool such as one village.

Endogamy may also be based on location. Village endogamy is a basis of arranging marriages throughout the eastern Mediterranean among both Christians and Muslims. Village endogamy is the preferred pattern among Muslims throughout India and among Hindus of southern India. Hindus of northern India, in contrast, forbid village endogamy and consider it a form of incest. Instead, they practice village **exogamy** ("marriage out"). For them, a preferred spouse should live in a far-off village or town. Thus, marriage distance is greater in the north than the south, and brides are far less likely to maintain regular contact with their natal kin in the north. Many songs and folktales of North Indian women convey sadness about being separated from their natal families, a theme that may not make much sense in a situation of village endogamy, where the bride's parents are likely to be close by.

Status considerations often shape spouse selection. The rule of **hypergyny** requires the groom to be of higher status than the bride; in other words, the bride "marries up." Hypergyny is a strong rule in northern India, especially among upper-status groups. It is also implicitly followed among many people in the United States, where females "at the top" have the hardest time finding an appropriate partner because there are so few options "above them." Women medical students are a prime population experiencing an increased marriage squeeze because of status hypergyny. The opposite is **hypogyny,** when the female "marries down." Status hypogyny is rare cross-culturally, as is age hypogyny, in which the groom is younger than the bride. Age hypogyny, though rare as a preferred pattern, is increasing in the United States because of the "marriage squeeze" on women who would otherwise prefer a husband of equal age or somewhat older. **Isogamy,** marriage between equals, is preferred in cultures where male and female roles and status tend to be more equal.

Physical features, such as ability, looks, and appearance are factors that may be explicitly or implicitly recognized, or both. Features such as facial beauty, skin color, hair texture and length, height, and weight are variously defined as important, depending on the culture. Invariably, however, "looks" tend to be more important for females. Marriage advertisements placed in newspapers in India (similar to the "personal ads" in Western newspapers) that describe an available bride often mention that her skin color is "fair" or "wheatish" and may note that she is slender and tall—although she should not be too tall, that is, taller than a potential groom. Height hypergyny (in which the groom is taller than the bride) is more common in male-dominated contexts. Height isogamous marriages are common in cultures where gender roles are relatively equal and where sexual dimorphism (differences in shape and size of the female body compared to the male body), is not marked, as in much of Southeast Asia.

Physical ability is another feature affecting marriage options. Research shows that cross-culturally, people with disabilities, particularly women, face constraints in marrying nondisabled partners (Sentumbwe 1995). Nayinda Sentumbwe, a blind researcher, conducted fieldwork in 1987 and 1989 with participants in education and rehabilitation programs for blind people in Uganda. He became aware that all of the married women in his study had blind husbands, while the same was not true for the men. In exploring why there is a high degree of group in-marriage among blind women, Sentumbwe considered Ugandan perceptions of blind people and gender

The Taj Mahal, located in Agra, north India, is a seventeenth century monument to love. It was built by the Mughal emperor Shah Jahan as a tomb for his wife, Mumtaz Mahal, who died in childbirth in 1631.

relations, especially the housewife role. Most Ugandans consider blindness to be the worst of all physical disabilities. Parents treat blind children differently, as described by a thirty-two-year-old blind woman: "My parents have just realized that a blind daughter can be useful, too, simply because I am educated; otherwise their understanding has been very discriminating where I am concerned. For example, I have no share when my sisters get land in which to do their gardening activities. Nothing is allocated to me, simply because I am blind" (161).

The term "spread" refers to the association of the loss of one function with decreased capacity in other physical functions. It accounts for exclusion of the blind from many activities that they can in fact accomplish, in particular, to people's perception of blind women's decreased competence as wives and mothers and their reduced desirability as spouses. Ugandan housewives have many roles: mother, hostess, housekeeper, homestead-keeper, provider of meals, and provider of home-grown food, among others:

> A woman's ability to fulfill these roles is always tested at times of celebration or crisis—occasions like weddings or funeral ceremonies, which prompt neighborhood or family gatherings. It is at such events that criticism of a woman's physical appearance and ability to perform tasks expected of a housewife is expressed. Such criticism is an evaluation of a man's choice of a wife. (164)

It is important for men to have "competent" wives, so they do not select blind women as partners. Instead, blind women are often chosen as men's lovers. The relationship between lovers is private and does not involve social competence in the woman or societal approval.

The importance of romantic love as a requirement for marriage is a matter of debate between sociobiologists and cultural constructionists (see Chapter 1). Sociobiologists argue that feelings of romantic love are universal among all humans because they play an adaptive role in uniting males and females in offspring care. Cultural anthropologists, in contrast, argue that romantic love is far from universal, that it is an unusual, even "aberrant" factor influencing spouse selection (Little 1966, quoted in Barnard and Good 1984:94). In support of a cultural constructionist position, cultural materialists have examined differences in male and female economic roles to explain cross-cultural variations in an emphasis on romantic love. They say that romantic love is more likely to be an important factor in relationships in cultures where men contribute more to subsistence, and where women are therefore economically dependent on men.

These debates have prompted cultural anthropologists to devote more research to how romantic love is defined and constructed cross-culturally and within different microcultures. For example, Dorothy Holland and Margaret Eisenhart (1990) conducted a study of young American women just entering college in 1979–1981 and again in 1987 after they had graduated and begun their adult lives. Their research sites were two southern colleges in the United States, one predominantly attended by White Euro-Americans and the other by African Americans. They found a contrast between the women of the two colleges. The White women were much more firmly committed to notions of romantic love than the Black women. This pattern matched differences in career goals and expectations of future earning ability. White women were less likely to have strong and independent career goals and more likely to expect to be economically dependent on their spouse. The Black women expressed self-dependence and stronger career goals. Holland and Eisenhart suggest that the ideology of romantic love "derails" many young White women from competing with men in the job market. The theme of romantic love provides young women with a model of the heroic male provider as the ideal, with her role being one of attracting him and providing the domestic context for their married life. Black women are socialized to be more economically autonomous, a tradition that stems from African traditions in which women earn and manage their own earnings.

Whatever the cause of romantic love, it is the norm for marriage in North America, South America, and Europe (Levine, Sato, and Verma 1995). Arranged marriages, not based initially on romantic love between the bride and groom, are formed instead as a link between the two families involved and considerations of what constitutes a "good match" between the families. Arranged marriages are common in many contemporary Middle Eastern, African, and Asian countries. Some theorists have claimed that arranged marriages are "traditional" while love marriages are "modern," and thus believe arranged marriages will disappear with modernity. Japan presents a case of a highly industrialized economy with a highly educated population in which arranged marriages constitute a substantial proportion of all marriages, about 25 to 30 percent (Applbaum 1995). In earlier times, marriage partners would be found through personal networks, perhaps relying on an intermediary who knows both families. Now, in large cities such as Tokyo and Osaka, professional matchmakers have become important sources for finding marriage partners. One registers, pays a fee, and fills out forms about family background. The most common desirable characteristics in a spouse are the family's reputation and social standing, the absence of undesirable traits such as a case of divorce or mental illness in the family, and the potential spouse's education, income, and occupation.

Marriage Gifts

Most marriages are accompanied by some form of gift-giving of goods or services between the partners, members of their families, or friends. As Lévi-Strauss said long ago, exchange can be considered an essential aspect of marriage. In many societies, wedding prestations are the major economic transactions in a person's lifetime (Barnard and Good 1984:114). No one has been able to calculate how much the total flow of marriage prestations and the total cost of weddings is, as a percent of a given economic system, but it is likely to be significant in most contemporary cultures.

The major forms of marital exchanges cross-culturally are dowry and brideprice (Goody and Tambiah 1973). Dowry involves the transfer of goods, and sometimes money, from the bride's side to the new conjugal unit for their use. Common throughout the northern Mediterranean, this "classic" form of dowry includes household goods such as furniture and cooking utensils and sometimes rights to a house. Dowry is the predominant form of marriage prestation in a broad region of Eurasia, from Western Europe through the northern Mediterranean and into China and India (Goody 1976). In northern India, what is called "dowry" is more appropriately termed "groomprice" since the goods and money pass not to the new couple but rather to the groom's family (Billig 1992). In China during the Mao era, marriage gifts of any type were viewed as a sign of women's oppression and made illegal. Now, marriage gifts are becoming more common with the recent increase in consumerism (Whyte 1991).

Brideprice, or the transfer of goods or money from the groom's side to the bride's parents, is more common in horticultural and pastoral cultures, while dowry is associated with intensive agricultural societies. In cultures where dowry and brideprice are given, recent decades have brought an inflation in the required amounts, making it difficult in some cases for young people to marry. **Bride-service,** less common than brideprice, is still practiced in some horticultural societies, especially in the Amazon. Bride-service involves the groom working for his father-in-law for a certain period of time before returning home with the bride. Bride-service is brideprice paid in labor rather than in goods. Many marriages involve prestations from both the bride's and groom's sides. For example, a typical pattern in the United States is for the groom's side to be responsible for the rehearsal dinner the night before the wedding, while the bride's side is responsible for everything else.

Weddings

Creating a marriage can be accomplished merely by the couple spending a night together or with an elaborate and costly wedding ceremony that takes place over several days. Weddings vary cross-culturally and intraculturally in terms of the accompanying feasts and festivities, which may involve special food and music, secular or religious ceremonies, variation in duration, and numerous costs. The degree of simplicity or elaboration of weddings can be explained to some extent by differences in production systems and a family's economic status within socially stratified contexts. In low-consumption, foraging societies, marriage receives little formal marking and little expenditure of effort, time, or money. Marjorie Shostak (1983) describes the simplicity of first marriages among the Ju/wasi foragers as studied in the 1970s:

> The marriage ceremony is quite modest, although negotiations and gift exchanges are typically begun long before the actual marriage takes place. A hut is built for the couple by members of both families, and is set apart from the rest of the village. As sunset approaches, friends bring the couple to the hut. The bride, head covered, is carried and laid down inside; the groom, walking, is led to the hut and sits beside

VOICES

Nisa's Third Marriage

Among the Ju/wasi during the 1970s, most women stayed in one marriage for a long time. Nisa, in contrast, had five. Here she describes her marriage to her third husband, who is named Tashay. Tashay had seen Nisa and wanted to marry her. Although he was a stranger to her, the arrangements were made. Her description of the marriage emphasizes her feelings of *kua,* which means awe, fear, or respect, and which is associated with the intense emotion of this ritual event.

The day of the wedding everyone was there. All of Tashay's friends were sitting around, laughing and laughing. His younger brother said, "Tashay, you're too old. Get out of the way so I can marry her. Give her to me." And his nephew said, "Uncle, you're already too old. Now let *me* marry her." They were all sitting around, talking like that. They all wanted me.

I went to my mother's hut and sat there. I was wearing lots of beads and my hair was completely covered and full with ornaments.

That night there was another dance. We danced, and some people fell asleep and others kept dancing. In the early morning, Tashay and his relatives went back to their camp; we went to our huts to sleep. When morning was late in the sky, they came back. They stayed around and then his parents said, "Because we are only staying a short while—tomorrow, let's start building the marriage hut."

The next day they started. There were lots of people there—Tashay's mother, my mother, and my aunt worked on the hut; everyone else sat around, talking. Late in the day, the young men went and brought Tashay to the finished hut. . . .

I was still at my mother's hut. I heard them tell two of my friends to go and bring me to the hut. I thought, "Oohh . . . I'll run away." When they came for me, they couldn't find me. They said, "Where did Nisa go? Did she run away? It's getting dark. Doesn't she know that things may bite and kill her?" My father said, "Go tell Nisa that if this is what she's going to do, I'll hit her and she won't run away again. What made her want to run away, anyway?"

I was already far off in the bush. They came looking for me. I heard them calling, "Nisa . . . Nisa. . . ." I sat down at the base of a tree. Then I heard [my friend] Nukha, "Nisa . . . Nisao . . . my friend . . . a hyena's out there . . . things will bite and kill you . . . come back . . . Nisa . . . Nisao."

When Nukha finally saw me, I started to run. She ran after me, chasing me, and finally caught me. She called out to others, "Hey! Nisa's here! Everyone come! Help me! Take Nisa, she's here!"

They came and brought me back. Then they laid me down inside the hut. I cried and cried. People told me, "A man is not something that kills you; he is someone who marries you, who becomes like your father or your older brother. He kills animals and gives you things to eat. . . . Why are you so afraid of your husband and what are you crying about?"

I listened and was quiet. Later, we went to sleep. Tashay lay down beside the opening of the hut, near the fire, and I lay down inside; he thought I might try and run away again. He covered himself with a blanket and slept.

While it was dark, I woke up. I sat up. I thought, "How am I going to jump over him? How can I get out and go to mother's hut to sleep beside her?" I looked at him sleeping. Then came other thoughts, other thoughts in the middle of the night, "Eh . . . this person has just married me . . ." and I lay down again. But I kept thinking, "Why did people give me this man in marriage? The older people say he is a good person, yet. . . ."

I lay there and didn't move. The rain came beating down. It fell steadily and kept falling. Finally, I slept. Much later dawn broke.

In the morning, Tashay got up and sat by the fire. I was so frightened I just lay there, waiting for him to leave. When he went to urinate, I went and sat down inside my mother's hut.

That day, all his relatives came to our new hut—his mother, his father, his brothers . . . everyone! They all came. They said, "Go tell Nisa she should come and her in-laws will put the marriage oil on her. Can you see her sitting over there? Why isn't she coming so we can put the oil on her in her new hut?"

I refused to go. They kept calling for me until finally, my older brother said, "Uhn, uhn. Nisa, if you act like this, I'll hit you. Now get up and go over there. Sit over there so they can put the oil on you."

I still refused and just sat there. My older brother grabbed a switch from a nearby tree and started coming toward me. I got up. I was afraid. I followed him to where the others were sitting. Tashay's mother rubbed the oil on me and my aunt rubbed it on Tashay.

Then they left and it was just Tashay and me.

Source: Reprinted by permission of the publisher from *Nisa: The Life and Times of a !Kung Woman* by Marjorie Shostack, Cambridge, Mass.: Harvard University Press, pp. 153–155. Copyright © by Marjorie Shostack.

> the door. Coals from the fires of both families are brought to start the new fire in front of the marriage hut. The friends stay with them, singing, playing, and joking. The couple stay apart from each other, maintaining a respectful reserve, and do not join in the festivities. After everyone leaves, they spend their first night together in the hut. The next morning, oil is ceremonially rubbed on both of them—each by the other's mother. (130)

In the case of remarriage, the process is even simpler, although key elements are maintained. Nisa's description of her third marriage mentions the importance of kin in building the hut for the newly married couple and the new mother-in-law's ritual blessing (see the Voices box on page 206). In contrast, in socially stratified societies, substantial microcultural variation exists in weddings across class and ethnic groups. In the United States, this variation includes "common law marriage," an unmarked form that is achieved simply through the passage of time; secular weddings held in a court with minimal ritual; church weddings with or without much ritual and with or without expensive meals; and the fabulously expensive weddings of the very wealthy, followed by a costly honeymoon for the newlyweds (see the Multiple Cultural Worlds box).

Forms of Marriage

How Many Spouses Should a Person Have?

Cultural anthropologists distinguish two basic forms of marriage based on the number of partners involved. Monogamy, the simplest, is marriage between two people—a male or female if the pair is heterosexual, and two people of the same gender in the case of a homosexual pair. Heterosexual monogamy is the most common form of marriage cross-culturally, and in many nations, it is the only form of marriage al-

MULTIPLE CULTURAL WORLDS

Weddings American Style

Among the wealthy in the United States, spending a lot on a daughter's wedding is an important status symbol and social networking event. The 1995 wedding of Lizzie Grubman was an example of the weddings of the rich:

> "What do you think this cost?" shouts a member of the wedding coordination team over the chants of the Village People.
>
> "One-fifty," someone offers. But that's too low for the wedding of Lizzie Grubman, a daughter of Allen Grubman, the most powerful lawyer in the music business—and Eric Gatoff, a young associate of Grubman's firm says. "Higher. Between three-fifty and five." About $12,000 went for the beluga caviar, served from a lasciviously dripping sturgeon ice sculpture. An unknowable portion went into the Dom Pérignon. One assumes that the Village People, those paleo-disco icons, came cheap, since Grubman worked on their first record deal. Now he represents Madonna, Bruce Springstein, Elton John—and Martha Stewart, too, who is among tonight's 420 guests at the Pierre Hotel. . . . So what father wouldn't go all out for his little girl's wedding? "Elizabeth saw the room and said, 'Daddy, can we have it here?'" recalls Grubman. "I said, 'If you want it at the Pierre, you'll have it at the Pierre.'" She probably also wanted the 10,000 white roses, the ceiling covered with wild smilax and dendrobium orchids, even the custom-painted dance floor (*The New York Times Magazine*, November 19, 1995:110–113).

At the other end of the spectrum in the United States is the quick and simple option of drive-in marriages available in Las Vegas or a somewhat more formal affair at the local shopping mall. At a chapel installed in a mall in Le Sueur, Minnesota, one can arrange for a wedding by a pastor that is "almost like a church wedding" (*People* 2(9), 1994:88–89). The total cost of $395 includes an hour of planning from the chapel's consultant, a half hour in the chapel for vows, recorded music of the couple's choice, a garter for the bride, an 8" × 10" photograph of the event, two wine glasses, and a bottle of inexpensive champagne. For an additional fee, one can arrange for a cake, a horse and carriage outside the mall, a celebrity-look-alike singer, and fifteen extra prints of the wedding picture.

lowed by law. **Polygamy** refers to a marriage with multiple spouses, a pattern that is allowed by the majority of the world's cultures, even though the majority of people within such cultures may not practice plural marriage (Murdock 1965:24). Two forms of polygamous marriage exist. The predominant pattern is polygyny, marriage of one husband with more than one wife. Within cultures that allow polygyny, the majority of unions nevertheless are monogamous. **Polyandry,** or marriage between one woman and more than one man, is rare. However, it has been practiced among groups as diverse as the Kaingang of the Amazon, the Todas of southern India, and the Chukchee of Siberia. One region in which polyandry occurs over a large area includes Tibet, the high Himalayas of India and Nepal.

Given the cultural variation in the practice of polygyny, anthropologists have long been inspired to ask why it exists in some cultures and not in others (White and Burton 1988). Evolutionary theorists suggested that polygyny constituted a middle stage. Engels's three stages, for example, went from "group marriage" (in which everyone was supposedly married to everyone else, a hypothetical situation unknown ethnographically for the past or the present), polygyny, and then monogamy. Sociobiologists say that polygyny contributes to males' reproductive success by allowing them to maximize the spread of their genes in future generations. Neither the evolutionary nor sociobiological models offer insight into the cross-cultural variation in the distribution of polygyny. Economic theories have been proposed. One prominent economic hypothesis states that polygyny will be more likely in contexts where women's contribution to the economy is more important. Political and demographic factors have also been examined, especially the role of warfare in reducing the ratio of males to females, and the taking of female captives in warfare. Considering several of these theories in addition to ones that take into account ecology (does the environment favor expansion in land-holdings and other resources?), Douglas White and Michael Burton analyzed data for 142 societies. Strong support for a set of interrelated views emerges:

- Polygyny is part of an expansionist economic strategy favored in homogeneous and high-quality environments.
- Polygyny is associated with warfare for plunder and/or female captives.
- Polygyny is associated with the presence of **fraternal interest groups** (strongly bonded groups linked through ties between brothers).
- Polygyny is constrained in the context of plow agriculture or by high dependence on fishing.

Support was also found for the hypothesis about the effect of female contribution to subsistence, but not at such a strong level as for the above factors.

Similarly, theories accounting for the presence of polyandry focus heavily on economics, especially on the importance of male economic roles and relatively limited female economic roles. Melvyn Goldstein's (1987) analysis portrays the polyandrous household economy as benefiting from the "diversified portfolio" of having several contributing males. The domestic dynamics of this form of marriage are discussed in the following chapter.

Where to Live?

Residence rules often match the prevailing "direction" of descent rules (refer back to Figure 8.3). Thus, in most patrilineal societies, marital residence is patrilocal (with or near the male's kin). In most matrilineal societies, it is matrilocal (with or near the woman's kin) or **avunculocal** (with or near the wife's brother's household). Common in Western industrialized society is the practice of neolocality (in which the couple typically moves to a new and different location). These residence patterns have political, economic, and social implications. The combination of matrilineal descent and matrilocal residence, for example, is often found among groups that engage in long-distance warfare (Divale 1974). Strong female household structures maintain the domestic scene while the men are absent on military campaigns, as among the Iroquois of upstate New York and the Nayar of southern India (described earlier in this chapter). Patrilineal descent and patrilocal residence promote the development of cohesive male-focused lineages that are associated with frequent local warfare. In this case, local defense requires the presence of a force of fighting men on the home front.

Change in Marriage

Marriage continues to be a major basis of forming kinship bonds cross-culturally. While the institution of marriage in general remains prominent, many of its specific details are changing. Almost everywhere, the

A newly married husband and wife and their relatives in front of the church in Seoul, Republic of Korea.

age at first marriage is rising. This change is related to increased emphasis on completing a certain number of years of education before marriage and rising aspirations about the potential spouse's economic status before contemplating marriage. Marriages between people of different nations and ethnicity are increasing, caused partly by increased rates of international migration (Chapter 16). Migrants take with them many of their marriage and family practices. They also adapt to rules and practices in their area of destination. Pluralistic practices evolve, such as conducting two marriage ceremonies—one based on the "original" culture and the other conforming to norms in the place of destination.

Style changes in weddings abound. Globalization of Western-style "white weddings" promotes the adoption of many features that are familiar in the West: a white wedding gown for the bride, a many-layered wedding cake, and certain kinds of floral arrangements. What the bride and groom wear is an expression of both the bride's and groom's personal identity and also the cultural identity of their family and larger social group. Clothing choice reflects adherence to "traditional" values, or may reject those in favor of more "modern" values. Euro-American trends are prominent worldwide. Throughout much of East and Southeast Asia, advertisements and upscale stores display the Western-style white wedding gown (but not so much in India, where white clothing for women signifies widowhood and is inauspicious). On the other hand, some resurgence of local "folk" styles is occurring in some contexts, such as in Morocco, where there is a trend for "modern" brides to wear a Berber costume (long robes and jewelry characteristic of the rural, mountain people) at one stage of the wedding ceremony.

SUMMARY

The study of kinship systems was the central focus of early anthropology. This phase of research produced voluminous amounts of data on the formal aspects of kinship systems, especially kinship terminology. On the basis of these data, anthropologists were able to classify kinship systems into several major types. However, the actual dynamics of kinship behavior were neglected. For example, we knew relatively little about how an uncle and a niece related to each other on an every day basis in a particular society, or how uncles and nieces related to each other cross-culturally.

The three major bases for forming kinship attachments are descent, sharing, and marriage. Cultural anthropologists have done the most research on the first and last of these, but increasing attention is being paid to sharing-based systems.

Key differences in descent systems have been shown to exist between unilineal systems, which are predominant numerically, and bilineal systems. Within unilineal systems, patrilineal systems differ from matrilineal systems in terms of property division, residence rules, and their implications for the status of males and females. Attention to changing kinship patterns indicates that matrilineal kinship systems are declining in the face of Western influences, dating from the time of European colonial expansion in the 1500s. Some form of child transfers, from one primary caretaker to another, is probably a cross-cultural universal. In some cultures, such as in the United States, legalized options for child transfers through adoption are common and even allow for the transfer of children from one nation to another. Marriage continues to be an important basis of kinship formation, even though it often results in divorce in many contexts. Marriage preferences and arrangements reflect other aspects of the culture, such as the relative importance of males or females in the economy.

CRITICAL THINKING QUESTIONS

1. How much time (in hours, roughly) of your average week is involved in "kinship work"? What about during a key holiday period? What are the major activities involved during "normal" times and holiday times? Compare your self-rating with that of other students in the class. What accounts for some of the similarities and differences?
2. Do you know what the predominant inheritance patterns are in your family? If there is more than one child in the family, how is inheritance decided?
3. If you were to get married and have a wedding (rather than eloping in the dead of the night), how would you and your (potential) spouse work out paying for the wedding? Why?

KEY CONCEPTS

ambilineal descent, p. 195
avunculocality, p. 208
bilineal descent, p. 190
bilocality, p. 195
bride-service, p. 205
cross cousin, p. 202
descent, p. 186
double descent, p. 195
endogamy, p. 202
exogamy, p.203
extended family, p. 189
fraternal interest group, p. 208
genealogy, p. 187
generalized exchange system, p. 186
hypergyny, p. 203
hypogyny, p. 203
incest taboo, p. 202
isogamy, p. 203
kinsip diagram, p. 187
kinship system, p. 184
marriage, p. 201
matrifocality, p. 196
matrilineal descent, p. 186
matrilocality, p. 193
neolocality, p. 195
parallel cousin, p. 202
patrilineal descent, p. 186
patrilocality, p. 192
polyandry, p. 208
polygamy, p. 208
polygyny, p. 184
primogeniture, p. 201
restricted exchange system, p. 186
teknonymy, p. 193
unilineal descent, p. 190
virilocal, p. 193
Westermarck hypothesis, p. 199

SUGGESTED READINGS

John Borneman, *Belonging in the Two Berlins: Kin, State and Nation.* This book considers two levels of analysis: people's changing perceptions of the family and the government's policies related to the family. New York: Cambridge University Press, 1992.

Laurel Kendall, *Getting Married in Korea: Of Gender, Morality and Modernity.* Berkeley: University of California, 1996. The ethnographic study examines preferences about desirable spouses, matchmaking, marriage ceremonies and their financing, and the effect of women's changing work roles on their marital aspirations.

Nancy Tapper, *Bartered Brides: Politics, Gender and Marriage in an Afghan Tribal Society.* New York: Cambridge University Press, 1991. Based on fieldwork before the Soviet invasion, this study examines marriage among the Maduzai, a tribal society of Turkistan. The book looks at how marriage relates to productive and reproductive aspects of society and the role it plays in managing political conflict and competition.

Margaret Trawick. *Notes on Love in a Tamil Family.* Berkeley: University of California Press, 1992. This reflexive ethnography takes a close look at the daily dynamics of kinship in one Tamil (South Indian) family. Special attention is given to sibling relationships, the role of older people, children's lives, and the way love and affection are played out in a particularly Tamil way.

Michael Young and Peter Willmott. *Family and Kinship in East London.* New York: Penguin Books, 1979. This classic study of kinship relationships among the working class of "Bethnal Green" gives particular attention to the importance of married women's continued close relationships with their mothers as maintained through residential proximity and visiting.

CHAPTER 9

Domestic Groups

CHAPTER OUTLINE

THE HOUSEHOLD
- Household Forms
- Household Headship
  - *Critical Thinking:* Is Father-in-the-Household Best?

THE HOUSEHOLD AS AN ECONOMIC UNIT
- The Gender Division of Labor in Two Household Types
- Family Businesses
  - *Multiple Cultural Worlds:* Succession Problems in the Japanese Business Elite
- Remittances

INTRAHOUSEHOLD DYNAMICS
- Spouse/Partner Relationships
  - *Multiple Cultural Worlds:* "Love Hotels in Japan"
- Sibling Relationships
- Domestic Violence

DIVORCE, DEATH, AND REMARRIAGE
- Kinship Systems and Divorce
  - *Current Event:* Princess Diana's Divorce Settlement
- Gender and Divorce
- Widow(er)hood
- Remarriage

KIN NETWORKS BEYOND THE HOUSEHOLD
- Marital Roles and Social Networks
  - *Multiple Cultural Worlds:* The Importance of a Woman's Natal Kin in Working-Class London
- Networks and Poverty

SOCIAL CHANGE AND DOMESTIC LIFE
- International Forces of Change
- Changing Patterns of Domestic Life in the United States

SUMMARY

KEY CONCEPTS

CRITICAL THINKING QUESTIONS

SUGGESTED READINGS

◀ A Bedu household in Egypt's South Sinai region.

In casual conversation, North Americans might use the words "family" and "household" interchangeably to refer to people who live together. Social scientists have proposed a distinction between the two terms, both of which may refer to some sort of "domestic group," or people who live together. A **family** includes people who consider themselves related through kinship (as described in Chapter 8—descent, marriage, or sharing). In North American English, the term "family" includes both "close" or "immediate" relatives and more "distant" relatives. One may live with and see some members of one's family every day, but others only once a year on a major holiday, or less. People who are considered close family relatives may be scattered in several different residences, including grandparents, aunts, uncles, and cousins; children of divorced parents, who live with one parent and visit the other; and children of divorced parents, who may live with different parents. The notion of the family as a clearly defined unit with firm boundaries thus often misrepresents the fluidity of this category (Lloyd 1995).

In contrast, the term **household** refers to people who may or may not be related by kinship, and who share living space including perhaps a kitchen and certain budgetary items such as food and rent. Most households around the world consist of family members who are related through kinship. An example of a non-kin household is a group of friends who live in the same apartment. A single person living alone is also a household.

Typical Yanomami household: husband, wife, child, anthropologist

This chapter discusses anthropological findings about a variety of domestic groupings, including large extended households and the functioning of family groups as business enterprise. It also considers the content of the relationships of various family or household members and factors that lead to the break-up of domestic groups. Consideration of wider social ties that connect the family or household with larger groups is discussed in Chapter 10.

THE HOUSEHOLD

Household Forms

Ethnologists of household organization have categorized household forms into several groups according to how many married adults are involved. Single-person households comprise only one member, living alone. A single-parent household comprises an adult with offspring. The nuclear household (which many people call the **nuclear family**) contains one adult couple (married or "partners"), with or without children. Complex households include a variety of household forms based on the presence of more than two married adults. Polygynous (multiple wives) and polyandrous (multiple husbands) households are one form of complex household in which one spouse has multiple partners. They may all live together in one residence or, as is the case in many African polygynous households, each wife has a separate residential unit within the overall household compound. Extended households contain more than one adult married couple. These couples may be related through the father–son line (making a patrilineal extended household such as the Lims of Taiwan who were mentioned in Chapter 8), the mother–daughter line (a matrilineal extended household), or through sisters or brothers (called a collateral extended household).

The precise cross-cultural distribution of these various types is not known. However, some broad generalizations can be offered. First, nuclear household units are found universally, either as freestanding units or as the basic unit of more complex forms (Murdock 1965:2). But the nuclear household is the exclusive household type in a minority of cultures.

A cross-cultural analysis of nearly two hundred cultures found that the nuclear household as the only form was found in one-fourth of the total. Another quarter allowed polygamous marriages. One-half of the cultures were characterized by the presence of extended households. The distribution of nuclear versus complex household forms roughly corresponds with modes of production (refer back to Figure 8.3 on page 191). The nuclear form is most characteristic of economies at the two extremes of the continuum: in foraging groups and in industrialized societies. As noted in Chapter 8, the greater prevalence of nuclear households in these two modes of production reflects the need for spatial mobility and flexibility in making a living. Polygynous or polyandrous households and extended households constitute a substantial proportion of households in horticultural, pastoral, and preindustrial agricultural economies. Throughout Asia—China, Japan, India—in much of Africa, and among Native North Americans, some form of complex or extended households are the ideal and are found in substantial numbers.

In India, where extended households are the preferred form, the household may contain fifty or more members. The existence of extended households is correlated with settled agriculture and owning property. Property provides the material base to support many people. Having large land holdings requires a large labor force to work the land. In northern India, more households own property, compared to southern and eastern India where rates of landlessness are higher. In addition to property differences, the unbalanced sex ratio in the North means there are more sons available to bring in wives and establish patrilineal extended households (see Chapter 5). Logically, then, patrilineal extended households are more common in the northern part of the country (Kolenda 1968). (Recall, however, the existence of the relatively uncommon pattern in India of matrilineal extended households, mainly in the southern state of Kerala.)

Some anthropologists and sociologists argue that the frequency of extended households worldwide will decline with industrialization and urbanization, which are considered key factors of modernity. This argument is based on an assumed European model of reduced numbers of extended farming households and increased numbers of nuclear households. Taking the nuclear household as a key marker of modernity, though, has its problems. First, historical evidence indicates that nuclear households characterized preindustrial, premodern northwestern Europe (Goody 1996). So, the claimed transformation from extended households to nuclear households as modernity proceeded is not entirely correct, although it may have occurred in some contexts. Second, in terms of cross-cultural applicability of the link between modernity and nuclear households, Asian data do not fit the model. For example, in India, urban areas have a higher percentage of extended households than do rural areas, a fact that contradicts the equation of urbanization and modernity and nuclear household form (Freed and Freed 1969). Further, data from India on literacy rates, often taken as an indicator of modernity and exposure to change, again show contradictory findings. A study of three villages conducted in West Bengal state of eastern India, found that extended household heads are more likely to be literate than nuclear household heads (Dasgupta, Weatherbie, and Mukhopadhyay 1993).

Moving from India to Japan, we again find that the extended household structure has endured within the context of an industrial and urban economy. The *ie*, or "stem household," has a long history in Japan (Skinner 1993) and is still important (Bachnik 1983). A variant of an extended household, a **stem household** contains two (and only two) married couples related through the males. Thus, if more than one son is born, only one will remain in the household, bringing in his wife, who then is expected to perform the important role of caretaker for the husband's parents as they age. In Japan and in contemporary China, this patrilineal stem household is still a widely preferred form (Bachnik 1983).

These examples of the endurance of extended household formation in certain Asian contexts relate to the discussion, later in this chapter, of family businesses. It make sense that extended households have a greater chance of survival when they function as a "mini-corporation," with shared economic interests and a loyal set of managers and workers linked by kinship.

Household Headship

Defining Headship

One consideration in studying household formation is to look at who is the "head," or the primary person (or people) in charge of supporting the household financially and making decisions. Yet cultural anthropologists realize that the very concept of **household head** may be an ethnocentric one, reflecting a Euro-

American pattern of one "head" who makes most of the money, controls most of the decision making, and was traditionally a man. European colonialism contributed to spreading the concept of the male head of household around the world. It exported to many cultures its male-biased legal system that vests household authority in the father.

The model of one head (probably male) has influenced the way official statistics are gathered and reported worldwide. The result is that if a household has a coresident male and female, there will be an automatic tendency to report the household as "male-headed," regardless of the actual internal dynamics. We do not have information on who might actually be the household head in all cultures. Colonial influences on local systems have been a powerful determinant in masculinizing the way households are conceived and formalizing male rights to a greater degree than in the past. In Brazil, the official definition of the Brazilian Office of Geography and Statistics considers only a husband to be head of the household, regardless of his contribution to the household budget and the legal situation of the couple: "[S]ingle, separated or widowed women who house and feed their children, grandchildren and elderly or handicapped parents are deprived of the title of head of the family. If they have a partner with them on the day when the census official arrives, he is considered to be the head of the family, whether or not he is the father of any of the children, contributes to the family income, or has been living there for years or only a few months" (de Athayde Figueiredo and Prado 1989:41). A study conducted in the Philippines also indicates how misleading official statistics may be. According to official reports, 90 percent of households in the Philippines are headed by males (Illo 1985). Anthropological research shows that in everyday life, women play a prominent role in income generation and budgetary control, and both male and female domestic partners tend to participate jointly in decision making. In the Philippines, coheadship would be a more appropriate label for many households.

Matrifocal or Woman-Headed Households: Causal Factors

Many early anthropologists were also male-biased in their assessment of household headship. They overlooked household headship patterns that did not conform to their Eurocentric view of male headship. Beginning with the work of Nancie González, awareness of the prevalence and functioning of woman-headed households has increased. González was one of the first anthropologists to define and study matrifocality, a domestic pattern in which a female (or females) is the central, stable figure around whom other members cluster (1970:233). In matrifocal households, the mother is likely to be the primary, or only, income provider. The concept of matrifocality does not exclude the possibility that men may be part of the household. That is, a matrifocal household is under the control of a woman head who may or may not have a (male) partner.

There has been much public discussion in the United States recently about partnerless women as household heads. Concern has arisen because the number of such households is increasing, and they are more likely to be poorer than households containing a married couple. What causes the formation of partnerless woman-headed households? A woman-headed household can come about if a partner existed at one time, but for some reason—such as separation, divorce, or death—is no longer part of the household, or a partner exists but is not coresident because of long-term outmigration, imprisonment, or some other form of separate residence. (Most thinking about woman-headed households assumes a heterosexual relationship and thus does not account for woman-headed households formed by a single woman with children either adopted or conceived through artificial insemination, with or without a visiting woman partner.) Three theories are often proposed to account for the absence of a male spouse or partner.

- *Slavery:* The high frequency of woman-headed households among African Americans in the Western hemisphere is often said to be the heritage of slavery, which intentionally broke up conjugal ties. This theory has several problems. First, if slavery were the cause of woman-headed households, one would predict that all peoples who experienced slavery would have this household form. In Jamaica, which is populated mainly by descendants of African slaves, percentages of woman-headed households vary between rural and urban areas (Miller and Stone 1983). Yet both urban and rural people have the same heritage. In the United States, no generic "Black household" exists, just as there is no generic "White household:" "Black Americans count for more than 10 million households, ranging from young adults in condominiums to suburban couples with two children and a swimming pool" (Hacker 1992:67). Second, historically in the United States, homes with two coresiding parents were the norm among Black Americans following the Civil War through the mid-twentieth century. This makes it difficult to describe woman-headed households today as a "legacy" of slavery. It is true that the slave system denied legal standing to adult pairings since owners did not want their slaves committed to lifetime relationships. Slaves were subject to sale, and wives and husbands, parents and children, were separated. While such circumstances would seem to have led to a "break-up" of a conjugal [married] household tradition, it is now clear that the slaves themselves never accepted the arrangements imposed by the owners: "Once freed, blacks sought the durable unions they had been denied" (69). Third, in the United States, percentages of woman-headed households have increased in roughly the same proportion among Blacks and Whites. These parallels indicate that similar factors may underlie the changes for both populations. Last, the distribution of woman-headed households throughout the world is more widespread than the distribution of slavery. So, other factors must be involved in promoting the formation of this pattern.

- *Poverty:* Woman-headed households are said to be adaptations to poverty, because in many societies, the poor have a higher frequency of woman-headed households. If so, it is only one of many possible adaptations since not all low-income populations worldwide are characterized by high rates of woman-headed households. Within just the United States, significant ethnic differences exist: "Low-income Chinese, Japanese, and other Asiatic peoples generally have low frequencies of single-parent households, and many Mexican-American communities have a strong predominance of dual-parent families even though experiencing relatively low incomes and considerable unemployment" (Pelto et al. 1982:40). As an explanatory factor, poverty needs to be considered along with attention to male and female income-earning capabilities, other resources available, and other support systems.

In the Caribbean region and throughout Latin America, the association between poverty and woman-headed households is strong. But beneath this seemingly negative association, some positive findings appear. In the Caribbean region, about one-third of all households are woman-headed, and most of the women have never been married (Massiah 1983). Instead, they have "visiting unions" (involving a steady sexual relationship, but the maintenance of separate residences). Many women who were interviewed as part of a study conducted in several of the islands commented that they sometimes expect and hope for financial support from their male partner or "baby father." Numerous others emphasized the value they place on freedom from a husband or permanent partner. One woman said, "Being single fits in with my independent thinking" (41). Another commented on her visiting union: "I like freedom, so I'm keeping it like it is" (41). In much of African-Caribbean culture, economic conditions dictate that men are not dependable sources of financial support. Women in low-income groups in the Caribbean and throughout much of Latin America have an advantage over males in earning money. Rural women earn income, for example, from gardening and marketing their produce. Urban women work in service occupations, small businesses, domestic service, and light industry. Cities offer more opportunities for such salaried employment than rural areas, and thus they attract greater numbers of female migrants. When men do get

Members of a matrifocal household in rural Jamaica: two sisters and their children.

In urban areas of the Caribbean, employment options are more limited for men than for women among the low-income class. Women are more likely to find regular employment as domestic workers.

jobs, they are likely to be irregular or seasonal. On top of limited employment options, African-Caribbean men tend to withhold portions of their earnings for personal expenditures (Chant 1985). An earning male who contributes to household finances can be a plus for the household.

The differences in male-female employment opportunities affect women's preferences concerning location and household structure. In El Salvador, "a woman without a stable partner, regardless of her legal or religious marital status . . . generally preferred city to rural life; married women with working spouses like rural life (Nieves 1979:139). In addition to income generation, women have an advantage over men in mobilizing supplementary household support from kin and friends. Thus, women in these contexts are less dependent on men's income than in places where they do not have access to such jobs and resources. In fact, having a nonearning male around the house who consumes and does not contribute constitutes a net economic loss. Thus, a woman-headed household can be viewed as a positive adaptation to economic and social circumstances (see the Critical Thinking box).

- *Unbalanced sex ratio:* Woman-headed households are said to occur in contexts of high male out-migration or in other demographic situations causing a shortage of males. The sheer availability of partners may put constraints on marriage. In Spanish Galicia, the local economy, inheritance rules, and household formation are related (Kelley 1991). This coastal region has a high percentage of households headed by unmarried women. In the village of Ezaro, for example, about one-fourth of all baptisms were of illegitimate children in the latter half of the nineteenth century. The proportion has declined in the

CRITICAL THINKING

Is Father-in-the-Household Best?

Much Western popular thought places the nuclear family, comprising a coresident adult heterosexual couple and children, as "the best" type, and as "natural." Other forms, especially woman-headed households, are seen as less desirable. Woman-headed households are often viewed as "broken" versions of the nuclear household, and are said to be less adequate structures within which to raise children. Putting the "father" back into the "American" household is an important policy goal in the United States. Given the preceding discussion, what can be said about the household debate in the United States?

Critical Thinking Questions

- Is "putting the father back in the household" going to accomplish the goal of improved lives for children?
- What if there is more than one father for the children of one mother?
- What if the father has no job?
- What if the household has a coresident adult couple, but they are both males or both females?

twentieth century, but the Galician region still stands out from the rest of Spain in this respect. In Ezaro, households headed by unmarried mothers constitute over 10 percent of the total. The general Mediterranean kinship system puts high value on marriage and male honor through control of the sexuality of female family members. Yet little or no stigma is attached to unwed motherhood in Galicia. Women household heads often gain honored positions in their villages.

What accounts for this system? The answer lies in Galicia's high rates of male emigration. The scarcity of males promotes flexible attitudes toward unwed motherhood and other adaptive features not found elsewhere in the Mediterranean region. The women have important roles in production and property relations. In Ezaro, women are in charge of agricultural work. They inherit land and gain prestige and power from owning and managing agricultural land. Women's agricultural work is the basis of their reputation in the community: "Women's work is considered so critical to the prestige of the household in Ezaro that success at work is the single most important factor in the community's evaluation of a woman's character (and in her own self-evaluation). The good woman in Ezaro is the hardworking woman" (572). Her work is more important in this respect than her marital status.

Inheritance practices reflect the importance of women's agricultural work. The goal is to ensure continuity of the *casa,* the house, which includes both the physical structure and its members. Parents usually award one of their children with a *millora,* a larger share of the inheritance, making that child the principal heir. The rest is divided equally among siblings. Daughters are often chosen to receive the millora, and thus a single woman can become head of an estate. Her children ensure that the estate has continuity. In contrast, a man cannot become a household head and gain social status without being married.

The preceding theories about why woman-headed households exist can be labeled "compensatory theories." They suggest that a woman-headed household emerges as a default system when "something is wrong" or men are unavailable as spouses. This bias is based on the assumption that the heterosexual nuclear household is the "normal" pattern that occurs when everything is "okay." A cultural materialist view would say that a variety of household forms are expectable, depending on such factors as men's and women's economic roles, especially access to work, wages, and the distribution of productive resources such as property.

THE HOUSEHOLD AS AN ECONOMIC UNIT

Households can be examined from a variety of perspectives: as economic units, political units, and social groups. This section discusses the economic workings of households (power issues and social relations are discussed later). The focus is on what happens inside the household: the household gender division of labor, households as businesses, and the financial impact of remittances (money that is sent) from nonresident members.

The Gender Division of Labor in Two Household Types

The "Classic" Nuclear Household

The classic Euro-American model of the nuclear household involves a division of labor in which only one spouse (typically the male) works in the wage economy and the other (typically the female) does unpaid work in the domestic domain, including child care. This classic pattern is common in North America and Western Europe. An anthropological study of the classic nuclear household in South Wales, England, addressed women's and men's perceptions of their contributions and value (Murcott 1993 [1983]). In the classic nuclear household, the husband works outside the home for wages while the wife remains in the home doing work that is unremunerated, including bearing and raising children, preparing meals, and cleaning. The Welsh wives defined their domestic responsibility mainly in terms of their importance in providing "home cooking." Home cooking means preparation of a "cooked meal" of meat, potatoes, vegetables, and gravy: "[A] proper meal is a cooked dinner. This is one which women feel is necessary to their family's health, welfare, and, indeed, happiness. It is a meal to come home to, a meal which should figure two, three or four times in the week and especially on Sundays" (78). In contrast, the responsible husband goes out to work. At the end of his work day, he comes home for dinner. The responsible wife has prepared a cooked meal for him. As one woman commented: "When my husband comes home ... there's nothing more he likes I think than coming in the door and smelling a nice meal cooking. I think it's awful when someone doesn't make the effort.... I think well if I was a man I'd think I'd get really fed up if my wife never bothered" (79). Cooking a proper meal is a more important task for a married woman than for a single person. People who live alone tend to eat more casually, snacking or eating chips (fried potatoes). Cultural evaluations of the "good wife" or the "good husband" tend to fit with the prevailing economy, as the wage job market is the world primarily of men.

The Polyandrous Household

How is the gender division of labor organized in households with multiple spouses? As noted in Chapter 8, polyandrous households are rare cross-culturally, but relatively common in some areas of Asia, especially in the Himalayan region. Among Tibetan peoples, fraternal polyandry, in which one wife has several husbands who are related as brothers, is the ideal form of marriage (Goldstein 1987). Research among Tibetan people who live in an area of Nepal near the border with Tibet reveals the following:

> The mechanics of fraternal polyandry are simple. Two, three, four or more brothers jointly take a wife, who leaves her home to come and live with them. Traditionally, marriage was arranged by parents, with children, particularly females, having little or no say. This is changing somewhat nowadays, but it is still unusual for children to marry without their parents' consent. Marriage ceremonies vary by income and region and range from all the brothers sitting together as grooms to only the eldest one formally doing so. The age of the brothers plays an important role in determining this: very young brothers almost never participate in actual marriage ceremonies, although they typically join the marriage when they reach their midteens.
>
> The eldest brother is usually dominant in terms of authority, that is, in managing the household, but all the brothers share the work and participate as sexual partners. Tibetan males and females do not find the sexual aspect of sharing a spouse the least bit unusual, repulsive, or scandalous, and the norm is for the wife to treat all the brothers equally. (39)

The Tibetans' explanation of why they choose to marry polyandrously is economic: It prevents division of land and animals, and helps everyone achieve a higher standard of living. Anthropological analysis reveals other economic benefits such as the more diverse and flexible male labor force than would be available in a monogamous household. The wife will work in the fields and manage food processing and other household work. Of the husbands, one stays and works on the land, another may be away with the herds, and another may be involved in long-distance trade. In earlier times, before Tibet became controlled by China, its pattern of feudal serfdom required regular labor contributions from one male in each household. This posed yet another demand for male labor. In a monogamous system, this requirement would have serious negative effects on the household economy. Polyandry provides a male labor "safety net" and helps to maximize economic advantage in a difficult ecological context that requires diversification and flexibility.

Family Businesses

The subject of family businesses is important in anthropology and many other disciplines, including sociology, economics, business, and international development. Family businesses face a similar problem in all cultures: When the senior members of a family business die or decide to retire, who will succeed them? (see the Multiple Cultural Worlds box).

Family Businesses in Chinese Culture

In contemporary China, family businesses are regaining prominence, with the new economic policies that promote growth in the private sector. A multidisciplinary study using nationwide survey data sought to assess what the role of women has been in the trend toward establishing new, nonagricultural businesses (Entwisle et al. 1995). The sample covered about one-third of China's provinces and included 3,764 households. Results show that the number of adults and the gender composition of the adults affect whether a household enterprise will be launched. The more adults there are, and the more adult men there are, the greater is the likelihood that the family will start a business. "Working-age men are almost three times as likely than women to work in the household business, and working-age women are more than twice as likely as men to work exclusively in agriculture.... Household businesses appear to be an opportunity for men, not for women" (47–48).

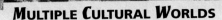

Multiple Cultural Worlds

Succession Problems in the Japanese Business Elite

Mathews Hamabata's experiences in gaining rapport and learning proper forms of reciprocity during his fieldwork in Japan were described in Chapter 2. His book, *Crested Kimono: Power and Love in the Japanese Business Family* (1990), offers insights into the workings of Japan's elite business families. It tells of the intricate interpersonal dynamics and power plays that have taken place in the "Moriuchi" family, beginning with the time when "Grandfather" and Grandmother" were both still alive. Struggles over succession are the major threads in this story.

> Grandmother had a strange hold on Grandfather. He resented her, yet found his life to be inseparable from hers. Grandfather's hidden despair was never expressed in any direct way to Grandmother. Instead, his angst transformed into a dislike of his eldest son, the *choonan* [pet] of the Moriuchi household and Grandmother's favorite child.
>
> While Grandfather tried to deny the very existence of the *choonan*, Grandmother denied him nothing. She loved the *choonan*, Tetsuo, deeply, looked after his interests, protected him from Grandfather's vengeance, spoiled him. While all the other children were given to wet nurses, she coddled him and personally looked after his every need. This child represented her power, as well as the dependence of Grandfather and almost five hundred years of Moriuchi history on that power. Her son would be the next head of the household.
>
> In 1955, Grandmother died at the age of fifty-six, just after seeing her beloved Tetsuo installed as president of the newly established Moriuchi Industrial Design and Construction, a *kogaisha* (subsidiary) of Moriuchi Industries. It was a coup for grandmother, for . . . the presidency of an important subsidiary would give Tetsuo power. . . . At the age of forty, Tetsuo was finally separated from his mother's guidance and protection. (95–96)

The story did not turn out that way at all. In Grandfather's view, setting up Tetsuo in the subsidiary was a way of shifting him out of the main family (*honke*) and into a branch family (*bunke*). Grandfather did not designate a successor as household head, but maintained that position himself. Grandfather acted against normal patterns in two ways: He did not name a successor to household headship before starting the process of branching, and he placed the logical successor in a branching position. In 1956, he retired and named Satoo-san as the next president of the Moriuchi Industries. Satoo-san was long Grandfather's right-hand man in the business, and he had arranged that he marry Kyoto, his eldest daughter. Satoo-san was to act as "regent" with Kyoko as heads of the business and the household. Then,

> Satoo-san would decide which of Grandfather's sons would be most worthy of assuming the household headship of the Moriuchi *ie*, as family and enterprise. After that decision, Satoo-san and Kyoko would abdicate their positions as household head and household wife, leaving the main family to establish a new branch family. (101)

While Grandfather was alive, things went according to plan, and Satoo-san's leadership was accepted. After his death, power struggles between him and Grandfather's sons over control of the household and business increased:

> Since Grandfather had so much personal power over his sons, he neglected to establish organizational channels of communication and centralized control between the main enterprise and the subsidiaries. He simply saw no need. After Grandfather's death, Satoo-san's lack of personal authority and weakened official authority could not serve as the basis for centralized control. Faced with constant opposition from Grandfather's sons, he could not establish a mechanism as the main enterprise to keep track of the subsidiaries. In fact, the Moriuchi *ie* split into competing factions, each replete with its own enterprise and family: Satoo-san and Kyoko heading one, while Grandfather's sons and their wives headed their own. (104)

Eventually one of the brothers aggressively gained control of his brothers' subsidiaries, reassumed centralized control of Moriuchi Industries, and moved into Grandfather's house.

The interpretation of this finding is that women's household roles in China have long been that of "filling in," by doing work that needed to be done while men pursue the "main" tasks. With the move toward privatization, agriculture is now secondary to business in importance. So women are left to "fill in" while men move out of agriculture into business. However, this pattern may change if the private sector continues to grow and the number of shops increases because women often work in the shops.

Cultural anthropologists have also studied "overseas" Chinese culture, often with attention to their entrepreneurship. One such study looks at Chinese families involved in the tanning industry in Calcutta, India (Oxfeld 1993). The business success of these families is to a large extent the result of the effective use of both male and female labor power in a way that differs from reported patterns for ethnically similar people of Taiwan. In the Calcutta Chinese tanning families, some tasks are reserved for men only, but many others involve both genders. This degree of overlap contrasts with the situation in Taiwan, with its more sharply defined gender division of labor (Cohen 1976). In rural Taiwanese families, the public–private distinction is adhered to, with men working outside and women inside. The often overlapping tasks of Chinese men and women in Calcutta's tanning industry can be explained by the fact that several aspects of the work can be done within the domestic domain. Men of the family take care of the few tasks that involve a high degree of interaction with unrelated males, such as buying rawhides. Rawhides are sold in two Muslim areas of the city where one rarely sees a woman in public. Buying rawhides also involves the "public sphere of hard-core bargaining" and sustained interaction with men, something from which women are excluded. Selling the finished leather is also men's work. Both male and female family members perform several tasks related to processing the leather, including mixing chemicals and packing the finished products.

Farming Family Businesses in the United States

In the United States, most family firms are either sold or liquidated after the retirement or death of their founders. This pattern exists in spite of the widespread preference of family business owners to pass them on to their offspring. Family analysts in the United States are trying to learn what processes within the family might promote successful succession. So far, the focus has been on the relationships between fathers and sons, since they tend to be most involved in the day-to-day operation of businesses (Marotz-Baden and Mattheis 1994). The roles of daughters are often overlooked.

In the United States, an interesting set of relationships emerges in two-generation family farming businesses. In two-generation farm families, daughters-in-law have higher stress levels than other adult family members. A daughter-in-law's stress level will be high if she wants to be integrated into the family business and perceives that she is not. Unresolved tensions between a dissatisfied daughter-in-law and the rest of the family may have more serious consequences for intergenerational continuity of the business than tensions between father and son. The prevailing gender division of labor in North American farm families designates men mainly as the farm operators, with women involved in bookkeeping, household organization, coordination of household and farm labor, and membership in community organizations. Transmission of the farm is generally patrilineal. Because starting up a farm on one's own is costly, most young farmers or ranchers work with or for their parents. Marriage, then, means that a daughter-in-law moves from her natal home into that of her husband and his parents.

> The patrilineal emphasis and the fact that farming is often facilitated by patrilocal residence places the in-marrying bride in a weak position. She is the newcomer into the extended family system and is probably viewed as an outsider to the farm family business . . . daughters-in-law are typically the most stressed family members in two-generation farm family businesses . . . [they] experience high stress around issues of equality, particularly with the amount of involvement or influence they experience concerning the farming operation. In addition, stress seems to emanate from competing demands of family and farm, financial concerns, and extended family differences about child rearing and the appropriate amount of contact time with extended family members. (133)

The mother retains substantial decision-making authority. One might assume that over time, the daughter-in-law and mother-in-law relationship would strengthen with shared experiences and greater sharing of decision making. A study of fifty-four daughters-in-law in two-generational farm families in Montana showed, instead, that daughters-in-law thought their relationship with their mother-in-law had worsened over time, especially as more children were born. Daughters-in-law who perceived their relationships to be most strained, experienced more stress, and were less involved in business decision making or transfer plans.

Remittances

Remittances (or money that is sent to someone else for their use) of nonresident members constitute an important part of many household economies.

Migrant laborers sometimes leave home for a specific period of time or to earn a specific amount of money before returning. In other cases, migrants leave and do not return, but continue to send money back home. An important stream of the international flow of remittances comes from the Gulf area, where men migrate primarily to work in the oil industry, and women migrate to work as domestic maids, nurses, and in other services. Intranational migration, particularly from rural to urban areas, is also common.

A less well-known source of remittance income for some households is through sex work, or prostitution, of one or more of their members. Contributions to the family economy from sex work varies. In the United States, **family disaffiliation** (feeling alienated from one's family) is a frequent motivation for a woman to enter prostitution, especially among the Euro-American population (McCaghy and Hou 1994). These girls and women tend to come from divorced homes; they frequently have been victims of familial abuse and neglect; and they have a poor relationship with their parents. They use their earnings for self-support and do not frequently send money home. But microcultures are important here. A study of African American sex workers in Milwaukee indicated that they often maintained contact with their families, and it is probable that they would share their income from sex work with their families. The generalization about family disaffiliation of sex workers in the United States appears to apply more strongly to Euro-American groups.

In Asia, family disaffiliation is uncommon for female sex workers, where kin support is a prominent motivation for doing sex work. In Thailand, a study found that only one of forty-six sex workers had broken ties with her family. Most visited their family once a year and sent regular remittances. In Taiwan, interviews with eighty-nine sex workers indicated that family obligation was the predominant motivation for doing sex work (Wang and Lin 1994). One-third of the women became prostitutes to earn money to help support their parents, thus helping to fulfill a daughter's intergenerational obligations. Another 30 percent took up sex work in order to help support their husbands (who had financial problems such as a failing business or gambling debts, or illness), thereby fulfilling a woman's conjugal obligations. About 17 percent became prostitutes for their own material self-gain. Six percent were the victims of fraud; in other words, they were deceived or tricked into becoming prostitutes. In Taiwan, less stigma is attached to sex work if it is done for kin support, given the strong norms of family obligation.

Cambodian sex-workers seek out customers in Phnom Penh. Cambodia is also a source of illegal transfer of sex-workers into neighboring Thailand.

INTRAHOUSEHOLD DYNAMICS

This section considers variations in how household members interact with each other, especially their emotional attachment, their rights and responsibilities, and power relationships between and among members of various categories such as spouses, siblings, and those of different generations. Kinship systems define what the content of these relationships should be. In everyday life, people may conform more or less to the ideal, as was apparent in the description of problems between mothers-in-law and daughters-in-law in extended farming households of the United States. The important dimension of how people may or may not diverge from ideal roles and relationships is, oddly enough, one that has been neglected for a long time by cultural anthropology and has only recently gained some attention.

Spouse/Partner Relationships

Studying relationships between spouses and partners can be approached from many directions: decision making, power relationships, the degree of attachment and commitment, duration of commitment, and the possibility of intimate relationships outside the primary relationship. This section presents findings on levels of emotional satisfaction between spouses and how they might relate to extramarital relationships.

Anthropologists, sociologists, and psychologists have done some research assessing spouses' level of emotional satisfaction within marriage. A landmark sociological study of marriages in Tokyo in 1959 compared marital satisfaction of husbands and wives in love marriages and arranged marriages (Blood 1967). In all marriages, marital satisfaction declined over time, but differences between the two types emerged. The decline was greatest for wives in arranged marriages and least for husbands in arranged marriages. In love-match marriages, husbands' satisfaction dropped dramatically and a bit later than their wives' satisfaction, but both husbands and wives have nearly equal levels of satisfaction by the time they had been married nine years and more. A related and more recent study conducted in Chengdu, Sichuan Province, China, gathered data only on wives' perceptions of marital satisfaction (Xiaohe and Whyte 1990). The Chinese results parallel those of the Tokyo study in that Chengdu wives in arranged marriages were less satisfied than wives in love marriages at all periods of their marriage. The Chengdu data also show that women's marital satisfaction is highest when they have been married between twenty to twenty-five years, but then it steeply declines. What could account for this pattern? One hypothesis is that it may be related to the kinship responsibilities that women face. At that point in the marriage, the children are getting married and moving out of the house. The aging parents-in-law are still fairly independent. Thus, for the wife, the stress of childrearing is over, and the responsibility of caring for the feeble aged has not yet begun.

Sexual activity of couples can be both an indication of marital satisfaction and a cause of marital satisfaction. Anthropologists have not studied this topic much at all, but help from sociologists working with survey data is available. As noted in Chapter 5, data on reported frequency of sex are not totally dependable, but they are better than no data at all. Analysis of reports of marital sex from the 1988 Survey of Families and Households in the United States shows that frequency per month declines with duration of marriage, from an average of twelve times per month for people aged nineteen to twenty-four years, to less than once a month for people seventy-five years of age and older (Call, Sprecher, and Schwartz 1995). Older married people have sex less frequently, as do those who report being less happy. Within each age category, sex is more frequent among three categories of people: those who are cohabiting but not married, those who had cohabited before marriage, and those who were in their second or later marriage. Cross-cultural data are not available to show how these findings for the United States might compare to other settings.

While historians have documented the existence of harems and other forms of extramarital sexual relationships especially of men, cultural anthropologists have largely neglected the study of extramarital relationships. We do know that extramarital sexual relationships are an example of widespread social practices that occur in defiance of accepted norms. For example, the Japanese corporate work ethic for men, as described in Chapter 7, promotes male bonding at work and minimizes husband–wife bonding. Within this context, both overworked husbands and their neglected wives may seek emotional and sexual satisfaction outside marriage, although precise data on how frequent this might be do not exist (see the Multiple Cultural Worlds box). The general fact of extramarital sexual relationships in the face of social disapproval raises the intriguing question of why societal rules don't change to reflect social reality.

Sibling Relationships

Sibling relationships are another understudied aspect of kinship dynamics. Suad Joseph (1994) provides an example of research on this topic in her study of a working-class neighborhood of Beirut, Lebanon, prior to the civil war. She got to know several families well and became especially close to Hanna, the oldest son in one of these families. Hanna was an attractive young man, considered a good marriage choice, with friends across religious and ethnic groups. He seemed peace-loving and conscientious. Therefore, the author reports: "I was shocked . . . one sunny afternoon to hear Hanna shouting at his sister Flaur and slapping her across the face" (50). Aged twelve, Flaur was the oldest daughter. "She seemed to have an opinion on most things, was never shy to speak her mind, and welcomed guests with boisterous laughter. . . . With a lively sense of humor and good-natured mischief about her, neighbors thought of her as a live wire"

Multiple Cultural Worlds

Love Hotels in Japan

To most Americans, renting a hotel room by the hour means a drive to the edge of town, an embarrassed check-in, a stained and threadbare wall, and grunts from the next room. That formula wouldn't work in Japan, though, where privacy, decorum, and hygiene are all held at a premium. Yet the demand for hourly rooms is much higher in Japan, thanks in part to a more chauvinistic society that doesn't frown as heavily on philandering husbands as well as to a living-space shortage that drives even married couples to seek occasional trysts outside their cramped, thin-walled apartments.

But in Japan every problem seems to have a technological solution. The result in this case is the multibillion-dollar "love hotel" industry.

It's hard to miss some love hotels. They can be astoundingly gaudy affairs on the outside, often done up to vaguely resemble such out-of-place icons as cruise ships, wedding cakes, or the Statue of Liberty. Otherwise, love hotels are paradigms of discretion. You drive into a parking lot whose entrance is covered with long cloth fringes to foil prying eyes. Various types of pull-down or clip-on devices are available for covering up your license plate, lest a jealous spouse take to cruising the lot in search of your car.

The most impressive concession to privacy offered by many love hotels, however, is the ability to check in and out without interacting with any staff. Just inside the entrance to the hotel is an electronic screen that tells you the numbers of the rooms that are vacant. You then make your way to one of the rooms and gain entrance by inserting yen notes (typically about $30 an hour) into a computerized lock. The door flies open, and that room number disappears from the screen at the entrance.

High-tech touches inside the neat, if small and slightly garish, rooms can include wide-screen-video karaoke and a remote-controlled sound system that offers not only dozens of music channels but also noises such as gongs and crowing roosters (hey, whatever turns you on) and even the sounds you would hear in a train station (to be played as background when you phone your boss or spouse from the room to say you're going to be late).

When you leave, maids are electronically summoned by the computerized door lock to thoroughly clean and sanitize the room. One hour and five minutes after you first walked in, the room number is back up on the board.

Source: Michael P. Cronin, "The Love Hotel," *Inc. Technology* 17(4):116, 1995. Reprinted with permission, *Inc. magazine,* Technology Summer 1995 issue. Copyright 1995 by Goldhirsch Group, Inc., 38 Commercial Wharf, Boston, MA 02110.

(50). Further consideration of the relationship between Hanna and Flaur indicated that Hanna played a fatherly role to Flaur. He would be especially irritated with her if she lingered on the street near their apartment building, gossiping with other girls: "He would forcibly escort her upstairs to their apartment, slap her, and demand that she behave with dignity" (51). Adult family members thought nothing was wrong and said that Flaur enjoyed her brother's aggressive attention. Flaur herself commented, "It doesn't even hurt when Hanna hits me" and that she hoped to have a husband like Hanna.

An interpretation of this common brother–sister relationship in Arab culture is that it is part of the socializing process that maintains and perpetuates patriarchal family relationships: "Hanna was teaching Flaur to accept male power in the name of love . . . loving his sister meant taking charge of her and that he could discipline her if his action was understood to be in her interest. Flaur was reinforced in learning that the love of a man could include that male's violent control and that to receive his love involved submission to control" (52). This close and unequal sibling relationship persists throughout life. Even after marriage, a brother maintains a position of responsibility toward his sister and her children, as does a married sister toward her brother and his children. This loyalty can lead to conflict between husband and wife as each vies for support and resources from their respective spouses in competition with siblings.

Domestic Violence

Violence between domestic partners, with males dominating as perpetrators and women as victims, seems to be found in almost all cultures, although in varying forms and frequencies (J. Brown 1992). A cross-cultural review of ethnographic evidence of wife beating revealed that wife beating is more common and more severe in societies where men control the wealth and less common and less severe where women's work groups are prominent (Levinson 1989). More research is needed to explore this correlation. For now, we can say only that the presence of women's work groups appears to be related to a greater importance of women in production and matrifocal residence. Both factors provide women with the means to leave an abusive relationship. For example, among the Garifuna, an African-Indian people of Belize, Central America, incidents of spouse abuse occur, but they are infrequent and not extended (Kerns 1992). Women's solidarity in this matrifocal society to a large extent limits male violence against women.

Increased domestic violence worldwide throws into question the notion of the house as a refuge or place of security. In the United States, for example, evidence exists for high and increasing rates of intrahousehold abuse of children (including sexual abuse), violence between spouses or partners, and abuse of aged family members. The topic of intrahousehold violence unites the work of cultural anthropologists, sociologists, legal experts, health care providers, social workers, and those who shape and implement public policy relating to the family.

DIVORCE, DEATH, AND REMARRIAGE

Divorce and separation, like marriage and other forms of long-term union, are cultural universals, even though they may be frowned upon or forbidden. Marriages can break up for several reasons: Voluntary separation or death of one of the partners are the most common. Globally, distinct variations exist in the legality and propriety of divorce. Some nations, such as the Republic of Ireland, and some religions, such as Roman Catholicism, prohibit divorce. In some cultures, such as Islamic societies, divorce is easier for a husband to obtain than for a wife. Important questions about marital dissolution include the causes for it, the reasons rates of divorce appear to be rising worldwide, and the implications for the welfare of children of divorced parents.

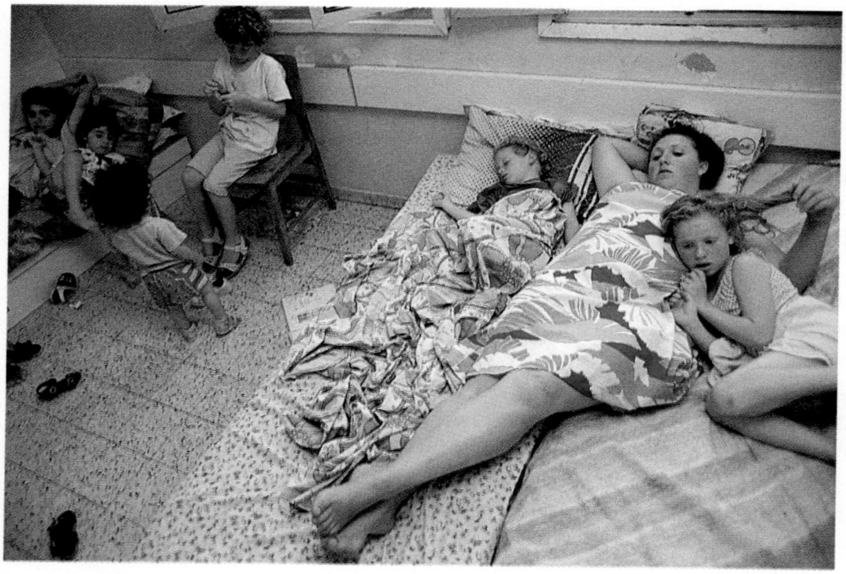

A shared bedroom in a battered woman's shelter, Tel Aviv, Israel. Many people wonder why abused women do not leave their abusers. Part of the answer lies in the unavailability and low quality of shelters throughout much of the world. Another factor is that a woman who leaves an abusive relationship is often in greater danger of serious injury (including death) than when she stays in the relationship.

Kinship Systems and Divorce

One hypothesis suggests that divorce rates will be lower in situations where a large descent group has control over offspring (Barnard and Good 1984:119). Patrilineal societies are most associated with vesting such rights in the larger group, compared to bilineal and matrilineal societies in which large "corporate" lineages are less likely to develop. Royal lineages, with their strong vested interests in maintaining the family line, are especially unlikely to favor divorce, particularly if it means losing control of offspring (see the Current Event box).

How does this theory hold up in the face of evidence? In foraging societies, couples generally have a fluid way both of joining

Current Event

"Princess Diana's Divorce Settlement"

- In 1996, Princess Diana agreed to a divorce from Prince Charles, thus ending a marriage that began nearly fifteen years earlier.
- Her statement said she would retain the title of Princess of Wales and continue to live at Kensington Palace in London. A spokesperson for Queen Elizabeth II remarked that there had been no agreement on retention of the title.
- Charles would get custody of the children because of William's status as heir to the throne. Diana had said she would "continue to be involved" with decisions concerning the couple's sons, William and Harry. The courts in England do not get involved in custody disputes involving future kings: It is the Queen's prerogative.
- In terms of the financial aspects of the settlement, a multimillion-dollar settlement was estimated.

Source: The Washington Post, February 2, 1996.

and then breaking up. The same is true for the contemporary United States with its (more or less) bilineal system. In contrast, Japan's kinship system is more patrilineal, and divorce rates in Japan are low (Cornell 1989). These low rates have risen only slightly since World War II: "The number of divorces per 1,000 population fluctuated around .85 in the 1950s and .80 in the 1960s, rose above 1.0 only in the 1970s, and reached 1.22 in 1980. . . . The United States centered around 2.4, 2.5, and 4.6 in the same periods and stood at 5.2 in 1980" (457). Patrilineal kinship systems of Pakistan and northern India seem related to the low divorce rates there.

Researchers have asked whether separation or divorce are more characteristic of some kinds of unions than others. In the United States, people in cohabiting relationships are more likely to split up than people who are formally married. In La Laja, a poor "barrio" or neighborhood in a city in Venezuela, three forms of marriage exist: church marriage, legal marriage, and common-law marriage through coresidence for a period of time (Peattie 1968:45). Church marriages are the least common form of marriage in La Laja. People say that they are expensive because of the costs for clothing and festivities required. Women in La Laja comment that a church marriage is bad because it permits no divorce: It is a contract with no escape clause in a society where separation often seems appropriate. Common-law marriages, the predominant form in La Laja, may be terminated by either party. For example, women said, "He left me for another woman." "He drank too much and I decided to spend the rest of my years in peace with my children" (46).

How durable are marriages with multiple spouses? Concerning the relationship between polygyny and divorce, a case study in Nigeria found that two-wife arrangements are the most stable, while unions with three or more wives have the highest rates of disruption (Gage-Brandon 1992).

Gender and Divorce

Two examples are provided here of how gender roles affect an individual's ability to obtain a divorce and the nature of the settlement, including child custody, that may result. Both the situation in Islamic law and the challenges faced in the United States by lesbian mothers indicate how the law favors males.

Throughout most of the Islamic world, the law grants men easy access to divorce. Turkey is the only Islamic nation in which the law allows women and men equal access to divorce. Elsewhere, for Islamic women, divorce is difficult, expensive, and usually unsuccessful. Variations in the requirements for divorce under Islam exist according to different schools of law. The branch called *Maliki law* is the most liberal (Mir-Hosseini 1993). It provides three modes of divorce. The first and most common is separation by *khul',* which is initiated by the husband. He secures his wife's consent and they come to an agreement about the compensation to be given to her. Khul' divorce does not require legal action.

The second type is the age-old form called *talaq* or "repudiation." This form is reserved for the husband, who simply says, "I divorce you" three times, with or without the knowledge or consent of the wife. The husband needs to get the talaq registered by two Notary Judges. Some limitations on talaq exist: A man cannot divorce a wife by talaq when he is intoxicated, in a fit of violence or anger, or when his wife is menstruating. The husband must pay a consolation gift whenever he repudiates his wife. The amount of compensation may be contested by the wife in court. It is not based on length of marriage, but more on the degree of harm to the wife, especially if the husband repudiated her on caprice; it is less if she is at fault or gave her consent. In Morocco, in 1987, 10 percent of the 1898 divorce cases filed were initiated by men who sought to reduce the dues set by the Notary Judge when they registered their talaq.

The third way to obtain a divorce is *tatliq,* a form pursued by women. Grounds for divorce under tatliq include the husband's failure to provide maintenance, the husband having an incurable disease injurious to the wife (such as insanity or leprosy, but only if she was not aware of the condition before marriage), the husband's ill treatment of the wife, the husband's absence for a period of at least one year and its effect of causing the wife harm, and the husband's abandonment of marital relations resulting from his taking an oath of sexual abstinence (he is given a period of four months to break the oath). Divorce by tatliq requires extensive written proof, including medical certificates, bank statements, and reports by witnesses. Of 156 tatliq divorces recorded in two Moroccan cities, the husband's absence was the most frequent grounds, totaling 73 cases, or nearly half of the total. Success rates for divorce by tatliq are low, with variation according to the grounds. Of the 73 cases based on the husband's absence, 48 were accepted by the court. Only 13 of the 64 combined harm cases were accepted. Divorce on the grounds of harm has the lowest rate of acceptance, because it is so difficult to prove, given the demanding requirements for written testimony from witnesses and other documentation.

Lesbian mothers in the United States face many barriers in getting a fair divorce settlement from a former heterosexual marriage (Lewin 1993). Child custody is a key issue, as revealed by an ethnographic study conducted in California: "At the core of the lesbian mother's predicament is her vulnerability to custody litigation. . . . Of the formerly married heterosexual women I interviewed, 24 percent had either experienced an actual custody action or been threatened by one. The proportion of lesbian mothers who reported such experiences rose to 41 percent" (163). Judges tend to view lesbian mothers as unsuitable custodial parents because of their sexual orientation. Lesbian mothers attempting to protect themselves from custody challenges from their husbands often adopt an "appeasement strategy." They keep a low profile—abandoning claims to marital property and to child and spousal support, and compromising on issues such as visitation. One lesbian mother arranged to live in a middle-class neighborhood and to appear "bourgeois." One mother gave up her share in the marital house, saying "He never really brought it into the negotiations directly. But he would like call me and harass me, and by innuendo suggest that there were many issues that he could bring up if he wanted to. . . . So basically, I traded my equity in the house for that issue not being raised at that time" (170). These strategies have important social consequences. They reinforce the mother's role as sole supporter of the household, limit contact between father and child, and reduce mother–father interaction and discussion about the child. On the surface, the father's stated custody claim seeks a positive role in raising the child; in fact it has the opposite effect.

Widow(er)hood

"Death involves, among other things, a rearrangement of kinship . . . among the living" (Barnard and Good 1984:119). In the case of a married or cohabiting couple, the survivor reaches a new status as widow or widower. The new position carries with it altered responsibilities and rights. The material or economic aspects of this change are important in shaping the person's new status. Given the prevalence of male dominance in most cultures and greater male access to wealth and property, women's status as widows tends to be lower than men's status as widowers. Women's position as widows is often marked symbolically. In Mediterranean cultures, a widow must wear modest, simple, and black-colored clothing, sometimes for the rest of her life. Her sexuality is supposed to be virtually dead. At the same time, her new "asexual" status allows her greater spatial freedom than before. She can go to public coffeehouses and taverns, something not done by women whose husbands are living.

Extreme restrictions on widows are recorded for parts of China and South Asia where social pressures on a widow strongly enforce self-denial and self-deprivation, especially among the propertied class. A widow should wear only a plain white sari, shave her head, eat little food, and live an asexual life. Many widows in India are abandoned, especially if they have no son to support them. They are considered polluting and inauspicious. In a similar fashion, widows experience symbolic and life-quality changes much more than do widowers in South Africa:

> A widower is encouraged to take on the challenge of picking up the pieces and to face life again. He is re-

A widow of Madeira, Portugal, wearing the typical black, modest clothing required in the Mediterranean region as a sign of widowhood.

> minded that he must be strong and swallow his pain. His body is not marked in any significant way except to have his head shaved, as is the custom in most African communities. He also is required to wear a black button or arm band. The period of mourning for widowers is generally six months, compared to at least one year for widows. . . . The fear of the ritual danger embodied in widows is expressed in terms of "heat," "darkness," and "dirt." . . . Her body is marked in different communities by some or all of the following practices: shaving her head, smearing a mixture of herbs and ground charcoal on her body, wearing black clothes made from an inexpensive material, and covering her face with a black veil and her shoulders with a black shawl. A widow may express her liminal status in a variety of ways, [by] eating with her left hand, wearing clothes inside out, wearing one shoe, or eating out of a lid instead of a plate (Ramphele 1996:100).

Spatial restrictions are imposed on widows in some South African communities. They should stay home except for essential business. They should not attend public ceremonies as they may pollute others.

Remarriage

Remarriage patterns are influenced by economic factors and gender-linked expectations that shape a person's desirability as a partner. In the United States, divorce frequently is followed by remarriage for both males and females, with a slight edge for men (Cornell 1989). In Japan, the tendency to remarry for males is significantly greater than for women. A marked age distribution in nonremarriage for women exists: "[W]hile divorced Japanese women, up to age 40, are already about 15% more likely to remain divorced than are their U.S. white female counterparts of the same age, after age 40 their situation grows rapidly more unfavorable for remarriage. In the subsequent decade it rises to 25% more divorced at age 45, 40% more at age 48, more than half again as many at age 50, and 65% more at age 51" (460). Older women's lower rates of remarriage are the result of age-hypergynous marriage and males' greater access to economic and political resources that increase their attractiveness as marriage partners in spite of their increasing age.

KIN NETWORKS BEYOND THE HOUSEHOLD

Local endogamy promotes more frequent and easy contact between natal kin than exogamy. Village endogamous marriages, as commonly practiced in southern India, mean that a married woman's kin are nearby and she can visit them without long-distance travel. That nearness may be a source of support and bargaining power for the woman in her marriage household (Dyson and Moore 1983). Likewise, women's status and autonomy may be a causal factor in determining how often and for how long a woman may visit her home (Niraula and Morgan 1996). For example, in Nepal's mountainous region, women's status and autonomy are higher than in the lowland region near India; likewise, women's visits home are more frequent in the mountainous region than in the lowland region (Fricke, Axinn, and Thornton 1993). This contrast relates to the fact that women are more important in the household economy and kinship system of the mountainous region in comparison to the lowlands, where the cultural system is more like that of northern India in which female labor is devalued.

Marital Roles and Social Networks

Elizabeth Bott (1957) conducted pioneering research on social networks in a sample of middle-class urban households in London. She defines a **social network** as social relationships of an individual that themselves do not form a composite group or organized group with distinctive aims (58–59). For example, "[S]upposing that a family, X, maintains relationships with friends, neighbors, and relatives, who may be designated as A, B, C, D, E, F . . . N, one will find that some but not all of these external persons know one another. They do not form an organized group" (58–59). Bott's sample included twenty families composed of husband and wife and children. She gathered interview data on marriage history, daily activities and work roles, annual and special events, and social ties outside the household.

Analysis of the data revealed two types of households based on activities of the conjugal pair. The first is households with "joint roles," in which husband and wife carry out activities together or either partner carries out the task at different times. The second is households with "segregated roles," in which activities of husband and wife are carried out separately with no reference to each other or husband and wife carry out different but complementary tasks. Households with husbands in semiprofessional work are more associated with joint roles. Households with husbands engaged in semiskilled manual work are more associated with segregated roles. A relationship also exists with type of social network. Segregated roles are associated with more close-knit social networks (see the Multiple Cultural Worlds box). Joint roles are more associated with loose-knit social networks. Are these merely correlations, or is there also a causal relationship? According to Bott, there is a causal dimension. The spouse brings his or her social network into the marriage, and this affects marital roles:

> Close-knit networks are most likely to develop when husband and wife, together with their friends, neighbors, and relatives, have grown up in the same local area and have continued to live there after marriage. Many people know one another and have known each other since childhood. Women tend to associate with women and men with men. The only legitimate forms of heterosexual relationship are those between kin

Multiple Cultural Worlds

The Importance of a Woman's Natal Kin in Working-Class London

In an area of London called "Bethnal Green," many newly married couples begin their marriage living with relatives, especially the wife's parents (Young and Willmott 1979:31). Of the 45 couples in the study, 21 co-resided with relatives, of which 15 lived with the wife's parents compared to 6 with the husband's:

> From what people told us it was clear that this is the preferred arrangement: if they have to share a house—and particularly a gas stove—it should be with the wife's parents. The reason is simply that mother and daughter are already used to each other, while mother-in-law and daughter-in-law are strangers, and, what is worse, rivals for a stove and a sink—and maybe for a man. (31–32)

This pattern is related to the more general issue of the retention of strong ties between mothers and daughters throughout their lives. Even when the couple is able to find a place of their own, it is far more likely to be located near the wife's family than the husband's. Visits between daughter and mother are frequent:

> Mrs. Wilkins is in and out of her mother's all day. She shops with her in the morning and goes round there for a cup of tea in the afternoon. "Then any time during the day if I want a bit of salt or something like that, I go round to Mum to get it and have a bit of a chat while I'm there." If the children have anything wrong with them, "I usually go round to my Mum and have a little chat. If she think's it's serious enough I'll take him to the doctor." Her mother looked after Marilyn, the oldest child, for about three years. . . . Mrs. Wilkins, and her husband for that matter, also see her two sisters frequently (44).

> and between husband and wife. Friendships between a man and woman who are not kin are suspect.
>
> In such a setting, husband and wife come to marriage each with his own close-knit network. . . . Each is engaged in reciprocal exchanges of material and emotional support with them. . . . The marriage is superimposed on these pre-existing relationships. (92)

Couples with loose-knit networks typically lived neolocally and made new friends in many different contexts during the course of their marriage. Their more interdependent conjugal roles fulfill the functions that are filled for those in close-knit networks by kin, friends, and others.

Networks and Poverty

Carol Stack's (1974) study of how kinship and friendship networks promote economic survival among low-income African Americans is a landmark contribution. Her research was conducted in the late 1960s in "The Flats," the poorest section of a Black community in a midwestern city. She found "extensive networks of kin and friends supporting, reinforcing each other—devising schemes for self help, strategies for survival in a community of severe economic deprivation" (28). Close friends, in fact, are called by kin terms. Strategies include maintaining exchange relationships with many people through "swapping" goods (food, clothing) needed by someone at a particular time, shared "child keeping," and food stamps and money as gifts or loans. Such gifts are part of a clearly understood exchange network—gifts go back and forth over time. One's network of exchange partners involves people mutually obligated to one another and who can be called on in time of need. In discussing the common practice of child keeping, Stack says:

> The exchange of children, and short-term fosterage, are common among female friends. Child-care arrangements among friends imply both rights and duties. Close friends frequently discipline each other's children verbally and physically in front of each other. In normal times, and in times of stress, close friends have a right to "ask" for one another's children. A woman visiting a friend and her children may say, "Let me keep your girl this week. She will have a fine time with me and my girls. She won't want to come back home to her mama." This kind of request among kin and friends is very hard to refuse.
>
> Temporary child-care services are also a means of obligating kin or friends for future needs. Women may ask to "keep" the child of a friend for no apparent reason. But they are, in fact, building up an investment for their future needs. (82)

In opposition to theories that suggest the breakdown of social relationships among the very poor, Stack's research documents how poor people strategize and cope through social networks.

SOCIAL CHANGE AND DOMESTIC LIFE

International Forces of Change

Changing economic opportunities in recent times have led to rapid change in household structures and dynamics. For example, employment of daughters in electronics factories in Malaysia has changed intra-household power structures (Ong 1987). The girls' mothers encourage them to take up factory work and urge them to contribute a proportion of their earnings to the household economy. This frees up daughters from their father's control (as is traditional among Malaysian Muslims), while giving greater control to the mother.

Migration is another major cause of change in family and household formations (Chapter 16). Dramatic changes can occur in one generation when members of a farming household in, for example, Taiwan or India, migrate to England, France, or the United States. In their homeland, having many children makes economic sense, but it does not in their new destination. Having come from large sibling sets and perhaps large, extended households, the migrants decide to have only one or two children and live in small, isolated nuclear households. Liberal education and women's movements for changing family styles are other factors creating change.

Changing Patterns of Domestic Life in the United States

Cultural anthropologists and sociologists have valuable insights to offer policy makers and concerned individuals about the current status of "the family" and future trends in family/household structure and dynamics in the United States. As of 1996, the United States registered its 100 millionth household, representing a doubling in number in less that forty years (Francese 1996:15). During the same period, household size shrank from an average of 3.3 persons to 2.6 persons, and the share headed by married couples declined from 74 percent to 55 percent. The current situation contains several seemingly contradictory patterns that were first noted in the early 1980s by two sociologists (Cherlin and Furstenberg 1992 [1983]):

- The number of unmarried couples living together has more than tripled since 1970.
- One out of four children is not living with both parents.
- About 80 percent of all adults in a recent national survey said they get "a great deal" of satisfaction from their family lives, and only 3 percent said "a little" or "none."
- Two-thirds of the married adults in the same survey said they were "very happy" with their marriages, and only 3 percent said they were "not too happy."
- At current rates, half of all American marriages begun in the early 1980s will end in divorce.
- In a survey of parents of children in their middle years, 88 percent said that if they had to do it over, they would choose to have children again.

What about domestic life in the next millenium? Basic outlines of the near future indicate the reduced economic dependence of women and the weakening of marriage in industrialized societies (Cherlin 1996: 478–480). These changes, in turn, will lead to increased movement away from nuclear household living and increased diversity in household forms. By the year 2000, three kinds of households will be most common in the United States: households composed of couples living in their first marriage, single-parent households, and households formed through remarriage (Cherlin and Furstenberg 1983:3). A new fourth category is the **intergenerational household,** in which an "adult child" returns to live with his or her parents. About one in three unmarried adults between the ages of twenty-five and fifty-five share a home with their mother or father or both (*Psychology Today* 1995 [28]: 16). Currently, in the United States, adult offspring spend over two hours a day doing household chores, with daughters contributing about 17 hours a week and sons 14.4 hours. The daughters spend most of their time doing laundry, cooking, cleaning, and washing dishes, while sons are more involved in yard work and car care. Even so, the parents still do three-quarters of the housework. Kinship and domestic arrangements are certainly not dull and static concepts. Just trying to keep up to date on their changing patterns in the United States is a daunting task, not to mention the rest of the world.

SUMMARY

Kinship rules and preferences state how people should live their lives in terms of certain people defined as kin. These rules and preferences set up a number of options, depending on cultural circumstances, for the arrangements of domestic life. Most people live in a unit that English-speakers refer to as a household. Households range from the smallest single-person household to large, extended households. Household form correlates generally with the dominant mode of economy. Foragers, like mobile industrialists, have small households of the nuclear type. People with more fixed asset bases, such as herds or land, tend to have larger domestic units, often comprising several nuclear units and having dozens of members.

Households can be examined from many perspectives—economic, political, and psychological, to name a few. As economic units, households may manage production, consumption, and distribution functions, depending on the context. In preindustrial societies, households often fulfill all of these functions, while in industrial societies they are more concerned with consumption and exchange since most production takes place outside the household. Intrahousehold dynamics is an area that merits more study from anthropologists. Studies thus far indicate that, in contrast to the Western notion that a home should be a place of refuge, many households are arenas of power conflicts and violence.

Two factors that lead to the break-up of domestic units are divorce or separation of cohabiting partners, or death of one spouse or partner. Gender roles in a society have much to do with options for marital separation and one's rights and responsibilities regarding offspring and property after the divorce. Likewise, in the case of spousal death, widows and widowers tend to have specific experiences, with the general cross-cultural pattern defining greater loss of status and social restrictions for widows than for widowers.

Relationships within the household, whether they are close and equal between spouses, how much time they demand, and more, affect a person's relationships with kin and non-kin beyond the household, as does economic standing. Studies have shown that members of low-income households are more likely to have strong networks outside the household, especially women, in terms of sharing child care and other domestic needs.

Marriage continues to be a prominent basis for household formation, although other options such as cohabitation continue to be important, and others are assuming increasing importance in some contexts, including single-parent or single-person households. Implication of these patterns for the care of dependent members, especially children and the aged, is a key question of our times.

CRITICAL THINKING QUESTIONS

1. Consider your current living situation. How would an anthropologist describe your family, or your household? How would the anthropologist deal with the possibility that you might be living away from home in a college dormitory for eight or nine months out of the year? Are you still a family member, or a household member? Are dormitories (like other large institutional living situations such as prisons or retirement homes) households?
2. Does poverty cause a particular form of household structure, or does household structure cause poverty? Or should we rephrase the question?
3. Given the fact that cultural anthropologists have been doing research in many settings for nearly one hundred years, what could explain their relative neglect of intrahousehold relationships and dynamics?

KEY CONCEPTS

family, p. 214
household, p. 214
household head, p. 215
intergenerational household, p. 232
nuclear family, p.214
social network, p. 230
stem household, p. 215

SUGGESTED READINGS

Dorothy Ayers Counts, Judith K. Brown, and Jacquelyn C. Campbell, *Sanctions and Sanctuaries: Cultural Perspectives on the Beating of Wives.* Boulder, CO: Westview Press, 1992. This book includes fifteen case studies plus an introductory overview and concluding comparative essay. One chapter considers possible the evolutionary origin of wife abuse. The wide range of cultural contexts studied include Australia, southern Africa, Papua New Guinea, India, Central America, the Middle East, and the Pacific.

Robert McC. Netting, Richard R. Wilk, and Eric J. Arnould, eds., *The Household: Comparative and Historical Studies of the Domestic Group.* Berkeley: University of California Press, 1984. Several comparative chapters on topics such as changing forms and functions of the household and case studies of contemporary Thailand, Niger, Belize, and the United States, and historic analyses of the Baltic and Sweden are included in this text.

Ellen Oxfeld, *Blood, Sweat, and Mahjong: Family and Enterprise in an Overseas Chinese Community.* Ithaca, NY: Cornell University Press, 1992. This ethnography addresses the Chinese immigrant community in Calcutta, India, and family involvement in the tanning industry; attention is given to the social history of the Hakka community, gender roles, and norms about family entrepreneurship.

Sulamith Heins Potter, *Family Life in a Northern Thai Village: A Structural Study in the Significance of Women.* Berkeley: University of California Press, 1977. This ethnography of matrifocal family life in rural Thailand focuses on work roles, rituals, and intrafamily relationships.

Debbie Taylor, *My Children, My God: A Journey to the World of Seven Single Mothers.* Berkeley: University of California Press, 1994. This narrative report by a journalist is based on interviews with seven single mothers in different countries: Uganda, Brazil, India, China, Australia, Egypt, and Scotland.

CHAPTER 10

Social Groups and Social Stratification

CHAPTER OUTLINE

SOCIAL GROUPS
- Friends
  - *Multiple Cultural Worlds:* Male and Female Friendship in Rural Spain
  - *Voices:* Memoirs from the Women's Prison
- Clubs and Fraternities
  - *Current Event:* "Alfalfa Club's Old Boys Bring in the Girls"
- Non-Mainstream Groups
- Work Groups
- Cooperatives
- Women's Rights and Human Rights Groups

SOCIAL STRATIFICATION
- The Concept of Status Groups
- Class: Achieved Status
- Race, Ethnicity, and Caste: Ascribed Status
  - *Critical Thinking:* What's Missing from This Picture?
  - *Voices:* Growing Up under Apartheid
  - *Multiple Cultural Worlds:* The Chinese Takeover of Tibetan Medicine

CIVIL SOCIETY: BETWEEN SOCIAL GROUPS AND GOVERNMENT
- *Current Event:* "Fragile Civil Society Takes Root in Chinese Reform"

SUMMARY

KEY CONCEPTS

CRITICAL THINKING QUESTIONS

SUGGESTED READINGS

◀ A north Indian village carpenter seated in front of his house. The status position of carpenters is middling, neither as high and powerful as landholding elites or brahman priests, nor as low as those who deal with polluting materials such as animal hides or refuse.

In the early 1800s, when French political philosopher Alexis de Tocqueville visited the United States and characterized it as a "nation of joiners," he implied that people in some cultures are more likely to join groups than others. Membership in some sort of social groups that unite people into clusters beyond the domestic group is an important aspect of life for everyone, except for those few who opt for complete isolation and solitude (Halpern 1992). The questions of what motivates people to join groups, what holds people together in groups, and how groups deal with leadership and participation have intrigued scholars in many fields for centuries.

This chapter focuses primarily on non-kin groups and relates to the issue of microculture formation. At the end of Chapter 1, several factors related to the formation of microcultures were defined: class, race, ethnicity, gender, age, region, and institutions such as prisons or retirement homes. Thus far, we have looked at how these factors affect fieldwork, and how they vary in different economies and in different reproductive systems. This chapter looks again at these and other key factors of social differentiation in order to see how they affect group formation and the relationships between groups in terms of hierarchy and power. It first examines a variety of social groups and then considers the issue of inequalities between certain key social categories.

SOCIAL GROUPS

A **social group** is a cluster of people beyond the domestic unit who are usually related on grounds other than kinship, although kinship relationships may exist between people in the group. Two basic categories exist: people who interact more or less regularly (**primary group**), and people who identify with each other on some common ground, but who may never meet with one another personally (**secondary group**) (Holy 1996:351). A social group thus can refer to a wide range of social clusters, including personal friendships, clubs, and institutions. Members of all social groups have some sense of rights and responsibilities in relation to the group which, if not maintained, could mean loss of membership in the group. Primary group membership involves more direct accountability about rights and responsibilities than secondary group membership because of its face-to-face characteristic. When discussing different kinds of groups, social scientists also draw a distinction between informal groups and formal groups (March and Taqqu 1986:5):

- Informal groups are smaller and less visible than formal groups.
- Members of informal groups have close, face-to-face relationships with one another, while members of formal groups may or may not know each other.
- Organizational structure is less hierarchical in informal groups than in formal groups.
- Informal groups do not have legal recognition, which formal groups are likely to have.

This section of the book begins with a discussion of informal groups and then moves to more formal groups. This transition parallels to some extent a shift from primary to secondary groups as well, although it should be remembered that even within large secondary groups, an individual may have close contacts with some of the members within the larger group.

The rich array of social groups found around the world seems to defy theoretical formulations. Modes of economies do seem to affect the proliferation of social groups, with the greatest variety being found in agricultural and industrial societies (see Figure 10.1). One theory has suggested that mobile populations, such as pastoralists, are less likely to develop enduring social groups beyond kin relationships. It may be true that foragers and pastoralists have less variety of social groups, but they are not completely without any social groupings. A prominent form of social group among foragers and pastoralists is an **age set,** which is a group of people close in age who go through certain rituals, such as circumcision, at the same time. A related hypothesis is that settled and densely populated areas will have more social groups as a way to organize society. Again, this may be generally true, but important variations and exceptions exist. Cross-culturally, both informal and formal groups appear to be more varied and active in Africa and Latin America than in South Asia (Uphoff and Esman 1984).

In Bangladesh, for example, a densely populated and agrarian country of South Asia, indigenous social groups are rare. The most prominent ties beyond the household are kinship-based: men's political linkages with their patrilineage (Miller and Khan 1986). Some examples of social cooperation are found in neighborhoods where groups informally undertake projects such as sponsoring religious celebrations, maintaining

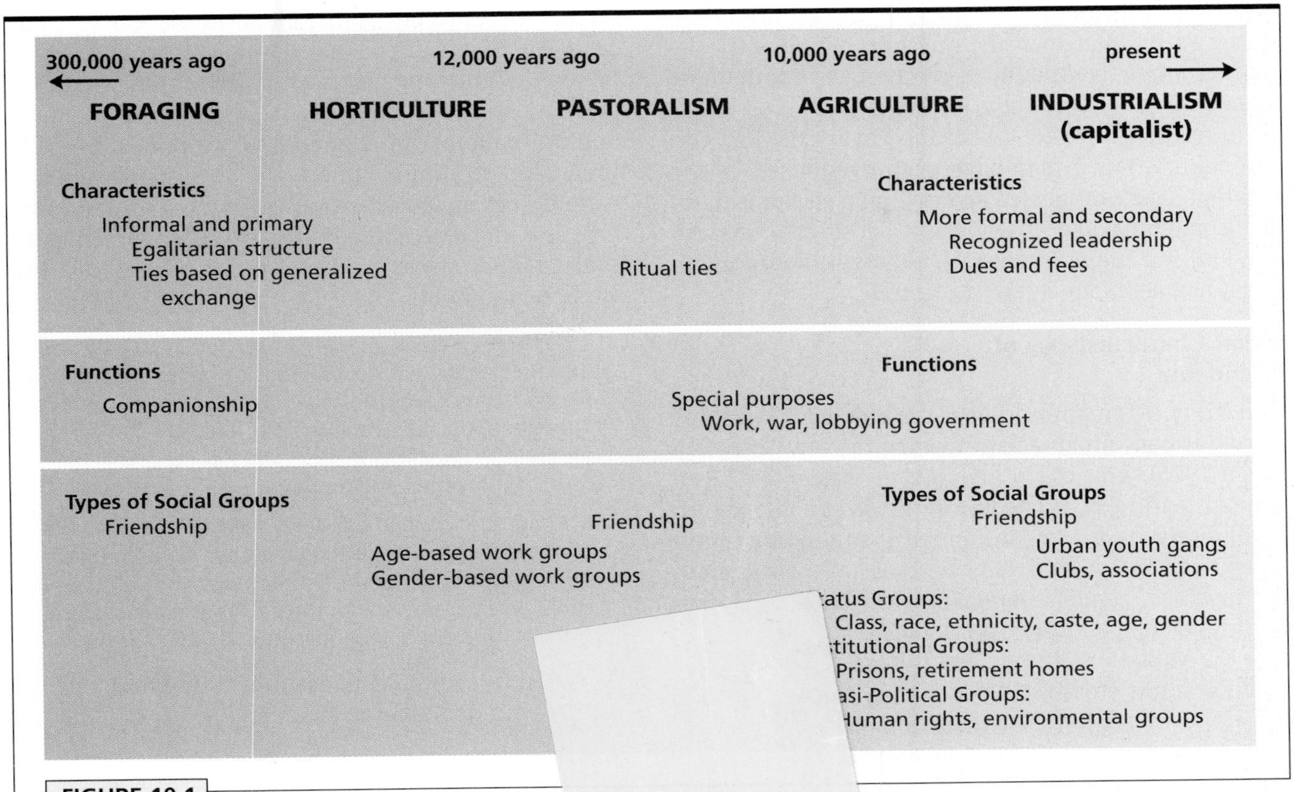

FIGURE 10.1
Economies and Social Groups

paths that lead to the mosque, and supporting Isla[...] schools. In spite of the lack of indigenous so[...] groups, however, Bangladesh has gained world[...] nown for its success in forming local credit groups for grassroots development through an organization called the Grameen Bank, which gives loans to poor people to help them start small enterprises.

In northern Thailand's Chiangmai region, in contrast, many local groups exist. One scholar has commented that a village itself is like a corporate group, jointly owning property that is maintained through funds and labor donated by the village as a whole (Potter 1976). Corporate village property includes the Buddhist temple and its grounds, the temple library, the monastery and school, the irrigation canals that crisscross the villages, the cremation grounds, and the village roads. Within this overall structure, several more formal and focused groups exist: the temple committee that organizes building new pavilions and arranges festivals; the school committee; the Young People's Club (all youth from about the age of fifteen until their marriage—they assist at village ceremonial [...] village dancers (about a dozen young [...]en who act as the host for intervillage [...]), the funeral society, which helps provide financial aid for funeral services and cremation; cooperative labor exchanges; neighborhood groups that take turns sending food to the temple for the monks; and, of course, irrigation groups. Members of all households participate in several of these groups at any one time. The precise reasons why some cultures have strong and enduring social groups beyond kinship affiliations await further exploration and explanation from social scientists.

Friends

Friendship, which fits in the category of a primary social group that is informal, has generated extensive research by sociologists and psychologists. While cross-cultural research by anthropologists is comparatively scant, some important studies have contributed to this area. One question that cultural anthropologists have asked is if friendship is a cultural universal. Unfortunately, at this point, insufficient cross-cultural research exists to answer the question definitively. The lack of data is compounded by the fact that defining friendship cross-culturally is problematic. For example, a relationship like "friendship" may exist in a certain culture, but it may have been overlooked by the anthropologists or labeled as something else. It is likely that something like "friendship" (close ties between non-kin) is a cultural universal, although shaped in different degrees from culture to culture.

Social Characteristics of Friendship

One study by an anthropologist examined friendships among urban, middle-class women in New York City (Yuan 1975). This study highlighted "selectivity" as a general feature of friendship: Friends are chosen on a voluntary basis. Yet, the broad parameters of who "qualifies" as a friend may be culturally structured. For instance, gender segregation will limit cross-gender friendships and promote same-gender friendships (see the Multiple Cultural Worlds box), and racial segregation limits cross-race friendships. Another characteristic of friendship is that friends are supportive of each other, psychologically and sometimes materially. Support is mutual, shared back and forth in an expectable way (as in generalized exchange, see Chapter 4). Friendship generally occurs between social equals, although there are exceptions such as between older and younger people, a supervisor and a staff worker, or a teacher and student. In the movie, *Dead Man Walking,* a friendship developed between Sister Prejean, a nun, and a prisoner on death row.

The study also showed the importance of maintaining balance in rights and responsibilities in friendship so that no one feels "used" or exploited. Among urban, middle-class women in New York City, friends often share child care. The women value sharing and strive to keep things equal, as two women comment:

> I don't keep track of every hour in our switching arrangements, but I do keep track of how much time I used. I don't want to take advantage of her. I feel strongly about this because she took my son when we went to Canada one time, and I know that is hard to do. I'll take her son anytime.
>
> If I had to leave my kids for a week, I'd leave them with my friend. I've taken care of her kid before, and she's indebted to me for two days for one child, so I could give her my two for three days at the most, and then I'd owe her some time. (92–93)

When debts accumulate, resentment does too, and the relationship could come to an end.

Friendships in Prison

Prisons, like colleges and universities, are social institutions with limited populations among whom relationships may develop. In the case of colleges and universities, people are there voluntarily and they

MULTIPLE CULTURAL WORLDS

Male and Female Friendships in Rural Spain

The prevailing gender division of labor and spatial gender segregation found in southern Spain shape differences in men's and women's friendship patterns (Uhl 1991). Women's lives are taken up mainly with unpaid household work within the domestic domain. Men's lives involve the two activities of work and leisure outside the house. This dichotomy is somewhat fluid, however, for women's domestic roles do take them into the public domain—markets, town hall, taking children to school—with some time for visiting friends.

Women often referred to their friends either with kin terms or as *vecina,* "neighbor," reflecting women's primary orientation to family and neighborhood. For men, an important category of friend is an *amigo,* a friend with whom one casually interacts. This kind of casual friendship is the friendship of bars and leisure-time male camaraderie. It grows out of work, school, common sports and hobbies, and drinking together night after night. Women do not have such friendships. Men also are more likely than women to have *amigos(as) de trabajo,* friendships based on work activities. Differences between men and women also emerge in the category of "true friends," or *amigo(as) de la verdad* or *de confianza.* True friends are those with whom one shares secrets without fear of betrayal. Most men claimed to have many more true friends than the women had, reflecting their wider social networks.

have a good idea about how long they will be there. It makes sense to form enduring bonds with friends and classmates. In the context of prisons, people are not there voluntarily, and the formation of social ties is limited in several respects. Nevertheless, depending on conditions, friendship and the formation of larger groups may arise out of a perceived need to resist conditions in the prison itself (see the Voices box on page 240).

One factor that affects the formation of friendship in prisons is the sheer duration of the sentence. A study that explored this issue first had to deal with the obvious difficulty of doing participant observation—learning by living in the culture. A research team of two people overcame this constraint by including an "insider" and an "outsider" (Schmid and Jones 1993). An inmate serving a short-term sentence did participant observation, conducted focused interviews, and kept a journal. The "outsider," a sociologist, met with him weekly to discuss findings and review the research strategy (the sociologist also did the analysis). The inmate researcher was a male, and so this study deals only with male prisoners. Furthermore, since his was a short-term sentence, its findings concern the effects of short-term sentencing (of one or two years) on social relationships among inmates. Having a short sentence means that inmates retain strong identification with the outside world and are less likely than long-term inmates to form strong or lasting friendships with other inmates.

Three stages of inmate adaptation are typical. First, inmates experience uncertainty and fear, based on their images of what life is like in prison. They avoid contact with other prisoners and guards as much as possible. The next stage involves the creation of a survival niche. The prisoner has selective interactions with other inmates and may develop a "partnership" with another inmate. Partners hang around together and watch out for each other. Partnerships are not likely to develop between short-term and long-term prisoners, as one short-term prisoner explained: "I was talking with [a long-term inmate] and he was telling me that he doesn't usually hang around short-timers because they are so preoccupied with time. He said it took him a long time to get over counting the days, weeks, and months, and that he doesn't really like to be reminded about it" (453). Even among the short-timers, maintaining a close tie with another inmate is difficult: "I think it would be almost impossible to carry on a relationship, a real close relationship, being here for two years or a year and a half. It's literally impossible. I think that the best thing to do is to just forget about it, and if the relationship can be picked up again once you get out, that's fine. And if it can't, you have to accept that" (453). In the third phase, the prisoner anticipates his eventual release, transfers to a minimum security area, and is thereby able to increase contact with outside visitors and begin the transition to the outside.

Friendship and Conflict

Friendship relationships, like other groups discussed in this chapter, provide cross-cutting alliances that can help reduce the possibility of social conflict among members of the in-group, but may shift conflict outward along new lines. Among foragers of the Kalahari desert of southern Africa who have been forced to settle down somewhere, friendship-based sharing networks are emerging (Kent 1995). One such group is the Basarwa, a Kalahari community who live in a settlement called Kutse. Kutse was initially established when the Central Kalahari Game Reserves told several families to leave a particular area that was to be set aside for tourists.

Settling down itself has not been easy for these people, who are used to periodic migration. Many camps have relocated since the beginning of the settlement period. A stable core of about twenty households emerged between 1987 and 1992. In this new context, several changes have occurred: divorce rates are higher, there are more fights, and the people suffer from new health problems. At the same time, people have begun to form links with each other through sharing networks that are based on the traditional camp ethos of collective goods distribution. Within one's sharing network, everything is shared, either on request or spontaneously. Feeling friendly toward someone is the basis for including that person in a sharing network. They may or may not be kin.

In camp locations, friendship is more important than kinship since equally close kin tend to locate their camps away from each other. Sharing partners locate their camps near each other, visit each other, and visit other camps together. They may go hunting or gathering together. As the Basarwa are increasingly forced to form larger settlements, sharing groups come into contact with people outside their network. Thus, "in-groups" and "out-groups" live in close contact with each other and the boundaries of exclusion from sharing become increasingly apparent. Newcomers to the community are not immediately absorbed into existing sharing networks. This leads to

VOICES

"Memoirs from the Women's Prison" by Nawal El Saadawi

Nawal El Saadawi is a leading Egyptian feminist, socialist, doctor, and novelist. While her writing has angered political and religious authorities in Egypt, she has helped mobilize women throughout the Middle East to press for their rights. In 1981, she was imprisoned by Anwar Sadat for alleged "crimes against the state" and was not released until after Sadat's assassination. Here she describes the emergence of women's solidarity behind bars.

The hardest part of any disaster to bear is its beginning and the most momentous event in the life of a prisoner is the unexpected transferral from one life to another, from habits of a lifetime to new patterns which must be learnt. The hardship increases to the extent that the individual has been living a life of contented ease, or has been pampered, always expecting others to serve.

But I have become accustomed to serving myself. I work a lot and eat sparely; I bathe in cold water in wintertime and have taken regular physical exercise since I was a child. I realised early that I needed two strong arms with which I could defend myself when necessary—in the street, or in a bus, whenever any man would try to turn my being into a female body which he could grab from behind or from the front. . . .

While a student at the university, when my female colleagues were priding themselves on the softness of their hands, the smallness of their feet, the gentleness of their small bodies and the laxness of their weak muscles, I was proud of my tall stature and my strong, taut muscles. How had that happened? I don't know. I sensed within myself a rejection of the notion of weakness as "feminine" or of femininity as weakness. I have never used powder on my face. However, I *was* used to washing my face every morning, brushing my teeth with toothpaste and doing my morning exercises, then exposing my body to the gushing water of the shower.

I opened my eyes the first morning in gaol and found no water in the tap, no toothbrush or toothpaste or soap or towel or shower. The toilet was a hole in the ground, minus door and flush, overflowing with sewage, water and cockroaches.

Noted feminist writer, Nawal El Saadawi (left) during an editorial meeting for the magazine "Moon" in Cairo, Egypt. Some of El Saadawi's work has been banned in Egypt.

We began our life in prison by repairing the state of the toilet. That was the first point of agreement and it was the beginning of a common ground between all cellmates, veiled and bareheaded.

It is fortunate that the human digestive system does not distinguish between right and left, or between one religious outlook and another. Whatever the difference in thought or politics between one individual and another, their need for the toilet is identical.

Our first meeting in the cell was attended by all the inmates. In fact, Boduur, who had refused at first to join even one session with those whom she labelled "atheistic infidels," was the most enthusiastic of any of us about this meeting. I had not seen her so worked up even when praying or reading the Qur'an. . . .

In this first meeting, we began to distribute jobs and responsibilities among ourselves so we could achieve a human existence inside the cell. We took a collective decision to stand firmly together in facing the prison administration.

Source: Nawal El Saadawi, *Memoirs from the Women's Prison.* pp. 41–43. Edited/translated by Marilyn Booth.

feelings of resentment and perceived injustices. The change from loosely structured and small groups whose members all know each other and share with each other, to larger, settled groups of strangers, has not yet generated new solutions of leadership and conflict resolution.

Clubs and Fraternities

Clubs and fraternities often define membership on some sense of shared identity. Thus, they may often, but not always, comprise people of the same ethnic heritage (such as the Daughters of the American Revolution in the United States), occupation or business, religion, or gender. Some groups appear to exist primarily to serve functions of sociability and psychological support rather than economic or political functions. Deeper analysis often shows that these groups do have economic and political roles.

Women's clubs in a lower-class neighborhood in Paramaribo, Suriname, have multiple functions (Brana-Shute 1976). Many clubs exist, each with its own name, flag, and color. The clubs raise funds to sponsor special events and support individual celebrations, meet financial needs, and send cards and flowers for funerals. All club members attend each other's birthday parties and death rites as a group. The clubs thus offer psychological support to the women, entertainment, and financial supports. A political aspect exists, too. Club members are often members of the same political party, and core groups of club members may attend political rallies and events together. These women constitute political interest groups that can influence political outcomes: "Interviews with politicians and party workers confirmed the existence of real pressure placed on them by women individually and in groups" (175). These clubs' activities, therefore, span the private and public domains.

College fraternities and sororities are highly selective groups that serve a variety of explicit functions such as entertainment and social service. They also form bonds between members that may help in securing jobs after graduation. Compared to sociologists, few anthropologists have studied the "Greek system" on American campuses. One exception is Peggy Sanday, who was inspired to study college fraternities after a gang rape of a woman student by several fraternity brothers at the campus where she teaches. In her book, *Fraternity Gang Rape: Sex, Brotherhood, and Privilege on Campus* (1990), she explores initiation rituals, the role of pornography, ritual dances, and heavy drinking at parties, and how they relate to a pattern of male bonding solidified by victimization and derision of women. Well aware that not all fraternities are the same nor all fraternity brothers the same, she nevertheless detects certain common features. Most shockingly, her interviews revealed the prevalence of gang rape, or a "train." Fraternity party invitations may even hint at the possibility of a "train." Typically, the brothers seek out a "party girl"—a somewhat vulnerable young woman who may be especially seeking of acceptance or especially high on alcohol or other substances (her drinks may even have been "spiked"). They take her to one of the brother's rooms where she may or may not agree to have sex with one man—often she passes out. Then a "train" of men have sex with her. Rarely prosecuted, the male participants reinforce their sense of privilege, power, and unity with one another through this group ritual involving abuse of a female outsider.

In a related study of a small, liberal arts college where about half of all students are affiliated with fraternities, researchers sought to identify fraternities that were high-risk or low-risk fraternities for rape (Boswell and Spade 1996). The research first involved interviews with forty college women about their perceptions of fraternity reputations. On the basis of these discussions, fraternities were ranked as high-risk or low-risk. The researchers collected interview data to detect possible behavioral differences between the two categories of fraternities. They spoke with fraternity men and men who were not in fraternities, women who attended fraternity parties, and self-identified fraternity rape victims. They also did participant observation at two fraternities every weekend during spring semester and at local bars.

Marked differences emerged in behaviors and attitudes in the two groups of fraternities. Men at parties in high-risk fraternities treated women less respectfully. Even the women's bathrooms in high-risk fraternities were in worse condition: "filthy, including clogged toilets and vomit in the sinks" (137). The atmosphere was "less friendly," with few one-on-one male-female conversations other than those that were obviously flirtatious. In fact, men appeared to be openly hostile toward women: "When a brother was told of the mess in the bathroom at a high-risk house, he replied, 'Good, maybe some of these beer wenches will leave so there will be more beer for us'" (137). Of many "rituals of disrespect" that fraternity men show toward women, is one called "chatter." When an unknown woman (not a steady girlfriend) sleeps over at the house, the brothers yell degrading remarks out the window at her as she leaves in the morning. Brothers also may observe or videotape a brother having sex with an unknown woman. Rape victims are most often women who were unknown to the brothers. In fact, brothers in high-risk fraternities mutually discourage each other from having steady girlfriends. Instead, they are urged to pursue the "hook-up" scene with unknown women.

Men's clubs in which strong male–male bonds are created and reinforced by the objectification and mistreatment of women are common, but not universal, cross-culturally (see the Current Event box). They are especially associated with cultures where male–male competitiveness is an important feature of society (Bird 1996) and in which warfare and group conflict are frequent. In many Amazonian groups, the men's house is fiercely guarded from being entered by women. If a woman were to trespass on male territory, she is subject to punishment by gang rape. One interpretation is that males have a high degree of anxiety about their identity as fierce warriors and as sexually potent males (Gregor 1985). Maintaining their identity as fierce males toward outsiders involves taking an aggressive position in relation to women of their own group. Parallels of gynophobic ("women-hating" or otherwise anti-woman) men's clubs among women do not exist. College sororities are not mirror images of college fraternities. Women's groups and organizations, even if vocally anti-male, do not involve physical abuse of males or ritualized forms of derision.

Current Event

"Alfalfa Club's Old Boys Bring in the Girls"

- For the first time in its history of over eighty years, the prestigious Alfalfa Club is admitting women members. Three were recently chosen: Sandra Day O'Connor (Supreme Court Justice), Katharine Graham (Washington Post Executive Committee Chair), and Elizabeth Dole (Red Cross President).
- At the same time, six new male members were admitted.
- Progress has been slow in opening the club to women. Since 1993, several prominent women—such as O'Connor and Cabinet members Donna Shalala and Attorney General Janet Reno, Hillary Clinton, and Tipper Gore—have been invited to the annual dinner.
- The club is named for the thirsty plant with long roots that always need refreshment. Its sole event is the annual "boys' night out," which attracts the most powerful players [men] in United States politics and business, and usually the President. Now, the President can bring the First Lady along with him.

Source: The Washington Post, January 7, 1994.

Non-Mainstream Groups

Several kinds of groups are formed by people who are, for some reason, excluded from "mainstream" culture or by people who seek consciously to resist conforming to the dominant cultural pattern, as in so-called "countercultural" groups and movements such as the "hippie" culture of the 1960s. This section considers examples of non-mainstream groups in different contexts. One similarity among these groups is the importance of bonding through shared rituals.

Youth Gangs

The term "gang" can refer to a variety of groups, such as one's friends, as in, "I think I'll invite the gang over for pizza" (Short 1996:325). The more specific term **youth gangs** refers to groups of young people, found mainly in urban areas, who are often considered a social problem by adults and law enforcement officials (Sanders 1994:5–15). While increasingly found throughout the world, they are not a new phenomenon. In sixteenth century France, for instance, groups called *charivaris* composed of young, unmarried males, were explicitly rebellious and mocking of existing traditions (Davis 1986).

Youth gangs vary in terms of how formally they are organized. In contrast to friendships, gangs—like clubs and fraternities—often have formalized rituals of initiation for new members, a recognized leader, and symbolic markers of identity such as tattoos or special clothing. An example of an informal youth gang with no formal leadership hierarchy or initiation rituals are the "Masta Liu," found in Honiara, the capital city of the Solomon Islands (Jourdan 1995). The primary unifying feature of the male youth who become Masta Liu is the fact that they are unemployed. Most have migrated to the city from the countryside to escape what they consider an undesirable lifestyle there: working in the fields under control of their elders. Yet, as a group, they have developed a distinct lifestyle and identity:

> Drifting in and out of jobs, in and out of hope, they are very often on the verge of delinquency. Many of them have had some brush with the law ... songs are being written about them, people talk about them.... The *liu* have become a significant segment of the urban population, not only because of their sheer numbers, but because of the influence they have on the development of the urban popular culture. Their life-style, the way they dress and talk, their taste in music and films, their outlook on life, all this gives a particular direction to social change in Honiara. (202)

Some liu live with extended kin in the city, others organize liu-only households. They spend their time wandering around town (*wakabaot*) in groups of up to ten: "They stop at every shop on their way, eager to look at the merchandise but afraid to be kicked out by the security guards; they check out all the cinemas only to dream in front of the preview posters ... not even having the $2 bill that will allow them to get in; they gaze for hours on end, and without moving, at the electronic equipment displayed in the Chinese shops, without saying a word: one can read in their gaze the silent dreams they create." (210)

"Street gangs" are a more formal variety of youth gang. They generally have leaders and a hierarchy of membership roles and responsibilities. They are named and their members mark their identity with tattoos or "colors." While many street gangs are involved in violence, not all are. An anthropologist who did research among nearly forty street gangs in New York, Los Angeles, and Boston learned much about why individuals join gangs, providing insights that contradict popular thinking on this subject (Jankowski 1991). One common stereotype is that young boys join gangs because they are from homes with no male authority figure with whom they could identify. This study showed that equal numbers of gang members were from homes with "intact" nuclear families as from families with an absent father (39).

Another common perception is that the gang replaces a missing feeling of "family" as a motive. This study, again, showed that the same number of gang members reported having close family ties as those who didn't. So, then, what might be the reasons behind joining a male urban gang? It seems that a particular personality type characterized many gang members, a type that could be called a "defiant individualist." The defiant individualist type has five traits: intense competitiveness, mistrust or wariness, self-reliance, social isolation, and a strong survival instinct. Cultural materialist theory would suggest that poverty, especially urban poverty, leads to the development of this kind of personality structure. With-

Members of two opposing youth gangs meet at a park in Los Angeles, California, in order to negotiate a truce.

in the context of urban poverty, such a personality structure becomes a reasonable response to the economic blockades and uncertainty. In terms of explaining the global spread of urban youth gangs, cultural materialists would again point to global economic changes in urban employment structures as the cause. In many countries, the declining urban industrial base has created persistent poverty in inner-city communities (Short 1996:326). At the same time, aspirations for a better life have been promoted through schooling and the popular media. Urban gang members, in this view, are the victims of large structural forces beyond their control. Yet, research with gangs shows that they are not just passive victims of structural forces: Strong entrepreneurial interests motivate much gang activity. Many of these youths want to "get ahead," but social conditions channel their interests and skills into illegal pursuits rather than into legal pathways of material achievement.

Body Modification Groups

Of the many non-mainstream movements in the United States, one includes people who have a sense of community strengthened through forms of body alteration. James Myers (1992) did research in California among people who feel they are a special group because of their interest in permanent body modification, especially genital piercing, branding, and cutting. He explains his choice of research topic:

> My original plan was to concentrate my research efforts on tattooing, but 4 months into the 24-month study period, I shifted my focus almost entirely to piercing, cutting, burning, and branding. The change was brought about by my increasing awareness of the growing popularity of nonmainstream modification other than tattoos and the realization that research on the subject was scant. I was also intrigued by the deep feelings of revulsion and resentment held by mainstream American society against these forms of body modification. (269)

Fieldwork involved participant observation and interviews. He was involved in six workshops organized especially for the San Francisco SM (sadomasochist) community by "Powerhouse," a San Francisco Bay Area SM organization; attended the Fifth Annual Living in Leather Convention held in Portland, Oregon, in 1990; and spent time in tattoo and piercing studios as well as talking with students and others in his home town who were involved in these forms of body modification. The study population included males and females, heterosexuals, gays, lesbians, bisexuals and SMers. The single largest group was SM homosexuals and bisexuals, a proportion similar to that found in a survey of subscribers to the magazine *Piercing Fans International Quarterly (PFIQ)*. The study population was mainly White, and most had either attended or graduated from college.

Myers witnessed many modification sessions at workshops: Those seeking modification go up on stage and have their chosen procedure done by a well-known expert. Whatever the procedure, the volunteers evidence little pain (usually a sharp intake of breath at the moment the needle passes through or the brand touches skin). After that critical moment, the audience breathes an audible sigh of relief. The volunteer stands up, adjusts clothing, and members of the audience applaud. Myers interprets this public event as a kind of initiation ritual that binds the expert, the volunteer, and the group together. Pain has long been recognized as an important part of rites of passage, providing an edge to the ritual drama. The audience in this case witnesses and validates the experience and also becomes joined to the initiate through witnessing.

A prominent motivation for seeking permanent body modification was a desire to identify with a specific group of people, and the body marking is thus a sign of affiliation. As one informant said,

> It's not that we're sheep, getting pierced or cut just because everyone else is. I like to think it's because we're a very special group and we like doing something that sets us off from others. . . . You see all the guys at the bar and you know they are pierced and tattooed, and it gives you a good feeling to know that you're one of them. . . . Happiness is standing in line at a cafeteria and detecting that the straight-looking babe in front of you has her nipples pierced. I don't really care what her sexual orientation is, I can relate to her. (292)

The experts who do the body modification are group heroes. Jim Ward, for example, is widely recognized as a "master piercer." He was the president of Gauntlet, Inc., one of the few firms worldwide that manufactures non-mainstream piercewear and is the editor of *PFIQ*. Ward's popularity at workshops is evidenced by the warm greetings he receives, through hand shaking, hugging, and kissing with both males and females. Myers does not discuss the emergence of a more formal leadership structure in this diverse and diffuse group, but the occurrence of annual conventions is an indication that some degree of formal structure may have emerged.

Work Groups

Work groups are organized to perform specific tasks, although they also may have other functions including sociality and friendship among members. They are found in all modes of production, but they tend to be more prominent in nonindustrialized horticultural and agricultural communities where land preparation, harvesting, or repair of irrigation canals requires large inputs of labor that exceed the capability of a single household unit. In her classic study of the Bemessi people of the Cameroon, West Africa, Phyllis Kaberry (1952) describes a labor group system (called a *tzo*, translated as "working bee") which:

> consists of women who are of about the same age and who are kin or friendly neighbors. For the preparation of corn beds there may be ten or twelve individuals; for weedings only three or four. About a week's notice is given and, once a woman has received help on her own plot, she is under an obligation to fulfill a similar duty to others on pain of being reported to the *Fon* (chief). The women usually work in pairs, chat, and urge each other on. Towards the end of the afternoon a small repast is provided, which includes a little fish contributed by the husband. (56)

Youth work groups are common in African regions south of the Sahara, particularly in settled, crop-growing areas. Such work groups are often composed of one or more age sets. Among the Wolof of Gambia, the *ton*, or work group, is formed separately for boys and girls, and comprises several age sets (Ames 1959:224–237). The major responsibility of the youth groups is providing field labor. The group works one or more days in the village chief's fields for no remuneration. They also maintain public paths and the public meeting area, construct and maintain roads between villages, build and repair canals, combat brush fires, maintain the village mosque, and prevent animals from grazing where they aren't allowed (Leynaud 1961). Girls' groups exist, but in patrilocal contexts they are less durable because their marriage and relocation breaks ties with childhood companions (Hammond 1966:133). As adults, however, women in African cultures have many types of associations such as mothers' groups, savings groups, and work groups.

Irrigation organizations are formal groups devoted to maintaining irrigation canals and dealing with the tricky issue of distributing the water. Indigenous irrigation organizations are common around the world and have been the focus of much anthropological and sociological attention. These organizations are responsible for a highly valued good, and they tend to develop leadership and membership rules and roles. Given the fact that watershed systems are connected across large regions, irrigation organizations often provide a link between local groups.

The important role these organizations play is illustrated by the case of the Chiangmai region of northern Thailand. At the village level, care of the irrigation canals is a constant concern (Potter 1976). Each year the main weir across the Ping River is washed away by floods and must be rebuilt. This task requires two weeks of concentrated labor by all the farmers who use the system. The entire length of the main canal has to be cleared at least once a year and the smaller ones must be cleared more often. These tasks require much more than labor: they also entail organization and administration. In the Chiangmai region, the administration has three tiers. At the highest level is the overall leader of the irrigation group, who is chosen by three local political leaders. The head was a wealthy man of high social status, who had been in the position for twenty years. He had two assistants. At the next lower tier are the heads of each major canal in the system. At the most local level was the village irrigation leader, chosen by the village farmers. Irrigation leaders have many duties, including keeping detailed records and arbitrating disputes. They receive some benefits, such as exemption from either furnishing irrigation labor or paying a proportion of their land tax, or they can keep part of the revenues from fines levied against those who are delinquent in providing labor.

Allocating the water from the systems also requires careful administration. As is often the case, water is allocated proportionally according to landholdings (Coward 1976, 1979). But farmers who are downstream are more likely to be deprived of their fair share than farmers who are upstream and can divert more water to their fields. In order to deal with conflicts that arise from this built-in inequity in one area of the Philippines, subgroups of farmers formed to meet and discuss distribution problems. Although irrigation organizations have been functioning around the world for decades and they are often efficient, they are by no means perfect systems. One of the biggest problems is corruption such as water theft, in which a particular farmer will tap off water out of turn (Price 1995).

Cooperatives

Cooperatives are a relatively recent form of economic group, with two key features: surpluses are shared among the members, and decision making follows the democratic principle of one person, one vote (Estrin 1996). Many kinds of cooperatives exist: consumer cooperatives, farmer cooperatives, credit cooperatives, and producer cooperatives. Agricultural and credit cooperatives are the most common forms of cooperatives worldwide, followed by consumer cooperatives. They bring together millions of people in a common cause. Cooperatives have become increasingly evident in Eastern European countries as a compromise form between pure socialism and pure capitalism.

Farmers' Cooperatives in Western India

In India's western state of Maharashtra, the sugar industry is largely owned and operated through farmer cooperatives (Attwood 1992). Most shareholders are small farmers, producing just one or two acres of sugar cane. Yet the sugar industry, owned and managed cooperatively, is huge, almost as large as the state's iron and steel industry. In contrast, in the northern states where sugar cane is grown, cooperatives are not prominent. How and why are sugar cooperatives are so successful in this region? The answer lies in the different pattern of social stratification. The rural social stratification system in Maharashtra is simpler than in northern India (see pp. 254–257). In most villages, the Marathas are the dominant caste, but they constitute even more of a majority and they control even more village land than is typical of dominant castes. They also have stronger local ties with each other because their marital arrangements are locally centralized. Thus, they have a better basis for cooperating with each other in spite of class differences among themselves. Large farmers dominate the elected board of directors of the cooperatives. These "sugar barons" use their position to gain power in state politics. However, within the cooperatives, their power is held in check. They do not form cliques that exploit the cooperatives to the detriment of the less wealthy. In fact, large farmers cannot afford to alienate the small and middle farmers, for that would mean economic ruin for the cooperative and the loss of their own profits. The technology of sugar cane processing requires wide participation of the farmers. Mechanization involves investing in expensive heavy equipment. The machinery cannot be run at a profit unless it is used at full capacity during the crushing season. If small and middle farmers were displeased with their treatment, they might decide to pull out of the cooperative and put their cane into other uses. Then capacity would be under-used and profits would fall. If the large farmers were to try to take advantage of the system, they would be "cutting their own throats." The success of cooperatives has much to do with the power balance between large farmers versus the middle and small farmers.

Craft Cooperatives in Panama

In Panama's east coastal region, Kuna women have long sewn beautiful *molas,* or cloth with appliqued designs. This cloth is made for their own use as clothing (Tice 1995). Since the 1960s, molas have been important items for sale both on the world market and to tourists who come to Panama. Revenue from selling molas is now an important part of the household income of the Kuna. Some women continue to operate independently, buying their own cloth and thread and selling their molas either to an intermediary who exports them or in the local tourist market. But many other women have joined cooperatives that offer them greater economic security. By the 1980s, several local cooperatives were in operation, with about 1,500 members in the San Blas region.

The cooperative buys cloth and thread in bulk and distributes it to the women. The women are paid almost the entire sale price for each mola, with only a small amount of the eventual sale prices being taken out for cooperative dues and administrative costs. Their earnings are thus more steady than what the fluctuating tourist season offers. As one Kuna woman commented,

> Without the cooperative I didn't have money to buy cloth to make *molas* and couldn't buy anything for my children. Also, sometimes molas didn't sell so well outside the cooperative. The cooperative helps us a lot. We save money so that if a member gets sick or something happens, and she doesn't have any money the cooperative can help. We bought twenty sacks of sugar and twenty sacks of rice to distribute on credit to all of the co-op members. If one day a member doesn't have anything to eat or drink she can come get food and cloth at the cooperative and pay back what she owes when she finishes her mola.

> The members say the cooperative is good for their families, and me.... I love the cooperative very much. (136)

Beyond the initial economic reasons for joining the cooperative, other benefits include the use of the cooperative as a consumer's cooperative (buying rice and sugar in bulk for members), as a source of mutual strength and support, and as a basis for women's greater leadership skills and opportunities for political participation in the wider society. One local chapter had the region-wide administrative responsibility for distributing and inventorying cloth supplies and for keeping financial records. Elected cooperative leaders attend regional meetings in different cities twice a year and thus gain wider exposure and experience.

Women's Rights and Human Rights Groups

Activist groups worldwide are protesting political repression, violence, and human rights violations. Many such groups are initiated and organized by women. Even in cultures where they are primarily involved in the domestic domain, women often have a significant impact in the public domain, too. The CO-MADRES of El Salvador is an important social movement in Latin America (Stephen 1995). CO-MADRES is a Spanish abbreviation for an organization called, in English, the Committee of Mothers and Relatives of Political Prisoners, Disappeared and Assassinated of El Salvador. It was founded in 1977 by a group of mothers in denunciation of the atrocities committed by the Salvadoran government and military. During the civil war that lasted from 1979 until 1992, a total of 80,000 people had died and 7,000 more had disappeared, or one in every 100 El Salvadorans.

The initial group comprised nine mothers. A year later, it had grown to between twenty-five and thirty, including some men. For two years, they had no office, but in time they secured a permanent space where they could set up files and an archive system. In 1979, they made their first international trip to secure wider recognition. This developed into a full-fledged and successful campaign for international solidarity in the 1980s, with support in other Latin American countries, Europe, Australia, the United States, and Canada. The increased organization and visibility brought with it government repression. Their office was first bombed in 1980 and then four more times after that. In addition, a majority of the most active CO-MADRES have been detained, tortured, and raped. Forty-eight members of the CO-MADRES have been detained since 1977; five have been assassinated. Harassment and disappearances continued even after the signing of the Peace Accords in January 1992: "In February 1993, the son and the nephew of one of the founders of CO-MADRES were assassinated in Usulutan. This woman had already lived through the experience of her own detention, the detention and gang rape of her daughter, and the disappearance and assassination of other family members" (814).

In the 1990s, CO-MADRES focused on holding the state accountable for human rights violations during the civil war, as well as some new areas, such as providing better protection for political prisoners, seeking assurances of human rights protection in the future, working against domestic violence, educating women about political participation, and developing some economic projects to help women attain financial autonomy. They are part of a coalition of women's groups that worked on the 1994 political

A march of the "Mothers of the Disappeared" in Argentina. This organization of women combines activism motivated by personal causes (the loss of one's child or children to political torture and death) and wider political concerns (state repressiveness in general).

platform to secure better rights and conditions for women. The work of CO-MADRES, throughout its history, has incorporated elements of both the "personal" and the "political," concerns of mothers and family members for lost kin and for exposing and halting abuses of the state and military.

SOCIAL STRATIFICATION

In this section, we look at the way certain key social categories define group membership and varying relations of inequality among groups. **Social stratification** refers the hierarchical relationships between different groups as if they were arranged in layers or "strata." Stratified groups may be unequal on a variety of measures, including material resources, power, human welfare, education, and symbolic attributes. People in groups in higher positions have privileges not experienced by those in lower groups, and they are likely to be interested in maintaining their privileged position. Social stratification emerged late in human history, most clearly with the emergence of agriculture. Now some form of social stratification is nearly universal. With few exceptions, egalitarian foraging groups have been incorporated within nations at the lowest level. Socialist states that sought to reduce social stratification are still saddled with inequalities. Post-socialist states that have relinquished socialist distributive principles in favor of capitalism are experiencing the emergence of a high degree of stratification.

Analysis of the categories—such as class, race, gender, and age—that form stratification systems reveals a crucial difference in the degree to which membership in a given category is an **ascribed position** (based on qualities of a person gained through birth) and those in which it is an **achieved position** (based on qualities of a person gained through action). Ascribed positions include one's race, ethnicity, gender, age, and physical ability. These factors are generally out of the control of the individual, although some scope for flexibility exists in gender through surgery and hormonal treatments and for certain kinds of physical conditions. Also, one can sometimes "pass" for being a member of another race or ethnic group. Age is an interesting ascribed category because an individual will pass through several different status levels associated with age. Achievement as a basis for group membership means that a person belongs on the basis of some valued attainment. Ascribed systems are thus more "closed" and achievement-based systems more "open" in terms of mobility within the system (either upward or downward). Some scholars of social status believe that increasing social complexity and "modernization" led to an increase in achievement-based positions and a decline in ascription-based positions.

The Concept of Status Groups

Societies place people into categories—student, husband, child, retired person, political leader, or member of Phi Beta Kappa—which are referred to as a person's **status** (position or standing in society) (C. Wolf 1996). Each status has an accompanying **role** (expected behavior for someone of a particular status), with a "script" for how to behave, look, and talk. Some statuses have more prestige attached to them than others (the word "status" can be used to mean prestige, relative value, and worth). Groups, like individuals, have status, or standing in society. Noted German sociologist Max Weber called lower-status groups "disprivileged groups." These include, in different contexts and in different times, physically disabled people, people with certain illnesses such as leprosy or HIV/AIDS, Blacks, Jews, low-caste Indians, women, and others. Moving from left to right on the production continuum (see Chapter 3) takes us from less complex social structures to more complex social structures and to more varied statuses. At the same time, social inequality increases, especially in intensive agricultural and capitalist industrialist systems.

Within societies that have marked status positions, different status groups are marked by a particular lifestyle, including goods owned, leisure activities, and even linguistic styles. The maintenance of group position by higher status categories is sometimes accomplished by exclusionary practices in relation to lower status groups through a tendency toward group inmarriage and socializing only within the group.

Class: Achieved Status

Class (as defined in Chapter 1) refers to a person's or group's position in society defined primarily in economic terms. In many cultures, class is a key determining factor of one's status, while in others it is less important than, for example, one's birth into a certain family. However, even in societies in which class can determine status, they do not always match. A rich person may have become wealthy in disreputable ways and never gain high status in society. Both status and class groups are secondary groups, since one person is unlikely to know every other member of the group, especially in large-scale societies. In most instances, they are also informal groups since there are no recognized leaders or elected officials of the "urban elite" or the "working class." Subsegments of these large categories do organize themselves into formal groups, such as labor unions or exclusive clubs for the rich and famous. Class can be both ascribed and achieved since a person who is born rich has a greater than average chance of living an upper-class lifestyle. In "open" capitalistic societies, the prevailing ideology is that mobility in the system is up to the individual. This view emphasizes the importance of human agency in the ability of an individual to overcome structural forces. Political economy theories, in contrast, argue that low class position severely inhibits upward mobility because of the constraints and hardships of life in poverty.

The concept of class was especially important to the theories of Karl Marx. Situated within the context of Europe's industrial revolution and the growth of capitalism, Marx wrote that class differences, exploitation of the working class by the owners of capital, class consciousness among workers, and class conflict are forces of change that would eventually bring the downfall of capitalism.

In contrast to Marx's approach, French sociologist Emile Durkheim viewed social differences (including class) as the basis for social solidarity (1966 [1895]). He distinguished two major forms of societal cohesion: **Mechanical solidarity** exists when groups that are similar join together, and **organic solidarity** prevails when groups with different abilities and resources are linked together in complementary fashion. Mechanical solidarity creates less enduring relationships because it involves little mutual need. Organic solidarity builds on need and creates stronger bonds. Durkheim placed these two concepts in an evolutionary framework, saying that in preindustrial times, the division of labor was only minimally specialized: Everyone did what everyone else did. With increasing social complexity and economic specialization, organic solidarity developed.

Race, Ethnicity, and Caste: Ascribed Status

Three ascribed systems of social stratification are based on divisions of people into large, unequally ranked groups on the basis of race, ethnicity (defined in Chapter 1) and **caste** (a ranked group, determined by birth, often linked to a particular occupation and to South Asian cultures). Like status and class groups, these three types of groups are also secondary social groups, since no one can have a personal relationship with all other members of the entire group. Some social scientists emphasize the differences among these three systems of social stratification, while others focus on similarities. Gerald Berreman (1979 [1975]) has long been writing about similarities in systems of social inequality and how "invidious distinctions" such as race and caste affect the welfare of much of humanity. He says,

> "Race" as the term is used in America, Europe, and South Africa, is not qualitatively different in its implications for human social life from caste, *varna* or *jati* as applied in India, *quom* in Swat and Muslim India, the "invisible race" of Japan, the ethnic stratification of Rwanda and Burundi. Racism and casteism are indistinguishable in the annals of man's inhumanity to man, and sexism is closely allied to them as man's inhumanity to woman. All are invidious distinctions imposed unalterably at birth upon whole categories of people to justify the unequal social distribution of power, livelihood, security, privilege, esteem, freedom—in short, life chances. Where distinctions of this type are employed, they affect people and the events which people generate in surprisingly similar ways despite the different historical and cultural conditions in which they occur. (213)

One thing is certain: In all hierarchical systems, powerful people and groups seek to maintain dominance. Marvin Harris has said that those in power face an "organizational challenge" of how to maintain their position (1971, quoted in Mencher 1974:469). Harris notes two ways to meet this challenge: (1) through institutions that control the content of ideology, and (2) through institutions that physically suppress the subversive. The following sections on race, ethnicity, and caste provide insights about how both ideological and physical control maintain systems of inequality.

Race

Roger Sanjek (1994) has pointed out that racial stratification results from the unequal meeting of two formerly separate groups through colonization, slavery, and other large-group movements. Europe's "age of discovery," beginning in the 1500s, ushered in a new era of global contact. In contrast, in relatively homogeneous cultures, ethnicity is a more important distinction than race. In contemporary Nigeria, for example, the population is relatively homogeneous, and ethnicity is the more salient term there (Jinadu 1994). A similar situation prevails in Rwanda.

A key feature of racial thinking is its insistence that behavioral differences among peoples are "natural," in-born, or biologically caused (in this, it resembles sexism, ageism, and casteism). Throughout the history of racial categorizations in the West, such features as head size, head shape, and brain size have been accepted as the reasons for behavioral differences. Franz Boas contributed to de-linking supposed racial attributes from behavior. He showed that people with the same head size but from different cultures behaved differently, and people with different heads sizes within the same cultures behaved similarly. For Boas and his followers, culture, not biology, is the key explanation for behavior. Thus, race is not a biological reality; there is no way to divide the human population into races on the basis of certain biological features. Yet, "social race" exists and continues to be a basis of social stratification. In spite of some progress in reducing racism in the United States in the twentieth century, racial discrimination persists (see the Critical Thinking box). Some would argue that racism is increasing in such forms as neo-Nazism.

Emic racial classifications in the Caribbean and Latin America are especially complicated systems of status classification. This complexity results from the variety of contact over the centuries between peoples from Europe, Africa, Asia, and indigenous populations. Skin tone is one basis of racial classification, but it is mixed with other physical features and economic status as well. In Haiti, for example:

> [S]kin texture and depth of skin tone, hair color and appearance, and facial features also figure in any categorization ... color categories embrace characteristics that go far beyond the perceived phenotype into the field of social relations. These can include income, social origin, level of formal education, customary behavior, ties of kinship or marriage ... and different combinations of these social traits can move a person from one category to a more or less proximate one. (Trouillot 1994:148–149)

Thus, two people of the same "color" can be classed in different categories because of other biological and social factors.

Several emic color-race labels also exist in Brazil, resulting in dozens of different possible named categories. Brazil has long prided itself on its racial harmony in the face of so much diversity. Yet, within this generally harmonic picture lies the fact that less-favored racial groups do exist with lower standards of human welfare (Byrne, Harris, Consorte, and Lang 1995). For example, when collapsing the many possible racial labels into just three groups, different levels of education are clear:

brancas (Whites): 6.8 years
pardas (mixed): 6.4 years
pretas (Blacks): 4.1 years

Racial Apartheid in South Africa. The South African policy of apartheid, which is legally sanctioned segregation between dominant Whites and non-Whites, was an example of extreme racial stratification. White dominance in South Africa began in the early 1800s with White migration and settlement. In the 1830s, slavery was abolished. At the same time, increasingly racist thinking developed among Whites (Johnson 1994:25). Racist images, including visions of Africans as lazy, uncontrolled, and libidinous, served as the rationale for colonialist domination in place of outright slavery. In spite of years of African resistance to White domination, the Whites succeeded in maintaining and increasing their control for nearly two centuries. In South Africa, Blacks constitute 90 percent of the population, a numerical majority dominated through strict apartheid by the White minority until only recently. Every aspect of life for the majority of Africans was far worse than for the Whites. Every measure of life quality—infant mortality, longevity, education—showed great disparity between the Whites and the Africans. In addition to physical deprivation, the Africans experienced psychological suffering through constant insecurity about raids from the police and other forms of violence (see the Voices box on page 252).

Since the end of apartheid in South Africa, many social changes are taking place that anthropologists are beginning to document. One study describes the early stages of the dismantling of apartheid in the city of Umtata, the capital of the Transkei (Johnson 1994). Before the end of apartheid, Umtata "was like other South African towns: all apartheid laws were in full force; public and private facilities were completely segregated; only whites could vote or serve in the town government; whites owned all the major economic assets" (viii). When the change came, Umtata's dominant Whites bitterly resisted at first. They did not want to lose their privileges and they feared reprisals by the Africans. These things did not happen, however. The initial stages of transition brought

CRITICAL THINKING

What's Missing from This Picture?

Read the following summary from a news item entitled "Baseball Team Members Who Used KKK Symbol Will Receive Multi-Cultural Training" (*Jet* 88(18): 39–40, 1996). Then consider how anthropological research could provide a fuller understanding of racism in its social context:

> A county school board in Virginia opted not to punish members of the state champion high school baseball team who used a Ku Klux Klan symbol. The team members drew the symbol in the dirt before games for good luck. Investigators believe that the symbol represents four hooded Klansmen looking down a hole, the last thing a Black victim would see after being dropped down a well by Klansmen. The school superintendent decided to reprimand the coaches and the school board voted to send the students for "multi-cultural training."

This brief news item tells us some things about the case, but provides little information that would lead to deeper understanding of the broader cultural context. If a cultural anthropologist decided to do in-depth fieldwork in the community, what kinds of research questions would be most important? Here are some examples:

- The racial composition of the team.
- The racial composition of the school leadership (superintendent), coaches, and other local leaders.
- The pattern of racial and class stratification in the community in which the school is located.

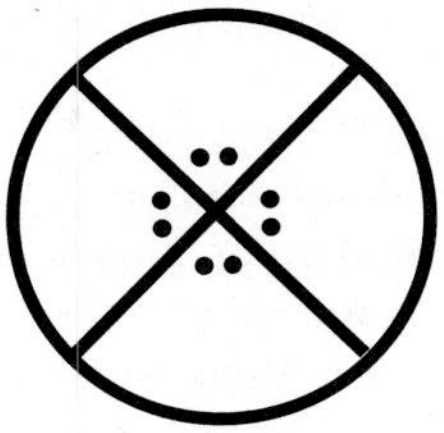

Ku Klux Klan symbol

- Other possible forms of racist thinking and behavior in the community.
- Any generational differences that might exist in racist thinking and behavior in this community.
- The reactions: of different community members to the behavior of members of the high-school baseball team; of the coaches; of the school superintendent's decision about how to treat the baseball players.
- Social programs in the schools and wider community that might reduce racism.

Critical Thinking Questions

- How does cultural anthropology differ from journalism in terms of research goals?
- In terms of research methods?
- In terms of research results and how they are presented?
- What are the comparative costs and benefits of each approach?

"neoapartheid," in which White privilege was not seriously threatened. Then members of the dominant group began to welcome the less tense, "nonracial" atmosphere.

Ethnicity

Ethnicity includes a shared sense of identity on some grounds and a set of relations to other groups (Comaroff 1987). Identity is formed sometimes on the basis of a perception of shared history, territory, language, or religion. As such, ethnicity can be a basis for claiming entitlements to resources such as land or artifacts, and a perceived basis for defending or regaining those resources.

States are interested in managing ethnicity to the extent that it does not threaten security. China has one of the most formalized systems for monitoring its many ethnic groups, and it has an official policy on ethnic minorities, meaning the non-Han groups (Wu 1990). The government lists a total of fifty-four groups other than the Han majority, which constitutes about 94 percent of the total. The other 6 percent of

VOICES

"Growing Up under Apartheid" by Mark Mathabane

I am always asked to explain what it felt like to grow up black under South Africa's system of legalized racism known as apartheid, and how I escaped from it and ended up in America. . . . The last thing I ever dreamed of when I was daily battling for survival and for an identity other than of inferiority and fourth-class citizen, which apartheid foisted on me, was that someday I would attend an American college, edit its newspaper, graduate with honors, practise journalism and write a book.

How could I have dreamed of all this when I was born of illiterate parents who could not afford to pay my way through school, let alone pay the rent for our shack and put enough food on the table; when black people in Alexandra lived under constant police terror and the threat of deportation to impoverished tribal reserves; when at ten I contemplated suicide because I found the burden of living in a ghetto, poverty-stricken and without hope, too heavy to shoulder; when in 1976 I got deeply involved in the Soweto protests in which hundreds of black students were killed by the police, and thousands fled the country to escape imprisonment and torture?. . .

Much has been written and spoken about the politics of apartheid: the forced removals of black communities from their ancestral lands, the Influx Control and Pass laws that mandate where blacks can live, work, raise families, be buried; the migrant labour system that forces black men to live away from their families eleven months out of a year; the breaking up of black families in the ghettos as the authorities seek to create a so-called white South Africa; the brutal suppression of the black majority as it agitates for equal rights. But what does it all mean in human terms?

When I was growing up in Alexandra it meant hate, bitterness, hunger, pain, terror, violence, fear, dashed hopes and dreams. . . . In the ghettoes black children fight for survival from the moment they are born. They take to hating and fearing the police, soldiers and authorities as a baby takes to its mother's breast.

In my childhood these enforcers of white prerogatives and whims represented a sinister force capable of crushing me at will; of making my parents flee in the dead of night to escape arrest under the Pass laws; of marching them naked out of bed because they did not have the permit allowing them to live as husband and wife under the same roof. They turned my father—by repeatedly arresting him and denying him the right to earn a living in a way that gave him dignity—into such a bitter man that, as he fiercely but in vain resisted the emasculation, he hurt those he loved the most.

The movies, with their lurid descriptions of white violence, reinforced this image of white power and terror. Often the products of abject poverty and broken homes, many black children, for whom education is inferior and not compulsory, have been derailed by movies into the dead-end life of crime and violence. It is no wonder that black ghettos have one of the highest murder rates in the world, and South African prisons are among the most packed. It was purely by accident that I did not end up a *tsotsi* (thug, murderer, mugger, gangster). . . . The turning point came when one day in my eleventh year I accompanied my grandmother to her gardening job and met a white family that did not fit the stereotypes I had grown up with. Most blacks, exposed daily to virulent racism and dehumanized and embittered by it, do not believe that such whites exist. From this family I started receiving "illegal books" like *Treasure Island* and *David Copperfield,* which revealed a different reality. . . . At thirteen I stumbled across tennis, a sport so "white" most blacks thought I was mad for thinking I could excel in it. . . . Through tennis I learned the important lesson that South Africa's 4.5 million whites are not all racists. As I grew older, and got to understand them more—their fears, longings, hopes, ignorance and mistaken beliefs, and mine—this lesson became the conviction that whites are in some ways victims of apartheid, too, and that it is the system, and not they, that has to be destroyed; just as it was Hitler's regime that had to be extirpated, not the German people. Such an attitude helped me survive the nightmare into which my life was plunged by the Soweto protests of 1976. A tennis scholarship to an American college, arranged by professional tennis player Stan Smith, in 1978, became my passport to freedom.

Source: Reprinted with the permission of Simon & Schuster from *Kaffir Boy* by Mark Mathabane, pp ix-xi.

the population is made up of the other fifty-four groups, about 67 million people. The non-Han minorities occupy about 60 percent of China's land mass and are located in border or "frontier" areas such as Tibet, Yunnan, Xinjiang, and Inner Mongolia. Basic criteria for defining an ethnic group include language, territory, economy, and "psychological disposition." The Chinese government establishes strict definitions of group membership and group characteristics, including setting standards for ethnic costumes and dances. The Chinese treatment of the Tibetan people is especially severe and can be considered an attempt at ethnocide or annihilation of the culture of an ethnic group by a dominant group. The Tibetans continue to resist the loss of their culture and absorption into the Han mainstream. The government's treatment of Tibetan traditional medicine over the past several decades illustrates how the Han majority uses certain aspects of minority cultures (see the Multiple Cultural Worlds box).

People of one ethnic group who move from one niche to another are at risk of exclusionary treatment from the local residents. Rom, or gypsies, are a **diaspora population** (dispersed group living outside their original homeland) scattered throughout Europe and the United States. Their history is one of mobility and marginality since they first left India around 1000 AD (Fonseca 1995). Everywhere they live, they are marginalized and looked down on by the settled populations. Traditional Rom lifestyle is one of movement, with temporary camps of their wagons often appearing overnight on the outskirts of a town. For decades, European governments have tried to force the Rom to settle down. In addition, Rom migration to cities in Eastern Europe is increasing because of the recent economic crisis, unemployment, and declining standard of living. In cities, high-status groups reside in areas segregated from others (Ladányi 1993). Low-status people must live where no one else wants to reside. In Budapest, Hungary, the Rom minority is the most disadvantaged ethnic group. Not all Rom in Budapest are poor, though. Some 1 percent has gained wealth, and they live in the high-status neighborhoods. However, the vast majority live in substandard housing, usually in areas where low-income Hungarians reside, in the slum inner areas of Pest.

MULTIPLE CULTURAL WORLDS

The Chinese Takeover of Tibetan Medicine

In 1951, Tibet became part of China, and the Chinese government undertook measures to bring about the social and economic transformation of what was formerly a decentralized, Buddhist feudal regime. This transformation has brought increasing ethnic conflict between Tibetans and Han Chinese, including demonstrations by Tibetans and crackdowns from the government. Traditional Tibetan medicine has become part of the Chinese–Tibetan conflicts because of its culturally significant and religiously important position in Tibetan society (Janes 1995:7).

Several policy swings of the Chinese state toward Tibetan traditional medicine occurred in the second half of the twentieth century: Between 1951 and 1962, it was tolerated but largely ignored; by 1962, it was officially included as a component of the public health system and given funds for clinical operations and training programs; in 1966, it was delegitimized; in 1978, it was near extinction; and in 1985, it re-emerged as a legitimate sector of the government health bureaucracy, having a major role in providing primary health care in the Tibetan region, with a substantial operating budget and over 1,200 physicians.

Linkage with a centralized medical system substantially transformed traditional Tibetan medicine. The training of physicians is one area of major change. Previously based on a model of apprenticeship training, it is now westernized and involves several years of classroom-based, lecture-oriented learning followed by an internship. At Tibet University, only half of all formal lecture-based instruction is concerned with traditional Tibetan medicine. Curriculum changes have reduced the integrity of Tibetan medicine: It has been separated from its Buddhist content, and parts of it have been merged with a biomedical approach. While one might say that overall, traditional Tibetan medicine has been "revived" in China, stronger evidence supports the argument that the state has co-opted it and transformed it for its own purposes.

A Rom encampment in Romania's Transylvania region. Not all European Rom are poor, however. Some urban Rom have become wealthy and have therefore attracted the jealousy of the non-Rom population.

Since the fall of state socialism, discrimination against Roms has increased. Rom houses have been torched, and their children have been harassed while going to school.

A less difficult but still not easy adjustment is being experienced by Indo-Canadians (immigrants from India to Canada). Research among a sample of nearly three hundred Indo-Canadians in Vancouver, British Columbia, revealed that about half of all the respondents reported experiencing some form of discrimination in the recent past (Nodwell and Guppy 1992). The percentage was higher among men (54 percent) than among women (45 percent). The higher level for men was consistent across the four categories: verbal abuse, property damage, workplace discrimination, and physical harm. Verbal abuse was the most frequent form of discrimination, reported by 40 percent of both men and women. Indo-Canadians of the Sikh faith who were born in India say that they experience the highest levels of discrimination in Canada. Apparently, however, their actual experience of discrimination is not greater than for other Indo-Canadians. The difference is that Sikhs who were born in India are more sensitive to discrimination than others. Sikhism, as taught and practiced in India, supports a strong sense of honor, which should be protected and, if wronged, avenged. This study helps explain differences in perception of discrimination among ethnic migrants. It does not explain why such high levels of discriminatory treatment exist in a nation committed to ethnic tolerance.

Caste

The caste system is a form of social stratification found in its clearest form in India, among its Hindu population, and in other areas of Hindu culture such as Nepal, Sri Lanka, and Fiji. It is particularly associated with Hindu peoples because ancient Hindu scriptures are taken as the foundational sources for defining the major social categories called *varnas* (a Sanskrit word meaning "color," or "shade"). The four varnas are: the *brahmans* who were priests, the *kshatriya* or warriors, the *vaishya* or merchants, and the *shudras* or laborers. Of these, men of the first three varnas could go through a ritual ceremony of "rebirth" and thereafter wear a sacred thread. These three categories are referred to as "twice-born," and their status is higher than that of the shudra varna. Beneath the four varna groups were people considered so low that they were outside the caste system itself (hence, the word "outcast"). Throughout history, these people have been referred to by many names in Indian languages and by the English term "untouchable." Mahatma Gandhi, himself a member of an upper caste, renamed them *harijans* (or "children of god") as part of his attempt to raise their status into that of the level above them. Currently, members of this category have adopted the term ***dalit*** (meaning "oppressed" or "ground down") as their favored name.

Each of the four varnas and the dalit category contains many locally named groups called *castes* or, more appropriately, *jatis*. The term "caste" is a Portuguese word meaning "breed" or "type" and was first used by Portuguese colonialists in the fifteenth century to refer to the closed social groups they encountered (Cohn 1971:125). Jati means "birth group," and conveys the meaning that a Hindu is born into his or her group. It is an ascribed status and cannot be changed under normal conditions. Just as the four varnas are ranked with each other, so are all the jatis within them. For example, the category of brahmans "may be subdivided into priestly and non-priestly subgroups, the priestly Brahmans into Household-priests, Temple-priests and Funeral-priests; the Household-priests into two or more endogamous circles; and each circle into its component clans and lineages ... non-priestly Brahmans are superior in relation to priestly ones, and Household-priests in relation to Funeral-priests" (Parry 1966:77).

Status levels also exist among dalits. In western Nepal, artisans such as basket-weavers and ironsmiths are the highest tier (Cameron 1995). They do not touch any of the people beneath them. The second tier includes leatherworkers and tailors. The bottom tier comprises people who are "untouchable" to all other groups including other dalits because their work is extremely polluting according to Hindu rules: musicians (some of their instruments are made of leather and they perform in public) and prostitutes.

Indian anthropologist M. N. Srinivas (1959) contributed the concept of the **dominant caste** to refer to the tendency for one caste in any particular village to control most of the land and, often, to be numerically preponderant as well. Although brahmans are at the top of the social hierarchy in terms of ritual purity, they are often, but not always, the dominant caste. Throughout northern India, it is common for jatis of the kshatriya varna to be the dominant village group. This is the case in "Pahansu" village, where a group called the Gujars is dominant (Raheja 1988). The Gujars constitute the numerical majority, and they control most of the land (see Table 10.1 on page 256). Moreover, they dominate in the **jajmani system,** a patron-provider system in which landholding patrons (*jajmans*) are linked through exchanges of food for services with brahman priests, artisans (blacksmiths, potters), agricultural laborers, and other workers such as sweepers (Kolenda 1978:46–54). In Pahansu, Gujars have power and status as the major patrons, supporting many different service-providers who are thus beholden to them.

Only a special category of brahman priests can officiate at the Chidambaraman temple in south India. Here, an age-mixed Chidambaraman group sit for a moment's relaxation.

Some anthropologists have described the jajmani service system as one of mutual interdependence (organic solidarity, to use Durkheim's term), which provides security for the less well-off. Joan Mencher (1974) and others argue that the system benefits those at the top to the detriment of those at the bottom. Mencher has done fieldwork among low caste people. This perspective, from "the bottom up," views the patron-service system and the entire caste system as one of exploitation by those at the top. Mencher says that the benign interpretation is based on research conducted among the upper castes who present this view. A more comprehensive look reveals that while both patrons and clients have rights and responsibilities, the relationship is not equal. Patrons have more power. Dissatisfied patrons can dismiss service providers, refuse them loans, or not pay them. Service providers who are dissatisfied with the treatment they receive from their patrons have little recourse. Male patrons often demand sexual privileges from low-caste females from service-providing households. Whatever one's perspective on whether the jajmani system is exploitative or supportive, it is clear that, throughout South Asia, it has declined in recent decades. Industrial manufacturing and marketing are the main factors leading to these changes. They have created less need for some service providers, especially craftspersons such as tailors, potters, and weavers. With less need for their skills in the countryside, many former service providers have left the villages to work in urban areas. This trend has been noted since the 1950s and 1960s (Elder 1970). The tie that remains the strongest is between patrons and

Table 10.1
Caste Ranking in Pahansu Village, North India

Caste Name	*Traditional Occupation*	*Number of Households*	*Occupation in Pahansu*
Gujar	agriculturalist	210	owner cultivator
Brahman	priest	8	priest, postman
Baniya	merchant	3	shopkeeper
Sunar	goldsmith	2	silversmith, sugar cane press operator
Dhiman (Barhai)	carpenter	1	carpenter
Kumhar	potter	3	potter, tailor
Nai	barber	3	barber, postman
Dhobi	washerman	2	washerman
Gadariya	shepherd	4	agricultural laborer, weaver
Jhivar	water-carrier	20	agricultural laborer, basket-weaver
Luhar	ironsmith	2	blacksmith
Teli	oil-presser	2	beggar, cotton-carder, agricultural laborer
Maniharan	bangle-seller	1	bangle-seller
Camar	leatherworker	100	agricultural laborer
Bhangi	sweeper	17	sweeper, midwife

Source: Adapted from Raheja 1988:19.

their brahman priests, whose ritual services cannot be replaced by machines.

Like all status hierarchies, the caste system involves several mechanisms that maintain it: marriage rules, spatial segregation, and ritual. These operate in addition to the basic material constraints that prevent low-caste people from obtaining property and skilled jobs—control of land markets and control of educational opportunities by dominant groups. Marriage rules strictly enforce jati endogamy. Marriage outside one's jati, especially in rural areas and particularly between a higher-caste female and lower-caste male, is cause for serious, even lethal, punishment by caste elders and other local power-holders. Indian newspapers frequently carry accounts of local action taken to punish offenders. They may be beaten to death or stoned. Sometimes the female's life is spared, but she may be branded, have her head shaved, and be subject to social scorn. Among urban educated elites, a trend to allow some degree of inter-jati marriages is in motion, but it is not preferred.

Spatial segregation functions to maintain the privileged preserve of the upper castes and to continually remind the lower castes of their marginal status. In many rural contexts, the dalits live in a completely separate cluster; in other cases, they have their own neighborhood sections into which no upper-caste person will venture. Ritual rules and practices also serve to maintain dominance. The rich upper-caste leaders sponsor important annual festivals, thereby regularly restating their claim to public prominence (Mines 1994). Processions of deities through particular parts of the village or city stamp a claim on that locale and tie residents to the sponsor in relationships of loyalty and respect. During public festivals that all castes may attend, folk epics and religious stories are recited and enacted in plays that contain plots substantiating the heroism and power of the ruling castes. Most notably, *The Ramayana,* which tells the story of the king Rama and his dutiful wife Sita, is a morality tale about good leaders and the value of being good followers.

Social mobility within the caste system has traditionally been limited, but instances have been documented of group "up-casting." Several strategies exist, including gaining wealth, affiliation or merger with a somewhat higher jati, education, migration, and political activism (Kolenda 1978). In all cases, a group that attempts to gain higher jati status takes on the behavior and dress of twice-born jatis. This process is termed **Sanskritization,** or the adopting of practices and values more associated with brahmanic culture. These include men's wearing the sacred thread, vegetarianism, non-remarriage of widows, seclusion of women from the public domain, and the giving of larger dowries for the marriage of a daughter. Some dalits have opted out of the caste system by converting to Christianity or Buddhism. Others are becoming politically organized through the Dalit Panthers, a social movement seeking greater power and improved economic status for dalits (Omvedt 1995).

Discrimination on the basis of caste was made illegal by the Indian constitution of 1949, but constitutional decree did not bring an end to these deeply structured inequalities. The government of India has instituted policies to promote the social and economic advancement of dalits, such as reserving places for them in medical schools, seats in the government, and public sector jobs. This "affirmative action" plan has infuriated many of the upper castes, especially brahmans who feel most threatened. Is the caste system on the decline? Surely, aspects of it are changing. Especially in large cities, people of different jatis can "pass" and participate more equally in public life—if they have the economic means to do so.

CIVIL SOCIETY: BETWEEN GROUPS AND GOVERNMENT

The concept of **civil society** refers to the social domain of diverse interest groups that function outside the government to organize economic and other aspects of life. It has a long history in Western philosophy, with many different definitions proposed by thinkers such as John Locke, Thomas Paine, Adam Smith, and Karl Marx (Kumar 1996:89). According to the German philosopher Georg Wilhelm Friedrich Hegel, civil society encompasses the social groups and institutions between the individual and the state. Italian social theorist Antonio Gramsci wrote that there are two basic types of civic institutions: those that support the state such as the Church and schools, and those that oppose state power such as trade unions, social protest groups, citizens' rights groups, and counterculture groups.

Among other issues in post-socialist states, concern about the environment has prompted the emergence of many nongovernmental groups (NGOs). In Poland, youth activism related to the environment grew in strength in the late 1980s (Glínski 1994:145). This was the first generation to come after Stalin that did not experience martial law, so they have less fear of organizing than their parents. Furthermore, the government's new policy of limited liberalization involves concessions to social groups and the interests they expressed. The mass media now has greater freedom of expression. Many of the ecological groups draw on countercultural values (values in opposition of the dominant culture) of the 1960s and 1970s: "This was evident in their quest for alternative values, their distance from the political system, and their gentle, if ironic, form of communicating with the surrounding world. The counterculture orientation also encouraged the non-violent posture adopted by the Polish youth environmental groups in the 1980s as well as the relative moderation of programs and activities" (146–147). Polish "green organizations" are distanced from the government.

This distance is related to several factors. First, the government itself has not incorporated environmental concerns into its agenda. Furthermore, political elites actively sought to marginalize youth and countercultural groups: "There was no dialogue between the government and environmentalists over controversial questions. On the contrary, old bureaucratic methods were employed: police units were dispatched against young people protesting the construction of a nuclear power plant in Żarnowiec (1989) and a dam at Czorsztyn (1990, 1991, 1992)" (151). All of this increased the youths' sense of alienation from political institutions. In the local elections of 1990, youth group participation was sporadic, and few members of ecology groups were elected to local bodies. The first fully democratic parliamentary election in 1991 did not seek to involve the youth ecological movement. On the other hand, "artificially green" political parties developed, using ecological names and slogans to win parliamentary seats, but chose candidates from outside the environmental movement. The activists saw through these ploys and did not support such ecological "pseudo-parties." As of the early 1990s, some preliminary movement toward dialogue with the Ministry of Environmental Protection had occurred, and the Ministry established a special office for contact with youth groups and held monthly meetings with them. The youth groups are evolving into a second stage: They are building effective, professional NGOs. Several foundations and ecological groups began to seek financial support for their activities, often from foreign sources. They have made efforts to coordinate the activities of different groups and organizations. Most youth ecological groups have participated actively in all of these processes.

International interest in the notion of civil society has increased recently, given the changes in government structure in many post-socialist states. There is now potential for growth of civil society in these transforming states, but the way civil institutions will emerge and develop is still unfolding (see the Current Event box).

Current Event

"Fragile Civil Society Takes Root in Chinese Reform"

- The Chinese bureaucracy regulates the formation of all clubs and social groups. Any group—a soccer team, music ensemble, women's advice center, labor union, or religious group—must obtain an official seal of approval.
- Nevertheless, in post-Mao China, civil society is beginning to grow in the gray area outside the structure of the state.
- By the late 1980s, Liaoning Province alone had over 2,000 peasant societies of a wide variety. For example, a rabbit-raising association boasted 3,200 members throughout China.
- Some of the economic groups occasionally express independent viewpoints, especially to defend their interests. In 1995, taxi drivers struck following the Beijing government's raising of a toll on the airport expressway. In spite of the strike, the toll hike remained in place.
- Decentralization and the diminishing power of the central government increase the need for groups outside the central structure. Because of recent reforms, the social safety net has deteriorated, so the government needs social groups to help solve problems and generate funds.
- The China Youth Development Foundation has raised enough money privately to pay the tuition for 540,000 children and to build 240 primary schools in underdeveloped areas.
- Wang Xingjuan, a retiree, founded the popular Women's Hot Line. Although it was under the women's federation umbrella, Wang raised the funds herself.
- Unlike civil society in Eastern Europe, which opposed the power of the state, China's civil society has a symbiotic relationship with the party-run state. . . . As one person active with nongovernmental organizations said, "In order to survive, you have to create an environment for playing a positive role . . . things like . . . human rights may be difficult."

Source: The Washington Post, June 4, 1996.

SUMMARY

Cultural anthropologists have documented the importance of social groups, the way they are formed, their functions, and how social groups communicate with other groups. Groups can be classified in terms of whether members all have face-to-face interaction with one another, whether membership is based on ascription or achievement, and how formal the group's organization and leadership structure is.

The fact of solidarity within a group necessarily means that other people and other groups are excluded from it. It may also mean that groups and their members have a particular status in relation to other groups and their members, something that is especially likely in more socially complex cultures. Prominent bases on which groups are formed with hierarchical intergroup relations are class, race, ethnicity, gender, age, and ability. The degree of social inequality between different status groups is especially marked in most agricultural and industrial societies, whereas status inequalities are not characteristic of foraging groups. India's caste system of social stratification is a particularly rigid form of social inequality that persists in importance in spite of legislation against discrimination on its basis. Marriage choices, job opportunities, and electoral politics are still influenced by caste considerations to a large degree.

In recent years, a trend toward emphasizing the concept of civil society in post-socialist states has brought new attention to the role of nongovernmental groups in fulfilling important social functions. Cultural anthropologists have a role to play in researching the existence of such groups and what they do, for example, in terms of providing social support services for the poor, contributing to educational institutions, and affecting government policy through lobbying.

CRITICAL THINKING QUESTIONS

1. What are the exchange relationships involved in different groups that you know or might belong to (in other words, what are members' responsibilities to each other and the group as a whole, and what do they get from other members and from the group as a whole)?
2. Why might certain social groups more strongly define and defend in-group/out-group differences? Why do some groups promote violence against out-groups?
3. How much of your own (or your family/household's) status and class positions are explained by either ascription or achievement?

KEY CONCEPTS

achieved position, p. 248
age set, p. 236
ascribed position, p. 248
caste, p. 249
civil society, p. 257
cooperative, p. 246
dalit, p. 254
diaspora population, p. 253
dominant caste, p. 255
jajmani system, p. 255
mechanical solidarity, p. 249
organic solidarity, p. 249
primary group, p. 236
role, p. 248
Sanskritization, p. 257
secondary group, p. 236
social group, p. 236
social stratification, p. 248
status, p. 248
youth gang, p. 243

SUGGESTED READINGS

Gerald Berreman, *Caste and Other Inequities: Essays on Inequality.* Delhi: Folklore Institute, 1979. These eighteen essays on caste and social inequality in India were written over a period of twenty years. Topics include caste and economy, caste ranking, caste and social interaction, and a comparison of caste with race in the United States.

Steven Gregory and Roger Sanjek, editors, *Race.* New Brunswick: Rutgers University Press, 1994. The editors each provide a useful introductory chapter. Seventeen other contributions cover aspects of racism in the United States and the Caribbean, how race articulates with other inequalities, and racism in higher education and anthropology.

Martín Sánchez Jankowski, *Islands in the Sun: Gangs and American Society.* Berkeley: University of California Press, 1991. This book includes attention to theories about street gang life, comparisons of different ethnic patterns of gang behavior in three cities in the United States, and variations in why youths join street gangs.

Kathryn March and Rachelle Taqqu, *Women's Informal Associations in Developing Countries: Catalysts for Change?* Boulder: Westview Press, 1986. This book provides an overview of various types of women's informal organizations and an assessment of their positive role in women's lives in developing countries. It also includes attention to credit, labor, ritual, and religious associations.

Karin Tice, *Kuna Crafts, Gender and the Global Economy.* Austin: University of Texas Press, 1995. This ethnographic study looks at how the tourist market has affected women's production of molas in Panama and how women have organized into cooperatives in order to improve their situation.

FEDER ACION
SINDICATO - AGRARIO
"EL-PALMAR"
GUARANI

Chapter 11

Politics and Leadership

CHAPTER OUTLINE

POLITICAL ANTHROPOLOGY
- Politics: The Use of Power, Authority, and Influence
- Politics: Species Universal, Human Universal?
  - *Multiple Cultural Worlds:* Socialization of Women Politicians in Korea
- Symbols of Power

POLITICAL ORGANIZATION AND LEADERSHIP
- Bands
- Tribes
- Chiefdoms
- States
  - *Multiple Cultural Worlds:* The Benefits of Citizenship in Kuwait
  - *Current Event:* "Who's Buried in Margarita's Tomb?"
  - *Critical Thinking:* How "Open" Are Democratic Electoral Politics?

CHANGE IN POLITICAL SYSTEMS
- Emergent Nations and Fractured States
- Democratization
- Women in Politics: New Directions?
- Fluctuating World-System Politics
  - *Viewpoint:* Václav Havel, "The Hope for Europe"

SUMMARY

CRITICAL THINKING QUESTIONS

KEY CONCEPTS

SUGGESTED READINGS

◀ A political rally of indigenous people in Bolivia.

- November 4, 1995: Prime Minister Itzak Rabin of Israel was assassinated by a radical Israeli law student, who opposed Rabin's attempts to forge a peaceful agreement in the Middle East.
- June 13, 1996: The United States's Board of Immigration Appeals ruled that a nineteen-year-old woman, Fauzuya Kasinga of Togo, West Africa, should be granted political asylum because she sought to avoid genital mutilation as practiced in her homeland.
- July 3, 1996: Seven hundred years after King Edward I of England took Scotland's "Stone of Scone," the sandstone-carved throne has been returned to Edinborough. This coronation "seat" of Scottish kings has long been a symbol to people in Scotland of the independence their nation once enjoyed.
- At midnight on June 30, 1997, the British flag came down in Hong Kong, to be replaced by the flag of the People's Republic of China. Six million people were transferred from living under a Western colonial power to a socialist state.

These headline events are cultural happenings related to public power and politics. Political anthropology addresses the area of human behavior and thought related to power: who has it and who doesn't; degrees of power; the bases of power; abuses of power; relationships between political and religious power; political organization and government; social conflict and social control; and morality and law. Several academic disciplines are concerned with these topics, especially political science, but also history, sociology, economics, public policy, and legal studies. Anthropologists in all four fields address political and legal topics. Archaeologists study the evolution of centralized forms of political organization and the physical manifestations of power in monumental architecture, housing, and material possessions. Primatologists do research on dominance relationships, coalitions, and aggression among nonhuman primates. Linguistic anthropologists analyze power differences in interpersonal speech, the media, political propaganda and more.

POLITICAL ANTHROPOLOGY

Lewis Henry Morgan's mid-nineteenth century study, *The League of the Iroquois* (1851), is considered the first "political ethnography" (Vincent 1996). As a separate subfield, political anthropology emerged about one hundred years later, in the mid-twentieth century, with the publication of *African Political Systems,* a book of essays compiled by British social anthropologists Meyer Fortes and E. E. Evans-Pritchard (Colson 1968:189). This book placed African ethnography at the center of both political anthropology and legal anthropology (the cross-cultural study of how law and order are defined and maintained). This new phase of anthropological research in Africa shifted attention from small-scale foraging and horticultural societies to the study of larger, settled populations and more complex levels of political organization. As field studies accumulated, anthropologists of the 1960s began to devise typologies and terminology for the variety of political systems encountered.

British anthropologists, especially Bronislaw Malinowski and A. R. Radcliffe-Brown, long dominated theory-making in political anthropology. Their approach, referred to as *functionalism,* emphasized how institutions such as political organization and law promote social cohesion. Later, the students of these two teachers developed divergent theories. For example, in the late 1960s, some scholars began to look at aspects of political organization that pull societies apart. The new focus on disputes and conflict prompted anthropologists to gather information on dispute "cases" and to analyze the actors involved in a particular conflict, "processual analysis." The processual approach to micropolitics has been countered by a swing toward a more macro view (Vincent 1996), which examines politics, no matter how local, within a global context (Asad 1973). This global perspective has prompted many studies of colonialism and neocolonialism in political anthropology and historical anthropology. Ann Stoler's book, *Capitalism and Confrontation in Sumatra's Plantation Belt, 1870–1979* (1985), on the history and cultural impact of Dutch colonialism in Indonesia, is a classic study in this genre. In the 1980s, the experiences of "subaltern" peoples (those subordinated by colonialism) and "subaltern movements" in former colonized regions attracted research attention, particularly from native anthropologists of decolonizing countries. The history of political anthropology in the twentieth century illustrates the theoretical tensions between the actor-as-agent approach (processual approach) and the structural, political economy perspective that sees actors as constrained in their choices by larger forces.

Politics: The Use of Power, Authority, and Influence

Politics usually refers to public power, as opposed to the more private, micropolitics of family and domestic groups. **Power** is the ability to bring about results, often through the possession or use of forceful means. Closely related to power are authority and influence. **Authority** implies "the right to take certain forms of action" (M. Smith 1966:3). It is usually based on a person's achieved or ascribed status, moral reputation, or other basis for respect. Authority differs from power in that power "is the capacity to take autonomous action in the face of resistance.... It is the capacity to pursue one's will effectively, if necessary, by imposing it on others" (3). Power is backed up by the potential use of force. **Influence** is another way of achieving a desired end, through exerting social or moral pressure, not force, on someone or some group. Compared to authority, influence may be reinforced by social position and status, but it may also be exerted from a low-status and marginal position. All three terms are relational. A person's power, authority, or influence exists in relation to others. Power implies the greatest likelihood of a coercive and hierarchical relationship, and authority and influence offer the most scope for consensual, cooperative decision making. Power, authority, and influence are all related to politics, with power being the strongest basis for action and decision making.

Politics: Species Universal, Human Universal?

A question that intrigues anthropologists, archaeologists, primatologists, political scientists, and historians is whether politics or political organization is found in other animals, especially nonhuman primates, and in all cultures throughout history.

Is politics a primate universal? Aristotle is credited with coining the still-popular phrase that "man is a political animal," implying that humans in general are innately aggressive; that is, they are naturally prone to seeking power and forming coalitions for maintaining dominance. Many ethologists and popular writers gathered evidence for this position, and a cluster of "man the animal" books appeared in the 1960s: Robert Ardrey's *African Genesis* (1961) and *The Territorial Imperative* (1966), Konrad Lorenz' *On Aggression* (1966), and Desmond Morris's *The Naked Ape* (1967). The gist of these books is that humans have inherited from their primate ancestors "instincts" for certain forms of political behavior, especially territoriality and aggressiveness.

These days, most scientists would replace the word "instinct" with "genes" as the motivating factor. Whether based on innate instincts or genetic coding, this kind of thinking promotes an "easy" and "simple" explanation for behaviors such as aggression, hierarchy, and dominance that are assumed to be universal and natural among humans, just as they are assumed to be universal and natural among nonhuman primates. One critic of such approaches comments: "What is most serious is that Ardrey and Lorenz [and other such writers, by implication] show themselves to be so enamored of their own theories that they overlook or evade bodies of fact that do not support their views" (Montagu 1973:xiii). Since the 1960s, counterevidence to humans being naturally aggressive and naturally political has accumulated. At the same time, evidence is accumulating that nonhuman primates often act in political ways, sometimes by developing persistent hierarchies. These two statements are not contradictory if one accepts the possibility that nonhuman primates also "learn" to be political through culture, as do humans.

Primatologist Frans de Waal (1989) studied "chimpanzee politics" in the Arnhem Zoo in Holland. He analyzed many hours of observation of interactions into the following themes:

- *Formalization of ranking:* When rank becomes unclear, a dominance struggle ensues, after which the winner is formally recognized.
- *Influence:* Positions of influence are not necessarily the same as positions of highest rank. The oldest male and female of the group are the most influential group members. Individuals build coalitions by intervening in conflicts to help friends or relatives. Coalitions are the basis of power.
- *Exchanges:* Social support is exchanged as favors. Support tends to flow to a central individual, who uses the prestige to provide social security to others.
- *Manipulation:* Individuals use others as social instruments.
- *Privilege:* High-ranking males copulate more frequently than low-ranking males (no mention is made of female ranking and copulation frequency). (210–212)

Gender differences in chimpanzee political behavior exist. Female dominance hierarchies are less prominent, while their support networks are stronger. Females sometimes mediate between males who are competing for status. On the basis of the similarities between these chimpanzee behaviors and human behavior, de Waal congratulates Aristotle for calling humans "political animals." Human political behavior is thus biologically driven, through inherited patterns of genes or hormones. He does not raise the possibility that nonhuman primates may have "human" traits, especially a capacity for culture and learning that might shape their behavior and be dependent on variables in the ecological and social environment. Furthermore, the nonhuman primate record contains several possible models for human evolution, and the human record, as this chapter shows, also contains a variety of models that cannot be explained by a single evolutionary line.

Thus primate studies reveal the existence of political behavior among nonhuman primates, but there is no doubt that most human cultures are more political and more aggressive than those of other primates. (For example, we have war and they they don't.) But is politics a human universal? Some anthropologists would say no. They point to instances of cultures with scarcely any institutions that can be called political, with no durable ranking systems and very little aggression. In fact, traditional foraging lifestyles, as a model for early human evolution, indicate that nonhierarchical social systems characterized human life for 90 to 99 percent of its existence. Only with the emergence of private property, surpluses, and other changes do ranking systems, government, formal law, and organized group aggression emerge. Also, many studies show how dominance-seeking and aggression are learned behaviors, emphasized in some cultures and among some segments of the population such as the military, and de-emphasized among others such as religious leaders, healers, and child care providers. Being a good politician, five-star general, or marine is a matter of socialization (see the Multiple Cultural Worlds box).

Multiple Cultural Worlds

Socialization of Women Politicians in Korea

Parental attitudes affect children's involvement in public political roles. Sarah Chunghee Soh's (1993) research in the Republic of Korea reveals how variation in paternal roles affects daughters' political leadership roles. Korean women members of the National Assembly can be divided into two categories: elected members (active seekers) versus appointed members (passive recipients). Korea is a strongly patrilineal and male-dominated society, so women political leaders represent "a notable deviance from the usual gender-role expectations" (54). This "deviance" is not stigmatized in Korean culture; rather it is admired within the category of *yŏgŏl.* A yŏgŏl is a woman with "manly" accomplishments. Her personality traits include extraordinary bravery, strength, integrity, generosity, and charisma. Physically, a yŏgŏl is likely to be taller, larger, and stronger than most women, and to have a stronger voice than other women. Why do some girls grow up to be a yŏgŏl?

Analysis of the life histories of elected and appointed women legislators offers clues about differences in their socialization. Elected women legislators were likely to have had atypical paternal experiences of two types: either an absent father, or an atypically nurturant father. Both of these experiences facilitated a girl's socialization into yŏgŏl qualities, or, in the words of Soh, into developing an androgynous personality combining traits of both masculinity and femininity. In contrast, the presence of a "typical" father results in a girl developing a more "traditional" female personality that is submissive and passive.

One intriguing question that follows from Soh's findings is: What explains the socialization of different types of fathers—those who help daughters develop leadership qualities and those who socialize daughters for passivity?

Representative Kim Ok-son greets some of her constituents who are members of a local Confucian club in Seoul, Republic of Korea. She is wearing a men's style suit and has a masculine haircut.

Other anthropologists argue that, despite a wide range of variation, politics is a human universal. Every society is organized to some degree by kinship relationships, and many anthropologists would not draw a clear boundary between kinship organization and political organization. Radcliffe-Brown supported the position that all human societies have something similar to politics or government that functions in the roles of politics or government (1964 [1922]). His research among a few hundred displaced and decculturated indigenous people in the Andaman Islands in 1906 and 1908 revealed nothing in the way of formal political institutions, but he argued that "political" or "governmental" functions existed and were informally fulfilled by the roles of respected elders.

This chapter takes the approach that there is a continuum of formalization and evolution of political structures, starting with the most minimal forms that are found among foraging groups.

Symbols of Power

Among nonhuman primates, the leader ("alpha male" or "alpha female") can be determined through observing social interactions. Deference behavior of followers to leaders is one clue. Sometimes leaders are distinguished by their larger size or their advanced age. Among humans, formalized leadership roles tend to involve deference behavior from followers and a wide range of symbols. Deference is conveyed through language with special terms of address and sometimes even special "high" forms of speech. Physically, cross-cultural prescriptions for deference include such actions as kneeling, prostrating oneself, being seated lower than the ruler, and keeping the head bowed and eyes lowered. Emphasis on status differences between ruler and ruled is accomplished through special dress and insignia for the rulers such as banners, ermine robes, tiaras, famous jewels, or gold-encrusted weaponry. Ceremonies and ritual events are regular public reminders of greatness. As the following section shows, the use of symbols of power varies dramatically from foraging groups, where power differences are minimal if not nonexistent, to the state systems with which readers of this book are familiar.

POLITICAL ORGANIZATION AND LEADERSHIP

Political organization refers to groups that exist for purposes of public decision making and leadership, maintaining social cohesion and order, protecting group rights, and ensuring safety from external threats. Power relationships situated in private, within the family for example, may be considered "political" and may be related to wider political realities, but they are not considered forms of political organization. Political organizations have several features that overlap with the groups and organizations discussed in the previous chapter:

- *Recruitment principles:* Criteria for determining admission to the unit.
- *Perpetuity:* Assumption that the group will continue to exist indefinitely.
- *Identity markers:* Particular characteristics that distinguish it from others, such as costume, membership card, or title.
- *Internal organization:* An orderly arrangement of members in relation to each other.
- *Procedures:* Prescribed rules and practices for behavior of group members.
- *Autonomy:* Ability to regulate its own affairs. (Tiffany 1979:71–72)

Cultural anthropologists cluster the many forms of political organization that occur cross-culturally into four major types (see Figure 11.1 on page 266). The four types of political organization correspond, generally, to the major economic forms (see Chapter 3). Recall that the categories of economies represent a continuum, suggesting that there is overlap between the different types rather than neatly drawn boundaries; this overlap exists between types of political organization as well.

Bands

Anthropologists use the term "band" to refer to the political organization of foraging groups. Since foraging has been the predominant mode of production for almost all of human history, the band has been the most longstanding form of political organization. A **band** comprises a small group of households, between twenty and a few hundred people at most, who are related through kinship. These units come together at certain times of the year, depending on their foraging patterns and ritual schedule.

Band membership is flexible: If a person has a serious disagreement with another person or a spouse, one option is to leave that band and join another. Leadership is also informal in most cases, with no one person being named as a permanent leader for the whole group at all times. Depending on the events

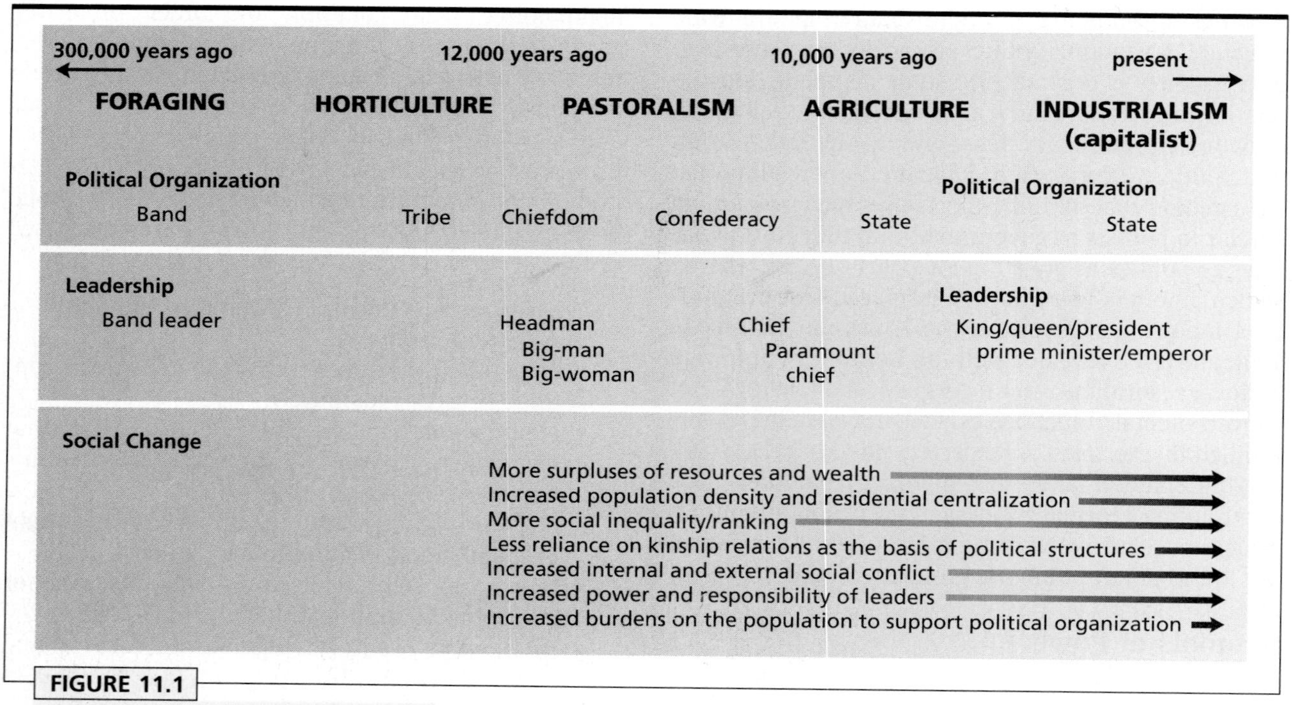

FIGURE 11.1
Economies and Political Organization

at hand, such as organizing the group to relocate or to send people out to hunt, a particular person may come to the fore as a leader for that time. That person's advice and knowledge about the task may be especially respected.

There is no social stratification between leaders and followers. Anthropologists refer to a band leader as a "first among equals." Leadership is informal and is based on the sheer quality of the individual's advice and personality. If a person gives bad advice, people will not continue to listen. Band leaders have limited authority or influence, but no power. They cannot enforce their opinions. Social leveling mechanisms prevent anyone from accumulating much authority or influence, since strong values of self-effacement prevail over self-aggrandizement. Political activity in bands involves mainly decision making about migration, food distribution, and interpersonal conflict resolution. External conflict between groups is rare since territories of different bands are widely separated and the population density is low.

The band level of organization barely qualifies as a form of political organization since groups are flexible, leadership ephemeral, and there are no signs or emblems of political affiliation. In fact, many anthropologists would say that "real" politics did not exist in undisturbed band societies such as the Ju/wasi of southern Africa, the Inuit of northern Canada and Alaska, and the Andaman Islanders of India.

Tribes

A tribe is a more complex form of political organization than the band. Typically associated with horticulture and pastoralism, tribal organization developed only about 12,000 years ago with the advent of these modes of production. A **tribe** is a political group that comprises several bands or lineage groups, each with similar language and lifestyle and occupying a distinct territory. These groups may be connected through a **clan** structure in which most people claim descent from a common ancestor, although they may be unable to trace the exact relationship. Kinship, as in the band, is the primary basis of membership. Tribal groupings contain from a hundred to several thousand people. Tribes are found in the Middle East, South Asia, Southeast Asia, the Pacific, Africa, and among Native Americans.

In terms of group leadership, a tribal headman (most are male) is a more formal and effective leader than a band leader. Key qualifications for this position are being hardworking and generous, and possessing good personal skills. A headman is a political leader on a part-time basis only. Like all other group members, he is primarily involved in production. Yet, this role is more demanding than being a band leader. Depending on the mode of production, a headman will be in charge of determining the times for hunting, moving herds, and planting and harvesting, and setting the time for seasonal feasts and celebrations. Internal and external conflict resolution is also his responsibility. A headman relies mainly on authority and persuasion rather than power. These strategies are effective because tribal members are all kin and have a certain loyalty to each other. Furthermore, exerting force on kinspersons is generally avoided.

Among horticulturalists of the Amazonian rainforest, tribal organization is the dominant political pattern. Each local tribal unit, which is itself a lineage, has a headman (or perhaps two or three). Each tribal group is autonomous, but recently many have united temporarily into larger groups, in reaction to threats to their environment and lifestyle from outside forces. Payakan, leader of the Kayapo tribe, overcame tribal separatism to organize a collective protest about the building of a dam on the Xingu River. He gained international renown for his efforts.

Chief Paul Payakan, leader of the Kayapo, a group of indigenous people living in the rainforest of the Brazilian Amazon. Paiakan was instrumental in mobilizing widespread political resistance in the region against the construction of a hydroelectric dam.

While it is relatively uncommon for horticultural tribes to join forces, pastoralist tribal formations are often linked into a confederacy, with local units or segments each maintaining substantial autonomy. The local segments meet together rarely, usually at an annual festival. In case of an external threat, the confederacy gathers together. Once the threat is removed, local units resume their autonomy. The overall equality and autonomy of each unit in relation to the others, along with their ability to unite and then disunite, is referred to as a **segmentary model** of political organization (a pattern of smaller units within larger units that can unite and separate depending on external threats). This more complex form of tribal organization is found among pastoralists from Morocco to Mongolia (Eickelman 1981). For example, the Qashqa'i, pastoralists of Iran, have three levels of political organization—subtribe, tribe, and confederacy:

> Leaders at all levels of the Qashqa'i political hierarchy dealt with wider authorities and external forces on behalf of the tribespeople and communicated information to higher and lower levels in the system. They possessed extensive political, economic, and social networks in the wider tribal system and in sedentary society which most other tribespeople did not, and they provided services for them in these realms. Tribespeople . . . were obliged to reciprocate these favors by paying taxes and providing other services. From the perspective of the Qashqa'i people, tribal and confederacy memberships brought benefits that the region's non-Qashqa'i peasants and pastoral nomads lacked. They gained relatively secure and protected access to pastures . . . and leaders assisted them in times of economic need. Relations with external powers were mediated for them . . . and they profited from the military power and political authority of their leaders. (Beck 1986:201)

Leadership combines both ascribed and achieved features. Subtribe headmen's positions were mainly based on achievement. Both *khans* (tribe leaders) and *ilkhanis* (confederacy leaders) were members of noble lineages and achieved their positions through patrilineal descent, with the eldest son favored. The role of the *ilkhani* merges into that of chiefs (described in the next section).

The increased power of the state in most places has reduced the role of pastoral leaders. Research among the Qashqa'i is the basis of Lois Beck's book (1991) about Borzu Qermezi, headman of one segment of the Qasqa'i tribe. She details the decreased role of headman during just one year:

> Borzu and the people of the Qermezi group faced many difficulties in 1970 and 1971. . . . Expected winter rains did not fall, and the pastures and crops on which the people depended did not grow. The drought caused their debts to urban merchants and moneylenders to mount. Iran's government was increasing its control over the Qashqa'i, and the Qermezi group could not escape the expanding jurisdiction of central authorities. The government's application of new policies concerning pastures, migratory schedules, animals, prices of pastoral products, and tribal leadership was jeopardizing the people's ability to conduct viable nomadic pastoralism. Non Qashqa'i agriculturalists and livestock investors were encroaching on land upon which the group depended. . . . Borzu's role as tribal headman shifted in response to political and economic changes in Iran as a whole. He gradually lost some of the political support upon which he had relied. . . . They withdrew from him because of outside pressures that not only affected economic conditions but also made part of his role as headman obsolete. (1–2)

The big-man system.

Big-Man Leadership

A form of political organization that fits midway between the tribe and the chiefdom is called the **big-man system,** which is distinguished by increased reliance on the leadership of key individuals who devote much of their efforts to developing a political following through a system of redistribution based on personal ties and grand feasts (as mentioned in Chapter 4). Anthropological research in Melanesia, a large region in the South Pacific, established the big-man type of politics, and most references to it are from this region (Sahlins 1963, Strathern 1971). Nevertheless, such personalistic, favor-based political groupings are found elsewhere and some anthropologists use the term "big-man politics" for them as well. A big-man's role has some characteristics of both a tribal headman and a chief (described next). Compared to a tribal headman, a big-man has an expanded following that includes people in several villages. A big-man tends to have greater wealth than his followers, although people continue to expect him to be generous. The core supporters of a big-man tend to be kin, with extended networks including non-kin. A big-man has heavy responsibilities in regulating both internal affairs—cultivation—and external affairs—intergroup feasts, exchanges of goods, and war. In some instances, a big-man is assisted in carrying out his responsibilities by a group of other respected men. These councils include people from the big-man's different constituencies.

Big-man political organization is common in Papua New Guinea. In several tribes in the Mount Hagen area of the New Guinea highlands, an aspiring big-man develops a leadership position through making *moka* (Strathern 1971). Making moka involves exchanging gifts and favors with individuals and sponsoring large feasts where further gift-giving occurs. A crucial factor in big-manship in the Mount Hagen area is having at least one wife. An aspiring big-man urges his wives to work harder than ordinary women in order to grow more food to feed more pigs. (Pigs are an important measure of a man's status and worth.) The role of the wife is so important that a man whose parents died when he was young is at an extreme disadvantage. He has impaired chances of getting a wife or wives since he lacks financial support from his parents for the necessary bridewealth.

Using his own wife's (or wives') production as an exchange base, the aspiring big-man begins to extend his moka relationships, first with kin and then beyond. By giving goods to people, he gains prestige over them. The recipient, later, will make a return gift of somewhat greater value: "One of the most striking features of the moka is the basic rule that to make moka

Table 11.1
Family Background of Big-Men in Mt. Hagen, Papua New Guinea

	Father Was a Big-Man	*Father Was Not a Big-Man*	*Totals*
Major Big-Men	27	9	36
Minor Big-Men	31	30	61
Total	58	39	97

Source: Strathern 1971:209.

one must give more than one has received. It is strictly the increment that entitles a man to say he has made moka" (Strathern 1971:216). The exchanges continue to go back and forth, over the years. The more one gives, and the more people in one's exchange network, the greater prestige the big-man develops. Degrees of big-manship exist throughout the Pacific region. In the Mt. Hagen region, there are "minor big-men" and a "major big-men." One well-known big-man of the Kawelka tribe, Ongka, worked for years to make a grand moka, which is documented in the film, *Ongka's Big Moka*.

Strictly speaking, big-manship is an achieved position. However, analysis of the family patterns of big-manship in the Mt. Hagen area shows that most big-men are the sons of big-men (see Table 11.1). This is especially true of major big-men, of whom over three-quarters were sons of former big-men. It is unclear whether this pattern is the result of the greater wealth and prestige of big-man families to begin with, socialization into big-manship through paternal example, or a combination of these aspects. This is what the Hageners have to say about sons of big-men and their political chances:

> The sons of a big-man may emulate him. We watch them as they grow up, and see if they are going to be big-men or not. Promising boys are those who speak well, learn quickly to make exchanges and to ask for things, and whose eyes are like a pig's, taking in everything around them. . . . It may turn out to be any one or none of a big-man's sons who will themselves become big-men. We decide by the skill they show in moka and speaking. (208–209)

Big-Woman Leadership

With few exceptions, the early anthropological literature about Melanesian tribal politics portrays men as dominating public exchange networks and the public political arenas. Women as wives are mentioned as being important in providing the material basis for men's political careers. Maria Lepowsky's (1990, 1993) recent study of Vanatinai, a Pacific island which is gender-egalitarian, reveals the existence of big-women as well as big-men. In this culture, both men and women can gain power and prestige by sponsoring feasts at which valuables are distributed, especially mortuary feasts (feasts for the dead):

> On Vanatinai, any individual, male or female, may choose to exert the extra effort to go beyond the minimum contributions to the mortuary feasts expected of every adult. He or she accumulates ceremonial valu-

Throughout much of the South Pacific, big-man politics has long involved the demonstration of generosity on the part of the leaders who are expected to be able to mobilize resources for impressive feasts such as this one on Tanna Island.

> ables and other goods both in order to give them away in acts of public generosity and to honor obligations to exchange partners from the local area as well as distant islands. These people are the giagia. . . .
>
> A woman may have considerably more prestige and influence than her husband due to her reputation for acquiring and redistributing valuables. There are more men than women who are extremely active in ceremonial exchange, but there are also some women who are far more active in exchange and feasting than the majority of men. . . . Vanatinai women may lead expeditions by sailing canoes to distant islands to visit their exchange partners, who are both male and female. . . . Women as well as men host mortuary feasts, mobilizing kin, affines, and exchange partners to plant extra large yam gardens to feed guests sumptuously. (41–42)

As in other parts of Melanesia, exchanging and feasting are not the only paths to power and leadership roles. On Vanatinai, big-women also include powerful sorcerers, famous healers, and successful gardeners. Sometimes these people are also *giagia,* big-women who accumulate wealth and redistribute valuables, and sometimes they are not.

Contact with European culture gave men a political edge that they had not had before on Vanatinai. The Europeans traded with men for goods and approached the women only for sexual relations. Formal government councils were established. Thus far, councilors from Vanatinai have all been male. Many officials from outside the area have a more patriarchal tradition and wish to deal with men only. In addition, some Vanatinai men have received some training in the English language, the language of government, and thus have another advantage. In other cases, European domination led to more political equality between men and women with the imposition of "pacification," which ended local warfare and thereby eliminated traditional paths to power for men.

Chiefdoms

A **chiefdom** is a political grouping of permanently allied tribes and villages under one recognized leader. Compared to most tribes, chiefdoms have larger populations, often numbering in the thousands, and are more centralized and socially complex. Heritable systems of social ranking and economic stratification are found in chiefdoms (Earle 1991) with social divisions existing between the chiefly lineage or lineages and non-chiefly groups. Chiefs and their descendants are considered to be superior to commoners, and intermarriage between the two strata is forbidden. Chiefs are expected to be generous, but they may have a more luxurious lifestyle than the rest of the people; they are not simply a "first among equals." The chiefship is an "office" that must be filled at all times. When a chief dies or retires, he or she must be replaced. In contrast, the death of a band leader or big-man or big-woman does not require that someone else be chosen as a replacement. A chief has more responsibilities than a band or tribal leader. He or she regulates production and redistribution, solves internal conflicts, and plans and leads raids and warring expeditions. Criteria for becoming a chief are more clearly defined. Besides ascribed criteria (birth in a chiefly lineage, or being first son or daughter of the chief), achievement is still important. Achievement is measured in terms of personal leadership skills, charisma, and accumulated wealth. Chiefdoms have existed in many places, including the Ashanti of West Africa and the Cahokia chiefdom in the area of present-day St. Louis, Missouri.

Why Chiefdoms?

Anthropologists and archaeologists are interested in how and why chiefdom systems evolved as an intermediary unit between tribes and states, and what the political implications of this evolution are (Earle 1991). Several political strategies support the expansion of power in chiefdoms: controlling more internal and external wealth and distributing feasting and gift exchanges that create debt ties; improving local production systems; applying force internally; forging stronger and wider external ties; and controlling ideological legitimacy. Research on many chiefdoms historically and in contemporary times shows that depending on local conditions, different strategies were employed. Internal control of irrigation systems was the most important factor in the emergence of chiefdoms in prehistoric southeastern Spain, while control of external trade was more important in the prehistoric Aegean region (Gilman 1991).

Gender and Leadership

Much evidence about leadership patterns in chiefdoms comes from historical examples. Prominent chiefs—men and women—are documented in colonial archives and missionary records. Many historic examples of women chiefs and women rulers come from West Africa, including the Queen Mother of the Ashanti of Ghana and of the Edo of Nigeria (Awe 1977). Oral histories and archival records show that Yoruba women had the institution of the *iyalode,* chief of the women. The iyalode was the women's political spokesperson in the "council of kingmakers," the highest level of government. She was a chief in her own right, with chiefly insignia including the necklace of special beads, wide-brimmed straw hat, shawl, personal servants, special drummers, and bell ringers. She had her own council of subordinate chiefs. The position of iyalode was completely based on achievement. The most important qualifications were her proven ability as a leader, economic resources to maintain her new status as chief, and popularity. Tasks included dispute settlement in her court and meeting with women to formulate women's stand on such policy issues as the declaration of war and the opening of new markets. Although she represented all women in the group and had massive support, she was outnumbered at the council of kingmakers because she was the only female and the only representative of half of the population.

The Iroquois of upstate New York provide a case of women's political importance in other than chiefly roles (J. K. Brown 1975). Men were chiefs, but women and men councilors were the appointing body. Most adult males were away for extended periods, waging long-distance war as far away as Delaware and Virginia. Women controlled production and distribution of the staple crop, maize. If the women did not want warriors to leave for a particular campaign, they would refuse to provide them with maize, thereby vetoing the plan. While some have said that the Iroquois are an example of a **matriarchy** (society in which women are dominant in terms of economics, politics, and ideology), most anthropologists would agree that the Iroquois are better characterized as an egalitarian society since women did not control the society to the exclusion of men nor did they oppress men as a group. Men and women participated equally on the councils.

It is not easy to explain why women play greater political roles in some chiefdoms than others. The most successful theories are based on women's economic roles as the primary basis for political power, as among the Iroquois and many African horticultural societies. In contrast, the dominant economic role of men in Native American groups of the prairies, following the introduction of the horse by the Spanish and the increased importance of buffalo hunting by men, supported male-dominated political leadership in such groups as the Cheyenne.

A marked change in leadership patterns among chiefdoms in the past few hundred years has been the decline of women's political status in many groups, mainly because of European and North American colonial and missionary influences (Etienne and Leacock 1980). For example, the British colonialists redefined the institution of iyalode in Nigeria. Now "she is no longer a member of any of the important councils of government. Even the market, and therefore the market women, have been removed from her jurisdiction, and have been placed under the control of the new local government councils in each town" (146). Ethnohistorical research on chiefdoms in Hawaii provides a similar view of formerly powerful women chiefs (Linnekan 1990). Following Captain Cook's arrival in 1778, a Western-model monarchy was established. By the time the United States annexed the islands in 1898, indigenous Hawaiians had been displaced from prominent economic and political roles by westerners.

Confederacies

An expanded version of the chiefdom occurs when several chiefdoms are joined in a confederacy, headed by a chief of chiefs, "big chief," or paramount chief. Many prominent confederacies have existed, for example, in Hawaii in the late 1700s, and in North America, the Iroquois league of five nations that stretched across New York state, the Cherokee of Tennessee, and the Algonquins who dominated the Chesapeake region in present-day Virginia and Maryland. In the Algonquin confederacy, each village had a chief, and the regional council was composed of local chiefs and headed by the paramount chief. Powhatan, father of Pocahontas, was paramount chief of the Algonquins when the British arrived in the early 1600s. Confederacies were supported financially by contributions of grain from each local unit. Kept in a central storage area where the paramount chief lives, the grain was used to feed warriors during external warfare that both maintains and expands the confederacy's borders. A council building existed in the central location, where local chiefs came together to meet with the paramount chief to deliberate on questions of internal and external policy.

States

A **state** is a centralized political unit encompassing many communities and possessing coercive power. Earliest evidence of the state form of political organization comes from Mesopotamia, China, India, and Egypt, perhaps as early as 4000 BCE. States emerged in these several locations with the development of intensive agriculture, increased surpluses, and increased population density. The state is now the form of political organization in which all people live. Band organizations, tribes, and chiefdoms still exist, but they are incorporated, to a greater or lesser degree, within state structures.

Origins of the State

Many scholars have proposed theories of why the state evolved (Trigger 1996). Marxist theory says that the state emerged to maintain ruling-class dominance. Demographic theory posits that population density drove the need for central mechanisms for social control. Economic theory argues that the state emerged in response to the increased surpluses of food production in the neolithic era, which produced sufficient wealth to support a permanent ruling class. Political theory would say that the state arose as a necessary arbiter as competition increased for arable land and access to food surpluses. Rather than emphasizing a single causal factor, most scholars now incorporate multiple causes in their theories. Another development is that scholars have moved from the "why" question to the "how" question (Trigger 1996). New areas of inquiry include the state's increased bases for central power, such as finances and information management.

Powers of the State

The state and its leaders have much more power and responsibility than leaders of other categories of political organization. The increased powers of the state include:

- *States define citizenship and its rights and responsibilities.* In complex nations, since early times, not all residents were granted equal rights as citizens (see the Multiple Cultural Worlds box).
- *States monopolize the use of force and the maintenance of law and order.* Internally, the state controls the population through laws, courts, and the police. Externally, the state uses force to defend the nation's borders and offensively to extend territory.
- *States maintain standing armies, militias, and police* (as opposed to part-time forces).
- *States keep track of their citizens in terms of number, age, gender, location, and wealth through*

MULTIPLE CULTURAL WORLDS

The Benefits of Citizenship in Kuwait

Following World War II, the oil boom contributed to major economic changes in the Middle East, especially the Gulf states. This "unprecedented prosperity" has been used to provide many social benefits, such as subsidized health, housing, and education (Longva 1993). In Kuwait, a major division in the distribution of the benefits of this wealth is between citizens and non-citizens. Foreign migrants are the majority of the population: In 1989, the population composition was 650,000 Kuwaitis, 1.3 million migrant workers, and about 250,000 bedouins (former or current pastoral nomads). Foreign migrants do not have citizenship.

Some state benefits are distributed to everyone living in Kuwait, including health care, subsidized water, electricity, and gasoline. Kuwaiti citizens receive additional benefits and pay no income taxes. Citizens receive free education and practically free housing. They are guaranteed a job in the government sector if they want one, and they are entitled to several state financial supports: living allowances, bridewealth grants for first marriages, and subsidies for wedding celebrations. Foreigners are subject to residence and labor laws that prevent them from settling permanently in Kuwait. They cannot own real estate or other permanent assets and they cannot join trade unions.

Throughout Kuwaiti society, the elevated status of Kuwaiti nationals is emphasized: "[I]n a queue, a Kuwaiti seldom expected, or was expected, to stand behind an expatriate; people would find it normal for him or her to go to the head of the line" (448). Even driving etiquette gives priority to Kuwaitis, with non-Kuwaiti drivers yielding the right of way at crossroads and roundabouts. The key signal for deference is the wearing of distinctive Kuwaiti national dress by the nationals. For men, this is the *dishdasha,* and for women the *abaya,* both of which convey the message of "Kuwaitiness" and signal social power and prestige.

census systems that are regularly updated. A census allows the state to develop formal taxation systems, military recruitment, and policy planning such as population settlement plans, immigration quotas, and social benefits like old-age pensions.

- *States have the power to extract resources from citizens through taxation.*

The financial base of state systems deserves some detailed attention. All political organizations are supported by contributions of the membership, but variations occur in terms of the rate of contributions expected, the form in which they are paid, and the "return" that members get in terms of services provided through public expenditures. In bands, people voluntarily give time or labor for "public projects" such as a group hunt or a planned move. Collective participation is a norm, not mandated by law. People who do not participate will be subject to social pressure either to change their ways or to leave the group.

Public finance in states is based on formal taxation that can take many forms. **In-kind taxation** is a system of mandatory, non-cash contributions to the state. For example, the Inca state used the *corvee,* a labor-tax, to finance public works projects such as roads and monuments and agricultural work on state lands. Another prominent form of in-kind taxation in early states required that farmers pay a percentage of their crop yield. Heavy tax burdens on peasants throughout history have caused farmers to become impoverished and have prompted many revolts (Scott 1976). Cash taxes, such as the income tax that takes a percentage of wages earned in the United States, emerged only in the past few hundred years. Tax policy may seek to affect behavior as well as accumulate wealth for the state. Taxes on such items as alcohol, cigarettes, or gasoline may be labeled "social-purpose taxes" since they supposedly may act as deterrents to people, prompting them to consume less either for their own good or for ecological reasons. In Canada, pronatalist taxation encourages people to have more babies: Large families pay reduced taxes. In China, anti-natalist taxation increases the tax burden on families with more than one or two children as a reproductive disincentive.

- *States manipulate information.* Control of information to protect the state and its leaders can be done directly through censorship and restricting access to certain information by the public and promotion of favorable images through propaganda, and indirectly through pressure on journalists and television networks to present information in certain ways. An example of a subtle but pervasive form of image-management that promotes loyalty to the king is found in Morocco, where photographs of the king appear everywhere (Ossman 1994).

Gender and Leadership

Most states are hierarchical and patriarchal. They exclude members of lower classes and women from equal participation with upper-class males. Some contemporary states are less male-dominated than others, but none are female-dominated (see the Current Event box on page 274). Marvin Harris (1993) suggests that increasing male dominance in politics with the evolution of the state is based on male control of the technology of production and warfare. Women in most cultures have been excluded from these areas of power, and they have not been able to reverse or equalize these longstanding power relationships except in states that are relatively peaceful such as Norway, Sweden, and Denmark. Strongly patriarchal contemporary states preserve male dominance through ideologies that restrict women's political power, such as purdah (female seclusion and segregation from the public world), as practiced in much of the Muslim Middle East, Pakistan, and north India. In China, scientific beliefs that categorize women as less strong and dependable than men have long been used to rationalize the exclusion of women from politics (Dikötter 1998). Socialist states usually pay some attention to increasing women's political roles, but not in the most elite positions. The proportion of female members of legislative bodies is higher in socialist states than in capitalist democracies.

Women's leadership roles can be direct (as leaders themselves) or indirect (as mothers or wives of male rulers such as Eva Peron in Argentina or Hillary Clinton in the United States). Among the Maya of Mexico and Central America, women royalty played key roles during the classic period kingdoms in the classic period from 600 to 900 AD (Freidel and Schele 1993). Many highly placed women gained powerful, but indirect, positions through their sons who would become heirs. Women's indirect political power through their sons is an understudied topic. One piece of information comes from contemporary Turkey, where

Current Event

"Who's Buried in Margarita's Tomb?"

- The richest tomb ever found at the ancient Maya city of Copán in Honduras is occupied by a woman, to the surprise of archaeologists. The 1,500 year-old Margarita tomb was originally thought to be that of Ruler II, Copán's first great builder and the son and successor of Yak K'uk' Mo' (Green Quetzal Macaw), who founded the Copán dynasty in AD 426.
- The tomb contains the remains of a fifty-year-old woman covered with thousands of shell pendants and jade ornaments, earflares, beads, and burned offerings of birds, turtles, and fish.
- The tomb was designed to remain accessible for many years. Evidence suggests that the tomb was reentered on several occasions, possibly to conduct rituals. Following the decomposition of the remains, red pigment continued to be sprinkled over the bones. This act may have involved the renewal of life forces symbolized by the blood-colored substance. Many of the offerings were rearranged after a partial collapse of the building, which may have been caused by an earthquake.
- What woman was worthy of such veneration? "Whoever this lady was," says archaeologist Robert Sharer, "she was long venerated and no doubt played a pivotal role in Copán's ruling dynasty." Physical anthropologist Jane Buikstra is currently conducting DNA analysis of the remains from several other burials in the same complex to determine possible kinship relationships.

Source: Schuster, 1996.

most parents consider politics an undesirable career for their children. However, in a recent survey, more women than men stated that they would say "yes" to their sons' political ambitions (Güneş-Ayata 1995: 238–239). The implication is that mothers of male leaders use their position as mothers to influence politics because more direct political roles are largely closed to them.

A handful of contemporary states have or have recently had women as prime ministers or presidents. Such powerful women include Indira Gandhi in India, Golda Meir in Israel, Margaret Thatcher in the United Kingdom, and Benazir Bhutto in Pakistan, among others. Female heads of state in Latin America and Asia are often related by kinship (as wife or daughter) to former heads of state. Indira Gandhi, for example, was the daughter of the popular first prime minister of independent India, Jawaharlal Nehru (she is not related to Mahatma Gandhi). It is unclear as to how much these women's leadership positions can be explained by their inheriting the role or through the political socialization they may have received, directly or indirectly, as a result of being born into political families. The United States has many well-known political families in which males are prominent. Rarely do wives step into a husband's position, although many have wielded indirect political power. Somewhat more common are political daughters, such as former senator Nancy Kassebaum (her father is Alf Landon, a former presidential candidate).

Symbols of State Power

Religious beliefs and symbols are often closely tied to the power of state leadership: The ruler may be considered to be a deity or part deity, or a high priest of the state religion, or may be closely linked with the high priest who serves as advisor. Architecture and urban planning remind the populace of the greatness of the state. In pre-Columbian Mexico, the central plaza of city-states, such as Tenochtitlán (founded in 1345), was symbolically equivalent to the center of the cosmos and thus the locale of greatest significance (Low 1995). The most important temples and the residence of the head of state were located surrounding the plaza. Other houses and structures, in decreasing order of status, were located on avenues in decreasing proximity to the center. The grandness and individual character of the leader's residence indicate power, as do monuments—especially tombs to past leaders or heroes or heroines. Egypt's pyramids, China's Great Wall, and India's Taj Mahal are a few of the world's great architectural reminders of state power.

In democratic states where leaders are elected by popular vote and in socialist states where political rhetoric emphasizes social equality, expense and elegance are "toned down" in some ways by the adoption of more egalitarian ways of dress (even though in private, these leaders may live relatively opulent lives in terms of housing, food, and entertainment). The earlier practice of all Chinese leaders wearing a "Mao jacket," regardless of their rank, was a symbolic statement of their anti-hierarchical philosophy. A quick glance at a crowd of people including the prime minister of Canada or Britain or president of the United

This expansive, and expensive, new mosque in Casablanca was constructed by and named after the king, Hassan II. It is a clear statement of his presence and power in Morocco.

States would not reveal who was the leader because dress differences are not used as markers by these secular, elected leaders. It is important for these leaders to avoid looking like they spend excessively on themselves. American presidents and their wives have been criticized by the press and the public for excessive expenditures on dresses, dishes, and haircuts. Members of British royalty also wear "street clothes" on public occasions where regalia is not required.

Local Power and Politics in Democratic States

The degree to which the state influences the lives of the citizens varies. So-called totalitarian states have the most direct control of local politics. In most other systems, local politics and local government are granted some degree of power. In highly centralized states, the central government controls public finance and legal institutions, leaving little power or autonomy in these matters to local governments. In decentralized systems, local governments are granted some forms of revenue generation (taxation) and the responsibility of providing certain services. Local politics continue to exist within state systems, with their strength and autonomy dependent on how centralized the state apparatus is. This section considers examples of village politics in Japan, factional politics in Belize and Taiwan that link different localities, and local electoral politics in France, as representing varying patterns of political goals and strategies.

In Japan, relatively egalitarian systems of local power structures exist in villages and hamlets. Families subtly vie for status and leadership roles through gift-giving, as is common in local politics worldwide (Marshall 1985). Egalitarianism prevails as a community value, but people strive to be "more than equal" by making public donations to the *buraku*, or hamlet. The custom of "giving a gift to the community" is a way that hamlet families can improve their positions in the local ranking system. In one hamlet, all thirty-five households recently gave gifts to the community on specified occasions: the forty-second birthday of male family members, the sixty-first birthday of male family members, the seventy-seventh birthday of male family members, the marriage of male family members, the marriage of female family members whose husband will be the household successor, the birth of the household head or successor couple's first child, and the construction of a new house. These occasions for public gift-giving always include an invited meal for members of all hamlet households:

> About a month before the meal is scheduled, the donor household notifies the hamlet head of its intentions and places with him the cash portion of its gift, from which provisions for the meal will be purchased. . . . The donor family and the hamlet head agree on a suitable date and time for the meal, usually a Sunday afternoon as a prelude to a general meeting of the hamlet as council for the discussion of hamlet affairs. . . . When the hamlet members are all seated in the hamlet hall and the meal has been placed before them . . . the hamlet head holds up the decorated envelope in which he received the cash gift and reads from it the donor household's name, the amount of the gift, and the nature of the occasion. During the meal the envelope is circulated from hand to hand around the tables and examined without comment as it travels around the hall. (169)

Since the 1960s, it has also become common to give an item that is useful for the hamlet, such as a set of fluorescent light fixtures for the hamlet hall, folding tables, space heaters, and vacuum cleaners.

Local politics within a democratic framework reveal another type of gift-giving and exchange in the interest of maintaining or gaining power. Here we see people in elected positions of power giving favors in expectation of political loyalty in return. In these cases, various **factions** vie with each other. A faction, a more formalized aspect of local politics, is a politically oriented conflict group whose members are mobilized and maintained by a leader to whom the main ties of loyalty and affiliation are lateral—from leader to follower—rather than horizontal between members (Brumfiel 1994b). Factions tend to be personalistic, transitory, lacking formal rules and meeting times, and lacking formal succession. Factional politics is not redistributive, however. It often leads to conflict and unequal resource distribution.

Two villages in Belize show a contrast in the development and role of factional politics (Moberg 1991). One village, Mt. Hope, is almost faction-free, while the other village, Charleston, has divisive factionalism. Economic differences in the two villages are important. In Mt. Hope, the government provided residents with land and established a marketing board to purchase villagers' crops. Farmers grow rice for the domestic market and citrus crops for export. Citrus-growers account for about half of Mt. Hope's households, receive more than three-fourths of its total income, and control about 87 percent of the land. In Charleston, most men work in small-scale fishing augmented by part-time farming. Lack of a road that would allow export of agricultural crops has inhibited the development of commercial agriculture. Start-up costs for citrus cultivation (fertilizer, insecticide, tractors) are prohibitive for most Charleston households. Charleston is "racked by intense intergroup conflict," and that includes factional conflict that divides kin groups: "One of the village's most acrimonious political conflicts exists between two brothers whose relationship deteriorated when the allies of one brother were excluded from a cooperative that the other had organized" (221). Factionalism in Charleston is sustained by outside political party patronage and favor-giving. Local faction leaders vie with one another to obtain grants and other benefits from the state. In return, national political parties look to Charleston as a base for developing political loyalties. The national parties have mainly bypassed Mt. Hope because economic development created less dependence on state favors for local projects such as a cooperative or a road. Charleston was ripe for political manipulation; Mt. Hope was not.

Factions in rural Taiwan resemble political machines that trade favors for votes in coordination with national political parties (Bosco 1992). Taiwanese factions appear to be incipient political parties, but have been prevented from forming themselves as such because of a government prohibition on forming new parties (this ban has been liberalized since 1987). Local faction leaders have the power to influence people by controlling some key government jobs. They also give small gifts around election time to remind faction members of their loyalty: soap, towels, china, small amounts of money, pens, paperweights, and watches. National party politicians expect local faction leaders to estimate their faction's voting strength and then "deliver" the vote at election time. The leader will read down the list of voters and estimate who will vote for each candidate, based on his personal knowledge of people's ties and associations. The faction leader's continued success rests on his ability to estimate accurately the number of votes before the election. Accuracy is important to determine if last-minute vote-buying (through cash gifts) will be needed. Although these practices may sound corrupt, in rural Taiwan they appear as an outgrowth of traditional guanxi connections.

In rural France, anthropological research reveals the importance of family ties and family reputation as influencing who becomes an elected local leader (Abélès 1991). The department of Yonne, located in the Burgundy region southeast of Paris, is the "provincial heartland of France." Fieldwork there was devoted to understanding how individuals gained access to local political office, and involved interviewing local politicians, attending town council meetings, and following local elections. France is divided into 36,000 communes that are grouped in 96 departments. Communes and departments are the major arenas for local politics. At the commune level, elected officials are the mayor and town councilors. Several political parties contest the elections—the Socialist party, the Union for French Democracy, and others, including scattered support for the Communist party. A successful candidate for either commune or department positions should have local roots and come from a "distinguished" family. Typically, the same family names recur again and again. In one town:

> For more than half a century the Truchots and the Rostains were the two families who dominated public life in Quarré: Ferdinand Rostain, who represented the moderate tendency . . . climbed the rungs of the ladder of electoral politics without any great difficulty. Originally assistant mayor, he succeeded the mayor on his death in 1908. He was constantly reelected mayor of Quarré and member of the General Council until his death in 1939, when his son Maurice replaced him at the head of the municipal

> council and on the General Council. Maurice continued as mayor throughout the war years. Like many elected representatives who lived through those troubled times, he was brushed aside after the war. The history of the Rostain family is one of economic prosperity as the reward of hard work. One of their ancestors, originally from the Alps, and a peddlar, like many migrants from that area, settled in the Côte-d'Or. His son moved to Quarré, where he set up a timber business, then extended his activities to the grain and wine trade. The business flourished. (31–32)

The Truchot family, which provided the major opponent to Rostain, was also a family of grain and wine merchants.

Another factor influencing electoral choice is a bias toward incumbents. The monopoly of political office by a certain family is perceived by local people to contribute to order and peace. Thus, local roots, reputation, and networks combined with a value placed on continuity as the ingredients for electoral success in rural France (see the Critical Thinking box). This combination is summed up in the concept of "legitimacy." "To enjoy legitimacy is to belong to a world of eligible individuals, those to whom responsibilities can be entrusted. Legitimacy is an elusive quality at first glance: certain individuals canvassing the votes of their fellow-citizens are immediately recognized as legitimate, while others, despite repeated efforts, are doomed to failure. . . . It is as though a candidate's legitimacy is something people instinctively recognize"(265).

CHANGE IN POLITICAL SYSTEMS

In the early days of political anthropology, researchers examined the varieties of political organization and leadership and created categories such as bands, tribes, chiefdoms, and states. Contemporary political anthropologists are more interested in political dynamics and change, especially in how the pre-eminent political form, the state, affects local people's lives. This section covers selected topics in the anthropological study of political change.

CRITICAL THINKING

How "Open" Are Democratic Electoral Politics?

In France, the only legal requirements for office are French citizenship and age. Other than that, elected positions are, in principle, "open" to anyone interested in contesting them. According to the perspective that emphasizes human agency in shaping behavior and events, one would hypothesize nearly complete openness in elections and low predictive value of "name" or "family" in determining electoral success. But such "openness" does not seem to be the case in rural Burgundy and may not exist elsewhere.

Critical Thinking Questions:

- How well does the human agency approach work in the case of rural Burgundy?
- How well does a political economy approach work?
- Does any other theory (perhaps sociobiology?) that seeks to explain human behavior account for the "family dynasty" effect?

In comparison, consider the structure of the local political system(s) in which you have lived.

Critical Thinking Questions

- Is your experience with an "open" electoral system?
- If yes, what are the criteria for eligibility for office?
- Do all eligible people appear to run for office on an equal basis?
- Do all eligible people appear equally successful in being elected?
- How do the electoral success patterns of candidates resemble or differ from that described for rural Burgundy?
- What other factors in the United States are bases for election by candidates who do not have "distinguished" family lines?
- What do various factors of electoral success have to do with actual competence to do the job?

Emergent Nations and Fractured States

It is not easy to explain clearly what a nation is and what the relationship of this concept is to the state since many different definitions exist for a "nation" and some of them overlap with definitions given for a "state" (Maybury-Lewis 1997b:125–132). Furthermore, popular usage often uses the two terms interchangeably. One basic definition says that a **nation** is a group of people who share a language, culture, territorial base, political organization, and history (Clay 1990). In this sense, a nation is culturally homogeneous, and, thus, the United States would not be considered a nation but rather a unit composed of many nations (as well as states!). Referring to "national policy" as something that relates to the unit as a whole is then a misnomer. According to this definition of nation, it should be noted that many indigenous groups can be referred to as nations, but not ethnic groups that lack a territorial base. Yet another related term is the "nation-state," which some people say refers to a state that comprises only one nation, while others think it refers to states that comprise many nations. A fairly clear example of a nation is the Iroquois nation of central New York state. The criteria of nationhood fits their case well and it is easy to see that they are a nation within a state. In the former USSR, ethnic and regional groups were referred to as "nationalities." In China, all but the Han peoples are referred to as "national minorities." In both cases, however, these groups lacked political organization.

Depending on their resources and power, nations may constitute a political threat to states. Anyone reading this book can easily think of several examples from historic and contemporary times. In response to this (real or perceived) threat, states seek to create and maintain a sense of unified identity. Political scientist Benedict Anderson, in his widely read book, *Imagined Communities* (1991 [1983]) writes about the efforts that state-builders employ to create a sense of belonging and commitment—"imagined community"—among diverse peoples. Strategies for building state identity among the many nations within a state include the imposition of one language as "the" national language; the construction of monuments and museums; and the creation of songs, poetry, and other media-relayed messages about the "motherland." Anderson points, for example, to the construction of tombs of "Unknown Soldiers" as major unifying symbols: "The public ceremonial reverence accorded these monuments precisely because they are deliberately empty or no one knows who lies inside them, has no true precedents in earlier times" (9). State control of such key areas of life as religion and language has been documented for many parts of the world. For example, the opposition to any form of religion in the former USSR and in contemporary China represents an attempt to form state unity and to divert people's loyalties from religion to the state. Strategies of repression to promote unification have also included media censorship, torture, and imprisonment.

The break-up of the former Soviet Union has led to the emergence of many new states facing varied challenges of identity formation and integration; language is often a key issue for many of them. In Ukraine, forging a new national identity is one of the major internal political challenges (Motyl 1993). Ukraine gained its independence from the former USSR in 1991. Its population is about 52 million, with roughly 73 percent Ukrainian and 22 percent Russian (Hodges and Chumak 1994:1). The western and central provinces are mainly Ukrainian. The eastern and southern provinces have higher percentages of Russians. The 100,000 or so minority peoples are Jews, Belarussians, Moldovans, Poles, Bulgarians, Hungarians, and Romanians who live mainly in the border regions (the word "Ukraine" itself means borderland, and the area's history is one of invasions and control by various outside powers). Language is a key aspect of Ukraine's attempt at unity. Under the USSR, Russian was promoted as the dominant language. It was used in politics, economics, mass media, theater, and literature, and was taught in most schools. People who spoke Ukrainian as their native language also learned some Russian, especially in cities of the east, central, and southern areas. Most Russians living in Ukraine did not attempt to learn Ukrainian. No matter what happens with its internal language policy—which is still unfolding, Ukraine will play a major role in global politics because of its size and resources, which make it the most powerful nation between Russia and Germany.

As emerging states seek to build and maintain a sense of belonging among their plural populations, those very groups are building their own solidarity and political momentum:

> These communities compete, sometimes by civic methods, sometimes by violence for hegemony (control of the state apparatus), for autonomy (ranging from regional self-government to succession), or for incorporation into the society and polity on more favourable terms. Inter-ethnic relations may vary

> from stratificational (one group dominating the others politically and economically), to segmentational (each party controlling significant resources and institutions). In the contemporary era, ethnic politics implicate the state, because the state has become the principal allocator of the values that affect the relative power, status, material welfare, and life-chances of ethnic collectivities, and their individual constituents. (Esman 1996:259)

Several major ethnic/national populations are seeking separate statehood or greatly expanded autonomy from the state. The Kurds are a large group of about 20 million people, most of whom speak some dialect of the Kurdish language (Major 1996). They live in a crescent-shaped region ("Kurdistan") that extends from Turkey into Iran, Iraq, and a bit of Syria. This area is mainly grasslands, interspersed with mountains, with no coastline. Oil reserves have been found in some places, but the main resource of international interest is the headland of the Tigris and Euphrates rivers: "These rivers give life to the surrounding region (including most of Iraq) and also provide power to Turkey, Syria, and Iraq, through hydroelectric generators built in and near Kurdistan" (C1). The approximately 12 million Kurds in Turkey constitute 20 percent of the total population and live mainly in the southeastern portion of the country (J. Brown 1995). They have been battling for a separate state for years, with no success, and with great suffering in terms of human rights violations against them. Suppression and oppression have been the major government strategies for dealing with the "Kurdish problem." In 1994, the Turkish government shut down the pro-Kurdish Democracy party and expelled its thirteen deputies from Parliament (Marcus 1996). A journalist who was tried, charged, and later acquitted by a Turkish security court for her reporting on the Kurds, says:

> The Turks are undecided about the Kurds, who have been in a state of unrest since the republic was founded in 1923. Some Turks talk of "our citizens of Kurdish origin," others refer to the need for "first-class treatment" to those who feel "second-class," and almost everyone speaks of "terrorism." But few talk of the Kurds as Kurds.
>
> It's really no surprise that most people are silent. Strict restrictions on freedom of expression make most discussion—that is, talk contrary to Ankara's position—against the law. People have been put on trial for saying Turkey oppresses the Kurds, for interviewing PKK rebels, for saying the Kurds should have an independent state, and for writing about army abuses against civilians. Mainstream newspapers usually figure it's safer to ignore the issue than face being labeled a traitor. . . . Those who still dare are put on trial. Among the most celebrated recent cases was the conviction of Yasar Kemal, perhaps the country's most famous author, who accused Turkey of both abusing Kurds and lying about it. Columnist Ahmet Altan received a suspended sentence for a satire imagining that Ataturk, the revered founder of the republic, had been a Kurd and it was Turks who were repressed. And I was put on trial last fall for a Reuters article that described soldiers throwing Kurds out of their villages. (105)

In a nutshell, the "Kurds want to be Kurds." They want the right to have Kurdish language schooling, and television and radio broadcasts; they would like to have their folklore recognized as well. The Kurds want other changes in the current authoritarian stance to their region: lifting of the state of emergency in the southeast, allowance of freedom of expression, and removal of the ban on ethnic-based political organizations. They are concerned about human rights issues—torture and mysterious killings—which occur more in the southeast than elsewhere in the country. Kurdish solidarity for years was found in the PKK, the only Kurdish organization (even though it was banned by the state), which followed a Marxist-Leninist philosophy of socialist revolution. Kurdish disaffection for the PKK is growing, however, because the rebel war is wearing them down. Much of Kurdish village life has been destroyed and many leading Kurdish activists have been killed.

One move toward a solution would be to adopt a policy of devolution of authority to localities. Local officials, health workers, and teachers would be appointed at the province level rather than in Ankara. Devolution has been used successfully elsewhere, notably in the policy of Spain toward its Basque region. It is increasingly considered as a possible solution that will both maintain state borders and allow for ethnic identity (J. Brown 1995).

World peace increasingly involves intrastate and cross-state ethnic politics and conflict. The Kurds are only one example. The Tibetans, the Chechens, the Kayapo, the Eritreans (whose war of liberation recently ended), the Palestinians, the Sikhs of northwestern India, and the Assamese of eastern India . . . the list goes on. Attempts by nationalistic states to force homogenization of ethnic groups will prompt resistance of varying degrees from those who wish to retain autonomy. Cultural anthropologists are becoming more involved in studying both local and global aspects of ethnic relations. Their data can contribute to the realm of "peace and conflict" studies and policy through providing case studies and theories based on comparative analysis.

Democratization

Democratization refers to the process of transformation from an authoritarian regime to a democratic regime. This process includes several features: the end of torture, the liberation of political prisoners, the lifting of censorship, and the toleration of some opposition (Pasquino 1996:173). In some cases, what is achieved is more a relaxation of authoritarianism rather than a true transition to democracy, which would occur when the authoritarian regime is no longer in control. Political parties reemerge, some presenting traditional interests and others oppositional. The variety of approaches to democratization is great and outcomes are similarly varied. Writing for the *New York Times,* correspondent Barbara Crossette reported in August 1996 that while "more than 100 nations now call themselves democratic, the definition has never been more blurred, with dramatically different societies trying to design systems that work for them" (August 4, 1996, 4–1). Of the twenty-seven nations created from the former Soviet Union, nineteen are democracies. All nations in Western Europe are democracies, as are thirty-one of thirty-five in the Americas. The percentage is about half in Asia and the Pacific. Africa has the lowest percentage, with only eighteen democracies among fifty-three countries.

Democracy movements have grown in resistance to authoritarian regimes in several countries. In Burma, Aung San Suu Kyi leads the democracy and human rights movement. The daughter of Burma's national hero, Aung San, who was assassinated just before Burma achieved its independence from the British, she has long spoken against the authoritarian socialist government that came to power in 1966. She was placed under house arrest on July 20, 1989 and not released until July 1995. During the time she was under house arrest, she was awarded the Nobel Peace Prize, the eighth woman in history to receive this award. Over the years, she has delivered thousands of speeches and has written many essays in support of democracy in Burma (some of these are collected in the book, *Freedom from Fear,* 1995).

The transition to democracy appears to be most difficult when the direction of change is from highly authoritarian socialist regimes. This pattern is partly explained by the fact that democratization implies a transition from a planned economy to one based on market capitalism (Lempert 1996).

Women in Politics: New Directions?

Two questions arise in the area of changing patterns of women in contemporary politics: Is the overall participation of women at varying political levels increasing? and Does the participation of women in politics bring more attention to women's issues such as the division of labor and wages, access to health care, and violence? While insufficient comparative research exists to allow for a full answer of these questions, some evidence at the international level can be considered. As of March 1996, 5 of a total of 190 world leaders were women (Petty 1996): Benazir Bhutto of Pakistan, Gro Harlem Bruntland of Norway, Violeta Barrios de Chamarro of Nicaragua, Chandrika Bandaranaike Kumaratunga of Sri Lanka, and Khaleda Zia of Bangladesh. In Turkey, Tansu Ciller, former prime minister of Turkey, was defeated for reelection and then became part of a two-person coalition in 1996. In terms of the second question, none of these leaders, with the exception of Bruntland of Norway, has a strong record on supporting women's issues. One interpretation of this pattern is that women polit-

Russians vote in their first democratic election following the breakup of the Soviet state.

ical leaders in male-dominated contexts become "like men" or, even more so, have to avoid "feminist issues" in order to maintain their position.

Women do not have political status equal to that of men in any country (Chowdhury et al. 1994:3). In general, women are still marginalized from formal politics and must seek to achieve their goals either indirectly (as wives or mothers of male politicians) or through channels other than formal politics such as grassroots movements.

In some Native American groups, evidence of a recovery of former political power is emerging (B. G. Miller 1994). In several communities, female participation in formal politics is increasing, along with attention to issues that face women. This change is occurring within the context of women's greatly decreased roles, which were the result of colonialist policies; for example, until recently, only Native American men were allowed to vote. One explanation for the change is that women are obtaining newly available managerial positions on reservations. These positions give women experience in dealing with the outside world and authority for assuming public office. In addition, they face less resistance from men than women in more patriarchal contexts do. Most Native Americans do not view "women's roles" as contradictory to public authority roles.

The resurgence in women's political roles among the Seneca of New York state and Pennsylvania echoes these themes (Bilharz 1995). From their precontact position of at least equal political power with men, Seneca women's status had declined in many ways. Notably, when the constitution of the Seneca nation was drawn up on a European model in 1848, men were granted the right to vote, but not women. In 1964, Seneca women finally gained the right to vote. Even before enfranchisement, women were politically active, and worked on committees formed to stop the building of Kinzua Dam in Pennsylvania. For Seneca women, job creation through the Seneca Nation of Indians (SNI) brought new employment opportunities. Although no woman has run for president of the Seneca Nation as yet and only two women have been head of a reservation, many women hold elective offices of clerk and judge, and many women head important service departments of the SNI such as Education and Health. Women of the Seneca nation still retain complete control over the "clearing" (the cropland), and "their primacy in the home has never been challenged" (112). According to the author, Seneca women have regained a position of "equality."

Fluctuating World-System Politics

World-systems theory proposes that since the seventeenth century, the world's nations have been increasingly linked in a hierarchical structure. This structure of power relations is largely regulated through international trade. In the seventeenth century, Holland was the one core nation, dominating world trade. It was then surpassed by England and France, which remained the two most powerful nations up to around 1900. In the early part of the twentieth century, challenges for world dominance were made by the United States and later Germany and Japan. The outcome of World War II placed the United States as leader of the "core" (see Chapter 3), and most recently, Japan has returned as the primary contestant for first place. Greater complexities in world-systems theory now allow for an additional category of semiperiphery states, intermediary between the core and the periphery. Cultural anthropology's traditional strength has been the study of small, bounded local groups, so anthropologists have had relatively little to say about international affairs. Now, more anthropologists have enlarged their focus to the international level, studying both how global changes affect local politics and how local politics affect international affairs. Worldwide communication networks facilitate global politics. Ethnic politics, although locally initiated, increasingly have international repercussions. Migrant populations promote interconnected interests across state boundaries.

One pioneering study in "the anthropology of international affairs" is that of Stacia Zabusky (1995), who did ethnographic research on patterns of cooperation among international scientists at the European Space Agency, the ESA. The European Space Agency involves people from different European nations seeking to cooperate in joint ventures in space and more indirectly to promote peaceful relations in Europe. Zabusky attended meetings and interviewed people at the European Space Research and Technology Centre, ESA's primary production site, in the Netherlands. Focusing on people's work roles, their style of reaching consensus at meetings, and the role of national differences in this cooperative effort, she found that language plays a key part in affecting cooperation. The official languages of the ESA are English and French, but most interactions take place in English. Some nonnative English speakers felt that this gave the British an automatic advantage, especially in meetings where skill in speech can win an argument. A major divisive

VIEWPOINT

"The Hope for Europe" by Václav Havel

Humanity is entering an era of multipolar and multicultural civilization. Europe is no longer the conductor of the global orchestra, but this does not mean it has nothing more to say to the world.... Europe's task is no longer, nor will it ever be again, to rule the world, to disseminate by force its own concepts of welfare and what is good, to impose its own culture upon the world or to instruct it in its proper course. The only meaningful task for the Europe of the next century is to be the best it can possibly be—that is, to revivify its best spiritual and intellectual traditions and thus help to create a new global pattern of coexistence. We shall do most for the world if we simply do as we are bidden by our consciences, that is, if we act as we believe everyone should act. Perhaps we will inspire others: perhaps we won't. But we should not act in the expectation of that outcome. It may be hard to abandon the belief that it makes no sense to live by an imperative from above as long as others do not live by it or are not prepared to do so. But it can be done. And it is not impossible that this is, in fact, the best thing Europe can do for itself, for the restoration of its own identity, for its own new dawning.

Source: Havel 1996, 38–41.

factor is the sheer geographic dispersal of the participants throughout Europe. This means that travel is a constant, as scientists and engineers convene for important meetings. Zabusky discovered that, despite logistical problems, meetings are an important part of the "glue" that promoted cooperation above and beyond just "working together." Conversations and discussions at meetings allow people to air their differences and work toward an agreement. Zabusky concludes that the ESA represents an ongoing "struggle" for cooperation that is motivated by more than just the urge to do "big" science. "In working together, participants were dreaming about finding something other than space satellites, other than a unified Europe or even a functioning organization at the end of their travails. Cooperation indeed appeared to participants not only as an achievement but as an aspiration" (197). (See the Viewpoint box.)

SUMMARY

Political anthropology addresses the area of human behavior and thought related to power, including who has it and who doesn't; degrees of power; bases of power; abuses of power; relationships between political and religious power; political organization and government; social conflict and social control; and morality and law.

Politics usually refers to public power, as opposed to the private, micropolitics of family and domestic groups. Power is the capacity to take action, if necessary, by force. Authority implies the right to take certain forms of action and is based on a person's status in society. Influence is another way of achieving a desired end through exerting social or moral pressure on someone or some group.

The evolution of political structures forms a continuum, starting with the band, the earliest and most minimal form. Band membership is flexible: If a person has a serious disagreement with another person or a spouse, one option is to leave that band and join another. Leadership is informal. A tribe is a more complex form of political organization than the band. A tribe comprises several bands or lineage groups. These groups may be connected through a clan structure. Big-man political systems are midway between the tribe and the chiefdom. Chiefdoms may include several thousands of people. Rank is inherited, and social divisions exist between the chiefly lineage or lineages and non-chiefly groups. A marked change in leadership patterns among chiefdoms in the past few hundred years has been the decline of women's political status in many groups; this is mainly the result of European and North American colonial and missionary influences.

A state is a centralized political unit encompassing many communities and possessing coercive power. Earliest evidence of the state form of political organization comes from Mesopotamia, China, India, and Egypt, as early as 4000 BCE. States came into existence in these several locations with the emergence of intensive agriculture, growing surpluses, and increased population density. Most states are hierarchical and patriarchal. Strategies for building nationalism include imposition of one language as "the" national language; construction of monuments and museums; and the creation of songs, poetry, and other media-relayed messages about the "motherland." Ethnic/national politics have emerged within and across states as groups seek to compete for increased rights within the state or autonomy from it.

Worldwide communication networks facilitate global politics. Ethnic politics, although locally initiated, increasingly have international repercussions. Cultural anthropologists have rarely addressed the topic of international affairs, but interest is increasing in this direction.

CRITICAL THINKING QUESTIONS

1. What are some similarities and differences between "politics" among nonhuman primates and humans?
2. Was the invention of the state "a terrible mistake"?
3. Choose one recent example of ethnic conflict. What issues do the media emphasize as creating the conflict? What would a cultural anthropological approach ask about causes? How do the two different approaches shape possible solutions?

KEY CONCEPTS

authority, p. 263
band, p. 265
big-man system, p. 268
chiefdom, p. 270
clan, p. 266
democratization, p. 280
faction, p. 275
influence, p. 263
in-kind taxation, p. 273
matriarchy, p. 271
nation, p. 278
political organization, p. 265
politics, p. 263
power, p. 263
segmentary model, p. 267
state, p. 271
tribe, p. 266

SUGGESTED READINGS

Mona Etienne and Eleanor Leacock, eds., *Women and Colonization: Anthropological Perspectives.* New York: Praeger, 1980. This classic collection examines the impact of Western colonialism and missionary intervention on women of several indigenous groups of North America and South America, Africa, and the Pacific.

A. W. Johnson and Timothy Earle, *The Evolution of Human Societies: From Foraging Groups to Agrarian State.* Stanford: Stanford University Press, 1987. This comprehensive synthesis of knowledge of links between ecology, economy, and political organization includes detailed case studies of over a dozen cultures as illustrations.

David H. Lempert, *Daily Life in a Crumbling Empire.* New York: Columbia University Press, 1996. This two-volume ethnography is based on fieldwork conducted in Moscow before perestroika. It is the first comprehensive ethnography of urban Russia and its economic, political, and legal systems and reforms.

Dan Rabinowitz, *Overlooking Nazareth: The Politics of Exclusion in Galilee.* New York: Cambridge University Press, 1997. This is an ethnographic study of Palestinian citizens in an Israeli new town. The book examines specific situations of conflict and cooperation and provides wider theoretical insights about nationalism and ethnicity. Biographical accounts of three Palestinians—a medical doctor, a basketball coach, and a local politician—are included.

Jack M. Weatherford, *Tribes on the Hill.* New York: Rawson, Wade Publishers, 1981. This engagingly written analysis of politics within the United States Congress gives attention to the effects of male privilege and seniority on ranking, lobbying tactics, and ritual aspects of the legislation process.

Joan Vincent, *Anthropology and Politics: Visions, Traditions and Trends.* Tucson: The University of Arizona Press, 1990. This text presents a definitive history of the emergence of political anthropology, with a detailed presentation of theories and findings through the late 1980s.

CHAPTER 12

Social Order and Social Conflict

CHAPTER OUTLINE

THE ANTHROPOLOGY OF ORDER AND CONFLICT
SYSTEMS OF SOCIAL CONTROL
- Norms and Laws
  - *Voices:* "Letter from the Birmingham Jail," Martin Luther King, Jr.
- Social Control in Small-Scale Societies
- Social Control in States
- Social Inequality and the Law
  - *Viewpoint:* "Something Nasty in the Tea Leaves" by Simon Courtald
- Change in Legal Systems

SOCIAL CONFLICT AND VIOLENCE
- Theoretical Issues
- Studying Conflict and Violence
- Types of Social Conflict
  - *Multiple Cultural Worlds:* Patriarchy, the Police, and Wife Abuse in Rural Kentucky
  - *Multiple Cultural Worlds:* The "Bandit Queen" of India
  - *Current Event:* "Burundi's Three-Year "Campaign of Terror" Leaves a Bloody Trail on University Campuses"
  - *Critical Thinking:* The Yanomami, "The Fierce People"?
  - *Current Event:* "Chinese Protest Finds a Path on the Internet"

MAINTAINING WORLD ORDER
SUMMARY
CRITICAL THINKING QUESTIONS
KEY CONCEPTS
SUGGESTED READINGS

◀ Yanomami men displaying their fierceness in the Venezuelan part of the Amazon rainforest. Conflict in the region between settlers from outside and the indigenous Yanomami has increased in recent years. A massive fire swept through the area in 1998, caused by the outside settlers' use of fire in clearing land.

Socially agreed-upon ways of behaving shape people's everyday life in countless ways. We wait for our turn to get on a bus rather than pushing to the head of the line, and we pay for a sandwich at the deli instead of stealing it. The first section of this chapter discusses options for maintaining peace and order, including informal arrangements that we hardly know exist and more formal laws and systems of crime prevention. The second section takes us away from the study of conformity and order to the study of situations in which normal expectations and laws are not followed and conflict and violence occur.

THE ANTHROPOLOGY OF ORDER AND CONFLICT

Anthropologists in all four fields have devoted attention to the subjects of social order and social conflict. Historical archaeologists, studying cultures that had writing, have traced the development of written law through time. Other archaeologists have examined artifacts such as weapons, remains of forts, and the waxing and waning of political centers in order to understand group conflict in the past. Many primatologists study nonhuman primate patterns of cooperation, coalitions, and conflict. Linguistic anthropologists have done research on social conflict related to national language policies and on how communication patterns within the courtroom influence outcomes. Legal anthropology is the subfield within cultural anthropology that is most directly concerned with the study of social control and social conflict.

Over the course of the twentieth century, the direction of legal anthropology has headed away from its original foundations in functionalism (the way a particular practice or belief contributed to social cohesion) toward a view that focuses on internal divisiveness. Helping to launch the subfield through his classic book, *Crime and Custom in Savage Society* (1962 [1926]), functionalist Malinowski wrote that in the Trobriand Islands, social ties themselves promoted mutual social obligation and harmony. No separate legal institutions existed throughout Melanesia; instead, law was embedded in social life. Thus, he made the important contribution that social relationships can perform the same functions as formal laws and courts.

Later, in the mid-twentieth century, Max Gluckman (1955, 1963) diverged from functionalism in studying disputes and conflict. His research in central African villages revealed how the court systems resolved conflict. Much early research on indigenous law and legal processes, including Gluckman's, was commissioned by colonial administrations. The colonialists wanted to learn about local customs in order to rule over the colonized peoples more effectively. This early work was mainly concerned with documenting how different cultures defined law, justice, and punishment.

By the 1960s, another new turn was established with the study of law in action. This transition brought an emphasis on collecting ethnographic data on the dispute event and the chain of events that followed it. June Starr's book, *Dispute and Settlement in Rural Turkey* (1978), exemplifies this approach of extended case analysis. Her book is built around thirty-two dispute cases including: two boys fighting at a wedding, a man's dog killing a chicken, the lighthouse keeper's wife taking a lover, and a dispute among siblings about dividing the family land. In examining each case, Starr provides information on the social relationships of the disputants, the cultural significance of the dispute, Turkish law in relation to the offense (for example, Turkish law says that it is a criminal offense to shoot a gun at a wedding), forms of resolution, and why particular resolutions emerged compared to others. This approach highlights rules of law and order, but situates them in the cultural context for interpretation.

Several new directions have emerged in legal anthropology: the study of legal discourse especially in courtroom settings, law and transnational processes in colonial and postcolonial settings, **critical legal studies** (an approach that examines how the law and judicial systems serve to maintain and expand the dominant power interests rather than protecting those who are marginal and less powerful), and law and human rights in cross-cultural perspective (Merry 1992). Research in critical legal studies is discussed in the section on Inequality before the Law.

SYSTEMS OF SOCIAL CONTROL

The concept of social control has several meanings depending on one's theoretical perspective. A generally accepted definition in anthropology is that **social control** is "the processes which help produce and maintain orderly social life" (Garland 1996:781). Scholars of the more critical bent would emphasize the negative aspects of social control systems as supporting hierarchy and domination, either directly or indirectly. Underlying both views are two premises:

- Social control systems exist to ensure a certain degree of social conformity to agreed-upon rules.
- Some people in all cultures may violate the rules and resist conformity (what sociologists refer to as "deviant behavior").

Social control systems include internalized social controls that exist through socialization for proper behavior, education, and peer pressure, and formal systems of codified rules about proper behavior and punishments for deviation. The Amish and Mennonites, Christian immigrant groups from Europe, rely on internalized social controls more than most microcultural groups in the United States and Canada. These groups have no police force or legal system; the way social order is maintained is through religious teaching and group pressure. If a member veers from correct behavior, punishment such as ostracism ("shunning") may be applied.

Norms and Laws

Cultural anthropologists distinguish two major instruments of social control: norms and laws. **Norms** are generally agreed-upon standards for how people should behave. All societies have norms. They are usually unwritten and learned unconsciously through socialization. Norms include, for example, the expectation that children should follow their parents' advice, that people standing in line should be orderly and not try to "jump" the line, and that an individual should accept an offer of a handshake (in cultures where handshakes are the usual greeting) when meeting someone for the first time. In rural Bali, etiquette dictates certain greeting forms between people of different status: "[P]ersons of higher status and power are shown very marked respect: they are greeted submissively and treated obsequiously; if seated, then others moving past them crouch . . . so as not to loom above them" (Barth 1993:114). Enforcement of norms tends to be informal; for example, a violation may simply be considered rude and the violator avoided in the future. In others, punishment may be involved, such as asking someone who is disruptive in a meeting to leave.

The categories of norm and law form a continuum in terms of how explicitly they are stated and how strongly they are enforced. A **law** is a binding rule created through enactment or custom that defines right and reasonable behavior. Laws are enforceable by threat of punishment. Systems of law are more common and more elaborate in state-level societies, but many non-state societies have formalized laws. Often the legitimacy and force of law are based on religion. For example, Australian Aborigines believe that law came to humans during the "Dreamtime," a time in the mythological past when the ancestors created the aboriginal world. Contemporary Islamic states explicitly link law and religion. Secular Western states consider their laws to be religiously neutral, but in fact, much Western legal practice is heavily influenced by Judeo-Christian beliefs. Critiques of law versus norms have focused on how, in some instances, laws are less morally sound than norms (see the Voices box on page 288).

Social Control in Small-Scale Societies

Anthropologists distinguish small-scale societies and large-scale societies in terms of prevalent forms of conflict resolution, social order, and punishment of offenses. Formal laws are rare among foraging groups, although Inuit and Australian Aborigines are notable for their more formalized, although unwritten, law systems. Because bands are small, close-knit groups, disputes tend to be handled at the interpersonal level through discussion or one-on-one fights. The group may act together to punish an offender through shaming and ridicule. Emphasis is on maintaining social order and restoring social equilibrium, not hurtfully punishing an offender. Ostracizing an offending member (forcing the person to leave the group) is a common means of formal punishment. Capital punishment has been documented, but is rare. For example, in some Australian Aboriginal societies, a law restricts access to religious rituals and paraphernalia to men who have gone through a ritual initiation. If an initiated man shared secrets with an uninitiated man, the elders would delegate one of their group to kill the offender. In such instances, the elders act like a court.

In pre-state societies, punishment is legitimized through belief in supernatural forces and their ability to affect people. Among the highland horticulturalists

VOICES

"Letter from the Birmingham Jail" by Martin Luther King, Jr.

How does one determine when a law is just or unjust? A just law is a man-made code that squares with the moral law or the law of God. An unjust law is a code that is out of harmony with the moral law.... An unjust law is a code that a majority inflicts on a minority that is not binding on itself. This is difference made legal. On the other hand a just law is a code that a majority compels a minority to follow that it is willing to follow itself. This is sameness made legal....

Who can say that the legislature of Alabama which set up the segregation laws was democratically elected? Throughout the state of Alabama all types of conniving methods are used to prevent Negroes from becoming registered voters and there are some counties without a single Negro registered to vote despite the fact that the Negro constitutes a majority of the population. Can any law set up in such a state be considered democratically structured?...

I hope you can see the distinction I am trying to point out.... We can never forget that everything Hitler did in Germany was "legal" and everything the Hungarian freedom fighters did in Hungary was "illegal." It was "illegal" to aid and comfort a Jew in Hitler's Germany. But I am sure that if I had lived in Germany during that time I would have aided and comforted my Jewish brothers even though it was illegal.

Source: King 1994 [1963]:11–15.

of the Indonesian island of Sumba, one of the greatest offenses is to fail to keep a promise (Kuipers 1990). Breaking a promise will bring on "supernatural assault" by the ancestors of those who have been offended by the person's misbehavior. The punishment may come in the form of damage to crops, illness or death of a relative, destruction of the offender's house, or having clothing catch on fire. When such a disaster occurs, the only choice is to sponsor a ritual that will appease the ancestors.

Conflict resolution among horticulturalists relies on many of the same methods as among foragers, notably public shaming and ridicule. In the Trobriands of the early twentieth century Malinowsy (1926) reports:

> The rare quarrels which occur at times take the form of an exchange of public expostulation (*yakala*) in which the two parties assisted by friends and relatives meet, harangue one another, hurl and hurl back recriminations. Such litigation allows people to give vent to their feelings and shows the trend of public opinion, and thus it may be of assistance in settling disputes. Sometimes it seems, however, to harden the parties. In no case is there any definite sentence pronounced by a third party, and agreement is but seldom reached then and there. (60)

Village fission (breaking up) and ostracism are other common mechanisms for dealing with unresolvable conflict. The overall goal in dealing with conflict in small-scale societies is to return the group to harmony.

Social Control in States

In societies that are more densely populated, more socially stratified, and have more wealth, increased stresses form around the distribution of surplus, inheritance, and rights to land. In addition, increased social scale means that not everyone knows everyone else, and face-to-face accountability may exist only in local neighborhoods.

Increased Specialization

As with all aspects of the division of labor, the specialization of tasks related to law and order—police, judges, lawyers—increases with the emergence of state organization. In pre-state societies, it is often society at large that determines right from wrong and punishes offenders, or the elders may have special authority and be called on for advice. In chiefdoms, special advisors, such as the so-called "leopard-skin chief" of the Nuer of Sudan, have had a leading role

A "Leopard-Skin Chief" among the cattle-herding Nuer of the Sudan acted as an intermediary between people and groups in conflict, including instances of murder. His power, however, is limited to negotiation and the ability to threaten punishment through supernatural means.

in decision making about crime and punishment. However, full-time professionals, such as judges and lawyers, emerged with the state. These professionals often come from powerful or elite social groups, a fact that perpetuates elite biases in the justice process itself. In the United States, the legal profession is committed to opposing discrimination on the basis of gender and race, but it is nonetheless characterized by a lack of representation of women and minorities. Minority women, who face a double bind, are especially underrepresented (Chanen 1995:105). **Policing** includes processes of surveillance and the threat of punishment related to maintaining social order (Reiner 1996). Police are the specific organization and personnel who discover, report, and investigate crimes. As a specialized group, police exist mainly in complex state societies.

Japan's low crime rate has attracted the attention of Western law-and-order specialists, who think that it may be the result of the police system there. They are interested in learning whether solutions to America's crime problems can be found in such Japanese policing practices as neighborhood police boxes staffed by foot patrolmen and volunteer crime prevention groups organized on a neighborhood basis. Debate exists as to whether these institutions are so embedded in Japanese culture that they cannot be transferred successfully to the United States (Steinhoff 1993:828). Fieldwork among police detectives in the city of Sapporo reveals several aspects of Japanese culture and policing that promote low crime rates and would not transfer easily to the United States (Miyazawa 1992). First, the police operate under high expectations that no false arrests should be made and all arrests should lead to confession. And, in fact, the rate of confession is very high. This may be because the police do a good job of targeting the guilty or because the police have nearly complete control of interrogation over isolated suspects for long periods of time, which can lead to wearing down resistance and potentially distorting the process of justice. In Japan, an "enabling legal environment" gives more power to the police and less to the defendant than in United States law. For example, the suspect's statements are not recorded verbatim or taped. The detectives write them up and the suspect is asked to sign them.

Trials and Courts

In societies where misdoing and punishment are defined by spirits and ancestors, a person's guilt is evidenced simply by the fact that misfortune has befallen him or her. If a person's crops were damaged by lightning, then that person must have done something wrong. In other instances, guilt may be determined through **trial by ordeal,** a form of trial in which the accused person is put through some kind of test that is often painful. In this case, the guilty person will be required to place a hand in boiling oil, for example, or to have a part of their body touched by a red-hot knife. Being burned is a sign of guilt, while not being burned means the suspect is innocent. The court system, with lawyers, judge, and jury, is used in many contemporary societies, although there is variation in how cases are presented and juries constituted. The goal of contemporary court trials is to ensure both justice and fairness. Analysis of actual courtroom dynamics and patterns of decision making in the United States and elsewhere, however, reveals serious problems in achieving these goals.

Punishment

As one commentator says, "Punishment is an intended evil" (Christie 1996:708). It involves doing something unpleasant to someone who has committed an offense. Studies of punishment have considered such questions as the bases or reasons for punishment, forms of punishment, effects of various forms of punishment, and the relationship between types of societies and levels of punishment. Some theories argue that the degree of punishment should match the crime; others say the punishment should be a means of getting people to obey the law in the first place and thus should be a deterrent. Little solid knowledge exists about the effectiveness of different forms of punishment, for example, between prison sentences of one versus two years, or long-term imprisonment versus the death penalty as crime deterrents. One result is clear: People who are imprisoned are stigmatized by it, become more marginalized, and therefore have an increased likelihood of committing further crimes.

The prison, as a place where people are forcibly detained as a form of punishment, has a long history. The dungeons and "keeps" of old forts and castles all over the world are vivid evidence of the power of some people to detain and inflict suffering on others (Millett 1994). In general, however, such prisoners were not detained for long periods—they were tried and punished and their cell emptied. Long-term detention of prisoners did not become common until the seventeenth century in Europe (Foucault 1977). The first penitentiary in the United States was built in Philadelphia in the late 1700s (Sharff 1995). Cross-nationally and through history, percentages of imprisoned people vary widely. The United States and Russia have high percentages compared to other contemporary Western countries: 550 and 470 prisoners per 100,000 inhabitants respectively. The British Isles rate is about 100, while the Scandinavian countries have among the lowest rates, under 60. In the United States, the prison population has tripled over the past one hundred years, in spite of fairly even levels of crime.

Interior scene of the Cellular Jail in India's Andaman Islands, which was so-named because all prisoners had single cells, arranged in long rows, in order to prevent them from any social interaction and possible collusion to escape or rebel.

The death penalty (capital punishment) is rare in pre-state societies because condemning someone to death requires a high degree of power. A comparison of capital punishment in the contemporary United States with human sacrifice among the Aztecs of Mexico of the sixteenth century reveals striking similarities (Purdum and Paredes 1989). Both systems involve the death of mainly able-bodied males who are in one way or another socially marginal. In the United States, most people who are executed are non-White, have killed Whites, are poor, and have few social ties. Aztec sacrificial victims were mainly male war captives from neighboring states, but Aztec children were also sometimes sacrificed. The deaths in both contexts have a political message: They communicate a message of the state's power and strength to the general populace, which is why they are highly ritualized and well publicized as events.

Social Inequality and the Law

Scholars working in the area of critical legal studies have examined discrimination against indigenous people, women, and minorities in various judicial systems around the world, including those of long-standing democratic societies (see the Viewpoint box). While one could draw examples from many countries about how racial biases and discrimination affect legal processes, this section presents instead one in-depth example from the Australian judicial system.

At the invitation of some Aboriginal leaders in Australia, Fay Gale and some colleagues (1990) conducted research comparing treatment of Aboriginal youth and White youth. The question posed by the Aboriginal leaders to the researchers was: Why are our kids always in trouble? Two directions can be pursued to find the answer. First, structural factors such as Aboriginal displacement from their homeland, poverty, poor living conditions, and bleak future prospects can be investigated. These factors make it more likely for Aboriginal youth to commit crimes than the relatively advantaged White youth. Second, the criminal justice system can be examined to see if it treats Aboriginal and White youth equally. The researchers decided to direct their attention to the judicial system because little work had been done

VIEWPOINT

"Something Nasty in the Tea-Leaves"
by Simon Courtauld

Gypsies have never been popular. In seventeenth-century Britain they were hanged automatically when apprehended; later many were sent into slavery in the West Indies. In more recent times they have been persecuted, and their nomadic way of life outlawed, both in Hitler's Germany and under communism in the former Soviet Union and eastern Europe. The . . . repeal of the Caravan Sites Act 1968 Act, contained in the new Criminal Justice Bill, seems to continue the same tradition. The Government may deny wanting to get rid of gypsies, but thousands of Romany gypsy families now fear for their future. . . .

Under the 1968 Act, county councils have a duty to provide sites for gypsy caravans, but the majority of councils have failed to allocate enough pitches for the number of caravans requiring them. In Avon, for instance, figures for 1992 showed that only 20 pitches had been provided, leaving 283 "unauthorized encampments" in the area.

Another problem has arisen through the Act's definition of gypsies as "persons of nomadic habit of life, whatever their race or origin"—which has encouraged "New Age" travellers to demand council pitches for themselves. Now that a High Court judge has recently ruled that New Age travellers are not gypsies, one might have thought that the Act could simply be amended on this point. At the same time it could surely be strengthened to ensure that all councils in the future carry out their legal obligations. But the Government has decided instead to repeal the law, so relieving councils of the duty to provide caravan sites, and to impose stiffer penalties on gypsies for whom councils have refused to make proper provision. . . .

If councils are no longer obliged to provide gypsy sites . . . the number of illegal encampments, followed by prosecutions and evictions will inevitably increase. Caravans in the future may be seized, and councils will then have to find bed and breakfast accommodation for gypsies, with consequent disruption to their lives and, possibly, to their children's health and education. Save the Children Fund and other organisations argue that the effect of mass evictions which are bound to result from the new legislation will be to contravene the Children's Protection Act by failing to protect the needs of gypsy children.

But the success of the legislation is likely to be judged by the number of gypsies forced off the roadside and into conventional housing. . . . One can argue about the advantages of a nomadic way of life; however, like the Romany language (a variation of Sanskrit) it is part of gypsy culture. Any law which makes gypsies into criminals and threatens their nomadic tradition . . . is oppressive and unacceptable.

Source: The Spectator, January 8, 1994, p. 16. Reprinted with the kind permission of *The Spectator.*

British Gypsies

on that area by social scientists. Australia, a former colony of England, adopted the British legal system, which claims to administer the law equitably. Gale's research assesses this claim in one state, South Australia.

Results show that Aboriginal youth are overrepresented at every level of the juvenile justice system from apprehension through pretrial processes to the ultimate stage of adjudication and disposition: "A far greater proportion of Aboriginal than other young people follow the harshest route. In other words, at each point in the system where discretion operates, young Aborigines are significantly more likely than other young persons to receive the most severe outcomes of those available to the decision-makers" (3). At the time of apprehension, the suspect can be either formally arrested or informally reported. A formal arrest is made to ensure that the offender will appear in court. Officers ask the suspects for a home address and if they have a job. Aboriginal youths are more likely than White youths to live in a poor neighborhood in an extended family, and they are more likely to be unemployed. Thus, they tend to be placed in a category of "undependable," and they are formally arrested more than nonaboriginal youths for the same crime (see Table 12.1). The next step determines whether the suspect will be tried in Children's Court or will be referred to Children's Aid Panels. The Children's Aid Panels in South Australia have gained acclaim worldwide for the opportunities they give to individuals to avoid becoming repeat offenders and take their proper place in society. But most Aboriginal youth offenders are denied access to them and instead have to appear in court, where the vast majority of youthful offenders end up pleading guilty. The clear and disturbing finding from looking at how Aboriginal youths fare in this system is that the mode of arrest tends to determine each subsequent stage in the system. The power hierarchy is thus "inverted," with most power at the lowest and least capable levels of the system, where decisions affect any later attempts to give equal opportunity to Aboriginal youth.

Change in Legal Systems

As with other cultural domains, law-and-order systems change over time. European colonialism since the seventeenth century has had major impacts on indigenous systems. On the other hand, law is often viewed as an instrument of social change. This section looks briefly at these two aspects of change.

European Colonialism and Indigenous Systems

Colonial governments, to varying degrees, attempted to learn about and rule their subject populations through what they termed "customary law" (Merry 1992). By seeking to codify customary law, colonial governments created fixed rules where former flexibility and local variation had existed. Leopold Pospisil (1979) reports on how his research on one Kapauku group's traditional law in New Guinea was erroneously co-opted by the Dutch for use throughout the entire Kapauku population:

Table 12.1

Comparison of Outcomes for Aboriginal and White Youth in the Australian Judicial System

	Aboriginal Youth (percent)	*White Youth (percent)*
Brought into system via arrest rather than police report	43.4	19.7
Referred to Children's Court rather than diverted to Children's Aid Panels	71.3	37.4
Proportion of Court appearances resulting in detention	10.2	4.2

Note: Most of these youths are males; data are from 1979–1984.
Source: Gale, Bailey-Harris, and Wundersitz 1990:4.

> The colonial administrator was often called upon to adjudicate a great variety of civil cases. . . . How did the Dutch officer in his new role as dispenser of civil justice discover what tribal law was? I was astounded to see my book *Kapauku Papuans and Their Law* (1958) being used by the administration official as a legal *codex*—as the "authorized version" of Kapauku law. Although I was amused, this was certainly not the reaction of all the Kapauku. As a matter of fact, my book was very unpopular with some of them for an obvious reason. My work dealt only with the legal system of the Ijaaj-Pigome confederacy of the southern part of the Kamu Valley, which differed from every other confederacy's legal system. By applying the Ijaaj-Pigome legal system to the whole of Kapauku society, the Dutch officer had invested the system with a status it had never previously held. The only amused people were my Ijaaj-Pigome friends, who joked about it or even poked fun at the other Kapauku. One of them, tongue in cheek, even mockingly threatened the others: "If you fellows don't behave we shall make our American big man write another and even tougher book." In an effort to undo the injustice, I explained the problem to the officer. He was surprised and admitted that he thought the opposition to his ruling was due to the stubborn nature of some of the litigants. (132)

Often the colonialists overrode customary law and imposed their own laws. Homicide, marriage, land rights, and indigenous religion were frequent areas of European imposition. Colonial governments everywhere banned headhunting and blood feuds. Among the Nuer of Sudan, British legal interventions resulted in substantial confusion among the Nuer about the issue of blood feuds (Hutchinson 1996). Nuer practices involved either the taking of a life in repayment for a previous homicide, or negotiated payments in cattle depending on the relations between the victim and the assailant, what type of weapon was used, and a consideration of current rates of bridewealth as an index of value. In contrast, the British determined a fixed (nonnegotiable) amount of indemnity. They imprisoned people for committing a vengeful murder. From the Nuer point of view, these changes were incomprehensible. They interpreted being put in prison as a way of protecting the person from a reprisal attack.

When European administrators and missionaries encountered polygamy and other aspects of kinship systems different from their own, they often tried to impose their own ways. Among the Akan of Ghana, for example, marriage was a fluid concept, a process, rather than a fixed "state of being" (Vellenga 1983). Strong ties with the matrikin were traditionally maintained by married adults. The British addressed both practices in their attempt to solidify monogamous marriage and to strengthen the conjugal bond over the matrilineage bond.

Any socially plural society will have the option of multiple legal solutions. Colonial imposition of European legal systems onto indigenous systems added another layer, and one that had pre-eminent power over others. **Legal pluralism** refers to a situation in which more than one kind of legal process might be applied to identical cases (Rouland 1994:50). For example, should a case of murder in the Sudan be tried according to indigenous Sudanese principles or European ones? Post-colonial nations are now in the process of attempting to reform their legal systems and develop more unified codes (Merry 1992:363).

SOCIAL CONFLICT AND VIOLENCE

All systems of norms and forms of social control have to deal with the fact that, more or less frequently, conflict and violence may occur. This section turns to a consideration of the causes and distribution of such social problems.

Theoretical Issues

Classical thinkers and writers such as Thucydides, Machiavelli, and Hobbes have approached the subject of social conflict. Key contributions of the nineteenth century, especially from Darwin and Marx, added new lines of thinking. Darwin's approach suggests that conflict is an inevitable and natural way that species compete and evolutionary advancement occurs. Marx said that society evolves through conflict based on unequal property relations, with the controlling class seeking to maintain dominance and the workers attempting to achieve equality. The question of why some societies and eras seem to have more social conflict than others is a basic theoretical problem. Social conflict and violence may be cultural universals because no society is completely free of them, but the degree to which they exist offers an opportunity for understanding causes and solutions. Conversely, the foundations of peace and harmony are also an important area of study.

Studying Conflict and Violence

No doubt it is safer and perhaps easier to study peaceful communities than violent ones. Recall Napoleon Chagnon's difficulties in adjusting to an aggressive style in male–male interactions. Special challenges facing anthropologists doing fieldwork in violent contexts include shock and bewilderment, how to deal with rumors, how to respond to unpredicted and accidental happenings, and requests from the people involved for help or even complicity (Robben and Nordstrom 1995:13–20). These themes appear in the account by Indian anthropologist Veena Das (1984), who worked with victims of the Delhi riots that erupted after the assassination of prime minister Indira Gandhi. Das, some colleagues, and other concerned citizens, became involved in research and public service after the riots subsided. She describes the context:

> Following the assassination of the Indian Prime-Minister, Indira Gandhi, in Delhi on 31 October 1984, there was widespread violence against the Sikhs for three days.... By 3 November, it became clear to civil-rights groups, university teachers and students, retired bureaucrats, journalists, and other concerned citizens, that they had to take the major responsibility for establishing relief camps, procuring food and medicines, and collecting information about the number of people dead or missing.... It was in this context that my colleagues and I decided to enquire into the pattern of riots by going into the affected localities rather than restricting ourselves to relief camps. (4)

In the most afflicted locality, over two hundred people were killed. The researchers were met with urgent requests by the victimized residents that the details of their suffering be made known: "One man, whose two sons had been killed, offered to raise fifty rupees later if we could have an account of their suffering published in a newspaper" (5). The writings of the academics received criticism from others that they would lead to vengeance and continued ethnic conflict. Das responds by saying that anthropologists have the responsibility to express "the ethnographic voice" and all its details even if they seem "gory" or "trivial." She points to another lesson that emerges from doing research in a time of violent crisis as compared to "reasonable normality":

> If one is working among victims of a collective tragedy, one's movements are naturally determined by the sole criterion of the needs of the people. Procuring rations, arranging for medical help, filling forms and establishing liaisons with police officers and administrators—these are the activities that define the trajectory of one's existence ... society seems to take control of the researcher, who simply has to lend himself or herself to become the anonymous space on which the hitherto suppressed knowledge of society inscribes itself. (5–6)

Types of Social Conflict

Conflict can occur at any social level, from the most private, microlevel of the household to the public, mass situation of all-out warfare. This section considers findings from anthropological research on conflict in a variety of domains, moving from interpersonal conflict in the domestic domain to public conflict such as revolution and war.

Interpersonal Conflict

Interpersonal conflict encompasses a wide range of behavior, from simple arguments and differences of opinion to murder. Anthropologists have studied interpersonal disputes in many social contexts. At the most microlevel, the household, interpersonal disputes are common. Some might say that it's easier to kill or be cruel to someone you don't know, an anonymous enemy. But abusive and lethal conflict between people who are intimately related as lovers or family members is frequent cross-culturally. Dating violence among high school and college students is a problem that has begun to receive attention from researchers (Makepeace 1997, Sanday 1996). Attempts to dissolve an unsatisfactory relationship may entail additional conflict as was found in rural Kentucky (see the Multiple Cultural Worlds box on pages 296 and 297). Beyond the household, interpersonal conflict occurs between neighbors and residents of the same town or village, often over resources or territory.

Since the 1970s, villagers of the Gwembe Valley in southeast Africa have kept diaries documenting economic and demographic information and reports of disputes (Colson 1995). Over the years, the number of disputes has increased. Two reasons could be behind this change: Either disputing is actually on the rise because of the increased availability of beer and guns, or the people have become even more willing to disclose "the seamy side" of their communities. One thing is clear: Disputes still occur over the same issues: "[P]eople argued about cattle damage to growing crops, land encroachment, inheritance, elopement and impregnation damages, marriage payments and marriage difficulties, slander, including implicit accusations of sorcery, theft, physical violence exploding at beer drinks, and the rights of senior people over the labour of younger men and women (73). These matters continue to engage the people, but they are now more likely to get into disputes about debts.

A different pattern of local conflict emerges from interviews with one hundred middle-class, American suburbanites (Perin 1988). While discussing a variety of subjects related to everyday life and neighborhood relationships, dogs emerged as a major basis of conflict:

> [I]n the first five minutes of listening to suburbanites discuss neighbors, it became clear that dogs are the most worrisome population.... "Dogs, like children, can be the glue or the solvent of the neighborhood," one man puts it. Says another: "Dogs seem to be a big problem in the suburbs. I think probably worse than kids, really. Because you can control the toilet habits of the kids." (108)

Problems include dogs roaming off the leash; barking; relieving themselves; chewing garbage bags; biting; and threatening children, joggers, and bicyclists. Using a leash is a workable solution, but many owners refuse to comply. Humane society officials report that about half of all dog owners see nothing wrong with dogs running loose; this is perhaps a conservative estimate.

How do American suburbanites deal with conflicts about dogs? Some opt for a face-to-face solution:

> When I'm standing in your driveway with a shovel and some stuff on it, and I dump it in front of your door and say, "I don't want it on my doorstep again." There are several people like me who do the same thing—go right to the people and say, "Your dog left this, it belongs to you, it ain't mine, and I don't want to see it on my property." So pretty soon when you have two or three people do it to you, you get the message. (112)

The relationship may subsequently have "a little more strain." Some people resort to the dog warden after trying to talk to the neighbor several times. In pursuing the issue to court, every complaint has to be substantiated. A building inspector in Houston said, "The barking dog isn't as cut and dried a thing as it might seem. We watch it for a week. If we're going to court, we have to prove it's excessive. We have to keep numbers. People's first reaction to a barking complaint is that they're not in violation. The same goes for dog-droppings" (113). Mutual hostility may continue for a long time. Even one case of mail box bombing and shooting each other's windows has been reported. The seriousness of dog-related conflicts has resulted in an expanded role of the courts. In Middlesex District Court in Massachusetts, one day each month is devoted to dog cases, while two days a month are needed in Portland, Oregon. In Santa Barbara, California, the city attorney's office will provide professional mediation for dog-related disputes.

MULTIPLE CULTURAL WORLDS

Patriarchy, the Police, and Wife Abuse in Rural Kentucky

Domestic violence in the United States is reportedly highest in the state of Kentucky. Neil Websdale (1995), a sociologist, used ethnographic techniques to study the role of the police in preventing and dealing with domestic violence in Kentucky. In an area of eastern Kentucky called "Lovelace," he conducted fifty focused interviews with battered women living in shelters, police officers, shelter employees, state troopers, sheriffs, sheriff's deputies, a district court judge, attorneys, and social workers. He rode with police officers and observed them as they dealt with domestic altercations. He became familiar with leaders and organizers of the Kentucky Domestic Association and worked with people who ran groups for men who battered their partners. He also observed domestic abuse cases in court. Most research in the United States on domestic violence has been conducted in urban areas, whereas Websdale's research revealed three categories of isolation that characterize domestic violence in rural Kentucky and make it particularly difficult to prevent:

- *Physical isolation:* "The most consistent factor in women's description of their lives was isolation" (106). Isolation and loneliness may be both a product of abuse and a cause of it. Abusers' tactics were more effective because of geographical isolation:

  > The batterer's strategies, according to the women, included removing the phone from the receiver (for example, when leaving for work) ... locking the thermostat, especially in winter, as a form of torture; disabling motor vehicles to reduce or eliminate the possibility of her leaving the residence; destroying motor vehicles; closely monitoring the odometer reading on motor vehicles (a simple yet effective form of control due to the lack of alternate means of transportation); driving recklessly to intimidate his partner; discharging firearms in public (for example, at a battered woman's pet).... These tactics might still be used in urban areas, but they would either have less impact or be more visible. (106–107)

  Studies have shown that a woman's greater dependence on the batterer is correlated with a greater likelihood that she will endure more extreme abuse. Women's isolation in rural Kentucky promotes their greater dependence on men. Women reported how difficult it is to leave an abusive home located many miles from the nearest paved road, especially if they have children. No public transportation serves even the paved road. The time involved in getting away exposes the woman to greater danger from her abuser. Between 20 and 30 percent of households in the study area had no phones. Getting to a phone to report abuse results in delay and gives police the impression that the call is less serious. Physical remoteness delays response time to calls for help and increases a woman's sense of hopelessness: "Sheriffs have acquired a very poor reputation among battered women in the region for not attending domestic calls at all. Of the 25 women interviewed, 18 expressed varying degrees of dissatisfaction with the police.... Only three women were satisfied with the police response in their cases" (109). State troopers are better trained for dealing with domestic violence, but they patrol a much wider area, thus delaying their response time.
- *Sociocultural isolation:* Aspects of rural family life and gender roles lead to a system of "passive policing." In rural Kentucky, men are seen as providers and women are strongly tied to domestic work and childrearing. When women do work, their wages are about 50 percent of men's wages. Residence is often in the vicinity of the husband's family, which creates isolation of a woman from the potential support of her natal family and restricts help-seeking in the immediate vicinity because the husband's family is likely to be nonsupportive. Police officers, especially local ones, view the family as a private unit, a man's world. They will be less inclined to intervene and arrest husbands whom they feel should be dominant in the family. In some instances, the police take the batterer's side, share the batterer's understandings of the situation, and have similar beliefs in a man's right to control his wife. Officer Davis viewed many victims of domestic violence as being manipulative and undeserving of police support:

  Davis: A lot of them were fabricated.... [T]hat man has taken all that he can take....

[T]hat's the way he lashes out . . . and boom. Call the State Police. I want his ass out of here. And I just don't really see that's right. . . . It's bullshit is what it is.

N.W.: As a rough guess, what would you say the percentage of bullshit ones is to legit ones?

Davis: Probably 70–30. (112)

- *Isolation from potentially supportive institutions:* Battered women in rural areas face special problems in using the limited services of the state. The fact that abused women often know the people who run the services ironically inhibits the women from approaching them, given values of family privacy. In addition, social services for battered women in Kentucky are scarce. Other institutional constraints include less schooling for rural women than urban women, lack of day care centers to allow mothers the option to work outside the home, inadequate health services with doctors appearing unfamiliar with domestic violence, and fundamentalist Christianity that supports patriarchal values that teach women that it is their duty to stay in a marriage, to "weather the storm."

Some policy recommendations emerge from the analysis. The most fundamental need is for changes in women's structural position. Women need more and better employment opportunities to reduce their dependency on abusive partners. Rural outreach programs and expanded telephone subscriptions might help decrease rural women's isolation. Police officers need better training. Because of the complexity of the social situation in Kentucky, no single policy solution will suffice. Instead, coordinated action and social change are needed.

Banditry

Banditry refers to a form of aggressive conflict that involves taking something that belongs to someone else. It is usually practiced by a person or group ("band") of persons who have become socially marginal and who gain a special social status from their illegal activity. Political scientists, sociologists, historians, and anthropologists have proposed various theories to explain why banditry appears at particular times and places more than others, why it is persistent in some contexts, and what sentiments inspire bandits. One theory says that bandits flourish in the context of weak states and decline as states grow stronger and increase their control of the use of violence (Blok 1972). Another view says that banditry is a form of protest, expressing a yearning for a prepolitical, just world (Hobsbawm 1969). Neither of these theories can explain, however, the surge of banditry in late nineteenth century Egypt during the time of British colonialism (Brown 1990). British control was not weak, nor was this banditry an expression of anti-British sentiment since banditry has a long heritage in Egypt. Instead, the answer appears to

Anthropologist Michael Herzfeld (far right) observes, and participates with, Glendiot men at a coffeehouse while doing fieldwork on male bonding and banditry in Crete.

be that the British chose to highlight the presence of banditry as a social problem so that they could justify their presence and role in creating "law and order."

One anthropologist has termed banditry "adventurist capital accumulation" (Sant Cassia 1993:793), but anthropological research shows that it is much more than that. For example, banditry, male identity and status, and the creation of social alliances are closely associated on the Greek island of Crete (Herzfeld 1985). In this sheepherding economy, manhood and male identity depend on a standardized local form of banditry—stealing sheep. "Coming out on the branch" is a metaphor for the attainment of manhood following a young male's first theft. This phrase implies that he is a person to be reckoned with. To not participate in sheep raids is to be an effeminate male. Each theft, however, requires a countertheft in revenge, and so the cycle goes on. For protection of his flock from theft and to be able to avenge any theft that occurs, a shepherd relies heavily on male kin (both patrilineal kin and kin through marriage). Another important basis for social ties is, however, sheep stealing itself. After a series of thefts and counterthefts and rising hostility between the two groups, a mediator will often be brought in to resolve the tension, with the result being that the enemies swear to be loyal friends from then on. According to Michael Herzfeld, the pattern of male identity formation through sheep stealing in this region of Crete is still strong, although it is declining somewhat as some shepherds begin to take up farming. Another force of change is from the government, which has sought, although largely unsuccessfully, to suppress the raiding and to define sheep-stealing as a crime rather than a source of social and personal status.

Analysis of many instances of banditry yields the finding that they often involve a process of "mythification" of bandits (Sant Cassia 1993). In this process, the "invented" or imagined character of the bandit becomes more significant than what the bandit actually did. The story of Phulan Devi, India's "Bandit Queen," contains many aspects of banditry mythification: her low socioeconomic status, traditions of pastoralism, and raiding as honorable. Villagers have composed songs praising her, and a world-class movie appeared in 1995 depicting her as a heroine who suffered, resisted, and ultimately triumphed (see the Multiple Cultural Worlds box).

Multiple Cultural Worlds

"The Bandit Queen of India"

Phulan Devi's story has been written on the basis of letters she dictated while in prison and interviews with her family and others involved in the case (Sen 1995). She was born into a poor herding family in a part of northern India famous for its bandits. She had an arranged marriage as a young girl to a man much older than she, who abused her. Attempting to escape this abuse, she ran back to her parents for shelter, something rarely done by an Indian bride who is supposed to submit docilely to whatever treatment her husband and his family hand out to her. In her natal village, she incurred the wrath of the local dominant caste, the Thakurs, in two ways. First, she refused the sexual advances of a Thakur youth and she vocally contested the Thakurs' taking over of her father's land. The Thakurs arranged to have her kidnapped by bandits as punishment. She was kidnapped and raped repeatedly by the leader until a second-in-command killed the leader in sympathy for her. He and she became lovers. He taught her to shoot, live in the ravines, and conduct village raids. After some time, he was killed and Phulan was captured. She was taken to a village where she was raped by several Thakurs and then thrown into the center of the village naked. She subsequently rejoined a bandit gang and became its leader. When twenty Thakur men were massacred by bandits in the same village where Phulan Devi was raped, she and her gang were suspected. The police finally succeeded in recapturing her. She was imprisoned for several years, but because she had become a heroine especially among the dalits, she was released and was elected as a member of Parliament. Most recently, her enemies have again attempted to re-try her for murder.

Feuding

Feuding, or long-term, retributive violence that may be lethal between families, groups of families, or tribes, is probably the most universal form of intergroup aggression. Its practice is motivated by a concept of revenge that leads to the pattern of long-term, back-and-forth violence between two groups. Feuding has long had an important role among the horticultural Ilongot people of the Philippine highlands (Rosaldo 1980). From 1883 to 1974, Ilongot feuds were structured around headhunting as the redress for an insult or offense. Manhood was defined by the taking of a first head, and fathers were responsible for transferring the elaborate knowledge of headhunting to their sons. In 1972, the government banned headhunting and attempted to stop the Ilongot from practicing shifting cultivation. The repercussion of these changes has been devastating:

> Ilongots perceive that the social fabric has been torn asunder. To give up dry rice horticulture and take up wet rice agriculture, for instance, is to surrender Ilongot ethnic identity for that of a Philippine lowlander.... In 1972, martial law brought the painful rupture in the transmission from father to son of the elaborate techniques of headhunting, and the Ilongots, by the time we were again living among them two years later, sometimes said they no longer were Ilongots. (60)

Sometimes contemporary change leads to the increase of feuding, as in the case of Thull, a Pakistani village of about 6,000 people (Keiser 1986). "Blood feuds" (which involve the death of someone in the enemy group) had increased in frequency and intensity over a fifteen-year period. Previously, there had been fights, usually expressing hostility between three local patrilineal clans, but they did not always involve deadly weapons. According to the honor code in this region, an act of avenging should not exceed the original act: A blow should answer a blow, a death a death. For a murder, a man prefers to kill the actual murderer, but a father, adult brother, or adult son is a permissible substitute; killing women and children is unknown. Wrongs committed against a man through his wife, sister, or daughter are special. Whatever the transgression, the most appropriate response is to kill the offender: "For example, staring at a man's wife or his daughter or sister (if she is of marriageable age) demands a deadly retaliation. Thus, according to some people in Thull, Diliwar Khan killed Said Omar because Said Omar had come to Diliwar Khan's door "not to bring food, but rather to catch a glimpse of Diliwar Khan's attractive young wife" (327).

Why did blood feuds increase in Thull? The answer lies in the effects of economic change on the area. A new road changed the economy from a balanced blend of herding and cultivation to increased cultivation, especially of potatoes as a cash crop. The government initiated large-scale logging operations in the region (the reason for building the road), which involved local men in wage work and greatly increased the amount of cash available. Tension increased between males, and men have grown more vigilant about defending their *ghairat* (honor). Along with the increased cash came a dramatic increase in the number of firearms owned. Now even poor men can afford rifles. More guns mean more lethal feuding.

Ethnic Conflict

Ethnic pluralism is a characteristic of most states in the world today. Ethnic conflict and grievances may result from an ethnic group's attempt to gain more autonomy or more equitable treatment (Esman 1996). It may also be caused by a dominant group's actions to subordinate, oppress, or eliminate an ethnic group by genocide or ethnocide. In the past few decades, political violence has increasingly been enacted within states rather than between states and constitutes the majority of "the 120-odd shooting wars in the world today" (Clay 1990). Political analysts and journalists often cite ethnicity, language, and religion as the causes of certain conflicts. Ethnic identities give people an ideological sense of commitment to a cause, but one must always look beneath these labels to see if deeper issues exist. Such deeper causes may include claims to land, water, ports, and other material resources.

The vast region of Central Asia is populated by many ethnic groups, none of whom has a pristine indigenous claim to the land. Yet, in Central Asia, every dispute appears on the surface to have an ethnic basis: "Russians and Ukrainians versus Kazakhs over land rights and jobs in Kazakhstan, Uzbeks versus Tajiks over the status of Samarkhand and Bukhara, conflict between Kirghiz and Uzbeks in Kyrghyzstan, and riots between Caucasian Turks and Uzbeks in the Fergana Valley of Uzbekistan" (Clay 1990:48).

Attributing all such problems to ethnic differences overlooks the fact that the concept of a functioning plural society is more firmly entrenched in the Central Asian states than anywhere else in the former Soviet Union. In contrast to the Baltic states, the Central Asian nations have granted citizenship to all inhabitants. This acceptance of diversity follows an old pattern: Different ethnic groups fit different economic slots. This could be called a "segmentational model," in which different groups control significant resources and institutions, as contrasted with a "stratificational model," in which one group dominates others (Esman 1996). A more illuminating way of analyzing the basis of conflict in Central Asia is to consider the division between centers and hinterlands and their different access to crucial resources. Uzbekistan has most of the cities and irrigated farmland, but small states like Kyrghyzstan and Tajikistan control most of the water. Turkmenistan has vast oil and gas riches. "No ethnic catalyst would be needed to provoke conflict in such situations; simple need or greed would more than suffice" (51).

Ethnic conflicts are waged in many different ways, from the cruelest and most gruesome killings and rapes to more subtle forms of power jockeying (see the Current Event box). An example of the latter type of conflict concerns whether Muslim girl students may wear head scarves in school in France. The Israeli–Palestinian situation in Israel encompasses many forms of conflict. In Israel, land that appears to be unused is said to belong to the state (Cohen 1993). Palestinians who live in areas near the expanding municipal border of Jerusalem attempt to prevent further encroachment by planting olive trees (their symbol) on the land, thus claiming the land as theirs. In turn, the Israelis have programs for planting pine trees around Jerusalem as part of the mayor's "greenbelt" plan, a strategy that claims the land as Israeli.

Current Event

"Burundi's Three-Year Campaign of Terror Leaves a Bloody Trail on University Campuses"

- Conflict between the Hutus and the Tutsis has resulted in the death of tens of thousands of civilians. In 1995, the conflict moved on to the campuses of the University of Burundi.
- Fewer than 100 students from the Hutu community, which makes up 85 percent of the national population, were studying there. The rest were Tutsis, members of the country's 14 percent minority. Some of the Tutsi students are said to have waged a campaign of terror against Hutu students at the university.
- In one incident, about 50 Hutus were killed. Reprisals followed. Over the following months, several more incidents occurred. While several Tutsis were killed, the number of Hutus killed was much larger.
- As of 1996, no Hutu students remained on campus.

Source: The Chronicle of Higher Education, August 16, 1996, p. A39.

Revolution

A **revolution** is a "political crisis propelled by illegal and usually violent actions by subordinate groups which threatens to change the political institutions or social structure of a society" (Goldstone 1996:740). Revolutions are sometimes called "wars," but they receive separate consideration here as within-state conflicts that are considered illegal by the state. Revolutions have occurred in a range of societies, including preindustrial monarchies, postcolonial Third World countries, and totalitarian states. Scholars who have compared revolutions in modern times—England 1640, France 1789, Mexico 1910, China 1911, Russia 1917, Iran 1979—say that interrelated factors, such as a military or fiscal crisis and a weak state military machine, may begin a revolution. The process of revolutions varies in terms of the degree of popular participation, roles of radicals and moderates, and leadership.

Theorists also argue about the different role of rural versus urban sectors in fomenting revolution. Many revolutions occurred in mainly agrarian countries and were propelled by rural participants, not urban radicalism (Skocpol 1979; E. Wolf 1969). Such agrarian-based revolutions include the French, Russian, and Chinese revolutions. A rural-based movement also characterizes many national liberation movements against colonial powers such as French Indo-China, Guinea-Bissau, Mozambique, and Angola (Gugler 1988). Algeria was a somewhat more urbanized country, but it was still about two-thirds rural in 1962 when the French finally made peace there. In all of these cases, the colonial power was challenged by a rural-based guerrilla movement that controlled crop production, processing, and transport and thus could strike at the heart of the colonial political economy.

On the other hand, some revolutions have been essentially urban in character, including Bolivia, Iran, and Nicaragua. The case of Cuba is mixed since rural-based guerrillas played a prominent role and the cities provided crucial support for the guerrillas. The importance of cities in these revolutions is related to the fact that the countries were highly urbanized. Thus, revolutionary potential exists where resources are controlled and where the bulk of the population is located. Given the rapid urban growth in Third World countries, it is possible that the world is entering "the age of urban revolutions" (Gugler 1988).

Warfare

Several definitions of war have been proposed (Reyna 1994). Is it open and declared conflict between two political units? This definition would rule out, for example, the American–Vietnam War because it was undeclared. Is it simply organized aggression? This definition is too broad since not all organized violence can be considered warfare. Perhaps the best definition is that **war** is "organized, purposeful group action, directed against another group . . . involving the actual or potential application of lethal force" (Ferguson 1994, quoted in Reyna 1994:30). A critical point is that lethal force during war is legal if it is conducted according to the rules of battle.

Cultural variation exists in the frequency and seriousness of wars. Intergroup conflicts between different bands of foragers are relatively rare. More often, they involve conflicts between individuals belonging to different groups, not group conflicts per se. Conflicts are usually fought out person-to-person, either with words or fists. The informal, nonhierarchical political organization among bands is not conducive to waging armed conflict. Bands do not have specialized military forces or leaders.

Archaeological evidence indicates that warfare emerged and intensified during the Neolithic era. Plant and animal domestication required more extensive land use, and they were accompanied by increased population densities. The combined economic and demographic pressures put more and larger groups in more direct and more intense competition with each other. Tribal leadership patterns facilitate mobilization of warrior groups for raids, but not all tribal groups have equal levels of warfare. At one extreme are the Yanomami of the Venezuelan and Brazilian Amazon, who have been typified as "the fierce people." Is this characterization correct, and, if so, what causes this behavior pattern? (see the Critical Thinking box on pages 302 and 303).

Many chiefdoms are characterized by relatively high rates of warfare and casualty rates. They have increased capacity for war in terms of personnel and surplus foods to support long-range expeditions. In many chiefdoms, the chief could call on his or her retainers as a specialized fighting force as well as the general members of society. Chiefs and paramount chiefs could be organized into more effective command structures (Reyna 1994:44–45). These levels of aggregation and potential for more extensive and massive campaigns continued to expand as chiefdoms and confederacies evolved into state-level organizations. In states, standing armies and complex military hierarchies are supported by the increased material resources under the control of leaders through taxation and other forms of revenue generation. Greater state power allows for more powerful and effective military structures, which in turn increase the state's power; thus, a mutually reinforcing relationship emerges between the military and the state. While states are generally highly militarized, not all are, nor are all states equally militarized. Costa Rica does not maintain an army, but Turkey has one of the world's largest armies.

The military as a subject has not attracted much attention from cultural anthropologists thus far. Issues that would benefit from anthropological analysis include the internal organization of the military, gender issues in military training and assignments, and militarism in child socialization (especially boys) through toys and games. Anthropologists have been somewhat more involved in studying the effects of war, such as the health and psychological status of survivors.

Examining the causes of war between states has occupied scholars in many fields for centuries. Some experts have pointed to common, underlying causes such as attempts to extend boundaries, secure more resources, ensure markets, support political and economic allies, and resist aggression from other states. Others point to humanitarian concerns that prompt participation in "good wars," to defend values such as freedom or to protect human rights as defined in

CRITICAL THINKING

Yanomami: The "Fierce People"?

The Yanomami are a horticultural people living in dispersed and mutually hostile villages composed of between 40 to 250 people each (M. Ross 1993:3–5). According to Napoleon Chagnon's estimates, about one-third of Yanomami males die violently, about two-thirds of all adults had lost at least one close relative through violence, and over 50 percent had lost two or more close relatives (Chagnon 1992 [1968]: 205). One village was raided twenty-five times during Chagnon's first fifteen months of fieldwork. Although village alliances are sometimes formed, they are fragile, and allies may turn against each other unpredictably.

The world for the Yanomami appears to be a dangerous place. Enemies, human and supernatural, are everywhere. Support from one's allies is uncertain. Autonomy, for the village and the individual, becomes the unattainable solution to this dilemma. It is sought in what Chagnon calls the *waiteri* complex: Men develop a fierce political and personal stance, and groups and individuals behave aggressively to communicate strength and independence to others. Fierceness is a dominant theme in the socialization of boys, who learn how to fight with clubs, participate in chest-pounding duels with other males, and use a spear. Males are aggressive and hostile toward females, and young boys learn to be aggressive toward girls from an early age.

Many anthropologists have been convinced that the Yanomami indeed are a "fierce people" and have relatively high levels of aggressive behavior, both within their own villages and between groups. If so, the question is why? The Yanomami have explained that the purpose of village raids and warfare is so that men may obtain wives. While there is a preference for village endogamy, there is a "supply" problem. The Yanomami practice female infanticide, creating a scarcity of women. While the Yanomami prefer to marry endogamously, a wife from another group is preferable to remaining a bachelor. Men in other groups, however, are unwilling to give up their women to provide brides for men in other groups. Hence, the necessity for raids. Suspicion of sorcery or theft of food are other valid reasons for raids.

Napoleon Chagnon provides a sociobiological explanation. He says that warfare contributes to reproductive success since successful warriors will be able to gain a wife or more than one wife (since polygyny is allowed). Thus, they will have higher rates of reproduction than unsuccessful warriors. This system leads to an overall higher survival rate of groups with high levels of male violence because their population will produce more and better warriors through genetic selection for fierceness. Male fierceness, in this view, is ecologically adaptive.

Marvin Harris (1984), from his cultural materialist perspective, says that protein scarcity and population dynamics in the area are the underlying cause of intergroup conflict. The Yanomami lacked sources of domesticated meat, which was highly valued. Harris suggests that when hunting in an area became depleted, pressure would rise to expand into the territory of neighboring groups, thus precipitating conflict. Such conflicts in turn resulted in a high rate of adult male mortality. Combined with the effects of female infanticide, this meat-warfare complex kept population growth rates down to a level that the environment could support.

R. Brian Ferguson's (1990) historical analysis supports the position that the high levels of violence were caused by the intensified Western presence through the preceding one hundred years. European-introduced diseases severely depopulated the Yanomami and other Amazonian groups, and must have greatly increased their fears of sorcery since that is how they explained much death and disease. The attraction to Western trade goods such as metal tools and guns would have increased intergroup rivalry. These changes increased the difficulty of finding wives. Thus, Ferguson suggests that the "fierce people" are a creation of world historical forces as much as factors internal to their society.

Critical Thinking Questions

- Is the characterization of the Yanomami as the "fierce people" accurate? (Are all Yanomami people equally fierce; are they *all* socialized into the waitiri complex?)

- Which theory appears most persuasive to you and why?
- Can you offer any alternative theories, and what evidence would you need to support your theory?
- What relevance does this case have for theories that violence is a universal human trait?
- What other tribal groups would provide good comparisons with the Yanomami—do you know of any tribal groups that could be called the "peaceful people"?

one nation and being violated in another. Experts also study the immediate causes of the war—the catalyst—such as the assassination of Archduke Ferdinand in sparking World War I.

Thomas Barfield (1994b) compared wars in Afghanistan since the seventeenth century. Warfare increasingly became a way that kings justified their power in terms of the necessity to maintain independence from outside forces such as the British and Czarist Russia (1994b). The last king was murdered in a coup in 1978. When the Soviet Union invaded in 1979, there was no centralized ruling group to meet it. The Soviet Union deposed the ruling faction and replaced it with one of their own and "then engaged in a wholesale war against the population. Three million Afghans fled to Pakistan and Iran, over one million were killed, millions of others were displaced internally" (7). Yet, in spite of having no central command, divided by ethnic and sectarian differences, and outmatched in equipment by Soviet forces, a war of resistance eventually wore down the Soviets, who withdrew in 1989.

This case suggests that war was a more effective tool of domination in the premodern period when war settled matters more definitively. "The number of troops needed after a conquest were relatively few because they were not expected to have to put down continual internal revolts, but to defend the new conquest from rival outsiders" (7). Success in the Soviet Union's holding Afghanistan would have required more extensive involvement and commitment, including: introduction of a new political ideology or economic structure that would win the population over, population transfer to remove opposition and immigration of allies into the area. Barfield notes that in contemporary times, "winning battles or wars becomes only the first stage in a much more complicated process with no guarantees of ultimate success" (10). His findings thus point us in new directions of research and analysis concerning state–state conflict.

Nonviolent Conflict

Mohandas K. Gandhi was one of the greatest designers of strategies for bringing about peaceful political change. Born in India, he was married at the age of twelve, and then began to study law in London when he was nineteen years old (Caplan 1987). After his studies, he went to South Africa, where he worked as a lawyer, serving the Indian community. He became active in organizing the Indians to protest racial injustices. In South Africa, he evolved his primary method of civil disobedience through nonviolent resistance. The two basic tenets of Gandhi's approach are the Hindu ethic of *ahimsa* (nonviolence) and the concept of *satyagraha* (truth force). In 1915, he returned to India, joined the nationalist struggle against British colonialism, and put into action his model of civil disobedience through nonviolent resistance, public fasting, and strikes, characterized in Gandhian politics by mass prayer and fasting.

Celibacy is another key feature of Gandhian philosophy because avoiding sex helps maintain one's inner strength and purity (recall the "lost semen complex" mentioned in Chapter 5). Regardless of whether one agrees with Gandhi's approach to food and sex, it is clear that the methods he developed of nonviolent civil disobedience have had a profound impact on the world. Martin Luther King, Jr., and his followers adopted many of Gandhi's tactics during the Civil Rights Movement in the United States, as did members of the Peace Movement of the 1960s and 1970s in the United States.

Political scientist James Scott (1985) used the phrase "weapons of the weak" as the title of his book on rural people's resistance to domination by land-

Mahatma Ghandi (left), leader of the Indian movement for freedom from British colonial control, on his famous "Salt March" of 1930, in which he led a procession to the sea to collect salt in defiance of British law. He is accompanied by Sarojini Naidu, a noted freedom fighter.

lords and government through tactics other than outright rebellion or revolution. Most subordinate classes throughout history have not had the "luxury" of open, organized political activity because of its danger. Instead, people have had to resort to ways of living with or "working" the system. Everyday forms of resistance include "foot dragging," desertion, false compliance, feigned ignorance, and slander, as well as more aggressive acts such as theft, arson, and sabotage. Many contemporary anthropologists have followed Scott's lead and contributed groundbreaking studies of everyday resistance. One form that Scott overlooked, however, is humor. Humor is an important part of Native American cultural resistance to complete domination by White society (Lincoln 1993). Instead of pitying themselves or lamenting the genocide that occurred as a result of European and Euro-American colonization, they have cultivated a sharp sense of humor. "Rez" (reservation) jokes travel like wildfire. Charlie Hill, for example, is notorious for his one-liners:

> The first English immigrants, he snaps, were illegal aliens—"Whitebacks, we call 'em." Hill imagines the Algonquians asking innocently, "You guys gonna stay long?" His Custer jokes are not printable ("Look at all those f---ing Indians!"—a barroom nude painting of Custer's last words). (4–5)

Or, what did Native Americans say at Plymouth Rock? Answer: "There goes the neighborhood." Obviously, humor has not been the only source of strength for Native Americans, but Lincoln is surely correct in adding humor to the list of "weapons of the weak." Most recently, the Internet has become a medium for political protest in China (see the Current Event box).

Current Event

"Chinese Protest Finds a Path on the Internet"

- In 1996, a Chinese student posted a message on one of the computer bulletin boards that link more than two hundred Chinese universities. The student called for a demonstration at the Japanese Embassy in Beijing to protest Japanese actions concerning five tiny East China Sea islands, the Diaoyu Islands. The possession of these islands is disputed by China, Japan, and Taiwan.
- The information campaign widened, and several demonstrations took place in Hong Kong. Hundreds of thousands of Chinese signed a petition expressing their outrage.
- The Chinese government responded by banishing a leader of the petition drive from Beijing to a remote province.
- The government is also seeking to tighten control of computer communication. For example, computer technicians censor university computer bulletin boards and delete messages on matters other than "education and research." Messages about politics, along with humorous messages, are erased.

Source: Mufson 1996b.

MAINTAINING WORLD ORDER

Computer-operated war missiles, e-mail, faxes, satellite television, and jet flights mean that the world's nations are more closely connected and able to influence each other's fate than ever before. Modern weaponry means that such influences can be even more lethal. In the face of these geopolitical realities, politicians, academics, and the public ponder the possibilities for world peace. Anthropological research on peaceful, local-level societies shows that humans are capable of living together in peace. The question is, can people living in larger groups that are globally connected also live in peace? Numerous attempts have been made, over time, to create institutions to promote world peace, of which the United Nations is the most established and respected. One of the UN's significant accomplishments was the creation of the world court, which is located at the Hague in Holland (Nader 1995). In 1946, two-thirds of the Court's judges were American or Western European. Now the Court has many judges from Third World countries and more sympathy for such nations. Despite this more balanced representation from a wide range of countries, there has been a decline in use of the International Court of Justice and an increased use of international negotiating teams for resolving disputes between nations. Laura Nader analyzed this decline and found that it follows a trend in the United States beginning in the 1970s to promote "alternate dispute resolution" (ADR). The goal was to move more cases out of the courts and to privatize dispute resolution. In principle, ADR seems a more peaceful and more dignified option. Deeper analysis of actual cases and their resolution shows, however, that this bilateral process tends to favor the stronger party. Nader looked at several cases of international river disputes. In each example, adjudication (formal decree by a judge) would have resulted in a better deal for the weaker party than bilateral negotiation did. Overall, less powerful nations are being negatively affected by the trend toward the move away from the International Court.

Is it possible that cultural anthropologists have the capacity to be involved in peace-keeping organizations? Robert Carneiro (1994) has a pessimistic response. During the long history of human political evolution from bands to states, Carneiro says that warfare has been the major means by which political units enlarged their power and domain. Foreseeing no logical end to this process, he predicts that war will follow war until superstates become ever larger and one megastate is the final result. He also considers the United Nations powerless in dealing with the principal obstacle to world peace, which is national sovereignty interests. Carneiro indicts the United Nations for its lack of coercive power and its poor record of only a few cases of resolving disputes through military intervention.

One positive point emerges, however. The United Nations does provide an arena for airing disputes. A more optimistic view suggests that international peace organizations play a major role by providing analysis of the interrelationships among world problems and helping others see what are the causes of violence (Vickers 1993:132). In addition, some people see hope for local and global peace-making through nongovernmental organizations and local grassroots initiatives that seek to bridge group interests, such as the Joint Palestinian/Israeli Women's Coordinating Committee.

If the belief exists that war is inevitable, that leaves little room for hope that anthropological knowledge might be applied to peace-making efforts. Despite Carneiro's views, cultural anthropologists have shown that war is not a cultural universal, and that different cultures have ways of solving disputes without resorting to killing. The cultural anthropological perspective of critical cultural relativism (review this concept, Chapter 1) can provide useful background on issues of conflict and prompt a deeper dialogue between parties.

SUMMARY

Social control can be based on rules that are either informal norms or formal laws. Social control in small-scale societies seeks to restore order more than to punish offenders. Social shaming and shunning are commonly applied methods. In state societies, capital punishment may exist, reflecting the greater coercive power of the state. Legal systems and different types of legal specialists are more associated with the state than any other form of social organization. Critical legal anthropology seeks to reveal power inequities in legal systems. Critical legal anthropologists have studied discrimination in court systems on the basis of race, ethnicity, and gender.

Legal systems are responsive to social change. Global colonialism and imperialism brought changes to indigenous systems of social control and law, often resulting in a situation of legal pluralism. As a culture's economic system changes, for example, from socialism to capitalism, different laws are needed.

Studying social conflict and violence poses particular problems for anthropological fieldworkers, in addition to safety issues. Particularly important are ethical questions about responsibility toward the people involved. Social conflict ranges from face-to-face conflicts, as among neighbors or domestic partners, to larger group conflicts between ethnic groups and states. Solutions that would be effective at the interpersonal level are often not applicable to large-scale, impersonalized conflict.

Although anthropologists have been less likely to study global interrelationships in the past, some are now turning their attention in this direction. Some key issues involve the role of cultural knowledge in dispute resolution and the way international or local organizations can help achieve or maintain peace.

CRITICAL THINKING QUESTIONS

1. What kinds of social control systems are in operation at your college or university? Consider both norms and laws. How are they made known? What happens to violators?
2. Find a recent news event that involves a legal issue. How might a critical legal anthropologist approach this case?
3. What are the major similarities and differences in disputes among the Gwembe villagers of southeast Africa and middle-class American suburbanites?
4. Consider an international dispute that is currently ongoing. How do the media present the issues and interests? What more would an anthropologist want to know? Would anthropological knowledge help to bring about a solution?

KEY CONCEPTS

banditry, p. 297
critical legal studies, p. 286
feuding, p. 299
law, p. 287
legal pluralism, p. 293
norm, p. 287
policing, p. 289
revolution, p. 300
social control, p. 286
trial by ordeal, p. 289
war, p. 301

SUGGESTED READINGS

R. Brian Ferguson and Neil L. Whitehead, eds., *War in the Tribal Zone: Expanding States and Indigenous Warfare.* Santa Fe: School of American Research Press, 1992. Essays on tribal and pre-state warfare include examples from pre-Columbian Mesoamerica, early Sri Lanka, West Africa, the Iroquois, the Yanomami, and highland New Guinea.

Thomas Gregor, ed., *A Natural History of Peace.* Nashville: University of Tennessee Press, 1996. This book contains essays on "What is Peace," reconciliation among non-human primates, the psychological bases of violent and caring societies, community-level studies on Amazonia and Native America, and issues of peace and violence between states.

Roger N. Lancaster, *Life is Hard: Machismo, Danger, and the Intimacy of Power in Nicaragua.* Berkeley: University of California Press, 1992. This ethnography of everyday life in a barrio of Managua, Nicaragua, gives attention to interpersonal violence as well as the wider issue of how living during a revolution affected people.

Sally Engle Merry, *Getting Justice and Getting Even: Legal Consciousness among Working-Class Americans.* Chicago: University of Chicago Press, 1990. Based on fieldwork among native-born, White, working class Americans in a small New England town and their experiences in the court system, this book considers how the court system is perceived by the litigants as more often controlling than empowering.

Carolyn Nordstrom and Antonius C. G. M. Robben, eds., *Fieldwork under Fire: Contemporary Studies of Violence and Survival.* Berkeley: University of California Press, 1995. After an introductory chapter that discusses general themes, several examples of fieldwork experiences in dangerous situations including Palestine, China, Sri Lanka, United States, Croatia, Guatemala, and Ireland are given.

俾善涉大水徯我后后来其蘇

CHAPTER 13

Religion

CHAPTER OUTLINE

WHAT IS RELIGION?
- Magic versus Religion
- Theories of the Origin of Religion

VARIETIES OF RELIGIOUS BELIEFS
- How Beliefs Are Expressed: Myth and Doctrine
- Beliefs about Supernatural Forces and Beings

BELIEFS IN ACTION: RITUAL PRACTICES
- Life-Cycle Rituals
- Rituals of Reversal
- Sacrifice
  - *Critical Thinking:* Why Did the Aztecs Practice Human Sacrifice...and Cannibalism?

RELIGIOUS SPECIALISTS
- Shamans and Priests
- Other Specialists

WORLD RELIGIONS
- Hinduism
- Buddhism
- Judaism
  - *Current Event:* Women Raise Their Voices for the Right to Pray Aloud at Wall
- Christianity
- Islam

AFRICAN RELIGIONS
- Features of African Religions
- Ras Tafari

DIRECTIONS AND CHALLENGES OF CHANGE
- Revitalization Movements
- Contested Sacred Sites
  - *Multiple Cultural Worlds:* Aboriginal Beliefs versus Mining at Guratba
- Socialism and Religion
- Religious Freedom as a Human Right

SUMMARY

KEY CONCEPTS

CRITICAL THINKING QUESTIONS

SUGGESTED READINGS

◀ A woman praying at a Buddhist pagoda in Ho Chi Minh City, Vietnam, is dwarfed by spiraled hanging incense. The temple is dedicated to Me Sanh, a fertility goddess. Both men and women, but especially women, come here to pray for children.

Cultural anthropology's approach to religion parallels its approach to every other domain of life. It examines the variety of religions within their cultural context and seeks to provide explanations for questions such as: Why do some religions advocate animal sacrifice? Why do some religions give greater room for women's participation? and How do different religions respond to changing conditions in the political economy? Most cultural anthropologists view religions as cultural constructions with long histories of evolution over time. The perspective of cultural relativism would suggest that no religion is better or worse than any other. This perspective is controversial to those who hold that a particular religion is divinely created and supreme.

Religion has been a cornerstone topic in cultural anthropology since its beginning. Over these many decades, a rich collection of material has accumulated. Early attention was focused on religions of nonstate societies, including the many localized traditions of particular groups and areas. More recently, anthropologists devoted attention to the major religions of state-level societies. Comparing religions across the production continuum reveals general differences in belief systems and variations in the complexity and hierarchy of religious organization. Attention to these differences is a major concern of this chapter.

WHAT IS RELIGION?

Since the earliest days of anthropology, various definitions of religion have appeared. One of the simplest, offered by Tylor in the late 1800s, is that religion is the belief in spirits. The definition favored by a cultural materialist approach is that **religion** is both beliefs and actions related to supernatural beings and forces (what Tylor referred to as spirits). In defining religion so that it fits the cross-cultural material, anthropologists avoid a narrow definition that says religion is the belief in a supreme deity. In many religions, no concept of a supreme deity exists, while others have multiple deities. Religion is not the same as a people's **world view,** or way of understanding how the world came to be, its design, and their place in it. World view is a broader concept and does not include the criterion of concern with a supernatural realm. An atheist has a world view, but not a religious one.

Magic versus Religion

In the late 1800s, E. B. Tylor wrote that magic, religion, and science are alike in that they are different ways people have tried to explain the physical world and events in it. For Tylor, the three systems were contradictory and incompatible. Tylor thought that magical laws were false and scientific laws were true, and that religion is based on the false assumption that the world operates under the control of supernaturals. James Frazer followed many of Tylor's ideas. He defined **magic** as the attempt to compel supernatural forces and beings to act in certain ways, in contrast to religion, which is the attempt to please supernatural forces or beings. After reviewing many practices cross-culturally that he considered to be magical, Frazer deduced two general principles of magic that correspond to two major categories of magic. First is the "law of similarity," the basis of what he called "imitative magic." It is founded on the assumption that if person or item X is like person or item Y, then actions done to person or item X will affect person or item Y. The most well-known example is a voodoo doll. By sticking pins into a doll X that represents person Y, then person Y will experience pain or suffering. The second is the "law of contagion," which is the basis for "contagious magic." The law of contagion says that persons or things once in contact with a person can still have an effect on that person. Common items for working contagious magic are a person's hair trimmings; nail clippings; teeth; spit or blood or fecal matter left carelessly beside a pathway; or the placenta of a baby. In cultures where contagious magic is practiced, people are careful about disposing of their personal wastes so that no one else can get hold of them.

Early scholars of religion posited an evolutionary model, with magic as the predecessor of religion. They evaluated magic as less spiritual and ethical than religion and therefore more "primitive." They assumed that, in time, magic would be completely replaced by the "higher" system of religion, and then ultimately by science as the most rational way of thinking. They would be surprised to see the widespread presence of magical religions in the modern world as evidenced, for example, by a recent ethnographic study of magic and witchcraft in contemporary London (Luhrmann 1989). Most anthropologists now think that magic remains prominent in all cultures. In different situations, people will turn to magic, religion, or science. For example, magic has a prominent place in sports (Gmelch 1997 [1971]). American baseball players repeat actions or use charms (including a special shirt or hat) to help them win on the assumption that if it worked before, it may work again. They are following Tylor's law of contagion. Such magical thinking is most common in contexts where uncertainty is greatest. In baseball, pitching and hitting involve more uncertainty than fielding, and pitchers and hitters are more likely to use magic. Besides sports, magical practices are prominent in farming, fishing, the military, and love.

Theories of the Origin of Religion

Why did religion come into being, and how did it come into being? (Smith 1995:816–819). The universal existence of some form of religion has prompted theorists concerned with the "why" question to emphasize religion's functions in fulfilling universal human needs. According to this view, religion provides ways of explaining and coping with the "imponderables of life" such as birth, illness, misfortune, and death. Others have suggested that religion grew out of people's attempt to understand nature and its changes, such as sunrise and sunset, the annual flooding of great rivers, the tides, drought, pestilence, and the changing positions of the stars.

Tylor's theory, as proposed in his book, *Primitive Culture* (1871), was based on his assumption that early people had a need for explanation, especially for the difference between the living and the dead. They therefore developed the concept of a soul that exists in all living things and departs from the body after death. Tylor named this way of thinking **animism,** the belief in souls or "doubles." He suggested that evidence for the soul is found in the fact that all people dream. (Scholars of human evolution point to the Neanderthal practice of intentional burials, often accompanied with flowers, as evidence that concepts of the soul or afterlife or some supernatural realm probably existed 50,000 years ago.) Eventually, Tylor speculated, the concept of the soul became personified until, later, human-like deities were conceived. For Tylor, religion evolved from animism to polytheism (the belief in many deities) to monotheism (the belief in one supreme deity). In contrast to Tylor, Frazer suggested that religion developed out of the failure of magic. Neither scholar suggested a place or time period during which these developments may have occurred, and both based their theories on speculation rather than archaeological or other empirical data.

Later, Emile Durkheim offered a functional explanation for how and why religion emerged in his book, *The Elementary Forms of the Religious Life* (1912). He reviewed ethnographic data on "primitive" religions cross-culturally and was struck by their social aspects: Durkheim speculated that early humans realized, through clan gatherings, that contact with one another made them feel uplifted and powerful. This positive feeling, arising from social solidarity, became attached to the clan totem, an emblem of their group that became the first of many future objects of worship. Religion therefore originated to serve society by giving it cohesion through shared symbols and group rituals.

Durkheim's focus on social solidarity represents a functional approach to religion in which religious beliefs and practices are interpreted as serving roles other than purely religious ones. Malinowski documented its psychological functions, writing about how rituals help reduce anxiety and uncertainty. Marx, taking a conflict approach rather than a functional one, emphasized religion's political and economic role in being an "opiate of the masses" and

The Origin of Religion

supporting oppressive power structures. A third major theoretical thread, symbolic analysis, informs Freud's theory of the role of the unconscious. Many anthropologists agree with Freud that religion is a "projective system" that expresses people's unconscious thoughts, wishes, and worries. Anthropologists have also applied Freudian analysis of symbols and their underlying or hidden meanings in dreams to the analysis of myths. A fourth theoretical theme, which can be seen to combine Durkheimian functionalism with symbolic analysis, comes from Clifford Geertz (1973) who proposed in his early writings that religions are primarily systems of meaning. In this view, religion offers a conception of reality, "a model of life," and a pattern for how to live, a "model for life."

VARIETIES OF RELIGIOUS BELIEFS

Religions comprise beliefs and behavior. Scholars of religion generally address belief systems first since they appear to inform patterns of religious behavior. Religious beliefs tend to be shared by a group, sometimes by very large numbers of people. Through the centuries, people have found ways to give their beliefs permanence. Elders teach children the group's songs and tales, artists paint the stories on rocks and walls, and sculptors create images in wood and stone that depict aspects of religious belief.

How Beliefs Are Expressed: Myth and Doctrine

Beliefs are expressed and transferred over the generations in two main formats: **myth,** narrative stories about supernatural forces or beings, and **doctrine,** direct and formalized statements about religious beliefs.

Myths are composed of language in the form of a narrative that has a plot with a beginning, middle, and end. The plot may involve recurrent motifs, the smallest units of narrative. Myths convey messages about the supernaturals indirectly, through the medium of the story itself, rather than by using logic or formal argument. Greek and Roman myths, such as the stories of Zeus, Athena, Orpheus, and Persephone, are world-famous. Some people would say that the Bible is a collection of mythology; others would object to that categorization as it suggests that the stories are not "real" or "sacred."

Myths are distinguished from folktales, which are largely secular stories, although borderline cases exist. For example, some people would classify "Cinderella" as a folktale, while others would quickly point out that the fairy godmother is not an ordinary human and so "Cinderella" should be considered a myth. These arguments are more entertaining than important. In earliest times, myths were part of people's oral tradition. Only with the emergence of writing were these stories recorded, and then only if they were of great importance, perhaps part of a royal or priestly tradition. Many of the world's myths, especially their local variants, are still unwritten.

Anthropologists have asked why societies have myth. The functionalist explanation is that myths help to maintain the society itself. Malinowski said that a myth is a "charter" for society in that it expresses core beliefs and teaches morality. French anthropologist Claude Lévi-Strauss, probably the most famous mythologist, says that myths are tribal peoples' form of philosophy, their way of explaining the world. The philosophical message does not lie on the surface of the myths. It is embedded in their underlying structure and the symbolism of key characters and events. Human beings, he says, think in terms of classifications, especially binary classification. He finds recurrent binary oppositions in myths, such as nature versus culture, life versus death, raw versus cooked food, wild versus tame animals, and incest versus exogamy. Such oppositions are philosophically uncomfortable for people to face—for example, the fact that life cannot exist without death. Myths help people deal with the deep puzzles and discomforts of life by presenting the oppositions along with a third position that mediates between the two extremes and provides a solution. For example, many Pueblo Indian myths juxtapose grass-eating animals (vegetarians) with predators (carnivores). The mediating third character is the raven, who is a carnivore but, unlike other creatures, does not have to kill to eat meat.

Epics tend to be longer than myths and focus more on heroic traditions. Many epics are firmly associated with particular ethnic groups or nations, such as the *Odyssey* and the *Iliad* of Greece. Less well-known in North America, but just as good reading are India's two great Hindu epics, the *Mahabharata* and the *Ramayana*. Iceland's *eddas* of the thirteenth century

A stone sculpture at Mamallapuram (Mahaballipuram), south India, dating from the eighth to ninth centuries, depicts the impending triumph of the goddess Durga (riding the lion, on the left) over the bull-headed demon Mahishasmura. The story of her creation by the gods and her ultimate saving of the world through the killing of Mahishashura has inspired countless works of art in India.

are grouped into two categories: mythic (dealing with gods) and heroic (dealing with humans). Eddas of other Nordic countries share similar motifs and patterns.

Doctrine, the other major form in which beliefs are expressed, explicitly defines the supernaturals—who they are, what they do, and how to relate to them through religious practice; the world and how it came to be; and people's roles in relation to the supernaturals and to other humans. Doctrine, which is written and formal is close to law in some respects because it makes direct links between incorrect beliefs and behaviors and the punishments for each. Many religious scriptures incorporate both myth and doctrine.

Doctrine is associated more with institutionalized, large-scale religions than with localized, small-scale "folk" religions. Thus, the major world religions discussed later in this chapter all have established doctrine to which followers should adhere. Doctrine, however, can and does change (Bowen 1998:38–40). Over the centuries, various Popes have pronounced new doctrine for the Catholic church. A papal declaration of 1854, given with the intent of reinvigorating European Catholicism, gave authenticity to the concept of the Immaculate Conception, an idea with substantial popular support.

Muslim doctrine is expressed in the Qu'ran, the basic holy text of the Islamic faith that consists of revelations made to the prophet Muhammed in the seventh century, and the *hadith*, collections of Muhammed's statements and deeds (Bowen 1998:38). Ongoing debates throughout the Muslim world continue to refer to these sources for justification and guidance about contemporary practices. In Kuala Lumpur, Malaysia, a small group of highly educated women called the Sisters in Islam regularly debate with members of the local *ulama* (male religious authorities who are responsible for interpreting Islamic doctrine especially concerning families, education, and commercial affairs) (Ong 1995). In recent years, the debates have concerned such issues as polygamy, divorce, women's work roles, and women's clothing.

Beliefs about Supernatural Forces and Beings

In all cultures, some concept of otherworldly beings or forces exists, even though not all members of the culture believe in their existence. Supernaturals range from impersonal forces to those that look just like humans. **Animatism** refers to belief systems in which the supernatural is conceived of as an impersonal power. A well-known example is *mana*, a concept widespread throughout the Melanesian region of the South Pacific. Mana is a force outside nature that works automatically; it is neither spirit nor deity. It manifests itself in objects and people and is associated with personal status and power since some people accumulate more of it than others. Some supernaturals are **zoomorphic** (deities that appear in the shape, or partial shape, of animals). No satisfactory theory has appeared to explain why some religions develop zoomorphic deities, and for what purposes, and why others do not. Religions of classical Greece and Rome and ancient and contemporary Hinduism are especially rich in zoomorphic supernaturals.

Anthropomorphic supernaturals (deities in the form of humans) are common, but not universal. Allah, the supreme deity of Islam, is not anthropomorphized and can be represented only in the form of writing his name. The human tendency to perceive of supernaturals in their own form was noted 2,500 years ago by the Greek philosopher Xenophanes (who lived sometime between 570 and 470 BCE). He said: "If cattle and horses, or lions, had hands, or were able to draw with their feet and produce the worlds which men do, horses would draw the forms of gods like horses, and cattle like cattle, and they would make the gods' bodies the same shape as their own" (*Fragment* 15). But why some religions do and others do not have anthropomorphic deities is another question that is impossible to answer, although such deities seem more common in sedentary societies than among foragers. Anthropomorphic supernaturals, like humans, can be moved by praise, flattery, and gifts. They can be tricked. They have emotions: They get irked if neglected, they can be loving and caring, or they can be distant and nonresponsive. Most anthropomorphic supernaturals are adults. Few are very old or very young. Humans and supernaturals have similar marital and sexual patterns. Divine marriages tend to be heterosexual. In societies where polygyny occurs, male gods also have multiple wives. Deities have sexual intercourse, within marriage and sometimes extramaritally. Gods of the Greek and Roman pantheon (the entire collection of deities) often descended to earth and kidnapped and raped human women. So far, however, legal divorce has not occurred among supernaturals, although separations have. While many supernaturals have children, grandchildren are not prominent.

In complex pantheons, a division of labor exists by which certain supernaturals are responsible for particular domains. This greater specialization among the supernaturals reflects the greater specialization in human society. There may be a deity of forests, rivers, the sky, wind and rain, agriculture, childbirth, disease, warfare, and marital happiness. Some gods are more effective for material wealth and others for academic success. The supernaturals have political roles and hierarchies. High gods, like Jupiter and Juno of classical Roman religion, are distant from humans and hard to contact. The more approachable deities are below them on the hierarchy. Next, one finds a miscellaneous collectivity of spirits, good and bad, often unnamed and uncounted, in the lowest tier. This discussion clearly applies to polytheistic religions, but it is also relevant to monotheistic religions, such as Islam and Catholicism, that incorporate lesser supernaturals such as saints.

Deceased ancestors can also be supernaturals. In some religions, spirits of the dead can be prayed to for help, and in turn they may require respect and honor from the living (Smith 1995:46). Many African, Asian, and Native American religions have a cult of the ancestors, as did religions of ancient Mesopotamia, Greece, and Rome. In contemporary Japan, ancestor veneration is the principal religious activity of many families. Three national holidays recognize the importance of the ancestors: the annual summer visit of the dead to their home and the visits by the living to graves during the two equinoxes. Important ancestors sometimes evolved into deities with wide popularity. This process, by which a human who once lived is transformed into a deity, is called **euhemerism**, named after the philosopher Euhemerus of Messene (ca. 340–260 BCE), who suggested that the many classical Greek deities had once been earthly people.

BELIEFS IN ACTION: RITUAL PRACTICES

Ritual, as used in this book, refers to patterned forms of behavior that have to do with the supernatural realm. Many rituals are the enactment of beliefs expressed in myth and doctrine, such as the Christian ritual of communion. The term "ritual" is distinguished from "secular rituals" such as a sorority or fraternity initiation or a common-law wedding, all patterned forms of behavior with no connection to the supernatural realm. It is not always easy to distinguish ritual from secular ritual. Consider the American holiday of Thanksgiving, which originated as a sacred meal, with its primary purpose to give thanks to god for the survival of the pilgrims (Siskind 1992). Its original Christian meaning is not maintained by everyone who celebrates the holiday with a special meal. It may even be rejected, for example, by Native Americans who are not likely to consider the arrival and survival of the pilgrims a cause for thankfulness.

Anthropologists and scholars of religion have categorized rituals in many ways. One division is based on how regularly the ritual is performed. Regularly performed rituals are called *periodic rituals.* Many periodic rituals are performed annually to mark a seasonal event like planting or harvesting, or to commemorate some important event. For example, an important periodic ritual in Buddhism, Visakha Puja or Buddha's Day, commemorates the birth, enlightenment, and death of the Buddha (all on one day!). On this day, Buddhists gather at monasteries, hear sermons about the Buddha, and perform rituals such as pouring water over images of the Buddha. Calendrical events such as the shortest or longest day of the year, or the new moon or full moon, often shape ritual cycles. Nonperiodic rituals, in contrast, occur irregularly, at unpredictable times, in response to unscheduled events such as a drought or flood, or to events in a person's life such as illness, infertility, birth, marriage, or death.

Life-Cycle Rituals

Belgian anthropologist Arnold van Gennep (1960 [1908]) first proposed the category of life-cycle rituals in 1909. **Life-cycle rituals,** or rites of passage, mark a change in status from one life stage to another of an individual or group. Victor Turner's (1969) fieldwork among the Ndembu, horticulturalists of Zambia, provided insights about the phases of life-cycle rituals. Among the Ndembu, and cross-culturally, life-cycle rituals have three phases: separation, transition, and reintegration. In the first phase, the initiate (the person undergoing the ritual) is separated physically, socially, or symbolically from normal life. Special dress may mark the separation, for example a long white gown for a baby that is to be baptized in a church. In many cultures of the Amazon and in East and West Africa, adolescents are secluded for several years in separate huts or areas away from the village. The transition phase, or the "liminal phase," is the time when the person is no longer in their previous status, but is not yet a member of the next stage. Liminality often involves the learning of specialized skills that will equip the person for the new status. Reintegration, the last stage, occurs when the initiate emerges and is welcomed by the community in the new status.

Cross-cultural data on life-cycle rituals has prompted theorizing about variations in the occurrence and amplification of such rituals. Ritual marking of a baby's entry into society as a human is a common practice, but it varies in terms of how soon after birth the ceremony is done. Where infant mortality rates are high, the ceremony tends to be done late, when the baby is a year old or older. Until the ceremony has been performed, the baby is not named and is not considered "human." This timing may be a way of ensuring that the baby has gotten through the most dangerous period and is likely to survive. This late timing contrasts with the increasingly common practice in the United States of pregnant women paying for an ultrasound video of their unborn fetus, a secular ritual that declares the "personhood" of the fetus before it is born. This early ritual is conducted within the context of low infant mortality.

Differences in the distribution of puberty rituals for boys and girls have been interpreted as reflecting the value and status of males and females within society. Most societies have some form of puberty ceremony for boys, but puberty ceremonies for girls are less common. A cross-cultural analysis using HRAF data

An Apache girl's puberty ceremony. Cross-cultural research indicates that the celebration of girls' puberty is more likely to occur in cultures in which adult women have valued productive and reproductive roles.

found that this difference is related to the mode of production and gender division of labor (J. Brown 1978). In societies where female labor is important and valued, girls have elaborate (and sometimes painful) puberty rites. Where their labor is not important, menarche is unmarked and there is no puberty ceremony. Female puberty rites function to socialize the female labor force. Girls going through initiations often receive training related to their expected adult economic roles. For example, among the Bembe of southern Africa, a girl learns to distinguish thirty or forty different kinds of mushrooms and to know which ones are edible and which are poisonous.

Pilgrimage

Pilgrimage is round-trip travel to a sacred place or places for purposes of religious devotion or ritual. Prominent pilgrimage places are Varanasi in India (formerly called Banaras) for Hindus; Mecca in Saudi Arabia for Muslims; Bodh Gaya in India for Buddhists; Jerusalem in Israel for Jews, Christians, and Muslims; and Lourdes in France for Christians. Pilgrimage often involves hardship, with the implication that the more suffering that is involved, the more merit the pilgrim accumulates. Compared to a weekly trip to church or synagogue, pilgrimage removes a person further from everyday life, is more demanding and therefore potentially more transformative. Victor Turner has applied his three sequences of life-cycle rituals to pilgrimage as well: the pilgrim first separates from everyday life, then enters the liminal stage during the actual pilgrimage, and finally returns to be reintegrated into society in a transformed state. Indeed, in many pilgrimage traditions, a person who has done certain pilgrimages gains enhanced public status, for example, the status of *haji* (someone who has done the *haj*, or pilgrimage to Mecca) in the Islamic faith.

Connections between myth and pilgrimage are strong. For example, in the Hindu goddess tradition, the story of Sati is the basis for the sanctity of four major and forty-six minor pilgrimage sites in India (Bhardwaj 1973). Because of an argument with her father over whether or not her husband Shiva was welcome at a big sacrifice her family was holding, the unhappy Sati committed suicide. When Shiva heard about her death, he was distraught. He picked up her body and carried it over his shoulder as he wandered across India, grieving. Along the way, parts of her body fell to the ground. The places where they dropped became holy. Some of these include her tongue at Jwala Mukhi and her throat at Vaishno Devi, both in the Himalayas, and her genitals in the eastern state of Assam.

Pilgrimage, especially in India, may involve bathing in a sacred river or in a pond near a temple, or even in the ocean (Gold 1987). Flowing water is believed to have great powers of purification in the Hindu tradition. Many of India's most famous pilgrimage sites are located on rivers, such as Varanasi (Banaras), the most prominent place of Hindu pilgrimage, which is located on the Ganges River.

Rituals of Reversal

Some rituals involve an element of reversal, in which normal social roles and order are temporarily inverted. Scholars say these rituals allow for social "steam" to be let off temporarily and they also may provide a reminder about the propriety of normal, everyday roles and practices to which people must inevitably return once the ritual is over.

These rituals, called **rituals of reversal,** are common cross-culturally, with one of the most well-known in the West being Carnival. Carnival is celebrated throughout the northern Mediterranean region, North and South America, and the Caribbean. It is a period of riotous celebration before the Christian fast of Lent (Counihan 1985). Carnival begins at different times in different places, but always ends at the same time on Mardi Gras (or Shrove Tuesday), the day before Lent begins. The word "carnival" is derived from Latin and means "flesh farewell," referring to Lent. In Bosa, a town in Sardinia, Italy, Carnival involves several aspects of social role reversal and relaxing of usual social norms: "The discotheques extend their hours, and mothers allow their daughters to attend more often and longer than at other time of the year. Men and women play sexually, fondling and flirting with each other in the discotheques and masquerades that are totally illicit at other times of the year" (14). Carnival in Bosa has three major phases. The first is impromptu street theater and masquerades that take place over several weeks, usually on Sundays. The theatrical skits are social critiques of current events and local happenings. The masquerades mainly involve men dressing up as exaggerated women:

> Young boys thrust their padded breasts forward with their hands while brassily hiking up their skirts to reveal their thighs.... A youth stuffs his shirt front with melons and holds them proudly out.... The high school gym teacher dresses as a nun and lifts up his habit to reveal suggestive red underwear. Two men wearing nothing but bikinis, wigs, and high heels feign a stripper's dance on a table top. (15)

The second phase occurs during the morning of Mardi Gras when hundreds of Bosans, mostly men, dress in black like widows and flood the streets. They accost passersby, shaking in their faces dolls and other objects that are maimed in some way or bloodied. They shriek at the top of their lungs as if mourning, and they say, "Give us milk, milk for our babies.... They are dying, they are neglected, their mothers have been gallivanting since St. Anthony's Day and have abandoned their poor children" (16). The third phase, called *Giolzi,* takes place during the evening. Men and women dress in white, wearing sheets for cloaks and pillow cases for hoods. They blacken their faces. Rushing into the street, they hold hands and chant the word "Giolzi." They storm at people, pretending to search their bodies for Giolzi and then say "Got it!" It is not clear what Giolzi is, but whatever it is, it represents something that makes everyone happy. How does an anthropologist interpret these events? Carnival allows people to act out roles that are normally closed off to them, for a short time, before they have to go back to their normal positions. It also provides a time in which everyone has fun for a while. In this way, rituals of reversal can be seen to function as mechanisms of maintaining social order: After the allotted days of revelry, everyone returns to their original places for another year.

Sacrifice

Many rituals involve some form of **sacrifice,** or offering of something for transference to the supernaturals. Sacrifice has a long history throughout the world and may be one of the oldest forms of ritual. It may involve the killing and offering of animals, or human offerings (of whole people, parts of a person's body, or even bloodletting), vegetables, fruits, grains, flowers, or other products. One anthropologist has suggested that flowers are symbolic replacements for former animal sacrifices (Goody 1993).

Scholars have highlighted four key focus points in sacrifice: the person who does the sacrificing, the act of sacrifice itself, the mode of transference of the offering to the supernaturals, and the recipient of the sacrifice (Smith 1995:948). Throughout the Aztec region of Mesoamerica, sacrifice (not just human sacrifice) has long been practiced. State-level sacrifices were performed by trained priests, ostensibly to "feed" the gods on behalf of the welfare of the state. Apparently the gods were fond of human blood—as well as other items such as quails, crocodiles, jaguars, ducks, salamanders, and cakes made from the amaranth plant—because one of the most widely offered items for important events like a coronation or naming newborn babies was a limited amount of ritually induced bleeding. Symbolic anthropologists would accept the religious logic involved in pleasing the gods as a sufficient explanation for blood sacrifice. Cultural materialists are inclined to propose an ecological explanation for the practice (see the Critical Thinking box on page 318).

RELIGIOUS SPECIALISTS

Not all rituals require the presence of a religious specialist, or someone with special and detailed training, but all require some level of knowledge on the part of the performer(s) about how to do them correctly. Even the daily, household veneration of an ancestor requires some knowledge gained through informal learning. At the other extreme, many rituals cannot be done without a highly trained specialist.

Shamans and Priests

General features of the categories of shaman and priest illustrate some key differences between these two types of specialists (as with all types, many specialists fit somewhere in between). Shamans or shamankas (the female form with the "-ka" ending derives from the original Siberian usage) are part-time religious specialists who gain their status through direct relationships with the supernaturals, often by being "called." A potential shaman may be recognized by special signs, such as the ability to go into a trance. Anyone who demonstrates shamanic abilities can become a shaman; in other words, this is an openly available role. Shamans are more associated with pre-state societies, yet in many ways, faith healers and evangelists of the United States could be considered to fit in this category. One of the most important functions of shamanic religious specialists is

CRITICAL THINKING

Why Did the Aztecs Practice Human Sacrifice...and Cannibalism?

Documentation of state-sponsored human sacrifice and cannibalism of the victims among the Aztecs of Mexico comes from accounts written by the Spanish conquistadors (Harris 1977, 1989; Sanday 1986). The Aztec gods required human sacrifice—they "ate" human hearts and "drank" human blood. Most of the victims were prisoners of war, but many others were slaves, and sometimes young men and women, and even children. The victims were marched up the steep steps of the pyramid, held lying on their backs over a stone altar, and slit open in the chest by a priest, who wrenched out the heart (said to be still beating), which was then burned in offering to the gods. The body was rolled down the other side of the temple, where it was retrieved by butchers and prepared for cooking. The skull would be returned to the temple area to be put on display racks. Although no one knows for sure how many victims were sacrificed over all, estimates are in the hundreds of thousands. At a single site, a chronicler reported that the display racks contained more than one hundred thousand skulls (Harris 1977:106). At an especially grand event, victims were arranged in four lines, each two miles long. Priests worked for four days straight to complete the sacrifices. Human sacrifice and cannibalism of any scale might seem to invite the question "Why?" Certainly one must ask "why" about sacrifice and cannibalism as practiced on the grand scale of the Aztecs. Of the many attempted explanations, two are compared here: cultural materialist theory and symbolic theory.

Michael Harner (1977) and Marvin Harris (1977, 1989) propose that the combination of mass human sacrifice and mass cannibalism can be explained only in reference to local ecology and the politics of Aztec expansionism. The region of the Aztec empire was marked by its lack of sufficient amounts of animal sources of protein to satisfy its growing population. While the ruling classes managed to maintain their own supply of delicacies such as dog, turkey, duck, deer, rabbit, and fish, little was available for the poor. Yet the rulers needed to support and retain the loyalty of their army in order to protect and expand the empire's boundaries, and they needed to keep the masses happy. Providing the gods with human hearts and blood was a powerful statement of the empire's strength, but it had the indirect benefit of yielding huge amounts of flesh for soldiers and commoners to eat. Harris comments that "cannibal redistribution" could be manipulated by the state to reward particular groups and to compensate for periodic shortages in the agricultural cycle.

Peggy Sanday (1989) rejects the cultural materialist theory. Offering a symbolic analysis, she argues that the explanation for Aztec human sacrifice and cannibalism can be found only by carefully examining the Aztec explanation for these practices. Sacrifice and cannibalism, she says, followed religious logic and symbolism and were practiced to satisfy the gods' hunger, not human hunger. Aztec religion says that the gods require certain sacrifices in order for the universe to continue to operate. Human flesh was not consumed as an "ordinary meal," but as part of a religious identification with the gods, just as people would wear the skins of sacrificed victims in order to participate in their sacredness. Sanday says that the cultural materialist explanation, in focusing on the "business" aspects of Aztec sacrifice and cannibalism, has missed the tradition's true meaning for the Aztecs.

Critical Thinking Questions

- Do the materialist and symbolic interpretations differ in the kind of data they use?
- Which of these theories do you find more appealing, and why?
- Is there any other way to explain Aztec human sacrifice and cannibalism?
- If Aztec human sacrifice and cannibalism were still practiced today, what would a cultural anthropologist need to research in order to test these two theories?

in healing, usually upon request from an afflicted individual, as described in Chapter 7 on medical anthropology.

In states, the more complex occupational specialization in religion means that there is a wider variety of types of specialists, especially what anthropologists refer to as "priests," (not the same as the specific modern role of the Catholic priest) and the development of religious hierarchies and power structures. The terms **priest** or **priestess** refer to a category of full-time religious specialists whose position is based mainly on abilities gained through formal training. A priest may receive a divine call, but more often the role is hereditary, passed on through priestly lineages. In terms of ritual performance, shamans are more involved with nonperiodic rituals. Priests perform a wider range of rituals, including periodic state rituals. In contrast to shamans, who rarely have much secular power, priests and priestly lineages often do.

Other Specialists

Certain other specialized roles are widely found. Diviners are specialists who are able to discover the will and wishes of the supernaturals through techniques such as reading animal entrails. Palm readers and tarot card readers fit into the category of diviners. Prophets are specialists who convey divine revelations usually gained through visions or dreams. They often possess charisma (a specially attractive and powerful personality) and may be able to perform miracles. Prophets have founded new religions, some longlasting and others shortlived. Witches use psychic powers and affect people through emotion and thought. Mainstream society often condemns witchcraft as negative. Some scholars of ancient and contemporary witchcraft differentiate between positive forms that involve healing and negative forms that seek to harm people.

WORLD RELIGIONS

The term **world religions** was coined in the nineteenth century to refer to religions with many followers that crossed national borders and had a few other specific features, such as a concern with salvation (the belief that human beings require deliverance from an imperfect world). At first, the term referred only to Christianity, Islam, and Buddhism. It was later expanded to include Judaism, Hinduism, Confucianism, Taoism, and Shintoism. The category of world religions is even less appropriate now because many more religions cross national boundaries and therefore have "world" reach. Nonetheless, since college religion courses teach entire semesters of material on these "world religions," this chapter provides an anthropological perspective on five of them.

Cultural anthropologists emphasize that no world religion exists as a single ("monolithic") entity, but rather each is composed of many variants such as regional and class variations, and doctrinal differences between reformist and fundamentalist interpretations. The five religions considered here are presented roughly in order of their age, although no one can say for sure whether Judaism or Hinduism predates the other. These five religions are discussed in terms of their general history, distribution, and teachings. Then examples are given of how they vary in different contexts to show how the same texts and teachings are localized.

Hinduism

Over 650 million people in the world are Hindus (Hiltebeitel 1995). The majority live in India, where Hinduism accounts for about 80 percent of the population. The other 20 million, the Hindu diaspora, live in the United States, the United Kingdom, Malaysia, Fiji, Trinidad, Guyana, and Hong Kong. What makes a Hindu a Hindu? First, one is born a Hindu. Hinduism is not a proselytizing religion—it does not actively seek converts. The four Vedas, composed in Sanskrit in northern India between 1200 and 900 BCE, are the core texts of Hinduism. Many other scholarly texts and popular myths and epics, especially the Mahabharata (the story of a war between two lineages, the Pandavas and the Kauravas) and the Ramayana (the story of king Rama and his wife Sita), also serve as unifying scriptures. Throughout India, a multiplicity of local traditions exist, some of which carry forward elements from pre-Vedic times. Thus, Hinduism incorporates a diversity of ways to be a Hindu. It offers a rich polytheism and at the same time a philosophical tradition that reduces the multiplicity of deities into oneness. Deities range from simple stones (in Hinduism, stones can be gods) placed at the foot of a tree to elegantly carved and painted icons of gods such as Shiva, Vishnu, and the goddess Durga. Everyday worship of a deity involves lighting a lamp in front of the god, chanting hymns and mantras (sacred phrases), and taking *darshan* (sight of) the deity (Eck 1985). These acts bring blessings to the worshipper.

While certain "standard" features of Hinduism exist (as noted above, acceptance of key texts and worship of important, well-known deities), many localized versions of Hinduism throughout India involve the worship of deities and practice of rituals unknown elsewhere. For example, fire-walking is an important part of goddess worship in southern and eastern India (Freeman 1981; Hiltebeitel 1988) and among some diaspora groups, notably in Fiji (C. Brown 1984), but it is not done in the northern and western parts of the country. Besides regional variations, caste differences in beliefs and practices even within the same area or village are marked. Lower-caste deities prefer offerings of meat sacrifices and alcohol, while upper-caste deities prefer offerings of flowers, rice, and fruit. Temple structures range from magnificent buildings to a simple canopy placed over the deity for shade. Yet the "unity in diversity" of Hinduism has long been recognized as real, mainly because of the shared acceptance of elements of Vedic thought.

A Nayar Fertility Ritual

The matrilineal Nayars perform a nonperiodic ritual as a remedy for the curse of the serpent deities who cause infertility in women (Neff 1994). This ritual exemplifies the "unity in diversity" of Hinduism; certain ritual elements such as the use of camphor and the importance of serpent deities are commonly known and understood. Yet it is locally specific as well, being shaped to the needs of Nayars matrilineal culture. Among the Nayars, a woman's natal kin—uncles, brothers, mother—are responsible for helping to ensure that her desires for motherhood are fulfilled. Her kin are also concerned that she bear children in order to maintain the matrilineage. A one night version of the ritual goes like this:

> After dark, a large, sacred floor drawing . . . is "painted" on the earth. Then, several hours of Hindu rituals are performed to "feed" and propitiate the deity, rituals which include powerful aesthetic media—camphor, incense, flowers, colored powder, and glitter (for the sacred drawing), drumming, singing, cymbals, fire, and dance—offered to please the deity and to thereby invoke its presence. In a successful ritual, the deity's presence is achieved when two Nāyar women go into trance. . . . During the trance, . . . [matrilineal family] members may pray to and speak with the god, and, afterward, receive the deity's blessing. The ritual centerpiece and main offering . . . is a large, colored powder drawing of churning, intertwined serpents, which has been "painted" on the earth, covered above by coconut palm birds and flowers hung from a small red canopy. (479)

An important social outcome results from what the women say during the trance. They typically draw attention to family disharmonies or neglect of the deities. This diverts blame from the infertile woman for whom the ritual is being held. It also reminds family and lineage members of their responsibilities for each other and that an infertile woman should not be neglected by her family. Such ritual behavior can be seen as a form of human agency acting to affect larger structural forces, in this case, reproductive patterns believed to be under the control of the supernaturals.

Hindu Women and Karma in Great Britain

One of Hinduism's key concepts is that of *karma*, translated as destiny or fate. A person's karma is determined at birth on the basis of his or her previous life and how it was conducted. The karma concept has prompted many outsiders to judge Hindus as exceptionally fatalistic. Exactly how it affects everyday behavior has not been studied in detail. One insightful study looked at women's perceptions of karma among Hindus living in Britain (Knott 1996). No single answer emerges: Some Hindu women are fatalistic in their attitudes and behavior, while others are not. One woman who had a strongly fatalistic view of karma said:

> [W]hen a baby's born . . . we have a ritual on the sixth day. That's when you name the baby, you know. And on that day, we believe the goddess comes and writes your future . . . we leave a blank white paper and a pen and we just leave it [overnight], and a pair of brand new clothes. . . . So I believe that my future—whatever happens—is what she has written for me. That tells me [that] I have to do what I can do, and if I have a mishap in between I have to accept that. (24)

Other women did not share this view. One said that her sufferings were caused by the irresponsibility of her father and the "bad husband" to whom she had been married. She challenged her karma and left her husband: "I could not accept the karma of being with Nirmal [her husband]. If I had done so, what would have become of my children?" (25). Since Hindu women's karma dictates being married and having children, leaving one's husband is a major act of resistance. For some young women informants, questioning the role of karma was the same as questioning their parents' authority. Such intergenerational conflicts create feelings of ambiguity and confusion. Options for women seeking support for their struggle to sort out their roles can be either religious (praying more and fasting) or secular (seeking the advice of a psychological counselor or social worker). Some Hindu women in Britain have become counselors and are helping support other women's independence and self-confidence. This involves clear subversion of the traditional rules of karma for women and demonstrates that a single doctrine, in this case the doctrine of karma, is variously accepted by religious followers. Obviously, these findings for a diaspora population cannot be generalized to other Hindus, but they do suggest the need for comparative studies to highlight the role that cultural context may offer in allowing for varieties of interpretation.

Buddhism

Buddhism originated in a founding figure, Siddhartha Gautama (ca. 566–486 BCE), revered as the Buddha or Awakened One (Eckel 1995:135). It began in northern India, where the Buddha grew up. From there, it spread throughout the subcontinent, into Inner Asia and China, to Sri Lanka and on to Southeast Asia. In the past two hundred years, Buddhism has spread to Europe and North America. Buddhism's popularity subsequently faded in India, and Buddhists now constitute less than one percent of India's population. Its global spread is matched by a great diversity of doctrine and practice, to the extent that it is difficult to point to a single essential feature (for example, no single text is accepted as authoritative for all forms of Buddhism), other than the importance of Gautama Buddha. Many Buddhists worship the Buddha as a deity, while others do not—they honor his teachings and follow the pathway he suggested for reaching nirvana, or release from worldly life.

Buddhism first arose as a protest against certain features of Hinduism, especially caste inequality, yet it retained and revised several Hindu concepts such as karma. In Buddhism, everyone has the potential for achieving nirvana (enlightenment and the overcoming of human suffering in this life), the goal of Buddhism. Good deeds are one way to achieve a better rebirth with each incarnation until, finally, release from samsara (the cycle of birth, reincarnation, death, and so on) is achieved. Compassion toward others, including animals, is a key virtue. Branches of Buddhism have different texts that they consider their canon. The major division is between the Theravada Buddhism practiced in Southeast Asia and Mahayana Buddhism of Tibet, China, Taiwan, Korea, and Japan. Buddhism is associated with a strong tradition of monasticism through which monks and nuns renounce the everyday world and spend their lives meditating and doing good works. Buddhists have many and varied annual festivals and rituals. Some events bring pilgrims from around the world to India—to Sarnath, where he gave his first teaching, and Gaya, where he gained enlightenment.

Buddhism and Indigenous Spirits in Burma

One theory says that wherever Buddhism exists outside India, it is never the exclusive religion of the devotees because it arrived to find established religions already in place (Spiro 1967). In any particular context, Buddhism and the local traditions may have blended (such blending is called religious **syncretism**), both may coexist in a pluralistic fashion, or Buddhism may have taken a major role and incorpo-

Buddhism gained an established footing in Japan in the eighth century. The city of Nara was an important early center of Buddhism. Here, the emperor sponsored the casting of a huge bronze statue of the Buddha, housed in the Todaiji, the "Great Eastern Temple."

rated the indigenous traditions. The situation in Burma fits in the second category. Indigenous Burmese beliefs remained strong because they offer a more satisfying way of explaining and dealing with everyday problems. According to Burmese Buddhism, a person's karma (as in Hinduism) is a result of previous births and determines his or her present condition. If something bad happens, it's because of karma and the person can do little but suffer through it. Burmese supernaturalism, on the other hand, says that the bad thing happened because of the actions of capricious spirits called *nats*. Ritual actions can combat the influence of nats. In other words, nats can be dealt with, karma cannot.

Buddhism, however, became an important cultural force and the key basis for social integration in Burma. One village, for example, had three Buddhist monasteries, with four resident Buddhist monks and several temporary monks. Every male child was ordained as a temporary member of the monastic order. Almost every villager observed Buddhist holy days. While Buddhism is held to be the supreme truth for everyday problems such as a toothache or a monetary loss, the spirits retain control.

Buddhism and Abortion in Japan

Buddhist teachings about the "fluidity" of the supernatural and human realms have found a particularly important niche in contemporary Japan in relation to the widespread practice of abortion there. In Japanese Buddhism, fetuses, like newborn infants, are not considered to be full-fledged, solid lives (LaFleur 1992). They are fluid creatures who can be "returned" through abortion (or, in previous centuries, infanticide) to the supernatural realm. People believe that a "returned" fetus may come back at a more convenient time. Women who have had an abortion commonly go to a Buddhist temple and perform a special ritual in which they pray for the good fortune of the rejected fetus. They dedicate a small statue to it that may be placed, along with hundreds of other such statues, in a cemetery-like setting. It is periodically adorned with clothing, cheap jewelry, and trinkets. These practices may have a positive psychological effect on the parents by diverting possible feelings of sadness. Thus, religious doctrine fits with the "family planning" goals of many Japanese families to have few children (given that abortion is the predominant way of limiting the number of offspring available in Japan).

Judaism

Like all world religions, Judaism has multiple versions that have evolved over time and across cultures. Followers of Judaism share in the belief in the Torah (the Five Books of Moses, or Pentateuch) as the revelation of god's truth through Israel, a term for the "holy people" (Neusner 1995:598–607). The Torah explains the relationship between the supernatural and human realms and guides people in how to carry out the world view through appropriate actions. A key feature of all forms of Judaism is the identification of what is wrong with the present and how to escape, overcome, or survive that situation. Jewish life is symbolically interpreted as a tension between exile and return, given its foundational myth in the exile of the Jews from Israel and their period of slavery in Egypt. Contemporary varieties of Judaism range from conservative Hasidism to Reform Judaism, which emerged in the early 1800s. One difference between these two perspectives concerns the question of who is Jewish. Jewish law traditionally defined a Jewish person as someone born of a Jewish mother. In contrast, reform Judaism recognizes as Jewish the offspring of a Jewish father and non-Jewish mother.

Judaism is monotheistic, teaching that god is one, unique, and all-powerful. Humans have a moral duty to follow Jewish law, to protect and preserve life and health, and to follow certain duties such as observing the Sabbath. The high regard for human life is reflected in the general opposition to abortion within Jewish law and opposition to the death penalty. Words, both spoken and written, have high importance in Judaism: There is an emphasis on truth-telling in life and the use of established literary formulas at precise times during worship. These formulas are encoded in a *sidur* or prayer book. Dietary patterns also distinguish Judaism from other religions; for example, rules of kosher eating forbid the mixing of milk and milk products with meat.

Who's Who at the Kotel

The most sacred place to all Jews is the kotel, or Western Wall in Jerusalem. Since the 1967 war, which brought Jerusalem under Israeli rule, the kotel can be considered the most important religious shrine and pilgrimage site of Israel. The kotel is located at one edge of the Temple Mount (or Haram Sharif), an area sacred to Jews, Muslims, and Christians. According to Jewish scriptures, god asked Abraham to sacrifice his

The kotel (or Western Wall) in Jerusalem is a sacred place of pilgrimage especially for Jews. Males pray at a section marked off on the left while women keep to the area on the right. Both men and women should cover their heads, and women should take care when leaving the wall area, to keep their faces toward it and avoid turning their backsides to it.

son Isaac on this hill. Later, King Solomon built the First Temple here in the middle of the tenth century BCE. It was destroyed by Nebuchadnessar in 587 BCE, when the Jews were led into captivity in Babylon. Around 500 BCE, King Herod built the Second Temple on the same site. The kotel is a remnant of the Second Temple. Jews of all varieties and non-Jews come to the kotel in vast numbers from around the world. The kotel plaza is open to everyone, pilgrims and tourists. The wall is made of massive rectangular stones weighing between two and eight tons each. At its base is a synagogue area, partitioned into men's and women's sections (see the Current Event box on page 324).

An ethnographic study of what goes on at the kotel included attention first to the "regulars" (Storper-Perez and Goldberg 1994). Regulars are people who provide regular services, both official and unofficial, spiritual and material, such as the Arab workmen who hose down the area in preparation for the Sabbath; police who provide security by checking handbags and parcels at the entrance; and kotel guards in the synagogue area who make sure that men wear a skullcap when entering the synagogue area and that women wear a scarf or shawl. In spite of plaques that state the prohibition against begging, there are beggars who offer to "sell a blessing" to visitors. They may remind visitors that it was the poor who built the wall in the first place. Another category of regulars is young men in search of prospective "born again" Jews who "hang around" looking for a "hit" (in their words). Most of the hits are young Americans who are urged to take their Jewishness more seriously and, if male, to be sure to marry a Jewish woman. Other regulars are Hebrew-speaking men who are available to organize a prayer service. One of the most frequent forms of religious expression at the kotel is the insertion of written prayers into the crevices of the wall.

There is great diversity among the visitors, evident in the various styles of dress and gesture:

> The Hasid . . . with a fur *shtreimel* on his head may enter the synagogue area alongside a man in shorts who utilizes a cardboard skullcap available for "secular" visitors. American youngsters in jeans may ponder Israeli soldiers of their own age, dressed in uniform, and wonder what their lot might have been if they were born in another country. Women from Yemen, wearing embroidered trousers under their dresses, edge close to the Wall as do women accoutred in contemporary styles whose religiosity may have been filtered through a modern education. . . . The North African-born Israeli, uttering a personal prayer with his forehead against the Wall becomes an object of comment for a European tourist. Pious women, with their heads covered for modesty, instruct their children in the decorum appropriate to the prayer situation. People from many parts of the country, nay the world, meet unexpectedly. (321)

The social heterogeneity of the Jewish people is brought together in a single space, creating some sense of what Victor Turner (1969) called *communitas,* a sense of collective unity out of individual diversity.

Passover in Kerala

The Jews of the Kochi area (formerly called Cochin) of Kerala, South India, have lived there for about

Current Event

Women Raise Their Voices for the Right to Pray Aloud at Wall

- A group called "Women of the Wall" that comprises over 100 women, is trying to change the rule against women praying aloud at the Western Wall in Jerusalem while men are allowed to do so. Regulation 13 prohibits any act at the Wall that offends worshippers. A member of Women of the Wall said that women's voices have been claimed to be provocative and lewd.
- Members of Women of the Wall have been testing the legality of Regulation 13 and tempting arrest by gathering monthly at the Wall and reading scriptures aloud.
- Anat Hoffman, member of the group and a Jerusalem city council member, said that the movement has been fueled by Western feminism: "Sure it's an American idea. And it's a fine idea.... Most Israeli women couldn't care less. We are designed from a very early age to feel that we have no role. Silencing women is rooted in Israeli society."
- So far, the issue has been shuffled from the Knesset, Israel's parliament, to the courts and then to a ministerial study committee. No resolution has been found.

Source: Doug Struck, *The Washington Post,* March 23, 1998:A13.

1,000 years (Katz and Goldberg 1989). The Maharaja of Kochi had good relations with and respect for the Jewish people, who were mainly merchants. He relied on them for external trade and contacts. In recognition of this, he allowed a synagogue, which is still standing, to be built next to his palace. Syncretism is apparent in Kochi Jew lifestyle, social structure, and rituals. Crucial aspects of Judaism are retained, along with adoption of many aspects of Hindu practices. Three aspects of syncretism with Hinduism are apparent in passover, one of the most important annual rituals of the Jewish faith. First, compared to the typically joyous Western/European passover celebration, the Kochi version has adopted a tone of austerity and is called "the fasting feast." Kochi passover, secondly, allows no roles for children who, at a traditional *seder* (ritual meal) usually ask four questions as a starting-point of the narrative. The Kochi Jews chant the questions in unison. This change relates to the fact that in Hinduism, children do not have solo roles in rituals. Third, a Kochi seder stresses purity even more than standard Jewish requirements. Standard rules about maintaining the purity of kosher wine usually mean that no gentile (non-Jew) should touch it. But Kochi Jews say that if the shelf or table on which the wine sits is touched by a gentile, the wine is impure. This extra level of "contagion" is influenced by Hindu concepts of pollution.

Christianity

Christianity has many ties with Judaism, from which it sprang, especially in terms of the Biblical teachings of a coming savior, or messiah. It began in Palestine and the eastern Mediterranean in the second quarter of the first century (Cunningham 1995:240–253). Most of the early believers were Jews who took up the belief in Jesus Christ as the "messiah" (annointed one) who came to earth in fulfillment of prophesies contained in the Hebrew scriptures. Today, Christianity is the largest of the world's religions with about 1.5 billion adherents or nearly one-third of the world's population. It is the majority religion of Australia, New Zealand, the Philippines, Papua New Guinea, most countries of Europe, and North and South America, and about a dozen southern African countries. Christianity is a minority religion throughout Asia, but Asian Christians constitute 16 percent of the world's total Christians and are thus a significant population. Christians accept the Bible (Old and New Testaments) as containing the basic teachings, the belief that a supreme god sent his son to earth as a sacrifice for the welfare of humanity, and the importance of Jesus as the model to follow for moral guidance. The three largest branches of Christianity are Roman Catholic, Protestant, and Eastern Orthodox. Within each of these branches, various denominations exist. Christianity has existed the longest in the Near East and Mediterranean regions. In contemporary times, the greatest growth in Christianity is occurring in sub-Saharan Africa, parts of India, and Indonesia. It is currently experiencing a resurgence in Eastern Europe.

A celebration of the Christian holy day of Palm Sunday in Port-au-Prince, Haiti. European colonialism brought thousands of Africans as slaves to the "New World" and it also exported Christianity through missionary efforts. Many forms of Christianity are now firmly entrenched in the Caribbean region as well as in Central and South America.

Protestantism among White Appalachians

Studies of variants of protestantism in Appalachia describe local traditions that outsiders who are accustomed to standard, urban versions may view as "deviant." For example, churches in rural West Virginia and North Carolina, called Old Regulars, emphasize in their worship three obligatory rituals: footwashing, communion (a ritual commemorating the "Last Supper" that Jesus had with his disciples), and baptism (Dorgan 1989). The footwashing ceremony occurs once a year in conjunction with communion, usually as an extension of the Sunday service. An elder is called to the front of the church, and he "introduces" the service. He preaches for about ten to twenty minutes, and then there is a round of handshaking and embracing. Two deaconesses come forward to "prepare the table" by uncovering the sacramental elements placed there earlier under a white tablecloth (unleavened bread, serving plates for the bread, cups for the wine, a decanter or quart jar or two of wine). The deacons come forward to prepare the bread by breaking it into small pieces while the moderator pours the wine into the cups. By now, the men and women have formed separate groups as the deacons serve the bread and wine (a few groups have allowed deaconesses to serve the women's side; this issue has caused conflicts and splits among traditional groups). After the deacons serve each other, it is time for the footwashing. The moderator may begin this part of the service by quoting from the New Testament (the book of John, chapter 13, verse 4): "He riseth from supper, and laid aside his garments; and he took a towel and girded himself." While speaking these lines he removes his coat and then ties a long towel around his waist. He takes a basin from the piles of basins by the communion table and puts water in it, selects a senior elder and removes his shoes and socks, then washes his feet slowly and attentively. Other members come forward and take towels and basins. Soon "the church is filled with crying, shouting, and praising as these highly poignant exchanges unleash a flood of emotions. A fellowship that may have remained very solemn during the communion will now participate in a myriad of intense expressions of religious enthusiasm and literally scores of high-pathos scenes will be played out" (106). Participants take turns washing and being washed. A functional interpretation of the ritual of footwashing is that it helps maintain interpersonal harmony in small religious communities.

Another feature of worship in many small, Protestant subdenominations of Scotch-Irish descendants in West Virginia involves the handling of poisonous snakes. This practice also finds legitimation in the New Testament (Daugherty 1997 [1976]). According to a passage in Mark (16:15–18): "In my name shall they cast out devils; they shall speak with new tongues; they shall take up serpents; and if they drink any deadly thing, it shall not hurt them; they shall lay hands on the sick, and they shall recover." Members of "Holiness-type" churches believe that the handling of poisonous snakes is the supreme act of devotion to god. They are Biblical literalists and have chosen serpent-handling as their way of celebrating life, death, and resurrection, and proving that only Jesus has the power to deliver them from death. During their services, the Holy Ghost (not the Holy Spirit) enables them to pick up serpents, speak in tongues, testify to the lord's greatness, and drink strychnine or lye. Most serpent handlers have been bitten many times, but few have died. One interpretation says that the risks of handling poisonous rattlesnakes and copperheads mirrors the risks of the environment. The people are poor, with high rates of unemployment and few prospects for improvement.

Are these people psychologically troubled? Apparently not. Psychological tests indicate they are more emotionally healthy than members of mainline Protestant churches.

Christian Syncretism

Wherever Christianity has gone, local people have adopted and adapted different aspects of its teaching and practice. In many places in Latin America, the Christian concept of the devil has been syncretically merged with local beliefs. Among Bolivians, the devil has been assimilated with that of Tio. For Bolivian miners:

> The Tio is a figure of power: he has what everybody wants, in excess. Coca remains lie in his greedy mouth. His hands are stretched out, grasping the bottles of alcohol he is offered. His nose is burned black by the cigarettes he smokes down to the nub. If a Tio is knocked out of his niche by an extra charge of dynamite and survives, the miners consider him to be more powerful than the others. (Nash 1997 [1972]:243)

Among Christians in Fiji, the image of the "Last Supper" is a dominant motif (Toren 1988). This scene, depicted on tapestry hangings, adorns most churches and many houses. People say, "Christ is the head of this household, he eats with us and overhears us" (697). The image's popularity is the result of its fit with Fijian notions of commensality (communal eating) and kava drinking. Seating rules at such events place the highest status people, such as the chief, and others close to him, at the "above" side of the room, away from the entrance. Others sit at the "lower" end, facing the highly ranked people. Intermediate positions are located on either side of the person of honor, in ranked order. Da Vinci's rendition of the Last Supper places Jesus Christ in the position of a chief, with the disciples in an ordered arrangement around him. "The image of an ordered and stratified society exemplified in people's positions relative to one another around the kava bowl is encountered virtually everyday in the village" (706). The disciples and the viewers "face" the chief and eat and drink together, as is appropriate in Fijian society.

Syncretism happens when features of two cultures match each other in some way. Many situations of non-fit can also be provided. Christian missionaries have had difficulty translating the Bible into indigenous languages because of lack of matching words or concepts, and because of differing kinship and social structures. Some Amazonian groups, for example, have no word that fits the Christian concept of "heaven" (Everett 1995, personal communication). In other cases, matrilineal peoples have found it difficult to understand the significance of the Christian construct of "god the father."

Islam

Islam is based on the teachings of the prophet Muhammed (AD 570–632), and is thus the youngest of the world religions (Martin 1995:498–513). The Arabic word, Islam, means "submission" to the will of the one god, Allah, through which peace will be achieved. Islam also implies acceptance of Muhammed as the last and final messenger of god, "the seal of the prophets." Muslim majority nations are located in northern Africa; the Middle East, including Afghanistan, Pakistan, and Bangladesh in South Asia; and several nations in Central Asia and Southeast Asia. In fact the majority of the world's Muslims (60 percent) live either in South Asia or Southeast Asia. While Islam originally flourished among pastoral nomads, only 2 percent of its adherents now are in that category.

A common and inaccurate stereotype of Islam is that, wherever it exists, it is the same. This erroneously monolithic model tends to be based on some imagined version of Arab Islam as practiced in Saudi Arabia. A comparison of Islam in highland Sumatra, Indonesia, and Morocco, North Africa, reveals culturally constructed differences (Bowen 1992). The annual Feast of Sacrifice is celebrated by Muslims around the world. It commemorates god's sparing of Abraham's son Ishmael (Isaac in Christian and Jewish traditions). It takes place everywhere on the tenth of the last month of the year, also called Pilgrimage Month. The ritual reminds Muslims of their global unity within the Islamic faith. One aspect of this event in Morocco involves the king publicly plunging a dagger into a ram's throat, a reenactment of Muhammad's performance of the sacrifice on the same day in the seventh century. Each male head of household follows the pattern and sacrifices a ram. Size and virility of the ram are a measure of the man's power and virility. Other men of the household stand to witness the sacrifice, while women and children are absent or in the background. After the ram is killed, they come forward and dab its blood on their faces. In some villages, women play a more prominent role before the sacrifice by daubing the ram with henna (red dye), thus sanctifying it, and using its blood afterward in rituals to protect the household. These national and household rituals are highly symbolic of male power in the public and private domains—the power of the monarchy and the power of patriarchy. Is this the standard, universal way of celebrating the Feast of the Sacrifice?

The degree of local adaption to Moroccan culture becomes clear when compared with the ritual's enactment in Sumatra, which has a less patriarchal culture and a political structure that does not emphasize monarchy. In Isak, a traditionalist Muslim village, people have been Muslims since the seventeenth century. They sacrifice all kinds of animals, including chickens, ducks, sheep, goats, and water buffalo. As long as the throat is cut and the meat is eaten, it satisfies the demands of god. Before cutting the victim's throat, the sacrificer dedicates it to one or more relatives. In contrast to Morocco, most sacrifices receive little notice and are done mainly in the back of the house with little fanfare. Both women and men of the household refer to it as "their" sacrifice, and there are no signs of male dominance. Women may sponsor a sacrifice, as did one wealthy woman trader who sacrificed a buffalo (the actual cutting, however, is done by a man). The Moroccan ritual emphasizes fathers and sons. The Isak ritual includes attention to a wider range of kin on both the husband's and wife's side, daughters as well as sons, and dead relatives, too. In the Indonesian context, no centralized dynastic meanings are given to the ritual. The differences are not because Moroccans know the scriptures better than Sumatrans. The Isak area has many Islamic scholars who consult the scriptures and discuss issues. Rather, the cultural context into which the same scriptural tradition is placed shapes it to local interests and needs.

AFRICAN RELIGIONS

The distinction between the world religions and "local religions" is blurry because many local religions are now practiced by people who have migrated to other nations. This is true for African religions, many of which spread outside Africa through the enforced movements of people as slaves, and for other religions such as Confucianism that have been diffused by voluntary migration. This section attempts to summarize some key features of African religions and then provides an example of a new religion with African roots, Ras Tafari.

Features of African Religions

As of 1994, Africa's total population comprised 341 million Christians, 285 million Muslims, and about 70 million practicing indigenous religions (Smith 1995:15–16). With its diverse geography, cultural variation, and history, Africa encompasses a wide range of indigenous religions. Some common, but not universal features, of indigenous African religions include: a mythology of rupture that once occurred between the creator deity and humans; a high god and a plurality of secondary supernaturals ranging from powerful gods to lesser spirits; elaborate initiation rituals; rituals involving animal sacrifices and other offerings, meals, and dances; altars within shrines as focal places where humans and deities meet; and close links with healing and divination. While these general features are fairly constant and are also found in many African American religions, one should not assume that African indigenous religions are frozen in time. Like all religions, they are rethought and reshaped, sometimes in response to external pressures such as colonialism and sometimes because of their own traditions of questioning and debate (Gable 1995).

Ras Tafari

Also called Rastafarianism, Ras Tafari is a relatively new religion of the Caribbean, the United States, and Europe. Numbers of Rastafarians are unknown because they refuse to be counted (Smith 1995:23). Ras Tafari is an unorthodox, protest religion that shares few of the features of African religions mentioned above. Ras Tafari traces its history to several preachers of the early twentieth century who taught that Ras ("Prince") Tafari, then the Ethiopian emperor Haile Selassie, was the "Lion of Judah" who would lead Blacks to the African promised land. Rastafarianism does not have an organized set of doctrines and there are no written texts or enforced orthodoxy. Shared beliefs of the many diffuse groups include the belief that Ethiopia is heaven on earth and Haile Selassie is a living god, and that all Blacks will be able to return to the homeland through his help.

Since the death of Haile Selassie in 1975, a greater emphasis has been placed on pan-African unity and Black power, and less on Ethiopia. Rastafarianism is particularly strong in Jamaica, where it is associated with reggae music, dreadlocks, and *ganja* (marijuana) smoking. Variations within the Rastafarian movement in Jamaica range from beliefs that one must fight oppression to the position that living a peaceful life brings victory against evil.

DIRECTIONS AND CHALLENGES OF CHANGE

All religions have established mythologies and doctrines that provide a certain degree of continuity and, often, conservativism in religious beliefs and practices. Yet, nowhere are religions frozen and unchanging. Cultural anthropologists have traced the resurgence of religions that seemed to have been headed toward extinction through colonial forces, and they have documented the emergence of seemingly new religions. Likewise, they are observing the contemporary struggle of once-suppressed religions in socialist states to find a new position in the post-socialist world. Religious icons, once a prominent part of Russian Orthodox churches, were removed and placed in museums. Now, the churches want them back. Indigenous people's beliefs about the sacredness of their land are an important part of their attempts to protect their territory from encroachment and development by outside commercial interests. The world of religious change offers these examples, and far more, as windows into wider cultural change.

Revitalization Movements

Revitalization movements are organized movements that seek to construct a more satisfying culture, either through reestablishing all or parts of a religion that has been threatened by outside forces or by adopting new practices and beliefs. Such movements often arise in the context of rapid cultural change and appear to represent a way for people to try to make sense of their changing world and their place in it. One such movement that emerged as a response of Native Americans to the invasion of their land by Europeans and Euro-Americans was the Ghost Dance movement (Smith 1995:385). In the early 1870s, a shaman of the Paiute tribe named Wodziwob declared that the world would soon be destroyed and then renewed: Native Americans, plants, and animals would come back to life. He instructed people to perform a circle dance at night. This movement spread to other tribes in California, Oregon, and Idaho, but ended when the prophet died and his prophecy was unfulfilled. A similar movement emerged in 1890, led by another Paiute prophet, Wovoka, who had a vision during a total eclipse. His message was the same: destruction, renewal, and the need to perform circle dances in anticipation of the impending event. The dance spread widely and with differing effects. Among the Pawnee, it provided the basis for a cultural revival of old ceremonies that had fallen into disuse. The Sioux altered Wovoka's message and adopted a more overtly hostile stance toward the government and White people. Newspapers began to carry stories about the "messiah craze," referring to Wovoka. Ultimately, the government took action against the Sioux, killing Chief Sitting Bull and Chief Big Foot and about three hundred Sioux at Wounded Knee. In the 1970s, the Ghost Dance was revived by the American Indian Movement, an activist organization seeking to improve Native American rights.

Men march with bamboo sticks representing guns as part of a cargo cult on Tanna Island in the South Pacific. This procession imitates that of foreign soldiers and is intended to help bring the arrival of "goods" associated with the foreign presence.

Cargo cults are a variety of revitalization movements that sprang up in much of Melanesia (including Papua New Guinea and Fiji), and in New Zealand among the indigenous Maori peoples, in response to Western influences. Most prominent in the first half of the nineteenth century, they are characterized by their emphasis on the acquisition of Western trade goods, or "cargo" in local terms. Typically, a prophetic leader emerges with a vision of how the cargo will arrive. In one instance, the leader predicted that a ship would come, bringing not only cargo, but also the dead ancestors. Followers set up tables for the expected guests, complete with flower arrangements. Later, after World War II and the islanders' experiences of aircraft arrivals bringing cargo, the mode of arrival changed to planes. Once again, people would wait expectantly for the arrival of the plane. The cargo cults emerged as a response to the disrupting effects of new goods being suddenly introduced into indigenous settings. The outsiders imposed a new form of exchange system that emphasized the importance of Western goods and denied the importance of indigenous valuables such as shells and pigs. This transformation undermined traditional patterns of status-gaining through the exchange of indigenous goods. Cargo cult leaders sought help, in the only way they knew, in obtaining Western goods so they could gain social status in the new system.

Contested Sacred Sites

Religious conflict often becomes focused on sacred sites. One place of recurrent conflict is Jerusalem, where many religions and sects within religions compete for control of sacred terrain. Three major religions claim they have primary rights: Islam, Judaism, and Christianity. Among the Christians, several different sects vie for control of the Church of the Holy Sepulchre. In India, frequent conflicts occur between Hindus and Muslims over sacred sites. Hindus claim that Muslim mosques have been built on sites sacred to Hindus. On some occasions, the Hindus have proceeded to tear down the mosques. In the United States, White racists burned several African American churches in the south during 1997. Conflicts also occur between religious and secular interests. In the Middle East, some Jewish leaders in Israel resist archaeological research because the ancient Jewish burial places should remain undisturbed. The same situation exists for Native Americans, whose burial grounds have often been destroyed for the sake of urban development in the United States. Around the world, large-scale development projects such as dams and mines have destroyed indigenous sacred areas. Resistance to such destruction is growing, for example, among Australian Aborigines (see the Multiple Cultural Worlds box).

Socialism and Religion

Uneven steps toward religious tolerance have been recently taken in some socialist and post-socialist states. Religion, especially Eastern Orthodox Christianity, is re-emerging in Russia and other post-

Multiple Cultural Worlds

Aboriginal Beliefs versus Mining at Guratba

Guratba, or "Coronation Hill," is located in Australia's Northern Territory. It was registered as a sacred site under legislation at the same time that a mining company was surveying the area for gold and other valuable ore (Keen 1993). The hill lies within the country of the Jawoyn peoples, who opposed mining in their area on the basis of its sacredness to them. The mining company persisted in trying to cast doubts on the validity of that claim. The pro-mining position included arguments that the area did not really belong to the Jawoyn people, but rather to two extinct tribes, and that it was not a "valid" sacred site or certainly not one of any "significance." Ian Keen, an Australian anthropologist, and a colleague served as consultants in the case and wrote a report on the significance of the area to the Aboriginal people. They learned that the Jawoyns believe Guratba is the place where the supernatural Bula made a "wild rope," and that the gold in the mountain is the bodily essence of Bula and other ancestral figures, the Ngalenjilenji sisters. Mining and increased tourist development in the area would pose a threat of injury to the sacredness of the place. The issue became a political one, debated in Parliament, but Jawoyn voices were little heard. As of 1998, the area remains under protection as a national park (Keen 1998 personal communication).

Soviet states of Eastern Europe. At the same time, anti-Semitism has grown. Newspaper reports about China suggest that the government is adopting more tolerant measures toward religious practice. One impetus for restoring religious sites, especially Buddhist ones, is international tourism. On the other hand, Chinese repression of Tibetan Buddhism appears to remain strong.

Religious Freedom as a Human Right

According to a United Nations Declaration, freedom from religious persecution is supposed to be a universal human right. Violations of this right by nations and by competing religions are common. Sometimes people who are being persecuted on religious grounds can seek and obtain sanctuary in other places or nations. Thousands of Tibetan Buddhist refugees, including their leader the Dalai Lama, fled Tibet after it was taken over by the Chinese. Several Tibetan communities have been established in exile in India, the United States, and Canada, where the Tibetan people attempt to keep their religion, language, and heritage alive. Currently, a resurgence of interest in studying religion is occurring among cultural anthropologists in North America, after several decades of relative neglect. Some of this new interest, it is hoped, will be directed at the issue of religious freedom, human rights, and the implications for human welfare in this changing world.

SUMMARY

Early anthropologists collected information on religions of non-Western cultures and constructed theories about the universality, origin, and functions of religion. Over the decades, ethnographic studies have documented a range of beliefs represented indirectly in myths and, in state-level religions, directly through doctrine. Anthropologists have also recorded and analyzed ritual behavior, the "action" component of religion that is guided by the principles and teachings of myths or doctrine. Major categories of rituals are life-cycle rituals, pilgrimage cleansing rituals, rituals of reversal, and sacrifice. In some sense, all rituals are transformative for the participants.

Many rituals, but not all, require the participation of a trained religious specialist such as a shaman/shamanka or priest/priestess. In pre-state societies, religious specialist roles are fewer and less formalized, and they carry less secular power and status. In states, religious specialists are often organized into hierarchies, and many specialists gain substantial secular power.

The five "world religions" are all based on a coherent and widely agreed upon set of teachings, but in different cultures they have been contextualized into local variants. When a new religion moves into a culture, it may be blended with indigenous systems, coexist in a pluralistic fashion, or may take over and obliterate the original beliefs.

Cultural anthropologists have documented and sought to explain why and how religious change occurs. Religious movements of the past two centuries have often been prompted by colonialism and other forms of social contact. In some instances, indigenous religious leaders and cults arise in an attempt to resist unwanted outside forces of change; in other cases, they are ways of incorporating selected outside elements.

CRITICAL THINKING QUESTIONS

1. Choose a well-known myth and try to apply to it a Lévi-Straussian perspective (look for oppositions and mediators). What insights does this exercise yield? What does it exclude as possible explanatory tools?
2. Think of the life-cycle ceremonies that you have attended, such as weddings or baptisms or funerals, and try to apply Victor Turner's three stages to them.
3. How do different modes of production shape religious beliefs and practices?
4. What are some examples of links between religion and politics that have appeared recently in the news?

KEY CONCEPTS

animatism, p. 313
animism, p. 311
anthropomorphic, p. 314
cargo cult, p. 328
doctrine, p. 312
euhemerism, p. 314
life-cycle ritual, p. 315
magic, p. 310
myth, p. 312
priest/priestess, p. 319
religion, p. 310
revitalization movement, p. 328
ritual, p. 314
ritual of reversal, p. 316
sacrifice, p. 317
syncretism, p. 321
world religion, p. 319
zoomorphic, p. 313

SUGGESTED READINGS

Thomas D. Blakely, Walter E. A. van Beek, and Dennis L. Thompson, *Religion in Africa: Experience and Expression.* Portsmouth, NH: Heinemann, 1994. This book contains an introductory overview and twenty chapters on topics including the impact of Islam and Christianity on African religious systems, women's spirit cults, myth and epic, and new religious movements.

Holly Beachley Brear, *Inherit the Alamo: Myth and Ritual at an American Shrine.* Austin: University of Texas Press, 1995. This book treats the story of the Alamo as a Texan creation myth involving sacrifice, death, and rebirth.

Karen McCarthy Brown, *Mama Lola: A Vodou Priestess in Brooklyn.* Berkeley: University of California Press, 1991. The life story of Mama Lola, a Vodou practitioner, is set within an ethnographic study of a Haitian community in New York.

Klara Bonsack Kelley and Harris Francis, *Navajo Sacred Places.* Bloomington: Indiana University Press, 1994. The authors report on the results of a research project to learn about Navajo cultural resources, especially sacred sites, and the stories associated with them in order to help protect these places.

Anna S. Meigs, *Food, Sex, and Pollution: A New Guinea Religion.* New Brunswick, NJ: Rutgers University Press, 1983. This book provides an analysis of taboos surrounding food, sex, and vital bodily essences among the Hua people of Papua New Guinea.

Fatima Mernissi, *Beyond the Veil: Male-Female Dynamics in Modern Muslim Society.* Bloomington: Indiana University Press, revised edition, 1987. The author considers how Islam perceives of female sexuality and seeks to regulate it on behalf of the social order. This edition contains a new chapter on Muslim women and fundamentalism.

CHAPTER 14

Communication

CHAPTER OUTLINE

INTRODUCING LINGUISTIC ANTHROPOLOGY
- Connections with the Other Fields
- ● *Current Event:* "Easter Island Decipherment"
- Fieldwork Challenges

HUMAN VERBAL LANGUAGE
- Key Characteristics: Productivity and Displacement
- Formal Properties of Language
- Multiple Levels of Language
- Origins and Change

LANGUAGE, THOUGHT, AND BEHAVIOR
- Opposing Models: Sapir-Whorf versus Sociolinguistics
- ● *Multiple Cultural Worlds:* Indexing Motherhood in Western Samoa and the United States

DISCOURSE, IDENTITY, AND POWER
- Children's Disputes
- Adolescent Girls' "Fat Talk"
- Cultural Cuing in the Medical Interview

HUMAN PARALANGUAGE
- Silence as Communication
- Kinesics
- Dress and Looks

MASS MEDIA
- The Media Process: Studying War Correspondents
- ● *Critical Thinking:* A Tale of Two Stories: Assessing Institutional Influence on News Reporting
- Television Studies
- Orientalism in American Popular Culture

LANGUAGE AND SOCIAL CHANGE
- ● *Voices:* On Decolonising the Mind, by Ngũgĩ wa Thiong'o

SUMMARY

KEY CONCEPTS

CRITICAL THINKING QUESTIONS

SUGGESTED READINGS

◀ Aini women, members of one of China's many minority groups, converse with each other, in Yunnan province.

People are in almost constant communication with other people, with supernaturals, with pets, or with other domesticated animals. Many animals and insects such as chimpanzees, lions, and bees have sophisticated ways of communicating about where food is available or warning about an impending danger. **Communication** refers to the conveying of meaningful messages from one person or animal or insect to another. Major means of communication among humans include eye contact, body posture, position and movements of limbs, and language. **Language** refers to a form of communication that is a systematic set of arbitrary symbols shared among a group and passed on from generation to generation. It may be spoken, signed, or written.

This chapter presents material mainly from linguistic anthropology, one of general anthropology's four fields. It discusses key characteristics of human language that set it apart from communication among other animals and considers what we know about the origins of languages. Then the role of language in our multicultural worlds is discussed: how language relates to thought in general, language learning, different styles and patterns of languages used by different groups of people and the way they relate to questions of identity, and the growing importance of communication via the mass media in shaping intercultural perceptions and relations.

INTRODUCING LINGUISTIC ANTHROPOLOGY

Linguistic anthropology is devoted to the study of communication, mainly, but not exclusively, among humans. Linguistic anthropology began in the United States, inspired by the realization that Native American languages were rapidly disappearing through population decline and assimilation (becoming culturally merged) into Euro-American culture. Franz Boas gained eminence for recording many of the languages, myths, and rituals of these disappearing cultures. Another force driving the development of linguistic anthropology was the discovery through cross-cultural fieldwork that many existing non-Western languages had never been written down. Study of non-Western languages revealed a wide range of different phonetic systems (pronunciation of various sounds) and exposed the inadequacy of Western alphabets to represent such sounds. This gap prompted the development of the "International Phonetic Alphabet," which contains symbols to represent all known sounds, such as the symbol "!" to indicate a click sound common in southern African languages. More recently, linguistic anthropologists have begun to explore new areas of research, including the relationship between nationalism and language, the role of language in the mass media, and language and politics. Many anthropologists are designing practical applications of research findings to promote improved language learning among school children, migrants, and refugee populations. Modifications of standardized tests to reduce bias against children from varied cultural backgrounds is an area where applied linguistic anthropologists are increasingly active.

From the above description, it is clear that cultural anthropology and linguistic anthropology have similar and overlapping interests. This is true for all of anthropology's four fields to a certain extent. A particular anthropologist working in any one of the fields, however, chooses to emphasize a certain aspect of human life for study. In the case of linguistic anthropology, communication is the primary distinguishing emphasis.

Connections with Other Fields

Archaeologists work closely with linguists in searching for the origins, spread, and changes in language and deciphering ancient languages, thereby shedding light on human history. Some early forms of writing continue to defy translation, such as the script used in the Mohenjo-daro civilization of present-day Pakistan that is dated around 3500 BCE. Even a more recently used language of Easter Island, in the Pacific, was, until recently, a mystery in terms of its use and meaning in society (see the Current Event box).

Some physical anthropologists and human geneticists use linguistic data to complement their attempts to trace genetic relationships of populations throughout history (Cavalli-Sforza, Menozzi and Piazza 1994). Communication among nonhuman primates is also of great interest to physical anthropologists. Attempts to teach chimpanzees to talk have been largely unsuccessful. Chimpanzees lack a crucial anatomical part, the pharynx, a resonating chamber that is crucial for the formation of many sounds (Harris 1989: 77).

Current Event

"Easter Island Decipherment"

- A major breakthrough has occurred in the decipherment of *rongorongo,* Easter Island's enigmatic script. Stephen Fischer, a New Zealand scholar, believes most of the inscriptions represented the islanders' creation myths. The script consists of parallel lines of characters engraved on twenty-five wooden tablets that are now housed in European and American museums.
- The writing developed after the Spanish took over the island in 1770. The last aristocratic or priestly islanders who could understand the tablets died off in a smallpox epidemic of the 1860s. Since then, their content has remained a mystery.
- Fischer says that *rongorongo* was a sophisticated writing system, the only indigenous script in Oceania before the twentieth century. He believes that *rongorongo* was a mixed writing system incorporating both logograms (symbols denoting words) and semasiograms (symbols denoting actions).

Source: Paul G. Bahn, *Archaeology* 49(4):18, 1996.

A fascinating area of research involves teaching nonhuman primates to understand and use arbitrary symbols. Symbolic understanding has long been held to constitute a major dividing line between communication abilities of nonhuman primates and human language. In 1966, a female chimpanzee named Washoe began learning how to use American Sign Language (ASL). She acquired the use of 160 signs in about five years, and she was able to use them to generate novel combinations. Another chimp, Sarah, learned abstract principles such as choosing a red chip when asked the question "what is an apple the same as?" Signing chimpanzees can pass sign language on to their offspring. So far, competence levels have been at about that of a three-year-old child. Studying these rudimentary signing systems may shed light on the early stages of human communication.

Chimpanzees have demonstrated a remarkable ability to learn aspects of human language. Here, trainer Joyce Butler signs "Nim" and Nim signs "Me."

This chapter presents findings in both linguistic and cultural anthropology, with some attention to research in archaeology and physical anthropology. It includes a wide range of topics related to human communication, from anthropologists' attempts to trace the origins and spread of language to analyses of everyday human speech events and the power issues involved in media representations of "other" people.

Fieldwork Challenges

The anthropological study of communication shares many methods with cultural anthropology, but its more specialized areas have unique approaches to data gathering and analysis. The study of language **pragmatics,** or language in use, relies on tape recordings or video recordings of people and events. The tapes are then analyzed qualitatively or quantitatively. Video recordings, for example, may be subjected to a detailed "frame analysis" that can pinpoint when communication breaks down or misunderstandings occur. Linguistic anthropologists argue that the analysis of recorded data is best done when situated within broader knowledge about the culture. This approach derives from Malinowski's view that communication is "embedded" in its social context and that it must therefore be studied in relation to that context. An example of such a contextualized approach is a study of speech in Western Samoa that gathered many hours of tape-recorded speech along with long-term fieldwork in the area (Duranti 1994). Analysis of the transcriptions of the recorded talk revealed two major findings about how speech is related to social status as used in village council meetings. First, turn-taking patterns reflected and restated people's power positions in the group. Second, people used particular grammatical forms and word choices that indirectly either praised or blamed others, thus shaping and reaffirming people's moral roles and status relations. Nonlinguistic data that assisted in forming these interpretations included observation of seating arrangements and the order of the distribution of kava (a ritually shared intoxicating beverage). The findings about the role of language in creating and maintaining social and moral order contribute to a richer understanding of the wider social context of status formation in Samoa.

Most anthropologists face the challenge of translation. One has to understand more about a language than just vocabulary in order to provide a reliable and meaningful translation. An anthropologist once translated a song that occurred at the end of a play in Zaire (Fabian 1995). The play was presented in the Swahili language, so he assumed that the final song was, too. Thus, he assumed that the repeated use of the word *tutubawina,* a Swahili word, indicated that it was a fighting song. But a Swahili speaker assisting the anthropologist said, no, it was a soccer song. The puzzled anthropologist only later learned, by writing to the theater performers, that the word *tutubawina* as used in this song was not a Swahili word. From a different language, it indicates a marching song.

Linguistic anthropologists who seek to study ordinary language use all face the problem of the **observer's paradox** (the impossibility of doing research on "natural" communication events without affecting the "naturalness" sought) (McMahon 1994: 234). The mere presence of the anthropologist with a tape recorder tends to make the speaker concentrate on speaking "correctly" and more formally. Several options exist for dealing with the paradox: recording informants in a group, observing and recording speech outside an interview situation, or using structured interviews in which the informant is asked to perform various speech tasks at varying levels of formality. In this last technique, the informant is first asked to read a word list and a short passage. The next stage is a question-and-answer session. Last, the interviewer encourages the informant, who may be more relaxed by now, to produce informal conversational speech by asking about childhood rhymes and sayings, encouraging diversions to get the informant to talk for longer periods, and posing questions that are likely to prompt an emotional response. Another strategy is to use "role plays" in which informants are asked to act out a particular scene, such as arguing about something. Data from such semistructured techniques can be compared with the more casual styles of "natural" speech to assess the possible bias created.

HUMAN VERBAL LANGUAGE

Most anthropologists agree that nonhuman primates share some abilities with humans to communicate through sounds and movements, and that some can be trained to recognize and use arbitrary symbols that humans use. Whatever progress will be made in teaching nonhuman primates aspects of sign language, it is unlikely that they could ever develop the range of linguistic ability that humans possess because of the vastly greater reliance on two features of human language that depend on the richness of the arbitrary symbols used in language.

Key Characteristics: Productivity and Displacement

Human language is said to have infinite **productivity,** or the ability to communicate many messages efficiently. In contrast, consider gibbon communication in the wild. Gibbons have nine calls that convey useful messages such as "follow me," "I am angry," "here is food," "danger," and "I am hurt." If a gibbon wants to communicate particular intensity in, say, the danger at hand, the only option is to repeat the "danger" call several times and at different volumes: "danger," "*danger,*" "*DANGER,*" and so on. This variation allows some productivity, but with greater degrees of danger, the system of communication becomes increasingly inefficient. By the time twenty danger calls have been given, it may be too late. In comparison, human language's capacity for productivity makes it extremely efficient. Different levels of danger can be conveyed in these ways:

I see a movement over there.
I see a leopard there.
A leopard—Help!
HELP!!

phonemes is called **phonetics** (these are "within the circle"). Sharon Hutchinson comments on her attraction to phonemes of the Nuer language spoken in the Sudan:

> As a native English speaker, I find the seeming airy lightness and rich melodic qualities of the Nuer language to be attractive. The language contains few "hard" consonants—and those that do exist are often softened or silenced at the ends of words. A terminal "k," for instance, often slides into a breathy "gh" sound . . . or a lighter "h" sound or is suppressed entirely. . . . Similarly, the letter "c" in Nuer is never pronounced like the English "c" in "cat" but, rather, as a soft "ch" sound that often softens to either a "sh" . . . or an "i" sound when serving as the terminal consonant of various words and stems. Another softening feature of the Nuer language—as perceived, of course, by a native English speaker—is the existence of four different "n"-like consonants. . . . The apparent "airiness" of the language stems from the fact that many Nuer vowels are heavily aspirated—that is, they are released with an audible bit of breath as in the English "hi" and "hea" in "behind" and "ahead." Indeed, one of the earliest obstacles I faced in trying to learn the language was to hear and to control the voice's "breathiness" or "nonbreathiness" in the pronunciation of various Nuer vowels. The pronounced and fluctuating intonation patterns of the language also presented hidden challenges: Nuer is "tonal" in that the relative musical pitches of words and particles can bear both lexical and grammatical significance. (1996:xv–xvi)

A native English-speaker trying to learn the North Indian language called Hindi is challenged to learn to produce and recognize several new sounds. For example, four different "d" sounds exist. None are the same as an English "d," which is usually pronounced with the tongue placed on the ridge behind the upper front teeth (try it). One "d" in Hindi, which linguists refer to as a "dental" sound, is pronounced with the tongue pressed firmly behind the upper front teeth (try it). Next is a dental "d" that is also aspirated (pronounced "with air"); making this sound involves the tongue being in the same position and a puff of air expelled during pronunciation (try it, and try the reg-

"I see a movement over there."
"I see a leopard there."
"A leopard—help!"
"Help!"

Human language also uses the feature of **displacement,** which allows people to talk about displaced domains—events in the past and future—as well as the immediate present. According to current thinking, displacement is not a prominent feature of nonhuman primate communication. A wild chimpanzee is unlikely to be able to communicate the message "Danger: there may be a leopard coming here tonight." Instead, it communicates mainly what is experienced in the present. Even if nonhuman primates can learn to use displacement, it is still true that its use among humans is far more prevalent. Among humans, the majority of language use relates to displaced domains, including reference to people and events that may never exist at all, as in fantasy and fiction.

Formal Properties of Language

Besides the above general characteristics, human language can be analyzed in terms of its formal properties: sounds, vocabulary, and grammar, features that lie "inside the circle" of formal linguistics (Agar 1994). Outside the circle lies the more exciting area of actual language use (the focus of most of this chapter). Learning a new language usually involves the discovery that other languages have different sets of sounds. The sounds that make a difference for meaning in a language are called **phonemes;** the study of ular dental "d" again with no puff of air at all). Next is what is referred to as a "retroflex sound," accomplished by flipping the tongue back to the central dome of the roof of the mouth (try it, with no puff of air). Finally, there is the aspirated retroflex "d" with the tongue again in the center of the roof of the mouth and a puff of air. Once you can do this, try the whole series again with a "t," because Hindi follows the same pattern with this letter as with the "d." Several other sounds in Hindi require careful use of aspiration and placement of the tongue for communicating the right word. A puff of air at the wrong time can produce a serious error, for example, saying the word for "breast" when you want to say the word for "letter."

Grammar refers to the patterns and rules by which words are organized to make sense in a string. All languages have a grammar, although they vary in form. Even within the languages of contemporary Europe, German is characterized by its placement of the verb at the end of the sentence (try to compose an English sentence with the verb at the end). Phonemes, vocabulary, and grammar are the formal building blocks of language.

The presence of both French and Arabic cultural influences in Morocco results in the frequent use of bilingual shop signs.

Multiple Levels of Language

A characteristic of contemporary language is the proliferation of people who speak more than one language and the existence of intralanguage variation in such matters as word choice, intonation, and even grammar, that is tied to social variation of the users.

Bilingualism

Global culture contact since the era of colonial expansion beginning in 1500 has meant that people have been increasingly exposed to more than one language. One result is that more people are bilingual. Bilingualism simply refers to the capacity to speak two languages. A true bilingual has "native speaking abilities" in two languages. Bilingualism is often the result of migration from one language area to another. Many world populations are bilingual because their country was colonized and a second language was introduced. As the result of the close proximity and high exposure to many languages, Europeans often grow up learning more than one language. The emergence of large populations speaking multiple languages has led to heated debates about the value of more than one "standard" language. The question arises of how linguistic pluralism (tolerance of linguistic diversity within a particular context) can be realized both in terms of the educational system and costs. The effort to make a second language codominant arises out of the belief that, if a large percentage of the population speaks a second language, they will have equal access to education, jobs and services as people speaking the first language.

Language testing of bilingual people seems to support the contention that even if people are fluent in their "adopted" language, they still are at a disadvantage. According to one theory, a person who has to use two languages to communicate everyday does not really have full capabilities in either language because each one fills in for the other to create a unitary whole out of two partial languages (Valdés and Figueroa 1994:7). Thus, if such a person is evaluated in one of these languages, he or she will appear to have a low level of linguistic competence: "When a bilingual individual confronts a monolingual test, developed by monolingual individuals, and standardized and normed on a monolingual population, both the test taker and the test are asked to do something that they cannot. The bilingual test taker cannot perform like a monolingual. The monolingual test cannot "measure" in the other language" (87). Given the monolingual content of existing tests, bilingual students are likely to test lower than monolingual students. This appears to be the reason why so many more Hispanic bilingual children are rated as mentally retarded compared to Euro-Americans. Schools in several states are "overrepresented" with Hispanic students in special education classes. This pattern has a long history in the United States. In New York City at the turn of the century, it was Italian American children who were said to have the highest rate of mental retardation.

Dialects

A standing joke in linguistics is that a dialect is a language without an army, suggesting power differentials between speakers of a language versus speakers of a dialect. The basic definition of a **dialect** is that it is a way of speaking in a particular place, or, more precisely, a subordinate variety of a language arising from local circumstances (R. Williams 1983:105). Thus, there is standard English and there are dialects of English. Standard forms of a language will have the stamp of authority of the nation and will be taught using standardized textbooks. Dialects may appear in literature or films as a way of adding "local color." It is often difficult for dialect speakers to avoid being considered somehow second class because they do not speak the standard language. For example, the British singing group, the Beatles, originated in the city of Liverpool known for its distinct dialect called "Scouse." Cockney, spoken in London, is another prominent dialect. Speakers of both dialects would be able to understand each other, but with some difficulty.

For many years, language experts have argued about whether Black English is a dialect of standard English. In the contemporary United States, race, ethnicity, and language are of key importance in child development and schooling, access to employment and job advancement, and other status-bearing domains such as the media. Black English has been looked down on by conservative bearers of a standard English tradition. Black English was judged by them to be a broken, haphazard, ungrammatical form of English that needed to be "corrected." Many educators now say that Black children in the United States learn one language at home and are then confronted with another language in school. Effectively, they are expected to be bilingual elementary school children because they must develop proficiency in standard English. Political scientist Andrew Hacker says that recognition of this issue is mainly what is needed, not having Black English taught in schools, as was proposed by the city of Oakland in early 1997, with its promotion of teaching in "Ebonic" or Black English (1992:171).

Another area that needs understanding from White teachers is that Black children may have culturally distinct styles of expression that can be valued. For example, Black children should be given more opportunities for expressive talking since, as Hacker notes, Black culture gives as much attention to style as to substance. In terms of narrative style, Black children tend to use a spiral pattern, seemingly skipping around to various topics before addressing the theme, while White children use a more linear style. In terms of literature assignments, if more Black authors were read in classrooms, this would help provide a cultural anchor to their heritage for Black children, offer respect for their traditions, and at the same time enrich White children, who might otherwise not get such exposure.

Language Codes

Even within a single language, particular subcultures are likely to have distinctive **codes,** or ways of speaking that may include marked vocabulary, grammar, and intonation depending on age, gender, occupation, class, region, and family role of the speaker and listener (many codes are hard to separate from a dialect). Most people know more than one such code and are able to **code-switch,** or move from one code to another as needed. For example, consider how you talk to your college friends when you are in a group, compared to how you might speak to a physician or potential employer. Code-switching can be an intentional strategy used to further the interests of the speaker. Generally, code-switching follows status lines, with a dominant language or code being used to make a statement of power or authority. This may be the rationale for American TV ads for diapers using a speaker with a British accent. In the decolonizing nations, people may wish to make a statement of resistance to the colonial powers by avoiding complete switching to the colonial language, but instead using **code-mixing.** In code-mixing, the speaker starts in the native language and then introduces strands of the colonial language (Myers-Scotton 1993:122).

Gender codes are common in most languages. Usually, males avoid code-switching into a female register, and females who adopt a male register may be judged by traditionalist males as "too" aggressive or unfeminine. More often than not, males and females are speaking in codes of which they are not even aware. Studies of North American gender codes have pointed to several features of the female code: more politeness, rising intonation at the end of sentences, and the frequent use of **tag questions,** which are questions seeking affirmation that are placed at the end of sentences, such as: "It's a nice day, *isn't it*?" (Lakoff 1973). Male codes are less polite, maintain a flat assertive tone in a sentence, and do not use tag questions. One conversational characteristic is that men interrupt women far more than women interrupt men. In general, the female code is a subservient, complementary, "weak" form, while the male code is dominating, hierarchical, and "strong." Separate versions of a language for males and females cause, reflect, and reinforce women's unequal status. They can also lead to miscommunication. Sociolinguist Deborah Tannen's popular book, *You Just Don't Understand* (1990), shows how differences in male and female communication styles in the United States lead to miscommunication. She says that "women speak and hear a language of connection and intimacy, while men speak and hear a language of status and independence" (42). Sometimes men and women use similar linguistic styles, such as indirect response, but their differing motivations create different meanings that are embedded in their speech. For example, many husbands saw their role as one of protector in explaining why they used an indirect rather than direct response to a question:

Michele: What time is the concert?
Gary: You have to be ready by seven-thirty. (289)

Michele feels that Gary is withholding information by not answering her directly, thus maintaining a power position. He feels that he is simply "watching out for her" by getting to the real point of her question. A similarly indirect response given by a wife to a husband is shaped around her goal of being helpful by anticipating the husband's real motivation:

Ned: Are you just about finished?
Valerie: Do you want to have supper now? (289)

Gender codes in spoken Japanese also reflect and reinforce gender differences and hierarchies (Shibamoto 1987). Certain words and sentence structures convey femininity, humbleness, and politeness. A common contrast between male and female speech is the attachment of the honorific prefix "o-" to nouns by females (see Table 14.1). This addition gives female speech a more refined and polite tone. Japanese women frequently use honorific and humble verb forms. Younger women, especially, use these forms when flirting. Tone also differentiates male and female speech: Female speech is more high pitched than male speech, and female sentences tend to have rising intonation.

Table 14.1
Male-Unmarked and Female-Marked Nouns in Japanese

	Male	*Female*
Box lunch	bentoo	obentoo
Money	kane	okane
Chopsticks	hasi	ohasi
Book	hon	ohon

Source: Shibamoto 1987:28.

Language Origins and Change

Did the first people have language, and if so, what was it like? Did grunts and exclamations evolve into words and sentences? Did early humans attempt to imitate the sounds of nature? Did a committee meet and decide to put together a set of arbitrary symbols with meanings that everyone would accept? No one knows, nor will we ever know, how language started in the first place. The prevailing view is that early humans began to develop language around 50,000 years ago, using the basic components of calls, body postures, and gestures. Human **paralanguage** (a category that includes all forms of nonverbal communication such as body posture, voice tone, touch, smells, and eye and facial movements) is thus considered the earliest aspect of human language.

No contemporary human language can be considered a "primitive" model of early human language. That would defy the principle of **linguistic relativism,** which says that all languages have passed through thousands of years of change, and all are equally successful forms of communication. Languages differ in their structure and in the meaning they attribute to various concepts (or "semantics"), but all are equally capable of conveying subtle meanings and complex thoughts. There is no such thing as a "simple" language—one that is easy to learn because it is less complex than others. Early scholars of comparative linguistics were sometimes misled by ethnocentric assumptions that language structures of European languages were normative and that languages that did not have the same structure were somehow deficient. Chinese was thus considered to be "primitive" on these grounds, as were Native American languages. Now we know that different languages have complexity in different areas—sometimes verb forms, sometimes noun formations.

Writing Systems

Gesture and speech have no way of being recorded in the archaeological record. Attempts to trace the beginnings of language are thus limited to working with the data we do have, which is records of written language. Evidence of the earliest written languages comes from Mesopotamia, Egypt, and China (Postgate, Wang and Wilkinson 1995). Current opinion dates the oldest writing system as being in use by the fourth millennium BCE in Mesopotamia. Some scholars say that symbols found on pottery in China dated at 5000 to 4000 BCE should be counted as the earliest writing. At question here is the definition of a writing system: Does the presence of symbolic markings on pots constitute a "writing system" or not? Most scholars say that a symbolic mark that could refer to a clan name is not necessarily evidence of a writing system that involves the use of words in relation to each other in a systematic way. A similarity of forms in all early writing systems is the use of logographs (symbols that convey meaning through a form or picture that resembles what is being referred to). Over time, some logographs were kept with their original meaning, others were kept but given more abstract meaning, and other non-logographic symbols were added (see Figure 14.1).

The emergence of writing is associated with the political development of the state. Some scholars take writing as a key diagnostic feature that distinguishes the state from earlier political forms because recordkeeping was an essential task of the state. The Inca state is one exception to this generalization; it used *quipu*, or cords of knotted strings of different colors for keeping accounts and recording events. Two interpretations of early writing systems exist. One says that the primary use of early writing was ceremonial because of the prevalence of early writing on tombs, bone inscriptions, or temple carvings. The other says that the primary function of early writing was utilitarian, for government recordkeeping and trade. The archaeological record, in this view, is naturally biased toward durable substances. This bias favors the amount of ceremonial writing preserved because durable substances such as stone would have been more likely to be used for ceremonial writing since it was intended to last. Utilitarian writing would more likely have been done on perishable materials since people would be less concerned with permanence—somewhat like the way we treat shopping lists. Thus, perhaps much more utilitarian writing existed than what has been preserved.

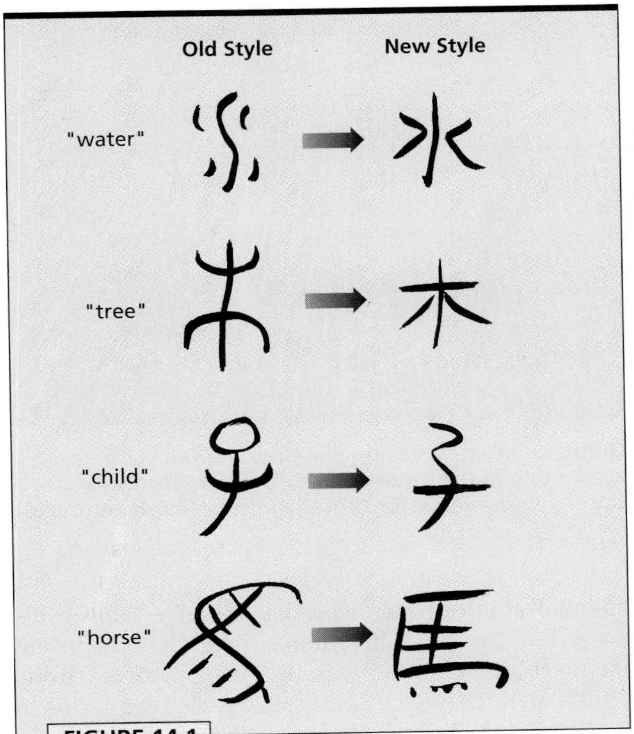

FIGURE 14.1
Logographic and Current Writing Styles

Historical Linguistics

Historical linguistics is the study of language change through history using formal methods that compare shifts over time and across space in formal aspects of language such as phonetics, grammar, and semantics. This approach originated in the eighteenth century with a discovery made by Sir William Jones, a British

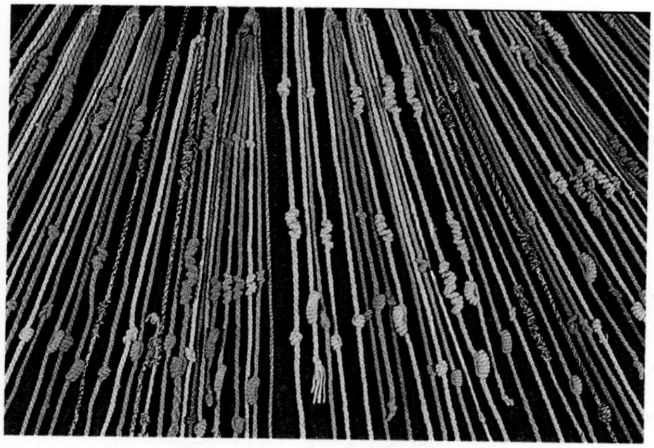

Quipu, or knotted strings, were the basis of state-level accounting in the Incan empire. The knots convey substantial information for those who could interpret their meaning.

colonial administrator working in India. During his spare time in India, he studied Sanskrit, the ancient language of India. He was the first to notice strong similarities between Sanskrit, Greek, and Latin in vocabulary and grammar. For example, the Sanskrit word for "father" is *pitr,* in Greek it is *patér,* and in Latin, *pater.* This was an astounding discovery for the time, given the prevailing European mentality that placed its cultural heritage firmly in the classical Graeco-Roman world (Bernal 1987).

Following Jones's discovery, other scholars began comparing lists of words and grammatical forms in different languages, for example, French: *père,* German: *Vater,* Italian: *padre,* Old English: *faeder,* Old Norse: *fadhir,* Swedish: *far.* With these lists, scholars could also determine degrees of closeness and distance in their relationships, for example, that German and English are closer to each other, and French and Spanish are closer to each other. Later scholars contributed the concept of "language families," or clusters of related languages. Attempts to reconstruct the ancient ancestral languages of family trees was a major research interest of the nineteenth century. Comparison of contemporary and historic Eurasian languages and shifts in sound, vocabulary and meaning, yielded a model of a hypothetical early parent language called Proto-Indo-European (PIE). For example, the hypothetical PIE term for "father" is p#ter (the "#" symbol is pronounced like the "u" in "mutter"). The PIE homeland has not been located and may never be, since PIE-speakers were probably pastoralists whose lifestyle left few remains in the archaeological record. Linguistic evidence suggests that PIE was located somewhere in Eurasia, perhaps in or near Turkey. The PIE language is dated as existing by 4000 BCE or earlier. Dating is based on the evidence of linguistic divergence. From its area of origin, PIE speakers subsequently spread out in waves toward Europe, central and eastern Asia, and South Asia. The farther they moved from the PIE center in terms of time and space, the more their language diverged from original PIE.

Similar reconstructions of language relationships and change through time have been done for other world regions. One classification places the languages of Africa into four families, those of New Guinea into two families, and those of North and South America into three families (Ruhlen 1994). The much-debated issue of relationships between these families divides linguists into two broad groups informally termed "lumpers" and "splitters." Lumpers favor a theory of linguistic *monogenesis,* which claims that, ultimately, all languages derive from an ancient ancestor language used by the earliest humans in Africa. Merritt Ruhlen, leading spokesperson for the lumpers, has amassed substantial data on etymology (changes in words over time in form or meaning) to support his position. Splitters argue that the data to support monogenesis are weaker than is claimed. Splitters also argue that our original African ancestors are unlikely to have had a true "language" during their early evolution since their cranial capacity may not have been able to support complex symbolic thought and their vocal tracts did not have the capacity for human speech as we know it. Splitters disagree among themselves about how far they will go in aggregating languages into larger families. Most linguists accept at least the following clusters: Indo-European, Afro-Asiatic (including the Semitic languages and most North African languages), and Uralic (Finnish and Hungarian).

Pidgins and Creoles

A **pidgin** is a contact language that emerges when different cultures with different languages come to live in close proximity and therefore need to communicate (McMahon 1994:253). Pidgins are generally limited to highly functional domains, such as trade, since that is what they were developed for. A pidgin therefore is no one's first language. Many pidgins of the Western hemisphere developed out of slavery, where owners needed to communicate with their slaves. A pidgin is always learned as a second language. Tok Pisin, the pidgin language of Papua New Guinea, consists of a mixture of many languages, some English, Samoan, Chinese, and Malayan. Tok Pisin has been declared one of the national languages of Papua New Guinea, where it is transforming into a **creole,** or a language descended from pidgin with its own native speakers and involving linguistic expansion and elaboration. About two hundred pidgin and creole languages exist today, mainly in West Africa, the Caribbean, and the South Pacific.

LANGUAGE, THOUGHT, AND BEHAVIOR

We now turn toward studies that concern communication in contemporary society. During the twentieth century, two major theoretical perspectives have been influential in considering how language, thought, and behavior are related. They are presented here as opposing models, but careful reading of all the writings of each founder and subsequent research would reveal that the contrasts are not really this simple and neat (Hill and Mannheim 1992). Nonetheless, the "extreme" forms have persisted in the literature over several decades.

Opposing Models: Sapir-Whorf versus Sociolinguistics

The Sapir-Whorf Hypothesis

Edward Sapir and Benjamin Whorf formulated an influential model, called the **Sapir-Whorf hypothesis,** which claims that language determines thought. For example, if a language has no word for what in English is called "snow," then a person who has been brought up in that language cannot think of "snow" as it is meant in English. Whorf first began developing this theory through study of different languages' vocabulary and grammar. He was so struck by the differences that he is often attributed with saying that people who speak different languages inhabit "different worlds." This catchy phrase became the basis for what is called **linguistic determinism,** which states that language determines consciousness of the world and behavior. Extreme linguistic determinism implies that the frames and definitions of a person's primary language are so strong that it is impossible to learn fully another language or understand another culture (Agar 1994:67).

Sociolinguistics

An alternative model to the Sapir-Whorf hypothesis is proposed by scholars working in the area of **sociolinguistics,** who argue that culture and society and a person's social position determine the content and form of language, and devote their research to showing how this is so. William Labov's (1962) research of the 1960s was foundational in this approach. Labov conducted several famous studies of the use of particular speech sounds among people of different classes in New York City. He hypothesized that class differences would be reflected in the use of certain sounds. For example, pronunciation of the consonant "r" in words such as car, card, floor, and fourth is more associated with upper-class people, while its absence ("caw," "cawd," "flaw," "fawth") is associated with lower-class people. In order to obtain data on discourse without the formalizing effects of taped interviews, Labov relied on use of rapid and anonymous observations of sales clerks' speech in three Manhattan department stores. The stores were chosen to represent three class levels: Saks, the highest, then Macy's, then S. Klein. His assumption is that clerks in each store represent, even though roughly, different class levels and statuses. Labov would approach a clerk and inquire about the location of some item that he knew was on the fourth floor. The clerk would respond, and then Labov would say, "excuse me?" in order to prompt a more emphatic repeat of the word "fourth." His analysis of the data confirmed the hypothesis. The higher-status "r" was pronounced both the first and second times by 44 percent of the employees in Saks, 16 percent of the employees in Macy's and 6 percent of the employees in S. Klein. In the rest of the cases, some of the clerks used the "r" in the emphatic, repeat response, but most uses were without the "r." The following section reviews major contributions in the area of sociolinguistics and its study of language pragmatics.

Focal Vocabularies

Focal vocabularies are clusters of related words that refer to important features of a particular culture. Studying focal vocabularies can contribute to understanding both how language is a thought-world (according to the Sapir-Whorf hypothesis) and how language is also a social construction that is responsive to a par-

Ski enthusiasts use a more elaborate set of terms to differentiate forms of snow than most English speakers, among whom "powder," for example, is not a familiar concept for snow.

ticular social context. For example, Inuit languages of the polar north recognize many different forms and have many specific terms for varieties of what most people in the United States refer to with one word: snow. Environmental conditions that make snow such an important factor, in conjunction with economic adaptations, drive this amplification and, therefore, shape how Inuit people actually think about the weather. In a similar way, English speakers of the United States who are avid skiers are likely to have a more amplified focal vocabulary related to forms of cold-weather precipitation than someone who grew up in Florida and has never lived in snow or gone skiing. Studying a culture's focal vocabularies provides insights into the culture and useful ways to compare cultures cross-culturally.

Language Socialization

Language socialization, or language learning through everyday interactions, is another area that links the two models described in this section. Language socialization includes two processes: socialization to *use* language and socialization *through* language (Ochs 1990:287). The first part of the definition refers to language acquisition, how child speakers learn to be native speakers. Language acquisition concerns people in many fields, especially psychology and education. Anthropological study of language acquisition adds an important comparative element, showing how children acquire aspects of different languages within a variety of cultures.

Analyses of children's acquisition of different languages can be used as a test for the presence of the Sapir-Whorf effect. Some languages, such as Hungarian, Turkish, and Japanese, place key grammatical cues either at the ends of words or sentences, a feature that should make it easier for children to discover the actor and spatial and temporal relations than for children learning languages without such clear cues (Slobin 1990). Thus, child speakers of Hungarian, Turkish, and Japanese should have a better grasp of such features of a story than child speakers of other languages. A comparative analysis of children's readings of the same story revealed, however, a striking similarity in the content and functions of children's early speech across the three languages and cultures: "The child's eye view of the world seems to transcend peculiarities of language and culture" (234). In a related study, comparative research on children's storytelling abilities in the United States, Spain, West Germany, Turkey, and Israel was conducted by showing children pictures and asking them to tell what was occurring. Children speaking different languages organized narratives differently, but not to the degree that distinct "thought-worlds" emerged. Each language accomplished the task at hand, and all the narrators understood the connections. Language affected verbal style differences, but not cognition. These studies appear to indicate the fairly limited applicability of the Sapir-Whorf hypothesis, at least for children.

Changing the perspective now to the second aspect of language socialization, we can see the important role of language in socializing children into a culture. Research shows again, though, that culture shapes the content and process of such socialization. Language has the characteristic of **indexicality** by which certain linguistic features "index," or point to, the identities, actions, or feelings of the speaker and convey important social information. For example, two ways of making requests exist in Samoan (Ochs 1990).

MULTIPLE CULTURAL WORLDS

Indexing Motherhood in Western Samoa and the United States

Elinor Ochs (1993) compared hundreds of hours of mother–infant "conversations" among Western Samoans and White middle-class (WMC) North Americans. Among the WMC Americans, mothers used three basic verbal strategies: baby talk or other forms of simplification, guessing and negotiating meaning of messages that the child conveys, and praising of the child's accomplishments. Baby talk is culturally widespread, but it is not universal (Helfrich 1979). It shares features with other "simplified registers" such as "teacher talk," "foreigner talk," and talk to the elderly, lovers, and pets. The WMC American mothers' baby talk included restricted vocabulary, baby talk words (the child's own version of words), shorter sentences, simplification of sounds (for example, avoiding consonant clusters in favor of consonant-vowel pairs), avoidance of complex sentences, topical focus on the here-and-now, exaggerated intonation, slower pace, repetition, and providing sentence frames for the child to complete.

Baby talk is particularly amplified in WMC American society because the culture is so child-centered, yet it is primarily a register used by mothers and female caretakers. This child-centeredness also promotes use of mothers' second strategy, strong verbal accommodation of the adult to the child. The WMC mothers, for example, often participated in conversation-like interactions with tiny infants, including greeting exchanges with a newborn. This pattern indicates the mother's willingness to take on the conversational work of both infant and mother. The WMC mothers also responded to children's unintelligible speech by attempting to guess at the meaning: "Guessing involves attempting to formulate the child's intended message, which in turn may entail taking into consideration what the child is looking at, holding, what the child has just said and other clues" (162). In the third strategy, WMC mothers praised their children for activities beyond their competence, things they could not have done without the mother. For example, in joint activities such as a mother and child building a block tower together, the mother praised the child as the sole accomplishing agent, thus denying her participation, and raising the position of the child.

Western Samoan mothers do not use a simplified register when talking with their infants and young children. Samoan has a simplified register used toward foreigners, who historically were missionaries, government representatives, and other people in high social positions. Thus linguistic accommodation is appropriate, "just as a host accommodates to a guest" (160). In the case of a child's unintelligible utterances, Western Samoan mothers ignore them or point out that they are unintelligible. In terms of praising:

> [I]n WMC American interactions, praising is typically unidirectional, in Samoan interactions, praising is typically bidirectional. There is a strong expectation that the first one to be praised will in turn praise the praiser. Typically the praise consists of the phrase "*Maaloo!*" ("Well done!"). Once the first maaloo is uttered, a second *maaloo* is to be directed to the producer of the original *maaloo*. . . . Children in Western Samoa households are socialized through such bidirectional praising practices to articulate the contributions of others, including mothers. (164)

Samoan women have a position of prestige in their relationships with their children. They are accommodated to by their children.

One, the imperative "Give it to me," uses the neutral form of "me" (*Mai ia te a'u*) and sets the meaning of the construction as a demand. The second uses the sympathy-marked form of "me" (*Mai taita*) and indexes that the speaker is begging. How do children gain knowledge of indexes? The answer lies in participation in recurrent communicative events. In contrast to formal language learning in school, learning indexicality is indirect and unconscious (see the Multiple Cultural Worlds box).

Gender codes are also learned through socialization patterns that differ for boys and girls in most cultures. Commonly, in the United States, boys tend to play outside in large groups that are hierarchically structured; their groups have a leader who tells others what to do and how to do it. Boys vie for center stage by telling stories and jokes and by sidetracking or challenging the stories and jokes of others. Boys' games have winners and losers and elaborate systems of rules that are frequently the subjects of arguments.

Preschool children already know much about gender roles and strategies. A boy (center) seeks to dominate a girl in the play area of a day care center in the United States.

Boys often boast of their skill and argue about who is best. Girls play in small groups or in pairs. Within the group, intimacy is the key goal. Sharing turns equally in games, such as jump-rope or hopscotch, is the norm. Many of girls' activities, such as playing house, have no winner or loser. Girls are less likely than boys to be boastful, they don't give orders, and they express their preferences as suggestions. A boy will say, "Gimme that!" and "Get outta here!" A girl will say, "Let's do this, " and "How about doing that?" (Tannen 1990:43–44). This scheme is highly generalized, and exceptions to the two patterns among both boys and girls are common enough to warrant separate attention. Nevertheless, for many boys and girls, it seems to hold true and to have effects on their discourse. Girls grow up learning to use "assimilative" codes that create connections among similarities, traditions, and contexts. Boys learn speech that is more task-oriented and assertive. Girls use more indirect speech and boys use more direct speech.

DISCOURSE, IDENTITY, AND POWER

The work of many sociolinguists has involved studying discourse (or talk) in particular domains in terms of power dynamics, how people of different groups convey meaning, and how miscommunication occurs. Discourse styles and content provide clues about a person's social background, age, gender, and status. Consider what cultural information can be gleaned simply from the following a bit of a conversation:

"So, like, you know, Ramadan?"

"Yeah."

"So I'm like talking to *X,* you know, and like she goes, 'Hey Ramadan starts next week.'

"And I'm like, what do you say, Happy Ramadan, Merry Ramadan?" (Agar 1994:95)

If you thought that the speakers were college students, you were correct. They were young women who were probably born in the United States, native English speakers likely to be White, and non-Muslim. Anthropologists have studied such conversations in varied contexts, from cursing someone out to telephone conversations to chiefly speeches.

Children's Disputes

Children's dispute styles in different cultures reveal how argumentation is learned and how power dynamics are played out. Comparative research on children's disputes shows that argument style is culturally learned. For example, among Hindi-speaking Indian children of Fiji, overlapping is the norm, with little regard for strict turn-taking (Lein and Brenneis 1978). Other work on turn-taking versus overlapping styles indicates that offended feelings can arise when turn-takers try to converse with overlappers. The turn-taker feels that the overlapper is rude, and the overlapper feels that the turn-taker is distant and unengaged.

An article entitled "You Fruithead!" presents an analysis of children's arguments using data gathered among White, middle-class children of western Massachusetts (Brenneis and Lein 1977). The children were asked to do role plays, for example, arguing about giving back a ball or discussing who is smarter. Comparison of the role-play data with natural arguments showed a high level of congruence, although the role plays did have somewhat greater formality and rule-following. Prominent stylistic strategies during an argument included use of volume, speed, and stress and intonation. Elevated volume was prominent, although sometimes an echo pattern of a soft statement followed by a soft response would occur. Acceleration of speed was common among older children, and less so among younger children. Strict adherence to turn-taking was followed, with no overlapping. Stress and intonation are used in rhythmical patterns, sometimes with a demand for rhyming echoes as in:

You're skinny.
You're slimmy.
You're scrawny.
You're ... I don't know.

The last line indicates defeat because the child was unable to come up with a meaningful term that echoed the word "scrawny. " In terms of content, most arguments began with an assertion such as "I'm stronger," which calls for an identical or escalated assertion such as "*I'm* Stronger," or "I'm the strongest in the world." Many of the children's arguments involved insults and counterinsults. Often the argument ends with the loser being placed at a loss for a response.

Adolescent Girls' "Fat Talk"

In the United States, Euro-American adolescent girls' conversations exhibit a high level of concern with their body weight and image through talk (Nichter and Vuckovic 1994). A study of 253 girls in the eighth and ninth grades in two urban high schools of the southwest reveals the contexts and meanings of "fat talk." Fat talk usually starts with a girl commenting, "I'm so fat." The immediate response from her friends is, "No, you're not." Girls in the study say that fat talk occurs frequently throughout the day. The following representative conversation between two fourteen-year-olds was recorded during a focus-group discussion:

Jessica: I'm so fat.
Toni: Shut up, Jessica. You're not fat—you know how it makes you really mad when Brenda says she's fat?
Jessica: Yeah.
Toni: It makes me really mad when you say that cuz it's not true.
Jessica: Yeah, it is.
Toni: Don't say that you're fat. (112)

Girls who use fat talk are typically not overweight and are not dieting. The weight of the girls in the study was within "normal" range, and none suffered from a serious eating disorder. Fat talk sometimes functions as a call for positive reinforcement from friends that the initiator is an accepted group member. In other cases, it occurs at the beginning of a meal, "especially before eating a calorie-laden food or enjoying a buffet-style meal where an individual is faced with making public food choices" (115). In this context, fat talk is interpreted as functioning to absolve the girl from guilt feelings and to give her a feeling that she is in control of the situation.

Cultural Cuing in the Medical Interview

Subtle differences in linguistic patterns between speakers of different languages or dialects can lead to serious miscommunication. For example, health care providers who speak standard English often misinterpret messages conveyed to them by speakers of Mohawk English (Woolfson et al. 1995). Linguistic cues are words or phrases that preface a remark to give the speaker's attitude toward what is being said, especially the degree of confidence in it. Standard English includes cues such as "maybe" and "in my opinion." Three functions of cuing exist in Mohawk English. They may indicate the speaker's unwillingness or inability to verify the certainty of a statement; respect for the listener; or the view of Mohawk religion that health is in the hands of the creator and any statement about health must acknowledge human limitations. A striking feature of medical interviews conducted among the Akwesasne (St. Regis) of upper New York was the presence of cuing. Here is a typical example:

Interviewer: What were the other kinds of diseases that people talked about in the past?
Informant: Hmm ... That [tuberculosis] ... was mostly, it well ... they always said cirrhosis.... *It seems* like no matter what anybody died from ... if they drank, it was cirrhosis. *I don't know* if anybody *really* knew a long time ago what anybody *really* died from. Even if the doctor requested an autopsy, the people would just say no ... you know ... it won't be done. So *I don't* think it was ... you know ... it was just what the doctor thought that would go down on the death certificate. (506)

The many cues may appear to health care practitioners as indecisiveness or noncooperation. These interpretations are incorrect, given the rules that the speakers are following about the validity of statements, humility, and religious belief.

HUMAN PARALANGUAGE

Human communication involves a range of nonverbal forms, including tone of voice, silence, and the full gamut of body language from posture to dress to eye movements. Referred to collectively as paralanguage, these ways of communication follow patterns and rules just like verbal language. Like verbal language, they are learned—often unconsciously—and, without learning, one will be likely to experience communication errors, sometimes funny and sometimes serious. Like verbal language, they vary cross-culturally and intraculturally.

Silence as Communication

The use of silence can be an effective form of communication, but its messages and implications differ cross-culturally. In Siberian households, the lowest status person is the in-marrying daughter, and she tends to speak very little (Humphrey 1978). However, silence does not always indicate powerlessness. In American courts, comparison of speaking frequency between the judge, jury, and lawyers shows that lawyers, who have the least power, speak most, while the silent jury holds the most power (Lakoff 1990:97–99). Native Americans tend to be silent more often than Euro-American speakers. Many outsiders, including social workers, have misinterpreted this as either reflecting their sense of dignity, or, more insultingly, a lack of emotion or intelligence.

How wrong and ethnocentric such judgments are is clearly revealed by a study of silence among the Western Apache of Arizona (Basso 1972 [1970]). The Western Apache use silence in four contexts. First, when meeting a stranger, someone who cannot be identified, especially at fairs, rodeos, or other public events, it is considered bad manners to speak right away. That would indicate interest in something like money, or work, or transportation: possible reasons for exhibiting such bad manners. Second, silence is important in the early stages of courting. Sitting in silence and holding hands for several hours is appropriate. Speaking "too soon" would indicate sexual willingness or interest. That would be immodest. Third, when children come home after a long absence at boarding school, parents and children should meet each other with silence for about fifteen minutes rather than rushing into a flurry of greetings. It may be two or three days before sustained conversations are initiated. Last, a person should be silent when "getting cussed out," especially at drinking parties. An underlying similarity of all these contexts is the uncertainty, ambiguity, and unpredictability of the social relationships. Rather than chattering to "break the ice," the Apache response is silence. The difference between the Apache style and the Euro-American emphasis on quick and continuous verbal interactions in most contexts can cause cross-cultural misunderstandings. Outsiders, for example, have misinterpreted Apache parents' silent greeting of their returning children as bad parenting or as a sign of child neglect.

Kinesics

Kinesics refers to the study of communication that occurs through body movements, positions, facial expressions, and spatial behavior. Just like verbal language, nonverbal language has rules for correct usage, possibilities for code-switching, and cross-cultural variation. Serious misunderstandings of body language can easily happen because, like verbal language and international forms of sign language, it is based on arbitrary symbols. Different cultures may emphasize different "channels" more than others: some are more touch-oriented than others, for example, or use facial expressions more. Eye contact is something valued in Euro-American conversations, but in many

Nonverbal communication in Japanese culture is especially marked by the frequent use of bowing. Two Japanese men in business suits meet each other, bow, and exchange business cards.

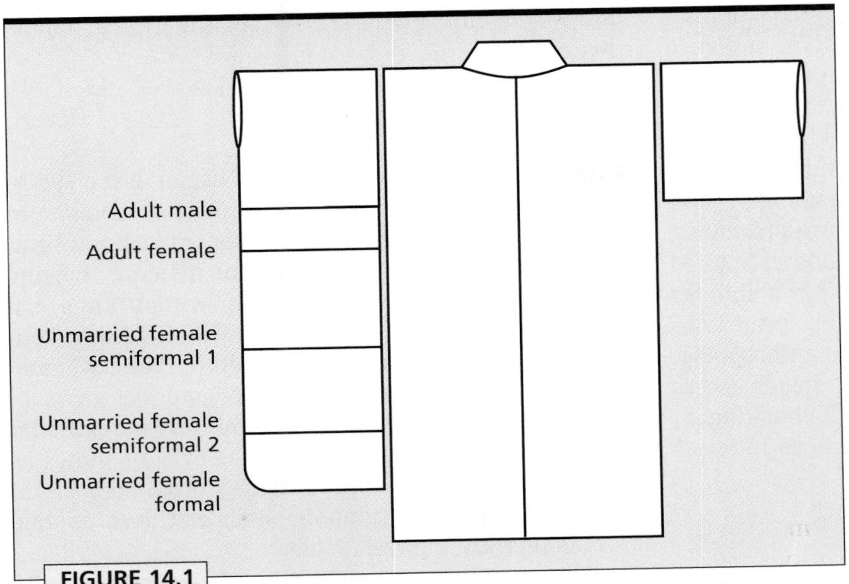

FIGURE 14.1

The Meanings of Kimono Sleeve Length.
(*Source:* From Liza Dalby, *Kimono*. New Haven: Yale University Press, 1993. © Yale University Press. Used with permission.)

Asian contexts, direct eye contact could be considered rude or possibly also a sexual invitation. Nonverbal communication is important in indexing social relationships, especially dominance and accommodation, or positive versus negative feelings.

Dress and Looks

Manipulation of the body is a way of sending messages. Marks on the body, clothing, and hair styles convey a range of messages about age, gender, sexual interest or availability, profession, wealth, and emotions. In the United States, gender differentiation begins in the hospital nursery with the color coding of blue for boys and pink for girls. In Japan, the kimono carries an elaborate system for coding gender, life cycle stage and formality of the occasion (see Figure 14.2):

> Ceremonial kimonos worn by unmarried women stand out by virtue of their sleeves, vivid colors, and busy designs. Kimono length of sleeve refers to a dimension that Western clothing lacks. For us, long or short sleeves mean the total length of the tube of sleeve material. For kimono the dimension is standardized just above the wristbone; the 'depth' of the bag of the sleeve is the important, variable part. Miss's ceremonial kimono takes its name, furisode, from its deep fluttering sleeves. In full-blown furisode, sleeves reach to the ankles. There are also ko- (little) and chū- (mid) versions of furisode, reflecting lesser degrees of formality.... The cultural dimension of social responsibility varies in inverse proportion to the depth of one's kimono sleeve—the more responsibility (adult males), the shorter the sleeve (Dalby 1993:195–196).

Messages conveyed through dress, like other linguistic cues, have the property of arbitrariness. Consider the different meaning of the new veiling in Egypt and Kuwait. The new veiling of Kuwaiti women is a nationalist message that distinguishes wealthy, leisured, and honorable Kuwaiti women from poor, laboring, immigrant women workers. Consider, in contrast, the practice and meaning of veiling in Egypt, a comparatively "moderate" nation in terms of Muslim values. In 1962, women gained the right to vote and they increasingly entered the work force. Recent economic decline, however, has put pressure on women to retreat to the domestic domain. The new veiling movement in Egypt emerged in the late 1970s as the economy declined (MacLeod 1992). Egyptian women who are veiling, like Kuwaiti women, have adopted the head scarf rather than full traditional veiling. But the new veiling in Egypt is done mainly by women from the lower and middle economic levels, where it has been adopted as a way for working-class women to accommodate to pressures from Islamic fundamentalism to veil, while preserving their right to keep working outside the home. The scarf says, "I am a good Muslim and a good wife/daughter."

MASS MEDIA

Mass media usually refers communication via electronic media such as radio, television, film, and recorded music or the print media of newspapers, magazines, and popular literature (Spitulnik 1993). Media anthropology is an important emerging area in cultural anthropology, with a research and applied focus (Allen 1994). In terms of research, media anthropologists study the media process, content, audience response, and social effects of media presentations. Media anthropology seeks to bring together the interests and goals of both anthropology and the media by promoting a contextualized view. In journalism, for example, media anthropology promotes going beyond the reporting of crises and other events to presenting a more holistic, contextualized story. Another applied goal is to disseminate more of anthropology's findings to the general public via radio, television, print journalism, magazines, and the Internet. An anthropological critique of mass media asks to what degree access to its messages are mind-opening and liberating or propagandizing and controlling, and whose interests the media are serving.

The Media Process: Studying War Correspondents

Anthropologist Mark Pedelty has devoted attention to the media process (meaning the study of who creates media messages and how they are disseminated) in his book, *War Stories* (1995), in which he examines the culture of war correspondents in El Salvador. He finds that their culture is highly charged with violence and terror: "War correspondents have a unique relationship to terror, however, a hybrid condition that combines voyeurism and direct participation.... They need terror to realize themselves in both a professional and spiritual sense, to achieve and maintain their culture identity as 'war correspondents'" (2). Pedelty researched a range of topics, including status differences between regular staff correspondents and "stringers" (freelancers who sell their stories where they can), events such as press conferences, the way reporters track down stories, news censorship, cultural differences in attachment to the ideal of objective reporting, and war correspondents' mental health (they tend to have frequent bad dreams and burnout). He probes the psychological ambivalence of war correspondents who are often accused of making a living from war and violence and who become dependent on the continuation of war for their livelihood. Even the Salvadoran correspondents, whose country was being racked by violence, worried that the end of the war would also mean the end of their ability to support their families. Pedelty also addresses media censorship, direct and indirect, and how it affects what stories readers receive and the way events are described (see the Critical Thinking box).

Television Studies

Ethnographic studies of television began in the 1980s. Along with related research done by scholars in English, comparative media studies, and communication studies, a substantial body of material is being amassed that situates television within its social context. A major question is how television both determines culture and reflects culture. The basic theoretical tension between structure and agency is of key importance in this area. Most anthropological and related studies of television treat television shows as "texts" that can be approached through analysis of content, dominant symbols, and plot just as one would analyze a novel or play.

Ethnographic research within a Japanese television station provided one anthropologist with insights into the social organization of the workplace and how it mirrors the messages put forth through television programming (Painter 1996). Gender dynamics form the basis of his analysis, although Painter explains that was not his original research plan:

> At the beginning of my research on how producers and directors create television in Japan, I envisioned a rather macho sort of political analysis that would identify influential individuals and groups, study factions and schisms, and chart the symbols and strategies that made up everyday life in the television station hereafter referred to as "ZTV"). However, this approach soon showed gender to be a key feature of company life. Fascinated, I paid close attention to the many ways men and women deployed representations of gender within the television station, and I tried to make sense of Japanese television programming in reference to this ethnographic grounding. (46)

At ZTV, men outnumber women, with close to 90 percent of the full-time employees (*shain*) being men. Shain women rarely occupy positions of power or even minimal authority. At the time of the research, no woman had reached the level of section manager, the lowest managerial position in the company. A pervasive ideology exists among the male employees, especially the senior ones, that depicts women as inherently inferior workers. As the president of ZTV commented one afternoon, "[B]asically, compared to men, women are less intelligent, they have less phys-

CRITICAL THINKING

A Tale of Two Stories: Assessing Institutional Influence on News Reporting

During the early period of Mark Pedelty's (1995) fieldwork, he talked with an experienced European reporter about how she alters her story depending on which newspaper she is writing for. She showed him computer printouts of two reports she had recently written about the same event, one for a European news institution and the other for a U.S. newspaper. She pointed out that the two reports were strikingly different.

The U.S. Report

Leftist rebels in El Salvador have admitted that one of their units may have executed two U.S. servicemen after their helicopter was shot down last Wednesday. An official FLMN rebel statement issued yesterday said two rebel combatants had been detained, "under the charge of suspicion of assassinating wounded prisoners of war."

The U.S. helicopter was downed in the conflictive eastern province of San Miguel as it was flying back to its base in Honduras. One pilot was killed in the crash, but a Pentagon autopsy team concluded that the other two servicemen in the helicopter were killed execution-style afterwards. Civilians confirmed that the two servicemen had survived the crash, although no one actually saw the actual execution.

"The FMLN has concluded that there are sufficient elements to presume that some of the three, in the condition of wounded prisoners, could have been assassinated by one or various members of our military unit," said the rebel statement. It also said that their investigations had determined that their initial information from units on the ground was false.

At first the guerrillas said the bodies of the Americans had been found in the helicopter. Then they said that two of the three had survived the crash but later died of wounds. Salvadoran officials have said that if the Americans were executed the guerrillas should hand over those responsible. The call was echoed by Rep. Joe Maokley (D-Mass), the Chairman of a congressional special task force on El Salvador.

"We should expect and we should demand that the FMLN turn over to the judicial authorities those responsible, if not this lack of action will have serious consequences," he said.

But the rebel statement made no promises to do that. "If responsibility for the crime is proved, the FMLN will act with all rigor, in conformity with our normal war justice," read the statement. The rebels said that because of the nationality of the victims, the investigations would be carried out publicly. The rebels also defended shooting down the helicopter which they said was flying in "attack position" in a conflicted zone. The UH1H Huey helicopter is the same model as those used by the Salvadoran army and was flying very low to evade anti-aircraft missiles.

The rebel statement did not say whether those detained were in charge of the guerrilla unit which shot down the helicopter. Western diplomats believe it unlikely the unit would have time to radio for orders. The hilly terrain also made radio communication over any distance difficult.

A U.S. embassy spokesman in San Salvador said State Department and embassy officials are studying the rebel statement.

In the last few days the rebels have privately sounded out United Nations officials about the possibility of setting up an independent commission made up of U.S. and U.N. investigators as well as the FMLN, according to a senior rebel source. However, no public proposal has been made.

The killings have opened up a debate in Washington as to whether another $42.5 million in military aid to El Salvador, frozen by Congress last October, should be released. The money was withheld in protest at the lack of progress in investigating the murders of six Jesuit priests by elite army soldiers a year ago. (The final four paragraphs concern the Jesuit murder case.)

The European Report

Nestled amid the steep mountains of Northern Chalatenango province, a simple wooden cross on a hill marks the grave of a teenage guerrilla fighter. There is no name on the grave. None of the villagers from the nearby settlement of San Jose Las Flores who buried his body two years ago knew what he was called. In life the young guerrilla had little in common with three North American servicemen who were killed last month after the rebels shot down their helicopter. They were enemies on opposite sides of a bitter war. But they shared a common death. They were all killed in cold blood after being captured.

When the young rebel was killed two years ago, I remember taking cover behind the wall of the church of San Jose Las Flores. One moment I was watching two adolescent guerrilla fighters sipping from Coke bottles and playing with a yo-yo. Then I remember seeing soldiers running, crouching, and shooting across the square. The crack of automatic rifle fire and the explosion of grenades was deafening in the confined space.

The whole incident lasted about twenty minutes. As soon as the soldiers left, whooping and yelling victory cries, we ran across the square to find the body of one of the teenage guerrillas still twitching. The villagers said that he had been wounded and surrendered. The soldiers had questioned him—and then finished him off at close range in the head. The bullet had blown off the top of his skull.

I remember clearly the reaction of the then U.S. ambassador when asked about the incident. "That kind of incident cannot be condoned," he said, "but I was a soldier, I can understand—it happens in a war." In a country where tens of thousands have been killed, many of them civilians murdered by the U.S. backed military or by right wing death squads, there was no suggestion of any investigation for the execution of a prisoner.

At the beginning of January of this year a U.S. helicopter was shot down by rebel ground fire in Eastern El Salvador. The pilot died in the crash. But two other U.S. servicemen were dragged badly wounded from the wreckage by the rebels. Before the guerrillas left they finished off the two wounded Americans execution style with a bullet in the head.

The present U.S. ambassador referred to the guerrillas in this incident as "animals." The killings made front page news internationally and provided the climate needed by President Bush to release forty-two and a half million dollars of military aid, which was frozen last October by Congress. U.S. lawmakers wanted to force the Salvadoran army to make concessions in peace talks and clean up its human rights record.

The two incidents highlight a fact of political life in El Salvador, recognized by all, that it is not worth killing Americans. Until the helicopter incident, in more than a decade of civil war the rebels have killed only six U.S. personnel. They have a deliberate policy of not targeting Americans, despite the fact that most guerrillas have a deep hatred of the U.S. government. As many have been killed by the U.S.' own allies. Extreme groups in the military, who resent U.S. interference, murdered four U.S. church workers and two government land reform advisers in the early 1980s.

In fact the rebels, because of the outcry and the policy implications in Washington have had to admit guilt in the helicopter incident. They have arrested two of their combatants and say they will hold a trial. They have clearly got the message.

Up until the Gulf War El Salvador has easily seen the most prolonged and deepest U.S. military commitment since Vietnam. However, it is a commitment for which few Americans have felt the consequences.

Source: Mark Pedelty, *War Stories: The Culture of Foreign Correspondents* pp. 9–12. New York: Routledge Inc, 1995. Used with permission.

Critical Thinking Questions

- What are the differences in content between the U.S. and the European news reports? (Consider the use and order of "facts," writer's voice, frame, use of quotations.)
- Are these two reports giving the same message in two different ways, or are they contradictory?
- What might be the audience response to each, and how might the writing of each report lead to a possibly different response?
- Would an anthropologist have interpreted and reported the helicopter incident differently from the journalist's reports?

ical strength, even their bodily structures are different—that is the philosophy I hold to—but in order to show that the company president is *not* a male chauvinist, we are also hiring women. They are people too, after all. While they may have certain limitations, there must also be 'territories' where they can make use of their abilities, too" (47). Many of the female employees at ZTV are temporary workers, pretty women who "adorned every office, tending the three pseudo-domestic zones of the Japanese workplace: the copy machine, the tea area, and the word processors" (51). These "flowers of the workplace" were occupied with answering the phone, sorting postcards from viewers, serving tea, and generally making the male employees feel important. Their behavior was consistently pleasant and subservient, and their dress stylish (compare this with the discussion of Japanese hostess clubs described in Chapter 6). Although these women had the lowest status in the station, they also had some freedom to joke about social hierarchies in a way that no shain woman would.

A temporary worker named Tami was unusual in having been at the station for eight years, since most temps leave after a few months or a year. Tami is the star of the "elevator incident." One of the company elevators made a loud buzz whenever when it was too full. That was a signal for the lowest-ranking person to get off. Painter comments, "I was struck by the alacrity with which the hierarchies were computed and enacted at such times; figuring out who was lowest on the totem pole was done quickly and automatically" (53). But the "elevator incident" was different:

> One day Tami-*chan* was riding the elevator up towards the production department. When it stopped at the second floor, our department manager, Mr. Ohira, got on. The elevator sounded BZZZZZ. Before we could decide who was to get off the elevator, Tami-*chan* accused in a loud voice, "Wasn't it you, Mr. Ohira?"... As if by reflex, the startled *buchō* jumped off the elevator and began the long walk up to the sixth floor. The doors closed and the elevator began to rise in stunned silence until, all together, we burst out in laughter!! (53)

A strong parallel appears between the way female temporary workers are employed to compliment and serve men and be harmonious and beautiful, and the way women are used on Japanese television to listen to and agree with men. Women on television provide harmony through their roles in maintaining warm human relations, not (like men) struggling for dominance and superiority. But, like the temporary workers, some women presented on television make fun of the status quo through parody and play—as long as it does not go too far. The limits are clearly defined.

The primary audience for Japanese television is the category of *shufu,* housewives. People at ZTV were preoccupied with the characteristics and preferences of shufu. They had devised six categories, ranging from the strongly self-assertive "almighty housewife" to the "tranquil and prudent" housewife. A popular form of programming for housewives is the *hōmu dorama,* the "home drama" or domestic serial. These serials consistently represent traditional values such as filial piety and the proper role of the daughter-in-law in regard to her mother-in-law. Caring for the aged has become a prominent theme that supplies the central tension for many situations in which women have to sort out their relationships with each other. In contrast, television representations of men emphasize their negotiation of social hierarchies within the workplace and other public organizations. While the dominant mode of representation puts women in traditional domestic roles, many women in contemporary Japan are rejecting such shows. In response, producers are experimenting with new sorts of dramas in which women are shown as active workers and aggressive lovers—anything but domesticated housewives. One such show is a ten-part serial aired in 1992 called *Selfish Women.* The story concerns three women: an aggressive single businesswoman who faces discrimination at work, a young mother who is raising her daughter alone while her photographer husband lives with another woman, and an ex-housewife who divorced her husband because she found home life empty and unrewarding. There are several male characters, but except perhaps for one, they are depicted as less interesting than the women. The show's title is ironic. In Japan, women who assert themselves are often labeled "selfish" by men. The lead women in the drama use the term in a positive way to encourage each other: ... "Let's become even more selfish!"... Painter comments that, "though dramas like *Selfish Women* are perhaps not revolutionary, they are indicative of the fact that telerepresentations of gender in Japan are changing, at least in some areas." (69)

Similar issues arise in the study of film-making and content analysis of the films themselves. A particular genre of Hollywood films is discussed next.

Orientalism in American Popular Culture

Literary critic Edward Said's books *Orientalism* (1979 [1978]) and *Culture and Imperialism* (1993) exposed the links between English and French colonial expansion of the eighteenth century in the Middle East and Asia and the way the colonialists represented colonized peoples in literature, art, and music. His term orientalism, a form of racism, refers to the highly reductionist stereotypes that were employed:

- The Orient (including the Middle East and Asia) was depicted as irrational, childlike, depraved, over-fertile and "different."
- The Orient is passive and voiceless; it cannot depict or present itself.
- The Orient is timeless and uniform.
- The Orient, while desirable, is also to be feared—for example, China as the Yellow Peril, the Mongol hordes—or controlled by pacification, research and development, or outright occupation if necessary.

In sum, Orientalist representations were self-serving for colonial enterprise. They were also inaccurate, totalizing, and projections of Europeans' repressed desires. Colonialism, strictly speaking, is largely something of the past. However, neocolonialism, through which certain world powers control other states through economic and political ties, replicates in many ways the colonialism that existed before World War II. After World War II, a turning point in global power relations, the United States eclipsed the United Kingdom and France as the world's primary dominating Western power. Said's approach says that dominating powers tend to depict "others" that they seek to conquer and control in Orientalist ways, as listed above. Is the United States representing other countries and cultures in Orientalist ways? A look at examples of popular culture reveals that they are, in fact, full of Orientalist themes.

Since World War II, Hollywood films that depict Asia or relations between Americans and Asians conform to Said's model and create a mythic image of Asia that empowers the West and rationalizes Euro-American authority over the Asian "other" (Marchatti 1993). Romance and sexuality provide the metaphoric justification for this domination. Films of the twentieth century that have Asian themes can be categorized into the following types:

- *Rape fantasy:* These films feature the rape or threat of rape of a White woman by a villainous Asian man.
- *Threat of captivity:* The major theme is the abduction of a woman by an alien and villainous Asian culture; subthemes are White slavery, a captive forced into prostitution, or a captive (missionary or nurse) who is threatened by a bandit or warlord
- *The seductive East:* The entire continent of Asia is metaphorically feminized and becomes an exotic, veiled, beckoning woman who can satisfy the male Westerner's desires. The female is the metaphor for the land that is available for Western penetration.
- *The White knight:* A White man rescues the Asian woman from a stifling or confining situation; examples include "Love is a Many-Splendored Thing" and "The World of Suzie Wong."

Lurking beneath these themes is the overarching message of Asia as both desirable and dangerous.

Orientalism has also been located in American rock and roll. Ellie Hisama, an Asian American scholar, analyzed the contents of several popular songs of the 1980s. Orientalist images abound. She comments on one: "Listening to John Mellencamp's 'China Girl,' a pop song in which a white male narrator attempts to woo an Asian female, I, an Asian-American female, am feeling fairly troubled ... [but] many people will not share my discomfort.... [They would say]: "So it's a love song sung by a white guy to a Chinese girl, but what's wrong with a little interracial romance?" (1993:91). In the song, the white male narrator asks a Chinese "girl" to take him to her "jasmine place" and thereby cool him. Likening her to a china doll, he assures her that he won't break her if she takes him into her world.

American comic books are Orientalist to a high degree. An analysis of 215 American comic books for Arab stereotypes found 218 Arab-type characters, but not one of these was a hero or heroine (Shaheen 1994). Some are "moderates" who play passive and minor roles, but overall, Arabs are villains of three types: the repulsive terrorist, the sinister sheikh, and the rapacious bandit. At least fifty instances of terrorism were found. For example, in "Batman: A Death in the Family":

> This four-part series begins as the Joker escapes from a mental hospital. He plans to sell Arab terrorists a nuclear Cruise missile and concludes a nuclear arms deal with Jamal, the terrorist leader. One of the Joker's entourage asks, "You got the money from these BANDITS-IN-BEDSHEETS?" Jamal appears overweight and double-chinned, his mouth permanently fixed in a sneer. Jamal is prepared to fire his new toy missile immediately. His intended target? Tel Aviv! (124)

In the United States, comic books are read weekly by more than 150 million children and young adults. More than just entertainment, comic books are an important part of children's political socialization.

LANGUAGE AND SOCIAL CHANGE

Languages change constantly, sometimes slowly and in small ways, other times rapidly and dramatically. Most of us are scarcely conscious of such changes. Colonialism was a major force of change. Not only did colonial powers declare their own language as the language of government, business, and higher

VOICES

On Decolonising the Mind, by Ngũgĩ wa Thiong'o

I was born into a large peasant family: father, four wives and about twenty-eight children.... We spoke Gĩkũyũ in and outside the home. I can vividly recall those evenings of story-telling around the fireside.... Our appreciation of the suggestive magical power of language was reinforced by the games we played with words through riddles, proverbs, transpositions of syllables, or through nonsensical but musically arranged words....

And then I went to school.... English became the language of my formal education. In Kenya, English became more than a language: it was *the* language ... one of the most humiliating experiences was to be caught speaking Gĩkũyũ in the vicinity of the school. The culprit was given corporal punishment—three to five strokes of the cane on bare buttocks—or was made to carry a metal plate around the neck with inscriptions such as I AM STUPID or I AM A DONKEY. Sometimes the culprits were fined money they could hardly afford.... The attitude to English was the exact opposite: any achievement in spoken or written English was highly rewarded; prizes, prestige, applause....

So what was the colonial imposition of a foreign language doing to us children? The real aim of colonialism was to control the people's wealth.... But its most important area of domination was the mental universe of the colonised.... The images of this world and his place in it implanted in a child take years to eradicate, if they ever can be.

Source: Hirschberg, *One World, Many Cultures,* 402–409.

education, but often direct steps were taken to suppress indigenous languages and literatures (see the Voices box).

National policies of cultural assimilation of minorities have also led to the extinction of many ethnic languages. The Soviet attempt to build a national commitment to communism after the 1930s included mass emigration of Russian speakers into remote areas, where they eventually outnumbered indigenous peoples (Belikov 1994). In some cases, Russian officials visited areas and burned books in local languages. Children were forcibly sent away to boarding schools, where they were taught in Russian. The Komi, an indigenous group who spoke a Finno-Ugric language, traditionally formed the majority population in their area north of European Russia on the banks of the lower Pechora River. Russian immigration brought in greater numbers of people than the original population and with it the use of Russian in schools. All Komi became bilingual. The Komi language was so heavily influenced by Russian that it now may be extinct.

Efforts to revive or maintain local languages face a difficult challenge. Political opposition often comes from national governments that may fear local identity movements and may not wish to support administratively or financially bilingual or multilingual policies and programs. The English-only movement among political conservatives in the United States is an example of attempts at suppressing linguistic diversity (Neier 1996). Because language is such a vital part of culture, linguistic suppression is equivalent to cultural suppression or ethnocide.

SUMMARY

The origins of linguistic anthropology as a field of anthropology lie in the late eighteenth century attempts to document disappearing Native American languages. Contemporary linguistic anthropologists are more likely to be engaged in studying the formal properties of language, historical linguistics, or the relationship between culture and communication.

One theory of the relationship between culture and language gives primacy to language in determining how speakers think and behave. An alternate view reverses the arrow of causality and says that culture shapes language. Research on human communication strategies and patterns in diverse cultural contexts provides substantial evidence for the latter view. People's use of particular styles of discourse, even their choice of code or dialect, is culturally constructed.

Besides verbal communication, human paralanguage is a prominent aspect of communication and often a source of miscommunication if cultural cues are not understood. The use of silence, body posture, dress and adornment, all convey culturally shaped messages.

Anthropological research on the media process offers insights into the way that messages are chosen and produced for popular consumption. Analysis of images in such popular media as Hollywood movies and comic books reveals pervasive cultural stereotyping.

Global forces in recent times, such as colonialism and neocolonialism, have promoted the spread of powerful languages, notably English, often to the detriment of local languages. Most anthropologists would support a position of linguistic pluralism, which reflects and supports cultural pluralism.

CRITICAL THINKING QUESTIONS

1. In the United States, amplification of terms for "money" is perhaps a parallel to Inuit focal vocabularies for snow. How many terms for money can you think of, and what are their different meanings? What are other possible focal vocabularies in English or other languages you know?
2. Is "fat talk" more characteristic of certain ethnic groups in the United States than others? How might American girls' "fat talk" be related to the fairly recent emergence of anorexia nervosa and bulimia among adolescent girls?
3. Listen to and watch men's and women's conversations in some context. Is men's speech less polite than women's speech? Are there nonverbal markers of politeness?
4. Greetings are a coded area of nonverbal communication. How many culturally different greetings do you know? How might these differences generate misunderstanding?

KEY CONCEPTS

code, p. 339
code-mixing, p. 339
code-switching, p. 339
communication, p. 339
creole, p. 343
dialect, p. 339
displacement, p. 337
focal vocabulary, p. 343
grammar, p. 338
historical linguistics, p. 341
indexicality, p. 344
kinesics, p. 348
language, p. 334
linguistic determinism, p. 343
linguistic relativism, p. 340
observer's paradox, p. 336
paralanguage, p. 340
phoneme, p. 337
phonetics, p. 337
pidgin, p. 342
pragmatics, p. 335
productivity, p. 336
Sapir-Whorf hypothesis, p. 343
sociolinguistics, p. 343
tag question, p. 340

SUGGESTED READINGS

Joy Hendry. *Wrapping Culture: Politeness, Presentation and Power in Japan and Other Societies.* New York: Oxford University Press, 1993. This book explores the pervasive idiom and practice of "wrapping" in Japanese culture, including verbal language, gift-giving, and dress. In verbal language, wrapping involves the use of various forms of respect, indicating social levels of the speakers, and the use of linguistic forms of beautification, which have the effect of adornment.

Robin Toimach Lakoff, *Talking Power: The Politics of Language in Our Lives.* New York: Basic Books, 1990. Lakoff explores strategies of communication and language power-plays in English in the United States, providing examples from courtrooms, classrooms, summit talks, and joke-telling.

William A. Smalley. *Linguistic Diversity and National Unity: Language Ecology in Thailand.* Chicago: University of Chicago Press, 1994. This book describes levels of linguistic variation in Thailand, paying attention to standard Thai in relation to regional languages and local dialects. Also, a detailed analysis of changes in sounds and vocabulary as part of wider processes of social change such as migration and urbanization is provided.

Catherine A. Lutz and Jane L. Collins, *Reading National Geographic.* Chicago: University of Chicago Press, 1993. This study presents the way National Geographic's editors, photographers, and designers select text and images of Third World cultures and how middle-class American readers interpret the material.

Susan U. Philips, Susan Steele, and Christine Tanz, ed., *Language, Gender and Sex in Comparative Perspective.* New York: Cambridge University Press, 1987. An introductory essay, followed by eleven chapters, explores women's and men's speech in Japan, Western Samoa, and Mexico; children's speech in American preschools and in Papua New Guinea; and sex differences in how the brain is related to speech.

CHAPTER 15

Expressive Culture

CHAPTER OUTLINE

WHAT IS ART?
- *Viewpoint:* Seeing Fine Art in Vietnam, by Susan Brownmiller
- *Critical Thinking:* Probing the Categories of Art

STUDYING ART IN SOCIETY
- Focus on the Artist
- Ethnicity, Gender and Power
  - *Multiple Cultural Worlds:* Invisible Hands Crafting Israeli Souvenirs

PERFORMANCE ARTS
- Music and Gender: Balance among the Temiar
- Theater and Myth: Ritual Dance-Drama in India

ARCHITECTURE AND DECORATIVE ARTS
- Architecture and Mode of Production
- Interior Decoration
- Gardens and Flowers

THE ANTHROPOLOGY OF MUSEUMS
- *Multiple Cultural Worlds:* Art Museums and Society in France and the United States
- *Current Event:* "Bilbao to Bid for Guernica"

PLAY AND LEISURE
- Games and Sports as Cultural Microcosm
  - *Voices:* "Childhood Tales of the Hammam," by Fatima Mernissi
- Leisure Travel

CHANGE IN ART AND PLAY
- Effects of Westernization
- Effects of Tourism
- Contemporary Cultural Revival: Return of the Hula
- Post-Communist Transitions

SUMMARY

CRITICAL THINKING QUESTIONS

KEY CONCEPTS

SUGGESTED READINGS

◀ In South Africa, women paint colorful designs on the outside of houses.

The anthropological study of **expressive culture** includes the areas of artistic and leisure activities. Encompassing such topics as cave paintings of paleolithic Europe, architectural styles of Africa, interior decoration in Japan, and basketball in the Caribbean, expressive culture comprises a vast domain. This chapter discusses theoretical approaches in the anthropology of expressive culture, examples of cross-cultural art and play, and directions of change. It should provide many questions to consider when you visit a museum, go to a concert, hear a joke, or attend a sports event in the future.

Archaeologists, linguistic anthropologists, and cultural anthropologists have longstanding and complementary interests in the study of expressive culture. Important questions about prehistory include: When did symbolic thought begin? and What can be considered the first art? Expressive culture, like language, is a form of communication, so strong connections exist between linguistic anthropology and the studies mentioned in this chapter. Physical anthropologists have worked less on this topic, but some have suggested a possible relationship between expressive culture and biology. One argument is that body art and decoration function in a Darwinian way to enhance the reproductive success of people who adorn themselves most attractively (Dissanayake 1992). Dance can be also be viewed as functioning to facilitate in attracting mates. Another area of interest is the question of whether nonhuman primates have an artistic sense. Clear evidence exists that other animals indulge in playful behavior, although not team sports, as far as we know.

But is it "art"?

WHAT IS ART?

Are ancient rock carvings art? Is subway graffiti art? An embroidered robe? A painting of a can of Campbell's soup? Philosophers, art critics, anthropologists, and art lovers have all struggled with the question of what art is. The question of how to define art involves more than mere word games. The way art is defined affects the manner in which a person classifies, values, and treats artistic creations and those who create art. Anthropologists propose broad definitions of art to take into account emic definitions cross-culturally. One definition says that **art** is the application of imagination, skill, and style to matter, movement, and sound that goes beyond the purely practical (Nanda 1994:383). The anthropological study of art considers both the process and the products of such human skill, the variation in art and its preferred forms cross-culturally, and the way culture constructs and changes artistic traditions. The skill that is involved is defined and recognized as such in a particular culture. Such culturally judged skill can be applied to any number of substances and activities and can be considered art: for example, a beautifully presented meal, a well-told story or joke, or a perfectly formed basket. In this sense, art is a human universal, and no culture can be said to lack artistic activity.

Within the general category of art, subcategories exist, sometimes denoting certain eras such as palaeolithic or modern art. Important subcategories are based on medium of expression, for example, graphic or plastic arts (painting, drawing, sculpture, weaving, basketry, and architecture); the decorative arts (interior design, landscaping, gardens, costume design, and body adornment such as hairstyles, tattooing, and painting); performance arts (music, dance, and theater); and verbal arts (poetry, writing, rhetoric, and telling stories and jokes).

A longstanding distinction in English exists between "fine art" and "folk art." The distinctions are based on a Western-centric judgment that defines fine art as rare, expensive art produced by artists usually

VIEWPOINT

Seeing Fine Art in Vietnam, by Susan Brownmiller

Susan Brownmiller was a network television newswriter during the Vietnam/American war and has traveled extensively in Asia. She was commissioned by a travel magazine to write her book on Vietnam, *Seeing Vietnam: Encounters of the Road and Heart* (1994:36–37), from which this passage is taken.

"Fine art" is a hallowed Western European concept rooted in snobbery and defined at its most basic as art that is definitely not practical or useful, or applied decoratively to something that has a utilitarian function, like a pot, a bowl, a chair, a paneled screen, or even a religious icon, if one is a strict purist. It is art for art's sake, created, at least originally, for the pure esthetic enjoyment of aristocratic patrons who could afford to commission and buy the work. . . .

Fine art, however, is a slippery term. It loses meaning when we explore the ruling esthetics of Eastern traditions, of deeply artistic cultures that didn't paint with oils on canvas or make sculptures from blocks of marble. Adding to the confusion, there have been moments in history when the definition of fine art was deliberately exploded, most vividly, after the Russian Revolution, when artists undertook a mission to educate and propagandize, producing Soviet socialist realism. Fine art or not fine art? The debate is not over.

"Skip it," an experienced traveler had said when I'd mentioned Hanoi's Fine Arts Museum. "It's all derivative."

"Go to the Fine Arts. You'll get a great overview of their handicrafts," advised another traveler, who'd been on a Vietnamese-American reconciliation tour.

From the *Lonely Planet* guidebook, an exhaustive, user-friendly tome produced in Australia, I learned that the museum was housed in an old colonial building that used to be the French Ministry of Information. One current highlight, according to the guidebook, was "an incredibly intricate embroidery of Ho Chi Minh reading."

Armed with these tips, I had pretty much eliminated the Fine Arts from my must-see list until I spoke with an assistant curator at the Freer and Sackler Galleries in Washington, a professional in the field of Asian art who had toured the museum with selective eyes, and who showed me how to decode its contents.

I arrived at the stately building, traversed the folk arts, and climbed to the second floor. There they were! Watercolors, pastels, and oils from the 1930s and 1940s, executed during French colonial rule in the French impressionist manner—the poignant, dutiful, and charming results of the *mission civilisatrice* in Indochina. I walked through a roomful of Vietnamese Cézannes, canvas after canvas of romantic, hazy, pastoral visions of calm, sleepy villages and virgin forests in the languorous tropics. Moving to an adjoining room, I found some Vietnamese Mary Cassatts, well-to-do, thoroughly Europeanized ladies posing among the comforts of home in cool summer frocks with their perfectly groomed children.

Down on the first floor, the museum's style and contents underwent a sea change. Here were the large, strident oils from the 1960s and 1970s, the Vietnamese adaptations, under Soviet patronage, to the artistic credo of socialist realism. Sturdy, heroic peasants laboring in the fields. Sturdy, heroic soldiers moving forward in battle, hauling heavy artillery up a mountain. Now and again, on both floors, luminous touches of gold lacquer, a traditional Viet technique that I'm as reluctant as they are to say came from China, highlighted the paintings with a lyrical, otherworldly effect.

So how do you adjudicate the fine arts debate when the overriding influence, in every decade, is cultural imperialism?

Source: Excerpt from *Seeing Vietnam* by Susan Brownmiller.

trained in the Western classical tradition. This is the kind of art that is included in college courses called "Fine Art." The implication is that all other art is less than fine and more appropriately called folk or "ethnic art" or "primitive art" or "crafts" (see the Viewpoint box). Characteristics of Western fine art are: It is created by a formally schooled artist, the product is made for the market (for sale or on commission), the product is clearly associated with a particular artist, the product's uniqueness is valued, and the product is not primarily utilitarian but is rather "art for art's sake." In contrast, all the rest of the world's art that is non-Western and nonclassical is supposedly characterized by the opposite features: It is created by an artist who has not received formal training, it is not produced for the market, the artist is anonymous and does not sign or individually claim the product, and it is made primarily for use in food storage and preparation, ritual, or war. These two categories prompt further thinking as to their adequacy.

Just as all cultures have art, all cultures have a sense of what makes something art versus non-art. The term "esthetics" refers to agreed-upon notions of quality (Thompson 1971:374). Before anthropologists proved otherwise, Western art experts considered that esthetics did not exist or was poorly developed elsewhere. We now know that established criteria for artistic quality exist everywhere regardless of whether they are written down and formalized. Franz Boas, from his wide review of many forms of art in pre-state societies, deduced principles that he claimed were universal for these cultures, especially symmetry, rhythmic repetition, and naturalism. (Jonaitis 1995: 37). These principles do apply in many cases, but they are not as universal as Boas thought they were.

Ethno-esthetics indicates local variations in esthetic criteria. The set of standards concerning wood carving in West Africa illustrates the importance of considering cultural variation (Thompson 1971). Among the Yoruba of Nigeria, esthetic guidelines include the following:

- Figures should be depicted midway between complete abstraction and complete realism so that they resemble "somebody," but no one in particular (portraiture in the Western sense is considered dangerous).
- Humans should be depicted at their optimal physical peak, not in infancy or old age.
- There should be clarity of line and form.
- The sculpture should have the quality of luminosity achieved through a polished surface, the play of incisions and shadows.
- The piece should exhibit symmetry.

A few anthropological studies have also documented intracultural differences in esthetic standards. For example, one anthropologist showed computer-generated graphics to the Shipibo Indians of the Peruvian Amazon and learned that men liked the abstract designs, while the women thought they were ugly (Roe in Anderson and Field 1993:257). If you are wondering why this difference would exist, consider the interpretation of the anthropologist: Shipibo men are the shamans and take hallucinogenic drugs that may give them familiarity with more "psychedelic" images (see the Critical Thinking box).

Yoruba wood carving is done according to esthetic principles that require clarity of line and form, a polished surface that creates a play of light and shadows, symmetry, and the depiction of human figures that are neither completely abstract nor completely realistic and that are shown as adults and never very young or very old.

STUDYING ART IN SOCIETY

The anthropological study of art seeks to understand more than just the products of art, but also who makes it and why, its role in society, and its wider social meanings. Franz Boas was the first anthropologist to emphasize the importance of studying the artist in society. A significant thread in general anthropology's theoretical history—functionalism—also dominated work of the early twentieth century on art. Anthropologists wrote about how paintings, dance, theater, and songs serve to socialize children into the culture; provide a sense of social identity and group boundaries; and promote healing. Art may legitimize

CRITICAL THINKING

Probing the Categories of Art

Probably every reader of this book, at one time or another, has looked at an object on display in a museum or in an art book or magazine and exclaimed, "But that's not art!" (The same applies to music.) As a research project on "what is art," go to the library and take out some books on art from different parts of the world, or go to an art museum and a natural history museum and compare what is on display, or find some recordings of music from different countries. Look carefully at or listen carefully to several pieces. In addition to looking and listening, try to find out something about the objects or songs, who created them, and why they were created.

Critical Thinking Questions

- Which objects or pieces of music would you classify as art or not-art, and why?
- Did some items seem more like fine art and others more like folk art? Which ones? On what did you base your classification?
- Was an artist identified with each object or musical piece?
- Was the object or song created for a particular purpose? If yes, what?
- Did objects or songs from Western traditions fit more in any one category?
- Did you locate any objects or songs from non-Western traditions that seemed to be fine art? If so, what were their characteristics?
- Did you locate any Western objects or songs that could be classified as folk art? If so, what were their defining features?
- Suggest some better ways of classifying these objects and musical pieces, or justify why the categories of fine art and folk art are useful.

political leaders and enhance efforts in war through magical decorations on shields and weapons. Art may serve as a form of social control, as in African masks worn by dancers who represent deities visiting humans to remind them of the moral order. Art, like language, can be a catalyst for political resistance or grounds for ethnic solidarity in the face of the state.

With its breadth of topical interest, the anthropology of art relies on a range of methods in data gathering and analysis. For some research projects, participant observation provides most of the necessary data. In others, participant observation is complemented by collecting and analyzing oral or written material such as video and tape recordings. Some anthropologists have become apprentices in a certain artistic tradition. For example, in undertaking one of the earliest studies of Native American potters of the Southwest, Ruth Bunzel (1972 [1929]) learned how to make pottery and thereby gained important data on what the potters thought constituted good designs. For John Miller Chernoff (1979), learning to play African drums was an important part of gaining rapport during his fieldwork in Ghana.

In contrast, anthropologists who study past traditions, such as palaeolithic art, cannot do participant observation or talk to the artists. They have to rely on indirect interpretation of silent symbols, shapes, colors, and contexts. Ethno-archaeology helps in this endeavor by providing clues about the past from the

In Sumba, Indonesia, Joel Kuipers interviews a ritual speaker who is adept at verbal arts performance.

present. Sheer creative thinking may lead to a new interpretation. One example of this is a recent interpretation of the "Venus" figurines, the first human images from the European Upper Palaeolithic period between 27,000–21,000 BCE (McDermott 1996). Little is known about why these palm-sized statuettes were made or who made them. Stylistically, the figurines have large breasts, abdomens, and buttocks, and small heads, arms, and legs. Past interpretations of this characteristic shape have seen it as intentional distortion to emphasize sexuality and fertility. A new theory proposes that women, especially pregnant women, sculpted these figurines as self-representations. A woman who used herself as a model would have a view of her body very much like that of the figurines (McCoid and McDermott 1996). Some anthropologists trace motif history and diffusion, similar to historical linguistics: Changes in the use of and variation in a particular motif can help expose cultural histories just like sound shifts or grammatical changes. For example, analysis of many stories from Asia about oppressed stepdaughters who end up triumphant and also have small feet has led researchers to believe that the Cinderella tale began in China (given its history of bound feet in certain areas) and spread out from there. Much anthropological interpretation of the products of art (drawings, performance, songs, folktales) and sports has relied on symbolic analysis.

This section presents findings in two important areas of the anthropological study of art: first, the artist, and then a more "functionalist" area—how art, gender, ethnicity, and power are related.

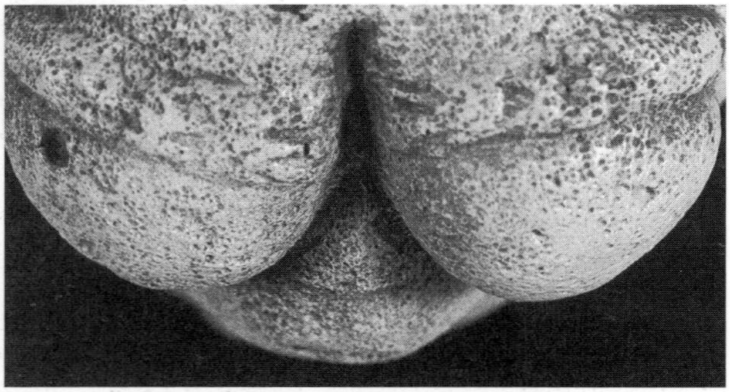

A top-down view of the "Venus" figurine, one of the first human images known. These small statues have often been interpreted as fertility goddesses on the basis of the large breasts, abdomen, and buttocks and small head and arms. These features are said to be intentional distortions of the artist done to emphasize fertility.

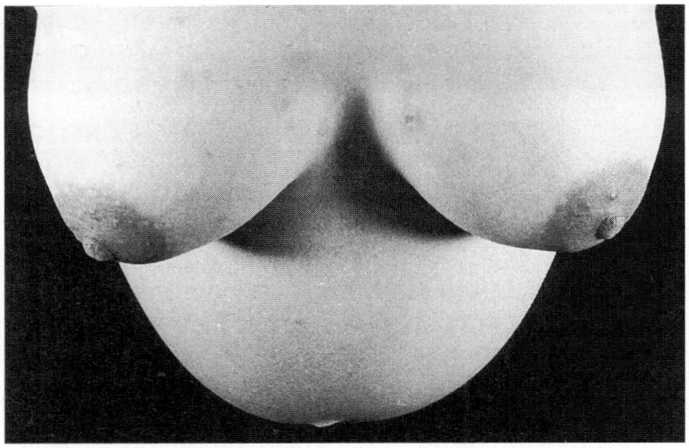

A new theory about the Venus figurines claims that they were self-portraits, crafted by women. A photograph of a pregnant woman looking down at herself presents a shape very like that of the Venus figurines—but the shape is actual, not a distortion.

Focus on the Artist

In the early twentieth century, Boas urged his students to go beyond the study of the products of artistic endeavor and study the artists. The special role of the anthropologist is to add to the understanding of art by studying the process of creating art both within its social context and from the artist's perspective. Ruth Bunzel's (1972 [1929]) study of Pueblo potters is an example of this tradition. She paid attention to the variety of pot shapes and motifs employed and also interviewed individual potters about their personal design choices. One Zuni potter commented, "I always know the whole design before I start to paint" (49). A Laguna potter said, "I made up all my designs and never copy. I learned this design from my mother. I learned most of my designs from my mother" (52).

The social status of artists varies widely. Artists may be revered and wealthy as individuals or groups, or stigmatized and economically marginal. In ancient Mexico, goldworkers were a highly respected group. In Native American groups of the Pacific Northwest coast, male carvers and painters had to be initiated into a secret society, and they had higher status than other men. Often a gender division of artistic involvement exists. Among the Navajo, women weave, while men do silversmithing. In the Caribbean, African-descent women are noted for their carvings of calabashes (large gourds). In the contemporary United States, most famous and successful graphic artists are male, although the profession includes many women. The lives of artists and performers are often are outside the boundaries of mainstream society or challenging the social boundaries.

In Morocco, a *shikha* is a female performer who sings and dances at festivities, including rites-of-passage ceremonies such as birth, circumcision, and marriage (Kapchan 1994). Shikhat (the plural ending is a "t") usually appear in a group of three or four with accompanying musicians. Their performance involves suggestive songs and body movements, including reaching a state of near-possession when they loosen their hair buns. With their long hair waving, they "lift the belt," a special technique accomplished through an undulating movement that rolls the abdomen up to the waist. Their entertainment at these mixed-gender events creates a lively atmosphere as they dance, sing, and draw participants into dancing with them: "[S]hikhat dominate and dictate the emotional tenor of celebrations. Through the provocative movements and loud singing of the shikhat, the audience is drawn up and into a collective state of celebration, their bodies literally pulled into the dance" (93).

In their private lives, shikhat are on the social fringes, leading "loose" lives as single women who transgress rules for proper females. They own property, drink alcohol, smoke cigarettes, and may have several lovers. Most of the shikhat have been rejected by their natal families, and they live alone or in groups. Middle- and upper-class women consider them vulgar and generally distance themselves from them. Shikhat who become successful, widening their performance spheres to larger towns and cities, manage to save money and become landowners and gain economic status. The modern mass media is contributing to an increased status of shikhat as performers. Videocassette recordings of shikhat music are popular, and the Moroccan term *mughanniyya* (singer), is being used to refer to them, implying more status. State-produced television broadcasts carry performances of regional shikhat groups as a way of presenting the diverse cultures of the nation. All of these forces are leading to a reevaluation of the social standing of this ancient art form.

As with other occupations, artists are more specialized in state-level societies. In foraging groups, some people may be singled out as especially good singers, storytellers, or carvers. Generally, however, among foragers, artistic activity is open to all, and artistic products are shared equally by all. With increasing social complexity and a market for art, specialized training is required to produce certain kinds of art and the products are sought after by those who can afford them. Class differences in artistic styles and preferences emerge along with the increasingly complex division of labor (Bourdieu 1984).

Ethnicity, Gender and Power

Art forms and styles, like language, are often associated with particular ethnic groups' identity and sense of pride. For example, the Berbers of highland Morocco are associated with carpets, the Navajo with woven blankets, and the Inuit with stone carving. One anthropological study has revealed how political interests affect "ownership" of ethnic artistic expression (see the Multiple Cultural Worlds box on pages 366 and 367). Another study that looked at a form of popular performance art in a Florida town, male strip dancing, shows how societal power relations between men and women are reinforced in this form of leisure activity (Margolis and Arnold 1993). Advertisements in the media tell women that seeing a male strip dancer is "their chance," "their night out." Going to a male strip show is thus presumably a time of reversal of traditional gender roles in which men are dominant and women submissive. The researchers asked if gender roles are reversed in a male stripper bar, and their answer was "no." Women customers are treated like juveniles, controlled by the manager who tells them how to tip as they stand in line waiting for the show to open, and symbolically humbled in relation to the dancers, who take on the role of lion-tamers, for example. The "dive-bomb" is further evidence that the women are not in charge. The dive-bomb is a particular form of tipping the dancer. The woman customer gets on her hands and knees and tucks a bill held between her teeth into the dancer's g-string.

Not all forms of popular performance are mechanisms of social control and hierarchy maintenance, however. In the United States, for example, urban Black youths' musical performance through rap music can be seen as a form of protest through performance. Their lyrics report on their experience of economic oppression, the danger of drugs, and men's disrespect for women.

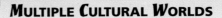

Multiple Cultural Worlds

Invisible Hands Crafting Israeli Souvenirs

Tourists who buy arts and crafts souvenirs rarely learn much about the people who actually made the items. Yet they probably have some mental image of, for example, a village potter sitting at the wheel or a silversmith hammering at a piece of metal in a quaint workshop. Souvenir shops come in different varieties, from basic street stalls that may specialize in a few items such as embroidered clothing or "ethnic" jewelry to carefully designed national emporiums that seek to represent the full range of arts and crafts. An upscale store of the latter category in Israel, called Maskit, caters mainly to tourists (Shenhav-Keller 1993:183). Ethnographic study shows how the sellers "put Israeli society on display via its sovenirs." It also reveals how certain artists and craftspeople are selectively rendered invisible.

The tourist artifact, or souvenir, can be analyzed like a "text" that contains social messages (Clifford 1988; Graburn 1976; Jules-Rosette 1984). Looking at souvenirs this way reveals what people choose to "preserve, value, and exchange" (Clifford 1988:221). Examining the contents of a shop catering to tourists seeking ethnic artifacts and souvenirs exposes the set of choices that have been made about what to display. In the Maskit stores, three central themes in Israeli society are expressed in the choice and presentation of souvenirs: Israel's attitudes toward its ancient and recent past, its view of its religion and culture, and its approach to Arab Israelis and Palestinians. Shelly Shenhav-Keller (1993) conducted participant observation in the original Maskit store in Tel Aviv and had interviews with Jewish Israeli, Arab Israeli, and Palestinian artists and artisans whose crafts were sold there. She provides some historical background on the shop:

> The name "maskit" means "ornament" or "beautiful and aesthetically exciting object" [and] is taken from the Bible. Maskit—The Israel Center for Handicrafts—was founded by Ruth Dayan (then the wife of Moshe Dayan) as a Ministry of Labor project in 1954, shortly after the period of mass immigration when Israel more than doubled its population. Its stated purpose was "to encourage artisans to continue their native crafts in the new surrounding . . . to retain and safeguard the ancient crafts." (183)

Maskit was a success, and a chain of shops was eventually opened. Its status increased and Maskit came to be perceived as an "ambassador of Israel." Dignitaries and delegations who traveled from Israel abroad were equipped with gifts from the shop. Official guests were given Maskit gifts during their visits. The original shop had two floors. The top floor, where the entrance was located, had five sections: fashion (women's clothing, wedding gowns, and dresses with three different styles of Arab embroidery), jewelry, ritual articles (candlesticks, goblets, incense burners), decorative items, and books. The larger lower floor had five thematic sections: the Bar-Mitzvah Corner with prayer-books and other ritual items, the children's corner (with clothing, games, toys, and T-shirts), embroidery section (tablecloths, linens, pillow covers, wallets, eyeglass cases), the carpet section, and a large area for ceramics, glassware, and copperware. Over the years, changes have occurred in who is producing the art sold in Maskit. Many of the original Jewish Israeli artists gained eminence and opened their own shops. Those that continue to supply Maskit specialize in ceramics, jewelry, carpet design, and ritual articles. These pieces are considered to have the status of art and may be displayed as an "individual collection" within the store. The amount of Jewish ethnic art—mainly Yemenite and Bukharan—has diminished as the older artists have aged and their descendants have not taken up the craft. This is most marked in Yemenite embroidery and silversmithing, the crafts that once dominated Maskit. Now, Arab embroidery is sought as a replacement. After the 1967 Six-Day War, Arab Israeli and Palestinian craftsmanship became increasingly available with the incorporation of new areas within Israel, including the Occupied Territories. Most of the Arabs who were absorbed into the souvenir industry became hired laborers in factories and workshops owned by Maskit or by Israeli artisans who sold their works to Maskit:

> An example is the large carpet factory founded by Maskit in one of the Arab villages in Galilee. The plant employed women and men predominantly from this and neighboring villages, mainly in the handweaving of carpets according to patterns prepared by Israeli designers. Other examples include workshops for ritual articles set up in the West Bank, in which Palestinians were employed in artistic work but classified as laborers. (188)

Maskit provides no information about the role of Israeli Arabs or Palestinians. The carpets, for example, are presented as handwoven Israeli carpets. It is not mentioned that Arab Israelis wove them. This lack of acknowledgment can be interpreted as a form of cultural imperialism in which a dominant culture appropriates or transforms the traditions of a less powerful group in its own interests.

PERFORMANCE ARTS

Anthropological study of the variety and patterns of the world's music gives rich insights into many aspects of culture as well as providing enjoyment of the music itself. **Ethnomusicology** is an established field of study linking cultural anthropology and music; it is concerned with musical traditions and change worldwide. Ethnomusicologists study a wide range of topics in addition to music itself: performers of various genres, social status of performers, their training, symbolism of music, the history of music, and issues of power and music.

Music and Gender: Balance among the Temiar

An important topic is the gender differences in access to performance roles in music (for readers interested in approaching this topic as a research question, see Table 15.1). A cultural materialist analysis of this issue would predict that in cultures where gender roles and relationships in society are more egalitarian, access to and meanings in music would be egalitarian as well. This seems to be the case, for example, among the Temiar, a group of Orang Asli forager-hunters of highland Malaysia, whose musical traditions emphasize balance and complementarity between males and females (Roseman 1987). Kinship and marriage rules are relatively flexible and open. Temiar marriages are not arranged, but are based on the mutual desires of each spouse. Marriage may be either village endogamous or exogamous. Descent is bilineal, and marital residence follows no particular rule following a period of bride service. Marriages often end in separation, with the usual pattern for everyone being serial monogamy. Men have a certain edge over women in political and ritual spheres. Men dominate as headmen and as spirit mediums who sing the songs that energize the spirits (although historical records indicate that women have been spirit mediums in the past). In most performances, individual male singers are the nodes through which the songs of spirit-guides enter the community, but women's performance role is significant. For example, the delegation of gender roles as male ini-

Table 15.1
Ten Ethnographic Questions about Gender and Music

1. Are musical materials equally accessible to all members of a culture? Are men encouraged to use certain instruments and repertoires and women others?
2. How is access to power sources within music defined and achieved? Training? Inheritance? Exposure? Ordination? Birthright by gender? Is musical training available to all?
3. Do male and female repertoires overlap, where, and for what reasons?
4. Do performances by women or men achieve different goals? Are they motivated by the same culturally perceived needs?
5. Are the performances of women public, private, or both? Under what conditions? Are women and men allowed to perform together? In what circumstances? To what ends? In co-performance, how are decisions made?
6. How is power wielded in performance? Who manipulates whom? How? How does the "acting out" of values in performance reflect divisions of labor, spirituality, and power? How are these connections rationalized by different groups within a social setting?
7. Do women control their own performances? Do they behave and perform differently among each other than they do in the presence of men? Do women shield parts of their knowledge from men? Why?
8. Are the performances of men and women given equal value? Are they critiqued or praised in the same way? By whom? Based on what criteria?
9. Do women seek to change the balance of power in their communities? Do they accomplish or define these changes through performance?
10. Is dissent acted out through performance? Through what means? With what effect?

Source: Adapted from Robertson 1987.

tial singer and female chorus is sometimes varied when the female chorus itself transforms into a self-contained initiator-respondent unit. One woman sings, and the others respond chorally. Overall, the male spirit medium role is not necessarily of higher priority or status. The leader/chorus distinction establishes "temporal" priority, but overall gender distinctions are blurred through substantial overlap between phrases and through repetition. The performance is one of intergender, community participation with integrated male and female complementary roles as in Temiar society in general.

Theater and Myth: Ritual Dance-Drama in India

Theater is a "form of enactment," related to other forms such as dance, music, parades, competitive games and sports, and verbal art (Beeman 1993). These forms seek to entertain through conscious forms of acting, movement, and words. Cross-culturally, strong connections exist between myth, ritual, and performance. Of the many forms of theater that anthropologists have studied, several combine the use of facial makeup, masks, and costumes to transform an actor into someone (or something) else.

One theatrical tradition that combines these elements in an exuberant blend of mythology, acting, and music is Kathakali ritual dance-drama of southern India (Zarrilli 1990). Stylized hand gestures, elaborate makeup, and costumes contribute to the attraction of these dramas, which dramatize India's great Hindu epics, especially the Ramayana and the Mahabharata. Appreciation of Kathakali cuts across all social classes. Performances were traditionally staged outdoors in a family compound or near a temple, but they are now often held as well in cities on Western-style stages.

Costumes and makeup transform the actor into one of several well-known characters from Indian mythology. The audience can easily recognize the basic character types at their first entrance by "reading" the costuming and makeup. Six basic makeup types exist to depict characters ranging from the most refined to the most vulgar, going along a continuum. Characters such as kings and heroes have green facial makeup, reflecting their high degree of refinement and moral uprightness. The most vulgar characters are associated with black facial makeup and occasionally black beards. Female demons are in this category: Their black faces are dotted with red and white, and they are the most grotesque of Kathakali characters. (One might find parallels to Kathakali in European opera: The performers wear makeup, costumes, and sometimes masks. Opera-goers can recognize themes in the opera based on the use of certain musical instuments that signal particular emotions.)

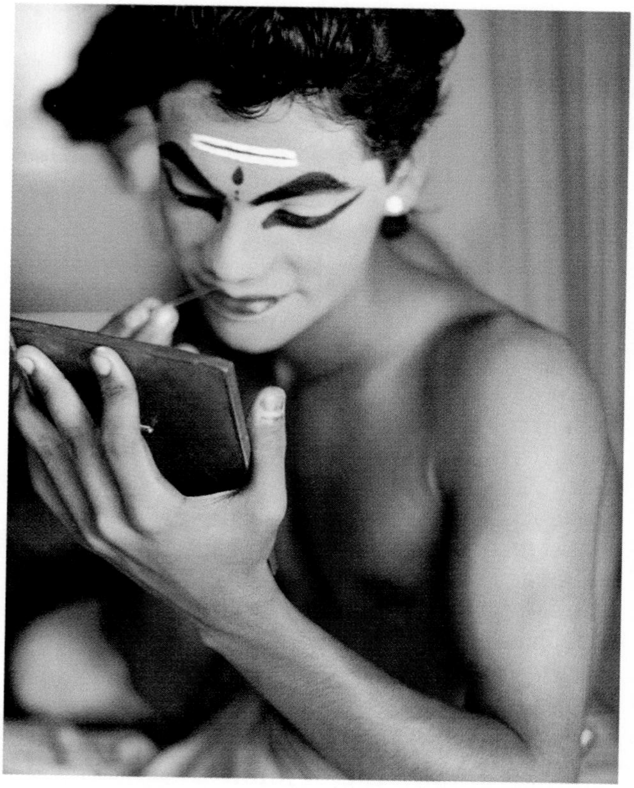

A Kathakali dancer applying makeup before a performance, Kerala, south India.

ARCHITECTURE AND DECORATIVE ARTS

Like other forms of art, architecture is interwoven with other aspects of culture. Architecture may reflect and protect social rank and class differences as well as gender, age, and ethnic differences (Guidoni 1975). Decorative arts—including interior decoration of homes and buildings, and external design features such as gardens—likewise reflect people's social position and also stand as statements of their status and "taste." Local cultures have long defined preferred standards in these areas of expression, but global influences from the West as well as from Japan and, increasingly, non-Western cultures, have been adopted and adapted by other traditions.

Architecture and Mode of Production

Foragers, being nomadic, build dwellings as needed, and then abandon them. Owning little and having few surpluses means that permanent storage structures are not needed. The construction of dwellings does not require the efforts of groups larger than the family unit. Foragers' dwellings are an image of the family and not of the wider society. The dwellings' positioning in relation to each other reflects the relations between families. More elaborate shelters and greater social cohesiveness in planning occur as foraging is combined with horticulture, as in the semipermanent settlements in the Amazon rainforest. People live in the settlement part of the year, but break up into smaller groups that spread out into a larger area for foraging. Important decisions concern location of the site in terms of weather, availability of drinking water, and defensibility. The central plaza must be elevated for drainage, and drainage channels must be dug around the hearths. The overall plan is circular. In some groups, separate shelters are built for extended family groups; in others, they are joined into a continuous circle with connected roofs. In some cases, the headman has a separate and larger shelter.

Pastoralists have designed ingenious portable structures such as the teepee and yert. The teepee is a conical tent made with a framework of four wooden poles tied at the top with thongs, to which are joined other poles to complete the cone; this frame is then covered with buffalo hide. A yert is also a circular, portable dwelling, but its roof is flatter than that of a teepee. The covering is made of cloth. This extremely lightweight structure is easy to set up, take down, and transport, and is highly adaptable to all weather conditions. Encampments often involved the arrangement of the teepees or yerts in several concentric circles, with social status as the structuring principle placing the council of chiefs and the head chief in the center.

In settled agricultural communities where permanent housing is the norm, decoration is more likely to be found in homes. Wall paintings, sculptures, and other features may distinguish the homes of more wealthy individuals. With the development of the state, around 10,000 BCE, urban areas grew larger and showed the effects of centralized planning and power (for example, in grid-style street planning rather than haphazard street placement). The symbolic demonstration of the power, grandeur, and identity of states was—and still is—expressed architecturally through the construction of impressive monuments: temples, administrative buildings, memorials, and museums.

Most world capitals have some character that distinguishes them from others. However, some areas of new construction lack any kind of local identity. Interpretations of urban identity through architecture show that Hong Kong is a good example of the latter category (Abbas 1994). Hong Kong, according to one observer, is having difficulty finding and maintaining some sort of architectural identity and has a dominant look, instead, that is "placeless." Two factors underlie the growth of placeless architecture in Hong Kong. First, Hong Kong has been highly receptive to adopting architectural styles, especially from the metropolitan West. Second, rapid economic development has brought about constant building and rebuilding, retaining little of even the recent past. Such placeless architecture can be found almost anywhere in the world. In the face of such urban development, local forms and styles are declining because of economic pressures for land; in particular, the formerly important small-scale fishing and marketing enterprises are being driven out as they have become less remunerative than before.

Interior Decoration

Studying the way people design and decorate the interior of buildings and homes links cultural anthropologists with people working in other professions and disciplines, including interior design, advertising, and consumer economics. Cultural anthropologists, however, have only recently begun to study seriously the subject of interior decoration, perhaps because of their earlier emphasis on preindustrial cultures in which interior decoration is relatively minor. Mobile foragers obviously have the least interest in, or use for, decorating the interior of shelters that are impermanent and in which people spend little time. Sedentary lifestyles and the increase of surplus goods are important contributing factors to the emergence of attention to interior decoration. In socially stratified societies, the way a home is decorated is often an important statement of status and identity.

One anthropological study of interior decoration that focuses on Japan uses as data the contents of home decorating magazines and observations within homes to see what choices people make (Rosenberger 1993). A recurrent thread is the way certain aspects of Western decorating styles are incorporated and localized (given a particularly Japanese flavor). Home decorating magazines target middle- and upper-class housewives who are guided in seeking to identify their status through new consumption styles. A general trend is the abandonment of three key features of traditional Japanese design: *tatami, shoji,* and *fusama.* Tatami are two-inch thick mats, about three feet by six feet. Room size is measured by the number of tatami mats they hold. Shoji are the sliding screen doors of tatami rooms, one covered with glass and the other with translucent rice paper often printed with a design of leaves or waves. Fusama are sliding wall panels made of thick paper; they are removable so that rooms can be enlarged for gatherings. Nancy Rosenberger (1993) describes the importance of the traditional tatami room:

> In a traditional Japanese house, a series of concentric circles go from inside to outside, signifying private to public and pure to impure. Inner tatami rooms have a symbolic purity because no footwear is worn there. These rooms are bounded by areas of wood flooring where slippers are worn—halls, kitchen, veranda, and sometimes a guest parlor. These areas in turn are bordered by stone and dirt in the entryway and the garden. A fence and gate form the perimeter of the household. Advisors on auspicious directions place the tatami rooms in the south so that good spirits and sunlight can flow in, and the impure kitchen and toilet in a dark northeasterly direction. (109)

The tatami room usually contains a low table with pillows for seating on the floor. A special alcove may contain a flower arrangement, ancestors' pictures, and a Buddhist altar. Futons are stored in closets around the edges and brought out at night for sleeping.

In seeking to distance themselves from the old style, the Japanese have made several changes: The kitchen is given a central rather than marginal location and is merged with a space called the DK (dining-kitchen) or LDK (living-dining-kitchen), with wood, tile, or carpeting on the floor. Western goods and products are used to cover old surfaces: Housewives remove the fusuma, cover the tatami with carpet, and hang curtains in place of shoji. Westernness is stated in the addition of a couch, dining set, VCR, and stereo, and an array of small Western items—Western-style teapots with cups and saucers, potted plants, French lithographs, cuckoo clocks, and knickknacks such as the Seven Dwarfs.

According to Rosenberger, these changing surfaces accompany deeper social changes involving new aspirations about marriage and family relationships. The home decorating magazines promote the idea that the new style brings with it happier children with better grades, and closer husband–wife ties. Tensions exist, however, between these ideals and the realities of middle- and upper-class life in Japan. Women feel compelled to work either part time or full time to be able to contribute to satisfying their new consumer needs. Simultaneously, Japanese women are discouraged from pursuing careers and are urged to devote more time to domestic pursuits, including home decorating and child care in order to provide the kind of life portrayed in the magazines. Children are placed in the conflicting position of being indulged as new consumer targets, while the traditional value of self-discipline still holds as well. Husbands are put in the conflicting position of needing to be more "attentive" to wife and home while the corporate world calls them for a "7–11" working day. Furthermore, the Western-style, happy nuclear family image contains no plan for the aged. The wealthiest Japanese families manage to satisfy both individualistic desires and filial duties because they can afford a large house in which they dedicate a separate floor for the husband's parents, complete with traditional tatami mats. Less wealthy people have a more difficult time dealing with this complex and conflicting set of values.

Gardens and Flowers

Gardens for use, especially for food production, can be differentiated from gardens dedicated to decoration and beauty. Not all cultures have developed the concept of the decorative garden. Inuit peoples cannot construct gardens in the snow. Purely nomadic peoples have no gardens since they are on the move. The decorative garden seems to be a product of state-level societies, especially in the Middle East, Europe, and Asia (Goody 1993). Variation exists in what is considered to be the appropriate contents, design, and purpose of a garden. A Japanese garden may contain no blooming flowers, focusing instead on the shape and placement of trees, shrubs, stones, and bodies of water (Moynihan 1979). Elite Muslim culture, with its core in the Middle East, has long been associated with formal decorative gardens. A garden, enclosed with four walls, is symbolically equivalent to the concept of "paradise." The Islamic garden pattern involves a square design with symmetrical layout, fountains, waterways, straight pathways, all enclosed within walls through which symmetrically placed entrances allow access. Islamic gardens were often used to surround the tombs of prominent people, with the usual plan placing the tomb in the center of the garden. India's Taj Mahal, built by a Muslim emperor, follows this pattern, with one modification in the landscaping: The tomb was placed at one edge of the garden rather than in the center. The result is a dramatic stretch of fountains and flowers leading up to the monument from the main gate.

The contents of a garden, like a fancy dinner menu with all its special ingredients or a personal collection of souvenirs from around the world with all their memories and meanings, makes a statement about its owner's identity and status. For example, in Europe during the heydey of colonialism, imperial gardens contained specimens from remote corners of the globe, collected through scientific expeditions. Such gardens are created through the intentional collection and placement of otherwise diverse plants in one place, creating a **heterotopia,** or the pulling together of different "places" into one (Foucault 1970). Gardens are thus the botanical counterpart to art museums or private art collections.

In contemporary times, cut flowers have become important garden products. Cut flowers, providing income for gardeners throughout the world where climates allow their production, are material goods to their producers, but important exchange items for those who purchase them. In France, women receive flowers from men more than any other kind of gift (Goody 1993:316). In much of the world, "special occasions" require gifts of flowers: In the West, as well as in East Asia, funerals are times for special displays of flowers. Ritual offerings to the deities in Hinduism may be single flowers or flowers such as marigolds woven into a chain or necklace. Flowers are often important as motifs in Western and Asian secular and sacred art, although less so in African art. In his comparative study of the use of flowers in ritual and art, Jack Goody (1993) tried to understand the relative absence of flowers in the religion and graphic arts of Africa (except for in Islamicized cultures of Africa where flowers are prominent). Some possible answers include ecological and economic factors. Eurasia possesses a greater variety of blooming plants than Africa. African horticulture, in general, is more limited in terms of space for the production of luxury items. In many African kingdoms, luxurious goods included fabrics of various design, gold ornaments, and wooden carvings rather than flowers.

THE ANTHROPOLOGY OF MUSEUMS

A museum is an institution that collects, preserves, interprets, and displays objects on a regular basis (Kahn 1995:324). Its purpose may be esthetic or educational. The idea of gathering and displaying objects goes back at least to the Babylonian kings of the sixth century BCE (Maybury-Lewis 1997a). The term comes originally from a Greek word referring to a place for the muses to congregate, where one would have philosophical discussions or see artistic performances. In Europe, the concept of the museum developed into a place where art objects were housed and displayed. Ethnographic and science museums came later, inspired by Europe's emerging interests in exploration in the 1500s and the accompanying scientific urge to gather specimens from around the world and classify them into an evolutionary history. The concept of the museum and its several forms has now diffused to most parts of the world. As a topic within anthropology, "museum anthropology" emerged in the 1980s as a subfield concerned with studying how and why museums choose to collect and display particular objects (Ames 1992; A. Jones 1993; Stocking 1985). Museum anthropologists are now at the forefront of serious debates about who gets to represent whom, the ownership of particular objects, and the public service role of museums versus elitism (see the Multiple Cultural Worlds box on page 372). The political aspects of museums have always existed, but now they are part of explicit discussion.

Another area of debate is whether objects from non-Western cultures should be exhibited, like Western art objects, with little or no ethnographic context (Watson 1997:24). Most anthropologists would support the need for context, not only for non-Western objects, but for all objects on display. The important point that all forms of expressive culture are context-

Multiple Cultural Worlds

Art Museums and Society in France and the United States

Many contemporary nations, both democracies and authoritarian states, are committed to making previously elite art forms available to the wider public (Zolberg 1992). But are museums being used by members of all social classes? Research on the social composition of museum-goers indicates a bias in those attending toward people with higher education. Within this generalization, what does a closer look at the situation in the United States and France indicate?

American museums range from huge public institutions to smaller galleries. Some encompass an encyclopedic array of objects, while others focus on the works of a single school, period, or even artist. They also vary in terms of how much information they convey about the objects: "[S]ome American art museums merely provide walls, lighting, and labels for pictures, and others have institutionalized elaborate programs . . . and lecture series" (189). Most were founded by wealthy men as their personal possessions. In return for public support, they have adopted a more service-oriented approach. On the whole, most large museums in America have a good record in education. However, the simple fact of large and increasing numbers of visitors to American museums since World War II cannot be taken as evidence of social barrier reduction. Studies show that art museum attenders tend to be better educated, better off, older, and more likely to be professionals than those who visit history, science, or other museums. In contrast to theater performances, though, art museums attract a wider social spectrum.

Outreach in European museums has generally lagged behind the United States. France, especially since World War II, has attempted to expand the reach of art museums to the public. Cultural anthropologist Pierre Bourdieu and some associates were asked to undertake a massive study of French people's taste in art and other matters (Bourdieu et al. 1969). They inquired as to whether the large number of museum-goers following World War II indicated that art was being more valued, sought after, and understood, and more available to "deprived strata" than in the past. Their answer was no because, in fact, highly educated people were overrepresented in the total number of museum-goers. They came to the museum well-informed and they remained longer than other visitors. They were eager to learn, read guide books, and they used tour guides. Lower-class visitors, in contrast, often found the experience unsettling, feeling like they were in some austere and uninviting cathedral. This research prompted some museums to incorporate a wider variety of items for display, such as furniture and ceramics, along with "high art" paintings. In addition, some French museums now advertise on television.

bound and can be better understood and appreciated within their social context is unfortunately a rare view among Western art historians and critics (Best 1986). For example, the labeling of Andy Warhol's hyperrealistic painting of a can of Campbell's soup should include information on the particular social moment in which such art was produced and some background on the artist.

Conflicts and debates also exist about who should have control of objects in museums that may have been claimed through colonial and neocolonial domination. The issue of returning objects to their original homes is a matter of international and intranational concern. Even the sharing of objects through museum lending and traveling displays may involve local or international politics (see the Current Event box). The break-up of the Soviet Union has prompted claims from several independent states that wish to retrieve artistic property that originated in their locale but was taken to Soviet national museums in Moscow and St. Petersburg. For example, Central Asian republics lost medieval carpets to Moscow and St. Petersburg museums; there are Georgian arms in the Armory of the Moscow Kremlin; and Ukrainians seek the return of objects of historical interest, such as the ceremonial staff of their national hero, the *hetman* [headman] Mazepa, who fought for Ukrainian independence against Peter the Great (Akinsha 1992a). In all, Ukraine is demanding the return of about two million art objects that originated in Ukrainian territory and are currently housed in Russian museums (Akinsha 1992b). Many of these objects are the pride of Russ-

Current Event

"Bilbao to Bid for Guernica"

- Which museum can borrow Picasso's "Guernica"? This powerful painting commemorates the Basque city that suffered massive German air attacks at the beginning of the Spanish Civil War.
- The painting belongs to the Reina Sofía Museum in Madrid. In the past, the Reina Sofía has declined every loan request on grounds of its fragile condition. The Guggenheim Museum Bilbao, in Spain's Basque country in which the village of Guernica is located, wanted to borrow the painting for its 1998 opening.
- The painting symbolizes Basque separatist longings. At the same time, the Basques are currently strong supporters of the ruling coalition in Spain, so political pressures may promote chances for the loan.

Source: Stoltz 1997.

ian museums, particularly the Scythian Gold Treasure, which is in the Hermitage in St. Petersburg. These gold objects, discovered in the Crimean area of Ukraine, date from the first millennium. A nomadic people, the Scythians buried their rulers in elaborate graves along with weapons, jewelry, vessels, and ornaments, often made of solid gold and of superb workmanship.

Another dimension of dispute about art in Russia concerns the state and the church. The Soviet state put many icons and other religious objects in museums and turned churches into museums. Now the Russian Orthodox Church is campaigning for the return of church property. A recent document adopted by a congress of churches demands that "all sacred objects of the church, all church buildings, and masterpieces of church art that were confiscated by the state after 1917 must be returned without exception to the ownership of the Russian Orthodox Church" (Akinsha 1992a:102). Art historians and museum officials protest that the churches have neither the resources nor the experience to care for these treasures. They wonder what will happen to all the icons. On the other hand, there are threats of theft and violence from those who wish to return the icons to churches and monasteries. In response, some museums have removed certain pieces from display.

In the United States and Canada, many Native American groups are lobbying successfully for the return of ancestral bones, grave goods, and potlatch goods. In 1990, the United States passed the Native American Graves Protection and Repatriation Act (NAGRPA) after two decades of lobbying by Native American groups (Bray 1996; Rose, Green, and Green 1996). This act requires universities, museums, and federal agencies in the United States to inventory their archaeological holdings in preparation for repatriating skeletons to their Native American descendants. One survey indicates that museums alone hold over 14,000 Native American skeletons (not including Hawaii), while unofficial estimates go as high as 600,000. Unknown numbers of other items are being inventoried as well, a process that is stretching thin museum resources (Watson 1997). An additional challenge exists in defining precise connections between particular remains and objects and their descendants. One clear lesson of the repatriation debates in North America is that museums and archaeologists have long had a poor record of dealing with indigenous peoples concerning their cultural property rights (Bray and Killion 1994). Discussion of new forms of partnerships among indigenous peoples, museums, and scientists is now taking place.

PLAY AND LEISURE

This section turns to another area of expressive culture: what people do "for fun." It is impossible to draw a clear line between the concepts of play and leisure as compared to art or performance, however, since they often overlap. For example, a person could paint watercolors in her leisure time, yet simultaneously be creating a work of art. In most cases, though, play and leisure can be distinguished from other activities by the fact that they have no direct, utilitarian purpose for the participant.

Dutch historian Johan Huizinga, in the 1930s, offered some features of play: It is unnecessary and thus free action; it is outside of ordinary life; it is closed and limited in terms of time; it has rules for its execution; and it contains an element of tension and chance (as summarized in Hutter 1996).

Leisure activities often overlap with play, but many leisure activities, such as reading or lying on a beach, would not be considered play because they lack rules, tension, or change. Often, the same activity, depending on the context, could be considered work instead of play. For example, gardening as a hobby would be classified as a leisure activity, even though weeding, pruning, and watering are the same activities that could be considered work for someone else. Playing a game with a child might be considered recreational, but if one has been hired as the child's babysitter, then it is work. Professional sports are an area where the line between play and work breaks down completely since the "players" are paid to "play." Further, while play and leisure may be pursued from a nonutilitarian perspective, they are often surrounded by a wider context of commercial and political interests. For example, nonprofessional athletes competing in the Olympic games are part of a wider set of powerful interests, from advertisers to host cities to athletic equipment companies.

Within the broad category of play and leisure activities, several subcategories exist, including varieties of games such as sports (institutionalized games), various hobbies or other individual pursuits (even watching television), and recreational travel. Cultural anthropologists have approached the study of play and leisure activities from several theoretical perspectives, from cultural materialism to Freudian symbolic analysis. But, regardless of their theoretical perspective, all cultural anthropologists study play and leisure within their cultural contexts and as part of holistic social systems. Why, for example, do some activities involve teams rather than individuals; what are the social roles and status of people involved in particular activities; what are the "goals" of the games and how are they achieved; how much danger or violence is involved; how are certain activities related to group identity; and how do such activities link or separate different groups within or between societies or nations?

Susan Brownell (1995) attended Beijing University in the mid-1980s in order to study Chinese and lay the groundwork for future dissertation research on sports in China. During the course of her studies, she also participated on the University's track team, having been a nationally ranked athlete in the United States in the heptathalon. Part of her ethnographic findings involve the importance of the theme of "winning glory" for one's university, province, or nation as part of the Chinese drive for sports excellence.

Games and Sports as Cultural Microcosm

Games and sports, like religious rituals and festivals, can be interpreted as reflections of broader social relationships and cultural ideals. In Geertz's terms, they are both "models of" a culture, depicting in miniature, key ideals, and "models for" a culture, through socializing people into certain values and ideals. American football can be seen as a model for corporate culture in that it relies on a clear hierarchy with leadership vested in one key person (the quarterback), and the major goal is to expand territorially by taking over areas from the competition.

A comparison of baseball as played in the United States and Japan reveals core values about social relationships (Whiting 1979). These differences emerge dramatically when American players are hired by Japanese teams. The American players bring with them an intense sense of individualism, which promotes the value of "doing your own thing." This conflicts with a primary value that influences the playing style in Japan: *wa,* meaning discipline and self-sacrifice for the good of the whole. In Japanese baseball, players must seek to achieve and maintain team harmony, so extremely individualistic, egotistical plays and strategies are frowned upon.

Sports and Spirituality: Male Wrestling in India

In many non-Western settings, sports are closely tied with aspects of religion and spirituality. Asian martial arts, for example, require forms of concentration much like meditation, leading to spiritual self-control. Male wrestling in India, a popular form of entertainment at rural fairs and other public events, also involves a strong link with spiritual development and even asceticism (Alter 1992). In some ways, these wrestlers are just like other members of Indian society. They go to work, and they marry and have families, but their dedication to wrestling involves important differences. A wrestler's daily routine is one of self-discipline. Every act—defecation, bathing, comportment, devotion—is integrated into a daily regimen of discipline.

Wrestlers come to the *akhara* (equivalent to a gymnasium) early in the morning for practice under the supervision of a guru or other senior akhara member. An akhara is a shady compound, with an earthen pit in the center about ten by fifteen meters, often with a

Indian wrestlers in the village of Sonepur. These wrestlers follow a rigorous regimen of dietary restrictions and exercise in order to keep their bodies and minds under control. Like Hindu ascetics, they seek to build up and maintain their inner strength through such practices.

tin or thatch roof. The earth of the pit is special. It is brought from a riverbed or pond bottom because that provides softer earth; then it is mixed with oil, turmeric, sometimes rose water, and buttermilk, to make it smooth and give it healing properties and fragrance. Surrounding the pit is an area of flat earth where the wrestlers practice. They practice moves repeatedly with different partners for two to three hours. In the early evening, they return for more exercise, which consists of two primary exercises: jack-knifing push-ups and deep knee-bends. A strong young wrestler will do around 2,000 push-ups and 1,000 deep knee-bends a day in sets of 50 to 100.

The wrestler's diet is prescribed by the wrestling way of life. Wrestlers are mainly vegetarian and avoid alcohol and tobacco, although they do consume *bhang*, a beverage made of blended milk, spices, almonds, and concentrated marijuana. In addition to regular meals, wrestlers consume large quantities of milk, *ghee* (clarified butter), and almonds. These substances are sources of strength as they help to build up the body's semen, according to traditional dietary principles.

Several features about the wrestler's life are similar to those of a Hindu *sannyasi*, an ascetic who has renounced life in the normal world. The aspiring sannyasi studies under a guru and learns to follow a strict routine of discipline and meditation called *yoga*, and has a restricted diet to achieve control of the body and its life force. Both wrestler and sannyasi are chosen life roles that focus on discipline as a way of achieving a controlled self. Thus, Indian wrestling does not involve the stereotype of the "dull-witted sportsman"; rather, the image is of perfected physical and moral health.

Play, Pleasure, and Pain

Many leisure activities fit in a border area between pleasure and pain, since they may involve physical discomfort as well. Serious injuries may result from mountain climbing, horseback riding, or playing touch football in the backyard. A more intentionally dangerous category of sports is **blood sports,** competition that explicitly seeks to bring about a flow of blood or even death, either between human contestants or with animal competitors, or in animal targets of human hunting (Donlon 1990). In the United States and Europe, professional boxing is an example of a highly popular blood sport that has not been analyzed yet by anthropologists. Cultural anthropologists have looked more at the use of animals in blood sports such as cockfights and bullfights. Interpretations of these sports range from seeing them as forms of sadistic pleasure or vicarious self-validation (usually of males) through the triumph of their representative pit bull or fighting cock, or as the triumph of culture over nature in the symbolism of bullfighting.

Even the seemingly pleasurable experience of a Turkish-style bath can involve discomfort and pain. One phase of the process involves scrubbing the skin roughly several times with either a rough natural sponge, a pumice stone, or a piece of cork wood wrapped in cloth (Staats 1994). The scrubbing removes layers of dead skin and "opens the pores" so that the skin will be beautiful. In Turkey, an option for men is a massage that can be quite violent, involving deep probes of leg muscles, cracking of the back, and being walked on by the (often hefty) masseur. In Ukraine, being struck repeatedly on one's bare skin

VOICES

"Childhood Tales of the Hammam"
by Fatima Mernissi

Fatima Mernissi (1995), a sociologist, grew up in a harem (pronounced "hareem," the part of the household reserved for women and children) in Fez, a traditional Islamic city of Morocco. A trip to the *hammam* was an occasion when those living in the harem could leave their secluded quarters for several hours. Before going to the *hammam,* the women would devote many hours to a first stage—preparing clay and other solutions for facial masks and putting *henna* (a reddish-orange dye used as a cosmetic and for hair coloring and conditioning) in their hair, all of which would be rinsed off in the *hammam.* Male and female children go with their mothers to the female *hammam* until boys are about ten, when they then start to go with the men to their separate hammam.

> The *hammam* that we went to in order to bathe and wash off our beauty treatments was all white marble walls and floors, with a lot of glass in the ceilings to keep the light flowing in. The combination of ivory light, mist, and nude adults and children running around made the *hammam* seem like a steamy-hot, exotic island that had somehow become adrift in the middle of the disciplined Medina. Indeed, the *hammam* would have been paradise, if it had not been for its third chamber.
>
> The first chamber of the *hammam* was steamy, yes, but nothing exceptional, and we passed through it quickly, using it mainly as a way to get used to the steamy heat. The second chamber was a delight, with just enough steam to blur the world around us into a sort of extraterrestrial place, but not enough to make breathing difficult. In that second chamber, women would get into a cleansing frenzy, sloughing off dead skin with *mhecca,* or round pieces of cork wrapped up in hand-crocheted woolen covers.
>
> To wash out the henna and the oils, the women used *ghassoul,* a miraculous clay shampoo and lotion which made your hair and skin feel incredibly smooth. "The *ghassoul* is what transforms your skin into silk," claimed Aunt Habiba. "That's what makes you feel like an ancient goddess when you step out of the *hammam.*" . . .
>
> *Ghassoul* was used in the second chamber of the *hammam* as a shampoo, and in the third and hottest chamber, where the most compulsive cleansing took place, as a smoothing and cleansing cream. Samir and I hated that third room, and even called it the torture chamber, because it was there that the grownups insisted on "seriously" taking care of us children. In the first two chambers of the *hammam,* the mothers would forget about their offspring, so involved were they with their beauty treatments. But in the third chamber, just before undertaking their own purification rituals, the mothers felt guilty about neglecting us, and tried to make up for it by turning our last moments in the *hammam* into a nightmare. It was then and there that everything suddenly went wrong, and we started sliding from one misfortunate experience to the next.
>
> First of all, the mothers filled buckets of cold and hot water directly from the fountains, and poured it over our heads before testing it properly first. And they never succeeded in getting the right temperature. The water was either scaldingly hot or ice cold, never anything in between. . . . Some would manage to escape from their mother's grip for a moment, but since the marble floor was slippery with water and clay, and the room so crowded, they never got away for very long. Some would try to avoid going in the third chamber in the first place, but in that case, which was often what happened to me, they would just be picked up by their feet and forced in, despite their shrill screams.
>
> Those were the few terrible moments that practically erased the whole delightful effect of the *hammam* session. (234–238)

Source: Fatima Mernissi, *Dreams of Trespass* (pages 234–238). Text © 1994 Fatima Mernissi. Reprinted by permission of Addison-Wesley Longman, Inc.

with birch branches is the final stage of the bath. However, violent scrubbing, scraping, and even beating of the skin, combined with radical temperature changes in the water are combined with valued social experiences at the bathhouse (see the Voices box).

Leisure Travel

Anthropologists who study leisure travel, or tourism, have often commented that their work is taken less seriously than it should be because of the perspective that they are just "hanging out" at the beach or at five-star hotels. Anthropological research on tourism and its impact is revealing that this is a serious subject, and can involve conflict and danger as much as any other topic. Violence is not unknown in tourist destinations, as for example, in Sri Lanka in the 1980s and 1990s, and in the former Yugoslavia in the 1990s.

Tourism is now one of the major economic forces in the world, it is growing, and it has dramatic effects on people and places in tourist destination areas. Expenditure of money, time, and effort for nonessential travel is nothing new. In the past, pilgrimage to religious sites has been a major preoccupation of many people (Chapter 13). A large percentage of worldwide tourism involves individuals from the industrialized nations of Europe, North America, and Japan traveling to the less industrialized nations. Ethnic tourism, cultural tourism, and off-the-beaten-path tourism are attracting increasing numbers of travelers. These new kinds of tourism are often marketed as providing a view of "authentic" cultures. Images of indigenous people as the "Other" figure prominently in travel brochures and advertisements (Silver 1993). They are reinforced by the contents of films, documentaries, and widely read "informational" publications such as *National Geographic, Natural History Magazine,* and *Smithsonian Magazine,* and glossy travel magazines such as *Condé Nast.*

The travel industry tends to promote images that are likely to be verified during travel—people want to see what the brochures show. Tourist promotional literature often presents a "myth" of other peoples and places (Silver 1993:304) and offers travel as a form of escape to a mythical land of wonder. In fact, research on Western travel literature shows that, from the time of the earliest explorers to the present, it has been full of "primitivist" images about indigenous peoples (Pratt 1992). They are portrayed as having static or "stone age" traditions and remaining largely unchanged by the forces of Western colonialism, nationalism, economic development, and tourism itself (Bruner 1991). As Kathleen Adams (1984) has written, on the basis of her research in Indonesia, tourists often seek to find the culture that the tourist industry defines rather than gaining a genuine, more complicated, and perhaps less photogenic version of a culture. For the traveler, obtaining these desired cultural images through mass tourism involves packaging the "primitive" with the "modern" because most tourists want comfort and convenience along with their "authentic experience." Thus, advertisements may minimize the foreignness of the host country noting, for example, that English is spoken, that the destination is remote yet accessible. Primitivist imagery attracts tourists, while a dash of similarity offers enough of the comforts of home to make it all acceptable. For example, "The Melanesian Discoverer" is a ship that cruises the Sepik River in Papua New Guinea, providing a way for affluent tourists to see the "primitive" while traveling in comfort.

So far, the anthropology of tourism has focused most of its attention on the impact of global and local tourism on indigenous peoples and places. Such impact studies are important in exposing the degree to which tourism helps or harms local people. For example, the formation of Amboseli National Park in Kenya affected the access of the Maasai to strategic water resources for their herds (Honadle 1985, as summarized in Drake 1991). The project staff promised certain benefits to the Maasai if they stayed off the reserve, but many of those benefits (including shares of the revenues from the park) never materialized. In contrast, local people in Costa Rica were included in the early planning stages of the Guanacaste National Park and have played a greater role in the park management system there.

CHANGE IN ART AND PLAY

Nowhere are forms and patterns of art and play frozen in time. Change is universal, and much change is influenced by Western culture. However, influence does not occur in only one direction. African musical styles have transformed the American musical scene since the days of slavery. Japan has provided a strong influence on upper-class garden styles in the United States. Cultures in which tradition and conformity have been valued in pottery-making, dress, or theatre may find themselves having to make choices about whether to innovate, and if so, how. Many contemporary artists (including musicians and playwrights) from Latin America to China are fusing ancient and "traditional" motifs and styles with more contemporary themes and messages.

Western interest in indigenous arts as "art" is quite recent, since their asethetic value was not widely recognized until the early twentieth century. Before that, the typical Western reaction to non-Western art was often one of either horror or curiosity (Mitter 1977). Given current global exchanges and influences in art and play (especially organized sports), it is easy to distinguish between those activities and products made for internal consumption versus those made for the external world (Graburn 1976:5).

Changes occur in the use of new materials and technology and in the incorporation of new ideas and tastes. These changes are often accompanied by social change.

Effects of Westernization

Cricket in the Trobriands

Western colonialist powers often acted directly to change certain indigenous art and leisure practices. In the Trobriand Islands, now part of Papua New Guinea, British administrators and missionaries sought to eradicate the frequent tribal warfare as part of its pacification process. One strategy was to replace it with intertribal competitive sports (Leach 1975). In 1903, Reverend Gilmore, a British missionary, introduced the British game of cricket in the Trobriands as a way of promoting a new morality, separate from the former warring traditions. As played in England, cricket involves particular rules of play and a very "proper" look of pure white uniforms. In the early stages of the adoption of cricket in the Trobriands, the game followed the British pattern closely. As time passed and the game spread into more regions, it became increasingly localized. Most importantly, it was merged into indigenous political competition between big-men. Big-men leaders would urge their followers to increase production in anticipation of a cricket match since the matches were followed by a redistributive feast. The British missionaries had discouraged traditional magic in favor of Christianity, but the Trobriand Islanders transferred war-related magic into cricket. For example, spells are used to help one's team win, and the bats are ritually treated in the way that war weapons were. Weather magic is also important. If things are not going well for one's team, a spell to bring rain and force cancellation of the game is a possibility.

Other transformations occurred. The Trobrianders stopped wearing the crisp white uniforms and instead donned paint, feathers, and shells. They announced their entry into the opposing village with new songs and dances, praising their team in contrast to the opposition. Many of the teams, and their songs and dances, draw on Western elements such as the famous entry song of the "P-K" team. (P-K is the name of a chewing gum. This team chose the name because the stickiness of gum is likened to the ability of their bat to hit the ball.) Other teams incorporated sounds and motions of airplanes, objects that they had never seen until World War II. Songs and dances are explicitly sexual and enjoyed by all, in spite of missionary attempts to suppress such "immoral" aspects of Trobriand culture. The Trobrianders have changed some of the rules of play as well. The home team should always win, but not by too many runs. In this way, guests show respect to the hosts. Winning, after all, is not the major goal. The feast after the match is the climax for the Trobrianders.

Machine-Made Tapa in Tonga

A Peace Corps worker on the island of Tonga in the South Pacific, who introduced a machine to beat tapa (a kind of bark) into cloth, has raised basic questions about gender relations (Teilhet-Fisk 1991). Tapa cloth holds an important place in many South Pacific societies. Made only by women, the cloth was long displayed in ritual ceremonies as a mark of women's power and status. When the machine was introduced, women's labor in making the cloth was greatly reduced. The Tongans were concerned that future generations of girls would therefore not learn how to beat tapa. Some women avoided using the machine, fearing public ridicule for using foreign technology or seeming to place themselves above others. Others advocated use of the machine since men had access to machines in their work; thus, women should also. Esthetically, it is difficult to distinguish hand-beaten tapa from machine-processed tapa, but the former continues to hold much higher symbolic value among the Tongans. The machine has been abandoned.

Effects of Tourism

Global tourism has had varied effects on indigenous arts. Often, tourist demand for ethnic arts and souvenirs has led to mass production of sculpture or weaving or jewelry of a less high quality than was created before the demand. Tourists' preferences for certain colors has sometimes had an effect on an indigenous art form. Also, tourists' interests in seeing an abbreviated form of a traditionally long dance or theater performances has led to the presentation of "cuts" rather

A water puppet performance in Hanoi, Vietnam. Water puppet shows are far more popular among international tourists than among the Vietnamese.

than an entire piece. Some scholars say, therefore, that tourism leads to the decline and transformation of indigenous arts in a negative sense. Evidence exists to support an alternative argument, too. Tourist support of traditional art, with or without certain modifications, is important throughout much of the world.

Often, tourist support for indigenous arts is the sole force maintaining them, since local people in a particular culture may be more interested in foreign music, art, or sports themselves. Vietnamese water puppetry is an ancient performance mode, dating back at least to the Ly Dynasty of 1121 AD (Contreras 1995). Traditionally, water puppet shows took place in the spring during a lull in the farm work, or at special festival times. During writer Susan Brownmiller's (1994) stay in Hanoi, she saw a performance of the water puppets. Unseen humans operate puppets with long poles hidden underwater: "Sailing into view, the doll-size wood puppets skim the water's surface, planting and harvesting rice, catching fish, chasing ducks, and each other in frantic confusion. Fire-breathing dragons! The Dance of the Lions! Magnificent sea battles amid popping firecrackers, billowing smoke, and churning waves!" (65). After the performance, her rickshaw driver asked her how she liked the performance. She responded with an enthusiastic "yes" and returned the question to him. His reply: "I like videos."

Contemporary Cultural Revival: Return of the Hula

In many cultures worldwide, one response to outside influences such as colonialism, neocolonialism, and tourism is a vigorous renaissance or reinvention of precontact forms of expressive culture. (Recall the discussion of similar responses in the area of religion in Chapter 13.) One example of indigenous revival of artistic forms as a counterstatement to outside influence is the resurgence of the hula, or Hawaiian dance (Stillman 1996). Beginning in the early 1970s, the "Hawaiian Renaissance" grew out of political protest; specifically, Hawaiian youth spoke out against encroaching development from the outside that was displacing the indigenous people from their own land and resources. Hula and other practices such as canoe paddling and the Hawaiian language were the focus of revival. Over the past two decades, hula schools have proliferated and hula competitions between many islands have become widely attended events. Since 1992, hula competitions have reached a level of international dissemination, with the first World Invitational Hula Festival held in Honolulu. This event is less popular, however, with indigenous Hawaiians since they feel that international competitors are not of comparable quality. The hula competitions have helped ensure the continued survival of this ancient art form. The format of competitions, however, has also brought changes to the older styles in performance style and presentation. Timing is one crucial factor. Most competitions deduct points if a performer uses more than the allotted time. Traditional dances cannot be completely performed within these limits, so entry and exit dances and interlude dances have had to be cut.

Post-Communist Transitions

Major changes are occurring in the arts in the post-communist states for two reasons: loss of state financial support and removal of state controls over subject matter and creativity. "A new generation of talented young artists has appeared. Many are looking for something new and different—art without ideology" (Akinsha 1992c:109). Art for art's sake—art as independent from the socialist project—is now possible. A circle of artists called the Moscow Conceptualists has been the dominant "underground" (nonofficial) school of art. These artists focused on political subject matter and poverty. In contrast, the new underground finds its inspiration in nostalgia for the popular culture of the 1950s and 1960s, a pack of Yugoslav chewing gum, or the cover of a Western art magazine. Commercial galleries are springing up, and a museum of modern art in Moscow may become a reality in the near future.

Theater in China is passing through a difficult transition period with the recent development of some features of capitalism. Since the beginning of the People's Republic in 1949, the arts have gone through different phases, from being suppressed as part of the old feudal tradition to being revived under state control. Now, nearly all of China's theater companies are in financial crisis (Jiang 1994:72). The Anhui troupe of nearly one hundred people had not put on any plays one year, although they still got paid each month—but not much. Steep inflation means that actors can no longer live on their pay. Theater companies are urging their workers to find jobs elsewhere, such as by making movies or videos, but this is not an option for provincial troupes. Traditional theater troupes are surviving by going on tours. Foreign tourist audiences are one source of support for traditional theater. Another factor is that audience preferences have changed: "People are fed up with shows that 'educate,' have too strong a political flavor, or convey 'artistic values.' They no longer seem to enjoy love stories, old Chinese legends, or Western-style theater. Most of the young people prefer nightclubs, discos, or karaokes. Others stay at home watching TV" (73). The new materialism in China means that young people want to spend their leisure time having "fun." For the theater, too, money now comes first. One trend is toward the production of Western plays.

For example, Harold Pinter's *The Lover* was an immediate success when it was performed in Shanghai in 1992. Why was it so successful?

> Sex is certainly a big part of the answer. Sex has been taboo in China for a long time; it is still highly censored in theater and films. The producers warned, "no children," fueling speculation about a possible sex scene. . . . Actually, *The Lover* contains only hints of sexuality, but by Chinese standards the production was the boldest stage show in China. The actress's alluring dress, so common in the west, has seldom, if ever, been seen by Chinese theatregoers. Also, there was lots of bold language—dialog about female breasts, for example. (75–76)

Another important feature is the play's focus on private life, on interiority, thoughts, and feelings. This emphasis corresponds with increasing interest in private lives in China. Change in the performing arts in China definitely is being shaped by underlying changes in the global and local political economy.

SUMMARY

Anthropologists share with philosophers, art critics, and others an interest in defining the concept of art. Anthropologists choose a broad definition that takes into account cross-cultural variations. In the anthropological perspective, all cultures have art and all cultures have a concept of what is good art. Franz Boas, a foundational figure in the anthropology of art, insisted that art should be studied in its social context and that attention should be given to the process of making art, the artist, and the finished product.

Art may serve a range of social functions, including social control, entertainment, and education. Art grows out of particular economic, political, and social contexts and, to an extent, art's content and form are likely to be products of those factors. Art may serve to reinforce social patterns, but it may also be a vehicle of protest and resistance.

Museums are collections of objects placed together on the basis of some culturally shaped organizing principles. The earliest ethnographic museums were established in Europe as the result of scientific and colonialist interest in learning about other cultures.

Anthropological studies of play and leisure also pay attention to these activities within their social context. Games can be seen to reflect and reinforce dominant social values and have thus been analyzed as cultural microcosms. Sports and leisure activities, while themselves done for nonutilitarian purposes, are often tied to economic and political interests. In some cultures, sports are also related to religion and spirituality.

Major forces of change in expressive culture include Western colonialism and international tourism. The effects of change are not exclusively shown on the "receiving" culture's side, however, because art and play in colonial powers and in contemporary core states have also changed through exposure to other cultures.

CRITICAL THINKING QUESTIONS

1. Is Western culture the only one that distinguishes between fine art and non-fine art?
2. What is the status of artists in North America and Europe? Are there gender differences?
3. Do different kinds of museums (e.g., natural history, science, art) attract different social groups?
4. What are some similarities and contrasts between blood sports and religious sacrifice?

KEY CONCEPTS

art, p. 360
blood sport, p. 375
ethno-esthetics, p. 362
ethnomusicology, p. 367
expressive culture, p. 360
heterotopia, p. 371
theater, p. 368

SUGGESTED READINGS

Richard L. Anderson and Karen L. Field, eds., *Art in Small-Scale Societies: Contemporary Readings.* Englewood Cliffs, NJ: Prentice-Hall. Thirty-four essays cover fieldwork, functions of art, symbolism, artists, the psychology and philosophy of art, and aspects of change. Attention is given to sculpture, painting, pottery, weaving, music, poetry, dance, architecture, and photography.

John Miller Chernoff, *African Rhythm and African Sensibility: Aesthetics and African Musical Idioms.* Chicago: University of Chicago Press, 1979. This book describes shared features of music style and musical performance throughout Africa, and presents links to key African cultural values.

Nelson H. H. Graburn, ed., *Ethnic and Tourist Arts: Cultural Expressions from the Fourth World.* Berkeley: University of California Press, 1976. Organized regionally, twenty chapters explore the survival, revival, and reinvention of the arts of indigenous peoples in North America, Mexico and Central America, South America, Asia, Oceania, and Africa. Graburn's introduction to the book and his introductory essays preceding each section provide theoretical and comparative insights.

Jay R. Mandle and Joan D. Mandle, *Caribbean Hoops: The Development of West Indian Basketball.* Amsterdam: Gordon and Breach Publishers, 1994. This concise description and analysis of the emergence of basketball (mainly men's basketball) as a popular sport in several Caribbean nations also explores regional differences within the Caribbean.

Timothy Mitchell, *Blood Sport: A Social History of Spanish Bullfighting.* Philadelphia: University of Pennsylvania Press, 1991. Based on fieldwork and archival study, this book presents a well-rounded view of bullfighting within the context of annual Spanish village and national fiestas, consideration of the role of the matador in society, and a psychosexual interpretation of the bullfight, with comparison to blood sports in ancient Rome.

Stuart Plattner, *High Art Down Home: An Economic Ethnography of a Local Art Market.* Chicago: University of Chicago Press, 1996. Based on participant observation and interviews with artists, art dealers, and collectors in St. Louis, Missouri, this book explores concepts of value related to contemporary art and constraints that the market places on artists.

CHAPTER 16

People on the Move

CHAPTER OUTLINE

ANTHROPOLOGY AND MIGRATION

WHAT IS MIGRATION?

- Internal Migration
  - *Multiple Cultural Worlds:* Urban Migration of Girls in Ghana
- International Migration
  - *Current Event:* "Free Trade Leads to Bolivians Seeking Jobs in Argentina"

CATEGORIES OF MIGRANTS

- Labor Migrants
  - *Critical Thinking:* Haitian Cane-Cutters in the Dominican Republic—Two Views on Human Rights
- Displaced Persons
  - *Multiple Cultural Worlds:* Palestinian Refugees in Lebanon—Uncounted and Unwanted
- Institutional Migrants
- Soldiers on Assignment
- Spouse/Partner Migration

THE NEW IMMIGRANTS

- *Multiple Cultural Worlds:* The New Immigrants and FGM in the United States
- The New Immigrants from Latin America and the Caribbean
- The New Immigrants from East Asia
  - *Voices:* "Saying Goodbye" by Marie G. Lee
- The New Immigrants from Southeast Asia
- The New Immigrants from South Asia: Asian Indians in New York City Maintain Their Culture
- The New Immigrants from Eastern Europe
  - *Multiple Cultural Worlds:* Bosnian Trauma Testimonies and Recovery

THE POLITICS AND POLICIES OF INCLUSION AND EXCLUSION

- *Viewpoint:* "The Immigration Wars" by Bart Laws

SUMMARY

CRITICAL THINKING QUESTIONS

KEY CONCEPTS

SUGGESTED READINGS

◀ Religion provides an important source of social cohesion and psychological support for many new immigrant groups whose places of worship attract both worshipers and cultural anthropologists interested in learning how religion fits into migrants' adaptation. This is a scene at a Lao Buddhist temple in Virginia.

The current generation of American youths will experience more moves during their lives than previous generations. College graduates are likely to change jobs an average of eight times during their careers, and these changes may require relocation. Ecological, economic, familial, and political factors are causing population movements at seemingly all-time high levels. Research in anthropology has shown, however, that frequent moves during a person's life and mass movements of peoples are nothing new; they have occurred throughout human evolution. Foragers and pastoralists relocate frequently as a normal part of their lives. Population movements account for the past and present dispersion of the world's cultures:

> When we look at population maps of any part of the world, we are looking at the results of migration. Some maps represent major permanent moves, such as the spread of Native Americans from the Bering Sea to Tierra del Fuego, or the spread of Bantu-speaking peoples into the southern half of the African continent. Major moves may be brought on by necessity (the potato famine in Ireland), by population pressure (as befell the San and the Khoi), or by extreme force (the African diaspora in which ten million people were removed from their home communities and scattered throughout the New World). (du Toit 1990:305)

Migration is the movement of a person or people from one place to another (Kearney 1986:331). It is related to other aspects of life such as job and family status, and it may also affect mental health and social relationships. Thus, many academic subjects and professions have some relevance to its study. Historians; economists; political scientists; sociologists; and scholars of religion, literature, art, and music have studied migration. Migration is one of three core areas of demography, along with fertility and mortality. The professions of law, medicine, education, business, architecture, urban planning, public administration, and social work have specialties that focus on the process of migration and the period of adaption following a move. Experts working in these areas share with anthropologists an interest in such issue as: people who migrate, causes of migration, processes of migration, psychosocial adaptations to new locations, and implications for planning and policy.

ANTHROPOLOGY AND MIGRATION

The subject matter of migration is related to all four fields of general anthropology. Archaeologists have reconstructed population movements through space and history and examined their relation to language change. They have studied urban growth in the past, much of which is accounted for by migration of people from the countryside to the city. Physical anthropologists examine migratory patterns of nonhuman primates and attempt to understand the reasons for movements of groups, especially in relation to carrying capacity of the environment. They have conducted nutritional and medical assessments of human populations in different environments, comparing, for example, foragers to settled populations. A growing area of linguistic anthropology is second language acquisition among migrants. Because the movement of people is interrelated with so many other aspects of culture, many chapters of this book have included information on migrant groups in relation to their subject matter.

Cultural anthropologists have addressed a wide range of issues related to migration, and it is their work that forms the basis of this chapter. They have studied *why* people move as well as their adjustments to living in a new place, especially the challenges and opportunities of maintaining their culture or constructing a new cultural identity. Given the breadth of

A food vendor at the Brazilian Independence Day street festival celebrated on West 46th Street in Manhattan, an area known as "Little Brazil."

migration studies, cultural anthropologists have used the full range of methods available, from individual life histories to large-scale surveys. Three differences distinguish migration studies in cultural anthropology. First, anthropologists studying migration are more likely to have fieldwork experience in more than one location in order to understand the places of origin and destination. Maxine Margolis (1994), for example, first did fieldwork in Brazil, then later studied Brazilian immigrants in New York City. Second, a greater emphasis on using macro and micro perspectives characterizes anthropology's approach to migration studies. Studying migration has challenged traditional cultural anthropology's focus on one village or neighborhood and created the need to take into account national and global economic, political, and social forces (Basch, Glick Schiller and Szanton Blanc 1994; Lamphere 1992). Third, anthropologists who work with migrants are more likely to be involved in assisting them, often as English language teachers. Nancy Donnelly (1994), through her work teaching English as a Second Language (ESL), became interested in learning more about the adaptation of Hmong refugees from Laos in Seattle.

WHAT IS MIGRATION?

Migration, or a spatial move, also involves cultural change, to varying degrees. A new situation requires individuals to learn new rules, roles, and expectations and adjust to them. Migration encompasses many categories depending on the distance of the move, its purpose, duration, degree of voluntarism (was the move forced or more a matter of choice?), and the migrant's status in the new destination. There is a major difference between internal migration (movement within national boundaries) and international migration. Moving between nations is likely to create more challenges both in the process of relocation and in adjustment after arrival.

Internal Migration

Rural-to-urban migration has been the dominant stream of internal population in most countries during the twentieth century. A major reason for people migrating to urban areas is the availability of work. According to the **push-pull theory** of labor migration, rural areas are increasingly unable to support population growth and rising expectations about the quality of life (the push factor). At the same time, cities (the pull factor) attract people, especially youth, for employment and lifestyle reasons. The push-pull model makes urban migration sound like a simple function of the rational decision making of freely choosing human agents who have information on the costs and the benefits of rural versus urban life, weigh that information, and then opt for going or staying (recall the approach to understanding culture that emphasizes human agency, Chapter 1). But many instances of urban migration are more the result of structural forces (economic need or political factors such as war) that are beyond the control of the individual (see the Multiple Cultural Worlds box on page 386).

The anonymity and rapid pace of city life and the likelihood of "psychosocial discontinuity" caused by relocation pose special challenges for migrants from rural areas. Research has shown that urban life increases the risk of hypertension (elevated blood pressure through stress or tension), and hypertension is related to coronary heart disease. For example, an anthropological study of urban migrants in comparison to rural dwellers in the Philippines found that hypertension, as defined by high blood pressure, is more prevalent in urban migrant populations than in settled rural groups (Hackenberg et al. 1983). This finding applied to both men and women. (Other social factors such as income level, education, age at migration, and social support systems can be important in affecting health outcomes of migration; some of these are discussed below). The relationship between elevated health risks resulting from psychosocial adjustment problems in rural-urban migration exists among international immigrant groups as well, for example, among Samoans living in California (Janes 1990).

In the United States, migration out of cities has been primarily to suburban locations. A recent trend is for relatively affluent city-dwellers to relocate to desirable rural areas, especially for retirement. These migrants often incur the ire of local people, who feel invaded and see their traditional lifeways changing rapidly. In Three Forks, Montana, for example, the population grew by 50 percent between 1990 and 1996, from somewhat over 1,000 people to 1,600 (McDonald 1996). At the same time, median home prices more than doubled from $30,000 to $70,000. Local people stereotype the newcomers as "Californians":

Multiple Cultural Worlds

Urban Labor Migration of Girls in Ghana

Child fostering is common throughout sub-Saharan Africa. Parents foster out children to enhance their chances for formal education or to help them learn a skill such as marketing through apprenticeship. The predominant direction of fostering is from rural to urban areas and from poorer to better-off families. Roger Sanjek (1990b) conducted a study of household composition in Adabraka, a middle-class neighborhood in Ghana's capital city of Accra. The neighborhood comprises people of different Ghanaian ethnic groups, but most are from the southern region, Christian, literate, and "modern." Child fostering is common. Of forty adults in the study, more than half had been fostered, with the proportion higher among women than men.

About one-fourth of the resident children in the fieldwork neighborhood were in-fostered. Striking gender differences emerge in this group of in-fostered children. First, there were twice as many girls as boys. School attendance rates were biased toward boys: All of the seventeen boys were attending school, but only four of the thirty-one girls were. The others worked as maids or assisted in market trade. As a whole, 80 percent of the children were kin of their sponsors, but this percentage was only 50 percent for girls. Girls sponsored by kin are less likely to be mistreated than other girls. Maids who are not kin are secured by making a cash payment to the parents. Payments to the girl are at the discretion of the "employer." All maids help in cooking and housecleaning. They may also assist in selling items from in front of their employer's building. Market helpers transport goods, take care of the trade location when the market woman is off on business or shopping, and run errands in the marketplace.

The number of girl maids and helpers in Accra as a whole is in the tens of thousands. This form of "hidden" child labor migration provides cheap labor for the better-off urban population. It subsidizes the education of city boys and girls by replacing their labor contribution to the household. Does urban fostering of poor rural girls offer them a path to social mobility? The research findings contradict this as a general conclusion. Rather, the labor of these girls is tapped mainly to benefit others, and "the life chances of many Ghanaian girls have been used up by the time they are 8 or 9 years old" (58).

> When residents of this town aren't talking about the Unabomber or the Freemen, they're complaining about Californians. Not the corporate executives who visit each summer to flyfish in the trout-rich rivers and spend money in Three Forks, but the new arrivals who have come to stay. Like many rural towns throughout the West, Three Forks . . . is in the midst of a major economic and cultural transformation, as urban refugees buy property, drive up the cost of housing, and turn productive agricultural land into subdivisions and upscale ranches. (A7)

To the contrary, anthropological survey research in Three Forks showed that the major source of immigrants is not California: Out of 400 households surveyed, one was from California and two were from Arkansas. The rest were from Montana. The study revealed several commonalities and shared values between the local people and the immigrants. Both groups are politically conservative. Both are concerned about not destroying agriculture and the environment, although the very presence of so many newcomers is an obvious threat to those interests. The ways small, rural communities will learn to cope with the new form of migration will be interesting to study in the coming years.

International Migration

International migration has grown in volume and significance since 1945, especially since the mid-1980s (Castles and Miller 1993). No one knows how many international migrants there are, although it is estimated that nearly 2 percent of the world's population lives abroad (thus, the vast majority resides in their home countries). This amounts to about 100 million people, including legal and illegal immigrants. Migrants who move for work-related reasons constitute the majority of people in this category. At least 35 million people from developing countries have migrated to the industrialized countries in the past three decades. International migration is likely to be one of the key factors in global social change through the first decade of the twenty-first century. Driving forces behind this trend are economic and political changes that affect labor demands and human welfare.

The "classic" countries of early international immigration are the United States, Canada, Australia, New Zealand, and Argentina. The first waves of European immigrants largely destroyed and dispossessed the indigenous peoples in each case. These countries' populations are now formed mainly of descendants of the European immigrants. The immigration policies of these nations in the early twentieth century have been labeled "White immigration" because they explicitly limited non-White immigration (Ongley 1995). In the 1960s in Canada, for instance, changes made immigration policies less racially discriminatory and more focused on skills and experience. Through the 1980s, further liberalization occurred and family reunification provisions were widened. The "White Australia" policy was formally ended in 1973. In both the Canadian and Australian cases, a combination of changing labor needs and interest in improving their international image prompted these reforms. During the 1980s, increased refugee flows inspired greater attention to humanitarian concerns.

During the 1980s and the 1990s, the United States, Canada, and Australia experienced large-scale immigration from new sources, especially Asia, and—to the United States—from Mexico, Latin America, and the Caribbean (Castles and Miller 1993). In addition, new destination countries have joined these "classic" countries. Long-time areas of out-migration of Northern, Western, and Southern Europe are now receiving many immigrants (often refugees from Asia). Some Central European states, such as Hungary, Poland, and Czechoslovakia, are new migrant destinations. Population flows in the Middle East are complex, with some nations such as Turkey experiencing substantial movements in both directions. Millions of Turks have emigrated to Germany, while ethnic Turks in places such as Bulgaria have returned to Turkey. Turkey has also received Kurdish and Iranian refugees. Several million Palestinian refugees now live mainly in Jordan and Lebanon. Israel has attracted Jewish immigrants from Europe, northern Africa, the United States, and most recently the former Soviet Union, through its attempt to build a Jewish nation. The Persian Gulf states draw thousands of labor migrants from elsewhere in the Middle East and Asia. Throughout Africa, labor migrants frequently go to their former colonial countries—for example, Moroccan and Algerian migrant workers go to France—and millions of refugees live outside their native countries. Industrialized Asian nations have also become immigration destinations. The complicated stratification of migration in and out of South American countries involves refugees and foreign workers entering Venezuela, Brazil, the Dominican Republic, and Argentina, and out-migration from Haiti, the Dominican Republic, and Mexico (see the Current Event box).

Current Event

"Free Trade Leads to Bolivians Seeking Jobs in Argentina"

- Latin American demographers predict that differences in economic growth and development in the region will spur cross-border migration and force countries to deal with the political and social consequences. For example, the 1991 census of Argentina counted 146,460 Bolivians. That figure more than doubled between 1992 and 1994 after amnesty was granted to illegal immigrants.
- About 200,000 undocumented Bolivians now live in Argentina. This increase is in part a response to the increasing demand for a cheap and unregulated labor force. The Bolivians are willing to accept almost any kind of work. One worker said that he would rather be exploited than not have a job.
- More recently, Argentina has begun to close its doors. Reasons include national security interests, high unemployment, and the latent racism of Argentinians toward brown-skinned peoples.

Source: Gabriel Escobar, *The Washington Post*, September 15, 1996, A21.

CATEGORIES OF MIGRANTS

Labor Migrants

Thousands of people migrate to work for a specific period of time. They do not intend to establish permanent residence and are often explicitly barred from doing so. This form of migration, when legally contracted, is called **wage labor migration.** The period of work may be brief or it may last several years, as among rural Egyptian men who go to other Middle Eastern countries to work for an average period of four years (Brink 1991). Asian women are the fastest growing category among the world's 35 million migrant workers (International Labour Office 1996: 16–17). About 1.5 million Asian women are working abroad; most are in domestic service jobs, and some work as nurses and teachers. Major sending countries are Indonesia, the Philippines, Sri Lanka, and Thailand. Main receiving countries are Saudi Arabia and Kuwait, and to a lesser degree, Hong Kong, Japan, Taiwan, Singapore, Malaysia, and Brunei. Such women are usually alone and are not allowed to marry or have a child in the country where they are temporary workers. International migrant workers are sometimes illegally recruited and thus have no protection in their working conditions. The illegal recruitment of female prostitutes, a growing problem worldwide, is especially serious in Thailand, where young women are offered the prospect of migrating to the United States and elsewhere under pretenses of receiving work, for example, as restaurant hostesses.

Circular migration refers to a common form of labor migration involving movement in a regular pattern between two or more places. Circular migration may occur either within or between nations. In the latter case, it is also referred to as **transnational migration.** The undocumented workers who go back and forth between Mexico and the United States each year are international circular migrants (Chavez 1992), as are many Haitian cane-cutters who work in the Dominican Republic (see the Critical Thinking box on pages 389–390). Internal circular migrants include, for example, female domestic workers throughout Latin America and the Caribbean. These women have their permanent residence in the rural areas, but work for long periods of time in the city for better-off people. They tend to leave their children in the care of their mother in the country and send regular remittances for their support.

Displaced Persons

Displaced persons are people who, for one reason or another, are "evicted from their houses, farms, and communities and forced to find a living elsewhere" (Guggenheim and Cernea 1993:1). Colonialism, slavery, war, persecution, natural disasters, and large-scale mining and dam-building are major causes of population displacement. **Refugees,** a category of displaced persons, are forced to relocate because they are victims or potential victims of persecution because of race, religion, nationality, ethnicity, gender, or political views (Camino and Krulfeld 1994:vii). In contrast to much labor migration, migration caused by these factors is involuntary and often traumatic.

Refugees constitute a large and growing category of displaced persons. An accurate count of all categories of refugees globally is unavailable. The lack of accurate data is compounded by political interests seeking, in some cases, to inflate numbers, and in others, to deflate numbers (see the Multiple Cultural Worlds box on page 391). In the past, most refugees have left their homes for political or economic reasons. The Love Canal residential area in western New York state and the Chernobyl area created a new subcategory of displaced persons called **ecological refugees,** or people who have to relocate because their home area has become unfit for habitation from pollution, a nuclear disaster, or environmental devastation from war.

The manner in which displaced persons are relocated has serious impacts on how well they will adjust to their new lives. Displaced persons in general have little choice about when and where they move, with refugees typically having the least of all.

Cultural anthropologists have done substantial research with refugee populations, especially those related to war (Camino and Krulfeld 1994; Hirschon 1989; Manz 1988). They have helped discover the key factors that ease or increase relocation stresses. One major issue is the extent to which the new location resembles or differs from the home place in several features such as climate, language, and food (Muecke 1987). Generally, the more different the places of origin and destination are, the greater will be the adaptational demands and stress. Other major factors are the refugee's ability to get a job equivalent to his or her training and experience, the presence of family members, and whether people in the new location are welcoming or hostile to the refugees.

The relatively successful case of Karelian refugee resettlement following World War II illustrates these points. One of the largest movements following the war was the displacement of over 400,000 Finnish Karelians from their homeland in Eastern Finland because the area was ceded by Finland to the Soviet Union (Mustanoja and Mustanoja 1993). The resettle-

CRITICAL THINKING

Haitian Cane-Cutters in the Dominican Republic—Two Views on Human Rights

The circulation of male labor from villages in Haiti to sugar estates in the Dominican Republic is the oldest and perhaps the largest continuing population movement within the Caribbean region (Martínez 1996). Beginning in the early twentieth century, Dominican sugar cane growers began to recruit Haitian workers, called *braceros.* Between 1952 and 1986, an agreement between the two countries' governments regulated and organized labor recruitment. Since then, recruitment became a private matter, with men crossing the border on their own or with recruiters working in Haiti without official approval.

Many studies and reports have addressed the system of labor recruitment from Haiti to the Dominican Republic. Two competing views exist. The human rights activists (View 1) focus on evidence of forced and fraudulent labor recruitment and take the position that this system violates the human rights of the Haitian laborers and is neo-slavery. The academics (View 2), while not completely unified in their views, use ethnographic data to support their position that it is inaccurate to consider the braceros as slaves because they have evidence that, more often, braceros migrate voluntarily.

View 1

Interviews with Haitian braceros in the Dominican Republic have exposed a consistent pattern of labor rights abuses:

> Men and boys as young as seven in rural Haiti are accosted by Haitian Creole-speaking recruiters making promises of easy, well-paid employment in the Dominican Republic. Those who agree are taken to the frontier on foot and are either taken directly to a farm in the Dominican Republic or perhaps more often are turned over by the recruiter to Dominican soldiers for a fee of a few pesos per recruit. Inside the Dominican Republic, soldiers and policemen also detain undocumented Haitians at highway checkpoints and in roundups conducted mostly in rural areas. Contrary to common international practice, the Dominican authorities generally do not deport undocumented Haitian entrants but hand them over, again for a fee, to agents of state-owned sugar estates, for shipment to company compounds.
>
> The recruits are transported from the frontier under armed military guard in buses that stop infrequently on the way east to minimize the risk of their Haitian passengers absconding.
>
> Once on the sugar estates, the recruits are given only one means of earning money for survival, cutting sugar cane. Cutting cane is very physically debilitating labor, and in the Dominican Republic only the strongest and most experienced cane cutters can earn more than the equivalent of US$2 a day. Given the horrible labor conditions on the estates and the

A Haitian migrant laborer. It is a matter of academic debate as to how much choice such a laborer has in terms of whether he will migrate to the neighboring Dominican Republic for short-term work cutting cane, given the fact that he cannot find any kind of work in Haiti.

availability of lighter and better-paying work elsewhere in the Dominican Republic, it is not surprising that cane growers take measures to try to prevent their Haitian recruits from leaving. For example, armed guards patrol estate grounds on the lookout for any bracero who tries to leave in the night.

At work, too, the braceros are subjected to open coercion. On ordinary work days, they are obliged to go out to the cane fields before dawn, sometimes even if they are too sick to work. Company overseers may also force them to work on Sundays or after dark, to help ensure a constant supply of cane to the mill.... As if all these abuses were not bad enough, a many-branched system of pay reductions and petty corruption deprives the braceros of a large fraction of the wages to which they are legally entitled. Many Haitians on the sugar estates say they have never been able to save enough money to return home. (19–29)

View 2

Anthropological studies based on long-term fieldwork in Haiti provide observations that appear to contradict the neo-slavery interpretation. They find instead that most Haitian labor migrants cross the border to the Dominican Republic of their own volition. Martínez comments that "Recruitment by force in Haiti seems virtually unheard of. On the contrary, if this is a system of slavery, it may be the first in history to have to *turn away* potential recruits" (20). Some recruits have even paid bribes to be hired. Most people, even young people, are aware of how terrible the working conditions are in the Dominican Republic. They therefore choose to go, understanding what they will face. Repeat migration is common and is also taken as evidence of free choice. In the cane fields, the major means of maintaining labor discipline is not force but wage incentives: The piece-work system ensures long and hard work. The life histories of braceros show that many of them move from one sugar estate to another, discrediting the view of the estates as being like "concentration camps."

Samuel Martínez adds a more focused understanding to View 2 by giving emphasis to the importance of the driving force of poverty in shaping the braceros' decisions to migrate. In this way, we can see, perhaps, a link between View 1 and View 2, since "neo-slavery" could be defined to include economic systems in which choice is so severely limited by economic needs that "freedom" is scarcely a factor in decision making:

> Both economically and legally, the bracero finds his freedoms narrowly restricted . . . poverty and the dearth of income opportunities and credit at home for the young, land-poor, and the unskilled leave many rural Haitians little or no choice about whether to emigrate. For example, the prevailing wage for a six-to-eight hour "day" of farm labor in rural Haiti is less than one dollar. Even at this wage, paid employment for poorer folk is scarce, because few Haitian farmers have the means to hire much labor.... Faced with such daunting obstacles to economic advancement at home, a man who lacks money, social support, and human capital to go to a more desirable urban or overseas destination may turn to the Dominican Republic, in hope of bringing home at least a small cash surplus. The typical migrant brings home savings of US$25 to $75, but many fail to save even this much. The fact that such meager and uncertain rewards exert an important attraction suggests that most migrants leave home not so much to optimize their incomes as to grasp at any chance that may present itself . . . poverty drives dependent young men and male heads of poorer households to go to the Dominican Republic and thus opens the door to the labor rights abuses so amply documented. (21–22)

Critical Thinking Questions

- How might the research methods of the activists and the academic anthropologists differ?
- How do these differences influence their results? Is either perspective more "biased" than the other in terms of presenting an accurate picture of the bracero system?
- What does each view offer in terms of policy reform?

Source: Martinez 1996. Reproduced by permission of the American Anthropological Association from American Anthropologist 98:1, March 1996. Not for further reproduction.

ment plan for these people was successful for the following reasons: it provided land to farmers quickly; it involved household welfare support during the time of transition; entire villages were resettled together as much as possible; new social organizations were formed to facilitate adaptation; and there was cultural similarity between the Karelians and the local Finnish population in the resettlement area. Important shared cultural features included farming practices, religion, and women's status.

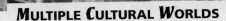

Multiple Cultural Worlds

Palestinian Refugees in Lebanon—Uncounted and Unwanted

Hundreds of thousands of Palestinians fled or were driven from their homes during the 1948 war (Zureik 1994). They went mainly to Jordan, the West Bank/East Jerusalem, Gaza, Lebanon, Syria, and other Arab states. Jordan and Syria have granted Palestinian refugees equal rights. Their situation in Lebanon is much worse because Lebanon refuses them the right to settle there. There is no official census count of the number of Palestinians who entered Lebanon following the 1948 formation of Israel. Estimates vary from about 200,000 to 600,000 (Salam 1994). The lower count is claimed to be accurate by the Israelis in order to downgrade the importance of the refugee problem. The higher count is favored both by the Palestinians, to highlight the seriousness of their plight, and by the Lebanese government, to emphasize its inability to absorb them. According to a 1987 estimate, only 30,000 had become Lebanese citizens. The rest are caught between resettlement and repatriation (return to one's homeland).

The Lebanese government does not extend civil rights, including the right to work or own property, to the Palestinians (*The Economist* 1995:4). The refugees are excluded from public services such as health care and education. They are spatially restricted to a limited number of camps that are threatened by expansion and development in Beirut. Palestinians believe that the Lebanese are trying to force them to migrate out, but they cannot go back to Israel. Israel refuses them "right of return" (Salam 1994). The right of return says that:

- refugees who wish to return home and live at peace should be allowed to do so
- they may accept either repatriation or compensation for losses
- they have the right to compensation for damages suffered whether or not they wish to return.

The right of return, considered a basic human right in the West since the time of the Magna Carta, is included in the United Nations General Assembly Resolution 194 passed in 1948. The right of return was elevated by the UN in 1974 to an "inalienable right." Israel responds to Palestinian claims by saying that its acceptance of Jewish immigrants from Arab countries constitutes an exchange. Some scholars and government officials say that the 1948 exodus from Israel was either voluntary or largely instigated by leaders of neighboring Arab countries—thus the Palestinians, they claim, were not true "refugees." Egypt and several Gulf states are following Lebanon's lead and denying rights to Palestinians. These governments consider the Palestinian presence a threat to internal stability.

Institutional Migrants

Institutional migrants include people who move into a social institution, either voluntarily or involuntarily. They include monks and nuns, retirees, prisoners, and boarding school or college students. This section considers only some examples of students as a category of migrants.

Studies of student adjustment reveal similarities with many other forms of migration, especially in terms of risks for mental stress. Ethnographic research conducted among adolescent boarding school children in Ambanja, a town in Madagascar, showed that girls experience more adjustment strains than boys (Sharp 1990). Ambanja is a "booming migrant town" characterized by rootlessness and anomie. Boarding school children in this town constitute a vulnerable group because they have left their families and come alone to the school. Many of the boarding school girls, who were between the ages of thirteen and seventeen, experienced bouts of spirit possession. Local people say that it is the "prettiest" girls that become possessed. The data on possession patterns showed, instead, that possession is correlated with a girl's being unmarried and pregnant. Many of these school girls become the mistresses of older men, who shower them with expensive gifts such as perfume and gold jewelry. Such girls attract the envy of both other girls and school boys, who are being passed over in favor of adult men. Thus, the girls have little peer support among their schoolmates. If a girl becomes pregnant, school policy requires that she be expelled. If the baby's father refuses to help her, she faces severe hardship. Her return home will be a great disappointment to her parents. Within this context, a girl's spirit possession may be understood as an expression of distress. Through the spirits, girls act out their difficult position between country and city and girlhood and womanhood.

International students also face serious challenges of spatial and cultural relocation. Like the school girls of Madagascar, they are at greater risk of adjustment stress than are local students. Many international students report mental health problems to varying degrees depending on age, marital status, and other factors. Spouses who accompany international students also suffer the strains of dislocation. The issue of international student adjustment is of increasing importance in the United States, where about a half million international students are enrolled in institutions of higher education, and that number is growing (Oei and Notowidjojo 1990).

United States marines wear gas masks as protection from fumes of the oil fires during the war with Kuwait.

Soldiers on Assignment

Soldiers are often sent on distant assignments for long periods of time. Their destination may have negative physical and mental health effects on them, in addition to the fact that they may face combat. During the British and French colonial expansion, thousands of soldiers were assigned to "tropical" countries (Curtin 1989). Colonial soldiers faced new diseases in their destination areas. Their death rates from disease were twice as high as soldiers who stayed home, with two exceptions—Tahiti and Hawaii—where soldiers experienced better health than at home. Most military personnel were male, but in some colonial contexts, many wives accompanied their husbands. In India, mortality rates were higher for females than males. This finding may be explained by the fact that the men had to pass a physical exam before enlisting, while their dependents did not. In addition to facing added risks while overseas, soldiers and their families experience adjustment difficulties when they return home.

Spouse/Partner Migration

When a relationship is initiated, patrilocal or matrilocal rules about residence may mean that one partner relocates while the other stays in place. The preponderance of patrilocal residence cross-culturally means that in heterosexual unions, women more often have a greater adjustment burden than men. In international marriage migration, one partner or both may lack language abilities and have poor job prospects. Staying at or near one's home location is relatively empowering because it allows the person to capitalize on local knowledge (of agricultural conditions or the best places to gather food) and social support. "Mail-order brides," women whose marriage to an American citizen is arranged through a mail-order service, are particularly at risk of difficult adjustments. The new husband typically has expectations of a subservient and dependent wife. The wife's expectations for living in the United States may not match her husband's, and she may be unable to find wage-paying work that would increase her autonomy. Frequent reports of wife abuse in "mail-order marriages" have brought attention to this system, although no clear solutions have emerged.

Another facet of spouse/partner migration occurs when a couple migrates to take up a new economic opportunity for one member of the couple. The second member is called a **trailing spouse** or **trailing partner.** The trailing spouse or partner moves in order to keep the relationship intact (Bayes 1989). In the United States, men are the primary wage-earners in 74 percent of two-earner couples, and so, when relocation occurs, it is usually a female who is the trailer (in heterosexual couples). The leading partner tends to adjust to a new location more easily because the new job is fulfilling. For the trailing partner, adjustment takes longer and is accompanied by loneliness and depression. Former roles and relationships, and even the physical attributes of the previous place of residence are missed, and the new location seems to have little with which to replace them. It can be a period of social and psychological "mourning" for a lost identity (Boire 1992).

THE NEW IMMIGRANTS

The term **new immigrants** refers to international migrants who have moved since the 1960s and later. New immigrants worldwide include increasing proportions of refugees, many of whom are destitute and desperate for asylum. Three trends are apparent in the new international migration of the 1990s, and they are likely to continue:

- *Globalization:* More countries are involved in international migration, leading to increased cultural diversity in sending and receiving countries.
- *Acceleration:* Quantitative growth of migration in all major regions has occurred.
- *Feminization:* Women are playing a greater role in migration to and from all regions and in all types of migration, with some forms having a majority of women.

These three trends merit scholarly attention and raise new issues for policy makers and international organizations as the cultural practices of immigrant groups and the areas of destination increasingly come in contact and, sometimes, in conflict, with each other (see the Multiple Cultural Worlds box).

Globalization, acceleration, feminization.

In the United States, the category of "new immigrants" refers to people who arrived following the 1965 amendments to the Immigration and Nationality Act. This change made it possible for far more people from developing countries to enter, especially if they were professionals or trained in some desired skill. Later, the "family reunification" provision allowed permanent residents and naturalized citizens to bring in close family members. Most of the new immigrants in the United States are from Asia, Latin America, and the Caribbean, although increasing

MULTIPLE CULTURAL WORLDS

The New Immigrants and FGM in the United States

About 7,000 women and girls immigrate to the United States annually from countries where people practice female genital mutilation (FGM) (see Chapter 6) (Burstyn 1995). Most live in California, New York, and the Washington DC area. Estimated rates of FGM in their home countries range from around 90 percent in Somalia and Ethiopia to 50 percent in Egypt. One commentator said, "Even if only a small percentage of newly arrived families from these countries maintain the tradition of FGM, these figures suggest that hundreds of young girls either brought here or born here are in danger each year" (33).

Canada, England, France, Belgium, Denmark, Switzerland, and Sweden have made FGM illegal. As of 1997, the United States had passed no specific legislation against FGM. Medical associations in most Canadian provinces have strict penalties for FGM and reinfibulation after childbirth. They have also begun educational efforts among communities where FGM is most likely in the hopes of discouraging the practice rather than punishing parents. Within the "legal vacuum" of the United States, many activist groups have sought to raise public awareness against FGM. Working one-on-one with families to prevent FGM is another strategy. For example, Mimi Ramsay, an Ethiopian-born nurse who lives in San Jose, California, makes many home visits to talk with mothers, trying to convince them to protect their daughters from FGM.

numbers are from Eastern Europe, especially Russia. The United States offers two kinds of visas for foreigners: immigrant visas (also called residence visas) and nonimmigrant visas for tourists and students (Pessar 1995:6). An immigrant visa is usually valid indefinitely and allows its holder to be employed and to apply for citizenship. A nonimmigrant visa is issued for a limited time period and usually bars its holder from paid employment. Some immigrants are granted visas because of their special skills related to labor market needs, but most are now admitted under the family unification provision.

The New Immigrants from Latin America and the Caribbean

Since the 1960s, substantial movements of the Latino population (people who share roots in former Spanish and Portuguese colonies in the western hemisphere) have occurred, mainly but not entirely in the direction of the United States. Compared to numbers of legal immigrants in the 1960s, numbers doubled or tripled in the 1980s and then declined in the 1990s. For example, legal immigrants from Central America numbered about 100,000 in the 1960s, nearly 900,000 in the 1980s, and about 270,000 in the 1990s (Parrillo 1997:398). Excluding the residents of Puerto Rico, Latinos totaled about 2.4 million people, or about 9 percent of the United States population in the 1990 census (Mahler 1995:xiii). In the United States, Latinos will be the largest minority early in the twenty-first century. In some cities, such as Los Angeles, Miami, San Antonio, and New York, they are already the largest minority. Within the category of Latino new immigrants, the three largest subgroups are Mexicans (13.5 million in the 1990 census), Puerto Ricans (2.7 million), and Cubans (1 million). Large streams also come from the Dominican Republic, Colombia, Ecuador, and more recently refugees from El Salvador, Nicaragua, and Peru.

Chain Migration of Dominicans

The Dominican Republic has ranked among the top ten source countries of immigrants to the United States since the 1960s (Pessar 1995). Dominicans are one of the fastest-growing immigrant groups in the United States. They are found clustered in a few states, with their highest concentration in New York. Within New York City, Washington Heights is the heart of the Dominican community. Unlike many other new immigrant streams, the Dominicans are mainly middle and upper class. Most have left their homeland "in search of a better life." Many hope to return to the Dominican Republic, saying that in New York, "There is work but there is no life."

Patricia Pessar conducted fieldwork in the Dominican Republic and in New York City, and thus she has a transnational view. She studied the dynamics of departure (such as getting a visa), the process of arrival, and adaptation in New York. Like most anthropologists who work with immigrant groups, she became involved in helping many of her informants: "Along the way I also endeavored to repay people's help by brokering for them with institutions such as the Immigration and Naturalization Service, social service agencies, schools, and hospitals" (xv). For Dominican immigrants, as for most other immigrant groups, the *cadena,* or chain, links one immigrant to another. **Chain migration** is the process by which a first wave of migrants then attracts relatives and friends to join them in the destination place. Most Dominicans who are legal immigrants have sponsored other family members, so most legal Dominicans have entered through the family unification provision. The U.S. policy defines a family as a nuclear unit, and thus, it excludes important members of Dominican extended family networks such as cousins

A Dominican Day parade in New York City.

and ritual kin (compadres). To overcome this barrier, some Dominicans (and other ethnic groups) use the technique of the "business marriage." In a business marriage, an individual pays a legal immigrant or citizen a fee of perhaps $2,000 to enter into a "marriage." He or she then acquires a visa through the family unification provision. Such an arrangement does not involve cohabitation or sexual relations; it is meant to be broken.

Dominicans have found employment in New York's manufacturing industries, including the garment industry. Dominicans are more heavily employed in these industries than any other ethnic group. Recent declines in the numbers of New York City's manufacturing jobs and the redefining of better positions into less desirable ones through restructuring has disproportionately affected them. Dominicans also work in retail and wholesale trade, another sector that has declined since the late 1960s. Others have established their own retail businesses or *bodegas.* A problem with this line of work is that many bodegas are located in unsafe areas and some owners have been killed. Declining economic opportunities for Dominicans have also been aggravated by arrivals of newer immigrants, especially from Mexico and Central America, who are willing to accept even lower wages and worse working conditions.

Although many families of middle and high status in the Dominican Republic initially secured fairly solid employment in the United States, they have declined economically since then. Dominicans now have the highest poverty rate in New York City, 37 percent, compared with an overall city average of 17 percent. Poverty is concentrated among women-headed households with young children. The gender gap in wages is high, and women are more likely to be on public assistance than men. On the other hand, Dominican women in the United States are more often regularly employed than women in the Dominican Republic. This pattern upsets a patriarchal norm in which the nuclear family depends on male earnings and female domestic responsibilities. A woman's earning power means that husband-wife decision making is more egalitarian. A working Dominican woman is likely to obtain more assistance from the man in doing household chores. All of these changes help explain why Dominican men are more interested in returning to the Dominican Republic than the women are. As one man said, "Your country is a country for women; mine is for men" (81).

Salvadorans: Escaping War to Struggle in Poverty

Salvadorans are the fourth largest Latino population in the United States, numbering 565,000 people in the 1990 census. The civil war in El Salvador, which began in 1979 and continued for a decade, was the major stimulus for Salvadoran emigration (Mahler 1995). Most of the refugees from the war came to the United States, and many settled in New York City. About 60,000 chose to live on Long Island, where they represent a rarely studied form of international migration to suburban areas. Middle- and upper-class Salvadorans were able to obtain tourist or even immigrant visas relatively easily, but the poor could not. Many entered the United States illegally as *mojados,* wetbacks, or undocumented immigrants. Like Mexicans, they use the term *mojado* to describe their journey, but for the Salvadorans there were three rivers to cross instead of one. These three crossings are a prominent theme of their escape stories, which are full of physical and psychological hardship, including hunger, arrests, and women being beaten and raped along the way. Sarah Mahler comments:

> After talking to Salvadorans about their trips, I always concluded our conversations by asking whether they would recommend that their friends or relatives come to the United States, knowing all that they had learned during their journeys and experiences. Nearly everyone answered the same way. They did not know that the trip would be so difficult; women particularly assert their desire never to repeat the experience. (51)

Once they arrive, things are not easy either, especially in the search for work and housing. Lack of education and marketable skills limit the job search. For those who are undocumented immigrants, getting a decent job is even harder. All of these factors make it more likely that Salvadorans will work in the informal sector, where they are easy targets for economic exploitation. Salvadorans who find work on Long Island are in the blue-collar sector, where they receive low wages and work in poor conditions. Jobs involve providing services to better-off Long Island households. Men do outside work such as gardening, landscaping, construction, and pool cleaning. Women work as nannies, live-in maids, house cleaners, restaurant help, and caregivers for the elderly. They often work a mix of these jobs, for example, working at a McDonalds in the morning and doing house cleaning in the afternoon. Men's pride prevents them from taking lowly (and to them female) jobs such as washing dishes. Women are comparatively more flexible and more likely to find work than men. For the poorest of Salvadoran refugees, even exploitative jobs may be an economic improvement compared to back home, where they could not support their families.

The Salvadorans were attracted to Long Island by its thriving informal economy, a sector where checking for visas was less likely to occur. Unfortunately, the cost of living on Long Island is higher than in many other places. The combination of low wages and high costs of living has kept most Salvadorans in the category of the working poor, with few prospects for improvement. They attempt to cope with high housing costs by crowding many people into units meant for a nuclear family. Compared to El Salvador, where most people except for the urban poor owned their own homes, only a few Salvadorans on Long Island own homes. Residential space and costs are shared among extended kin and non-kin who pay rent. This situation causes intrahousehold tension and stress.

The refugees carry with them memories of the war and their escape from it. As of the mid-1990s, response from the American health care system to these refugees' needs was minimal, and they were largely marginalized from normal benefits. On a more positive note, the Catholic church has begun to address the fact that the Salvadorans are now a substantial population and it has started to hold services in Spanish as an outreach for this new community of refugees. In spite of all these difficulties, most of the Salvadorans that Mahler knew evaluated their experience in the United States positively.

The New Immigrants from East Asia

Koreans: Economic Achievement and Political Identity

In 1962, the South Korean government began encouraging massive emigration (Yoon 1993). This change was motivated by perceived population pressure and an interest in gaining remittances from persons working abroad. Before 1965, most Korean immigrants were wives of American service men and children being adopted by American parents. After 1965, most immigrants were members of intact nuclear families or family members being unified with earlier pioneer migrants already in the United States. During the peak years of 1985 and 1987, more than 35,000 Koreans immigrated to the United States annually, making South Korea the largest immigrant source nation after Mexico and the Philippines. Many of the migrants were displaced North Koreans who had fled their homeland to avoid communist rule there between 1945 and 1951. They had difficulty gaining an economic foothold in South Korea. When the opportunity arose to emigrate to South America or the United States, they were more willing to do so than many established South Koreans.

In 1981, North Koreans constituted only 2 percent of the population of South Korea, but they were 22 percent of the Korean population of Los Angeles. Most of these immigrants were entrepreneurial, Christian, and middle class. In recent years, the number of lower-class migrants has increased in the migration stream from Korea. Many lower-class Korean immigrants moved to Los Angeles, the second largest city in the United States and one that is racially and ethnically diverse (Sonenshein 1996). Whites are less than 40 percent of the population, while Asian Americans and Hispanics together account for 50 percent. The proportion of Blacks is 14 percent. Electoral politics are mainly a matter of Blacks and Whites, with Hispanics involved to a lesser degree. The majority of eligible voters are Black or White. In the 1993 mayoral election, 72 percent of the voters were White, 12 percent Black, 10 percent Hispanic, and 4 percent Asian American. In the area called South Central, a low-income section of the city shared by Blacks, Hispanics, and Korean Americans, the Blacks are the only politically active group. Their views are liberal and they are mainly Democratic.

A wide gap separates Black politics from interests of the Korean Americans. While the Korean Americans are arguably exploited by larger economic interests, especially in their role as small shop owners, within South Central, they are seen by other people as exploitative. One issue over which conflict has arisen, especially between Blacks and Korean Americans, is liquor store ownership. Over the years, many bank branches, large grocery stores, and movie theaters have left South Central. The gap was filled by stores in which the most valuable commodity sold is liquor. In South Central there are 17 liquor licenses per square mile compared to 1.7 for the rest of Los Angeles County. Given this background, it is perplexing that no one foresaw the 1992 riots in which thou-

Korean Americans clean up the debris from attacks on their businesses after the Los Angeles riots of May 1992.

sands of Korean businesses were damaged, including 187 liquor stores. (The Hispanic population also suffered severe losses. One-third of all deaths resulting from the riot were Hispanic people). For the Koreans, one outcome has been an increased sense of ethnic unity and political awareness (see the Voices box on page 398). Prospects for a coalition between Blacks and Korean Americans in South Central appear dim. Each feels dominated by the other: Blacks feel economically dominated by Korean Americans and Korean Americans feel politically dominated by Blacks.

Changing Patterns of Consumption among Hong Kong Chinese

Studies of how international migrants change their behavior in the new destination have addressed, among other things, the question of whether consumption patterns change and, if so, how, why, and what effects such changes have on other aspects of their culture. Three models have emerged about the degree of change:

- Migrants assimilate to majority culture norms (the melting pot model).
- Migrants reject majority norms and seek to maintain their original habits.
- Migrants selectively adapt to majority practices.

An immigrant's education, class, gender, language, and exposure to the mass media play important roles affecting the degree of assimilation to the dominant culture.

A study conducted in Canada focused on the topic of consumption patterns among four groups: Anglo-Canadians, new Hong Kong immigrants (who had arrived within the previous seven years), long-time Hong Kong immigrants, and Hong Kong residents (Lee and Tse 1994). In anticipation of the transfer of Hong Kong to China, about 60,000 Hong Kong Chinese left Hong Kong for Canada, New Zealand, the United Kingdom, the United States, and Singapore. Since 1987, Hong Kong has been the single largest source of immigrants to Canada. The new immigrant settlement pattern in Canada is one of urban clustering. They have developed their own shopping centers, television and radio stations, newspapers, and country clubs. Because of their overall high incomes, the Hong Kong immigrants have greatly boosted Canadian buying power. In 1992, the estimated 35,797 immigrants resulted in an increase of $110 million in buying power.

For most migrants, however, the move has brought a lowered economic situation, which is reflected in their consumption patterns. New immigrants reduce their spending especially on entertainment and expensive items. Primary needs of the new immigrants include items that about half of all households owned: car, VCR, carpets, microwave oven, family house, and multiple TVs. Items in the second product category were dining room set, barbecue stove, deep freezer, and dehumidifier. Long-time immigrants tend to have a fuller complement of secondary products, suggesting that, with time and increased economic standing, expanded consumption occurs.

Trends suggest a gradual adoption of Anglo-Canadian product acquisition for such items. At the same time, businesses in Canada have responded to immigrant tastes by providing Hong Kong style restaurants, Chinese branch banks, and travel agencies. Supermarkets have specialized Asian sections. So, to some extent, traditional patterns and ties can be selectively maintained. Two characteristics of

VOICES

"Saying Goodbye" by Marie G. Lee

Marie G. Lee has published articles in a number of magazines and newspapers and written two children's novels. In this excerpt, Ellen Sung explores her Korean heritage during her freshman year at Harvard.

"Ellen, Koreans—and other immigrants—come to this country believing the myth that if they work hard, they can be just as good as any white American."

"Why do you call that a myth?" I say. "Look, your parents came to the U.S. with so little and here you are at Harvard."

"But that's just it—we're made to think we're equal, but in reality we're treated differently. Koreans have been here long enough that we should have tons of Korean American senators, writers, CEOs, but we don't. We have the highest education levels of any immigrant group, but no one seems to notice that our poverty rates, our family income levels, put us not on the level with whites, but with other oppressed minority groups."

"Jae," I say, "In Arkin, my father, the doctor, was one of the richest people in town. My best friend, Jessie, is really smart, but she could never afford to go someplace like this."

"But that's definitely not the norm for Korean American families." Jae says wearily. "Koreans are second-class citizens in this country."

"I didn't realize you were so militant about this," I say, a little uneasily.

"I have a reason to be. Remember, I grew up in L.A. During the riots, I saw with my own eyes how the cops and the National Guard were immediately dispatched in force to Beverly Hills while Koreatown was ignored until two days after the place burned down. We paid our taxes, obeyed the law—and what did the government do? They basically handed us over to the looters as sacrificial lambs to protect the white areas."

"Is that why so many Koreans defended their stores with guns?" I ask.

"There was no other way," Jae says. "When the police abandoned Koreatown and South Central, the Korean community had to take things into its own hands. A network was set up so store owners could radio for help, and people risked their lives defending other people's stores."

I wonder if Jae was one of those gun-toting Koreans. But there I go again: one of those. When I'm with Jae, everything's so easy. He's another human being, a guy, a friend, maybe even a lover. I feel I know him so well, yet this episode at KASH (Korean American Students of Harvard) proves that I don't. What effect did it have on him to be one of the Koreans involved in the riot instead of one who watched the carnage via the satellite safety of CNN, far, far away from Koreatown?

"I'm sorry I don't agree with you about all this KASH stuff," I say. "I want to, but I can't."

Jae puts his hand on my back, a touch that is unmistakably loving.

"I don't want you to pretend you agree with me," he says. "That's what I like about you. If we're honest with each other, we'll get through it, okay?"

"Okay," I say, but despite it all, I feel troubled.

Source: Excerpt from *Saying Goodbye,* pp. 134–135, by Marie Lee.

these migrants distinguish them from other streams: their relatively secure economic status and their high level of education, exceeding that of the average Canadian. Still, in Canada, they often have a difficult time finding suitable employment. Some have nicknamed Canada "Kan Lan Tai," meaning a difficult place to prosper, a fact that leads many to become "astronauts" or transnational migrants who have strong roots in two cultures at the same time.

The New Immigrants from Southeast Asia

Three Patterns of Adaptation among the Vietnamese

Over one and a quarter million refugees have left Vietnam since the 1970s. Although most were relocated to the United States, many went to Canada, Australia, France, Germany, and Britain (Gold 1992).

Vietnamese immigrants in the United States will constitute the nation's third largest Asian American minority by the year 2000. Three distinct subgroups are: the 1975-era elite, the boat people, and the ethnic Chinese. While they interact frequently, they have retained distinct patterns of adaptation.

The first group avoided many of the traumatic elements of flight. They were U.S. employees and members of the South Vietnamese government and military. They left before having to live under the communist regime, and they spent little time in refugee camps. Most came with intact families and received generous financial assistance. Using their education and English language skills, many found good jobs quickly and adjusted rapidly.

The boat people began to enter the United States after the outbreak of the Vietnam–China conflict of 1978. Mainly of rural origin, they lived for three years or more under communism, working in reeducation camps or "new economic zones." Their exit, either by overcrowded and leaky boats or on foot through Cambodia, was dangerous and difficult. Over 50 percent died on the way. Those who survived faced many months in refugee camps in Thailand, Malaysia, the Philippines, or Hong Kong before being admitted to the United States. Many more males than females escaped as boat people; thus, they are less likely to have arrived with intact families. They were less well educated than the earlier wave, half had no competence in English, and they faced the depressed American economy of the 1980s. By the time of their arrival, refugee cash assistance had been cut severely and other benefits canceled. They have had a much more difficult time adjusting to life in the United States than the 1975-elite.

The ethnic Chinese, traditionally a distinct and socially marginalized class of entrepreneurs in Vietnam, arrived mainly as boat people. Following the 1978 outbreak of hostilities between Vietnam and China, the ethnic Chinese were allowed to leave Vietnam. Some have used contacts in the overseas Chinese community and have been able to reestablish their roles as entrepreneurs, but most have had a difficult time in the United States since they did not have a Western-style education. They were also sometimes subject to discrimination from other Vietnamese in the United States.

The general picture of Vietnamese refugee adjustment in the United States shows high rates of unemployment, welfare dependency, and poverty, even after several years. Interviews with Vietnamese refugees in southern California reveal generational change and fading traditions:

> Most older Vietnamese live in America with the memories of these old traditions. Mr. Phuong Hoang, the elderly boat person who escaped with his family to the Philippines in 1978, recalls with nostalgia his instruction as a child to train him to be a good citizen, to respect teachers and old people, as well as brothers and sisters.
>
> "Ours was an education based on custom. We learned how citizens should pay taxes to the government, rules of politeness and respect, and the proper rules of relationship between young men and women, who should never touch or shake hands. If a man wanted to marry a particular woman, his parents should find an old friend or relative of the woman to serve as a matchmaker." (Freeman 1995: 115–116)

Many Vietnamese teenagers in southern California have taken on the lifestyle of other low-income American teenagers. Their American friends are of more significance in defining their identities than their Vietnamese heritage. Given the social variations and regional differences in adaptation throughout the United States, however, generalizations about "Vietnamese Americans" can be made only with caution for the present and, even more so for the future given the possibilities of cultural revival.

Khmer Refugees' Interpretation of Their Suffering

Since the late 1970s, over 150,000 people from Kampuchea (formerly called Cambodia) have come to the United States as refugees of the Pol Pot regime (Mortland 1994). These people survived years of political repression, a difficult escape, and time in a refugee camp before arriving in the United States. One question anthropologists ask is how people who have been through such terror and loss reconstruct their understanding of how the world works and their place in it. Most Khmer refugees were Buddhist when they lived in Kampuchea. They have attempted to understand why they experienced such disasters within the Buddhist framework of karma. According to their beliefs, good actions bring good to the individual, family, and community; bad actions bring bad. Thus, many Khmer Buddhists blame themselves for the suffering endured under the Pol Pot regime. They think that perhaps they did something wrong in a previous life. Self-blame and depression character-

Immigrants learning English at Evans Community Adult School.

ize many Khmer refugees. Others feel that Buddhism failed, and so they turned in large numbers to Christianity, the dominant faith of the seemingly successful Americans. In recent years, however, a resurgence of Khmer Buddhism has occurred. Many temples have been constructed, and popular public rituals and celebrations are held in them. For these reviving Buddhists, Christianity either becomes a complementary religion, or is rejected and avoided as a threat to Buddhism. Changing interpretations arise over time and with the new generations. Given the diversity within the Khmer immigrant population, it is difficult to say what the future holds for either the adults who are still trying to make sense of their suffering or for the new generation being raised outside Kampuchea.

The New Immigrants from South Asia: Asian Indians of New York City Maintain Their Culture

With the 1965 change in legislation in the United States, a first wave of South Asian immigrants dominated by male professionals arrived (Bhardwaj and Rao 1990). Members of this first wave settled primarily in eastern and western cities. Subsequent immigrants from India have been less well educated and wealthy, and they tend to be concentrated in New York and New Jersey. New York City has the largest population of Asian Indians in the United States, with 106,000 in 1990 or 1.2 percent of the city's population, and about one-eighth of the total number of documented Asian Indians in the United States (Mogelonsky 1995). In some parts of New Jersey, Asian Indians constitute over 2 percent of the total population. Members of the highly educated first wave are concentrated in professional fields such as medicine, engineering, and management (Helweg and Helweg 1990). Members of the less educated, later wave find work in family-run businesses or service industries. Asian Indians dominate some trades such as convenience and stationery stores. They have penetrated the ownership of budget hotels and motels and operate nearly half of the total number of establishments in this niche. More than 40 percent of New York City's 40,000 licensed Yellow Cab drivers are Indians, or Pakistanis or Bangladeshis (Mogelonsky 1995).

In general, the Asian Indian population in the United States is one of the better-off immigrant groups, and they are considered an "immigrant success story." Asian Indians place high value on their children's education and urge them to pursue higher education in fields such as medicine and engineering. In the United States, they tend to have small families and to invest heavily in their children's schooling and social advancement.

A continuing concern of many members of the first wave is the maintenance of Hindu or Muslim cultural values in the face of conflicting patterns prevalent in mainstream American culture such as dating, premarital sex, drinking, and drugs. The Hindu population has increasingly supported the construction of Hindu temples that attract pilgrims from around the nation and from India. These temples offer Sunday school classes and cultural events as a way of passing on the Hindu heritage to the next generation. Johanna Lessinger (1995) describes the growth of the Hindu congregation of the Ganesha Temple in New York:

> [T]he institution was founded in 1977 under the leadership of Indians from southern India. The temple's rituals still reflect South Indian ritual practice.

> At present, however, the temple is engaged in an effort to broaden its appeal to other Hindus. Over the years its congregation has grown, its physical structure continues to be expanded and improved. The daily and yearly cycle of rituals has become more extensive and elaborate. Today worshippers come to this temple from the entire New York metropolitan area.... The temple is now also a regular pilgrimage destination for Indian immigrants on holiday in New York from other parts of the U.S., and for visitors from India. (49–50)

The New Immigrants from Eastern Europe

The breakup of the Soviet Union into fifteen separate countries spurred the movement of over 9 million people throughout Eastern Europe and Central Asia. Many of these immigrants are people of Slavic descent who had lived in Central Asia during the time of the former Soviet Union and are seeking to return to their homelands. Another large category includes people who were forcibly relocated to Siberia or Central Asia. Many Soviet Germans have migrated from Siberia to Germany, and Crimean Tatars are shifting from Uzbekistan back to Crimea. Since 1988, people from the former Soviet Union have been the largest refugee nationality to enter the United States (Littman 1993, cited in Gold 1995).

Soviet Jews: Refugees Fleeing Religious Persecution

A sizable proportion of the refugees from the former Soviet Union are Soviet Jews. They have relocated to Israel, some countries of Western Europe, and the United States. The largest number of Soviet Jews lives in Israel, but since the mid-1960s, about 325,000 have settled in the United States. Steven Gold (1995) has studied different refugee groups in California for many years and speaks from a comparative perspective when he points out unique features of the experience of Soviet Jewish refugees. First, their origins in the Soviet Union accustomed them to the fact that the government controlled almost every aspect of life, "from the production of butter and the administration of summer camps to the shaping of ideology" (xi). These emigres are used to a wide range of government services, including jobs, housing, day care, and other basic needs. They have had to find new ways of meeting these needs in a market economy. Second, Soviet Jews, as White Europeans, are members of the dominant racial majority group in the United States. While Soviet Jews have suffered centuries of discrimination in Eastern Europe, they are much closer to the racial mainstream in the United States. Their education also places them in the elite of new immigrant groups. Third, they have access to established and prosperous communities of American Jews. They have well-connected sponsors when they arrive. Most other new immigrant groups do not have these advantages.

California is their major destination. Los Angeles has the second largest Jewish community in the United States and the San Francisco Bay area has the seventh. California's mild climate, relatively robust economy, wide range of social services, and good universities attracted Soviet Jews. The economic downturn of the 1990s, however, prompted a wave of anti-immigrant sentiment of which Soviet Jewish immigrants are "keenly aware" (xiii).

Soviet Jewish immigrants face other challenges as well. Depending on their area of relocation, many have a difficult time finding a job commensurate with their education and previous work in the Soviet Union. In the depressed economy of Pittsburgh, many Soviet Jewish immigrants remain unemployed or are forced to accept menial labor jobs far beneath their qualifications. This is especially true for women emigres who were employed, often as professionals, in the Soviet Union, but who can find no work in the United States other than house cleaning or baby sitting. In the early 1990s, this population constituted a major increase in admissions to the psychiatric unit at the university hospital, and attempts were being made to translate the psychiatric intake interview into Russian. Another major challenge relates to marriage options. Cultural norms promote interethnic marriage, and few Soviet Jews are interested in marrying Americans. However, the number of Soviet Jews in the marriage pool is small. As a result, marriage brokerage businesses have developed that pair young women in Russia with established emigres in America.

Bosnian Refugees: Rebuilding Their Lives after War

The Serbian policy of ethnocide or "ethnic-cleansing" in former Yugoslavia involved the claiming of territory and driving out of all "non-Serbs" through outright murder, mass rape of women, imprisonment, and torture (Stiglmayer 1994). The recent war in Bosnia-Herzegovina created the greatest refugee cri-

MULTIPLE CULTURAL WORLDS

Bosnian Trauma Testimonies and Recovery

Clinical experience and research with refugee survivors of massive psychological trauma indicate that these people are especially prone to suffer from post-traumatic stress disorder (PTSD); depression; and changes in memory, consciousness, identity, and personality. In terms of treatment, several approaches have been used, including the testimony method in conjunction with supportive therapy. While long-term effects have yet to be assessed, one study has examined the "trauma testimonies" (narrative accounts of their experiences of terror and suffering) of twenty Bosnian refugees who have been resettled in the United States (Weine et al. 1995). The testimony method involves asking the individual "to tell in detail the story of what happened to them and recording their narrative account verbatim . . . many clinicians agree that having individuals tell the story of their traumatic experiences in a safe and caring interpersonal setting helps them to live better with traumatic memories" (536–537).

Ten of the refugees in the study were male and ten were female. They belonged to six families and ranged in age from thirteen to sixty-two years. All but one were Muslims, and all adults were married and had worked either inside or outside the home. Analysis of the testimony showed that all had experienced a high number of traumatic events, with the frequency increasing with a person's age. Number of traumatic events did not differ by gender, but the qualitative aspects of the trauma did:

> Adult men were more likely to be separated from their families and to be held in concentration camps where they suffered extreme deprivation and atrocities. Adult women (as well as adolescents of both genders) were often held briefly in detention camps and then they spent months fleeing from capture or being held in occupied territory where they were subjected to violence. (537)
>
> Almost all the refugees experienced the destruction of their homes, forced evacuation, food and water deprivation, disappearance of family members, exposure to acts of violence or death, detainment in a refugee camp, and forced emigration: "Nearly all the refugees emphasized the shock that came with the sudden occurrence of human betrayal by neighbors, associates, friends, and relatives (538).

The testimonies document the genocidal nature of the traumas that were directed at the entire Muslim Bosnian population. The traumas experienced were "extreme, multiple, repeated, prolonged and communal" (539). Some of the survivors carry with them constant images of death and atrocity. One man describes them as "films" that play in his head. In contrast, others have lost their memories of the events, and one woman was later unable to remember the trauma story she told three weeks earlier: "All kinds of things come together. Being expelled. Things we lost. Twenty years of work—then suddenly being without anything. . . . All the memories come at the same moment and it's too much" (541). The massiveness of their suffering, the psychiatrists report, extends beyond the bounds of the current diagnostic category of PTSD.

sis in Europe since World War II. More than 3 million former Yugoslavians were displaced. Of these, about 13,000 were resettled in the United States by 1994. They are thus the most recent refugee arrivals. They share with other refugees from war and violence the memories of extreme suffering and loss experienced within the context of direct genocide (see the Multiple Cultural Worlds box).

THE POLITICS AND POLICIES OF INCLUSION AND EXCLUSION

National policies that set quotas on the quantity and types of immigrants welcomed and that determine how they are treated are largely dictated by political and economic interests. Even in the cases of seemingly humanitarian quotas, governments undertake a cost-benefit analysis of how much will be gained and how much will be lost. Politically, governments show either their support or disapproval of other governments through their immigration policies. One of the most obvious economic factors affecting policy is labor flow. Cheap, even illegal, immigrant labor is used around the world to maintain profits for businesses and services for the better-off. Flows of such labor undermine labor unions and the status of established workers.

In the United States, immigration law is an important area determining who will be allowed entry and what benefits the government will provide. A court case from 1915 presents issues that still prevail today (*Gegiow* v. *Uhl,* 1915). The case concerned a number of Russian laborers seeking to enter the United States. Only one member of the group spoke some English, and all had very little money. Their intention was to settle in Portland, Oregon. The acting commissioner of immigration in the port of New York denied them entry on the grounds that they were "likely to become public charges" because employment conditions in Portland were such that they probably would be unable to obtain work. The "aliens" seeking entry obtained legal counsel and the case eventually went to the Supreme Court, where the decision was handed down by Chief Justice Oliver Wendell Holmes. He focused on "whether an alien can be declared likely to become a public charge on the ground that the labor market in the city of his immediate . . . destination is overstocked." The relevant statute, Holmes declared, deals with admission to the United States, not to a particular city within it. Further, Holmes commented that a commissioner of immigration is not empowered to make decisions about possible overstocking of labor in all of the United States, for that is a matter in the hands of the President.

National immigration policies are played out in local communities. In some instances, local resentments are associated with a so-called **lifeboat mentality,** which seeks to limit enlarging a particular group because of perceived resource constraints (see the Viewpoint box).

Influxes of immigrants who compete for jobs have led to hostility in many parts of Europe and North America. Some observers have labeled this *working-class racism* because it emerges out of competition with immigrants for jobs and other benefits (Cole 1996). The number of immigrants has grown substantially in southern Italy since the early 1980s. In the city of Palermo, with a total population of 800,000, there are now between 15,000 and 30,000 immigrants from Africa, Asia, and elsewhere. Does the theory of working-class racism apply to the working class in Palermo? Two conditions seem to predict that it would: large numbers of foreign immigrants and a high rate of unemployment. However, instead of expressing racist condemnation of the immigrants, working-class residents of Palermo accept the immigrants as fellow poor people. One critical factor may be the lack of competition for jobs, which derives from the fact that working Palermitans and immi-

VIEWPOINT

"The Immigration Wars" by Bart Laws

Bart Laws is director of research and evaluation at the Latino Health Institute in Boston, and is a community organizer and health care reform activist.

> One argument for limiting immigration [to the United States] that has some weight is that there is probably some cost to low-wage workers from immigration, illegal immigration in particular. Illegal immigrants are highly exploitable workers. Their presence in the labor force may displace some native-born people and help keep wages down for unskilled jobs. [But] immigration, legal or illegal, makes only a tiny contribution to the erosion in earning power . . . this phenomenon is driven by technological change. We need to solve this problem, but stopping immigration won't do it. . . .
>
> There is another argument that must be considered. An ad has been appearing in magazines lately by an organization called Negative Population Growth. They write: "NPG urges a drastic reduction in immigration solely because of its contribution to the disastrous growth of the U.S. population. . . . NPG has adopted what's called a "lifeboat ethic." We're all safe in the lifeboat, but we can't stay seaworthy if we let anyone else on board. . . . The rest will have to swim or, preferably, sink on their own.
>
> The problem with this is that you can't live for very long on a lifeboat. We are completely interdependent with other nations, economically and environmentally. Our urgent challenge is not to keep people out, but to help make it possible for them to stay where they are, which most people, after all, would prefer to do if they could. . . .

Source: Laws 1996: 31–34.

grants occupy different niches. Immigrant jobs are less desirable, more stigmatized, and less well-paying. African immigrant men work in bars and restaurants, as building cleaners, or as itinerant street vendors. African and Asian women work as domestic servants in the better-off neighborhoods. Sicilians do refer to immigrants by certain racial/ethnic names, but they seem to be used interchangeably and imprecisely. For example, a common term for all immigrants, Asian or African, is *tuichi,* which means *Turks.* The word can be applied teasingly to a Sicilian as well and in conversation may connote alarm as in "Mom, the Turks!" Other loosely applied terms are the Italian words for Moroccans, Blacks, and Tunisians. In a questionnaire given to school children, the great majority agreed with the statement that "a person's race is not important." The tolerance among Palermo's working class may be only temporary. Nonetheless, it suggests that researchers take a closer look at cases elsewhere that require a loosening up of the theory of determined working-class racism against immigrants.

Recent politically conservative trends in the United States have succeeded in rolling back more progressive policies about immigration and minorities. Police raids in areas known to have many undocumented migrants have brought mass expulsion. Reversals of affirmative action in college admissions, initiated in California in the late 1990s, have gained widespread support among "nativist" Americans. This lifeboat mentality of exclusiveness and privilege is held mainly by the dominant White majority and others who have "made it."

SUMMARY

Population movements have been an important feature of human adaptation since the earliest times. Reasons for migration include the search for productive resources, for marriage and other domestic partnerships, or because of "push" factors such as warfare or natural disasters. People's adjustment to their new situations depends on the degree of voluntarism involved in the move, the degree of cultural difference between the place of origin and the destination, and how closely expectations about the new location are met especially in terms of making a living and establishing social ties.

Displaced persons are one of the fasted growing categories of migrants. Refugees, fleeing from political persecution, warfare, displacement by development projects, and ecological problems constitute an increasing number of all migrants. They face the most serious adjustment challenges since they often leave their home countries with few material resources and frequently have experienced much psychological suffering.

Worldwide, the "new immigrants" are contributing to growing transnational connections and the formation of increasingly multicultural populations within states. In the United States, the new immigrants from Latin America are the fastest growing category. The immigrants from East and South Asia, who were more likely to immigrate to the United States voluntarily, have achieved greater levels of economic success than most other new immigrant groups. Immigrant groups throughout the world are likely to face certain forms of discrimination in their new destinations, although the degree to which it occurs varies depending on perceived resource competition from already settled residents.

CRITICAL THINKING QUESTIONS

1. Have you ever moved, or known someone who did (if you moved to attend college, that counts as a move). Assess the degree of voluntarism in the move in terms of your motivation to move and choice of destination. Did this affect the migrant's adaptation to the new situation in any way?
2. Think of a movie you have seen or a novel you have read that involves characters who have migrated. Analyze the kinds of information presented and the way the migrants are portrayed—in a positive or negative light—and why.
3. Might there be a connection between current high rates of divorce in the United States and stresses related to migration for employment? How would a cultural anthropologist conduct research to answer to this question?

KEY CONCEPTS

chain migration, p. 394
circular migration, p. 388
displaced person, p. 388
ecological refugee, p. 388
internal migration, p. 385
lifeboat mentality, p. 403
new immigrants, p. 393
push-pull theory, p. 385
refugee, p. 388
trailing spouse/trailing partner, p. 392
transnational migration, p. 388
wage labor migration, p. 388

SUGGESTED READINGS

Linda Basch, Nina Glick Schiller, and Christina Blanc Szanton, *Nations Unbound: Transnational Projects, Postcolonial Predicaments, and Deterritorialized Nation-States*. Langhorne, PA: Gordon and Breach Science Publishers, 1994. Eight chapters explore theoretical issues in transnational migration and present detailed analysis of cases of migration from the Caribbean including St. Vincent, Grenada, and Haiti.

Colin Clarke, Ceri Peach, and Steven Vertovic, eds., *South Asians Overseas: Migration and Ethnicity*. New York: Cambridge University Press, 1990. The text includes fifteen chapters plus introductory essays that place the case studies in a broader context. Chapters are divided into two sections: South Asians in colonial and postcolonial contexts and South Asians in contemporary Western countries and the Middle East.

Sherri Grasmuck and Patricia R. Pessar, *Between Two Islands: Dominican International Migration*. Berkeley: University of California Press, 1991. Based on fieldwork in the Dominican Republic and New York City, this volume focuses on social ties and networks facilitating migration from rural areas in the Dominican Republic to Santo Domingo and from the Dominican Republic to the United States, and how employment opportunities shape the migration experience.

Beatriz Manz, *Refugees of a Hidden War: The Aftermath of Counterinsurgency in Guatemala*. Albany: State University of New York Press. This study was conducted to assess whether conditions would allow the return to Guatemala of 46,000 Indian peasant refugees living in camps in Mexico. It pays attention to aspects of family and community life in the camps and in resettled villages in Guatemala where the Indians face discrimination and harassment from the military.

Jennifer Robertson, *Native and Newcomer: Making and Remaking a Japanese City*. Berkeley: University of California Press, 1991. This text studies the social and symbolic adjustments of native residents of Kodaira city and the many residents who moved to Kodaira beginning in the 1950s. Detailed attention is given to the role of a community festival in expressing links between the natives and newcomers, while also stating and maintaining group boundaries.

CHAPTER 17

Development Anthropology

CHAPTER OUTLINE

ANTHROPOLOGY AND THE STUDY OF CHANGE
- Invention
  - *Critical Thinking:* Social Impacts of the Green Revolution
- Diffusion
  - *Multiple Cultural Worlds:* Snowmobiles and Sami Reindeer Herding
- Theories of Cultural Change
  - *Multiple Cultural Worlds:* The Effectiveness of Redistribution as a Development Strategy in Nadur Village
  - *Multiple Cultural Worlds:* The Shan-Dany Museum and the Construction of Community in Mexico

ORGANIZATIONAL APPROACHES TO DEVELOPMENT
- Large-Scale Institutions
  - *Current Event:* "Largest-Ever World Bank Loan Mistrusted in India"
- The "Development Apparatus"
- Grassroots Approaches

THE DEVELOPMENT PROJECT
- Anthropologists and the Project Cycle
- Comparative Studies
- The Anthropological Critique of Development Projects

METHODS IN DEVELOPMENT ANTHROPOLOGY
- Rapid Research Methods
- Participatory Appraisal

INDIGENOUS PEOPLE'S DEVELOPMENT
- Indigenous People as Victims of Development
  - *Voices:* "They Told Us That Indian Ways Were Bad" by Tulto
- From Victimization to Indigenous People's Development
  - *Current Event:* "Online in the Outback"

WOMEN AND DEVELOPMENT
- The Male Bias
- Women's Organizations for Change
- Human Rights and Development

SUMMARY

KEY CONCEPTS

CRITICAL THINKING QUESTIONS

SUGGESTED READINGS

◀ International tourism is a huge and growing part of the global and local economies of many countries. Many tourists are increasingly interested in "cultural" tourism through which they are able to see and participate in certain aspects of the culture they visit. Safari tour groups in Africa, as in the case of a trip to Maasailand shown here, combine exposure to wildlife and Maasai culture.

The usual goal of cultural anthropology is to provide informed description and analysis, with minimal influence on the people being studied. In applied anthropology, in contrast, the goal is to use knowledge to provide solutions to practical problems. (As mentioned in Chapter 1, all of anthropology's four fields have applied aspects.) The subfield of cultural anthropology called *development anthropology* seeks to understand how cultures change and how anthropologists can inform and transform the process of **international development** (directed change to achieve improved levels of human welfare in so-called developing countries, often through promoting economic growth).

The first part of the chapter considers general processes of cultural change and then reviews approaches in international development and anthropological views and findings related to them. In the second part of the chapter, three interrelated issues of great contemporary concern are considered in more depth: indigenous peoples' development, women and development, and human rights.

ANTHROPOLOGY AND THE STUDY OF CHANGE

All cultures change, but the causes and processes of change are varied. Cultural change can be intentional or accidental, forward-looking or backward-looking, rapid or gradual, obvious or nearly invisible, beneficial or harmful. Physical anthropology's interest in human evolution has long prompted a view of change that goes back millions of years into prehistory, even before the time when humans emerged. Archaeology's study of human cultural remains encompasses both prehistory and history, as does the work of linguistic anthropologists in reconstructing the evolution of language. In contrast to these three fields, early work in cultural anthropology took a **synchronic,** or "one-time" view in describing a particular culture with minimal or no attention to its past. This approach led to a static view of culture, fixed in what was called the "ethnographic present," a phrase referring to the period during which the anthropologist was in the field. Such cultural "snapshots" were erroneously assumed to have enduring validity until the 1970s, when anthropologists began to realize how dated these ethnographies were. Because cultural anthropology was originally devoted to conducting synchronic studies, its theories and methods have had to be revised to allow for the study of change. This process is still in motion, with much work to be done to improve **diachronic** ("across-time") analyses.

According to this book's theoretical position, the first step in theorizing about and researching change is to examine the infrastructural base (modes of production and reproduction), its links with transformations in political and power structures, and finally the way production and power influence social organization and ideology. The logic is that the deepest causal explanations are to be found in the base rather than in social structure and superstructure. Of course, social structure and ideas (superstructure) cause change as well. For example, higher education changes one's knowledge level (in other words, creating ideational change at the level of superstructure) and can lead to a better-paying job. In this example, it appears that change in the superstructure causes change in infrastructure. However, the cultural materialist would suggest a closer look toward the possible infrastructural factors that led, in the first place, to the person being able to get a higher education. In sum, a holistic, cultural materialistic view of change attempts to encompass all aspects of change, but gives priority to looking at material causal factors and outcomes. Within this broad framework of change, two basic processes are at work: invention and diffusion.

Invention

Cultural change may be prompted by the invention of something new. Inventions usually evolve gradually, through step-wise experimentation and accumulation of knowledge, but some appear rather surprisingly. We can all name many technological inventions that have created cultural change, for example the printing press, gun powder, polio vaccine, and satellite communication. Concepts such as Jeffersonian notions of democracy are also spread through diffusion. According to cultural materialism, ideological inventions are rooted in particular political economies and, through diffusion, are most likely to be adopted in similar contexts.

Research by cultural anthropologists and other social scientists has shown that not all inventions have positive social outcomes. Even innovations inspired by a socially positive goal often turn out to have mixed or even negative effects (see the Critical Thinking box). Along these lines, cultural anthropol-

CRITICAL THINKING

Social Impacts of the Green Revolution

Agricultural research scientists of the 1950s were inspired by the laudable goal of eliminating world hunger to try to develop genetic variations of wheat, rice, and corn. They succeeded. Adoption of these high-yielding varieties (HYV) of seeds was promoted to farmers throughout the developing world as part of the "Green Revolution" that would feed the world by boosting production per acre. In most places where Green Revolution agricultural practices were adopted, grain production did increase. Was world hunger conquered? The answer is no, because world hunger is not merely a problem of production; it also involves distribution.

Analyses of the social impact of the Green Revolution in India reveal that one of its results was to increase disparities between the rich and the poor (Frankel 1971). How did this happen? Green Revolution agriculture requires several expensive inputs: purchased seeds (HYV seeds cannot be harvested from the crop and saved until the next year since they are hybridized), the heavy use of commercial fertilizers, and the need for dependable irrigation sources. Thus, farmers who could use HYV seeds successfully were, in the first place, better-off because the innovation was selected for those who could afford such inputs. Small farmers who tried planting HYV seeds but could not provide these inputs experienced crop failure, went deeper into debt, and ended up having to sell the small amounts of land they had. Larger and better-off farmers took advantage of these new openings in the land market to accumulate more land and expand their holdings. With the acquisition of tractors and other mechanized equipment, large farmers became even more productive. Small farmers were unable to compete and continued to be squeezed out financially. They became hired day laborers, dependent on seasonal employment by large farmers, or they migrated to cities where they became part of the urban underclass.

Looking at the Green Revolution from a critical thinking perspective, we may see more clearly whose interests were served, whether this was the original intention or not. The big winners included the companies involved in selling chemical fertilizers (largely petroleum-based) and HYV seeds, companies that manufacture and sell mechanized farm equipment, the larger farmers whose income levels improved, and the research scientists themselves who gained funding for their research and world fame for their discoveries. In retrospect, it is difficult to imagine that early planners in the 1950s could have been so naive as to not realize who they would be helping and who they might end up hurting.

Critical Thinking Questions

- Is it likely that the original innovators of HYV grains considered what social transformations might occur in developing country agriculture as a result of their invention?
- Would they have been likely to stop their research if they had realized that it would lead to the "rich getting richer and the poor getting poorer"? Should they have done so?
- Would involvement of anthropologists in the approach to solving world hunger have offered other possible solutions instead of HYV grains?

ogists have made substantial contributions to improving development by telling the stories of the "victims" of change (examples of this approach are provided throughout this chapter).

Diffusion

Diffusion is the spread of culture—including technology and ways of behaving and thinking—through contact. It is logically related to invention and innovation because new discoveries are likely to spread. Diffusion can occur in several ways. First, in mutual borrowing, two roughly equal societies exchange aspects of their culture with each other. Second, diffusion may occur between unequal societies and involve a transfer from a dominant culture to a less powerful culture. This process may occur through force or more subtly through education or marketing processes that promote adoption of new practices and beliefs. Third, a more powerful culture may

Services for photocopying and sending faxes, invented in the West, have been recently diffused to most parts of the world, including the formerly remote capital of India's Andaman Islands, Port Blair. A popular restaurant at the same location also evidences diffusion of cuisine: South Indian, Chinese, and Continental.

appropriate aspects of a less powerful culture (the latter process is called *cultural imperialism*).

In each of these types of diffusion, the result is some degree of acculturation, or change in one culture as a result of contact with another culture. At one extreme, a culture may become so completely acculturated that it has become **assimilated,** no longer distinguishable as having a separate identity. In many cases, cultural change through diffusion has led to extreme change in the "receiving" culture, which becomes "deculturated" or extinct. Such deculturation has occurred among many indigenous people as the result of the introduction of new technology (see the Multiple Cultural Worlds box). Other responses to acculturative influences include partial acceptance of something new with reformulation and reshaping, like cricket in the Trobriands (Chapter 15), or resistance and rejection. The study of international development is, in fact, concerned with the dynamics and results of a particular form of diffusion—that of Western goods, behavior, and values through international aid.

Theories of Cultural Change

Two basic theories of cultural change dominate thinking from top leaders to local entrepreneurs in out-of-the-way settings: modernization and development. These two related concepts are heavily influenced by Western economics and lifestyles. In recent history, however, criticism of and several variations on these approaches have been proposed.

Modernization

Modernization is a process of change marked by industrialization, consolidation of the nation-state, bureaucratization, market economy, technological innovation, literacy, and options for social mobility. It derives from a period in Western European history beginning in the seventeenth century, which emphasized the importance of secular rationality and the inevitable advance of scientific thinking (Norgaard 1994). Modernization appears as almost an inevitable process that will, given the insights of science and rationality, spread throughout the world and lead to improvement in people's lives everywhere. Overall, the emphasis of modernization is on material progress and individual betterment.

Supporters and critics of modernization are found in both rich and poor countries. Supporters claim that the benefits of modernization (improved transportation; electricity; domestic comforts such as air conditioning; and technology such as washing machines, biomedical health care, and telecommunications) are worth the costs—whether those costs are calculated in terms of environmental or social costs. Other scholars in many disciplines—from literary studies to anthropology—regard modernization as a failure. Most cultural anthropologists are critics of modernization as a general process of social change because it leads to increased social inequality, the destruction of indigenous cultures, ecological ruin, and the overall decline in global cultural diversity (selected aspects of modernity, however, such as electricity and antibiotics may be accepted as positive). In spite of strong cautionary critiques from anthropologists and environmentalists about the negative impacts of modernization, nations around the world have not slowed their attempts to achieve it. China is a stunning example of a country that is now pursuing a massive modernization program, especially in its eastern cities such as Shanghai. A current joke is that the national bird of China is the crane—the construction crane. As one anthropologist has commented, "the god of wealth" has returned to China in full force (Ikels 1996).

Growth-Oriented Development

International development emerged as a prominent theory about change after World War II, at the same

MULTIPLE CULTURAL WORLDS

Snowmobiles and Sami Reindeer Herding

The question of how adoption of a new belief or practice may benefit or harm a particular culture and its various members is difficult to answer, but it must always be asked. Pertti Pelto's (1973) classic study of the "snowmobile disaster" among a Sami group in Finland offers a careful response to this question in a context of rapid technological diffusion. In the 1950s, Pelto went to Finland to study the Sami (previously referred to by outsiders as Lapps, which, in the Sami language, is a derogatory term). Their economy was based on fishing and reindeer herding, which provided most of the diet. Reindeer had several other important economic and social functions. They were used as draught animals, especially for hauling wood for fuel. Their hides were made into clothing and their sinews used for sewing. Reindeer were key items of exchange, both in external trade and internal gift-giving. A child was given a reindeer to mark the appearance of its first tooth. When a couple became engaged, they exchanged a reindeer with each other to make the commitment. Reindeer were the most important wedding gift. Each summer the herds were let free and then rounded up in the fall, a time of communal festivity.

Ten years later, all this had changed dramatically because of the introduction of the snowmobile in the early 1960s. Previously, the men had tended the reindeer herds on skis. Introduction of snowmobiles in herd management had several results. The herds were no longer kept closely domesticated for part of the year, during which they became tame. Instead they were allowed to roam freely all year and thus became wilder. On snowmobiles, the men would cover larger amounts of territory at round-up time to bring in the animals, and sometimes several round-ups occurred instead of one. Herd size declined dramatically. Reasons for the decline included the stress caused to the reindeer by the extra distance traveled during round-ups, the multiple round-ups instead of a single one, and the fear aroused by the noisy snowmobiles. Round-ups were now held at a time when the females were near the end of their pregnancy, another factor causing reproductive stress. As the number of snowmobiles increased, the number of reindeer decreased. Another economic change involved the dependence on the outside through links to the cash economy. Cash was needed in order to purchase a snowmobile, gasoline, and to pay for parts and repairs. This delocalization of the economy led to social inequality, which had not existed previously:

- The cash cost of effective participation in herding exceeded the resources of some families, who had to drop out of serious participation in herding.
- The use of snowmobiles drastically changed the role requirements of reindeer herding in favor of youth over age; thus, older herders were squeezed out.
- The snowmobile pushed many Sami into debt.
- The dependence on cash and indebtedness forced many Sami to migrate to cities for work.

Pelto terms these transformations a "disaster" for Sami culture. He offers some recommendations that might be helpful for the future: The lesson of the Sami, and other groups, should be presented to other communities before they adopt new technology so they understand better the potential consequences; any group facing change should have a chance to weigh evidence on the pros and cons and make an informed judgment, something that the Sami had no chance to do. Pelto's work is thus one of the early warnings from anthropology about the need for **social impact assessments** to gauge the potential social costs and benefits of particular innovations before the change is undertaken.

time that the United States began to increase its role as a world leader. One can think of development as the attempt, through conscious planning and intervention, to bring the benefits of modernization to the developing world. Indeed, international development, as conceived by major development institutions such as the World Bank, is similar to modernization in terms of its ultimate goals. The process, however, emphasizes economic growth as the most crucial element in development. Investments in economic growth in some sectors of the population will subsequently support (through the "trickle-down" effect) wider achievement of improved human welfare, such as health and education. Since the 1950s, the United States has emphasized economic development in its foreign aid packages, especially the transfer of Western economic expertise (in the form of advisors) and technology (such as agricultural equipment) to developing countries. Promoting growth-oriented development in poor nations, as followed by most large-scale development organizations, includes two major economic strategies:

- Recommendations for increasing economic productivity and trade such as new forms of agriculture, irrigation, and markets.
- Recommendations for reducing government expenditures on public services such as schools and health in order to reduce debt and reallocate resources to uses perceived to be more directly related to increased production; this strategy, called **structural adjustment,** has been vigorously pursued by the World Bank since the 1980s.

Distributional Development

In contrast to this growth-oriented approach, a distributional approach to development views poverty as the result of global economic and political factors such as world trade imbalances between nations and unequal distribution of entitlements within nations and communities (recall the discussion of entitlements in Chapter 4). In taking a structural view, this approach rejects the implicit claim of other approaches that poverty is caused by some inadequacy on the part of poor people or poor countries themselves (Rahnema 1992). In terms of poverty reduction, its position is based on evidence that growth-oriented strategies without concern for distribution result in increased social inequality with the "rich getting richer and the poor getting poorer." The distributional approach takes a strongly critical view of structural adjustment as promoted by those favoring the growth model since it worsens welfare of the poor by removing the few entitlements they had in the form of services. Advocates of the distributional model insist on the need to readjust access to crucial resources within countries in order to allow the poor to have a greater ability to produce and provide for their own needs. Within a particular country, this perspective involves the following strategies that differ markedly from the growth approach (note that the first two require asking questions of local people and then proceeding to formulate a plan that is contextually based):

- *Entitlement assessment:* This step produces an understanding of who has access to which life-supporting resources. Two anthropologists who support this approach note that, while "unequal distribution may appear to be an obvious and a crucial issue, planners often forget that in the communities where they are working, people's access to resources and decision-making power is rarely equal . . . those who plan from the outside tend to assume that 'the poor' are all the same and thus have the same interests" (Gardner and Lewis 1996:79). Entitlement assessment should pay attention to entitlement differences, depending on the context, that are related to constructions of race, gender, class and age, and perhaps others. Particular groups are not always disadvantaged to the same degree in all contexts. Women-headed households, for example, are often, but not always, disadvantaged, and male-headed households are not necessarily advantaged. (See Table 17.1 for key questions to ask in entitlement assessment.)
- *Assessing the cultural effects of development:* This stage is related to entitlement assessment, but it adds the dimension of determining the effects of outside intervention on the baseline of entitlements. Using the example of a resettlement project, Table 17.2 presents the key questions involved in assessing the cultural effects of such forms of development. This step highlights, again, the social complexity involved in devel-

Table 17.1
Key Questions in Assessing Entitlements

What are the most important resources available in the society?

How is access to these resources organized?
- Are key resources shared in the community, or do some people or groups have greater access than others?
- Are there obvious economic differences within the community? If so, what are they?
- Are key resources shared within the household, or do some members have greater access than others?

What is the distribution of decision-making power?
- Are some people or groups denied a voice?
- Do some people or groups have particular interests? If so, what are they?

Are these factors taken into consideration in the development policy or project?

Source: Adapted from Gardner and Lewis 1996:86.

Table 17.2
Key Questions in Assessing a Resettlement Project

How are local property relations organized in the original location?
- What access do different groups have to property or other key resources?
- What goods are highly valued?
- What are the inheritance patterns?

How is work organized?
- What are the main tasks done and during what seasons?
- What is the division of labor by gender and age?
- What is the role of kinship in allocating labor?

How is the household organized?
- Who lives where and with whom?
- How is decision making allocated within the household?
- Are there notable differences in household organization within the community? If so, what are they and how do they change over time?

What is the local political structure?
- Do some people or groups monopolize power?
- Are some groups marginalized?

How suitable is the proposed relocation site and plan, given the above economic, social, and political findings?

Source: Adapted from Gardner and Lewis 1996:89.

opment impact assessment and helps overcome the tendency of outside planners to homogenize "the poor."

- *Redistribution of crucial resources, especially land:* While generally unpopular with rich and powerful members of society, successful land reform programs have been undertaken by some nations, such as Japan and Taiwan. Such programs require substantial political will to achieve success.
- *Assistance programs:* As carried out in welfare states, such programs may serve as forms of redistribution. Health and education services, for example, seek to raise the quality of "human capital" without a radical redistribution of productive resources. Eventually, the recipients would gain independence from such assistance.

Many neoliberal economists argue on economic grounds that redistribution is not a realistic or a feasible strategy. Nevertheless, anthropologists have reported many cases in which the redistribution model has worked. One instance of successful development through redistribution comes from India's southern state of Kerala (see the Multiple Cultural Worlds box on page 414).

Human Development

Yet another alternative to "growth-first" strategies is called **human development,** the strategy of first investing in human capital. The United Nations coined this term in order to emphasize the need for improvements in human welfare in terms of health, education, and personal security and safety. According to this approach, improvements in human welfare will lead to overall development of the nation. We know that the reverse is not true: the level of economic growth of a country (or region within a country) is not necessarily correlated with its level of human development. Obviously, the relationship between poverty and development is more complex than what one might assume. Some poor countries, and areas within countries such as India's Kerala state, have achieved higher levels of human development than their GNP or GDP would predict. Thus, economic growth need not be considered an end in itself. The goal of development should be improved levels of human welfare.

Sustainable Development

A fourth position tempers the pursuit of economic growth in terms of its long-term viability both environmentally and financially. According to this view, the economic growth achieved by the wealthy nations has occurred at great cost to the environment and cannot be sustained at its present level. Since the 1980s, the term **sustainable development,** or forms of development that do not destroy nonrenewable resources and are financially supportable by the host country, has gained prominence in international development circles. This approach sounds like a step forward, but some experts say that it is just another buzzword. They point out that **development rhetoric** (the patterned way of speaking of development experts and policy makers) may change, but what actually goes on in terms of development aid does not (Escobar 1995; Ferguson 1994).

Anthropology's Four Fields and International Development

Each of general anthropology's four fields is relevant to an improved understanding of both the impacts of international development on people and the way these impacts might be improved. Consider the mul-

Multiple Cultural Worlds

The Effectiveness of Redistribution as a Development Strategy in Nadur

Anthropological research in Nadur village, Kerala, posed the question of whether redistribution was an effective and realistic development strategy (Franke 1993). The answer, based on extensive household interviews and surveys, is yes. Kerala's per capita income is low in comparison to the rest of India and to the rest of the world. Yet, while income remained low and stagnant, substantial material improvements occurred in many people's lives, including some of the poorest of the poor. How did this happen? Redistribution was not the result of a socialist revolution; it took place through democratic channels—protests and pressure on the government by people's groups and labor unions. These pressure groups forced the state to reallocate land ownership, shifting some land to the landless and thereby reducing inequality (although not eradicating it completely). In other instances, people pressured government leaders to improve village conditions by improving the schools, providing school lunches for poor children, and increasing attendance by dalit children. Throughout the 1960s and 1970s, Nadur village did become a better place to live, in many ways for many people. The question remains: Would the same improvements have occurred, or even more, if Kerala had followed a strategy of economic growth rather than redistribution? Without a "controlled" case study of two villages—one in a context of redistribution and another in a growth context—it is impossible to say for sure, but, generally, growth-led development does inevitably lead to increased social inequality as some people get ahead and others fall behind.

tiple angles in which archaeology is involved. First, development projects—for example, construction of roads and dams—may lead accidentally to the discovery of important new sites. Second, such projects may also destroy both known and unknown sites in their path. At the present time, the World Bank has no guidelines for countries to follow in terms of how to conduct appraisals of possible site destruction, but such consideration should be considered important and urgent. Third, archaeological sites can be sources of revenue generation for countries and a focus of pride for local populations and nations (see the Multiple Cultural Worlds box on page 415).

Physical anthropologists can contribute their expertise in many areas of project design and evaluation. Those who work on primate conservation, for example, can advise planners about how to construct reserves that will protect animals from the incursions of development. Such work also may contribute to tourism development, given international interest in visiting primate reserves and other protected areas where endangered species of flora and fauna may be found. Other physical anthropologists have assessed how urban poverty affects nutritional levels and have indicated some of the most high-risk groups for nutritional deficiencies (Dufour et al. 1997). Development projects often change people's health and nutrition in the project-affected area—sometimes for the better and sometimes adversely. For example, some studies have shown that relocation of people to a new area has had adverse effects on their nutrition since they have been exposed to radical dietary changes. Threats to global biodiversity are a concern of many biological anthropologists who are assessing the impacts of logging and large-scale deforestation throughout the world (Primack 1991).

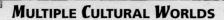

Linguistic anthropologists also have a vital role to play in several areas of development. First, they document language change that results from development, especially the continued trend toward language loss as people increasingly adopt more "cosmopolitan" dialects and languages (Kulick 1992). Additionally, their expertise in understanding communication patterns is helpful in showing how local people perceive of and interpret development aid. For example, Don Kulick's study of the village of Gapun in New Guinea reveals that the villagers have their own term for development, *kam-ap* (meaning "come up") in Tok Pisin. The villagers also interpret development in their own way that is related to cargo cults (Chapter 13). For them, the goal of kam-ap is to gain Western-style goods, and the pathway is through religion, not

MULTIPLE CULTURAL WORLDS

The Shan-Dany Museum and the Construction of Community in Mexico

The Shan-Dany museum, a local effort begun in 1986, houses artifacts that document the history, ritual practices, and traditional arts of Santa Ana, a rural indigenous community of about 3,000 people in Oaxaca, Mexico. As Jeffrey Cohen, an anthropologist involved in studying the role of the museum in the community, comments:

> The Shan-Dany is more than simply a treasury of artifacts and heirlooms: it is a living part of the community, a focus of Santañero energy and a key structure in the village's continual process of growth and development . . . it is through the museum's programs and projects that villagers define themselves and deal with many economic, social and political changes they collectively face as a community. (1997:37)

The village of Santa Ana is currently in the midst of rapid social change through involvement in global markets for their woven goods, wage labor migration within Mexico, and increasing levels of transnational migration. The Mexican state plays an increasing role in the area through government programs and education. The villagers themselves seek improved services, especially better roads and other infrastructure and access to consumer goods. The older generation is concerned about the loss of "tradition" in the face of all this change. The young generally glorify new technology and music. As Cohen comments, the challenge for Santa Ana is to bridge this gap.

What he found in Santa Ana was a successful response, actually a renaissance of local culture, of which one central feature is the Shan-Dany museum. The museum has grown from its original role as a place to store artifacts to a dynamic place where local culture is celebrated in terms of the past and the future. The museum took on the role of promoting economic development through strengthening the local weaving industry. Its exhibits document the historical development of weaving and showcase local traditions such as natural dying. In conjunction with the museum's efforts, weavers established a craft cooperative to share risks and profits. The museum actively sought to attract buyers to the village and thus played a role in market development.

The museum has taken on several other activist roles that enhance development in the village, including programs in the schools ranging from documenting village rituals to asking children to design campaigns for improving water. This case study shows how archaeological artifacts can be a basis for futurist thinking about community, identity, and improved lifestyles.

development projects. And, last, linguistic anthropologists can offer insights relevant to national policies on bilingualism and languages taught in schools in multiethnic contexts.

ORGANIZATIONAL APPROACHES TO DEVELOPMENT

Cultural anthropologists have become increasingly aware of the importance of examining the institutions and organizations involved in international development. This knowledge will help cultural anthropologists have a greater impact on how development is done. They have studied the management systems of large-scale institutions such as the World Bank as well as "local" management systems found in diverse settings; they have also examined several aspects of behavior within the institutions themselves: internal hierarchies and inequalities, social interactions, symbols of power, and institutional discourse. This section first describes some of the major development institutions and then offers an example of an anthropological study of development discourse of large-scale institutions.

Large-Scale Institutions

Large-scale development institutions can be separated into the "multilaterals" (those that include several nations as donors) and the "bilaterals" (those that involve a relationship between only two countries, a donor and a recipient). The major multilaterals are the United Nations and the World Bank, each constituting a vast and complex social system. The United Nations, established in 1945, includes some

160 member states, each contributing an amount of money assessed according to its ability and each given one vote in the General Assembly (Hancock 1989). The United States, Germany, and Japan are major contributors. Several UN agencies exist, fulfilling a range of functions (see Table 17.3). In all its units combined, the UN employs about 50,000 people.

The World Bank is supported by contributions from over 150 member countries. Founded in 1944 at a conference called by President Roosevelt in Bretton Woods, New Hampshire, "the Bank" is dedicated to promoting the concept of economic growth and expanded purchasing power throughout the world (Rich 1994). The main strategy is to promote international investment through loans. The World Bank is guided by a Board of Governors made up of the Finance Ministers of member countries. Rather than following the UN's approach of one country-one vote, in the World Bank system, the number of votes is based on the size of a country's financial commitment: "There is no pretence of equality—the economic superpowers run the show" (Hancock 1989:51).

Two major units within the World Bank are the International Bank for Reconstruction and Develop-

Table 17.3
Major Agencies within the United Nations Related to International Development

Agency	*Headquarters*	*Function*
UNDP (The United Nations Development Program)	New York City	UNDP provides many different services designed to help a country in planning and managing its own development: groundwater and mineral exploration, computer and satellite technology, seed production and agricultural extension, and research. UNDP does not itself implement projects; that is done through 29 "executing agencies," some of which are listed here.
FAO (The Food and Agricultural Organization)	Rome, Italy	FAO implements agricultural field projects that receive funding from the UNDP as well as "host governments."
WHO (The World Health Organization)	Geneva, Switzerland	WHO has four goals: developing and organizing personnel and technology for disease prevention and control; eradication of major tropical diseases; immunization of all children against major childhood diseases; and establishing primary health care services.
UNICEF (The United Nations Children's Emergency Fund)	Joint headquarters New York City and Geneva, Switzerland	UNICEF is complementary to WHO and has nearly 90 field offices in developing countries (the largest is in India). UNICEF is concerned with basic health care and social services for children. UNICEF receives about three-fourths of its funding from UN member governments and the other one-fourth from the sale of greeting cards. It is the only UN agency that receives money directly from the general pub lic.
UNESCO (The United Nations Educational, Scientific, and Cultural Organization)	Paris, France	UNESCO is dedicated to enhancing world peace and security through education, science, and culture, to promoting respect for human rights and the rule of law and fundamental freedoms. One of UNESCO's practical concerns is to promote literacy.
UNHCR (The United Nations High Commission for Refugees)	New York City	UNHCR is dedicated to promoting the rights and safety of refugees.
UNIFEM (The United Nations International Development Fund for Women)	New York City	UNIFEM promotes projects directed toward raising the status of women.
UNFPA (The United Nations Fund for Population Activities)	New York City	UNFPA supports family planning projects.

Source: Hancock 1989.

ment (IBRD) and the International Development Association (IDA). Both are administered at the World Bank headquarters in Washington, DC. They both lend for similar types of projects and often in the same country, but their conditions of lending differ. The IBRD provides loans to the poorest nations, which are generally regarded as "bad risks" on the world commercial market. Thus, the IBRD is a source of interest-bearing loans to countries that otherwise would not be able to borrow. The IBRD does not allow rescheduling of debt payments. It has recorded a profit every year of its existence, so it stands in an interesting position as a profit-making aid institution. Most of its loans support large infrastructure projects and, more recently, sectoral development in health and education (see the Current Event box). The IDA is the "soft-loan" side of the World Bank because it provides interest-free loans (although there is a .75 percent annual "service charge") and a flexible repayment schedule averaging between 35 and 40 years (Rich 1994:77). These concessional loans are granted to the poorest countries for projects of high development priority.

Critics of the multilaterals have emerged from many directions, including politicians, scholars, and people whose lives have been affected negatively by their projects. Politicians in the United States who oppose foreign aid to developing countries in any form point to the overlapping and wasteful organization of these institutions and the fact that they seem to have accomplished too little in comparison to the funds required by member countries to support them. Others argue that, too often, the projects supported by these institutions have failed to help the poor, but instead provide thousands of jobs for the people in their employment and are good business investments for first-world countries. Such critics point especially to the biased lending and aid policies that are shaped more by political factors than by economic need. The slogan "Fifty Years is Enough" is used by critics to convey the World Bank's failure to bring about broad-based development and the view that it should be abolished.

Some prominent bilateral institutions are the United States Agency for International Development (USAID), the Canadian International Development Agency (CIDA), Britain's Overseas Development Administration (ODA), the Swedish Agency for International Development (SIDA), and the Danish Organization for International Development (DANIDA). These agencies vary in terms of the proportion of aid disbursed as loans that have to be repaid or as grants that do not require repayment. Another variation is whether the loans or grants are "tied" to supporting specific projects that also provide for substantial donor country involvement in providing goods, services, and expertise versus being "untied," or allowing the recipient country the freedom to decide how to use the funds. The USAID generally offers more aid in the form of loans than grants, and more in tied than untied aid, especially in comparison to the bilateral agencies of Sweden, the Netherlands, and Norway. Another difference among the bilaterals is the proportion of their total aid that goes to the poorest of countries. The United Kingdom's ODA sends more than 80 percent of its aid to the poorest countries, while the largest chunk of U.S. foreign aid goes to Egypt and Israel (Hancock 1989:165). Emphasis on certain types of aid also varies from bilateral institution to bilateral institution. Cuba has long played a unique role in bilateral aid, although this fact is scarcely known in the United States. Rather than offering assistance for a wide range of development projects, Cuba has concentrated on health-related aid for training health care providers and promoting preventive health care (Feinsilver 1993). Most of Cuba's development assistance goes to socialist countries, including many in Africa.

Current Event

"Largest-Ever World Bank Loan Mistrusted in India"

- The World Bank announced that its largest-ever health-sector loan of US$350 million will go toward health-care reform in India.
- The loan is intended to reform the health-care system in three states. The plan to levy user charges (fees) for treatment and diagnostic services has become a source of controversy. Such moves have invoked criticism for introducing "commercialisation and indirect privatisation through the back door."
- Increased dependence of health programs on World Bank loans has drawn criticism from several nongovernmental organizations.

Source: Kumar, 1996: 1109.

The USAID has funded many development projects worldwide, such as this improved road in rural Bangladesh. It has a toll gate from which proceeds will be used to help pay for maintenance. The rickshaws are parked while their drivers pay their toll. The large white vehicle belongs to USAID and was being used by American researchers.

The "Development Apparatus"

It should be clear from what has been said already that international aid, while being presented to the public in largely humanitarian terms, often serves political ends related to international power relations. An anthropologist who took a close look at the details and dynamics of large-scale development institutions' involvement in Lesotho (pronounced Le-SOO-thoo), a small country in southern Africa, reveals the political features hidden behind what he calls the "development apparatus," or how development institutions conceptualize and describe their roles (Ferguson 1994). James Ferguson examined project documents relating to Lesotho and shows convincingly that development discourse about Lesotho differs substantially from academic descriptions. The development writings portray Lesotho as isolated and "virtually untouched by modern economic development" and still "basically a traditional peasant society" (25). In contrast, an entry in the *Encyclopedia Britannica* of 1910 describes Lesotho as "one of the greatest grain-growing countries of South Africa" with rich tracts of land, abundant export crops, trade networks via rail with South Africa, substantial labor migration to and from South Africa, and, in sum: "The social condition of the people is higher than that of the majority of South African natives" (26–27). Ferguson takes the position that the latter view is more accurate and that the former view is biased in the direction of justifying outside intervention by aid agencies. In other words, development discourse creates a country profile that is needy and dependent on foreign intervention.

Ferguson goes on to analyze the specific projects undertaken by many development agencies in Lesotho, most of which were related to agriculture and herding. He finds that they were universally unsuccessful in achieving their intended purpose of increased production, especially in the case of herding since the project did not take into account local people's value system about the importance of having large herds even if they are unproductive. Instead, an outcome that was achieved was the increased power of the bureaucracy in the rural areas and increased leverage of international agencies and their governments in Lesotho. Thus, while humanitarian development aid was the primary message of the agency's self-representation, the true result was political change. Ferguson points out that it is extremely difficult to know how much development experts are conscious of "goal displacement." Some must be, but many development experts are obviously motivated by humanitarian goals and really believe in the value of their work.

Grassroots Approaches

Many countries have experimented with what are sometimes called "grassroots" approaches to development, or locally initiated "bottom-up" projects. This alternative to "top-down" development as pursued by the large-scale agencies is more likely to be culturally appropriate, locally supported through participation, and successful. During the 1970s, Kenya sponsored a national program whereby the government committed itself to provide teachers if local communities would build schools (Winans and Haugerud 1977). This program was part of Kenya's promotion of *harambee,* or self-help, in many sectors, including health, housing, and schooling. Local people's response to the schooling program, especially, was overwhelmingly positive. They turned out in large numbers to build schools, which was their part of the bargain. Given the widespread construction of schools, the government found itself hard pressed to respond to its end of the bargain: paying the teachers' salaries. This program shows that self-help movements can be highly successful in terms of mobilizing local contributions, if the target—in this case, children's education—is something that is highly valued.

Many nongovernmental, grassroots organizations have existed for several decades. Prominent international examples include Britain's Oxfam, CARE, and Feed the Children. Churches also sponsor grassroots development. In Bangladesh, for example, the Lutheran Relief Agency has played an important role in helping local people provide and maintain small-scale infrastructure projects such as village roads and canals. With the Reagan administration's push toward privatization in the 1980s and a similar approach under various leaders in the United Kingdom, an emphasis on supporting development efforts through nongovernmental organizations (NGOs) emerged. This trend prompted the formation of many NGOs in developing countries that then often became beneficiaries of foreign aid to support local projects.

A parallel process took place in Washington, DC, with the massive downsizing of the USAID and the "restructuring" and job-trimming at the World Bank of the late 1990s. A simultaneous proliferation of NGO offices occurred, with their personnel taking on many of the former tasks of former USAID and World Bank employees. These private firms submit proposals for United States government contracts and then carry out the work with their own teams of experts and part-time consultants. Given the fact that the emergence of NGOs as a main institutional factor in international development is quite recent, anthropological studies of their work are just beginning to emerge. It is still not possible to form generalizations about their relative success and what factors are most crucial for project success. As discussed earlier in the chapter, however, such factors are likely to be sociocultural fit and a high level of local participation.

THE DEVELOPMENT PROJECT

Development institutions, whether they are large multilaterals or small, local NGOs, all rely on the concept of the development project as the specific set of activities that put policies into action. For example, let's say a government sets a policy of increased agricultural production by a certain percent within a certain period. Development projects put in place to achieve the policy goal might include the construction of a specified number of irrigation canals that would supply a certain amount of water to a number of farmers.

Anthropologists and the Project Cycle

While details vary between organizations, all development projects have a basic **project cycle,** or the full process of a project from initial planning to completion (Cernea 1985). These steps include:

- *Project identification:* Selecting a project to fit a particular purpose.
- *Project design:* Preparing the details of the project.
- *Project appraisal:* Assessing the project's budgetary aspects.
- *Project implementation:* Putting the project into place.
- *Project evaluation:* Assessing whether the project goals were fulfilled.

Since the 1970s, cultural anthropologists have been hired to offer insights into the project cycle at different stages, and with differing impacts. In the early phase of involvement, anthropologists tended to be primarily hired to do project evaluations, the last step in the project cycle, to see whether the project had achieved its goals. Unfortunately, many evaluations reported the projects to be dismal failures (Cochrane 1979). Some of the most frequent findings were: (1) the target group, such as the poor or women, had not been "reached," but instead project benefits had gone to some other group; (2) the project was inappropriate for the context; and (3) the intended beneficiaries were actually worse off after the project than before (as in the case of dam construction, for example). These problems are discussed further below.

One reason for these failures was that projects were typically identified and designed by Western economists located in cities far from the intended project site. These experts applied a "universal" formula, with little or no attention to the local cultural context. In other words, projects were designed by "people-distant" and culturally uninformed economists and planners, but were evaluated by "people-close" and culturally informed anthropologists. By demonstrating the weaknesses in project planning that led to failed projects, the victimization of people rather than their advancement through development, and the need to take local cultural context into account in projects, cultural anthropologists gained a reputation in development circles as trouble-makers and "nay-sayers"—people to be avoided by those who favored a "move-ahead" approach to getting projects funded and implemented.

Cultural anthropologists are still considered a "nuisance" by many development economists and policy planners, but sometimes, at least, a necessary nuisance. On a more positive note, cultural anthropologists have worked during the 1980s and 1990s to find a greater role earlier on in the project cycle, especially at the project identification and design stages (Cochrane 1979). Although still far less powerful than economists in defining development policy in the large-scale multilaterals, a few anthropologists have made notable strides in this direction, including having leadership roles in smaller-scale development organizations. Their role as watch-dogs and critics should not be discounted because it serves an important function in drawing attention to new and continuing problems.

Comparative Studies

We now have nearly fifty years of data on development projects that can be analyzed in order to reveal key factors contributing to project success or failure. Results of a few selected studies are reviewed here in terms of their insights on, first, project design and, then, project implementation.

Project Design

A comparative study by Conrad Kottak (1985) reviewed evaluations for sixty-eight development projects to see if economic success of projects was related to **sociocultural fit,** or how well a project meshes with the target culture and population. Results showed a strong correlation between the two factors. Through the years, anthropologists have provided many examples of projects that were culturally inappropriate, some amusing and others not. All were a waste of time and money. One glaring case of non-fit is a project to improve nutrition and health in the South Pacific through promoting increased milk consumption (Cochrane, class lecture 1974). The project involved the transfer of large quantities of American powdered milk to an island community. The inhabitants, however, were lactose intolerant (unable to digest raw milk) and everyone soon had diarrhea. Realizing what caused this outbreak, the people used the powdered milk to whitewash their houses. Beyond wasting resources, inappropriately designed projects can result in the exclusion of the intended beneficiaries, such as when a person's signature is required among people who cannot write, or a photo identification card is requested from Muslim women, whose faces should not be shown in public.

A clear role for anthropologists is to expose areas of non-fit and provide insights about how to achieve sociocultural fit and enhance project success rates. In one such case, Gerald Murray (1987) was able to play a positive role in redesigning a costly and unsuccessful reforestation project supported by the USAID in Haiti. Since the colonial era in Haiti, deforestation has been dramatic, with estimates of around 50 million trees cut annually. Some of the deforestation is driven by the market for wood for construction and for charcoal in the capital city of Port au Prince. Another aspect is that rural people are farmers and need cleared land for growing crops and grazing their goats. The ecological consequences of so much clearing, however, have been substantial soil erosion and declining fertility of the land. The USAID sent millions of tree seedlings to Haiti and the Haitian government attempted to urge rural people to plant them. The project fell flat: The farmers refused to plant the seedlings on their land and instead used them as goat fodder. Gerald Murray, who had done his doctoral dissertation on rural Haitian land tenure practices, was called in by the USAID to suggest an alternative approach. He advised that the kind of seedling promoted be changed from fruit trees, in which the rural farmers saw little benefit because they are not to be cut, to fast-growing trees such as eucalyptus which could be cut in as early as four years after planting and then sold in Port au Prince. This option was quickly accepted by the farmers since it would not tie up their farmland forever and would yield some profits in the foreseeable future,

A tree nursery in Haiti established as part of a reforestation project funded by the USAID.

and they could see that losses from food production would be offset by the income. The basic incompatibility had been that the USAID wanted trees planted that would stay in place for years to come while the Haitian farmers viewed trees as things that were meant to be cut.

Project Implementation

Another comparative study looked at twenty-four projects funded by the USAID in terms of problems of project implementation (Gow and Morss 1988). The most frequent problems encountered at the local level were:

- lack of in-country administrative and personnel capacity;
- lack of popular participation;
- timing (delays and inappropriate phasing of activities);
- need for better information management systems for project assessment; and
- conflicting interests of the groups and individuals involved.

Not all of these problems affect all projects, but they are common enough to warrant attention. Overall, local commitment and a collaborative approach between all groups involved are crucial to getting a project put in place and operational. Obviously, if project identification and design take the social context into account and achieve popular approval of and participation in the project, many of the problems listed above in implementation will be reduced. In fact, "participation" has become a buzzword of recent years, something that development experts acknowledge as important even while they may be unsure as to how it is to be achieved.

The Anthropological Critique of Development Projects

The early decades of development anthropology were dominated by what I call **traditional development anthropology (TDA).** In TDA, the anthropologist accepts the role of helping to make modernization-development work better. I call this the "add an anthropologist and stir" approach to development. It is an option that economists and others realize can help make their plans more effective. For example, an anthropologist familiar with a local culture could provide information about what kinds of consumer goods would be desired by the people, or what might induce them to relocate with less resistance. This kind of participation by anthropologists could be either positive or negative for the local people, depending on the project being undertaken.

More recently, concern has increased among anthropologists (and others) that simply helping make large-scale development projects work can be disastrous for local people and their environments (Bodley 1990; Horowitz and Salem-Murdock 1993; Taussig 1978). For example, a study of the welfare of local inhabitants of the middle Senegal valley (in the country of Senegal, West Africa) before and after the construction of a large dam shows that their level of food insecurity has increased (Horowitz and Salem-Murdock 1993). Formerly, the periodic flooding of the plain helped support a dense human population dependent on agriculture, fishing, forestry, and herding. Productivity of the wetlands had remained high for a long period of human occupation, with no signs of deterioration. The current practice of water control by the dam managers does not allow for periodic flooding. Instead, water is released less often and with disregard for the needs of the people downstream. In some years, they do not have enough water for their crops, and fishing has become a less rich source of food. At other times, a large flood of water will be released, damaging crops. As a result, many residents have become forced to leave the area—becoming, in fact, "development refugees," people who must leave home because of the effects of a development project.

The awareness of the socially negative impact of many supposedly positive development projects has led to the emergence of what I call **critical development anthropology (CDA).** In this approach, the anthropologist does not simply accept a supportive role, but rather takes on a critical-thinking role. The question is not: What can I do to make this project successful? Instead, the anthropologist asks: Is this a good project from the perspective of the target population? After long and careful thinking, if the answer is yes, then that is a green light for a supportive role. If careful thinking reveals areas where revisions in the project would make it beneficial, then the anthropologist can intervene with this information. If all evidence suggests that the project will harm the target population, either in the short run or the long run, then the anthropologist should assume the role of whistle-blower and either try to stop the project completely or substantially change the design. In the case of the Senegal Valley dam project, anthropologists working with engineers and local inhabitants devised an alternative management plan of regular and controlled amounts of released water that would reduce the harm done to people downstream and help restore some of the area's former fertility.

METHODS IN DEVELOPMENT ANTHROPOLOGY

Many full-scale anthropological studies of cultural change and development are based on long-term fieldwork and standard research methods as described in Chapter 2. However, often a development agency needs input from an anthropologist that requires faster turnaround than what long-term fieldwork would allow. Specialized methods have emerged to respond to the short time frame and provide answers to the often specific questions at hand in a way that planners and policy-makers can use. Key differences in methods used in development anthropology, compared to standard long-term fieldwork, are:

- more focused, less holistic research agenda.
- more use of multidisciplinary research teams.
- reliance on specialized methods such as rapid research methods and participatory research methods.

These three differences relate to the need to gather dependable data within a relatively short time period. Focusing the topic(s) of research is crucial and best achieved when the researchers already have some familiarity with the culture. The addition of multiple researchers working on different aspects of the problem from different angles at the same time can intensify the research process and help make up for the lack of duration of observation. The particular approaches that development anthropologists have found useful in responding to the need for short-turnaround time in generating research results are discussed next.

Rapid Research Methods

British development expert Robert Chambers is a founding figure of rapid research methods (RRMs). These methods include strategies such as going to the field with a prepared checklist of questions, conducting focus group interviews (talking to several people at the same time rather than one by one), and conducting "transect" observations (walking through a specific area with key informants and asking for explanations along the way) (Bernard 1995:139–140). Since the early 1980s, Chambers (1983) has written about the pros and cons of RRMs, and he has devised ways to correct some of the apparent gaps, particularly their potential superficiality. When used correctly, RRMs can provide useful data for assessing the problems and opportunities related to development. According to H. Russell Bernard (1995), author of a widely-used textbook in anthropological research methods, an anthropologist can do effective rapid research in just a few days, including participant observation, as he explains in the following analogy:

> Assuming you've wasted as much time in laundromats as I did when I was a student, you could conduct a reasonable participant observation study of one such place in a week. You'd begin by bringing in a load of wash and paying careful attention to what's going on around you.
>
> After two or three nights of observation, you'd be ready to tell other patrons that you were conducting research and that you'd appreciate their letting you interview them. The reason you could do this is because you already speak the native language and already picked up the nuances of etiquette from previous experience. (140)

An example of an effective mix of rapid research methods was used for preproject planning in rural Bali (Mitchell 1994). The research sought to identify environmental and social stresses that might be caused by economic development and then make recommendations to the government in preparing its next five-year development plan. Anthropologists and graduate students at the University of Windsor in Canada and an Indonesian university designed an eight-village study to provide data on ecological, economic, and social features. Each village was studied by a four-member team. Teams consisted of Indonesian and Canadian researchers, both men and women. All team members could speak Bahasa Indonesian (the national language) and at least one could also speak Bahasa Bali (the local language). Researchers lived in the village for four weeks. Several teams were involved, but each team spent some time in at least two villages. The fieldwork was preceded by a pilot study in a different village, which led to revisions in the questions and procedures to be used in the eight-village research.

Several methods were used for data collection: background data from provincial documents and village records, and interviews with key informants representing the village administration, religion, women, youth, school teachers, health clinic personnel, and agricultural extension workers. Household interviews were conducted with fifteen men and fifteen women from different neighborhoods in the village, and with a sample of primary school children. Other observations included general conditions of the village and villagers' daily activities. For each village, the research generated a fairly rich profile of relevant biophysical features; production and marketing; local government; health and welfare; and expressive culture. Their findings offered a range of issues for the government's consideration, including the apparent environmental and social stresses being caused by external development such as urbanization and tourism.

Participatory Appraisal

Building on the RRM approach, in the late 1980s, a method that involves more involvement of the local people, called **participatory appraisal (PA)**, emerged. Participatory appraisal responds to two factors: the need for more and better data than could be generated by rapid research methods, and the growing awareness that when the target population is involved in a development project, it is more likely to be successful in the short run and sustainable over the long run. Moreover, PA seeks to promote community empowerment in relation to the development project rather than dependency. Its value lies both in its use of innovative data collection methods and through "initiating a process that empowers the local community by providing it with vital data and other information that can be used for designing and implementing grassroots development initiatives" (Kabutha, Thomas-Slayter, and Ford 1993:76). Participatory appraisal proceeds by involving key community members at all stages of the research, and not only as informants. The best PA work teaches local people how to collect and analyze important kinds of data themselves. For example, local people know about such things as field size and soil quality. Barely literate villagers understand seasonal changes and can therefore participate in considering alternate strategies for improving food supplies during lean times. Such people can learn how to prepare maps and charts that will be used in project identification.

Participatory appraisal thus rests heavily on the anthropological assumption that local knowledge should not be bypassed, but instead should be the foundation of development work. Local people can also be involved in gathering and collecting data useful for project evaluation. While quantitative computer analysis of large data sets is still out of reach for most villagers, the day may not be far off when such capacities exist. Currently, workers in central project offices in provincial capitals throughout the world are becoming increasingly involved in learning how to do project analyses without foreign assistance. Besides data gathering and analysis, a crucial feature of PA is feedback from community members in project selection. Using large visual displays and charts with information on various projects and how they would be undertaken, a high degree of involvement and discussion can be achieved. In one case, in a rural Kenyan community of 4,000 adults, about 300 to 400 people were involved in the research and project selection which, while not total participation, was substantial. Local people can be trained to carry on data collection and analysis after the team has left the village. Two important effects of PA are the fostering of local autonomy in planning and a greater chance that the projects put in place will be maintained and adjusted to changing conditions.

Having looked at some of the general features of development and anthropology's role in it, this chapter now turns to a consideration of three interrelated problems in international development: indigenous peoples, women and development, and human rights and development. The particular insights in these areas provided by cultural anthropologists reveal lessons from the past and present that can be applied to improvements in the future.

INDIGENOUS PEOPLE'S DEVELOPMENT

Like colonialism, the pre–World War II process of global transformation, international development has deeply affected the world's indigenous people who have become marginalized by incoming, dominant cultures. **Indigenous people** are those who "self-identify as members of small-scale cultures and consider themselves to be the original inhabitants of the territories that they occupy" (Bodley 1994:365). The United Nations distinguishes between indigenous people and minority groups such as the Rom, the Tamils of Sri Lanka, and African Americans. While this distinction is useful in some ways, it should not be taken as a hard-and-fast difference since some groups cannot be defined as either and some groups seem to fit in both categories (Maybury-Lewis 1997; Plant 1994). David Maybury-Lewis explains that it is most useful to think of all these groups as forming a continuum from more purely indigenous groups to minority/ethnic groups that may not be geographically "original" to a place but that share many problems with indigenous people as a result of being encapsulated within a majority culture.

Regardless of the definitional debate, it is clear that indigenous people and minority people are urgently concerned with redressing basic entitlement inequalities. For indigenous people, this issue may most often take the form of land rights claims, while for minorities—especially those who live in cities—issues may focus more on employment and access to education. Language rights are an important shared issue.

Indigenous people differ from most national minorities by the fact that they often occupy (or occupied) remote areas and were, until the era of colonial expansion, less affected by outside interests. Now governments and international businesses have recognized that their lands often contain valuable natural resources such as natural gas in the polar region and gold in Papua New Guinea and the Amazon. Different governments have paid varying degrees of attention to "integrating" indigenous people into "mainstream" culture in the interests of fostering nationalism at the expense of pluralism. Recall the Chinese government's policy toward its many national minorities, many of whom can be considered indigenous people (Chapter 10).

Accurate demographic statistics on indigenous people are rare. No one agrees exactly on who to count as indigenous; there are questions about their spatial mobility in some cases, and there are political reasons in others. Governments may not bother to conduct a census of indigenous people, or if they do, they may report undercounts of indigenous people in order to downplay recognition of their very existence as a group (Baer 1982:12). A more positive reason for "demographic neglect" is the wish to avoid disturbing indigenous populations that the government is seeking to protect from excessive outside contact. A few island populations in India's Andaman Islands in the Bay of Bengal remain uncounted because Indian officials cannot gain access to them (Singh 1994). Given the difficulties involved in defining and counting indigenous people, therefore, it is possible only to provide very rough information on their number. It is estimated that, globally, indigenous people make up about 5 percent of the total world population. (Bodley 1990: 365). (See Table 17.4.)

Table 17.4
Population Estimates of Indigenous Peoples

Western Hemisphere
- less than one million in Canada
- 1.75 million in the United States
- less than 13 million in Mexico and Central America
- 16 million in South America

Europe
- 60,000 in Greenland
- 60,000 in Norway, Sweden, Finland and Russia
- 28 million within the former Soviet Union

Middle East
- 5 million

Africa
- 14 million

Asia
- 52 million in India
- 31 million in China (the government terms them *national minorities*)
- 26.5 million in Southeast Asia
- 50,000 in Japan and the Pacific combined
- 550,000 in Australia and New Zealand

Total: About 5 percent of the world's total population.

Source: Mayburg-Lewis 1997:10–11.

Indigenous People as Victims of Development

Many indigenous people and their cultures have been exterminated completely as a result of contact with outsiders (recall the discussion of diseases of contact in Chapter 7). Besides death and decline through contagious disease, political conflicts within indigenous people's territory often threaten their survival. In the Peruvian Andes, armed conflict between the Peruvian guerrillas, the Shining Path, drug traffickers, and U.S.-backed police and army units is taking a heavy toll on Native American populations:

> Not only do the warring factions attempt to enroll them by force, particularly as guides, but some of the natives, such as the Lamistas, also pay a price for the coca boom. They have always grown small crops of coca because they traditionally chew the leaves. To seize Indian land, the drug lords denounce them as illegal producers to draw down repression on them. (Jean 1991:101)

Indigenous people have also suffered from intentional efforts to take over their land by force, to prevent them from practicing their traditional lifestyle, and to integrate them into the state (see the Voices box). John Bodley (1988) has examined the effects of loss of autonomy for indigenous people that results from the unwillingness of the state to tolerate the presence of politically sovereign tribes within its boundaries. States intervene to prevent and quell armed resistance by indigenous people, even though such resistance may be critical to the maintenance of indigenous culture and the people's welfare. Indicators that an indigenous group has lost its autonomy are: inability to expel outside intruders or use force to regulate its internal affairs; introduction of formal schooling and national court systems; appointment of state-sanctioned political leaders; the institution of compulsory military service; and enforcement of payment of taxes. These changes undermine the previous quality of life and set in motion changes that indirectly lead to the peoples' further impoverishment. Such a situation is clearly and poignantly described in the life story of Rigoberta Menchú, a young Guatemalan Indian woman who, with other Indian groups of the highlands, fought for years to help maintain their land, their autonomy, and their values in the face of heavy military repression (Burgos-Debray 1997). Her brother, father, and mother were killed by the military;

VOICES

"They Told Us That Indian Ways Were Bad" by Tulto

Tulto, or Sun Elk, was born about 1870 in Taos Pueblo in New Mexico. He was the first from the pueblo to go to Carlisle Indian School in Pennsylvania, where he lived for seven years. In conversations with historian Edwin Embree, published in 1939, he describes how the lessons he learned—that Indian ways were "bad,"—resulted in the leaders of Taos Pueblo rejecting him after his return to the pueblo. His only choice, then, was to re-enter White society. He moved to a nearby town and took up work in a printing shop, having been excluded from the group by the pueblo leaders for his loss of Indian ways.

> Seven years I was there.... They said we must get civilized.... It means "be like the white man."... We all wore whiteman's clothes and ate whiteman's food and went to whiteman's churches and spoke whiteman's talk ... we also began to say Indians were bad. We laughed at our own people and their blankets and cooking pots and sacred societies and dances....
>
> [A]fter seven years I came home [to] my father and my mother and many brothers and cousins. They all began hugging me, and we all cried and were very happy.... My family loved me and I was at home ... [but the] chiefs did not want me in the pueblo....
>
> [T]he governor of the pueblo and the two war chiefs and many of the priest chiefs came into my father's house.... The chiefs said to my father, "Your son who calls himself Rafael has lived with the white men. He has been far away from the pueblo. He has not lived in the kiva nor learned the things that Indian boys should learn. He has no hair. He has no blankets. He cannot even speak our language and he has a strange smell. He is not one of us."
>
> My father was very sad.... I walked out of my father's house and out of the pueblo. I did not speak. My mother was in the other room cooking.... Some children were on the plaza and they stared at me, keeping very still as I walked away.

Source: Hirschfelder, 1995: 244–245.

she managed to stay alive, often in hiding, while participating in a continuing resistance campaign. Rigoberta Menchú was winner of the Nobel Peace Prize in 1992, a sign that the world appreciates her efforts. But anti-Indian violence continues throughout southern Mexico and central America.

Many indigenous people have long earned their living by foraging, pastoralism, or horticulture. These modes of production are similar in that they all require access to relatively large amounts of space if they are to remain sustainable: rotating use of territory for gathering, hunting, and fishing; shifting pasturage for herds; and rotating plots in horticulture. Many aspects of development are also space-extensive, and thus development and indigenous people's lifeways often come into direct conflict. Resource exploitation, especially the search for minerals and petroleum, has brought the destruction of human habitats and displacement of thousands of people. Tourism has displaced indigenous people in many parts of the world as reserves are set aside for the use of outsiders and the generation of revenues for the state. Environmentalism has created conflicts between its goals of animal preservation and indigenous people's traditional hunting and fishing rights. As noted earlier, development projects such as dams have altered the downstream environment and forced out horticulturalists and fishing peoples from their longstanding pursuits.

A Hmong woman and child, northern Thailand. The Hmong people of highland Southeast Asia have suffered decades of war in their homeland. Many have migrated to other parts of the world, including the United States and Canada, where they are classified as refugees.

An anthropological analysis of government policies in Thailand for development of the highlands reveals the complex interplay between outside interests and the welfare of the *chao khao*, or "hill people" (Kesmanee 1994). The hill people include the Karen, Hmong, Mian, Lahu, Lisu, Akha, and others, totaling about half a million people or one percent of the total Thai population. International pressures are for the hill people to replace opium cultivation with other cash crops. The Thai government's main concerns are with political stability and national security in this area, which borders on Burma and Laos. It therefore has promoted development projects to establish more connections between the highlands and the lowlands through transportation and marketing. Thus far, efforts to find viable substitute crops especially among the Hmong, who have traditionally been most dependent on opium as a cash crop, have been unsuccessful. Crops that have been introduced have required extensive use of fertilizers and pesticides, which have greatly increased environmental pollution. Efforts have been made to relocate hill horticulturalists to the plains, but there they have been provided plots with poor soil and the economic status of the people has declined. In the meantime, commercial loggers have gained access to the hills and done more damage to the forests than the traditional patterns of shifting horticulture. Increased penetration of the hill areas by lowlanders, international tourism, and communications have also promoted the increase of HIV/AIDS rates, prostitution, and opium addiction throughout the area. The loss of cultural identity of the hill peoples has been a logical consequence of these changes. Altogether, the effects of twenty years of development have been disastrous for the hill people, and awareness of this fact calls for a major change in how development is being approached by international agencies and the Thai government.

The situation in Thailand is not unique. In case after case, indigenous people have been subjected to loss of the rights they once had, increased impoverishment, and widespread despair. While active resistance to their disenfranchisement has taken place throughout history, it appears that more effective and highly organized forms of protest and reclamation of rights have become prominent since the 1980s. Many indigenous groups have acquired legal advice and expertise and have confronted power-holders in world capitals, insisting on changes. One of the most basic claims of all groups is recognition of their land rights. As Rigoberta Menchú mentions, having reflected on the condition of the Indians of highland Guatemala, "everything stemmed from the ownership of land. The best land was not in our hands. It belonged to the big landowners. Every time they see that we have new land, they try to throw us off it or steal it from us in other ways" (Burgos-Debray 1997:116).

From Victimization to Indigenous People's Development

Much evidence attests to the value of "development from within," or efforts to increase people's welfare and livelihood promoted by indigenous organizations rather than exogenous organizations. Basic components of indigenous people's development include rights to resources, local initiatives in planning through local organizations, and local leadership. The following sections consider, first, resource issues (especially land) and indigenous organizations for change.

Reclaiming Resources

The many land and resource claims being made by indigenous people are a direct response to their earlier losses and a major challenge to many states. Depending on how these disputes are resolved, they can be and sometimes are a basis for conflicts, ranging from fairly benign litigation to attempts at secession (Plant 1994).

The majority of Latin America's indigenous people are small peasant farmers, or, as landless laborers, workers on commercial farms. Yet, in no Latin American country does the government provide protection against encroachment on their land. Throughout Latin America, increasing numbers of Indians have been forced off the land and have had to seek wage labor. Those who remain live in extreme poverty. In response, a strong resurgence of activity by indigenous people and groups that support them has occurred in the 1990s (Plant 1994). Some of this activity has taken the form of physical resistance. Violence continues to erupt between indigenous people and state-supported power structures, especially in the southern Mexican state of Chiapas, with the most massacres of indigenous people occurring in the late 1900s.

Indigenous claims and pressures have had some positive effects, with Bolivia, Brazil, Colombia, and Paraguay adopting new legislation about indigenous lands. In these countries, however, more achievements have been made in demarcating lands of the forest-dwelling peoples of the Amazon compared to the highland, horticultural groups. Brazil's early policies provided for reservations, granting indigenous people's use of the land. Unfortunately, this did not include ownership because they were considered to be "minors" and thus not entitled to own property. Recently, even these meager advances in Brazil have been rolled back by new government policies unfavorable to the indigenous peoples. Peru, in contrast to Brazil, titled large areas of forest lands to communal ownership by indigenous groups. However, free access to these areas is allowed for oil and mineral exploration, so the meaning of holding a "title" is no protection against encroachment and environmental destruction.

In Canada, the law distinguishes between two different types of Native Americans and their land claims (Plant 1994). These forms of claims are: "specific claims" that concern problems arising from previous agreements or treaties, and "comprehensive claims" made by Native Americans who have not been displaced and made no treaties or agreements. Most of the former claims have led to monetary compensation. In the latter category, government interests in oil and mineral exploration have led to negotiations with indigenous people seeking to have their native claims either relinquished or redefined. The first such claim settled was the 1975 James Bay and Northern Quebec Agreement. Traditional hunting and fishing lands of several thousand Cree and Inuit were to be affected by a large hydroelectric project. It was agreed that the indigenous people would receive $225 million in partial compensation for the extinguishment of their original title. A reserve was set aside for hunting, fishing, and trapping, but the agreement said that the government of Quebec and several corporations had the right to develop resources on those lands. So far, of the forty-six comprehensive claims filed, only four have been settled. In some provinces, especially British Columbia, current claims affect most of the province.

Most Asian countries have been reluctant even to recognize the concept of special land rights of indigenous people (Plant 1994). In Bangladesh, for example, the formerly protected area of the Chittagong Hill Tracts is being massively encroached upon by settlers from the crowded plains. Nonindigenous settlers now occupy the most fertile land. A large hydroelectric dam built in 1963 displaced 100,000 hill dwellers because they could no longer practice horticulture in the flooded areas. A minority received financial aid, but most did not. Tribal opposition groups began emerging, and conflict, although suppressed in the news, has been ongoing for decades. Three other Asian sites of serious contestation with the state over land and resources in Asia include the Moros of the southern Philippines, the people of Irian Jaya in western Papua New Guinea, and the East Timorese, both of whom are under control of Indonesia and are being subject to colonization through massive immigration and resource extraction (Anderson 1997). In each of these cases, the indigenous people are waging a costly battle in terms of their lives to fight for secession from the state that controls them.

In Africa, political interests of state governments in establishing and enforcing territorial boundaries have created difficulties for indigenous people, especially pastoralists who are, for example, accustomed to moving their herds freely. Pastoralists in the Sahel region of Africa have been particularly affected by this process. Many formerly autonomous pastoralists have been transformed into refugees living in terrible conditions. The Tuareg people, for example, have traditionally lived and herded in a territory crossing what are now five different nations: Mali, Niger, Algeria, Burkina Faso, and Libya (Jean 1992:25). Given political conflict in the region, thousands of Tuareg people live in exile in Mauritania, and their prospects are grim. As elsewhere, resistance movements spring up, but states and local power interests move quickly to quell them. The death of Ogoni leader, Ken Saro-Wiwa, in 1995 is a stunning example of the personal price of resistance (Sachs 1996). Saro-Wiwa, a Nigerian writer, Nobel Peace Prize nominee, and supporter of minority people's rights, was executed by Nigerian military rulers. He had vigorously spoken out against the Nigerian regime and the oil development being pursued in Ogoniland by Royal/Dutch Shell. As president and spokesperson for the Movement for the Survival of the Ogoni People (MOSOP), he had asked the government to respect the Ogoni people's right to self-determination. He also had asked Shell to clean up oil spills and toxic waste pits that had ruined Ogoni farming and fishing communities along the Nile River delta. His message is one that applies worldwide: States tend to impose the costs of their economic growth on the people least able to cope with it—impoverished minorities—and then apply violent means of repression if such people raise serious objections to such treatment.

A ritual mask from the Ogoni people of Nigeria, whose way of life is seriously threatened by oil development being pursued in their region by international companies.

Forming Organizations

Many indigenous people have formed their own organizations for change in order to promote "development from within." In Mali, West Africa, a group named Tassaght ("The Link") is an example of an NGO established by indigenous people in response to a crisis. It began in 1985 when its founders, the Tamacheq people, obtained a grant to provide assistance to Tamacheq refugees stricken with drought. Tassaght was a facilitating organization:

> Translating, coordinating logistics and conducting research, the staff gained credibility within the NGO community and eventually obtained funding from several international partners.... Tassaght developed a reputation for the use of action research methods. The staff would first speak with settlement residents and the displaced populations around the city of Gao to better understand the dilemmas and possible solu-

tions. Information from these meetings determined the direction of development projects to improve literacy, agriculture, cereal storage, and herd management (Childs and Chelala 1994:20).

In many instances, organizations have been formed that cross over and link formerly separate groups (Perry 1996:245–246), as a response to external threats. In Australia, indigenous people have formed pan-Australian political organizations and regional coalitions such as the Pitjandjatjara Land Council that have had some success in land claim cases. In Canada, the Grand Council of the Cree has collaborated with the Inuit Tapirisat and other organizations over land issues. In this era of rapid change in telecommunications, many indigenous groups are taking advantages of new forms of communication in order to maintain links with each other over large areas (see the Current Event box).

Although it is tempting to see hope in the newly emerging forms of resistance, self-determination, and organizing among indigenous peoples, such hope cannot be generalized to all indigenous peoples. Many are making progress and their economic status

Online in the Outback

Current Event

"Online in the Outback"

- For several isolated Aborigine communities in the Australian outback, the technology has become the primary medium for personal and business communications. This medium effectively conveys the extensive system of hand gestures that Aborigines use while speaking. It is interactive and therefore facilitates the extensive consultations that Aborigine leaders traditionally employ in reaching ceremonial and community decisions.
- Since, 1993, Walpiri Aborigines in the Tanami region of Australia's Northern Territory have owned and operated a sophisticated rural videoconferencing network. The system, known as the Tanami Network, links four remote Walpiri settlements with each other and with videoconferencing sites in the cities of Sydney, Darwin, and Alice Springs.
- Connections to these urban areas provide the Walpiri with audio and video access to government services providers, other Australian Aborigines, business customers for Walpiri arts and crafts, and indigenous groups on other continents. In the popular network's first year of operation alone, community members logged 12,000 hours in personal or ceremonial videoconferences and made numerous contacts with government agencies providing services such as adult and secondary education, teacher training, remote health care, and social security and legal assistance.
- Videoconferencing improves the frequency and quality of family and community contacts for Aboriginal people. Regular communication among extended family and friends is important in Australian Aborigine communities, where social cohesion has been threatened by geographic isolation and the influence of Western culture.
- The Aborigines hope to create independent but interlinked regional videoconferencing networks throughout the country. The federal government recently decided to provide a grant to help establish a videoconferencing service in 20 remote Aborigine communities. Through projects such as these, Australia's Aborigines may soon offer the world an effective model for locally controlled rural telecommunications.

Source: Hodges, 1996:17–18.

is improving; others are suffering extreme political and economic repression, with little attention from the rest of the world.

WOMEN AND DEVELOPMENT

The category of women contrasts with that of the indigenous people discussed above because "women," in general, do not have a recognized territory and clear sense of identity as a group in relation to other groups. On the other hand, they are certainly more numerous than indigenous peoples. The effects of development on women share some features with that of indigenous people: Women have often lost power in their communities as well as former rights to property (recall the Multiple Cultural Worlds box in Chapter 3). One reason is that matrilineal kinship, a system that keeps property in the female line, is in decline throughout the world often as a result of westernization and modernization. Another is that Western experts have chosen to deal with men in the context of development projects. Women have been affected by development differently than men, within the same community and even household, because development has been pursued in an androcentric (male-centered) way.

The Male Bias

In the 1970s, feminist researchers began to notice and write about the fact that development projects were male-biased (Boserup 1970; Tinker 1976). Many projects completely bypassed women as beneficiaries, targeting men for such new initiatives as growing cash crops or learning about new technologies. This male bias in development targeting contributed to increased gender inequality and hierarchy by giving men greater access to new sources of income and depriving women of their traditional economic roles. The development experts' image of a farmer, for example, was male, not female. Women's projects focused on the domestic, ignoring their often important economic roles. Thus, women's projects were typically concerned with infant feeding patterns, child care, and family planning, and, over time, this has led to the increased "domestication" of women worldwide (Rogers 1979).

Another result of the male bias in development was an increased rate of project failure. In the West African nation of Burkina Faso, for example, a reforestation project included men as the sole participants, whose tasks would include planting and caring for the trees. Unfortunately, cultural patterns there dictate that men do not water plants; women do. So the men planted the seedlings and left them. Since the women were not included as project participants, the new young trees that were planted simply died.

Exclusion of women from positive forms of development continues to be a problem, in spite of over twenty years of work attempting to place and keep women on the development agenda. Currently, many large agencies speak of "gender fatigue," a phenomenon similar to what the news media has described as "famine fatigue," when television viewers simply tire of being interested in an issue, no matter how serious it is. As with television viewers, development specialists are subject to trendiness and an interest in new issues, even though the old ones have not been solved. Besides efforts to include women in development, another goal is to prevent further decline in women's status and welfare from development. While most large development institutions are supposed to include attention to the impact of any project on women, often the assessment is mere window-dressing. Ongoing attempts to place women's issues high on the development policy agenda are an uphill battle, especially in large institutions accustomed to focusing on issues of economic growth.

An example of an emerging development issue related to women's welfare is gender-based violence. This issue is gaining attention even among the large multilaterals, where experts now realize that women cannot participate in a credit program, for example, if they fear that their husbands will beat them for leaving the house. In September 1992, the United Nations Commission on the Status of Women formed a working group that drafted a declaration against violence against women (Heise, Pitanguy, and Germain 1994). The declaration was adopted by the General Assembly in 1993. Article 1 of the declaration states that violence against women includes "any act of gender-based violence that results in, or is likely to result in, physical, sexual or psychological harm or suffering to women, including threats of such acts, coercion or arbitrary deprivations of liberty, whether occurring in public or private life" (Economic and Social Council 1992). This definition cites "women" as the focus of concern, but it includes girls as well (see Table 17.5). A current weakness of programs that target issues of

Table 17.5
An Emerging Development Issue: Gender-Based Violence against Girls and Women throughout the Life Cycle

Prebirth	Sex-selective abortion, battering during pregnancy, coerced pregnancy
Infancy	Infanticide, emotional and physical abuse, deprivation of food and medical care
Girlhood	Child marriage, genital mutilation, sexual abuse by family members and strangers, deprivation of food and medical care, child prostitution
Adolescence	Dating and courtship violence, forced prostitution, rape, sexual abuse in the workplace, sexual harassment
Adulthood	Partner abuse and rape, partner homicide, sexual abuse in the workplace, sexual harassment, rape
Old Age	Abuse and neglect of widows, elder abuse

Source: Adapted from Heise, Pitanguy, and Germain 1994:5.

violence against girls and women is that they tend to deal with their effects, not the causes, often with disastrous results. For example, they may seek to increase personal security of women and girls in refugee camps by augmenting the number of guards at the camp when, in fact, it is often the guards who abuse refugee females.

Women's Organizations for Change

In many countries, women have made substantial gains in improving their status and welfare through forming organizations. These organizations range from "mothers' clubs" that help provide for communal child care to lending and credit organizations that provide women with the opportunity of starting their own businesses. Some are local and small-scale, others are global in reach, such as Women's World Banking, an international organization that grew out of credit programs for poor working women in India.

One community-based credit system in Mozambique, southern Africa, is supported by UNIFEM and allows farm women to buy seeds, fertilizers, and supplies on loan (Clark 1992:24). When the loan program was first started, thirty-two farm families in the village of Machel formed themselves into seven solidarity groups, each with an elected leader. The woman-headed farmer groups managed irrigation more efficiently and conferred on how to minimize use of pesticides and chemical fertilizers. Through their efforts, the women quadrupled their harvests and were able to pay off their loans. Machel women then turned their attention to getting additional loans to improve their herds and to buy a maize mill. Overall, in the midst of poverty, military conflict, the lack of government resources, and a drought, the project and the organization it fostered allowed many women farmers to increase their economic and household security.

A more informal system of social networks has emerged to help support poor women vendors in San Cristobal, Mexico (Sullivan 1992). Many of the vendors around the city square are women, and most of them have been expelled from highland Chiapas because of political conflicts there. The women vendors manufacture and sell goods to tourists and thereby provide an important portion of household income. In the city, they find support in an expanded social network that compensates for the loss of support from the extensive *compradrazgo* (god-parenthood system) of the highlands, which has broken down because of outmigration. Instead, the vendors have established networks encompassing relatives, neighbors,and church members, as well as other vendors, regardless of religious, political, economic, or social background.

These networks first developed in response to a series of rapes and robberies that began in 1987. The perpetrators were persons of power and influence, and so the women never pressed charges. Mostly single mothers and widows, they adopted a defensive strategy of self-protection: They began to group together during the slow period each afternoon. They travel in groups and carry sharpened corset bones and prongs: "If a man insults one of them, the group surrounds him and jabs him in the groin" (39–40). If a woman is robbed, the other women surround her, comfort her, and help contribute something toward her loss. The mid-afternoon gatherings have developed into support groups that provide financial assistance, child care, medical advice, and job skills. They have also publicly, and successfully, demonstrated against city officials' attempts to prevent them from continuing their vending. Through their organizational efforts, these women—poor, vulnerable refugees from highland Chiapas—have brought about important improvements in their lives.

Grameen Bank, a development project that began in Bangladesh to provide small loans to poor people, is one of the most successful examples of improving human welfare through "micro-credit." Professor Mohammed Yunnus (center) founded Grameen Bank and continues to be a source of charismatic leadership for it.

HUMAN RIGHTS AND DEVELOPMENT

Much of the preceding discussion of indigenous people and women and development intertwines with the question of human rights and development. In considering what cultural anthropologists have to contribute to the issue of human rights, we must first ask some basic and difficult questions:

- What are human rights?
- Is there a universal set of human rights?
- Are local cultural definitions of human rights that clash with those of other groups defensible?

Anthropologists' cross-cultural research and growing sense of the importance of advocacy as part of their role place them in a key position to speak to issues of global human rights (Messer 1993).

For nearly fifty years, the United Nations has been promoting human rights through its Declaration of Human Rights and other resolutions (Messer 1993). Difficulty in coming to a universal agreement on these rights is based in one sense on a split between capitalist and socialist states. The former emphasize political and civil rights such as freedom of speech as universally important. The latter emphasize socioeconomic rights such as employment and fair working conditions. Capitalist states do not acknowledge such socioeconomic rights as universal human rights and socialist states do not recognize political rights as valid. Developing states and indigenous people have added their voices, insisting on group rights to self-determination, indigenously defined paths of social change, and in some African states freedom from hunger. As Ellen Messer says, "[N]o state would go on record as being opposed to human rights.... Yet those from different states, and from different political, cultural, and religious traditions, continue to disagree on which rights have universal force and who is protected under them" (223). In spite of the array of differences, it is possible to discern certain shared features that may provide at least some overlapping, common ground that would include a minimum set of rights and freedoms, both political and socioeconomic.

Human rights are one of the latest conditions on foreign aid-giving (Tomasevski 1993). This condition means that aid will not be granted to states in which certain human rights are violated. Since the West equates human rights with democracy (free elections and free markets), Western aid is therefore denied to states defined as nondemocratic. This recent shift in United States foreign aid coincides with a decline in the sheer amount of foreign aid it gives. The new rhetoric of aid-giving linked to human rights may simply be a device for justifying giving less aid.

The connections between human rights, development, and cultural anthropology are multifaceted. We will discuss two examples of how development has negatively affected human rights.

A clear case of the use of military force in suppressing local resistance to dams and other projects has been documented in the mountain region of Northern Luzon (Drucker 1987; Kwiatkoski 1994).

Local political resistance first developed against the World Bank-funded Chico dams project, prompting the government to move in military troops to the region. Militarization in the region has resulted in numerous human rights violations, including torture, killings, imprisonment, and harassment of Cordillera people for suspected subversive activities. Members of local NGOs that support more appropriate forms of development that would benefit local people have been harassed since they oppose large-scale exogenous projects (Kwiatkoski 1994). These studies, and many others, attest to the seriousness of development and human rights abuse.

Development that leads to environmental degradation, such as pollution, deforestation, and erosion, should also be considered a form of human rights violation. Slain Ogoni leader Ken Saro-Wiwa made this point eloquently in a 1992 speech to the United Nations Working Group on Indigenous Populations:

> Environmental degradation has been a lethal weapon in the war against the indigenous Ogoni people.... Oil exploration has turned Ogoni into a wasteland: lands, streams, and creeks are totally and continually polluted; the atmosphere has been poisoned, charged as it is with hydrocarbon vapors, methane, carbon monoxide, carbon dioxide, and soot emitted by gas which has been flared 24 hours a day for 33 years in close proximity to human habitation.... The rainforest has fallen to the axe of the multinational companies ... the Ogoni countryside is no longer a source of fresh air and green vegetation. All one sees and feels around is death. [quoted in Sachs 1996:13–16]

Many social scientists are now arguing along with Saro-Wiwa that such forms of development constitute a violation of human rights since they undermine a people's way of life and threaten their continued existence (Johnston 1994).

Over the past few decades, cultural anthropologists have played an important role in defining and exposing a wide range of human rights abuses. While this role can lead to future change, Ellen Messer (1993) also calls for advocacy work directed toward prevention as well as reporting.

Human rights can be considered a core issue for cultural anthropology, pulling all its subject matter together. Human rights concern both individual and community-wide beliefs and behaviors about what is good and desirable and perceptions of violation, including people's natural environment, their livelihood, and patterns of consumption and exchange, family structure, social and political organizations, language and expressive culture, and religious beliefs.

Cultural anthropology is the only field of study that embraces all these areas and also speaks and acts in advocacy of increased respect for local knowledge and cultural diversity.

SUMMARY

Compared to anthropologists in the other three fields of general anthropology, cultural anthropologists have become seriously involved in the study of change mainly since the mid-twentieth century. In contrast, its role in applying anthropological knowledge for use dates from the very beginning of cultural anthropology when anthropologists worked for colonial administrations. International development, generally pursued as economic growth and the achievement of certain markers of modernization, emerged as a powerful theory of change following World War II. With its emergence has come the subfield of development anthropology which is devoted to the study of, and active involvement in, various forms of development and in improving its impact on the "target population."

Cultural anthropologists have often been hired as consultants on development projects, typically at the end of the project cycle, to provide evaluations. This work and its often negative results tended to give anthropologists a reputation among development experts as "nay-sayers" and "trouble-makers." More recently, some anthropologists have pushed for the earlier involvement of anthropologists in project design and implementation so that cultural knowledge can be incorporated in project planning to avoid many of the common errors.

In order to provide relevant information often in a short time-frame, cultural anthropology has adapted its traditional methods of long-term participant observation. So-called rapid research methods are intended to maximize data gathering during a short period with awareness of the greater limitations involved. The new method of participatory appraisal involves project beneficiaries in basic research before, during, and after the project.

The status of indigenous people and women and the complex issue of defining and protecting human rights are three urgent and interrelated areas of anthropological research and thinking. Research on the impact of development shows clearly that many indigenous people and women in comparison to men have suffered outright decline in their entitlements and level of living. Often, such losses are tied to violence and environmental degradation in their homelands, forcing them to become "development refugees." Such tragic occurrences can be seen to lead directly into the question of what human rights are and how development affects them. Here, cultural anthropologists are contributing much insight from different cultures about people's perceptions of their basic rights and values. No simple list of universal human rights may be available, but, at least, cross-cultural knowledge helps expose the complexities involved so that more informed debate can take place.

CRITICAL THINKING QUESTIONS

1. Consider and discuss why different countries give varying shares of foreign aid to the poorest countries, and why the countries vary in terms of the proportion of tied and untied aid.
2. Should anthropologists be involved in the applied aspects of international development at all?
3. What are some of the similarities and differences in the problems that indigenous peoples and women face in terms of the impact of large-scale development and their reactions to it?
4. What might be on a list of universal human rights?

KEY CONCEPTS

assimilation, p. 410
critical development anthropology, p. 422
development rhetoric, p. 413
diachronic, p. 408
diffusion, p. 409
human development, p. 413
indigenous people, p. 424
international development, p. 408
modernization, p. 410
participatory appraisal, p. 423
project cycle, p. 419
social impact assessment, p. 411
sociocultural fit, p. 420
structural adjustment, p. 412
sustainable development, p. 413
synchronic, p. 408
traditional development anthropology, p. 421

SUGGESTED READINGS

David H. Lempert, Kim McCarthy, and Craig Mitchell, *A Model Development Plan: New Strategies and Perspectives.* Westport, CT: Praeger, 1995. A group of university students from different disciplines (including one anthropologist, Lempert) spent six weeks in Ecuador, visiting nearly every province and studying development issues there as the basis for their development plan for Ecuador. A preface explains the background of the project. The rest of the volume consists of a detailed presentation of the plan.

Richard J. Perry, *... From Time Immemorial: Indigenous Peoples and State Systems.* Austin: University of Texas Press, 1996. This book provides a comparative examination of the history and status of indigenous peoples of Mexico, the United States, Canada, and Australia, with broader comparisons provided in a later section. The conclusion offers findings about state policies, state violence, resistance of the indigenous people, and efforts at self-determination.

Richard Reed, *Forest Dwellers, Forest Protectors: Indigenous Models for International Development.* The Cultural Survival Series in Ethnicity and Change. Boston: Allyn and Bacon, 1997. This is a fieldwork-based study of the Guaraní, indigenous people of Paraguay and Brazil, now occupying one of the world's largest remaining subtropical rainforests. Chapters consider social organization and production and consumption patterns. The text focuses on Guaraní practices and their ideas about use of forest resources.

Kalima Rose, *Where Women Are Leaders: The SEWA Movement in India.* Atlantic Highlands, NJ: Zed Books, 1992. Although not written by an anthropologist, this in-depth case study of a pioneering credit scheme for poor women of India stands as a useful contribution to the "success story" literature. The book provides a history of SEWA (Self-Employed Women's Association) and chapters describing different strategies of SEWA and its expansion throughout India and globally.

Michael French Smith, *Hard Times on Kairiru Island: Poverty, Development and Morality in a Papua New Guinea Village.* Honolulu: University of Hawaii Press, 1994. This is a fieldwork-based analysis of local understandings of poverty and development on a small island off the north coast of Papua New Guinea. Special attention is given to the stresses involved when the indigenous reciprocity economy meets up with profit-oriented capitalism.

References

Abbas, Ackbar. 1994
Building on Disappearance: Hong Kong Architecture and the City. Public Culture 6:441–459.

Abélès, Marc. 1991
Quiet Days in Burgundy: A Study of Local Politics. Trans. Annella McDermott. New York: Cambridge University Press.

Abu, Katharine. 1983
The Separateness of Spouses: Conjugal Resources in an Ashanti Town. In Female and Male in West Africa. Christine Oppong, ed. Pp. 156–168. Boston: George Allen & Unwin.

Abu-Lughod, Lila. 1993
Writing Women's Worlds: Bedouin Stories. Berkeley: University of California Press.

Adams, Kathleen M. 1984
Come to Tana Toraja, "Land of the Heavenly Kings": Travel Agents as Brokers in Ethnicity. Annals of Tourism Research 11:469–485.

Adams, Vincanne. 1988
Modes of Production and Medicine: An Examination of the Theory in Light of Sherpa Traditional Medicine. Social Science and Medicine 27:505–513.

Agar, Michael. 1994
Language Shock: Understanding the Culture of Conversation. New York: William Morrow and Company, Inc.

Akinsha, Konstantin. 1992a
Russia: Whose Art Is It? ARTNews 91(5):100–105.

___. 1992b
Whose Gold? ARTNews 91(3):39–40.

___. 1992c
After the Coup: Art for Art's Sake? ARTNews 91(1):108–113.

Allen, Catherine J. 1988
The Hold Life Has: Coca and Cultural Identity in an Andean Community. Washington, DC: Smithsonian Institution Press.

Allen, Susan. 1994
What is Media Anthropology? A Personal View and a Suggested Structure. In Media Anthropology: Informing Global Citizens. Susan L. Allen, ed. Pp. 15–32. Westport, CT: Bergin & Garvey.

Allison, Anne. 1994
Nightwork: Sexuality, Pleasure, and Corporate Masculinity in a Tokyo Hostess Club. Chicago: University of Chicago Press.

Alter, Joseph S. 1992
The Sannyasi and the Indian Wrestler: Anatomy of a Relationship. American Ethnologist 19(2):317–336.

Ames, David. 1959
Wolof Co-operative Work Groups. In Continuity and Change in African Cultures. William R. Bascom and Melville J. Herskovits, eds. Pp. 224–237. Chicago: University of Chicago Press.

Anderson, Benedict. 1991 [1983]
Imagined Communities: Reflections on the Origin and Spread of Nationalism. New York: Verso.

___. 1997
Survival By Nationalization? Paper presented at the annual meeting of the American Anthropological Association, Washington, DC, November.

Anderson, Richard L. and Karen L. Field. 1993
Chapter Introduction. Art in Small-Scale Societies: Contemporary Readings. In Richard L. Anderson and Karen L. Fields, eds. P. 247. Englewood Cliffs, NJ: Prentice Hall.

Appadurai, Arjun. 1986
Introduction: Commodities and the Politics of Value. In The Social Life of Things: Commodities in Cultural Perspective. Arjun Appadurai, ed. Pp. 3–63. New York: Cambridge University Press.

Applbaum, Kalman D. 1995
Marriage with the Proper Stranger: Arranged Marriage in Metropolitan Japan. Ethnology 34(1):37–51.

Ardrey, Robert. 1961
African Genesis. New York: Atheneum.

___. 1966
The Territorial Imperative. New York: Atheneum.

Arens, William. 1996
Incest. In The Social Science Encyclopedia. Adam Kuper and Jessica Kuper, eds. Pp. 393–395. Routledge: New York.

Ariès, Philippe. 1962
Centuries of Childhood: A Social History of Family Life. Trans. Robert Baldick. New York: Vintage Books.

Armstrong, Douglas V. 1990
The Old Village and the Great House: An Archaeological and Historical Examination of Drax Hall Plantation, St. Ann's Bay, Jamaica. Chicago: University of Illinois Press.

Asad, Talal, ed. 1973
Anthropology and the Colonial Encounter. London: Ithaca Press.

Attwood, Donald W. 1992
Raising Cane: The Political Economy of Sugar in Western India. Boulder: Westview Press.

Aung San Suu Kyi. 1995
Freedom from Fear. Revised edition. New York: Penguin Books.

Awe, Bolanle. 1977
The Iyalode in the Traditional Yoruba Political System. In Sexual Stratification: A Cross-Cultural View. Alice Schlegel, ed. Pp. 144–160. New York: Columbia University Press.

Bachnik, Jane M. 1983
Recruitment Strategies for Household Succession: Rethinking Japanese Household Organisation. Man 18:160–182.

Baer, Lars-Anders. 1982
The Sami: An Indigenous People in Their Own Land. In The Sami National Minority in Sweden. Birgitta Jahreskog, ed. Pp. 11–22. Stockholm: Almqvist & Wiksell International.

Bahn, Paul G., ed. 1996
The Cambridge Illustrated History of Archaeology. Cambridge: Cambridge University Press.

___. 1996
Easter Island Decipherment. Archaeology 49(4):18.

Barbash, Fred. 1996
And They'll Live Separately Ever After. The Washington Post, February 29:A1ff.

Bardhan, Pranab. 1974
On Life and Death Questions. Economic and Political Weekly, Special Number 9 (32–34):1293–1303.

Barfield, Thomas J. 1993
The Nomadic Alternative. Englewood Cliffs, NJ: Prentice-Hall.

___. 1994a
Establishing Legitimacy through Warfare in Archaic and Modern States. Paper presented at the annual meeting of the American Anthropological Association, Atlanta.
___. 1994b
Prospects for Plural Societies in Central Asia. Cultural Survival Quarterly 18 (2 & 3):48–51.
Barlett, Peggy F. 1980
Reciprocity and the San Juan Fiesta. Journal of Anthropological Research 36:116–130.
___. 1989
Industrial Agriculture. In Economic Anthropology. Stuart Plattner, ed. Pp. 253–292. Stanford: Stanford University Press.
___. 1990
Qualitative Methods in Rural Studies: Basic Principles. The Rural Sociologist 10(2):3–14.
Barley, Nigel. 1983
The Innocent Anthropologist: Notes from a Mud Hut. New York: Henry Holt and Company.
Barnard, Alan and Anthony Good. 1984
Research Practices in the Study of Kinship. New York: Academic Press.
Barth, Frederik. 1993
Balinese Worlds. Chicago: University of Chicago Press.
Basch, Linda, Nina Glick Schiller, and Christina Szanton Blanc. 1994
Nations Unbound: Transnational Projects, Postcolonial Predicaments, and Deterritorialized Nation-States. Langhorne, PA: Gordon and Breach Science Publishers.
Basso, Keith. H. 1972 [1970]
"To Give Up on Words": Silence in Apache Culture. In Language and Social Context. Pier Paolo Giglioni, ed. pp. 67–86. Baltimore: Penguin Books.
Bayes, Marjorie. 1989
The Effects of Relocation on the Trailing Spouse. Smith College Studies in Social Work 59(3):280–288.
Beals, Alan R. 1980
Gopalpur: A South Indian Village. Fieldwork Edition. New York: Holt, Rinehart and Winston.
Beatty, Andrew. 1992
Society and Exchange in Nias. New York: Oxford University Press.
Beck, Lois. 1986
The Qashqa'i of Iran. New Haven: Yale University Press.
___. 1991
Nomad: A Year in the Life of a Qashqa'i Tribesman in Iran. Berkeley: University of California Press.
Becker, Gary S. 1964
Human Capital: A Theoretical and Empirical Analysis, with Special Reference to Education. New York: National Bureau of Economic Research.
Beeman, William O. 1993
The Anthropology of Theater and Spectacle. Annual Review of Anthropology 22:363–393.
Belikov, Vladimir. 1994
Language Death in Siberia. UNESCO Courier 1994(2):32–36.
Benedict, Ruth. 1959 [1934]
Patterns of Culture. Boston: Houghton Mifflin Company.
___. 1969 [1946]
The Chrysanthemum and the Sword: Patterns of Japanese Culture. Rutland, VT: Charles E. Tuttle Company.
Berlin, Elois Ann and Brent Berlin. 1996
Medical Ethnobiology of the Highland Maya of Chiapas, Mexico: The Gastrointestinal Diseases. Princeton: Princeton University Press.
Bermann, Marc. 1994
Lukurmata: Household Archaeology in Prehispanic Bolivia. Princeton: Princeton University Press.
Bernal, Martin. 1987
Black Athena: The Afroasiatic Roots of Classical Civilization. New Brunswick, NJ: Rutgers University Press.
Bernard, H. Russell. 1995
Research Methods in Anthropology: Qualitative and Quantitative Approaches. Walnut Creek, CA: Altamira Press/ Sage.
Berreman, Gerald D. 1963
Hindus of the Himalayas. Berkeley: University of California Press.
___. 1979 [1975]
Race, Caste, and Other Invidious Distinctions in Social Stratification. In Caste and Other Inequities: Essays on Inequality. Gerald D. Berreman, ed. Pp. 178–222. New Delhi: Manohar.
___. 1993
Sanskritization as Female Oppression in India. In Sex and Gender Hierarchies. Barbara D. Miller, ed. Pp. 366–392. New York: Cambridge University Press.
Best, David. 1986
Culture Consciousness: Understanding the Arts of Other Cultures. Journal of Art & Design Education 5(1&2):124–135.
Beyene, Yewoubdar. 1989
From Menarche to Menopause: Reproductive Lives of Peasant Women in Two Cultures. Albany: State University of New York Press.
Bhardwaj, Surinder M. 1973
Hindu Places of Pilgrimage in India: A Study in Cultural Geography. Berkeley: University of California Press.
Bhardwaj, Surinder M. and N. Madhusudana Rao. 1990
Asian Indians in the United States: A Geographic Appraisal. In South Asians Overseas: Migration and Ethnicity. Colin Clarke, Ceri Peach, and Steven Vertovec, eds. Pp. 197–218. New York: Cambridge University Press.
Bilharz, Joy. 1995
First among Equals? The Changing Status of Seneca Women. In Women and Power in Native North America. Laura F. Klein and Lillian A. Ackerman, eds. Pp. 101–112. Norman: University of Oklahoma Press.
Billig, Michael S. 1992
The Marriage Squeeze and the Rise of Groomprice in India's Kerala State. Journal of Comparative Family Studies 23:197–216.
Bird, Sharon R. 1996
Welcome to the Men's Club: Homosociality and the Maintenance of Hegemonic Masculinity. Gender & Society 10(2): 120–132.
Bird-David, Nurit. 1993
Tribal Metaphorization of Human-Nature Relatedness: A Comparative Analysis. In Environmentalism: The View from Anthropology. Kay Milton, ed. Pp. 112–125. New York: Routledge.
Blackwood, Evelyn. 1995
Senior Women, Model Mothers, and Dutiful Wives: Managing Gender Contradictions in a Minangkabau Village. In Bewitching Women: Pious Men: Gender and Body Politics in Southeast Asia. Aihwa Ong and Michael Peletz, eds. Pp. 124–158. Berkeley: University of California Press.
Blaikie, Piers. 1985
The Political Economy of Soil Erosion in Developing Countries. New York: Longman.
Blanchard, Ray, Kenneth J. Zucker, Susan J. Bradley and Caitlin S. Hume. 1995
Birth Order and Sibling Sex Ratio in Homosexual Male Adolescents and Probably Prehomosexual Feminine Boys. Developmental Psychology 31(1):22–30.
Blau, Peter M. 1964
Exchange and Power in Social Life. New York: Wiley.
Bledsoe, Caroline H. 1983
Stealing Food as a Problem in Demography and Nutrition. Paper presented at the annual meeting of the American Anthropological Association.
Bledsoe, Caroline H. and Barney Cohen, eds. 1993
Social Dynamics of Adolescent Fertility in Sub-Saharan Africa. Washington, DC: National Academy Press.
Bledsoe, Caroline H. and Helen K. Hirschman. 1989
Case Studies Of Mortality: Anthropological Contributions. Proceed-

ings. International Union for the Scientific Study of Population, XXIst International Population Conference. Pp. 331–348. Liège: International Union for the Scientific Study of Population.

Bloch, Alexia. 1993
Personal communication.

Blok, Anton. 1972
The Peasant and the Brigand: Social Banditry Reconsidered. Comparative Studies in Society and History 14(4):494–503.

Blood, Robert O. 1967
Love Match and Arranged Marriage. New York: Free Press.

Boas, Franz. 1955 [1922]
Primitive Art. New York: Dover Publications.

Bodley, John H. 1988
Tribal Peoples and Development Issues: A Global Overview. Mountain View, CA: Mayfield Publishing Company.

___. 1990
Victims of Progress. 3rd edition. Mountain View, CA: Mayfield Publishing Company.

Bogin, Barry. 1988
Patterns of Human Growth. New York: Cambridge University Press.

Bohannan, Paul. 1955
Some Principles of Exchange and Investment among the Tiv. American Anthropologist 57(1):60–70.

Boire, Shelley Laforest. 1992
Relocation, Mental Health, and the Partnered Woman in the U.S. Unpublished term paper, Department of Anthropology, University of Pittsburgh.

Bosco, Joseph. 1992
Taiwan Factions: Guanxi, Patronage, and the State in Local Politics. Ethnology 31(2):157–184.

Boserup, Ester. 1970
Woman's Role in Economic Development. New York: St. Martin's Press.

Bossen, Laurel. 1989
Women and Economic Institutions. In Economic Anthropology. Stuart Plattner, ed. Pp. 318–350. Stanford: Stanford University Press.

Boswell, A. Ayres and Joan Z. Spade. 1996
Fraternities and Collegiate Rape Culture: Why Are Some Fraternities More Dangerous Places for Women? Gender & Society 10(2): 133–147.

Bott, Elizabeth. 1957
Family and Social Network: Roles, Norms, and External Relationships in Ordinary Urban Families. London: Tavistock.

Bottéro, Alain. 1991
Consumption by Semen Loss in India and Elsewhere. Culture, Medicine, Psychiatry 15:303–320.

Bourdieu, Pierre. 1984
Distinction: A Social Critique of the Judgement of Taste. Richard Nice, trans. Cambridge: Harvard University Press.

Bourdieu, Pierre, Alain Darbet et al. 1969
The Love of Art: European Art Museums and Their Relation to Culture. Richard Nice, trans. Chicago: The University of Chicago Press.

Bourgois, Philippe I. 1995
In Search of Respect: Selling Crack in El Barrio. New York: Cambridge University Press.

Bowen, Anne M. and Robert Trotter II. 1995
HIV Risk in Intravenous Drug Users and Crack Cocaine Smokers: Predicting Stage of Change for Condom Use. Journal of Consulting and Clinical Psychology 63:238–248.

Bowen, John R. 1992
On Scriptural Essentialism and Ritual Variation: Muslim Sacrifice in Sumatra. American Ethnologist 19(4):656–671.

___. 1998
Religions in Practice: An Approach to the Anthropology of Religion. Boston: Allyn and Bacon.

Brana-Shute, Rosemary. 1976
Women, Clubs, and Politics: The Case of a Lower-Class Neighborhood in Paramaribo, Suriname. Urban Anthropology 5(2):157–185.

Brandes, Stanley H. 1985
Forty: The Age and the Symbol. Knoxville: University of Tennessee Press.

Bray, Tamara L. 1996
Repatriation, Power Relations and the Politics of the Past. Antiquity 70:440–444.

Bray, Tamara L. and Thomas W. Killion, eds. 1994
Reckoning with the Dead: The Larsen Bay Repatriation and the Smithsonian Institution. Washington, DC: Smithsonian Institution Press.

Brenneis, Donald and Laura Lein. 1977
"You Fruithead": A Sociolinguistic Approach to Children's Dispute Settlement. In Child Discourse. Susan Ervin-Tripp and Claudia Mitchell-Kernan, eds. New York: Academic Press.

Brink, Judy H. 1991
The Effect of Emigration of Husbands on the Status of Their Wives: An Egyptian Case. International Journal of Middle East Studies 23:201–211.

Brinton, Mary C. 1993
Women and the Economic Miracle: Gender and Work in Postwar Japan. Berkeley: University of California Press.

Brison, Karen J. and Stephen C. Leavitt. 1995
Coping with Bereavement: Long-Term Perspectives on Grief and Mourning. Ethos 23:395–400.

Brooks, Alison S. and Patricia Draper. 1998 [1991]
Anthropological Perspectives on Aging. In Anthropology Explored: The Best of AnthroNotes. Ruth Osterweis Selig and Marilyn R. London, eds. Pp. 286–297. Washington, DC: Smithsonian Press.

Broude, Gwen J. 1988
Rethinking the Couvade: Cross-Cultural Evidence. American Anthropologist 90(4):902–911.

Brown, Carolyn Henning. 1984
Tourism and Ethnic Competition in a Ritual Form: The Firewalkers of Fiji. Oceania 54:223–244.

Brown, James. 1995
The Turkish Imbroglio: Its Kurds. Annals of the American Academy of Political and Social Science 541:116–129.

Brown, Judith K. 1970
A Note on the Division of Labor by Sex. American Anthropologist 72(5):1073–1078.

___. 1975
Iroquois Women: An Ethnohistoric Note. In Toward an Anthropology of Women. Rayna R. Reiter, ed. Pp. 235–251. New York: Monthly Review Press.

___. 1978
The Recruitment of a Female Labor Force. Anthropos 73(1/2): 41–48.

___. 1982
Cross-Cultural Perspectives on Middle-Aged Women. Current Anthropology 23(2):143–156.

___. 1992
Introduction: Definitions, Assumptions, Themes, and Issues. In Sanctions and Sanctuary: Cultural Perspectives on the Beating of Wives. Dorothy Ayers Counts, Judith K. Brown, and Jacquelyn C. Campbell, eds. Pp. 1–18. Boulder: Westview Press.

Brown, Nathan. 1990
Brigands and State Building: The Invention of Banditry in Modern Egypt. Comparative Studies in Society and History 32(2):258–281.

___. 1997
The Rule of Law in the Arab World: Courts in Egypt and the Gulf. New York: Cambridge University Press.

Brown, Paula. 1978
Highland Peoples of New Guinea. New York: Cambridge University Press.

Brownell, Susan. 1995
Training the Body for China: Sports in the Moral Order of the People's Republic. Chicago: University of Chicago Press.

Browner, Carole H. 1986
The Politics of Reproduction in a Mexican Village. Signs: Journal of Women in Culture and Society 11(4):710–724.
Browner, Carole H. and Sondra T. Perdue. 1988
Women's Secrets: Bases for Reproductive and Social Autonomy in a Mexican Community. American Ethnologist 15(1):84–97.
Browner, Carole H. and Nancy Ann Press. 1995
The Normalization of Prenatal Diagnostic Screening. In Conceiving the New World Order: The Global Politics of Reproduction. Faye D. Ginsberg and Rayna Rapp, eds. Pp. 307–322. Berkeley: University of California Press.
___. 1996
The Production of Authoritative Knowledge in American Prenatal Care. Medical Anthropology Quarterly 10(2):141–156.
Brownmiller, Susan. 1994
Seeing Vietnam: Encounters of the Road and Heart. New York: HarperCollins.
Bruce, Judith amd Daisy Dwyer. 1998
Introduction. In A House Divided: Women and Income in the Third World. Daisy Dwyer and Judith Bruce, eds. Pp. 1–19. Stanford: Stanford University Press.
Brumberg, Joan Jacobs. 1988
Fasting Girls: The Emergence of Anorexia Nervosa as a Modern Disease. Cambridge: Harvard University Press.
Brumfiel, Elizabeth M. 1994a
Ethnic Groups and Political Development in Ancient Mexico. In Factional Competition and Political Development in the New World. Elizabeth M. Brumfiel and John W. Fox, eds. Pp. 89–102. New York: Cambridge University Press.
___. 1994b
Introduction. In Factional Competition and Political Development in the New World. Elizabeth M. Brumfiel and John W. Fox, eds. Pp. 3–14. New York: Cambridge University Press.
Bruner, Edward M. 1991
The Transformation of Self in Tourism. Annals of Tourism Research 18:238–250.
Bunzel, Ruth. 1972 [1929]
The Pueblo Potter: A Study of Creative Imagination in Primitive Art. New York: Dover Publications.
Burgos-Debray, Elisabeth. 1997
I, Rigoberta Menchú: An Indian Woman in Guatemala. New York: Verso.
Burstyn, Linda. 1995
Female Circumcision Comes to America. Atlantic Monthly 276(4): 28–35.
Byrne, Bryan, Marvin Harris, Josildeth Gomes Consorte, and Joseph Lang. 1995
What's In a Name? The Consequences of Violating Brazilian Emic Color-Race Categories in Estimates of Social Well-Being. Journal of Anthropological Research 51:389–397.
Caldwell, John, Pat Caldwell and Bruce Caldwell. 1987
Anthropology and Demography: The Mutual Reinforcement of Speculation and Research. Current Anthropology 28(1):25–43.
Calhoun, Craig, Donald Light, and Suzanne Keller. 1994
Sociology. 6th edition. New York: McGraw Hill.
Call, Vaughn, Susan Sprecher and Pepper Schwartz. 1995
The Incidence and Frequency of Marital Sex in a National Sample. Journal of Marriage and the Family 57:639–652.
Cameron, Mary M. 1995
Transformations of Gender and Caste Divisions of Labor in Rural Nepal: Land, Hierarchy, and the Case of Women. Journal of Anthropological Research 51:215–246.
Camino, Linda A. and Ruth M. Krulfeld, eds. 1994
Reconstructing Lives, Recapturing Meaning: Refugee Identity, Gender and Culture Change. Basel: Gordon and Breach Publishers.
Cancian, Frank. 1989
Economic Behavior in Peasant Communities. In Economic Anthropology. Stuart Plattner, ed. Pp. 127–170. Stanford: Stanford University Press.
Caplan, Pat. 1987
Celibacy as a Solution? Mahatma Gandhi and Brahmacharya. In The Cultural Construction of Sexuality. Pat Caplan, ed. Pp. 271–295. New York: Tavistock Publications.
Carneiro, Robert L. 1995
War and Peace: Alternating Realities in Human History. In Studying War: Anthropological Perspectives. S. P. Reyna and R. E. Downs, eds. Pp. 3–27. Langhorne, PA: Gordon and Breach Science Publishers.
Carstairs, G. Morris. 1955
Medicine and Faith in Rural Rajasthan. In Health, Culture and Community: Case Studies of Public Reactions to Health Programs. Benjamin D. Paul and Walter B. Miller, eds. Pp. 107–134. New York: Russell Sage Foundation.
___. 1967
The Twice Born. Bloomington: Indiana University Press.
Carsten, Janet. 1995
Children in Between: Fostering and the Process of Kinship on Pulau Langkawi, Malaysia. Man (n.s.) 26:425–443.
Carter, William E., Mauricio Mamani P., and José V. Morales. 1981
Medicinal Uses of Coca in Bolivia. In Health in the Andes. Joseph W. Bastien and John M. Donahue, eds. Washington, DC: American Anthropological Association.
Castles, Stephen and Mark J. Miller. 1993
The Age of Migration: International Population Movements in the Modern World. New York: The Guilford Press.
Cátedra, María. 1992
This World, Other Worlds: Sickness, Suicide, Death, and the Afterlife among the Vaqueiros de Alzada of Spain. Chicago: University of Chicago Press.
Caudill, W. and David W. Plath. 1966
Who Sleeps by Whom? Parent-Child Involvement in Urban Japanese Families. Psychiatry 29:344–366.
Cavalli-Sforza, L., P. Menozzi and A. Piazza. 1994
History and Geography of Human Genes. Princeton: Princeton University Press.
Cernea, Michael M. 1985
Sociological Knowledge for Development Projects. In Putting People First: Sociological Variables and Rural Development. Michael M. Cernea, ed. Pp. 3–22. New York: Oxford University Press.
Cernea, Michael M. and Scott E. Guggenheim, eds. 1993
Anthropological Approaches to Resettlement: Policy, Practice, and Theory. Boulder: Westview Press.
Chagnon, Napoleon. 1992
Yanomamö. 4th edition. New York: Harcourt Brace Jovanovich.
Chalk, Frank and Kurt Jonassohn. 1986
Conceptualizations of Genocide and Ethnocide. In Famine in Ukraine: 1932–1933. Roman Serbyn and Bohdan Krawchenko, eds. Pp. 179–190. Edmonton, Canada: University of Alberta, Canadian Institute of Ukrainian Studies.
Chambers, Robert. 1983
Rural Development: Putting the Last First. Essex, United Kingdom: Longman.
Chanen, Jill Schachner. 1995
Reaching Out to Women of Color. ABA Journal 81 (May): 105.
Chant, Sylvia. 1985
Single-Parent Families: Choice or Constraint? The Formation of Female-Headed Households in Mexican Shanty Towns. Development and Change 16:635–656.
Chavez, Leo R. 1992
Shadowed Lives: Undocumented Immigrants in American Society. New York: Harcourt Brace Jovanovich.
Chen, Robert S. 1991
Estimating the Prevalence of World Hunger: A Review of Methods and Data. Providence, RI: Alan Shawn Feinstein World Hunger Program.

Cherlin. Andrew J. 1996
Public and Private Families: An Introduction. New York: McGraw-Hill Inc.

Cherlin, Andrew and Frank F. Furstenberg Jr. 1992 [1983]
The American Family in the Year 2000. In One World Many Cultures. Stuart Hirschberg, ed. Pp. 2–9. New York: Macmillan Publishing Company.

Chernoff, John Miller. 1979
African Rhythm and African Sensibility: Aesthetics and African Musical Idioms. Chicago: University of Chicago Press.

Childs, Larry and Celina Chelala. 1994
Drought, Rebellion and Social Change in Northern Mali: The Challenges Facing Tamacheq Herders. Cultural Survival Quarterly 18(4): 16–19.

Chiñas, Beverly Newbold. 1992
The Isthmus Zapotecs: A Matrifocal Culture of Mexico. New York: Harcourt, Brace, Jovanovich.

Chowdhury, Najma, Barbara J. Nelson, with Kathryn A. Carver, Nancy J. Johnson, and Paula O'Laughlin. 1994
Redefining Politics: Patterns of Women's Political Engagement from a Global Perspective. In Women and Politics Worldwide. Barbara J. Nelson and Najma Chowdhury, eds. Pp. 3–24. New Haven: Yale University Press.

Christie, Nils. 1996
Punishment. In The Social Science Encyclopedia. Adam Kuper and Jessica Kuper, eds. Pp. 708–709. New York: Routledge.

Clark, Gracia. 1992
Flexibility Equals Survival. Cultural Survival Quarterly 16:21–24.

Clark, Sam, Elizabeth Colson, James Lee, and Thayer Scudder. 1995
Ten Thousand Tonga: A Longitudinal Anthropological Study from Southern Zambia, 1956–1991. Population Studies 49: 91–109.

Clay, Jason W. 1990
What's a Nation: Latest Thinking. Mother Jones 15(7):28–30.

Cochrane, D. Glynn. 1979
The Cultural Appraisal of Development Projects. New York: Praeger Publishers.

Cohen, Jeffrey H. 1997
Popular Participation and Civil Society: The Shan-Dany Museum and the Construction of Community in Mexico. Practicing Anthropology 19:36–40.

Cohen, Lawrence. 1992
No Aging in India: The Use of Gerontology. Culture, Medicine, and Psychiatry 16:123–161.

Cohen, Mark Nathan. 1989
Health and the Rise of Civilization. New Haven, CT: Yale University Press.

Cohen, Mark Nathan and George J. Armelagos, eds. 1984
Palaeopathology at the Origins of Agriculture. New York: Academic Press.

Cohen, Mark Nathan and Sharon Bennett. 1993
Skeletal Evidence for Sex Roles and Gender Hierarchies in Prehistory. In Sex and Gender Hierarchies. Barbara Diane Miller, ed. Pp. 273–296. New York: Cambridge University Press.

Cohen, Myron. 1976
House United, House Divided. New York: Columbia University Press.

Cohen, Shaul. 1993
The Politics of Planting: Israeli-Palestinian Competition for Control of Land in the Jerusalem Periphery. Chicago: The University of Chicago Press.

Cohn, Bernard S. 1971
India: The Social Anthropology of a Civilization. New York: Prentice-Hall.

Cole, Jeffrey. 1996
Working-Class Reactions to the New Immigration in Palermo (Italy). Critique of Anthropology 16(2):199–220.

Colen, Shellee. 1995
"Like a Mother to Them": Stratified Reproduction and West Indian Childcare Workers and Employers in New York. In Conceiving the New World Order: The Global Politics of Reproduction. Faye D. Ginsberg and Rayna Rapp, eds. Pp. 87–102. Berkeley: University of California Press.

Comaroff, John L. 1987
Of Totemism and Ethnicity: Consciousness, Practice and Signs of Inequality. Ethnos 1987(3–4):301–323.

Committee on International Science, Engineering, and Technology (CISET) Working Group. 1994
Emerging and Re-Emerging Infectious Diseases: Global Microbial Threats in the 1990s. Report of the Committee on International Science, Engineering, and Technology (CISET) Working Group. Washington, DC: US Government, National Science and Technology Council.

Colson, Elizabeth. 1968
Political Anthropology: The Field. International Encyclopedia of Social Science. Pp. 189–202. New York: Macmillan.

___. 1995
The Contentiousness of Disputes. In Understanding Disputes: The Politics of Argument. Pat Caplan, ed. Pp. 65–82. Providence, RI: Berg Publishers.

Conklin, Beth A. and Laura A. Graham. 1995
The Shifting Middle Ground: Amazonian Indians and Eco-Politics. American Anthropologist 97(4):695–710.

Constable, Nicole. 1994
Christian Souls and Chinese Spirits: A Hakka Community in Hong Kong. Berkeley: University of California Press.

Contreras, Gloria. 1995
Teaching about Vietnamese Culture: Water Puppetry as the Soul of the Rice Fields. The Social Studies 86(1):25–28.

Cornia, Giovanni Andrea. 1994
Poverty, Food Consumption, and Nurition During the Transition to the Market Economy in Eastern Europe. American Economic Review 84(2):297–302.

Cornell, Laurel L. 1989
Gender Differences in Remarriage after Divorce in Japan and the United States. Journal of Marriage and the Family 51: 45–463.

Corrêa, Sonia. 1994
Population and Reproductive Rights: Feminist Perspectives from the South. Atlantic Highlands, NJ: Zed Press.

Costin, Cathy. 1993
Textiles, Women and Political Economy in Late Prehispanic Peru. Research in Economic Anthropology 14:3–28.

Counihan, Carole M. 1985
Transvestism and Gender in a Sardinian Carnival. Anthropology 9(1 & 2):11–24.

Counts, Dorothy Ayers. 1980.
Fighting Back is Not the Way: Suicide and the Women of Kaliai. American Ethnologist 7(2):331–351.

Courtald, Simon. 1994
Something Nasty in the Tea-Leaves. The Spectator 272 (January 8):16.

Courtless, Joan C. 1994
Alcohol Consumption in America: An Overview. Family Economic Review 7(1):22–31.

Coward, E. Walter, Jr. 1976
Indigenous Organisation, Bureaucracy and Development: The Case of Irrigation. The Journal of Development Studies 13(1):92–105.

___. 1979
Principles of Social Organization in an Indigenous Irrigation System. Human Organization 38(1):28–36.

Crandon-Malamud, Libbet. 1991
From the Fat of Our Souls: Social Change, Political Process, and Medical Pluralism in Bolivia. Berkeley: University of California Press.

Crapanzano, Vincent. 1980
Tuhami: Portrait of a Moroccan. Chicago: University of Chicago Press.

Crawford, C. Joanne. 1994
Parenting Practices in the Basque Country: Implications of Infant and Childhood Sleeping Location for Personality Development. Ethos 22(1):42-82.

Cronin, Michael P. 1995
The Love Hotels in Japan. Inc. Technology 17(4):116.

Crossette, Barbara. 1996
Globally, Majority Rules. The New York Times, August 4: 4–1ff.

Cunningham, Lawrence S. 1995
Christianity. In The HarperCollins Dictionary of Religion. Jonathan Z. Smith, ed. Pp. 240–253. New York: HarperCollins.

Curtin, Philip D. 1989
Death by Migration: Europe's Encounter with the Tropical World in the Nineteenth Century. New York: Cambridge University Press.

Dalby, Liza Crihfield. 1983
Geisha. New York: Vintage Books.

___. 1993
Kimono: Fashioning Culture. New Haven: Yale University Press.

Daly, Mary. 1978
Gyn/Ecology: The Metaethics of Radical Feminism. Boston: Beacon Press.

Daly, Martin and Margo Wilson. 1984
A Sociobiological Analysis of Human Infanticide. In Infanticide: Comparative and Evolutionary Perspectives. Glenn Hausfater and Sarah Blaffer Hrdy, eds. Pp. 487–502. New York: Aldine Publishing Company.

Dando, William A. 1980
The Geography of Famine. New York: John Wiley and Sons.

Dannhaeuser, Norbert. 1989
Marketing in Developing Urban Areas. In Economic Anthropology. Stuart Plattner, ed. Pp. 222–252. Stanford: Stanford University Press.

Das, Veena. 1985
Anthropological Knowledge and Collective Violence: The Riots in Delhi, November 1984. Anthropology Today 1:4–6.

Dasgupta, Satadal, Christine Weatherbie, and Rajat Subhra Mukhopadhaya. 1993
Nuclear and Joint Family Households in West Bengal Villages. Ethnology 32(4):339–358.

Daugherty, Mary Lee. 1997 [1976]
Serpent-Handling as Sacrament. In Magic, Witchcraft, and Religion. Arthur C. Lehmann and James E. Myers, eds. Pp. 347–352. Moutain View, CA: Mayfield Publishing Company.

Davis, John. 1992
Exchange. Minneapolis: University of Minnesota Press.

Davis, N. Z. 1986
Boundaries and the Sense of Self in Sixteenth Century France. In Reconstructing Individualism: Autonomy, Individuality and the Self in Western Thought. T. C. Heller, M. Sosna and D. E. Wellberry, eds. Pp. 53–63. Stanford: Stanford University Press.

Davis, Susan Schaefer and Douglas A. Davis. 1987
Adolescence in a Moroccan Town: Making Social Sense. New Brunswick: Rutgers University Press.

Davis-Floyd, Robbie E. 1987
Obstetric Training as a Rite of Passage. Medical Anthropology Quarterly 1:288–318.

___. 1992
Birth as an American Rite of Passage. Berkeley: University of California Press.

Davison, Jean and Martin Kanyuka. 1992
Girls' Participation in Basic Education in Southern Malawi. Comparative Education Review 36(4):446-466.

de Athayde Figueiredo, Mariza and Dando Prado. 1989
The Women of Arembepe. UNESCO Courier 7:38–41.

Deane, Phyllis. 1996
Capitalism. In The Social Science Encyclopedia. Adam Kuper and Jessica Kuper, eds. Pp. 71–73. New York: Routledge.

Deaton, Angus. 1987
The Allocation of Goods within the Household: Adults, Children, and Gender. Living Standards Measurement Study Working Paper No. 39. Washington, DC: The World Bank.

Delaney, Carol. 1988
Mortal Flow: Menstruation in Turkish Village Society. In Blood Magic: The Anthropology of Menstruation. Timothy Buckley and Alma Gottlieb, eds. Pp. 75–93. Berkeley: University of California Press.

Devereaux, George. 1976
A Typological Study of Abortion in Primitive Societies: A Typological, Distributional, and Dynamic Analysis of the Prevention of Birth in 400 Preindustrial Societies. New York: International Universities Press.

de Waal, Frans B. M. 1989
Chimpanzee Politics: Power and Sex among Apes. Baltimore: The Johns Hopkins University Press.

___. 1995
Bonobo Sex and Society. Scientific American, March 82–88.

DeWalt, Billie R. 1994
Using Indigenous Knowledge to Improve Agriculture and Natural Resource Management. Human Organization 53(2): 123–131.

Diamond, Jared. 1994 [1987]
The Worst Mistake in the History of the Human Race. In Applying Cultural Anthroplogy: A Reader. Aaron Podolefsky and Peter J. Brown, eds. Pp. 105–108. Mountain View, CA: Mayfield Publishing Company.

Dickemann, Mildred. 1975
Demographic Consequences of Infanticide in Man. Annual Review of Ecology and Systematics 6:107–137.

___. 1979
Female Infanticide, Reproductive Strategies, and Social Stratification: A Preliminary Model. In Evolutionary Biology and Human Social Behavior: An Anthropological Perspective. Napoleon Chagnon and William Irons, eds. Pp. 321–367. North Scituate, MA: Duxbury Press.

___. 1984
Concepts and Classification in the Study of Human Infanticide: Sectional Introduction and Some Cautionary Notes. In Infanticide: Comparative and Evolutionary Perspectives. Glenn Hausfater and Sarah Blaffer Hrdy, eds. Pp. 427–438. New York: Aldine Publishing Company.

Dikötter, Frank. 1998
Hairy Barbarians, Furry Primates and Wild Men: Medical Science and Cultural Representations of Hair in China. In Hair: Its Power and Meaning in Asian Cultures. Alf Hiltebeitel and Barbara D. Miller, eds. Pp. 51–74. Albany: State University of New York Press.

Di Leonardo, Micaela. 1984
The Varieties of Ethnic Experience: Kinship, Class, and Gender among California Italian-Americans. Ithaca: Cornell University Press.

Dissanayake, Ellen. 1992
Homo Aestheticus: Where Art Comes From and Why. Seattle: University of Washington Press.

Divale, William T. 1974
Migration, External Warfare, and Matrilocal Residence. Behavior Science Research 9:75–133.

Divale, William T. and Marvin Harris. 1976
Population, Warfare and the Male Supremacist Complex. American Anthropologist 78:521–538.

Donlon, Jon. 1990
Fighting Cocks, Feathered Warriors, and Little Heroes. Play & Culture 3:273–285.

Donnelly, Nancy D. 1994
Changing Lives of Refugee Hmong Women. Seattle: University of Washington Press.

Dorgan, Howard. 1989
The Old Regular Baptists of Central Appalachia: Brothers and Sisters in Hope. Knoxville: The University of Tennessee Press.

Dorris, Michael. 1993
Rooms in the House of Stone. Minneapolis, MN: Milkweed Editions.

Douglas, Cole. 1991
The History of the Kwakiutl Potlatch. In Chiefly Feasts: The Enduring Potlatch. Aldona Jonaitis, ed. Pp. 135-176. Seattle: University of Washington Press.

Douglas, Mary. 1962
The Lele: Resistance to Change. In Economic Anthropology. Paul Bohannan and George Dalton, eds. Pp. 211–233. Evanston: Northwestern University Press.

___. 1966
Purity and Danger: An Analysis of Concepts of Pollution and Taboo. New York: Penguin Books.
Douglas, Mary and Baron Isherwood. 1979
The World of Goods: Towards an Anthropology of Consumption. New York: W. W. Norton and Company.
Douglas, Mary and Aaron Wildavsky. 1985
Risk and Culture: An Essay on the Selection of Technical and Environmental Dangers. Berkeley: University of California Press.
Drake, Susan P. 1991
Local Participation in Ecotourism Projects. In Nature Tourism: Managing for the Environment. Tensie Whelan, ed. Pp. 132–155. Washington, DC: Island Press.
Drucker, Charles. 1988
Dam the Chico: Hydropower, Development and Tribal Resistance. In Tribal Peoples and Development Issues: A Global Overview. John H. Bodley, ed. Pp. 151–165. Mountain View, CA: Mayfield Publishing Company.
Dube, S. C. 1967
Indian Village. New York: Harper & Row.
Dufour, Darna, Lisa K. Staten, Julio C. Reina, and G. B. Spurr. 1997
Living on the Edge: Dietary Strategies of Economically Impoverished Women in Cali, Colombia. American Journal of Physical Anthropology 102:5-15.
Duncan, Margaret C. and Amoun Sayaovong. 1990
Photographic Images and Gender in Sports Illustrated for Kids. Play & Culture 3:91–116.
Durkheim, Emile. 1951 [1897]
Suicide: A Study in Sociology. New York: The Free Press.
___. 1965 [1985]
On the Division of Labor in Society. Trans. G. Simpson. New York: The Free Press.
___. 1965 [1915]
The Elementary Forms of the Religious Life. New York: The Free Press.
Duranti, Alessandro. 1994
From Grammar to Politics: Linguistic Anthrpology in a Western Samoan Village. Berkeley: University of California Press.
Durning, Alan Thein. 1993
Are We Happy Yet? How the Pursuit of Happiness is Failing. The Futurist 27(1):20–24.
du Toit, Brian M. 1990
People on the Move: Rural-Urban Migration with Special Reference to the Third World: Theoretical and Empirical Perspectives. Human Organization 49(4):305–320.
Dwyer, Daisy Hilse. 1977
Bridging the Gap between the Sexes in Moroccan Legal Practice. In Sexual Stratification: A Cross-Cultural View. Alice Schlegel, ed. Pp. 41–66. New York: Columbia University Press.
Dyson, Tim. 1994
World Population and Food Supplies. International Social Science Journal 46(3):361–385.
Dyson, Tim and Mick Moore. 1983
On Kinship Structure, Female Autonomy, and Demographic Behavior in India. Population and Development Review 9(1):35–60.
Earle, Timothy. 1991
The Evolution of Chiefdoms. In Chiefdoms, Power, Economy, and Ideology. Timothy Earle, ed. Pp. 1–15. New York: Cambridge University Press.
Eckel, Malcolm David. 1995
Buddhism. In The HarperCollins Dictionary of Religion. Jonathan Z. Smith. Pp. 135-150. New York: HarperCollins.
Economic and Social Council. 1992
Report of the Working Group on Violence against Women. Vienna: United Nations. E/CN.6/WG.2/1992/L.3.
The Economist. 1994a
South Korea: Not That Sort of Girl. April 23:35–36.
___. 1994b
Ghana: For Love of Gadgets. November 26:45.
___. 1995
Unwanted, Uncounted. June 24:33.
Eickelman, Dale F. 1981
The Middle East: An Anthropological Perspective. Englewood Cliffs, NJ: Prentice-Hall.
Elder, Joseph W. 1970
Rajpur: Change in the Jajmani System of an Uttar Pradesh Village. In Change and Continuity in India's Caste System. K. Ishwaran, ed. New York: Columbia University Press.
Ellis, Frank. 1988
Peasant Economics: Farm Households and Agrarian Development. New York: Cambridge University Press.
El Saadawi, Nawal. 1994 [1983]
Memoirs from the Women's Prison. Marilyn Booth, trans. Berkeley: University of California Press.
Elson, Diane. 1991
Male Bias in the Development Process. New York: St. Martin's Press.
Ember, Carol R. 1983
The Relative Decline in Women's Contribution to Agriculture with Intensification. American Anthropologist 85(2): 285–304.
Entwisle, Barbara, Gail E. Henderson, Susan E. Short, Jill Bouma, and Zhai Fengying. 1995
Gender and Family Businesses in Rural China. American Sociological Review 60:36–57.
Erhlich, Paul. 1968
The Population Bomb. New York: Ballantine.
Erhlich, Paul R. and Anne H. Erhlich. 1990
The Population Explosion. New York: Simon and Schuster.
Escobar, Arturo. 1995
Encountering Development: The Making and Unmaking of the Third World. Princeton: Princeton University Press.
Escobar, Gabriel. 1996
Free Trade Leads to Mobile Labor as Bolivians Seek Jobs in Argentina. The Washington Post, September 15:A21.
Esman, Milton. 1996
Ethnic Politics. In The Social Science Encyclopedia. Adam Kuper and Jessica Kuper, eds. Pp. 259–260. New York: Routledge.
Estioko-Griffin, Agnes. 1986
Daughters of the Forest. Natural History 95:36–43.
Estioko-Griffin, Agnes, Madeleine J. Goodman, and Bion Griffin. 1985
The Compatibility of Hunting and Mothering among the Agta Hunter-Gatherers of the Philippines. Sex Roles 12: 1199–1209.
Estrin, Saul. 1996
Co-operatives. In The Social Science Encyclopedia. Adam Kuper and Jessica Kuper, eds. Pp. 138-139. Routledge: New York.
Etienne, Mona and Eleanor Leacock, eds. 1980
Women and Colonization: Anthropological Perspectives. New York: Praeger.
Evans-Pritchard, E. E. 1933
Zande Blood-Brotherhood. Africa 6:131–161.
___. 1951
Kinship and Marriage among the Nuer. Oxford: Clarendon.
___. 1965 [1947]
The Nuer: A Description of the Modes of Livelihood and Political Institutions of a Nilotic People. New York: Oxford University Press.
Everett, Daniel. 1995
Personal communication.
Fabian, Johannes. 1995
Ethnographic Misunderstanding and the Perils of Context. American Anthropologist 97(1):41–50.
Fabrega, Horacio, Jr. and Barbara D. Miller. 1995
Adolescent Psychiatry as a Product of Contemporary Anglo-American Society. Social Science and Medicine 40(7): 881–894.
Fabrega, Horacio, Jr. and Daniel B. Silver. 1973
Illness and Shamanistic Curing in Zinacantan: An Ethnomedical Analysis. Stanford: Stanford University Press.
Fapohunda, Eleanor R. 1988
The Nonpooling Household: A Challenge to Theory. In A Home

Divided: Women and Income in the Third World. Daisy Dwyer and Judith Bruce, eds. Pp. 143–154. Stanford: Stanford University Press.

Farmer, Paul. 1990
Sending Sickness: Sorcery, Politics, and Changing Concepts of AIDS in Rural Haiti. Medical Anthropology Quarterly 4:6–27.

Feeley-Harnick, Gillian. 1991 [1960]
A Green Estate: Restoring Independence in Madagascar. Washington: Smithsonian Institution Press.

Feinsilver, Julie M. 1993
Healing the Masses: Cuban Health Politics at Home and Abroad. Berkeley: University of California Press.

Feldman-Savelsberg, Pamela. 1995
Cooking Inside: Kinship and Gender in Bangangté Idioms of Marriage and Procreation. American Ethnologist 22(3): 483–501.

Ferguson, James. 1994
The Anti-Politics Machine: "Development," Depoliticization, and Bureaucratic Power in Lesotho. Minneapolis: University of Minnesota Press.

Ferguson, R. Brian. 1990
Blood of the Leviathan: Western Contact and Amazonian Warfare. American Ethnologist 17(1):237–257.

Fiske, John. 1994
Radical Shopping in Los Angeles: Race, Media and the Sphere of Consumption. Media, Culture & Society 16: 469–486.

Fitchen, Janet M. 1990
How Do You Know If You Haven't Listened First?: Using Anthropological Methods to Prepare for Survey Research. The Rural Sociologist 10(2):15–22.

Fluehr-Lobban, Carolyn. 1994
Informed Consent in Anthropological Research: We Are Not Exempt. Human Organization 53(1):1–10.

Folbre, Nancy. 1986
Cleaning House: New Perspectives on Households and Economic Development. Journal of Development Economics 22:5–40.

___. 1995
Sexual Orientation Showing Up in Paychecks. Working Woman 20(1): 15.

Fonseca, Isabel. 1995
Bury Me Standing: The Gypsies and Their Journey. New York: Alfred A. Knopf.

Fortes, Meyer and E. E. Evans-Pritchard. 1987 [1940]
African Political Systems. New York: Routledge.

Fortune, Reo F. 1959 [1932]
Sorcerers of Dobu: The Social Anthropology of the Dobu Islanders of the Western Pacific. New York: E. P. Dutton & Co.

Foster, George. 1965
Peasant Society and the Image of the Limited Good. American Anthropologist 67:293–315.

Foster, George M. and Barbara Gallatin Anderson. 1978
Medical Anthropology. New York: Alfred A. Knopf.

Foucault, Michel. 1970
The Order of Things: An Archaeology of the Human Sciences. New York: Random House.

___. 1977
Discipline and Punish: The Birth of the Prison. New York: Pantheon Books.

Fox, Robin. 1995 [1978]
The Tory Islanders: A People of the Celtic Fringe. Notre Dame: University of Notre Dame Press.

Francese, Peter. 1996
The 100 Millionth Household. American Demographics 18(3):15–16.

Franke, Richard W. 1993
Life is a Little Better: Redistribution as a Development Strategy in Nadur Village, Kerala. Boulder: Westview Press.

Franke, Richard W. and Barbara H. Chasin. 1994 [1989]
Kerala: Radical Reform as Development in an Indian State. Oakland, CA: The Institute for Food and Development Policy.

Frankel, Francine R. 1971
India's Green Revolution: Economic Gains and Political Costs. Princeton: Princeton University Press.

Fratkin, Elliot. 1998
Ariaal Pastoralists of Kenya: Surviving Drought and Development in Africa's Arid Lands. Boston: Allyn and Bacon.

Fratkin, Elliot, Kathleen Galvin, and Eric A. Roth, eds. 1994
African Pastoralist Systems: An Integrated Approach. Boulder: Westview Press.

Frazer, Sir James. 1978 [1890]
The Golden Bough: A Study in Magic and Religion. New York: Macmillan.

Freed, Stanley A. and Ruth S. Freed. 1969
Urbanization and Family Types in a North Indian Village. Southwestern Journal of Anthropology 25:342–359.

Freedman, Diane C. 1986
Wife, Widow, Woman: Roles of an Anthropologist in a Transylvanian Village. In Women in the Field: Anthropological Experiences. Peggy Golde, ed. Pp. 333–358. Berkeley: University of California Press.

Freedman, Ronald. 1995
Asia's Recent Fertility Decline and Prospects for Future Demographic Change. Asia-Pacific Population Research Reports. Number 1, January. Honolulu: East-West Center, Program on Population, University of Hawaii.

Freeman, Derek. 1983
Margaret Mead and Samoa: The Making and Unmaking of an Anthropological Myth. Cambridge, MA: Harvard University Press.

Freeman, James A. 1979
Untouchable: An Indian Life History. Stanford: Stanford University Press.

___. 1981
A Firewalking Ceremony that Failed. In Social and Cultural Context of Medicine in India. Giri Raj Gupta, ed. Pp. 308–336. New Delhi: Vikas Publishing House.

___. 1989
Hearts of Sorrow: Vietnamese-American Lives. Stanford: Stanford University Press.

___. 1995
Changing Identities: Vietnamese Americans, 1975–1995. Boston: Allyn and Bacon.

Freidel, David and Linda Schele. 1993
Maya Royal Women: A Lesson in Precolumbian History. In Gender in Cross-Cultural Perspective. Caroline B. Brettell and Carolyn F. Sargent, eds. Pp. 59–63. Englewood Cliffs, NJ: Prentice Hall.

Fricke, Tom. 1994 [1984]
Himalayan Households: Tamang Demography and Domestic Processes. New York: Columbia University Press.

Fricke, T. E., W. G. Axinn, and A. Thornton. 1993
Marriage, Social Inequality, and Women's Contact with Their Natal Families in Alliance Societies: Two Tamang Examples. American Anthropologist 95(2):395–419.

Friedl, Ernestine. 1975
Women and Men: An Anthropologist's View. New York: Holt, Rinehart, and Winston.

___. 1986
Fieldwork in a Greek Village. In Women in the Field: Anthropological Experiences. Peggy Golde, ed. Pp. 195–220. Berkeley: University of California Press.

Frieze, Irene et al. 1978
Women and Sex Roles: A Social Psychological Perspective. New York: W. W. Norton.

Frisch, Rose. 1978
Population, Food Intake, and Fertility. Science 199:22–30.

Fuller, Christopher J. 1976
The Nayars Today. New York: Cambridge University Press.

Furst, Peter T. 1989
The Water of Life: Symbolism and Natural History on the Northwest Coast. Dialectical Anthropology 14:95–115.

Gable, Eric. 1995
The Decolonization of Consciousness: Local Skeptics and the "Will to Be Modern" in a West African Village. American Ethnologist 22(2): 242–257.
Gage-Brandon, Anastasia J. 1992
The Polygyny-Divorce Relationship: A Case Study of Nigeria. Journal of Marriage and the Family 54:282–292.
Gale, Faye, Rebecca Bailey-Harris, and Joy Wundersitz. 1990
Aboriginal Youth and the Criminal Justice System: The Injustice of Justice? New York: Cambridge University Press.
Galt, Anthony H. 1992
Town and Country in Locorotondo. New York: Harcourt Brace Jovanovich.
Galuszka, Peter. 1993
BMW, Mercedes, Rolls-Royce—Could This Be Russia? Business Week [330] August 2:40.
Gardiner, Margaret. 1984
Footprints on Malekula: A Memoir of Bernard Deacon. Edinburgh: The Salamander Press.
Gardner, Katy and David Lewis. 1996
Anthropology, Development and the Post-Modern Challenge. Chicago: Pluto Press.
Garland, David. 1996
Social Control. In The Social Science Encyclopedia. Adam Kuper and Jessica Kuper, eds. pp. 780–783. Routledge: New York.
Garreau, Joel. 1981
The Nine Nations of North America. New York: Avon Books.
Geertz, Clifford. 1962
The Rotating Credit Association: A "Middle Rung" in Development. Economic Development and Cultural Change 10(3): 241–263.
___. 1963
Agricultural Involution: The Processes of Ecological Change in Indonesia. Berkeley: University of California Press.
___. 1966
Religion as a Cultural System. In Anthropological Approaches to the Study of Religion. Michael Banton, ed. Pp. 1–46. London: Tavistock.
___. 1983
Local Knowledge: Further Essays in Interpretive Anthropology. New York: Basic Books.
Gegiow vs. Uhl. 1915
No. 340. Supreme Court of the United States.
Gevins, Adi. 1987
Tackling Tradition: African Women Speak Out Against Circumcision. In Third World, Second Sex. Vol 2. Miranda Davies, ed. Pp. 244–249. London: Zed Press.
Gifford-Gonzalez, Diane. 1993
You Can Hide, But You Can't Run: Representation of Women's Work in Illustrations of Palaeolithic Life. Visual Anthropology Review 9(1):23–41.
Gilbertson, Greta A. 1995
Women's Labor and Enclave Employment: The Case of Dominican and Colombian Women in New York City. International Migration Review 29(3):657–670.
Gill, Lesley. 1993
"Proper Women" and City Pleasures: Gender, Class, and Contested Meanings in La Paz. American Ethnologist 20(1):72–88.
Gilman, Antonio. 1991
Trajectories towards Social Complexity in the Later Prehistory of the Mediterranean. In Chiefdoms: Power, Economy and Ideology. Timothy Earle, ed. Pp. 146–168. New York: Cambridge University Press.
Ginsburg, Faye D. 1989
Contested Lives: The Abortion Debate in an American Community. Berkeley: University of California Press.
Ginsberg, Faye D. and Rayna Rapp. 1991
The Politics of Reproduction. Annual Review of Anthropology 20:311–343.
Gittelsohn, Joel. 1991
Opening the Box: Intrahousehold Food Allocation in Rural India. Social Science and Medicine 33(10):1141–1154.
Gladwin, Christina H. 1989
On the Division of Labor Between Economics and Economic Anthropology. In Economic Anthropology. Stuart Plattner, ed. Pp. 397–428. Stanford: Stanford University Press.
Glínski, Piotr. 1994
Environmentalism among Polish Youth: A Maturing Social Movement? Communist and Post-Communist Studies 27(2):145–159.
Gliotto, Tom. 1995
Paradise Lost. People Weekly 43(17):70-76.
Gluckman, Max. 1955
The Judicial Process among the Barotse of Northern Rhodesia. Manchester: Manchester University Press.
___. 1963
Order and Rebellion in Tribal Africa. London: Cohen and West.
Gmelch, George. 1997 [1971]
Baseball Magic. In Magic, Witchcraft, and Religion. Arthur C. Lehmann and James E. Myers, eds. Pp. 276–282. Mountain View, CA: Mayfield Publishing Company.
Godelier, Maurice. 1971
"Salt Currency" and the Circulation of Commodities among the Baruya of New Guinea. In Studies in Economic Anthropology. George Dalton, ed. Pp. 52–73. Anthropological Studies No. 7. Washington, DC: American Anthropological Association.
Goffman, Erving. 1963
Stigma: Notes on the Management of Spoiled Identity. Englewood Cliffs, NJ: Prentice-Hall.
Gold, Ann Grodzins. 1988
Fruitful Journeys: The Ways of Rajasthani Pilgrims. Berkeley: University of California Press.
Gold, Stevan J. 1992
Refugee Communities: A Comparative Field Study. Newbury Park: Sage Publications.
___. 1995
From the Workers' State to the Golden State: Jews from the Former Soviet Union in California. Boston: Allyn and Bacon.
Golde, Peggy, ed. 1986
Women in the Field: Anthropological Experiences. Berkeley: University of California Press.
Goldstein, Melvyn C. 1987
When Brothers Share a Wife. Natural History 96:38–49.
Goldstein, Melvyn C. and Cynthia M. Beall. 1994
The Changing World of Mongolia's Nomads. Berkeley: University of California Press.
Goldstone, Jack. 1996
Revolutions. In The Social Science Encyclopedia. Adam Kuper and Jessica Kuper, eds. Pp. 740–743. New York: Routledge.
González, Nancie L. 1970
Toward a Definition of Matrifocality. In Afro-American Anthropology: Contemporary Perspectives. Norman E. Whitten, Jr. and John F. Szwed, eds. New York: The Free Press.
Goodall, Jane. 1971
In the Shadow of Man. Boston: Houghton-Mifflin.
___. 1986
The Chimpanzees of Gombe: Patterns of Behavior. Cambridge, MA: Harvard University Press.
Goody, Jack. 1976
Production and Reproduction: A Comparative Study of the Domestic Domain. New York: Cambridge University Press.
___. 1977
Cooking, Cuisine and Class: A Study of Comparative Sociology. New York: Cambridge University Press.
___. 1993
The Culture of Flowers. New York: Cambridge University Press.

___. 1996
Comparing Family Systems in Europe and Asia: Are There Different Sets of Rules? Population and Development Review 22:1–20.
Goody, Jack and Stanley J. Tambiah. 1973
Bridewealth and Dowry. New York: Cambridge University Press.
Gow, David D. and Elliott R. Morss. 1988
The Notorious Nine: Critical Problems in Project Implementation. World Development 16(12):1399–1418.
Graburn, Nelson H. H., ed.
Ethnic and Tourist Arts. Berkeley: University of California Press.
Greenalgh, Susan. 1994
Controlling Births and Bodies in Village China. American Ethnologist 21(1):3–30.
Greenough, Paul R. 1982
Prosperity and Misery in Modern Bengal: The Famine of 1943–44. New York: Oxford University Press.
Gregor, Thomas. 1981
A Content Analysis of Mehinaku Dreams. Ethos 9:353–390.
___. 1982
No Girls Allowed. Science 82.
Gremillion, Helen. 1992
Psychiatry as Social Ordering: Anorexia Nervosa, a Paradigm. Social Science and Medicine 35(1):57–71.
Grenier, Guillermo J., Alex Stepick, Debbie Draznin, Aileen LaBorwit, and Steve Morris. 1992
On Machines and Bureaucracy: Controlling Ethnic Interaction in Miami's Apparel and Construction Industries. In Structuring Diversity: Ethnographic Perspectives on the New Immigration. Louise Lamphere, ed. Pp. 65–94. Chicago: University of Chicago Press.
Grinker, Roy Richard. 1994
Houses in the Rainforest: Ethnicity and Inequality among Farmers and Foragers in Central Africa. Berkeley: University of California Press.
Groce, Nora E. 1985
Everyone Here Spoke Sign Language: Hereditary Deafness on Martha's Vineyard. Cambridge: Harvard University Press.
Gross, Daniel R. 1984
Time Allocation: A Tool for the Study of Cultural Behavior. Annual Review of Anthropology 13:519–558.
Gross, Daniel R. George Eiten, Nancy M. Flowers, Francisca M. Leoi, Madeleine Lattman Ritter, and Dennis W. Werner. 1979
Ecology and Acculturation among Native Peoples of Central Brazil. Science 206(30):1043–1050.
Gross, Daniel R. and Barbara A. Underwoood. 1971
Technological Change and Caloric Costs. American Anthropologist 73:725–740.
Grossman, David C., B. Carol Milligan, and Richard A. Deyo. 1991
Risk Factors for Suicide Attempts among Navajo Adolescents. American Journal of Public Health 81(7):870–873.
Gudeman, Stephen. 1986
Economics as Culture: Models and Metaphors of Livelihood. London: Routledge & Kegan Paul.
Guggenheim, Scott E. and Michael M. Cernea. 1993
Anthropological Approaches to Involuntary Resettlement: Policy, Practice, and Theory. In Anthropological Approaches to Resettlement: Policy, Practice, and Theory. Michael M. Cernea and Scott E. Guggenheim, eds. Pp. 1–12. Boulder: Westview Press.
Gugler, Josef. 1988
The Urban Character of Contemporary Revolutions. In The Urbanization of the Third World. Josef Gugler, ed. Pp. 399–412. New York: Oxford University Press.
Guidoni, Enrico. 1987
Primitive Architecture. Robert Erich Wolf, trans. New York: Rizzoli.
Güneş-Ayara, Ayşe. 1995
Women's Participation in Politics in Turkey. In Women in Modern Turkish Society: A Reader. Sirin Tekeli, ed. Pp. 235–249. London: Zed Books.
Gutkind, Lee. 1990
One Children's Place: Inside a Children's Hospital. New York: Plume.
Guyer, Jane. 1988
Dynamic Approaches to Domestic Budgeting: Cases and Methods from Africa. In A Home Divided: Women and Income in the Third World. Daisy Dwyer and Judith Bruce, eds. Pp. 155–172. Stanford: Stanford University Press.
___. 1991
Female Farming in Anthropology and African History. In Gender at the Crossroads of Knowledge: Feminist Anthropology in the Postmodern Era. Micaela di Leonardo, ed. Pp. 257–277. Berkeley: University of California Press.
Hackenberg, Robert A. et al. 1983
Migration, Modernization and Hypertension: Blood Pressure Levels in Four Philippine Communities. Medical Anthropology 7(1):45–71.
Hacker, Andrew. 1992
Two Nations: Black and White, Separate, Hostile, Unequal. New York: Ballantine Books.
Hakamies-Blomqvist, Liisa. 1994
Aging and Fatal Accidents in Male and Female Drivers. Journal of Gerontology [Social Sciences] 49(6):5286-5290.
Hall, Thomas D. 1996
World System Theory. In The Social Science Encyclopedia. Adam Kuper and Jessica Kuper, eds. Pp. 922–923. New York: Routledge.
Halpern, Sue. 1992
Migrations to Solitude. New York: Pantheon Books.
Hamabata, Matthews Masayuki. 1990
Crested Kimono: Power and Love in the Japanese Business Family. Ithaca: Cornell University Press.
Hammerlsey, Martyn. 1992
What's Wrong with Ethnography: Methodological Explorations. London: Routledge.
Hammond, Peter B. 1966
Yatenga: Technology in the Culture of a West African Kingdom. New York: The Free Press.
Hancock, Graham. 1989
Lords of Poverty: The Power, Prestige, and Corruption of the International Aid Business. New York: The Atlantic Monthly Press.
Handwerker, W. Penn. 1990
Politics and Reproduction: A Window on Social Change. In Social Change and the Politics of Reproduction. Penn W. Handwerker, ed. Pp.1–38. Boulder: Westview Press.
Hannerz, Ulf. 1992
Cultural Complexity: Studies in the Social Organization of Meaning. New York: Columbia University Press.
Hardesty, Donald L. 1977
Ecological Anthropology. New York: John Wiley and Sons.
Harner, Michael. 1977
The Ecological Basis of Aztec Sacrifice. American Ethnologist 4: 117–135.
Harris, Marvin. 1968
The Rise of Anthropological Theory. New York: Thomas Y. Crowell Company.
___. 1971
Culture, Man and Nature. New York: Thomas Y. Crowell.
___. 1974
Cows, Pigs, Wars and Witches: The Riddles of Culture. New York: Random House.
___. 1975
Culture, People, Nature: An Introduction to General Anthropology. 2nd edition. New York: Thomas Y. Crowell.
___. 1977
Cannibals and Kings: The Origins of Culture. New York: Random House.
___. 1981
America Now: The Anthropology of a Changing Culture. New York: Simon and Schuster.

___. 1984
Animal Capture and Yanomamo Warfare: Retrospect and New Evidence. Journal of Anthropological Research 40(10): 183-201.
___. 1989
Our Kind: The Evolution of Human Life and Culture. New York: Harper & Row Publishers.
___. 1992
Distinguished Lecture: Anthropology and the Theoretical and Paradigmatic Significance of the Collapse of Soviet and East European Communism. American Anthropologist 94: 295–305.
___. 1993
The Evolution of Human Gender Hierarchies: A Trial Formulation. In Sex and Gender Hierarchies. Barbara D. Miller, ed. Pp. 57-80. New York: Cambridge University Press.
___. 1995
Cultural Anthropology. 4th edition. New York: HarperCollins.
Harris, Marvin and Eric B. Ross. 1987
Death, Sex and Fertility. New York: Columbia University Press.
Harrison, Michelle. 1982
A Woman in Residence. New York: Random House.
Harrison, Simon. 1993
The Commerce of Cultures in Melanesia. Man 28:139–158.
Hart, C. W. M., Arnold R. Pilling, and Jane C. Goodale. 1988
The Tiwi of North Australia. New York: Holt, Rinehart, and Winston.
Hartmann, Betsy. 1987
Reproductive Rights and Wrongs: The Global Politics of Population Control and Reproductive Choice. New York: Harper & Row.
Hastrup, Kirsten. 1992
Anthropological Visions: Some Notes on Visual and Textual Authority. In Film as Ethnography. Peter Ian Crawford and David Turton, eds. Pp. 8–25. Manchester: University of Manchester Press.
Havel, Václav. 1996
The Hope for Europe. The New York Review of Books, June 20:38–41.
Headland, Thomas N. and Lawrence A. Reid. 1989
Hunter-Gatherers and Their Neighbors from Prehistory to the Present. Current Anthropology 30(1):43–51.
Heider, Karl. 1976
Dani Sexuality: A Low Energy System. Man 11:188–201.
Helweg, Arthur W. and Usha M. Helweg. 1990
An Immigrant Success Story: East Indians in America. Philadelphia: University of Pennsylvania Press.
Herdt, Gilbert. 1987
The Sambia: Ritual and Gender in New Guinea. New York: Holt, Rinehart and Winston.
Herschfelder, Arlene, ed. 1995
Native Heritage: Personal Accounts by American Indians 1790 to the Present. New York: Macmillan.
Herzfeld, Michael. 1985
The Poetics of Manhood: Contest and Identity in a Cretan Mountain Village. Princeton: Princeton University Press.
Heise, Lori L., Jacqueline Pitanguy and Adrienne Germain. 1994
Violence against Women: The Hidden Health Burden. World Bank Discussion Papers No. 255. Washington, DC: The World Bank.
Helfrich, Hede. 1979
Age Markers in Speech. In Social Markers in Speech. Klaus R. Scherer and Howard Giles, eds. Pp. 63–107. New York: Cambridge University Press.
Hewlett, Barry S. 1991
Intimate Fathers: The Nature and Context of Aka Pygmy Paternal Care. Ann Arbor: University of Michigan Press.
Hiatt, Betty. 1970
Woman the Gatherer. In Woman's Role in Aboriginal Society. Fay Gale, ed. Pp. 2–28. Canberra: Australian Institute of Aboriginal Studies.
Hickey, Gerald Cannon. 1967
Village in Vietnam. New Haven: Yale University Press.
___. 1993
Shattered Worlds: Adaptation and Survival among Vietnam's Highland Peoples during the Vietnam War. Philadelphia: University of Pennsylvania Press.
Hill, Jane H. and Bruce Mannheim. 1992
Language and World View. Annual Review of Anthropology 21: 381–406.
Hill, Kim, Hillard Kaplan, Kristen Hawkes, and Ana Magdalena Hurtado. 1985
Men's Time Allocation to Subsistence Work among the Ache of Eastern Paraguay. Human Ecology 13(1):29–47.
Hiltebeitel, Alf. 1988
The Cult of Draupadi: Mythologies from Gingee to Kuruksetra. Chicago: The University of Chicago Press.
___. 1995
Hinduism. In The HarperCollins Dictionary of Religion. Jonathan Z. Smith, ed. Pp. 424–440. New York: HarperCollins Publishers.
Hirschon, Renee. 1989
Heirs of the Catastrophe: The Social Life of Asia Minor Refugees in Piraeus. New York: Oxford University Press.
Hirst, Paul. 1996
Socialism. In The Social Science Encyclopedia. Adam Kuper and Jessica Kuper, eds. Pp. 809–811. New York: Routledge.
Hisama, Ellie M. 1993
Postcolonialism on the Make: The Music of John Mellencamp, David Bowie and John Zorn. Popular Music 12(2):91–104.
Hobsbawm, Eric J. 1969
Bandits. 2nd edition. New York: Delacorte Press.
___. 1992
Nations and Nationalism since 1780. New York: Cambridge University Press.
Hodge, Robert W. and Naohiro Ogawa. 1991
Fertility Change in Contemporary Japan. Chicago: The University of Chicago Press.
Hodges, Linda and George Chumak. 1994
Ukraine Language and Travel Guide. New York: Hippocrene Books.
Hodges, Mark. 1996
Online in the Outback. Technology Review 99(3):17–18.
Hogan, Dennis P. and Takashi Mochizuki. 1988
Demographic Transitions and the Life Course: Lessons from Japanese and American Comparisons. Journal of Family History 13(3): 291–305.
Holland, Dorothy C. and Margaret A. Eisenhart. 1990
Educated in Romance: Women, Achievement, and College Culture. Chicago: The University of Chicago Press.
Holy, Ladislav. 1996
Groups. In The Social Science Encyclopedia. Adam Kuper and Jessica Kuper, eds. Pp. 351–352. Routledge: New York.
Hornbein, George and Marie Hornbein. 1992
Salamanders: A Night at the Phi Delt House. Video. College Park: Documentary Resource Center.
Horowitz, Irving L. 1967
The Rise and Fall of Project Camelot: Studies in the Relationship between Social Science and Practical Politics. Boston: MIT Press.
Horowitz, Michael M. and Muneera Salem-Murdock. 1993
Development-Induced Food Insecurity in the Middle Senegal Valley. GeoJournal 30(2):179–184.
Hostetler, John A. and Gertrude Enders Huntington. 1992
Amish Children: Education in the Family, School, and Community. New York: Harcourt Brace Jovanovich.
Howell, Nancy. 1979
Demography of the Dobe !Kung. New York: Academic Press.
___. 1986
Feedbacks and Buffers in Relation to Scarcity and Abundance: Studies of Hunter-Gatherer Populations. In The State of Population Theory: Forward from Malthus. David Coleman and Roger Schofield, eds. Pp. 156–187. New York: Basil Blackwell.
___. 1990
Surviving Fieldwork: A Report of the Advisory Panel on Health and

Safety in Fieldwork. Washington, DC: American Anthropological Association.
Howell, Signe. 1979
The Chewong of Malaysia. Populi 6(4):48–51.
Hughes, Charles C. and John M. Hunter. 1970
Disease and "Development" in Africa. Social Science and Medicine 3:443–493.
Humphrey, Caroline. 1978
Women, Taboo and the Suppression of Attention. In Defining Females: The Nature of Women in Society. Shirley Ardener, ed. Pp. 89–108. New York: John Wiley and Sons.
Hunte, Pamela A. 1985
Indigenous Methods of Fertility Regulation in Afghanistan. In Women's Medicine: A Cross-Cultural Study of Indigenous Fertility Regulation. Lucile F. Newman, ed. Pp. 44–75. New Brunswick: Rutgers University Press.
Hutchinson, Sharon E. 1996
Nuer Dilemmas: Coping with Money, War, and the State. Berkeley: University of California Press.
Hutter, Michael. 1996
The Value of Play. In The Value of Culture: On the Relationship between Economics and the Arts. Arjo Klamer, ed. Pp. 122–137. Amsterdam: Amsterdam University Press.
Ikels, Charlotte. 1996
Return of the God of Wealth: The Transition to a Market Economy in Urban China. Stanford: Stanford University Press.
Illo, Jeanne Frances I. 1985
Who Heads the Household? Women in Households in the Philippines. Paper presented at the Women and Household Regional Conference for Asia, New Delhi.
International Labour Office. 1996
Female Asian Migrants: A Growing But Vulnerable Workforce. World of Work 15:16–17.
Iyer, Pico. 1989
Video Night in Kathmandu: And Other Reports from the Not-So-Far East. New York: Vintage.
Janes, Craig R. 1990
Migration, Social Change, and Health: A Samoan Community in Urban California. Stanford: Stanford University Press.
___. 1995
The Transformations of Tibetan Medicine. Medical Anthropology Quarterly 9(1):6–39.
Jankowski, Martín Sánchez. 1991
Islands in the Street: Gangs and American Urban Society. Berkeley: University of California Press.
Jayawardena, Kumari. 1984
The Plantation Sector in Sri Lanka: Recent Changes in the Welfare of Children and Women. World Development 12(3): 317–328.
Jeffery, Patricia. 1979
Frogs in a Well: Indian Women in Purdah. London: Zed Press.
Jentoft, Sven and Anthony Davis. 1993
Self and Sacrifice: An Investigation of Small Boat Fisher Individualism and Its Implication for Producer Cooperatives. Human Organization 52(4):356–367.
Jet. 1995
Baseball Team Members Who Used KKK Symbol Will Receive Multi-Cultural Training. 88(18):39–40.
Jiang, David W. 1994
Shanghai Revisited: Chinese Theatre and the Forces of the Market. The Drama Review 38(2):72–80.
Jinadu, L. Adele. 1994
The Dialectics of Theory and Research on Race and Ethnicity in Nigeria. In "Race," Ethnicity and Nation: International Perspectives on Social Conflict. Peter Ratcliffe, ed. Pp. 163–178. London: University of College London Press.
Johnson, Walter R. 1994
Dismantling Apartheid: A South African Town in Transition. Ithaca: Cornell University Press.
Johnston, Barbara Rose. 1994
Environmental Degradation and Human Rights Abuse. In Who Pays the Price?: The Sociocultural Context of Environmental Crisis. Barbara Rose Johnston, ed. Pp. 7–16. Washington, DC: Island Press.
Jonaitis, Aldona. 1995
A Wealth of Thought: Franz Boas on Native American Art. Seattle: University of Washington Press.
Jones, Anna Laura. 1993
Exploding Canons: The Anthropology of Museums. Annual Review of Anthropology 22:201–220.
Joralemon, Donald. 1982
New World Depopulation and the Case of Disease. Journal of Anthropological Research 38:108–127.
___. 1999
Health and Disease: The Anthropological View. Boston: Allyn and Bacon.
Jordan, Brigitte. 1983
Birth in Four Cultures. 3rd edition. Montreal: Eden Press.
Joseph, Suad. 1994
Brother/Sister Relationships: Connectivity, Love, and Power in the Reproduction of Patriarchy in Lebanon. American Ethnologist 21:50–73.
Jourdan, Christine. 1995
Masta Liu. In Youth Cultures: A Cross-Cultural Perspective. Vered Amit-Talai and Helena Wulff, eds. Pp. 202–222. New York: Routledge.
Jules-Rosette, Bennetta. 1984
The Message of Tourist Art: An African Semiotic System in Comparative Perspective. New York: Plenum Press.
Kaberry, Phyllis. 1952
Women of the Grassfields: A Study of the Economic Position of Women in Bamenda, British Cameroons. London: Her Majesty's Stationery Office.
Kabutha, Charity, Barbara P. Thomas-Slaytor, and Richard Ford. 1993
Participatory Rural Appraisal: A Case Study from Kenya. In Rapid Appraisal Methods. Krishna Kumar, ed. Pp. 176–211. Washington, DC: The World Bank.
Kahn, Miriam. 1995
Heterotopic Dissonance in the Museum Representation of Pacific Island Cultures. American Anthropologist 97(2): 324–338.
Kapchan, Deborah A. 1994
Moroccan Female Performers Defining the Social Body. Journal of American Folklore 107(423):82–105.
Katz, Nathan and Ellen S. Goldberg. 1989
Asceticism and Caste in the Passover Observances of the Cochin Jews. Journal of the American Academy of Religion. 57(1):53–81.
Katz, Richard. 1982
Boiling Energy: Community Healing among the Kalahari Kung. Cambridge: Harvard University Press.
Kearney, Michael. 1986
From the Invisible Hand to Visible Feet: Anthropological Studies of Migration and Development. Annual Review of Anthropology 15:331–361.
Keen, Ian. 1993
Aboriginal Beliefs vs. Mining at Coronation Hill: The Containing Force of Traditionalism. Human Organization 52(4): 344–55.
___. 1998
Personal communication.
Keiser, R. Lincoln. 1986
Death Enmity in Thull: Organized Vengeance and Social Change in a Kohistani Community. American Ethnologist 13(3):489–505.
Kelley, Heidi. 1991
Unwed Mothers and Household Reputation in a Spanish Galician Community. American Ethnologist 18:565–580.
Kendall, Laurel. 1988
Healing Thyself: A Korean Shaman's Afflictions. Social Science and Medicine 27(5):445–450.
___. 1966
Getting Married in Korea: Of Gender, Morality, and Modernity. Berkeley: University of California Press.

Kent, Susan. 1995
Unstable Households in a Stable Kalahari Community in Botswana. American Anthropologist 97(2):297–312.
Kerns, Virginia. 1992
Preventing Violence against Women: A Central American Case. In Sanctions and Sanctuary: Cultural Perspectives on the Beating of Wives. Dorothy Ayers Counts, Judith K. Brown, and Jacquelyn C. Campbell, eds. Pp. 125–138. Boulder: Westview Press.
Kesmanee, Chupinit. 1994
Dubious Development Concepts in the Thai Highlands: The Chao Khao in Transition. Law & Society Review 28:673–683.
Kideckel, David A. 1993
The Solitude of Collectivism: Romanian Villagers to the Revolution and Beyond. Ithaca: Cornell University Press.
King, Martin Luther. 1994 [1963]
Letter from the Birmingham Jail. New York: HarperCollins Publishers.
Klass, Perri. 1987
A Not Entirely Benign Procedure: Four Years as a Medical Student. New York: Penguin Books.
Kligman, Gail. 1995
Political Demography: The Banning of Abortion in Ceausescu's Romania. In Conceiving the New World Order: The Global Politics of Reproduction. Faye D. Ginsberg and Rayna Rapp, eds. Pp. 234–255. Berkeley: University of California Press.
Knott, Kim. 1996
Hindu Women, Destiny and Stridharma. Religion 26:15–35.
Kolenda, Pauline M. 1968
Region, Caste, and Family Structure: A Comparative Study of the Indian "Joint" Family. In Structure and Change in Indian Society. Milton Singer and Bernard S. Cohn, eds. Pp. 339–396. New York: Aldine.
___. 1978
Caste in Contemporary India: Beyond Organic Solidarity. Prospect Heights, IL; Waveland Press.
Kondo, Dorinne. 1991
The Stakes: Feminism, Asian Americans, and the Study of Asia. CWAS Newsletter [Committee on Women in Asian Studies, Association for Asian Studies] 9(3):2–9.
___. 1992
The Aesthetics and Politics of Japanese Identity in the Fashion Industry. In Re-Made in Japan: Everyday Life and Consumer Taste in a Changing Society. Joseph J. Tobin, ed. Pp. 176–203. New Haven: Yale University Press.
___. forthcoming
Ethnography as Feminist and Minority Discourse. Cultural Critique.
Konner, Melvin. 1987
Becoming a Doctor: The Journey of Initiation in Medical School. New York: Penguin Books.
___. 1989
Homosexuality: Who and Why? New York Times Magazine. April 2:60–61.
Kopytoff, Igor. 1986
The Cultural Biography of Things: Commodification as Process. In The Social Life of Things: Commodities in Cultural Perspective. Arjun Appadurai, ed. Pp. 64–91. New York: Cambridge University Press.
Kottak, Conrad Phillip. 1992
Assault on Paradise: Social Change in a Brazilian Village. New York: McGraw Hill.
___. 1985
When People Don't Come First: Some Sociological Lessons from Completed Projects. In Putting People First: Sociological Variables and Rural Development. Michael M. Cernea, ed. Pp. 325–356. New York: Oxford University Press.
Krantzler, Nora J. 1987
Traditional Medicine as "Medical Neglect": Dilemmas in the Case Management of a Samoan Teenager with Diabetes. In Child Survival: Cultural Perspectives on the Treatment and Maltreatment of Children. Nancy Scheper-Hughes, ed. Pp. 325–337. Boston: D. Reidel.
Kriesberg, Louis. 1966
Conflict, Social. In The Social Science Encyclopedia. Adam Kuper and Jessica Kuper, eds. Pp. 122–125. New York: Routledge.
Kroeber, A. L. and Clyde Kluckhohn. 1952
Culture: A Critical Review of Concepts and Definitions. New York: Vintage Books.
Kuipers, Joel C. 1990
Power in Performance: The Creation of Textual Authority in Weyéwa Ritual Speech. Philadelphia: University of Pennsylvania Press.
___. 1991
Matters of Taste in Weyéwa. In The Varieties of Sensory Experience: A Sourcebook in the Anthropology of the Senses. David Howes, ed. Pp. 111–127. Toronto: University of Toronto Press.
Kulick, Don. 1992
"Coming Up" in Gapun: Conceptions of Development and Their Effect on Language in a Papua New Guinea Village. In Kam-Ap or Take-Off: Local Notions of Development. G. Dahl and A. Rabo, eds. Pp. 10–33. Stockholm: Stockholm Studies in Social Anthropology, Department of Social Anthropology, Stockholm University.
Kumar, Krishna. 1996
Civil Society. In The Social Science Encyclopedia. Adam Kuper and Jessica Kuper, eds. Pp. 88–90. Routledge: New York.
Kumar, Sanjay. 1996
Largest-ever World Bank Loan Mistrusted in India. The Lancet 347(April 20):1109.
Kurin, Richard. 1980
Doctor, Lawyer, Indian Chief. Natural History 89(11):6–24.
Kwiatkowski, Lynn. 1994
Development and Militarization in the Cordillera Region of the Philippines. Paper presented at the annual meeting of the American Anthropological Association.
Labov, William. 1966
The Social Stratification of English in New York City. Washington, DC: Center for Applied Linguistics.
Ladányi, János. 1993
Patterns of Residential Segregation and the Gypsy Minority in Budapest. International Journal of Urbana and Regional Research 17(1): 30–41.
Laderman, Carol. 1988
A Welcoming Soil: Islamic Humoralism on the Malay Peninsula. In Paths to Asian Medical Knowledge. Charles Leslie and Allan Young, eds. Pp. 272–288. Berkeley: University of California Press.
LaFleur, William. 1992
Liquid Life: Abortion and Buddhism in Japan. Princeton: Princeton University Press.
Lakoff, Robin. 1973
Language and Woman's Place. Language in Society 2: 45–79.
___. 1990
Talking Power: The Politics of Language in Our Lives. New York: Basic Books.
Lamphere, Louise. 1992
Introduction: The Shaping of Diversity. In Structuring Diversity: Ethnographic Perspectives on the New Immigration. Lousie Lamphere, ed. Chicago: University of Chicago Press.
Lappé, Francis Moore and Joseph Collins. 1977
Why Can't People Feed Themselves? In Food First: Beyond the Myth of Scarcity. Pp. 99–111. New York: Ballantine Books.
___. 1986
World Hunger: Twelve Myths. New York: Grove Press.
Larsen, Clark Spenser and George R. Milner. 1994
Bioanthropological Perspectives on Postcontact Traditions. In In the Wake of Contact: Biological Responses to Conquest. Clark Spenser Larsen and George R. Milner, eds. Pp. 1–8. New York: Wiley-Liss.
Laws, Bart. 1996
The Immigration Wars. Z Magazine 9(11):31–39.
Leach, Jerry W. 1975.
Trobriand Cricket: An Ingenious Response to Colonialism. Video. Berkeley: University of California Extension Media.

Leacock. Eleanor. 1978
Women's Status in Egalitarian Society: Implications for Social Evolution. Current Anthropology 19(2):247–255.
___. 1993
Women in Samoan History: A Further Critique of Derek Freeman. In Sex and Gender Hierarchies. Barbara D. Miller, ed. Pp. 351–365. New York: Cambridge University Press.
Leavy, Morton L. and R. D. Weinberg. 1979
Law of Adoption. Dobbs Ferry, NY: Oceana.
Lebra, Takie. 1976
Japanese Patterns of Behavior. Honolulu: University of Hawaii Press.
Lee, Gary R. and Mindy Kezis. 1979
Family Structure and the Status of the Elderly. Journal of Comparative Family Studies 10:429–443.
Lee, Marie G. 1994
Saying Goodbye. Boston: Houghton-Mifflin.
Lee, Raymond M. and Claire M. Renzetti. 1993
Researching Sensitive Topics. Newbury Park, CA: Sage Publications.
Lee, Richard Borshay. 1969
Eating Christmas in the Kalahari. Natural History: December.
___. 1979
The !Kung San: Men, Women, and Work in a Foraging Society. New York: Cambridge University Press.
Lee, Wai-Na and David K. Tse. 1994
Becoming Canadian: Understanding How Hong Kong Immigrants Change Their Consumption. Pacific Affairs 67(1):70–95.
Lein, Laura and Donald Brenneis. 1978
Children's Dispute in Three Speech Communities. Language in Society 7:299–323.
Lempert, David. 1996
Daily Life in a Crumbling Empire. 2 volumes. New York: Columbia University Press.
Lepowsky, Maria. 1990
Big Men, Big Women, and Cultural Autonomy. Ethnology 29(10): 35–50.
___. 1993
Fruit of the Motherland: Gender in an Egalitarian Society. New York: Columbia University Press.
Lessinger, Johanna. 1995
From the Ganges to the Hudson: Indian Immigrants in New York City. Boston: Allyn and Bacon.
Levine, Robert, Suguru Sato, Tsukasa Hashimoto, and Jyoti Verma. 1995
Love and Marriage in Eleven Cultures. Journal of Cross-Cultural Psychology 26:554–571.
Levinson, David. 1989
Family Violence in Cross-Cultural Perspective. Newbury Park, CA: Sage Publications.
Lévi-Strauss, Claude. 1967
Structural Anthropology. New York: Anchor Books.
___. 1968
Tristes Tropiques: An Anthropological Study of Primitive Societies in Brazil. New York: Atheneum.
___. 1969 [1949]
The Elementary Structures of Kinship. Boston: Beacon Press.
Levy, Jerrold E., Eric B. Henderson, and Tracy J. Andrews. 1989
The Effects of Regional Variation and Temporal Change in Matrilineal Elements of Navajo Social Organization. Journal of Anthropological Research 45(4):351–377.
Lew, Irvina. 1994
Bathing as Science: Ancient Sea Cures Gain Support from New Research. Condé Nast Traveler 29(12):86–90.
Lewin, Ellen. 1993
Lesbian Mothers: Accounts of Gender in American Culture. Ithaca: Cornell University Press.
Lewis, Oscar. 1966
The Culture of Poverty. Scientific American. 215:19–25.
Leynaud, Emile. 1961
Fraternités d'âge et sociétés de culture dans la Haute-Vallée du Niger. Cahiers d'Etudes Africaines 6:41–68.
Lieban, Richard W. 1977
The Field of Medical Anthropology. In Culture, Disease, and Healing: Studies in Medical Anthropology. David Landy, ed. Pp. 13–31. New York: Macmillan.
Lincoln, Kenneth. 1993
Indi'n Humor: Bicultural Play in Native America. New York: Oxford University Press.
Lindenbaum, Shirley. 1979
Kuru Sorcery: Disease and Danger in the New Guinea Highlands. Mountain View, CA: Mayfield Publishing Company.
Link, David. 1966
Gay Rites. Reason 27:28–33.
Linnekan, Jocelyn. 1990
Sacred Queens and Women of Consequence: Rank, Gender, and Colonialism in the Hawaiian Islands. Ann Arbor: University of Michigan Press.
Little, Kenneth. 1966
The Strange Case of Romantic Love. The Listener 7 (April).
Littman, Mark. 1993
Office of Refugee Resettlement Monthly Data Report for September 1992. Washington, DC: Office of Refugee Resettlement.
Lloyd, Cynthia B. 1995
Household Structure and Poverty: What Are the Connections? Working Papers, No. 74. New York: The Population Council.
Lock, Margaret. 1993
Encounters with Aging: Mythologies of Menopause in Japan and North America. Berkeley: University of California Press.
Lockwood, Victoria S. 1993
Tahitian Transformation: Gender and Capitalist Development in a Rural Society. Boulder: Lynne Reiner Publishers.
Loker, William. 1993
Human Ecology of Cattle-Raising in the Peruvian Amazon: The View from the Farm. Human Organization 52(1):14–24.
Longva, Anh Nga. 1993
Kuwaiti Women at a Crossroads: Privileged Development and the Constraints of Ethnic Stratification. International Journal of Middle East Studies 25:443–456.
Lorenz, Konrad. 1966
On Aggression. New York: Harcourt, Brace & World.
Low, Setha M. 1995
Indigenous Architecture and the Spanish American Plaza in Mesoamerica and the Caribbean. American Anthropologist 97(4):748–762.
Lozoff, Betsy, Abraham W. Wolf and Nancy S. Davis. 1984
Cosleeping in Urban Families with Young Children in the United States. Pediatrics 74:171–182.
Lu, Hanchao. 1995
Away from Nanking Road: Small Stores and Neighborhood Life in Modern Shanghai. Journal of Asian Studies 54(1):93–123.
Luhrmann, Tanya M. 1989
Persuasions of the Witch's Craft: Ritual Magic in Contemporary England. Cambridge: Harvard University Press.
Lutz, Catherine A. 1988
Unnatural Emotions: Everyday Sentiments on a Micronesian Atoll and Their Challenge to Western Theory. Chicago: University of Chicago Press.
Maclachlan, Morgan. 1983
Why They Did Not Starve: Biocultural Adaptation in a South Indian Village. Philadelphia: Institute for the Study of Human Issues.
MacLeod, Arlene Elowe. 1992
Hegemonic Relations and Gender Resistance: The New Veiling as Accommodating Protest in Cairo. Signs: The Journal of Women in Culture and Society 17(3):533–557.
Macpherson, Cluny and La'avasa Macpherson. 1984
Suicide in Western Samoa: A Sociological Perspective. In Culture, Youth and Suicide in the Pacific: Papers from an East-West Center Conference. Francis X. Hezel, Donald H. Rubenstein, and Geoffrey M. White, eds. Pp. 36–73. Pacific Island Studies Working Paper Series. Honolulu: Center for Asian and Pacific Studies, University of Hawaii.

Mahler, Sarah J. 1995
Salvadorans in Suburbia: Symbiosis and Conflict. Boston: Allyn and Bacon.
Major, Marc R. 1996
No Friends but the Mountains: A Simulation on Kurdistan. Social Education 60(3):C1–C8.
Makepeace, James M. 1997
Courtship Violence as Process: A Developmental Theory. In Violence between Intimate Partners: Patterns, Causes, and Effects. Albert P. Cardarelli, ed. Pp. 29–47. Boston: Allyn and Bacon.
Malinowski, Bronislaw. 1927 [1955]
Sex and Repression in Savage Society. New York: Meridien Books.
___. 1929
The Sexual Life of Savages. New York: Harcourt, Brace & World.
___. 1961 [1922]
Argonauts of the Western Pacific. New York: E. P. Dutton & Co.
___. 1962 [1926]
Crime and Custom in Savage Society. Paterson, NJ: Littlefield, Adams & Co.
Mamdani, Mahmoud. 1972
The Myth of Population Control: Family, Caste, and Class in an Indian Village. New York: Monthly Review Press.
Mandelbaum, David G. 1974
Human Fertility in India: Social Components and Policy Perspectives. Berkeley: University of California Press.
Manz, Beatriz. 1988
Refugees of a Hidden War: The Aftermath of Counterinsurgency in Guatemala. Albany: State University of New York Press.
March, Kathryn S. and Rachell L. Taqqu. 1986
Women's Informal Associations in Developing Countries: Catalysts for Change? Boulder: Westview Press.
Marchatti, Gina. 1993
Romance and the "Yellow Peril": Race, Sex, and Discursive Strategies in Hollywood Fiction. Berkeley: University of California Press.
Marcus, Aliza. 1996
Turkey, the Kurds, and Human Rights. Dissent, summer:104–106.
Margolis, Maxine. 1984
Mothers and Such: Views of American Women and Why They Changed. Berkeley: University of California Press.
___. 1994
Little Brazil: An Ethnography of Brazilian Immigrants in New York City. Princeton: Princeton University Press.
Margolis, Maxine L. and Marigene Arnold. 1993
Turning the Tables? Male Strippers and the Gender Hierarchy in America. In Sex and Gender Hierarchies. Barbara D. Miller, ed. Pp. 334–350. New York: Cambridge University Press.
Marotz-Baden, Ramona and Claudia Mattheis. 1994
Daughters-in-Law and Stress in Two-Generation Farm Families. Family Relations 43:132–137.
Marriott, McKim. 1965
Caste Ranking and Community Structure in Five Regions of India and Pakistan. Poona, India: Deccan College.
Marshall, Robert C. 1985
Giving a Gift to the Hamlet: Rank, Solidarity and Productive Exchange in Rural Japan. Ethnology 24:167–182.
Martin, Emily. 1987
The Woman in the Body: A Cultural Analysis of Reproduction. Boston: Beacon Press.
Martin, Linda G. 1990
Changing Intergenerational Family Relations in East Asia. Annals, AAPSS 510:102–114.
Martin, M. Kay and Barbara Voorhies. 1975
Female of the Species. New York: Columbia University Press.
Martin, Richard C. 1995
Islam. In The HarperCollins Dictionary of Religion. Jonathan Z. Smith, ed. Pp. 498–513. New York: HarperCollins.
Martínez, Samuel. 1996
Indifference with Indignation:Anthropology, Human Rights, and the Haitian Bracero. American Anthropologist 98(1): 17–25.
Marx, Karl and Friedrich Engels. 1964 [1848]
The Communist Manifesto. New York: Monthly Review Press.
Massiah, Joycelin. 1983
Women as Heads of Households in the Caribbean: Family Structure and Feminine Status. Paris: UNESCO.
Mathabane, Mark. 1986
Kaffir Boy: The True Story of a Black Youth's Coming of Age in Apartheid South Africa. New York: Plume.
Mathews, Holly. 1985
"We Are Mayordomo": A Reinterpretation of Women's Roles in the Mexican Cargo System. American Ethnologist 12(2):285–301.
Mauss, Marcel. 1967 [1925]
The Gift: Forms and Functions of Exchange in Archaic Societies. New York: W. W. Norton & Company.
Maybury-Lewis, David. 1997a
Museums and Indigenous Cultures. Cultural Survival Quarterly 21(1):3.
___. 1997b
Indigenous Peoples, Ethnic Groups, and the State. Boston: Allyn and Bacon.
Mayer, Adrian. 1960
Caste and Kinship in Central India: A Village and Its Region. Berkeley: University of California Press.
McCaghy, Charles H. and Charles Hou. 1994
Family Affiliation and Prostitution in a Cultural Context: Career Onsets of Taiwanese Prostitutes. Archives of Sexual Behavior 23:251–265.
McCoid, Catherine Hodge and LeRoy D. McDermott. 1996
Toward Decolonizing Gender: Female Vision in the Upper Paleolithic. American Anthropologist 98(2):319–326.
McDermott, LeRoy D. 1996
Self-Representation in Upper Paleolithic Female Figurines. Current Anthropology 37:227–275.
McDonald, Kim A. 1996
Crowding the Country: Montana State University Researchers Study Impact of Urban Refugees. Chronicle for Higher Education 42(37): A7, A10.
McElroy, Ann and Patricia K. Townsend. 1996
Medical Anthropology in Ecological Perspective. 3rd edition. Boulder: Westview Press.
McEwan, Colin, Chris Hudson, and Maria-Isabel Silva. 1994
Archaeology and Community: A Village Cultural Center and Museum in Ecuador. Practicing Anthropology 16(1):3–7.
McMahon, April M. S. 1994
Understanding Language Change. New York: Cambridge University Press.
Mead, Margaret. 1928 [1961]
Coming of Age in Samoa: A Psychological Study of Primitive Youth for Western Civilization. New York: Dell Publishing Company.
___. 1963 [1935]
Sex and Temperament in Three Primitive Societies. New York: William Morrow.
___. 1977
Letters from the Field 1925–1975. New York: Harper & Row.
___. 1986
Field Work in the Pacific Islands, 1925–1967. In Women in the Field: Anthropological Experiences. Peggy Golde, ed. Pp. 293–331. Berkeley: University of California Press.
Meigs, Anna S. 1984
Food, Sex, and Pollution: A New Guinea Religion. New Brunswick: Rutgers University Press.
Mencher, Joan P. 1965
The Nayars of South Malabar. In Comparative Family Systems. Meyer F. Nimkoff, ed. Pp. 163–191. Boston: Houghton Mifflin Company.
___. 1974
The Caste System Upside Down, or The Not-So-Mysterious East. Current Anthropology 15(4):469–49.

Mernissi, Fatima. 1987
Beyond the Veil: Male-Female Dynamics in Modern Muslim Society. Revised edition. Bloomington: Indiana University Press.

___. 1995
Dreams of Trespass: Tales of a Harem Girlhood. New York: Addison-Wesley.

Merry, Sally Engle. 1992
Anthropology, Law, and Transnational Processes. Annual Review of Anthropology 21:357–379.

Messer, Ellen. 1993
Anthropology and Human Rights. Annual Review of Anthropology 22:221–249.

Michaelson, Evalyn Jacobson and Walter Goldschmidt. 1971
Female Roles and Male Dominance among Peasants. Southwestern Journal of Anthropology 27:330–352.

Miller, Barbara D. [1997] 1981
The Endangered Sex: Neglect of Female Children in Rural North India. New Delhi: Oxford University Press.

___. 1987a
Social Patterns of Food Expenditure among Low-Income Jamaicans. In Papers and Recommendations of the Workshop on Food and Nutrition Security in Jamaica in the 1980s and Beyond. Kenneth A. Leslie and Lloyd B. Rankine, eds. Pp. 13–33. Kingston, Jamaica: Caribbean Food and Nutrition Institute.

___. 1987b
Female Infanticide and Child Neglect in Rural North India. In Child Survival: Anthropological Perspectives on the Treatment and Maltreatment of Children. Nancy Scheper-Hughes, ed. Pp. 95–113. Boston: D. Reidel Publishing Company.

___. 1993
Surveying the Anthropology of Sex and Gender Hierarchies. In Sex and Gender Hierarchies. Barbara D. Miller, ed. Pp. 3–31. New York: Cambridge University Press.

Miller, Barbara D. and Showkat Hayat Khan. 1986
Incorporating Voluntarism into Rural Development in Bangladesh. Third World Planning Review 8(2):139–152.

Miller, Barbara D. and Carl Stone. 1983
The Low-Income Household Expenditure Survey: Description and Analysis. Jamaica Tax Structure Examination Project, Staff Paper No. 25. Syracuse, NY: Metropolitan Studies Program, Syracuse University.

Miller, Bruce G. 1994
Contemporary Native Women: Role Flexibility and Politics. Anthropologica 36:57–72.

Miller, Daniel. 1993
Christmas against Materialism in Trinidad. In Unwrapping Christmas. Daniel Miller, ed. Pp. 134–153. New York: Oxford University Press.

Miller, Ron. 1995
Child Support. Psychology Today 28(5):16.

Millett, Kate. 1994
The Politics of Cruelty: An Essay on the Literature of Political Imprisonment. New York: Norton.

Mills, Mary Beth. 1995
Attack of the Widow Ghosts: Gender, Death, and Modernity in Northeast Thailand. In Bewitching Women, Pious Men: Gender and Body Politics in Southeast Asia. Aihwa Ong and Michael G. Peletz, eds. Pp. 44–273. Berkeley: University of California Press.

Milton, Katharine. 1992
Civilization and Its Discontents. Natural History 3/92:37–92.

Miner, Horace. 1965 [1956]
Body Ritual among the Nacirema. In Reader in Comparative Religion: An Anthropological Approach. William A. Lessa and Evon Z. Vogt, eds. pp. 414–418. New York: Harper & Row.

Mines, Mattison. 1994
Public Faces, Private Voices: Community and Individuality in South India. Berkeley: University of California Press.

Mintz, Sidney. 1974
A Note on the Definition of Peasantries. Journal of Peasant Studies 1(3).

___. 1985
Sweetness and Power: The Place of Sugar in Modern History. New York: Penguin Books.

Mir-Hosseini, Ziba. 1993
Marriage on Trial: A Study of Islamic Family Law: Iran and Morocco Compared. New York: I. B. Tauris & Co. Ltd.

Mitchell, Bruce. 1994
Sustainable Development at the Village Level in Bali, Indonesia. Human Ecology 22(2):189–211.

Mitter, Partha. 1977
Much Maligned Monsters: A History of European Reactions to Indian Art. Chicago: University of Chicago Press.

Miyazawa, Setsuo. 1992
Policing in Japan: A Study on Making Crime. Frank G. Bennett, Jr. with John O. Haley, trans. Albany: State University of New York Press.

Moberg, Mark. 1991
Citrus and the State: Factions and Class Formation in Rural Belize. American Ethnologist 18(20):215–233.

___. 1996
Myths that Divide: Immigrant Labor and Class Segmentation in the Belizean Banana Industry. American Ethnologist 23(2):311–330.

Modell, Judith S. 1994
Kinship with Strangers: Adoption and Interpretations of Kinship in American Culture. Berkeley: University of California Press.

Moerman, Daniel E. 1979
Anthropology of Symbolic Healing. Current Anthropology 20:59–80.

___. 1983
General Medical Effectiveness and Human Biology: Placebo Effects in the Treatment of Ulcer Disease. Medical Anthropology Quarterly 14:13–16.

___. 1992
Minding the Body: The Placebo Effect Unmasked. In Giving the Body Its Due. M. Sheets-Johnstone, ed. Pp. 69–84. Albany, NY: State University of New York Press.

Mogelonsky, Marcia. 1995.
Asian-Indian Americans. American Demographics 17(8): 32–39.

Montgomery, Sy. 1991
Walking with the Great Apes: Jane Goodall, Dian Fossey, Biruté Galdikas. New York: Houghton Mifflin Company.

Moore, Sally Falk. 1996
Law. In The Social Science Encyclopedia. Adam Kuper and Jessica Kuper, eds. Pp. 453–457. New York: Routledge.

Morgan, Lewis Henry. 1851
The League of the [Ho-de-ne-sau, or] Iroquois. New York: Russell Sage.

Morgan, William. 1977
Navaho Treatment of Sickness: Diagnosticians. In Culture, Disease, and Healing: Studies in Medical Anthropology. David Landy, ed. Pp. 163–168. New York: Macmillan.

Morris, Desmond. 1967
The Naked Ape: A Zoologist's Study of the Human Animal. New York: Dell Publishing Company.

Morris, Rosalind. 1994
Three Sexes and Four Sexualities: Redressing the Discourses on Gender and Sexuality in Contemporary Thailand. positions 2: 15–43.

Mortland, Carol A. 1994
Khmer Buddhism in the United States: Ultimate Questions. In Cambodian Culture Since 1975: Homeland and Exile. May M. Ebihara, Carol A. Mortalnd, and Judy Ledgerwood, eds. Pp. 72–90. Ithaca: Cornell University Press.

Mosher, Steven W. 1993
A Mother's Ordeal: One Woman's Fight against China's One-Child Policy. New York: HarperCollins.

Moynihan, Elizabeth B. 1979
Paradise as a Garden in Persia and Mughal India. New York: George Braziller.

Motyl, Alexander J. 1993
Dilemmas of Independence: Ukraine After Totalitarianism. New York: Council on Foreign Relations Press.
Ms. 1992
Ghana: Matrilineal Group Dumps Patriarchal Rite. 3(2):11.
Muecke, Marjorie A. 1987
Resettled Refugees: Reconstruction of Identity of Lao in Seattle. Urban Anthropology 16(3–4):273–289.
Mufson, Steven. 1996a
Fragile Civil Society Takes Root in Chinese Reform. The Washington Post, June 4:A1ff.
___. 1996b
Chinese Protest Finds a Path on the Internet. The Washington Post, September 17:A1ff.
Mull, Dorothy S. and J. Dennis Mull. 1987
Infanticide among the Tarahumara of the Mexican Sierra Madre. In Child Survival: Anthropological Perspectives on the Treatment and Maltreatment of Children. Nancy Scheper-Hughes, ed. Pp. 113–132. Boston: D. Reidel Publishing Company.
Munachonga, Monica. 1988
Income Allocation and Marriage Options in Urban Zambia. In A Home Divided: Women and Income in the Third World. Daisy Dwyer and Judith Bruce, eds. Pp. 173–194. Stanford: Stanford University Press.
Murcott, Anne. 1993 [1983]
"It's a Pleasure to Cook for Him": Food, Mealtimes and Gender in Some South Wales Households. In Gender in Cross-Cultural Perspective. Caroline B. Brettell and Carolyn F. Sargent, eds. Pp. 77–87. Englewood Cliffs, NJ: Prentice Hall.
Murdock, George Peter. 1965 [1949]
Social Structure. New York: The Free Press.
Murphy, Yolanda and Robert F. Murphy. 1985
Women of the Forest. New York: Columbia University Press.
Murray, Gerald F. 1987
The Domestication of Wood in Haiti: A Case Study of Applied Evolution. In Anthropological Praxis: Translating Knowledge into Action. Robert M. Wulff and Shirley J. Fiske, eds. Pp. 233–240. Boulder, CO: Westview Press.
Mustanoga, Ulla Marjata and Kari J. Mustanoga. 1993
Resettlement after Involuntary Displacement: The Karelians in Finland. In Anthropological Approaches to Resettlement: Policy, Practice, and Theory. Michael M. Cernea and Scott E. Guggenheim, eds. Pp. 87–108. Boulder: Westview Press.
Myerhoff, Barbara. 1978
Number Our Days. New York: Simon and Schuster.
Myers, James. 1992
Nonmainstream Body Modification: Genital Piercing, Branding, Burning, and Cutting. Journal of Contemporary Ethnography 21(3):267–306.
Myers-Scotton, Carol. 1993
Social Motivations for Code-Switching. New York: Oxford University Press.
Nader, Laura. 1974
Up the Anthropologist—Perspectives Gained from Studying Up. In Reinventing Anthropology. Dell Hymes, ed. Pp. 284–311. New York: Vintage Books.
___. 1995
Civilization and Its Negotiations. In Understanding Disputes: The Politics of Argument. Pat Caplan, ed. Pp. 39–64. Providence, RI: Berg Publishers.
Nag, Moni. 1963
Factors Affecting Human Fertility in Nonindustrial Societies: A Cross-Cultural Study. New Haven: Human Relations Area Files Press.
___. 1972
Sex, Culture and Human Fertility: India and the United States. Current Anthropology 13:231–238.
___. 1983
Modernization Affects Fertility. Populi 10:56–77.
Nag, Moni, Benjamin N. F. White, and R. Creighton Peet. 1978
An Anthropological Approach to the Study of the Economic Value of Children in Java and Nepal. Current Anthropology 19(2):293–301.
Nanda, Serena. 1990
Neither Man Nor Woman: The Hijras of India. Belmont, CA: Wadsworth Publishing Company.
___. 1994
Cultural Anthropology. Wadsworth, CA: Wadsworth Publishing Company.
Narayan, Kirin. 1989
Storytellers, Saints, and Scoundrels: Folk Narrative in Hindu Religious Teaching. Philadelphia: University of Pennsylvania Press.
Manning, Dennison. 1995
Prospects for Tourism Study in Anthropology. In The Future of Anthropology: Its Relevance to the Contemporary World. Akbar S. Ahmed and Cris N. Shore, eds. Pp. 179–202. Atlantic Highlands, NJ: Athlone.
Nash, June. 1997 [1972]
Devils, Witches, and Sudden Death. In Magic, Witchcraft, and Religion. Arthur C. Lehmann and James E. Myers, eds. Pp. 242–247. Mountain View, CA: Mayfield Publishing Company.
Neale, Walter C. 1976
Monies in Societies. San Francisco: Chandler & Sharp Publishers, Inc.
Neff, Deborah L. 1994
The Social Construction of Infertility: The Case of the Matrilineal Nāyars in South India. Social Science and Medicine 39(4):475–485.
Neier, Aryeh. 1996
Language and Minorities. Dissent (summer):31–35.
Nelson, Sarah. 1993
Sex and Gender Hierarchies. Barbara D. Miller, ed., Pp. 297–315. New York: Cambridge University Press.
___. 1998
Bound Hair and Confucianism in Korea. In Hair: Its Power and Meaning in Asian Cultures. Alf Hiltebeitel and Barbara D. Miller, eds. Pp. 105–122. Albany: State University of New York Press.
Netting, Robert Mc C. 1989
Smallholders, Householders, Freeholders: Why the Family Farm Works Well Worldwide. In The Household Economy: Reconsidering the Domestic Mode of Production. Richard R. Wilk, ed. Pp. 221–244. Boulder: Westview Press.
Neusner, Jacob. 1995
Judaism. In The HarperCollins Dictionary of Religion. Jonathan Z. Smith. Pp. 598-607. New York: HarperCollins.
Newell, William H. 1961
The Scheduled Castes and Tribes of the Brahmaur Tahsil of Chamba District. Census of India 1961, Report on Scheduled Castes and Scheduled Tribes. Delhi: Office of the Registrar General.
Newman, Lucile. 1972
Birth Control: An Anthropological View. Module No. 27. Reading, MA: Addison-Wesley.
Newman Lucile, ed., 1985
Women's Medicine: A Cross-Cultural Study of Indigenous Fertility Regulation. New Brunswick: Rutgers University Pres.
The New York Times. 1994
Arctic Tribe's Hard Life Unchanged for Centuries. November 22: C1ff.
___. 1997
As the World Intrudes, Pygmies Feel Endangered. June 16: A4ff.
Ngokwey, Ndolamb. 1988
Pluralistic Etiological Systems in Their Social Context: A Brazilian Case Study. Social Science and Medicine 26:793–802.
Nichter, Mark. 1992
Of Ticks, Kings, Spirits and the Promise of Vaccines. In Paths to Asian Medical Knowledge. Charles Leslie and Allan Young, eds. pp. 224–253. Berkeley: University of California Press.
___. 1996
Vaccinations in the Third World: A Consideration of Community Demand. In Anthropology and International Health: Asian Case

Studies. Mark Nichter and Mimi Nichter, eds. Pp. 329–365. Amsterdam: Gordon and Breach Publishers.
Nichter, Mark and Mimi Nichter, eds. 1996
Anthropology and International Health: Asian Case Studies. Amsterdam: Gordon and Breach Publishers.
Nichter, Mimi and Nancy Vuckovic. 1994
Fat Talk: Body Image among Adolescent Girls. In Many Mirrors: Body Image and Social Relations. Nicole Sault, ed. Pp. 109–131. New Brunswick: Rutgers University Press.
Nieves, Isabel. 1979
Household Arrangements and Multiple Jobs in San Salvador. Signs: Journal of Women in Culture and Society 5:134–142.
Niraula, Bhanu B. and S. Philip Morgan. 1996
Marriage Formation and Post-Marital Contact with Natal Kin and Autonomy of Women: Evidence from Two Nepali Settings. Population Studies 50:35–50.
Nodwell, Evelyn and Neil Guppy. 1992
The Effects of Publicly Displayed Ethnicity on Interpersonal Discrimination: Indo-Canadians in Vancouver. The Canadian Review of Sociology and Anthropology 29(1):87–99.
Nordstrom, Carolyn and Antonius C. G. M. Robben, eds. 1995
Fieldwork under Fire: Contemporary Studies of Violence and Survival. Berkeley: University of California Press.
Norgaard, Richard B. 1994
Development Betrayed: The End of Progress and the Coevolutionary Revisioning of the Future. New York: Routledge.
Norris, Ruth. 1992
Can Ecotourism Save Natural Areas? National Parks 66(1): 30–34.
Obeyesekere, Gananath. 1981
Medusa's Hair: An Essay on Personal Symbols and Religious Experience. Chicago: University of Chicago Press.
Ochs, Elinor. 1990
Indexicality and Socialization. In Cultural Psychology: Essays on Comparative Human Development. James W. Stigler, Richard A. Shweder, and Gilbert Herdt, eds. Pp. 287–308. New York: Cambridge University Press.
___. 1993
Indexing Gender. In Sex and Gender Hierarchies. Barbara D. Miller, ed. Pp. 146–169. New York: Cambridge University Press.
Oei, Tian P. S. amd Farida Notowidjojo. 1990
Depression and Loneliness in Overseas Students. The International Journal of Social Psychiatry 14:339-364.
Ohnuki-Tierney, Emiko. 1980
Shamans and Imu: among Two Ainu Groups. In The Culture-Bound Syndromes. Ronald C. Simons and Charles C. Hughes, eds. Pp. 91–110. Dordrecht: D. Reidel Publishing Company.
___. 1994
Brain Death and Organ Transplantation: Cultural Bases of Medical Technology. Current Anthropology 35(3):233–242.
Oinas, Felix J. 1993
Couvade in Estonia. Slavic & East European Journal 37(3):339–345.
Okely, Judith. 1993 [1984]
Fieldwork in the Home Counties. Talking about People: Readings in Contemporary Cultural Anthropology. In William A. Haviland and Robert J. Gordon, eds. Pp. 4–6. Mountain View, CA: Mayfield Publishing Company.
Okonjo, Kamene. 1983
Sex Roles in Nigerian Politics. In Female and Male in West Africa. Christine Oppong, ed. Pp. 211–222. Boston: George Allen & Unwin.
Omvedt, Gail. 1995
Dalit Visions: The Anti-Caste Movement and the Construction of an Indian Identity. Tracts for the Times/8. New Delhi: Orient Longman.
Ong, Aihwa. 1987
Spirits of Resistance and Capitalist Discipline: Factory Women in Malaysia. Albany: State University of New York Press.
___. 1995
State versus Islam: Malay Families, Women's Bodies, and the Body Politic in Malaysia. In Bewitching Women, Pious Men: Gender and Body Politics in Southeast Asia. Aihwa Ong and Michael G. Peletz, eds. Pp. 159–194. Berkeley: University of California Press.
Ongley. Patrick. 1995
Post–1945 International Migration: New Zealand, Australia and Canada Compared. International Migration Review 29(3):765–793.
Orlove, Benjamin S. and Henry J. Rutz. 1989
Thinking about Consumption: A Social Economy Approach. In The Social Economy of Consumption. Henry J. Rutz and Benjamin S. Orlove, eds. Monographs in Economic Anthropology No. 6. pp. 1–57. New York: University Press of America.
Ortner, Sherry B. 1974
Is Female to Male as Nature Is to Culture? In Woman, Culture and Society. Michelle Zimbalist Rosaldo and Louise Lamphere, eds. Pp. 67–88. Stanford: Stanford University Press.
Osborne, Robin. 1985
Indonesia's Secret War: The Guerrilla Struggle in Irian Jaya. Sydney: Allen and Unwin.
Ossman, Susan. 1994
Picturing Casablanca: Portraits of Power in a Modern City. Berkeley: University of California Press.
Pahl, Jan. 1980
Patterns of Money Management within Marriage. Journal of Social Policy 9(3):313–335.
___. 1983
The Allocation of Money and the Structuring of Inequality within Marriage. Sociological Review 31(2):1983.
Painter, Andrew A. 1996
The Telerepresentation of Gender. In Re-Imaging Japanese Women. Anne E. Imamura, ed. Pp. 46–72. Berkeley: University of California Press.
Pa'lsson, G'isli. 1991
Coastal Economies, Cultural Accounts: Human Ecology and Icelandic Discourse. New York: Manchester University Press.
Pandya, Vishvajit. 1990
Movement and Space: Andamanese Cartography. 17(4): 775–797.
Papanek, Hanna. 1990
To Each Less Than She Needs, From Each More Than She Can Do: Allocations, Entitlements, and Value. In Persistent Inequalities: Women and World Development. Irene Tinker, ed. Pp. 162–181. New York: Oxford University Press.
Papanek, Hanna and Laurel Schede. 1988
Women are Good with Money: Earning and Managing in an Indonesian City. In A Home Divided: Women and Income in the Third World. Daisy Dwyer and Judith Bruce, eds. Pp. 71–98. Stanford: Stanford University Press.
Pappas, Gregory. 1989
The Magic City: Unemployment in a Working-Class Community. Ithaca: Cornell University Press.
Parillo, Vincent N. 1997
Strangers to These Shores: Race and Ethnic Relations in the United States. Boston: Allyn and Bacon.
Park, Michael Alan. 1996
Biological Anthropology. Mountain View, CA: Mayfield Publishing Company.
Parker, Richard G. 1991
Bodies, Pleasures, and Passions: Sexual Culture in Contemporary Brazil. Boston: Beacon Press.
Parry, Jonathan P. 1966
Caste. In The Social Science Encyclopedia. Adam Kuper and Jessica Kuper, eds. Pp. 76–77. New York: Routledge.
Partridge, William L. and Elizabeth M. Eddy. 1978
The Development of Applied Anthropology in America. In Applied Anthropology in America. Elizabeth M. Eddy and William L. Partridge, eds. Pp. 3–48. New York: Columbia University Press.
Pasquino, Gianfranco. 1996
Democratization. In The Social Science Encyclopedia. Adam Kuper and Jessica Kuper, eds. Pp. 173–174. Routledge: New York.
Peacock, James L. and Dorothy C. Holland. 1993
The Narrated Self: Life Stories in Process. Ethos 21(4): 367–383.

Peattie, Lisa Redfield. 1968
The View from the Barrio. Ann Arbor: University of Michigan Press.
Pechman, Joseph A. 1987
Introduction: Recent Developments. In Comparative Tax Systems: Europe, Canada, and Japan. Joseph A. Pechman, ed. Pp. 1–32. Arlington, VA: Tax Analysts.
Pedelty, Mark . 1995
War Stories: The Culture of Foreign Correspondents. New York: Routledge
Peletz, Michael. 1987
The Exchange of Men in 19th-Century Negeri Sembilan (Malaya). American Ethnologist 14(3):449–469.
Pelto, Pertti. 1973
The Snowmobile Revolution: Technology and Social Change in the Arctic. Menlo Park, CA: Cummings.
Pelto, Pertti, Maria Roman, and Nelson Liriano. 1982
Family Structures in An Urban Puerto Rican Community. Urban Anthropology 11:39–58.
People Weekly. 1994
Mail-Order Brides. 42(9):88-89.
Perin, Constance. 1988
Belonging in America: Reading between the Lines. Madison: University of Wisconsin Press.
Perry, Richard J. 1996
... From Time Immemorial: Indigenous Peoples and State Systems. Austin: University of Texas Press.
Pessar, Patricia R. 1995
A Visa for a Dream: Dominicans in the United States. Boston: Allyn and Bacon.
Petras, James and Tienchai Wongchaisuwan. 1993
Free Markets, AIDS and Child Prostitution. Economic and Political Weekly March 13:440–442.
Petty, Jill. 1996
Only 5 of 190 World Leaders Are Women. How Are They Doing? Ms 6(5):20–23.
Piddocke, Stuart. 1969
The Potlatch System of the Southern Kwakiutl: A New Perspective. In Environment and Cultural Behavior: Ecological Studies in Cultural Anthropology. Andrew P. Vayda, ed. Pp. 130–156. Garden City, NY: The Natural History Press.
Pilisuk, Marc and Susan Hillier Parks. 1986
The Healing Web: Social Networks and Human Survival. Hanover, NH: University Press of New England.
Pillsbury, Barbara. 1990
The Politics of Family Planning: Sterilization and Human Rights in Bangladesh. In Births and Power: Social Change and the Politics of Reproduction. W. Penn Handwerker, ed. Pp. 165–196. Boulder: Westview Press.
Plant, Roger. 1994
Land Rights and Minorities. London: Minority Rights Group.
Plattner, Stuart. 1989
Markets and Marketplaces. In Economic Anthropology. Stuart Plattner, ed. Pp. 171–208. Stanford: Stanford University Press.
Poirier, Sylvie. 1992
"Nomadic" Rituals: Networks of Ritual Exchange between Women of the Australian Western Desert. Man 27:757–776.
Polednak, Anthony P. 1989
Racial and Ethnic Differences in Disease. New York: Oxford University Press.
Pollock, Donald. 1995
Masks and the Semiotics of Identity. Journal of the Royal Anthropological Institute (n.s.) 1:581–597.
Posey, Darrell Addison. 1990
Intellectual Property Rights: What Is the Position of Ethnobiology? Journal of Ethnobiology 10:93–98.
Pospisil, Leopold. 1979
Legally Induced Cultural Change in New Guinea. In The Imposition of Law. Sandra B. Bruman and Barbara E. Harrell-Bond, eds. New York: Academic Press.
Postgate, Nicholas, Tao Wang and Toby Wilkinson. 1995
The Evidence for Early Writing: Utilitarian or Ceremonial? Antiquity 69:459–480.
Potter, Jack M. 1976
Thai Peasant Social Structure. Chicago: The University of Chicago Press.
Potter, Sulamith Heins. 1977
Family Life in a Northern Thai Village: A Study in the Structural Significance of Women. Berkeley: University of California Press.
Povinelli, Elizabeth A. 1991
Organizing Women: Rhetoric, Economy, and Politics in Process among Australian Aborigines. In Gender at the Crossroads of Knowledge: Feminist Anthopology in the Postmodern Era. Micaela di Leonardo, ed. Pp. 235–256. Berkeley: University of California Press.
Pratt, Mary Louise. 1992
Imperial Eyes: Travel Writing and Transculturation. London: Routledge.
Prestwich, Michael. 1996
Feudalism. In The Social Science Encyclopedia. Adam Kuper and Jessica Kuper, eds. Pp. 301–302. New York: Routledge.
Price, David H. 1995
Water Theft in Egypt's Fayoum Oasis: Emics, Etics, and the Illegal. In Science, Materialism, and the Study of Culture. Martin F. Murphy and Maxine L. Margolis, eds. Pp. 96–110. Gainesville: University of Florida Press.
Primack, Richard B. 1991
Logging, Conservation and Native Rights in Sarawak Forests from Different Viewpoints. Borneo Research Bulletin 23: 3–13.
Prince, Raymond. 1985
The Concept of Culture-Bound Syndromes: Anorexia Nervosa and Brain-Fag. Social Science and Medicine 21(2):197–203.
Ptacek, James. 1997
The Tactics and Strategies of Men Who Batter: Testimony from Women Seeking Restraining Orders. In Violence between Intimate Partners: Patterns, Causes, and Effects. Albert P. Cardarelli, ed. Pp. 104–123. Boston: Allyn and Bacon.
Purdum, Elizabeth D. and J. Anthony Paredes. 1989
Facing the Death Penalty: Essays on Cruel and Unusual Punishment. Philadelphia: Temple University Press.
Putnam, Judith Jones. 1994
American Eating Habits Changing, Part 2: Grains, Vegetables, Fruit, and Sugars. Food Review 17(2):36–47.
Rabinowitz, Dan. 1997
Overlooking Nazareth: The Ethnography of Exclusion in Galilee. New York: Cambridge University Press.
Radcliffe-Brown, A. R. 1964 [1922]
The Andaman Islanders. New York: The Free Press.
Radin, Paul. 1963, orig. 1920
The Autobiography of a Winnebago Indian: Life, Ways, Acculturation, and the Peyote Cult. New York: Dover Publications.
Raheja, Gloria Goodwin. 1988
The Poison in the Gift: Ritual, Prestation, and the Dominant Caste in a North Indian Village. Chicago: University of Chicago Press.
Rahnema, Majid. 1992
Poverty. In The Development Dictionary: A Guide to Knowledge and Power. Wolfgang Sachs, ed. Pp. 159–176. Atlantic Highlands, NJ: Zed Press.
Ramesh, A., C. R. Srikumari, and S. Sukumar. 1989
Parallel Cousin Marriages in Madras, Tamil Nadu: New Trends in Dravidian Kinship. Social Biology 36(3–4):248–254.
Ramphele, Mamphela. 1996
Political Widowhood in South Africa: The Embodiment of Ambiguity. Daedalus 125(1):99–17.
Rao, Vijayendra and Francis Bloch. 1993
Wife Beating, Its Causes and Its Implications for Nutrition Alloca-

tions to Children: An Economic and Anthropological Case-Study of a Rural South Indian Community. Unpublished paper prepared for the World Bank.
Rapoport, Tamar, Yoni Garb, and Anat Penso. 1995
Religious Socialization and Female Subjectivity: Religious-Zionist Adolescent Girls in Israel. Sociology of Education 68:48–61.
Rapp, Rayna. 1993
Reproduction and Gender Hierarchy: Amniocentesis in America. In Sex and Gender Hierarchies. Barbara D. Miller, ed. Pp. 108–126. New York: Cambridge University Press.
Rappaport, Roy. 1968
Pigs for the Ancestors: New Haven: Yale University Press.
___. 1993
Distinguished Lecture: The Anthropology of Trouble. American Anthropologist 95(2):295–303.
Ratcliffe, John. 1978
Social Justice and the Demographic Transition: Lessons from India's Kerala State. International Journal of Health Services 8(1):123–144.
Rathje, William and Cullen Murphy. 1992
Rubbish! The Archaeology of Garbage. New York: Harper & Row.
Reid, Russell M. 1992
Cultural and Medical Perspectives on Geophagia. Medical Anthropology 13:337–351.
Reiner, R. 1996
Police. In The Social Science Encyclopedia. Adam Kuper and Jessica Kuper, eds. Pp. 619–621. New York: Routledge.
Renfrew, Colin. 1994
World Linguistic Diversity. Scientific American 270(1): 116–123.
Reyna, Stephen P. 1994
A Mode of Domination Approach to Organized Violence. In Studying War: Anthropological Perspectives. S. P. Reyna and R. E. Downs, eds. Pp. 29–65. Langhorne, PA: Gordon and Breach Science Publishers.
Rice, Don Stephen and Prudence M. Rice. 1984
Lessons from the Maya. Latin American Research Review 19(3):7–34.
Rich, Adrienne. 1980
Compulsory Heterosexuality and Lesbian Existence. Signs 5:631–660.
Rich, Bruce. 1994
Mortgaging the Earth: The World Bank, Environmental Impoverishment, and the Crisis of Development. Boston: Beacon Press.
Robb, John. 1993
A Social Prehistory of European Languages. Antiquity 67: 747–760.
Robben, Antonius C. G. M. and Carolyn Nordstrom. 1995
The Anthropology and Ethnography of Violence and Sociopolitical Conflict. In Carolyn Nordstrom and Antonius C. G. M. Robben, eds. Fieldwork under Fire: Contemporary Studies of Violence and Survival. Pp. 1–25. Berkeley: University of California Press.
Robertson, Carol E. 1987
Power and Gender in the Musical Experiences of Women. In Women and Music in Cross-Cultural Perspective. Ellen Koskoff, ed. Pp. 225–244. New York: Greenwood Press.
Robertson, Jennifer. 1991
Native and Newcomer: Making and Remaking a Japanese City. Berkeley: University of California Press.
Robson, Colin. 1993
Real World Research: A Resource for Social Scientists and Practitioner-Researchers. Cambridge, MA: Blackwell Publishers.
Rogers, Barbara. 1979
The Domestication of Women: Discrimination in Developing Societies. New York: St. Martin's Press.
Rosaldo, Renato. 1980
Ilongot Headhunting 1883–1974: A Study in Society and History. Stanford: Stanford University Press.
Roscoe, Will. 1991
The Zuni Man-Woman. Albuquerque: University of New Mexico Press.
Rose, Jerome C., Thomas J. Green, and Victoria D. Green. 1996
NAGPRA is Forever: Osteology and the Repatriation of Skeletons. Annual Review of Anthropology 25:81–103.
Roseman, Marina. 1987
Inversion and Conjuncture: Male and Female Performance among the Temiar of Peninsular Malaysia. In Women and Music in Cross-Cultural Perspective. Ellen Koskoff, ed. Pp. 131–149. New York: Greenwood Press.
Rosenberger, Nancy. 1992
Images of the West: Home Style in Japanese Magazines. In Re-made in Japan: Everyday Life and Consumer Taste in a Changing Society. James J. Tobin, ed. Pp. 106–125. New Haven: Yale University Press.
Rosenblatt, Paul C., Patricia R. Walsh, and Douglas A. Jackson. 1976
Grief and Mourning in Cross-Cultural Perspective. New Haven: HRAF Press.
Ross, Eric Barry. 1978
Food Taboos, Diet, and Hunting Strategy: The Adaptation to Animals in Amazon Cultural Ecology. Current Anthropology 19(1):1–16.
Ross, Marc Howard. 1993
The Culture of Conflict: Interpretations and Interests in Comparative Perspective. New Haven: Yale University Press.
Rouland, Norbert. 1994
Legal Anthropology. Philippe G. Planel, trans. Stanford: Stanford University Press.
Rubel, Arthur J., Carl W. O'Nell, and Rolando Collado-Ardon. 1984.
Susto: A Folk Illness. Berkeley: University of California Press.
Rubin, Gayle. 1975
The Traffic in Women: Notes on the "Political Economy" of Sex. In Toward an Anthropology of Women. Rayna R, Rapp, ed. Pp. 157–210. New York: Monthly Review Press.
Rubin, Joshua, Nancy M. Flowers, and Daniel R. Gross. 1986
The Adaptive Dimensions of Leisure. American Ethnologist 13(3): 524–536.
Ruhlen, Merritt. 1994
On the Origin of Languages: Studies in Linguistic Taxonomy. Stanford: Stanford University Press.
Rutter, Virginia. 1995
Adolescence: Whose Hell Is It? Psychology Today 28(1): 54–64.
Sachs, Aaron. 1996
Dying for Oil. WorldWatch June: 10–21.
Sahlins, Marshall. 1963
Poor Man, Rich Man, Big Man, Chief. Comparative Studies in Society and History 5:285–303.
___. 1972
Stone Age Economics. Chicago: Aldine-Atherton.
Said, Edward W. 1979 [1978]
Orientalism. New York: Vintage Books.
___. 1981
Covering Islam: How the Media and the Experts Determine How We See the Rest of the World. New York: Pantheon.
___. 1993
Culture and Imperialism. New York: Random House.
Saitoti, Tepilit Ole. 1986
The Worlds of a Maasai Warrior. New York: Random House.
Salam, Nawaf A. 1994
Between Repatriation and Resettlement: Palestinian Refugees in Lebanon. Journal of Palestine Studies 24(1):18–27.
Sanday, Peggy Reeves. 1973
Toward a Theory of the Status of Women. American Anthropologist 75:1682–1700.
___. 1986
Divine Hunger: Cannibalism as a Cultural System. New York: Cambridge University Press.
___. 1990
Fraternity Gang Rape: Sex, Brotherhood, and Privilege on Campus. New York: New York University Press.
___. 1996
A Woman Scorned: Date Rape on Trial. New York: Doubleday.
Sanders, William B. 1994
Gangbangs and Drive-Bys: Grounded Culture and Juvenile Gang Violence. New York: Aldine de Gruyter.

Sanjek, Roger. 1990a
A Vocabulary for Fieldnotes. In Fieldnotes: The Making of Anthropology. Roger Sanjek, ed. Pp. 92–138. Ithaca: Cornell University Press.
———. 1990b
Maid Servants and Market Women's Apprentices in Adabraka. In At Work in Homes: Household Workers in World Perspective. Roger Sanjek and Shellee Colleen, eds. Pp. 35–62. American Ethnological Society Monograph Series, Number 3. Washington, DC; American Anthropological Association.
———. 1994
The Enduring Inequalities of Race. In Race. Steven Gregory and Roger Sanjek, eds. Pp. 1–17. New Brunswick: Rutgers University Press.
Sanjek, Roger, ed. 1990
Fieldnotes: The Making of Anthropology. Ithaca, NY: Cornell University Press.
Sant Cassia, Paul. 1993
Banditry, Myth, and Terror in Cyprus and Other Mediterranean Societies. Comparative Studies in Society and History 35(4):773–795.
Sargent, Carolyn F. 1988
Born to Die: Witchcraft and Infanticide in Bariba Culture. Ethnology 27(1):79–95.
———. 1989
Maternity, Medicine, and Power: Reproductive Decisions in Urban Benin. Berkeley: University of California Press.
Sault, Nicole L. 1985
Baptismal Sponsorship as a Source of Power for Zapotec Women of Oaxaca, Mexico. Journal of Latin American Lore 11(2):225–243.
———. 1994
How the Body Shapes Parenthood: "Surrogate" Mothers in the United States and Godmothers in Mexico. In Many Mirrors: Body Image and Social Relations. Nicole Sault, ed. Pp. 292–318. Rutgers: Rutgers University Press.
Savishinsky, Joel S. 1974
The Trail of the Hare: Life and Stress in an Arctic Community. New York: Gordon and Breach.
———. 1991
The Ends of Time: Life and Work in a Nursing Home. New York: Bergin & Garvey.
Scheper-Hughes, Nancy. 1979
Saints, Scholars, and Schizophrenics: Mental Illness in Rural Ireland. Berkeley: University of California Press.
———. 1990
Three Propositions for a Critically Applied Medical Anthropology. Social Science and Medicine 30(2):189–197.
———. 1993
Death without Weeping: The Violence of Everyday Life in Brazil. Berkeley: University of California Press.
Schlegel, Alice. 1995
A Cross-Cultural Approach to Adolescence. Ethos 23(1):15–32.
Schlegel, Alice and Herbert Barry III. 1991
Adolescence: An Anthropological Inquiry. New York: Free Press.
Schmid, Thomas J. and Richard S. Jones. 1993
Ambivalent Actions: Prison Adaptation Strategies of First-Time, Short-term Inmates. Journal of Contemporary Ethnography 21 (4):439–463.
Schneider, David M. 1968
American Kinship: A Cultural Account. Englewood Cliffs, NJ: Prentice-Hall.
———. 1984
A Critique of the Study of Kinship. Ann Arbor: The University of Michigan Press.
Schuster, Angela M. H. 1996
Who's Buried in Margarita's Tomb? Archaeology 49(4):17.
Schwartz, Jeffrey H. 1987
The Red Ape: Orang-utans and Human Origins. Boston: Houghton Mifflin.
———. 1993
What the Bones Tell Us. New York: Henry Holt and Company.
Schuler, Sidney. 1987
The Other Side of Polyandry: Property, Stratification, and Nonmarriage in the Nepal Himalayas. Boulder: Westview Press.
Scott, James C. 1976
The Moral Economy of the Peasant: Rebellion and Subsistence in Southeast Asia. New Haven: Yale University Press.
———. 1985
Weapons of the Weak: Everyday Forms of Peasant Resistance. New Haven: Yale University Press.
Scrimshaw, Susan. 1984
Infanticide in Human Populations: Societal and Individual Concerns. In Infanticide: Comparative and Evolutionary Perspectives. Glenn Hausfater and Sarah Blaffer Hrdy, eds. Pp. 463–486. New York: Aldine Publishing Company.
Scudder, Thayer. 1973
The Human Ecology of Big Dam Projects: River Basin Development and Resettlement. Annual Review of Anthropology 2:45–55.
Sen, Amartya. 1981
Poverty and Famines: An Essay on Entitlement and Deprivation. New York; Oxford University Press.
Sen, Kasturi. 1994
Ageing: Debates on Demographic Transition and Social Policy. London: Zed Books.
Sen, Mala. 1995
India's Bandit Queen: The True Story of Phulan Devi. New Delhi: Indus/HarperCollins.
Sentumbwe, Nayinda. 1995
Sighted Lovers and Blind Husbands: Experience of Blind Women in Uganda. In Disability and Culture. Benedicte Ingstad and Susan Reynolds, eds. Pp. 159–173. Berkeley: University of California Press.
Shaheen, Jack G. 1994
Arab Images in American Comic Books. Journal of Popular Culture 28(1):123–133.
Shamgar-Handelman, Lea and Don Handelman. 1991
Celebrations of Bureaucracy: Birthday Parties in Israeli Kindergartens. Ethnology 30(4):293–312.
Sharff, Jagna Wojcicka. 1995
"We Are All Chickens for the Colonel": A Cultural Materialist View of Prisons. In Science, Materialism, and the Study of Culture. Martin F. Murphy and Maxine L. Margolis, eds. Pp. 132–158. Gainesville: University Press of Florida.
Sharp, Lauriston. 1952
Steel Axes for Stone-Age Australians. Human Organization 11: 17–22.
Sharp, Lesley. 1990
Possessed and Dispossessed Youth: Spirit Possession of School Children in Northwest Madagascar. Culture, Medicine and Psychiatry 14:339–364.
Shenhav-Keller, Shelly. 1993
The Israeli Souvenir: Its Text and Context. Annals of Tourism Research 20:182–196.
Shibamoto, Janet. 1987
The Womanly Woman: Manipulation of Stereotypical and Nonstereotypical Features of Japanese Female Speech. In Language, Gender, and Sex in Comparative Perspective. Susan U. Philips, Susan Steel, and Christine Tanz, eds. Pp. 26–49. New York: Cambridge University Press.
Shifflett, Peggy A. and William A. McIntosh. 1986–87
Food Habits and Future Time: An Exploratory Study of Age-Appropriate Food Habits among the Elderly. International Journal of Aging and Human Development 24 (1):2–15.
Short, James F. 1966
Gangs. In The Social Science Encyclopedia. Adam Kuper and Jessica Kuper, eds. Pp. 325–326. New York: Routledge.
Shostak, Marjorie. 1981
Nisa: The Life and Times of a !Kung Woman. Cambridge, MA: Harvard University Press.

Shu-Min, Huang. 1993
A Cross-Cultural Experience: A Chinese Anthropologist in the United States. In Distant Mirrors: America as a Foreign Culture. Philip R. DeVita and James D. Armstrong, eds. Pp. 39–45. Belmont, CA: Wadsworth Publishing Company.
Shweder, Richard A. 1986
Storytelling among the Anthropologists. The New York Times Book Review, September 21, pp. 1, 38–39.
Shweder, Richard A., Lene Arnett Jensen, and William M. Goldstein. 1995
Who Sleeps by Whom Revisited: A Method for Extracting the Moral Goods Implicit in Practice. In Cultural Practices as Contexts for Development: New Directions for Child Development. Number 67. Jacqueline J. Goodnow, Peggy J. Miller, and Frank Kessel, eds. San Francisco: Jossey-Bass Publishers.
Silver, Ira. 1993
Marketing Authenticity in Third World Countries. Annals of Tourism Research 20:302–318.
Simmons, William S. 1986
Spirit of the New England Tribes: Indian History and Folklore, 1620–1984. Hanover, NH: University Press of New England.
Simons, Ronald C. and Charles C. Hughes, eds. 1984
The Culture-Bound Syndromes: Folk Illnesses of Psychiatric and Anthropological Interest. Boston: D. Reidel.
Singer, Merrill. 1989
The Coming of Age of Critical Medical Anthropology. Social Science and Medicine 28(11):1193–1203.
Singh, K. S. 1994
The Scheduled Tribes. Anthropological Survey of India, People of India, National Series Volume III. Delhi: Oxford University Press.
Siskind, Janet. 1992
The Invention of Thanksgiving: A Ritual of American Nationality. Critique of Anthropology 12(2):167–191.
Skinner, G. William. 1964
Marketing and Social Structure in Rural China (Part 1). Journal of Asian Studies 24(1):3–43.
___. 1993
Conjugal Power in Tokugawa Japanese Families: A Matter of Life or Death. In Sex and Gender Hierarchies. Barbara D. Miller, ed. Pp. 236–270. New York: Cambridge University Press.
Skocpol, Theda. 1979
States and Social Revolutions: A Comparative Analysis of France, Russia, and China. New York: Cambridge University Press.
Slobin, Dan I. 1990
The Development from Child Speaker to Native Speaker. In Cultural Psychology: Essays on Comparative Human Development. James W. Stigler, Richard A. Shweder, and Gilbert Herdt, eds. Pp. 233–256. New York: Cambridge University Press.
Slocum, Sally. 1975
Woman the Gatherer: Male Bias in Anthropology. In Toward an Anthropology of Women. Rayna R. Reiter, ed. Pp. 36–50. New York: Monthly Review Press.
Smart, Carol. 1996
Divorce. In The Encyclopedia of Social Science. Adam Kuper and Jessica Kuper, eds. Pp. 193–194. New York: Routledge.
Smith, Jonathan Z., ed. 1995
The HarperCollins Dictionary of Religion. New York: HarperCollins.
Smith, Michael. G. 1966
Political Organization. International Encyclopedia of Social Sciences. Pp. 193–202. New York: Macmillan.
Smith, Stephen R. 1992
Drinking Etiquette in a Changing Beverage Market. In Re-Made in Japan: Everyday Life and Consumer Taste in a Changing Society. Joseph J. Tobin, ed. Pp. 143–158. New Haven: Yale University Press.
Smitherman, Geneva. 1986
Talkin and Testifyin: The Language of Black America. Detroit: Wayne State University Press.
Smuts, Barbara B. 1985
Sex and Friendship among Baboons. New York: Aldine.
Soh, Chunghee Sarah. 1993
Women in Korean Politics. 2nd edition. Boulder: Westview Press.
Sonenshein, Raphael J. 1996
The Battle over Liquor Stores in South Central Los Angeles: The Management of an Interminority Conflict. Urban Affairs Review 31(6):710–737.
Sperber, Dan. 1985
On Anthropological Knowledge: Three Essays. New York: Cambridge University Press.
Spiro, Melford. 1967
Burmese Supernaturalism: A Study in the Explanation and Reduction of Suffering. Englewood Cliffs, NJ: Prentice-Hall.
___. 1982
Buddhism and Society: A Great Tradition and Its Burmese Vicissitudes. Berkeley: University of California Press.
___. 1990
On the Strange and the Familiar in Recent Anthropological Thought. In Cultural Psychology: Essays on Comparative Human Development. James W. Stigler, Richard A. Shweder, and Gilbert Herdt, eds. Pp. 47–61. Chicago: University of Chicago Press.
Spitulnik, Deborah. 1993
Anthropology and Mass Media. Annual Review of Anthropology 22:293–315.
Srinivas, M. N. 1959
The Dominant Caste in Rampura. American Anthropologist 1:1–16.
Staats, Valerie. 1994
Ritual, Strategy or Convention: Social Meaning in Traditional Women's Baths in Morocco. Frontiers: A Journal of Women's Studies 14(3):1–18.
Stack, Carol. 1974
All Our Kin: Strategies for Survival in a Black Community. New York: Harper & Row Publishers.
Stannard, David E. 1992
American Holocaust. New York: Oxford University Press.
Starr, June. 1978
Dispute and Settlement in Rural Turkey: An Ethnography of Law. Leiden: E. J. Brill.
Stein, Gertrude. 1959
Picasso. Boston: Beacon Press.
Steinhoff, Patricia G. 1993
Pursuing the Japanese Police. Law & Society Review 27(4):827–850.
Stephen, Lynn. 1995
Women's Rights are Human Rights: The Merging of Feminine and Feminist Interests among El Salvador's Mothers of the Disappeared (CO-MADRES). American Ethnologist 22(4):807–827.
Stiglmayer, Alexandra, ed. 1994
Mass Rape: The War against Women in Bosnia-Herzegovina. Lincoln: University of Nebraska Press.
Stillman, Amy Ku'uleialoha. 1996
Hawaiian Hula Competitions: Event, Repertoire, Performance and Tradition. Journal of American Folklore 109(434): 357–380.
Stivens, Maila, Cecelia Ng, and Jomo K. S., with Jahara Bee. 1994
Malay Peasant Women and the Land. Atlantic Highlands, NJ: Zed Books.
Stocking, George W. Jr., ed. 1985.
Objects and Others: Essays on Museums and Material Culture. History of Anthropology Series, 3. Madison: University of Wisconsin Press.
Stoler, Ann Laura. 1985
Capitalism and Confrontation in Sumatra's Plantation Belt, 1870–1979. New Haven: Yale University Press.
___. 1989
Rethinking Colonial Categories: European Communities and the Boundaries of Rule. Comparative Studies in Society and History 31(1):134–161.
Stoltz, George. 1997
Bilbao to Bid for Guernica. ARTnews 96(1):47.

Storper-Perez, Danielle and Harvey E. Goldberg. 1994
The Kotel: Toward an Ethnographic Portrait. Religion 24: 309–332.

Strathern, Andrew. 1971
The Rope of Moka: Big-Men and Ceremonial Exchange in Mount Hagen, New Guinea. London: Cambridge University Press.

___. 1993
Landmarks: Reflections on Anthropology. Kent, OH: Kent State University Press.

Strathern, Marilyn. 1980
No Nature, No Culture: The Hagen Case. In Nature, Culture, and Gender. Carol P. MacCormack and Marilyn Strathern, eds. Pp. 174–222. New York: Cambridge University Press.

Struck, Doug. 1998
Women Raise Their Voices for the Right to Pray Aloud at the Wall. The Washington Post, March 23:A13.

Suggs, David N. and Andrew W. Miracle, eds. 1993
Culture and Human Sexuality: A Reader. Belmont, CA: Wadsworth Press.

Sundar Rao, P. S. S. 1983
Religion and Intensity of In-breeding in Tamil Nadu, South India. Social Biology 30(4):413–422.

Suttles, Wayne. 1991
The Traditional Kwakiutl Potlatch. In Chiefly Feasts: The Enduring Kwakiutl Potlatch. Aldona Jonaitis, ed. Pp. 71–134. Washington, DC: American Museum of Natural History.

Szabo, Joan C. 1988
Dwindling Numbers on the Farm. Nation's Business 76(4):16.

Talle, Aud. 1995
A Child is a Child: Disability and Equality among the Kenya Maasai. In Disability and Culture. Benedicte Ungstad and Susan Reynolds Whyte, eds. Pp. 56–72. Berkeley: University of California Press.

Tambiah, Stanley Jeyaraja. 1985
Animals Are Good to Think and Good to Prohibit. In Culture, Thought, and Social Action: An Anthropological Perspective. Stanley Jeyaraja Tambiah, ed. Pp. 169–211. Cambridge: Harvard University Press.

Tannen, Deborah. 1990
You Just Don't Understand: Women and Men in Conversation. New York: Morrow.

Tapp, Nicholas. 1989
Sovereignty and Rebellion: The White Hmong of Northern Thailand. New York: Oxford University Press.

Taussig, Michael. 1978
Nutrition, Development, and Foreign Aid: A Case Study of U.S.-Directed Health Care in a Colombian Plantation Zone. International Journal of Health Services 8(1):101–121.

Taylor, Sandra C. 1993
Jewel of the Desert: Japanese American Internment at Topaz. Berkeley: University of California Press.

Teilhet-Fisk, Jehanne H. 1991
To Beat or Not to Beat, That is the Question: A Study on Acculturation and Change in an Art-Making Process and Its Relation to Gender Structures. Pacific Studies 14(3):41–68.

Thomas, Duncan. 1991
Gender Differences in Household Resource Allocations. Living Standards Measurement Study, Working Paper No. 79. Washington, DC: The World Bank.

Thompson, Julia J. 1998
Cuts and Culture in Kathmandu. In Hair: Its Meaning and Power in Asian Cultures. In Alf Hiltebeitel and Barbara D. Miller, eds. Pp. 219–258. Albany: State University of New York Press.

Thompson, Robert Farris. 1971
Aesthetics in Traditional Africa. In Art and Aesthetics in Primitive Societies. Carol F. Jopling, ed. Pp. 374–381. New York: E. P. Dutton.

Thorne, Barrie. 1995
Gender Play: Girls and Boys in School. New Brunswick: Rutgers University Press.

Tice, Karin E. 1995
Kuna Crafts, Gender, and the Global Economy. Austin: University of Texas Press.

Tiffany, Walter W. 1979
New Directions in Political Anthropology: The Use of Corporate Models for the Analysis of Political Organizations. In Political Anthropology: The State of the Art. S. Lee Seaton and Henri J. M. Claessen, eds. Pp. 63–75. New York: Mouton.

Tinker, Irene. 1976
The Adverse Impact of Development on Women. In Women and World Development. Irene Tinker and Michele Bo Bramsen, eds. Pp. 22–34. Washington, DC: Overseas Development Council.

Tobin, Joseph J., David Y. H. Wu, and Dana H. Davidson. 1989
Preschool in Three Cultures: Japan, China, and the United States. New Haven: Yale University Press.

Tobin, Joseph J., ed. 1992
Re-Made in Japan: Everyday Life and Consumer Taste in a Changing Society. New Haven: Yale University Press.

___. 1992
Introduction: Domesticating the West. In Re-Made in Japan: Everyday Life and Consumer Taste in a Changing Society. Joseph J. Tobin, ed. Pp. 1–41. New Haven: Yale University Press.

Tobin, Joseph J., David Y. H. Wu, and Dana H. Davidson. 1989
Preschool in Three Cultures: Japan, China, and the United States: New Haven: Yale University Press.

Tomasevski, Katarina.
Development Aid and Human Rights Revisited. New York: St. Martin's Press.

Tooker, Elisabeth. 1992
Lewis H. Morgan and His Contemporaries. American Anthropologist 94(2):357–375.

Toren, Christina. 1988
Making the Present, Revealing the Past: The Mutability and Continuity of Tradition as Process. Man (n.s.) 23:696–717.

Torry, Saundra. 1996
ABA Panel Finds Sex Bias in Law Schools. The Washington Post, February 3.

Trawick, Margaret. 1988
Death and Nurturance in Indian Systems of Healing. In Paths to Asian Medical Knowledge. Charles Leslie and Allan Young, eds. Pp. 129–159. Berkeley: University of California Press.

___. 1992
Notes on Love in a Tamil Family. Berkeley: University of California Press.

Trelease, Murray L. 1975
Dying among Alaskan Indians: A Matter of Choice. In Death: The Final Stage of Growth. Elisabeth Kübler-Ross, ed. Pp. 33–37. Englewood Cliffs, NJ: Prentice-Hall.

Trigger, Bruce G. 1996
State, Origins of. In The Social Science Encyclopedia. Adam Kuper and Jessica Kuper, eds. Pp. 837–838. New York: Routledge.

Trotter, Robert T. II. 1987
A Case of Lead Poisoning from Folk Remedies in Mexican American Communities. In Anthropological Praxis: Translating Knowledge into Action. Robert M. Wulff and Shirley J. Fiske, eds. Pp. 146–159. Boulder: Westview Press.

Trouillot, Michel-Rolph. 1994
Culture, Color, and Politics in Haiti. In Race. Steven Gregory and Roger Sanjek, eds. Pp. 146–174. New Brunswick: Rutgers University Press.

Turnbridge, Louise. 1996
Burundi's 3-Year "Campaign of Terror" Leaves a Bloody Trail on Its Campuses. The Chronicle of Higher Education, August 16:A39.

Turner, Victor W. 1969
The Ritual Process: Structure and Anti-Structure. Chicago: Aldine Publishing Company.

Twose, Nigel. 1984
Drought and the Sahel. Oxford: Oxfam.

Tylor, Edward Burnett. 1871
Primitive Culture: Researches into the Development of Mythology, Philosophy, Religion, Art, and Custom. 2 volumes. London: J. Murray.

Uhl, Sarah. 1991
Forbidden Friends: Cultural Veils of Female Friendship in Andalusia. American Ethnologist 18(1):90–105.

United Nations Development Programme. 1994
Human Development Report 1994. New York: Oxford University Press.

Uphoff, Norman T. and Milton J. Esman. 1984
Local Organizations: Intermediaries in Rural Development. Ithaca: Cornell University Press.

Valdés, Guadalupe and Richard A. Figueroa. 1994
Bilingualism and Testing: A Special Case of Bias. Norwood, NJ: Ablex Publishing Company.

United Nations High Commissioner for Refugees. 1991
Guildelines on the Protection of Refugee Women. Geneva: Office of the United Nations High Commissioner for Refugees.

van der Geest, Sjaak, Susan Reynolds Whyte, and Anita Hardon. 1996
The Anthropology of Pharmaceuticals: A Biographical Approach. Annual Review of Anthropology 25:153–178.

van der Kwaak, Anke. 1992
Female Circumcision and Gender Identity: A Questionable Alliance? Social Science and Medicine 35(6):777–787.

Van Gennep, Arnold. 1960
The Rites of Passage. Chicago: University of Chicago Press.

Van Maanen, John. 1988
Tales of the Field: On Writing Ethnography. Chicago: University of Chicago Press.

Vatuk, Ved Prakash and Sylvia Vatuk. 1971
On a System of Private Savings among North Indian Village Women. Journal of Asian and African Studies 6(3–4): 179–190.

Veblen, Thorstein. 1953 [1899]
The Theory of the Leisure Class. New York: Mentor Books.

Velimirovic, Boris. 1990
Is Integration of Traditional and Western Medicine Really Possible? In Anthropology and Primary Health Care. Jeannine Coreil and J. Dennis Mull, eds. Pp. 51–778. Boulder: Westview Press.

Vellenga, Dorothy Dee. 1983
Who Is A Wife? Legal Expressions of Heterosexual Conflicts in Ghana. In Female and Male in West Africa. Christine Oppong, ed. Pp. 144–155. Boston: George Allen & Unwin.

Verdery, Katherine. 1996
What Was Socialism and What Comes Next? Princeton: Princeton University Press.

Vesperi, Maria D. 1985
City of Green Benches: Growing Old in a New Downtown. Ithaca: Cornell University Press.

Vickers, Jeanne. 1993
Women and War. Atlantic Highlands, NJ: Zed Books.

Vincent, Joan. 1990
Anthropology and Politics: Visions, Traditions, and Trends. Tucson: The University of Arizona Press.

___. 1996
Political Anthropology. In The Social Science Encyclopedia. Adam Kuper and Jessica Kuper, eds. P. 624. New York: Routledge.

Vincke, John, Ralph Bolton, Rudolf Mak, and Susan Blank. 1993
Coming Out and AIDS-Related High-Risk Sexual Behavior. Archives of Sexual Behavior 22(6):559–586.

Wallerstein, Immanuel. 1979
The Capitalist World-Economy. New York: Cambridge University Press.

Wang. Pair Dong and Ruey S. Lin. 1994
Sexual Activity of Women in Taiwan. Social Biology 41(3–4):143–149.

Ward, Martha C. 1989
Once Upon a Time. In Nest in the Wind: Adventures in Anthropology on a Tropical Island. Martha C. Ward, ed. Pp. 1–22. Prospect Heights, IL: Waveland Press.

Warren, Carol A. B. 1972
Identity and Community in the Gay World. New York: Wiley-Interscience.

___. 1988
Gender Issues in Field Research. Qualitative Research Methods, Volume 9. Newbury Park, CA: Sage Publications.

The Washington Post. 1994a
Test-Tube Babies Cost $60,000 to $110,000 Each. July 28:A18.

___. 1994b
Contraception the Natural Way. July 25:A3.

___. 1984c
Alfalfa Club's Old Boys Bring in the Girls. January 7:B3.

___. 1995
Consumerism Fuels Dowry-Death Wave. March 17:A35ff.

Watson, Rubie S. 1986
The Named and the Nameless: Gender and Person in Chinese Society. American Ethnologist 13(4):619-631.

___. 1997
Museums and Indigenous Cultures: The Power of Local Knowledge. Cultural Survival Quarterly 21(1):24–25.

Watson, Rubie S. and James L. Watson. 1997
From Hall of Worship to Tourist Center: An Ancestral Hall in Hong Kong's New Territories. Cultural Survival Quarterly 21(1):33–35.

Weatherford, J. 1981
Tribes on the Hill. New York: Random House.

Weber, Linda R., Andrew Miracle, and Tom Skehan. 1994
Interviewing Early Adolescents: Some Methodological Considerations. Human Organization 53(1):42–47.

Websdale, Neil. 1995
An Ethnographic Assessment of the Policing of Domestic Violence in Rural Eastern Kentucky. Social Justice 22(1):102–122.

Webster, Gloria Cranmer. 1991
The Contemporary Potlatch. In Chiefly Feasts: The Enduring Kwakiutl Potlatch. Aldona Jonaitis, ed. Pp. 227–250. Washington, DC: American Museum of Natural History.

Weine, Stevan M. et al. 1995
Psychiatric Consequences of "Ethnic Cleansing": Clinical Assessments and Trauma Testimonies of Newly Resettled Bosnian Refugees. American Journal of Psychiatry 152(4): 536–542.

Weiner, Annette B. 1976
Women of Value, Men of Renown: New Perspectives in Trobriand Exchange. Austin: University of Texas Press.

Weinstein, Jeff. 1993
I Always Cry at Weddings. The Village Voice 38(9):16.

Weismantel, M. J. 1989
The Children Cry for Bread: Hegemony and the Transformation of Consumption. In The Social Economy of Consumption. Monographs in Economic Anthropology No. 6. Henry J. Rutz and Benjamin S. Orlove, eds. Pp. 85–99. New York: University Press of America.

Werbner, Pnina. 1990
The Migration Process: Capital, Gifts, and Offerings among British Pakistanis. New York: St. Martin's Press.

White, Douglas R. and Michael L. Burton. 1988
Causes of Polygyny: Ecology, Economy, Kinship, and Warfare. American Anthropologist 90(4):871–887.

Whitehead, Tony Larry. 1986
Breakdown, Resolution, and Coherence: The Fieldwork Experience of a Big, Brown, Pretty-talking Man in a West Indian Community. In Self, Sex, and Gender in Cross-Cultural Fieldwork. Tony Larry Whitehead and Mary Ellen Conway, eds. Pp. 213–239. Chicago: University of Illinois Press.

Whitehead, Tony Larry and Mary Ellen Conway, eds. 1986
Self, Sex, and Gender in Cross-Cultural Fieldwork. Chicago: University of Illinois Press.

Whiting, Beatrice B. and John W. M. Whiting. 1975
Children of Six Cultures: A Psycho-Cultural Analysis. Cambridge: Harvard University Press.

Whyte, Martin King. 1993
Wedding Behavior and Family Strategies in Chengdu. In Chinese Families in the Post-Mao Era. Deborah Davis and Stevan Harrell, eds. Pp. 89–218. Berkeley: University of California Press.
Whyte, Susan Reynolds and Benedicte Ingstad. 1995
Disability and Culture: An Overview. In Disability and Culture. Benedicte Ungstad and Susan Reynolds Whyte, eds. Pp. 3–32. Berkeley: University of California Press.
Wikan, Unni. 1977
Man Becomes Woman: Transsexualism in Oman as a Key to Gender Roles. Man 12(2):304–319.
___. 1982
Behind the Veil in Arabia: Women in Oman. Chicago: University of Chicago Press.
Wilde, James. 1988
Starvation in a Fruitful Land. Time (December 5):43–44.
Williams, Alex. 1995
The Rituals that Still Matter to Them. The New York Times Magazine, November 19:110–113. Photographs by Larry Fink.
Williams, Brett. 1984
Why Migrant Women Feed Their Husbands Tamales: Foodways as a Basis for a Revisionist View of Tejano Family Life. In Ethnic and Regional Foodways in the United States: The Performance of Group Identity. Linda Keller Brown and Kay Mussell, eds. Pp. 113–126. Knoxville: The University of Tennessee Press.
___. 1988
Upscaling Downtown: Stalled Gentrification in Washington, D.C. Ithaca: Cornell University Press.
___. 1991
Good Guys and Bad Toys: The Paradoxical World of Children's Cartoons. In The Politics of Culture. Brett Williams, ed. Pp. 109–132. Washington, DC: Smithsonian Institution Press.
___. 1994
Babies and Banks: The "Reproductive Underclass" and the Raced, Gendered Masking of Debt. In Race. Steven Gregory and Roger Sanjek, eds. Pp. 348–365. Ithaca: Cornell University Press.
Williams, Melvin. 1992
The Human Dilemma: A Decade Later in Belmar. New York: Harcourt Brace Jovanovich.
Williams, Raymond. 1983
Keywords: A Vocabulary of Culture and Society. New York: Oxford University Press.
Williams, Walter. 1992
The Spirit and the Flesh: Sexual Diversity in American Indian Cultures. 2nd edition. Boston: Beacon Press.
Williamson, Nancy. 1976
Sons or Daughters: A Cross-Cultural Study of Parental Preferences. Beverly Hills, CA: Sage Publications.
Wilson, Richard. 1995
Maya Resurgence in Guatemala: Q'eqchi' Experiences. Norman, OK: University of Oklahoma Press.
Winans, Edgar V. and Angelique Haugerud. 1977
Rural Self-Help in Kenya: The Harambee Movement. Human Organization 36:334–351.
Winkler, Cathy, Renata McMullen and Kate Wininger. 1994
The Contexts of Meaning behind Rape Trauma. In Many Mirrors: Body Image and Social Relations. Nicole Sault, ed. Pp. 266–291. New Brunswick: Rutgers University Press.
Winzeler, Robert L. 1974
Sex Role Equality, Wet Rice Cultivation, and the State in Southeast Asia. American Anthropologist 76(3): 563–565.
Wolf, Arthur P. 1968
Adopt a Daughter-in-Law, Marry a Sister: A Chinese Solution to the Problem of the Incest Taboo. American Anthropologist 70(5):864–874.
___. 1995
Sexual Attraction and Childhood Association: A Chinese Brief for Westermarck. Stanford: Stanford University Press.
Wolf, Charlotte. 1966
Status. In The Social Science Encyclopedia. Adam Kuper and Jessica Kuper, eds. Pp. 842–843. New York: Routledge.
Wolf, Eric R. 1966a
Peasants. Englewood Cliffs, NJ: Prentice-Hall.
___. 1966b
Kinship, Friendship and Patron-Client Relations in Complex Societies. In The Social Anthropology of Complex Societies. IV. Michael Banton, ed. Pp. 1–22. London: Tavistock.
___. 1969
Peasant Wars of the Twentieth Century. New York: Harper & Row.
___. 1982
Europe and the People without History. Berkeley: University of California Press.
Wolf, Margery. 1968
The House of Lim: A Study of a Chinese Farm Family. New York: Appleton-Century-Crofts.
Woodrick, Anne C. 1995
Mother-Daughter Conflict and the Selection of Ritual Kin in a Peasant Community. Anthropological Quarterly 68(4): 219–233.
Woolfson, Peter, Virginia Hood, Roger Secker-Walker, and Ann C. Macaulay. 1995
Mohawk English in the Medical Interview. Medical Anthropology Quarterly 9(4):503–509.
World Press Review. 1993
Desperate Fainting. August:35.
Wright, Patricia Chapple. 1993
Variations in Male-Female Dominance and Offspring Care in Nonhuman Primates. In Sex and Gender Hierarchies. Barbara D. Miller, ed. Pp. 127–145. New York: Cambridge University Press.
Wu, David Y. H. 1990
Chinese Minority Policy and the Meaning of Minority Culture: The Example of Bai in Yunnan, China. Human Organization 49(1):1–13.
Xenophanes. translated by James H. Lesher. 1992
Xenophanes of Colophon: Fragments: A Text and Translation with a Commentary. Toronto: University of Toronto Press.
Xenos, Peter. 1993
Extended Adolescence and the Sexuality of Asian Youth: Observations on Research and Policy. East-West Center Reprints, Population Series No. 292. Honolulu: East-West Center.
Xiaohe, Xu and Martin King Whyte. 1990
Love Matches and Arranged Marriages: A Chinese Replication. Journal of Marriage and the Family 52:709–722.
Xizhe, Peng. 1991
Demographic Transition in China: Fertility Trends Since the 1950s. New York: Oxford University Press.
Yang, Mayfair Mei-hui. 1994
Gifts, Favors and Banquets: The Art of Social Relationships in China. Ithaca: Cornell University Press.
Yinger, John. 1995
Opening Doors: How to Cut Discrimination by Supporting Neighborhood Integration. Center for Policy Research, Policy Brief No. 3. 1995. Syracuse, NY: Syracuse University, Maxwell School of Citizenship and Public Affairs.
Yoon, In-Jin. 1993
The Social Origins of Korean Immigration to the United States from 1965 to the Present. Papers of the Program on Population, Number 121. Honolulu: East-West Center.
Young, Michael W. 1983
"Our Name is Women; We are Bought with Limesticks and Limepots": An Analysis of the Autobiographical Narrative of a Kalauna Woman. Man 18:478–501.
Young, Michael and Peter Willmott. 1979
Family and Kinship in East London. New York: Penguin Books.
Young, Roger and Caroline Van Bers. 1991
Death of the Family Farm. Alternatives 17(4):22-23.

Yuan, Ying-Ying. 1975
Affectivity and Instrumentality in Friendship Patterns among American Women. In Being Female: Reproduction, Power, and Change. Dana Raphael, ed. Pp. 87–98. The Hague: Mouton Publishers.
Zabusky, Stacia E. 1995
Launching Europe: An Ethnography of European Cooperation in Space Science. Princeton: Princeton University Press.
Zaidi, S. Akbar. 1988
Poverty and Disease: Need for Structural Change. Social Science and Medicine 27:119–127.
Zarrilli, Phillip B. 1990
Kathakali. In Indian Theatre: Traditions of Performance. Farley P. Richmond, Darius L. Swann, and Phillip B. Zarrilli, eds. Pp. 315–357. Honolulu: University of Hawaii Press.
Zihlman, Adrienne L. 1993
Sex Differences and Gender Hierarchies among Primates: An Evolutionary Perspective. In Sex and Gender Hierarchies. Barbara D. Miller, ed. Pp. 32–56. New York: Cambridge University Press.
Zolberg, Vera L. 1992
Barrier or Leveler? The Case of the Art Museum. In Cultivating Differences: Symbolic Boundaries and the Making of Inequality. Michèle Lamont and Marcel Fournier, eds. Pp. 187–209. Chicago: University of Chicago Press.
Zureik, Elia. 1994
Palestinian Refugees and Peace. Journal of Palestine Studies 24(1):5–17.

Index

Words in boldface type indicate key terms.

Abandonment, 158
Abbas, Ackbar, 369
Abélès, Marc, 276–277
Aborigines of Australia, 56, 60–61, 95, 291–293, 320, 329, 429
Abortion, 122–124, 322
Absolute cultural relativism, 12
Abu-Lughod, Lila, 46
Abuse (domestic) of children and women, 225–226
Acculturation
Achieved position (or status), 248
See also Class
Acquired immune deficiency syndrome, *see* HIV/AIDS
Adabraka, Ghana, 386
Adaptation, 15–16
Adams, Kathleen, 377
Adams, Vincanne, 176–178
Adolescence, 144
and industrialism, 145
and genital cutting, 145–147
and marking of the body, 145
and powerlessness, 24
and puberty, 144
and gender identity, 145–148
cultural versus biological explanations of, 10–11
Mead-Freeman controversy, 10–11
sexuality during, 38–39
whether or not universal, 144–145
Adoption, 196, 197–199
See also Fostering
Adulthood and personality, 150–153
Aerobic capacity, 69
Afghanistan, 122, 303
African Americans
and the informal economy, 77
anorexia nervosa cases, 163
Black English, 339
college women and romantic love, 204
condom use and HIV/AIDS risk, 158–159
household formation, 216–217
poverty and social networks, 231
prostitution and family affiliation, 223
racial conflict, 100–101, 396–397
African Brazilians, 165
African Genesis, 263
African Indians of Belize, 226
African Political Systems, 262
Agar, Michael, 337, 346
Age
and consumption, 89
and division of labor among foragers, 59
as a basis for microculture formation, 23–24
as a factor during fieldwork, 38–39
Age grades/age sets, 236
as elaborated in some African cultures, 24
Aged people (seniors), 152–153
Aging of populations, 115
Agency (individual will)
and karma, 320–321
and migration, 386
and political anthropology, 262
part of key debate in cultural anthropology, 14
Aggression
and "politics" among primates, 263–264
in infants, 139
See also Violence, Warfare
Agoraphobia, 163
Agriculture, 68
and kinship, 186
and reproduction, 114–115
collectivized, 73–75
family farming, 68–71
general characteristics of, 68
Green Revolution, 70, 409
industrialized, 72–73
sustainability, 75
Agta of the Philippines, 58
Ahimsa, 123
Aidoo, Ama Ata, 194
Ainu of Japan, 168
Aka of Central Africa, 151
Akinsha, Konstantin, 372–373, 379–380
Alcohol, 89, 94
Alfalfa Club, 242
Algonquins of the Chesapeake region, 271
Allen, Susan, 349–350
Allison, Anne, 136–137
Alter, Joseph, 374–375
Ambanja, Madagascar, 383–392
Ambilineal descent, 195
American Anthropological Association
attention to fieldwork safety, 50
code of ethics, 48
American kinship, 196
Ames, David, 245
Ames, Michael, 371
Amish of the United States, 41, 95
Analysis of data
qualitative data, 46-48
quantitative data, 45-46
Ancestors, as supernaturals, 314
Andaman Islands, 48–49, 59, 265, 424
The Andaman Islanders, 9
Anderson, Barbara, 160, 168
Anderson, Benedict, 278, 428
Anderson, Richard L., 362
Andrews, Tracy J., 194
Animatism, 313
Animism, 311
Anomie, 128
Anorexia nervosa, 163
Anthropology
fields within, 5–8
forensic, 8
four-field approach, 5
general anthropology, 4
holistic approach, 9, 15, 32
roots in colonialism, 5
See also Applied anthropology, Archaeology, Cultural anthropology, Linguistic anthropology, Physical anthropology
Anthropomorphic supernaturals, 214
Antinatalism, 118
Apache of Arizona, 348
Apartheid, 22, 89–90, 250–252
Apes, *see* Baboons, Chimpanzees, Orangutans, Physical anthropology
Appadurai, Arjun, 93
Appalachia, 122, 325–326
Applbaum, Kalman D., 204–205
Applied anthropology, 8
See also Clinical Medical Anthropology, Development Anthropology, Forensic Anthropology, Museum Anthropology
Arapesh of Papua New Guinea, 134–135
Archaeology
and community development, 415
and evidence of queens in early Honduras, 274
as a field of general anthropology, 5–6
and repatriation claims, 373
ethno-archaeology and the study of art, 363–364
Architecture, 368–369
Archives as data sources, 43, 159
Arnold, Marigene, 365
Ardrey, Robert, 263
Arens, William, 202
Argentina, 387
Ariaal of Kenya, 65, 147
Ariès, Philippe, 139
Armchair anthropology, 30
Armelagos, George, 6–7
Armstrong, Douglas V., 71
Argonauts of the Western Pacific, 9, 31, 33, 50
Army, standing, 273
Art, 360
and museums, 371–372
and power, 365
anthropological study of, 360, 363–364
architecture and decorative arts, 368–371
categories of, 360–361
change in post-communist societies, 379–380
claims to ownership, 372–373
ethno-esthetics, 362–363
fine art versus folk art, 360–362
performance arts, 367–368
play as art, 373–376
theater, 368
transnational change, 377–378

Art, *continued*
verbal arts, 363
See also Expressive culture
Artifacts, 5
Artists, 364–365
Arembepe, Brazil, 199
Asad, Talal, 262
Ascribed position (or status), 248
race, ethnicity and caste, 249–257
Ashanti of West Africa, 270, 271
Assault on Paradise, 9
Assimilation, 410
"A-Type" males, 18
Aung San Suu Kyi, 280
Australia, *see* Aborigines of Australia
Authority, 263
Avunculocality, 208
Awe, Bolanle, 271
Axinn, W. G., 229–230
Aymara of Bolivia, 20
Ayurvedic medicine, 170–171, 177
Aztecs of Mexico, 290, 317, 318

Baan Naa Sakae village of Thailand, 164
Baboons, 6
Bachnik, Jane, 215
Baer, Lars-Ander, 424
Balanced exchange, 97
Balanced reciprocity, 97
Balgo Hills region of Australia, 95
Bali, Indonesia, 20, 153, 422–423
Banaras, *see* Varanasi
Band, 265–266
Bandit Queen of India, *see* Phulan Devi
Banditry, 297–298
Bangangté of Cameroon, 195
Bangladesh, 120–121, 236–237, 428
Bantu of Congo, 54
Baraka, Eqbal, 142
Barberton, Ohio, 78
Barbie, 174
Bardhan, Pranab, 69
Barfield, Thomas J., 68, 303
Barley, Nigel, 34–35
Barlett, Peggy, 69, 72, 73, 94
Barnard, Alan, 199, 202, 204, 226, 228
Barry, Herbert III, 144
Barter, *see* Trade
Basarwa of the Kalahari, 239–240
Basch, Linda, 385
Baseball, 311, 374
Basic needs fund, 86
Basque region of Spain, 138, 279, 373
Basso, Keith, 348
Baths (public), 375–376
Beall, Cynthia M., 66–68
Beals, Alan, 40
Beatty, Andrew, 93–94
Beck, Lois, 64, 267–268
Becker, Gary, 90
Becoming a Doctor, 25, 174
Bedu [Bedouin], 46
Beirut, Lebanon, 224–225
Bell, Diane, 329
Belmar, Pennsylvania, 77
Below-replacement-level fertility, 115
Bemessi of Cameroon, 245
Benedict, Ruth, 135
Bennett, Sharon, 6–7
Berdache, 149–150
Berlin, Brent, 161
Berlin, Elois Ann, 161
Bermann, Marc, 5
Bernal, Martin, 342
Bernard, H. Russell, 40, 422
Berreman, Gerald, 9, 249
Best, David, 372
Bethnal Green, England, 230
Beyene, Yewoubdar, 41, 152
Bhardwaj, Surinder, 316
Bhutto, Benazir, 274
Bible, 324, 325
Big man politics, 268
Big woman politics, 269–270
Bilharz, Joy, 281
Bilineal (bilateral) **descent,** 190, 195–196
Bilingualism, 8, 338, 355
Billig, Michael, 205
Binary oppositions in structural analysis, 312
Biological anthropology, *see* Physical anthropology
Biological determinism, 13
Biomedicine (Western)
focus of critical medical anthropology, 173–174
training of medical students, 25
Bipedalism, 15
Bird, Sharon, 242
Bird-David, Nurit, 56
Birth, 137–138
Birth control, 122–124
See also Abortion, Contraception, Family Planning
Birth order
and homosexuality, 148
and marriage rules among the Nambudiri of India, 201
Birth rate, *see* Fertility
Black English, 339
Blacks, *see* African Americans, African Brazilians
Blackwood, Evelyn, 194
Bledsoe, Carolyn, 100, 124
Blindness, 203–204
Bloch, Alexia, 34
Blok, Anton, 297
Blood as a basis of kinship, 185, 196
Blood feuds, 299
Blood, Robert O., 224
Blood sports, 375
Boas, Franz, 43, 250, 334, 362, 363, 364
Bodh Gaya, India, 316
Bodley, John H., 421, 424–425
Body
body modification practices and groups, 244–245
hair, 20, 22
looks and partner selection, 203
marking during adolescence, 145
perceptions of in Mayan ethnomedicine, 160–161
Body fat and fertility, 114
Body language, *see* Paralanguage
Bogin, Barry, 137
Bohannan, Paul, 102
Bolivia, 5, 20, 326, 387
Bom Jesus, Brazil, 126, 138
Bonding theory (Western), 138
Borzu Qermezi, 268
Bosa, Italy, 316–317
Bosco, Joseph, 276
Boserup, Ester, 70, 194, 430
Bosnian refugees, 401–402
Boswell, A. Ayres, 242–242
Bott, Elizabeth, 230–232
Bourdieu, Pierre, 89, 365, 372
Bourgois, Philippe, 10, 36, 49, 77
Bowen, John, 152, 313, 326
Brahmans of India, 200–201, 254–255
Brandes, Stanley, 152
Branding, 244
Brando, Cheyenne, 127
Brazil
African Brazilians, 165
Arembepe, 199
attraction to Western goods among indigenous peoples, 103–104
Bom Jesus, 126, 138
child death and poverty, 125
household headship, 216
Kayapo, 267
medical pluralism, 165
Mehinaku, 134
Mundurucu, 63–64
race categories, 250
sexuality as a research topic, 48
sisal scheme, 104–105
See also Yanomami
Brazilian migrants, 385
Bray, Tamara, 373
Bread (white), 104
Breastfeeding
and fertility, 113
and kinship, 196–197
Breast talk, 136–137
Brenneis, Donald, 346–347
Brideprice, 128
as part of marriage arrangements, 205
Bride-service, 205
Bridewealth, *see* brideprice
Brink, Judith, 388
Britain
importance of women's natal kin in London, 230
karma concept among Hindu women, 320–321
Brooks, Alison, 152
Broude, Gwen, 150–151
Brow, James, 279
Brown, Carolyn H., 320
Brown, Judith K., 24, 62, 144, 225–226, 271, 315–316
Brown, Nathan, 297–298
Brownell, Susan, 374
Browner, Carole, 115, 119, 150
Brownmiller, Susan, 361, 379
Bruce, Judith, 91
Brumberg, Joan, 163
Bruner, Edward M., 377
Budapest, Hungary, 253–254
Buddha (Siddhartha Gautama), 321
Buddha's Day (Visakha Puja), 315
Buddhism
and adjustment of Khmer refugees, 399–400
and attitudes toward abortion in Japan, 123, 322
and suicide, 127
as a world religion, 321–322
in Burma, 321–322
in Japan, 322
Budgeting (household), 85, 90–92
Buikstra, Jane, 274
Bulgaria, 105
Bulimia, 163
Bunzel, Ruth, 363, 364
Burial of the dead, 5, 6, 311
Burkina Faso, 430
Burma, 321–322
Burton, Michael L., 208
Burundi, 300
Bushmen, *see* Ju/wasi
Byrne, Bryan, 250

Cahokia chiefdom, 270
Cairo Population Conference, 120
Cambodia, *see* Kampuchea
Cameron, Mary, 255
Cameroon, 245
Camino, Linda, 366
Canada, 42, 125, 397–398, 427
See also Inuit, Kwakwaka'wakw
Cancian, Frank, 71
Cannibalism, 318
Capital, 73
Capitalism, 54
and narcissism, 140
as a form of Western ethnocentrism, 12
market exchange, 98–99
Marx on, 249
world-economic system and, 56, 87–88
Caplan, Patricia, 303
Cargo cults, 328, and concepts of development, 414–415
Caribbean region
household formation, 216–219
Rastafarianism, 327–328

See also Belize, Cuba, Haiti, Jamaica
Carneiro, Robert, 305
Carnival, 49, 316–317
Carstairs, G. Morris, 117
Carsten, Janet, 194, 196–197
Cash crops, 104–105, 420–421, 426, 430
Caste, 249
and kinship in Central India, 9
in India, 254-257
Castration, 150
Cátedra, Maria, 33, 44
Catholicism
and infant and child mortality among the poor in Brazil, 126
and divorce, 226
and fertility, 120
and suicide, 127
doctrine of, 313
Cattle
as sacred in Hinduism, 14
as vectors in Kayasanur forest disease, 160
Caudill, W., 138
Causality, 125
Cavalli-Sforza, L., 335
Celibacy, 118, 303
Census, 273
Central Asia, 299–300
Ceremonial fund, 85
Cernea, Michael, 388, 419
Chagnon, Napoleon, 40, 62, 187, 294, 302–303
Chain migration, 394
Chambers, Robert, 422
Change, *see* Cultural change
Chant, Sylvia, 217
Charisma, 319
Chavez, Leo, 73, 388
Chen, Robert F., 88
Chengdu, China, 224
Chennai (Madras), India, 202
Cherlin, Andrew, 232
Chernoff, John Miller, 363
Chiangmai region of Thailand, 237, 245
Chiapas region of Mexico, 71, 161–163, 431
See also Maya
Chiefdoms, 270–271
Child(ren)
and food stealing among the Mende, 100
as a concept, 139
as sex workers, 77–78
as sources of security for parents, 118
changing consumption preferences in Ecuador, 104
costs and fertility, 118
disputes, 346–347
formal schooling, 141–143
infant and child mortality as affecting fertility, 118
informal learning, 141
labor value and fertility, 118
language, 344–346
malnutrition, 104–105
personality formation cross-culturally, 139–140
preschool child and personality, 140–141
work roles, 62, 65
See also Child care, Child neglect, Fertility, Fostering, Infanticide
Child care
among the Aka of Central of Africa, 151
and personality formation, 134–135
maternal and paternal roles, 151
Children of Six Cultures Study, 62–63, 70, 139–140
Childbirth, *see* Birth
Chimpanzees, 6, 158, 263–264
China
birth control policy, 112, 115, 123
emergence of civil society, 257
ethnic minorities, 251–253
family businesses, 220–221
female infant and child mortality, 112
guanxixue, 94
Internet use for protest, 304
kinship in, 185
markets and regional integration, 24
marital satisfaction, 224
marriage squeeze, 112
permanent markets in Shanghai, 99
preschool children, 140–141
sports in, 374
theater in, 379–380
treatment of Tibetan culture, 253
views on human evolution and race in, 22
writing system, 341
Cholera, 160
Christianity
and cricket in the Trobriands, 378
and fertility, 112
and potlatching, 82, 107
as a world religion, 324–326
in Appalachia, 325–326
in Haiti, 325
missionaries and European colonialism, 12
See also Catholicism
Chromosomes, 138
The Chrysanthemum and the Sword, 135
Cinderella, 312, 364
Circular migration, 388
Circumcision (male), 145–146
See also Female genital mutilation
Citizenship, 272
Civil society, 257
in post-socialist states, 257–258
Civilization
as defined by hairlessness in China, 22
in relation to culture, 15
Clan, 266
Clark, Gracia, 431
Clark, Sam, 118
Class, 20
and consumption, 89
as a basis of microculture formation, 20–21
as a factor during fieldwork, 37
as a form of social stratification, 248–249
Class struggle, 21
Clay (substance), 170–171
Clay, Jason, 278, 299–300
Clifford, James, 366
Clinton, Hillary, 242, 273
Clinical medical anthropology, 175
approaches to, 175–176
Clitoridectomy, 145–147
Clothing, *see* Dress
Clubs, 241–242
Coca, 169
Cochrane, D. Glynn, 419, 420
Codes (linguistic), 339
code-mixing, 339
code-switching, 339
gender codes, 339–340, 345–346
Cognatic descent
Cohen, Jeffrey, 415
Cohen, Mark Nathan, 6–7
Cohen, Shaul, 300
Cohn, Bernard, 254
Cole, Douglas, 107
Colen, Shellee, 120–121
Collado-Ardón, Rolando, 161–163
Collectivized agriculture, 73
labor patterns in, 74
Collins, Joseph, 88
Colombia, 173
Colonialism
and anthropology, 30
and cricket in the Trobriands, 378
and genocide of Native Americans, 130, 159–160
and indigenous legal systems, 292–293
and kinship change among the Minangkabau, 194
and orientalism, 354
and women's status, 70
and the Bengal famine of 1943–44, 88
attempts to suppress potlatching, 82
plantation mode of production, 72
topic in political anthropology, 262
Colson, Elizabeth, 118, 262, 295
CO-MADRES, 247–248
Comaroff, John, 251
Comic books, 354
Coming of Age in Samoa, 10–11, 145
Communication, 334
The Communist Manifesto, 73
Communitas, 323
Comparative approach, *see* Ethnology
Computers and data analysis, 46
Condom use, 158–159
Confederacies, 271
Conflict, *see* Social conflict
Congo, 54, 101, 118–119, 336
Consorte, Josildeth Gomes, 250
Consumerism, 84
Consumption, 54
general characteristics of, 83–84
of Hong Kong migrants to Canada, 397–398
See also Consumerism, Consumption funds, Minimalism, Modes of consumption
Consumption funds, 85
ceremonial fund, 85
entertainment fund, 85
recurrent cost fund, 85
tax/rent fund, 85
Contact with European culture
and dreams among the Mehinaku, 134
and women's political status, 270, 271
See also Colonialism
Contagious magic, 310
Contraception, 122–123
Cooperative, 246
of craftswomen in Panama, 246
of farmers in India, 246
Cornell, Laurel, 227, 229
Corporate farming, 72
characteristics of, 72–73
in the United States, 72–73
Costin, Cathy, 7
Counihan, Carol, 316–317
Cousin marriage
as practiced in South India, 202
forbidden between first cousins in the United States, 184
preferred form of marriage in some places, 184
Couvade, 150–151
Coward, E. Walter Jr., 245-256
Cows, *see* Cattle
Cranial capacity, 15
Crapanzano, Vincent, 47
Crawford, C. Joanne, 138
Credit cards, 106
Cree of North America, 56
Creole, 343
Crested Kimono, 36–37, 221
Crete, 298
Cricket, 378
Crime and Custom in Savage Society, 286

Critical cultural relativism, 12
Critical development anthropology, 422
Critical legal studies, 286
Critical medical anthropology, 172
approaches in, 172–174
Cross cousin, 202
Crossette, Barbara, 280
Cuba, 417
Cultural adaptation, 15–16
Cultural anthropology
as field of general anthropology 5, 8
distinctive features, 8–14
Cultural change
anthropology and the study of, 408–410
in Brazil, 9
theories of, 410–413
See also Development
Cultural configuration, 135
Cultural constructionism, 13
Cultural diversity as a value of cultural anthropology, 13
Cultural hegemony of the West, 20
Cultural imperialism, 12
Chinese takeover of Tibetan medicine, 253
diffusion and, 409–410
of whites over Native Americans, 425
See also Colonialism, Development
Cultural materialism, 14
and Aztec ritual, 318
and India's sacred cows, 14
and Yanomami warfare, 302–303
and youth gangs, 243–244
Cultural relativism, 12
and religion, 310
as a characteristic of cultural anthropology, 11–12
See also Absolute cultural relativism, Critical cultural relativism
Cultural Resource Management, 8
Cultural Survival Quarterly, 13
Culture, 4, 14–15
as adaptive, 15–16
as integrated, 19
as learned, 19
as related to nature, 16–18, 55–56
characteristics of culture, 15–20
Culture and Imperialism, 353
Culture and personality school, 134–136
Culture of poverty, 136–137
Culture-bound syndrome, 161
examples of, 161–162
Cuna Indians of Panama, 170
Curtin, Philip D., 392

Dalby, Liza, 38, 349
Dalits, 254–255, 414
Daly, Mary, 147
Dams, 160
Dance, 165–166
Dando, William A., 88
Danger in fieldwork, 49–50
Dani of Irian Jaya, 117
Dannhaeuser, Norbert, 98
Darshan, 319
Darwin, Charles/Darwinian theory, 15, 294, 360
See also Biological determinism, Sociobiology
Das, Veena, 294
Dating and violence, 295
Daugherty, Mary Lee, 325–326
Daughter preference, 118
Davidson, Dana, 141–141
Davis, Douglas A., 116
Davis, Susan Schaefer, 116
Davis-Floyd, Robbie, 137–138, 174–175
Dayak of Indonesia, 7
Deacon, Bernard, 49
Dead Sea, 169
Death, attitudes toward, 153
See also Burial of the dead, Mortality
Death penalty, 290
Deaton, Angus, 92
Deductive research approach, 31
Deforestation
and disease in India, 160
in Haiti, 420–421
Deities, *see* Supernaturals
Delaney, Carol, 145
Democratization, 280
Demographic transition model, 115
anthropological critique of, 115
Demography, 112
Descent, 186
various types of, 190–196
See also Family, Kinship
Detachment, of parents from children, 125–126
Development (of a person), *see* Life-cycle
Development (international), 408
and malnutrition in Colombia, 173
diseases of, 160
four-field approaches to, 413–415
human rights and, 432–433
indigenous peoples and, 424–430
organizational approaches, 415–419
research methods in, 422–423
theories of, 410–413
women and, 430–432
See also Development anthropology, Development apparatus, Development project, Development rhetoric
Development anthropology, 8, 408
Development apparatus, 418
Development project
anthropological critique of, 421–422
comparative studies of, 420–421
design, 420–421
male bias in, 70, 430
project cycle, 419–420
Development rhetoric, 413
Devereaux, George, 122–123
Devolution, 279
De Waal, Franz, 263–264
Diachronic analysis, 408
Diagnosis in medical systems, 164–164
Dialect, 339
Diana, Princess of Wales, 227
Diaspora population, 253
See also Displaced persons, Migration, Rom, New immigrants
Diarrhea, 165
Dickemann, Mildred, 125
Diet
and fieldwork adjustment, 39
cannibalism, 318
food preferences and taboos, 16
See also Malnutrition, Nutrition
Diffusion, 409
examples of, 409–410
Dikötter, Frank, 22, 273
Di Leonardo, Micaela, 185
Direct infanticide, 125
Discourse, 31, 336, 346–347
Discrimination
against Aboriginal youth in Australian courts, 291–293
against gypsies in England, 291
against women in development projects, 70, 430
as perceived by Indo-Canadians, 254
in the legal profession in the United States, 289
Disease
and colonial contact, 159–160
caused by development, 160
culture-bound syndromes, 161–162
infectious disease, 158–159
palaeopathology, 6
See also Eating disorders, HIV/AIDS, Malnutrition
Displaced persons, 388
Displacement (linguistic), 336
Dispute and Settlement in Rural Turkey, 286
Dispute resolution
international, 305
neighborhood/local, 295
Dissanayake, Ellen, 360
Distributional approach to development, 412–413
Divale, William T., 125, 126, 129, 208
Divination, 164
Diviners, 319
Division of labor
among family farmers, 68–70
among foragers, 57–59
among horticulturalists, 62–63
among pastoralists, 65
under socialism in Romania, 74
Divorce, 226–228
DNA, 6, 274
Doctrine, 312, characteristics of 312–313
Dogs, 295
Dole, Elizabeth, 242
Domestic violence, 129, 296–297, 430–431
Domestication, of plants and animals, 61
Dominant caste, 255
Dominican migrants, 394–395
Dominican Republic, 390–391
Donlon, Jon, 375
Dorgan, Howard, 325
Double descent (double unilineal descent), 195
Douglas, Mary, 92, 93, 96, 102
Dowayo of Cameroon, West Africa, 34–35
Dowry, 127–128
as groomprice in India, 127
Mediterranean type, 205
Dowry death, 129
Draper, Patricia, 152
Dress
and political symbolism, 275
and widowhood, 228–229
See also Body, Looks
Drinking, as culturally constructed, 16–17
Driving, gender differences in mortality from, 124–125
Drucker, Charles, 433
Drugs, 77, 363, 425
Dualist view of nature and culture in the West, 55
Dube, S. C., 9
Dufour, Darna, 414
Duranti, Alessandro, 336
Durga, 313
Durkheim, Emile, 127–128, 249, 255, 311
Du Toit, Brian, 281
Dwyer, Daisy, 91
Dyson, Tim, 69, 229

Earle, Timothy, 270
Easter Island, 334, 335
Eating, as culturally constructed, 16
See also Eating disorders, Flavor, Food preferences and taboos
Eating disorders, 163
Ebonic, 339
Eck, Diana, 319
Ecological/epidemiological approach in medical anthropology, 158
examples of, 158–160
Economic anthropology, 54
Economic growth model of development, 410–412
Economics as a discipline, 54
Economic system, 54
Ecuador, 94, 104

Eddas, 312
Edo of Nigeria, 271
Education *see* School, Socialization
Efe of Congo, 101
Ego, 187
Egypt, 142, 202, 240, 297–298, 349, 388
Eickelman, Dale, 267
Eisenhart, Margaret A., 204
Elder, Joseph, 255
El Saadawi, Nawal, 240
El Salvador, 218, 247–248, 350, 352–353
The Elementary Structures of Kinship, 186
Elimination, as culturally constructed, 18
Ember, Carol R., 68–69
Emic, 13
  analysis of Aztec cannibalism, 318
  and etic approaches in cultural anthropology, 13–14
  categories of disease, 161–162
  perceptions of culture and nature, 56–57
  racial classifications in Haiti and Brazil, 250
Emotion, and illness, 165
Enculturation, 19, 134
  See also Life-cycle, School
Endogamy, 202
  and women's kinship networks, 229
Engels, Frederick, 20–21, 73
The Elementary Forms of the Religious Life, 311
England, *see* Britain
Entitlements, 86–87, 412–413
  See also Famine
Environmentalism
  and indigenous peoples, 426
  and youth movements in Poland, 257–258
Epics, 312–313
Epidemiological approach in medical anthropology, 158
  examples, 158–160
Eskimo, *see* Inuit
Eskimo kinship system, 189
Esman, Milton, 236, 299, 300
Estioko-Griffin, Agnes, 58
Estioko-Griffin, Bion, 58
Estonia, 151
Estrus, 6
Ethics in research, 47–48
Ethnic conflict, 299–300, 396–397
Ethnicity, 22
  and art/expressive culture, 365–367
  as a basis of ascribed status, 251–251
  as a basis for microcultural formation, 22–23
  as similar to race and caste, 249
  See also Discrimination, Ethnic conflict, Race
Ethnoarchaeology, 363–364
Ethnobotany, 169
Ethnocentrism, 11–12
Ethnocide, 130
Ethnography, 9
Ethnology, 10
Ethnomedicine, 160
  diagnosis, 164–165
  disease concepts, 161–161
  healing modalities, 165–170
  perceptions of the body, 160–161
  preventive practices, 163–164
  See also Culture-bound syndrome
Ethnomusicology, 367
  example of, 367–368
Ethiopia, 327–328
Etic, 14
  and emic approaches in cultural anthropology, 13–14
Etienne, Mona, 194
Europe, 282
Euro-Americans
  college women and romantic love, 204
  condom use and HIV/AIDS risk, 158–159
  prostitution and family disaffiliation, 223
Euhemerism, 314
European Space Agency, 281–282
Evans-Pritchard, E. E., 64, 262
Everett, Daniel, 326
Evil eye, 162, 165
Exchange, 54
  balanced exchange, 97
  balanced reciprocity, 97
  exploitation, 101
  general characteristics of, 93–97
  generalized exchange in marriage, 186
  generalized reciprocity, 97
  in marriage arrangements, 127–128, 205
  market exchange, 97
  money-based, 96
  of people, 96–97
  redistribution, 97
  restricted exchange in marriage, 186
  sustained unbalanced exchange, 100–101
  theories of, 102
  See also Gift-giving, Kula, Modes of Exchange, Potlatch, Trade
Exogamy, 203
  and women's kinship networks, 229
Explanatory models in health care, 177–179
Expressive culture, 360
Extended household (or family), 189, 215
Extensive economic strategy, 57
Ezaro, Spain, 218–219

Fabian, Johannes, 336
Fabrega, Horacio Jr., 24, 144, 163
Factions, 276
  in Belize and Taiwan, 276
Factory studies, 76
Fallowing, 62
Family, 214
  See also Descent, Household, Kinship, Marriage
Family businesses, 220–222
Family disaffiliation, 223
Family farming
  as a form of agriculture, 68
  change in, 71
  labor patterns, 68–69
  property relations, 70–71
  public/private dichotomy in, 68
  relationships between daughter-in-law and mother-in-law in the United States, 222
Family planning, 114–115, 120–122
Famine, 87, 88
Farmer, Paul, 161
Fat talk, 347
Fatherhood, 150–151
Feast of the Sacrifice, 326–327
Feces, 5, 18
Feeley-Harnick, Gillian, 10
Feinsilver, Julie M., 417
Feldman-Savelsberg, Pamela, 195
Female genital mutilation/ Female genital surgery, 145
  in the United States, 393
  various types, 145–147
Female-headed household (matrifocal household), 91, 216–217
Femicide, 129
Ferguson, James, 418
Ferguson, R. Brian, 130, 301–303
Fertility, 112
  among Hutterites and Mennonites of North America, 112, 114
  and Hindu ritual, 320
  and Venus figurines, 364
  as affected by women's body fat and exercise, 114
  below-replacement-level fertility, 115
  family-level decision-making, 118–119
  highest among agriculturalists, 114–115
  low among foragers, 113–114
  politics of, 118–122
  replacement-level fertility, 115
  techniques of fertility control, 122–124
Feudalism, 54
Feuding, 299
Field, Karen L., 362
Field methods, *see* Fieldwork, Research methods
Field notes, 44
Fieldwork, 30
  and age, 38–39
  and class, 37
  and culture shock, 39–40
  and gender, 37–38
  and religion, 39
  fieldwork methods, 40–45
  funding for, 34
  gift-giving, 35–36
  multiple methods, 43
  participant observation, 30
  preparations for, 34
  race issues in, 37
  rapport, 35
  site selection, 34–35
  team approach, 43
Fiji, 326
Films, 354
Finland, 125
Fire-walking, 320
Fiske, John, 100–101
Fitchen, Janet, 41
The Flats, 102, 137, 231
Flavors, as culturally defined, 16
Fleuhr-Lobban, Carolyn, 48
Flowers, 370–371
Flutes (sacred), 23
Focal vocabulary, 343
Folbre, Nancy, 91
Fonseca, Isabel, 253
Food
  cooked meals in South Wales, 219–220
  eating as culturally constructed, 16
  exchange in Oman, 95
  preferences and taboos, 92–93, 150
  theft by children among the Mende, 100
  See also Diet, Famine, Malnutrition, Nutrition
Food gathering, *see* Foraging
Food production
  See also Agriculture, Animal Domestication, Family Farming, Horticulture, Plantation Agriculture, Collectivized Agriculture, Industrialism
Foraging, 56
  consumption funds and shares, 85
  general features, 56–57
  labor, 57–58
  political organization and, 265–266
  property relations, 59
  relatedness metaphor between humans and nature, 56
  reproduction and, 113–114
  sustainability, 59–60
Fore of Papua New Guinea, 89
Forensic anthropology, 8

Formal sector, 76
Fortes, Meyer, 262
Fortune, Reo, 9, 134
Forty, 152
Fossey, Dian, 4
Foster, George, 136, 160, 168
Fostering (of children)
and food theft among the Mende, 100
and poverty in The Flats, 231
as a basis of kinship, 197–199
Foucault, Michel, 290
Four-field anthropology
and art, 360
and cultural change, 408
and international development, 413–415
and migration, 384
and politics, 262
approach to kinship studies, 184–185
as a debated issue, 5
Fox, Robin, 184
Frame analysis, 335
France, 276–277, 300, 372
Franke, Richard W., 414
Frankel, Francine R., 409
Fraternities, 17, 241–242
Fraternity Gang Rape, 241
Fratkin, Elliot, 64, 147
Frazer, James, 30, 310, 311
Freed, Ruth, 215
Freed, Stanley, 215
Freedman, Diane, 39
Freedom from Fear, 280
Freeman, James, 42, 320
Freud, Sigmund/Freudian theory, 134, 151, 312
Fricke, Thomas E., 229–230
Friedl, Ernestine, 37
Friendship
among baboons, 6
and conflict among settled foragers in the Kalahari, 239–230
and exchange in New York City, 238
as a cultural universal, 237–238
in prisons, 238–239
in southern Spain, 238
Frisch, Rose, 114
Fuller, Christopher, 200
Functionalism, 82
and art, 363
and political anthropology, 262
and religion, 311
Funding field research, 33
Funerals, 371

Galdikas, Biruté, 7
Gale, Faye, 291, 293
Galt, Anthony, 71
Galvin, Kathleen, 64
Gambia, 245
Games, 141, 374
Gandhi, Indira, 274, 294
Gandhi, Mahatma, 254, 274, 303–304
Gang, *see* Youth gang
Gapun village of Papua New Guinea, 414–415
Garb, Yoni, 143
Gardener, Margaret, 49
Gardening (decorative), 370–371
See also Horticulture
Gardner, Katy, 412–413
Garifuna of Belize, 226
Garbage Project, 5
Garreau, Joel, 24
Gathering, *see* Foraging
Gaulin, Stephen
Geertz, Clifford, 5, 15, 31, 312
Generalized reciprocity, 97
Gender, 23, 138
and consumption, 89
and family businesses, 220–222
and ritual in Islam, 326–327
and television in Japan, 350–351
as a basis for microcultural formation, 23
as a factor during fieldwork, 37–38
codes (linguistic), 339–340, 345–346
differences in "chimpanzee politics," 263–264
differences in elimination patterns in India, 18
differences in sleeping patterns in India, 17–18
division of labor and household type, 219–220
identity in adolescence, 145–147
segregation, 68, 241–242
versus sex, 23
Geneaology, 188
General anthropology, 5
Generalized reciprocity, 97
Genghis Khan, 68
Genitals, 138
Genocide, 130
Geophagia (earth-eating), 169–170
Germany, 12
Gestures, *see* Paralanguage
Ghana, 84–85, 92, 194, 386
Ghost Dance, 328
Ghosts, 164
Gifford-Gonzales, Diane, 59
Gift-giving
and favors in China, 94
and fieldwork, 35–36
the pure gift, 99–100
See also Exchange
Gilman, David, 270
Ginsberg, Faye, 115, 117
Gittelsohn, Joel, 92
Glick Schiller, Nina, 385
Globalization, 19
Gluckman, Max, 286
Gmelch, George, 311
Godelier, Maurice, 96
Godparenthood, 196, 199, 431
Gods, *see* Supernaturals
Gold, Ann, 316
Gold, Stevan J., 398–399, 401
Goldberg, Harvey E., 323
Goldberg, Ellen S., 323–324
Golde, Peggy, 37
The Golden Bough, 30
Goldschmidt, Walter, 68
Goldstein, Melvyn C., 66–68, 208, 220
Goldstone, Jack, 300
Gonzalez, Nancie, 216
Good, Anthony, 199, 202, 204, 226, 228
Goodale, Jane C., 60–61
Goodall, Jane, 6, 158
Goodman, Madeleine J., 58
Goody, Jack, 24–25, 69, 104, 186, 205, 215, 317, 370–371
Gore, Tipper, 242
Gow, David D., 421
Graburn, Nelson, 366
Graham, Katharine, 242
Grameen Bank, 237
Grammar, 338
Grassroots approaches to development, 418–419
Greece, 37, 41, 152
Green, Thomas J., 373
Green, Victoria, D., 373
A Green Estate, 10
Green Revolution, 70, 409
Greenhalgh, Susan, 123
Greenough, Paul, 88
Gregor, Thomas, 134, 242
Gremillion, Helen, 163
Grenier, Guillermo, 76
Grinker, Richard, 101
Gross, Daniel, 40–41, 103, 104
Groups
age grades/age sets, 24, 236
body modifiers, 244–245
categories of, 236
civil society, 257–258
cooperatives, 246
indigenous people's organizations, 428–429
women's rights groups, 247–248
work groups, 245–247
Growing Up in Samoa, 10–11
Growth (economic) approach to development, 410–412
Growth (human), *see* Life-cycle
Grubman, Lizzie, 207
Guggenheim, Scott, 366
Gugler, Joseph, 300–301
Guidoni, Enrico, 368–369
Güneş-Ayata, Ayşe, 274
Guratba region in Australia, 329
Gusii of Kenya, 62–63, 139–140
Gutkind, Lee, 174
Gynophobia, 242
Gypsies
discrimination against in England, 291
fieldwork among in England, 42, 186
See also Rom

Hackenberg, Robert, 385
Hacker, Andrew, 22, 90, 216–217, 339
Hagen people of Papua New Guinea, 55–56, 268–269
Haile Selassie, 327–328
Hair, 20, 22
Haiti
braceros (migrant laborers), 390–391
Christianity in, 325
Haitian immigrants in the United States, 76
Haitians in New York City and amniocentesis, 124
HIV/AIDS as defined in, 161
race categories in, 250
reforestation project, 420–421
Haj, 315
Hamabata, Mathews, 36–37, 221
Hamman, 376
Hammersley, Martin, 40
Hammond, Peter, 245
Han people of China, 251–253
Hancock, Graham, 21, 416–417
Hand trembling as a diagnostic technique, 165
Harambee, 419
Hardon, Anita, 168–169
Harner, Michael, 318
Harris, Marvin, 15, 31, 92, 93, 113, 125, 126, 129, 249, 250, 273, 302–303, 318, 335
Harrison, Michelle, 174
Hart, C. W. M., 60–61
Hartmann, Betsy, 120
Hastrup, Kirstin, 45
Ha Tsuen village of Hong Kong, 193
Haugerud, Angelique, 419
Havel, Václav, 282
Hawaii, 271, 379
Hawthorne effect, 40
Headhunting, 19, 299
Headship (of household), 215
Healers, 167–168, 175
Healing
community healing among the Ju/wasi, 165–166
healing substances, 168–170, 175
humoral systems, 166–178
plural systems of, 176–179
See also Diagnosis, Healers, Medicine
Health communication, 175–176
Hearts of Sorrow, 42
Heider, Karl, 117
Heise, Lori, 430–431
Helweg, Arthur W., 400
Helweg, Usha M., 400
Henderson, Eric B., 194
Herding, *see* Pastoralism

Herdt, Gilbert, 145, 148
Herzfeld, Michael, 298
Heterotopia, 371
Hiatt, Betty, 58
Hijiras of India, 149–150
Hill, Jane H., 343
"The Hill," 24
Hiltebeitel, Alf, 319, 320
Hindi language, 337–338
Hindus of the Himalayas, 9
Hinduism
  and caste, 254–255
  and frequency of sexual intercourse, 117–118
  as a world religion, 319–321
  attitudes toward abortion, 123
  beliefs about sexuality as weakening, 112
  cattle as sacred, 14
  in New York City, 400–401
  pilgrimage in, 316
Hirschman, Helen K., 124
Hirschon, Renee, 388
Hisama, Ellie, 354
Historical linguistics, 341–342
History and cultural anthropology, 10, 43
HIV/AIDS, 32, 77–78, 116, 158–159, 161, 173, 426
Hobsbawm, Eric, 297
Hogan, Dennis P., 144–145
Holism, 9, 15, 32
Holland, Dorothy C., 203
Holocaust, 12
Homo sapiens, 6, 56
Homosexuality
  and economic discrimination in the United States, 148–149
  and marriage restrictions, 199–200
  as a research topic in Brazil, 48
  as biologically determined or culturally constructed, 148–149
  See also Gender identity, Lesbians, Third gender roles
Honduras, 274
Hong Kong, 163, 369
Hong Kong migrants, 397–398
Hormones, 138
Horowitz, Irving, 47
Horowitz, Michael, 44, 421–422
Horticulture, 61
  and change, 63–64
  and kinship, 186
  cycle of production, 61–62
  general characteristics, 61–62
  labor patterns, 62–63
  property relations, 62
  sustainability, 63
Hospitals as microcultures, 25
Hostetler, John A., 41, 69
The House of Lim, 192
Household, 214
  and family businesses, 220–222
  as an economic unit, 219–223
  forms of, 215
  gender division of labor in, 219–220
  headship, 215–216
  intergenerational household, 232
  unitary model of economists, 90–91
  woman-headed (matrifocal), 216–219
Housing, 369
Howell, Nancy, 49–50, 60, 113–114
Hua of Papua New Guinea, 23
Hughes, Charles C., 160
Huizinga, Johan, 373
Hula, 379
Human development approach, 413
Human Relations Area Files (HRAF), 144, 189
Human rights, 147, 330, 432–433
Humor, 304
Humphrey, Caroline, 348
Hunte, Pamela, 122
Hunter, John M., 160
Hunting, *see* Foraging
Huntington, Gertrude Enders, 41, 69
Hutchinson, Sharon, 293, 337
Hutter, Michael, 373
Hutterites of North America, 112
Hutu of Burundi, 300
Hypergyny, 203
Hypertension, 385
Hypogyny, 203

Iatrogenic, 152
Iceland, 44
Ideology (or superstructure), 14
Iliad, 312
Illness, *see* Culture-bound syndrome, Disease
Illo, Jeanne Frances I., 216
Ilongot of the Philippines, 299
Image of the limited good, 136–137
Imagined Communities, 278
In vitro fertilization, 115–116
Incan empire, 7, 341
Incest taboo, 202
  and marriage in Taiwan, 198–199
  as a basis for spouse selection, 202–203
Index culture, 20
Indexicality, 344
India
  Andaman Islands, 48–49, 59, 265, 424
  anorexia nervosa cases, 163
  Ayurvedic medicine, 171–172
  caste system, 249, 254–257
  cattle as sacred, 14
  class differences, 128
  dalits, 254–255, 414
  drinking practices, 16
  eating practices, 16
  elimination practices, 16, 18
  extended family/household, 215
  farmers' cooperatives, 246
  female infanticide, 127–128
  Hindu beliefs about sexual intercourse 112, 117–118
  intrahousehold allocation patterns, 127–128
  marriage payments, 127–128
  Nayar-Nambudiri marriages, 200–201
  Phulan Devi ("Bandit Queen"), 298
  puberty rituals in South India, 145
  redistribution as a development strategy, 414
  regional cultural variations, 127–128, 145
  restrictions on research, 48–49
  sleeping practices, 17–18
  theater, 368
  village studies, 9
  wrestling, 374–375
  See also Kerala
Indian (South Asian) migrants, 400–401
Indian Village, 9
Indigenous fertility control methods, 122–123
Indigenous people, 424
  as victims of development, 424–427
  organizations, 428–430
  population estimates, 424
  resource claims, 427–428
Indirect infanticide, 125–126
Indo-Canadians, 243
Indonesia, 7, 16, 20, 23, 93–94, 153, 287–288, 326–327, 422–423
Inductive research approach, 31
Industrial agriculture, 72
  in the United States, 72–73
  See also Corporate farming
Industrialism, 75
  and marriage patterns, 204–205
  formal sector, 76
  informal sector, 76–77
  mode of reproduction, 115
  sustainability, 78
Infancy and personality, 138–139
Infanticide, 113
  among the poor of Brazil, 126
  among the Tarahumara of Mexico, 125–126
  and child "fitness," 125–126
  and poverty, 126
  and religion, 123
  and warfare, 126–127
  direct infanticide, 125
  female infanticide, 125, 127–128
  in Pakistan and India, 123
  indirect infanticide, 125
  motivations, 125
  sex-selective infanticide, 119
Infant mortality rate, 126
Infectious diseases, 158
Infibulation, 145–147
Influence, 263
Informal sector, 76, examples, 76–77
Informed consent, 48
Infrastructure (in cultural materialism), 14, 112
Inheritance patterns, 191–195, 219
In-kind taxation, 273
In Search of Respect, 10
Initiation rituals, 244–245, 316
  See also Life-cycle rituals, Puberty
Institutional migrants, 389–392
Institutions as microcultures, 25
Intergenerational household, 232
Interior decoration, 369–370
International affairs and anthropology
  and human rights, 390–391, 432–433
  and international development, 408–433
  and international migration, 386–403
  and world conflict resolution, 305
  claims about art between nations, 372–373
  research on the European Space Agency, 281–282
International development, *see* Development
International students, 392
Interpretivism
  and key debates in cultural anthropology, 14
  in medical anthropology, 170–172
  interpretive ethnography, 46
Interview method, 40–41
Intrahousehold dynamics
  budgeting, 92
  domestic violence, 225–226
  marital satisfaction in Japan and China, 224
  sibling relationships, 224–225
  spouse/partner relationships, 223–224
Inuit of North America, 58, 153
Invention, 408–409
Ireland, 226
Irian Jaya, 117, 292–293
Iroquois of central New York, 31, 62, 208, 271
Iroquis kinship system, 189
Irrigation
  and disease, 160
  groups, 245–246
Islam
  and divorce, 227–228
  and gardens, 371
  attitudes of Muslims toward menstruation in Turkey, 145
  doctrine of, 313
  history and distribution of, 326
  taboos against eating pigs, 92
Israel, 143, 300, 366–367, 389

Italian Americans, 185
Italy, 71, 316–317, 403–404
Ituri rain forest of Congo, 101
Iyalode, 271
Iyer, Pico, 20

Jackson, Douglas A., 153
Jajmani system of India, 255
  characteristics and change, 255–256
Jamaica, 19, 21, 37, 46, 91
Janes, Craig, 253, 385
Jankowski, Martín Sánchez, 243
Japan
  abortion, 123, 322
  adolescence in, 144–145
  anorexia nervosa cases, 163
  arranged marriage, 205, 224
  baseball, 374
  cemeteries of "returned" fetuses, 123
  corporate male work ethic, 136–137, 224
  divorce rates, 227
  family businesses in, 221
  fertility patterns, 115
  fieldwork with geishas, 38
  gender codes in speech, 340
  gift-giving practices during fieldwork, 36–37
  infanticide, 119
  interior decoration, 370
  kimono, 349
  local politics in, 275–276
  love-match marriages, 224
  love hotels, 225
  national character study, 135
  personality of corporate males, 136–137
  preschool children, 140–141
  population ageing, 115
  research on the fashion industry, 37
  sleeping patterns, 138
  television studies, 350–351
  widow/widower remarriage, 229
Jati
  as subcaste, 254
  rules about marriage, 256
Java, 43, 70
Jawoyn of Australia, 320
Jerusalem, 316, 322–323, 300
Jesus, 325, 326
Jinadu, L. Adele, 250
Johnson, Walter R., 250
Jonaitis, Aldona, 362
Jones, A., 371
Jones, Richard S., 238–239
Jones, Sir William, 341–342
Joralemon, Donald, 158, 159
Jordan, Brigitte, 137
Joseph, Suad, 224–225
Jourdan, Christine, 243
Journalism, 350, 353–353
Judaism
  as a world religion, 322–324
  gender segregation at the kotel, 322–323
  taboo against eating pig, 92–93
  Zionist-Orthodox schooling for girls in Israel, 143
Jules-Rosette, Benetta, 366
Ju/wasi of southern Africa, 56, 59, 60, 84, 113–114, 166–167, 205–206

Kaberry, Phyllis, 245
Kahn, Miriam, 371
Kampuchea, 223, 399–400
  See also Khmer refugees
Kanwar, Rup, 125
Kapauku of Irian Jaya, 292–293
Kapchan, Deborah, 365
Karelians of Finland, 388–389
Karma, 320–322, 399–400
Kassebaum, Nancy, 274
Kathakali, 368
Katz, Nathan, 323–324
Kava, 326, 336
Kayapo of the Brazilian Amazon, 267
Kayasanur forest disease, 160
Katz, Richard, 165–166
Keen, Ian, 320
Keiser, R. Lincoln, 299
Kelley, Heidi, 218–219
Kent, Susan, 239–240
Kentucky, 296–297
Kenya, 62–63, 139–140, 147, 377, 419, 423
  See also Maasai
Kerala, India, 200–201, 208, 215, 320, 323–333, 414
Kerns, Virginia, 226
Khan, Showkat Hayat, 236–237
Khmer refugees, 399–400
Kideckel, David, 73–75
Kimono, 349
King, Martin Luther King Jr., 288, 303
Kingston, Jamaica, 19
Kinship
  based on descent, 190–196
  based on marriage, 199–209
  based on sharing, 196–199
  diagram, 187–189
  functions, 184
  gathering kinship data, 42, 186–187
  genealogy, 188
  kinship system, 184
  research on, 186–189
Kipling, Rudyard, 12
Klass, Perri, 174
Kligman, Gail, 120
Kluckhon, Clyde, 14–15
Knott, Kim, 320–321
Kolenda, Pauline, 216, 255, 256–257
Komi of Russia, 355
Kondo, Dorinne, 37
Konner, Melvin, 25, 148, 174
Korean migrants, 396, 398
Kotel, 322–323
Kottak, Conrad, 9, 199
Krantzler, Nora, 178
Kroeber, Alfred, 14–15
Krulfeld, Ruth, 366
Krupnick, Igor, 66
Kuala Lumpur, Malaysia, 313
Ku Klux Klan, 251
Kuipers, Joel, 16, 287–288, 363
Kula, 97–98
Kulick, Don, 414
Kuna of Panama, 246–247
Kurds of the Middle East, 278–279
Kurin, Richard, 35
Kuru, 89
Kuwait, 272, 349
Kwakiutl, *see* Kwakwaka'wakw
Kwakwaka'wakw of Canada, 82, 107, 135, 141
Kwiatkowski, Lynn, 433
Kyoto, Japan, 38

Labor exchange, 95–96
Labor migrants, 387–388
Labor patterns, *see* Division of labor
Labov, William, 343
Lactose intolerance, 420
Ladányi, János, 253–254
Laderman, Carol, 166–167
LaFleur, William, 123, 322
Lakoff, Robin, 340, 348
La Laja, Venezuela, 227
Lamphere, Louise, 385
Land ownership, *see* Property relations
Lang, Joseph, 250
Langkawi Island of Malaysia, 194, 196–197
Language, 334
  and gender, 339–340
  and identity and power, 346–347
  and social change, 354–355
  characteristics of, 336–337
  codes, 339–340
  dialects, 339
  formal properties of, 337–338
  multiple levels of, 338–340
  origins of, 340
  relation with thought and behavior, 343–346
  socialization, 344–345
  writing systems, 341
  See also Bilingualism, Communication, Creole, Grammar, Historical Linguistics, Mass Media, Paralanguage, Pidgin
Lappé, Francis Moore, 88
Larsen, Clark Spenser, 159
Latah, 162
Law, 287
  as a power of the state, 272
  as a topic in anthropology, 286
  See also Legal anthropology
Leach, Jerry, 378
Leacock, Eleanor, 11, 194
Lead poisoning, 175
Leadership
  and gender in chiefdoms, 270–271
  and gender in states, 273–274
  big-men/women, 268–270
  in bands, 265–266
  in tribes, 266–268
  resurgence of women in Native American politics, 281
  symbols of leadership in state, 274–275
  women in state politics, 280–281
The League of the Iroquois, 31, 262
Lebanon, 224–245, 389
Lebra, Takie, 127
Lee, James, 118
Lee, Marie G., 398
Lee, Richard B., 58, 60
Legal anthropology, 286
Legal pluralism, 293
Lein, Laura, 346–347
Leisure, 373–374, 376–377
Lele of central Africa, 96
Lempert, David, 105, 288
Leopard-skin chief, 288–289
Lepowsky, Maria, 193, 269–270
Leprosy, 159
Lesbians
  and birth order in the United States, 148
  and divorce in California, 228
  terms for in Thailand, 150
Lese of Congo, 101
Lesotho, 418
Lessinger, Johanna, 400–401
Levinson, David, 226
Lévi-Strauss, Claude, 12, 93, 96, 170, 186, 312
Levy, Jerrold E., 194
Lewin, Ellen, 228
Lewis, Oscar, 136
Leynaud, Emile, 245
Lieban, Richard W., 158
Lifeboat mentality, 403
Life cycle, 24, 137
Life cycle rituals, 315
Life history approach, 10, 42–43
Lim family of Taiwan, 192, 214
Limited-purpose money, 96
Lincoln, Kenneth, 304
Lindenbaum, Shirley, 89
Linguistic anthropology, 5, 7–8, 334–335
  Linguistic determinism, 343
  Linguistic pluralism, 338
  Linguistic relativism, 340
Linnekan, Jocelyn, 271
Little, Kenneth, 204
Lloyd, Cynthia, 214
Localization, 19
Locorotondo, Italy, 71
Lockwood, Victoria, 195
Logographs, 341
London, 230, 310
Long Island, 395–396
Longva, Anh Nga, 272

Looks (appearance), 203
Lorenz, Konrad, 263
Los Angeles, 100–101, 396–397
Lourdes, France, 316
Love, 204–205
Low, Setha, 274
Luhrmann, Tanya, 310
Lukurmata, Bolivia, 5

Maasai of Kenya and Tanzania, 144, 146, 182, 377, 406
Machel village, Mozambique, 431
Maclachlan, Morgan, 69
MacLeod, Arlene Elowe, 349
Macroculture, 15
Madagascar, 10, 389–390
Magic, 310
  compared to religion, 310
  in baseball, 311
  in cricket, 378
  varieties of, 310
Mahabharata, 312, 319
Mahler, Sarah, 394, 395–396
Major, Marc R., 279
Makepeace, James M., 295
Malaria, 159–160
Malawi, 142
Malaysia, 70, 166–167, 194, 196–197, 231, 313
Male strippers, 365
Malekula Island of the South Pacific, 49
Mali, 141, 428–429
Maliki law, 227
Malinowski, Bronislaw, 10, 31, 33, 47, 50, 116, 262, 286, 288, 335–336
Malnutrition, 104–105, 125, 173
Mamdani, Mahmoud, 114–115
Mana, 313
Mannheim, Bruce, 343
Man the Hunter model, 58–59
Manupur, North India, 114
Manz, Beatriz, 388
Mao Tse-Tung, 73
Marathas of India, 246
March, Kathryn, 236
Marchatti, Gina, 354
Marcus, Aliza, 279
Margolis, Maxine, 151, 385
Market exchange, 97
  among the Tiv, 102
  in Mexico, 98–99
  in Morocco, 98, 99
  in Shanghai, 99
Markets, 98–99
Marley, Bob, 19–20
Marriage, 201
  arranged, 204–204
  as exchange of people, 96–97
  based on love, 204–205
  between cousins, 202
  changes in, 208–209
  difficulty of defining, 199–201
  exchanges and gifts, 93–94, 205
  homosexual, 199–200
  Nisa's third marriage, 206
  number of spouses, 207–208
  residence patterns during, 208
  satisfaction during, 199, 224
  spouse selection, 201–205
Marshall, Robert C., 275–276
Martin, M. Kay, 62
Martínez, Samuel, 390–391
Marx, Karl, 20–21, 73, 249, 294, 311–312
Maskit, 366–367
Masks, 363
Massiah, Joycelin, 217
Masta Liu of the Solomon Islands, 243
Maté, 169
Maternity, Medicine and Power, 32
Mathabane, Mark, 252
Matrescence, 150
Matriarchy, 271
Matrifocality, 196
Matrilineal descent, 118, 186, 192–194, 320
Matrilocal residence, 193
Maya of Central America, 61, 71, 96, 137, 163–164, 199, 273–274, 425–427
Maybury-Lewis, David, 130, 278, 371, 424
McCoid, Catherine Hodge, 364
McDermott, LeRoy D., 364
McElroy, Ann, 166
McMahon, April M. S., 336, 342
Mead, Margaret, 10–11, 30, 38, 47, 134, 138, 145
Measles, 159–160
Meat, 101
Mecca, 316
Mechanical solidarity, 249
Mechanization, 72–73, 378
Media anthropology, 349–350
Medical anthropology, 158
Medical interview, 347–348
Medical pluralism, 176
  among the Sherpa of Nepal, 176–178
Medicalization, 172
  and matrescences in the United States, 150
  of menopause, 152
Medicine/medical systems
  Ayurvedic medicine, 171–172
  "traditional" medicines, 168–169
Medusa's Hair, 9–10
Mehinaku of Brazil, 134
Meigs, Anna, 23
Meir, Golda, 274
Melanesia, 268–269, 328–329
  See also Trobriand Islands, Vanatinai
Mellencamp, John, 354
Menarche, 116, 144
Mencher, Joan P., 200, 249, 255
Menchú, Rigoberta, 425–527
Mende of Sierra Leone, 100
Mennonites of North America, 112, 114
Menopause, 116, 152
Men's house/club, 23, 242
  See also Fraternities, Gender segregation
Menstruation, 116, 145
  See also Menarche, Menopause
Mernissi, Fatima, 144, 376
Merry, Sally Engle, 286, 292, 293
Messer, Ellen, 432–433
Mexican Americans, 175
Mexico
  birth practices among the Maya, 137
  child personality, 139–140
  culture of poverty, 136
  fertility preferences of men and women in Oaxaca, 119
  genocide due to European colonialism, 130
  godparenthood, 199
  markets, 98
  research on menopause, 41, 142
  Shan Dany Museum, 415
  women's organizations, 431
Miami, Florida, 76
Michaelson, Evelyn, 68
Microcultures
  and consumption, 89–90
  and illness, 158
  as units of analysis, 15, 20–25
Middle age, 24, 151–152
Midwife, 137
Migration, 112
  and marriage and household formation, 209, 231
  anthropology and, 384–385
  categories of, 387–393
  internal, 385–286
  international, 386–387
  migrant labor in the United States, 73, 76
  new immigrants, 393–402
  politics of exclusion, 402–404
Miller, Barbara D., 24, 32, 46, 91, 126, 127–128, 138, 144, 145, 163, 216, 236–237
Miller, Bruce G., 281
Mills, Mary Beth, 164
Milner, George R., 159
Milton, Katharine, 103–104
Minangkabau of Malaysia, 194
Miner, Horace, 4
Mines, Mattison, 256
Minimalism, 84
Mining, 329
Mir-Hosseini, Ziba, 227–228
Mitchell, Bruce, 422–423
Moberg, Mark, 276
Mochizuki, Takashi, 145
Mode of consumption, 84
  and microcultures, 89–90
  consumption funds, 85
  consumption inequality, 86–88
  See also Consumerism, Consumption, Minimalism
Mode of production, 54
  and architecture, 369
  and mode of reproduction, 112
  and political organization, 266
  as related to nature versus culture, 54–55
  historical appearance of different modes, 54–55
Mode of reproduction
  among agriculturalists, 114–115
  among foragers, 113–114
  in industrialism, 115
  three modes explained, 113
Modell, Judith, 198
Modernization, 410
Moerman, Daniel E., 171
Mohammad, *see* Muhammad
Mohawks of New York State, 347–348
Mohenjo-daro, 335
Moka, 98
Molas, 246–247
Moldova, 8
Money, 96
Mongolia, 66–68
Monogamy, 184, 207
Monogenesis (of language), 342
Monotheism, 311
Montagu, Ashley, 263
Montana, 222, 385–386
Moore, Michael, 69, 229
Morgan, Lewis Henry, 31, 185, 262
Morgan, S. Phillip, 229
Morgan, William, 165
Mormon religion, 184
Morocco, 98, 99, 116, 144, 209, 228, 273, 275, 326–327, 365, 376
Morris, Desmond, 263
Morris, Rosalind, 150
Morss, Elliott R., 421
Mortality, 112
  cultural construction of, 124–125
  domestic violence, 129
  gender and driving-related deaths, 124–125
  infanticide, 125–127, 127–128
  suicide, 33, 44, 127–129, 149
  warfare, 129–130
Mortland, Carol A., 399–400
Motherhood, 150–151
Motyl, Alexander J., 278
Moynihan, Elizabeth, 371
Mozambique, 431
Mt. Hagen area of Papua New Guinea, 55–56, 268–269
Muhammad, 326
Mull, Dennis, 125–126
Mull, Dorothy, 125–126
Multi-purpose money, 96
Mundugumor of Papua New Guinea, 134
Mundurucu of Brazilian Amazon, 63–64
Murcott, Anne, 219–220
Murdock, George Peter, 189, 214–215
Murphy, Robert F., 63
Murphy, Yolanda, 63

Murray, Gerald, 420–421
Museum anthropology, 371
Museums, 371–373, 415
Music, 365, 367–368
Muslims, *see* Islam
Myerhoff, Barbara, 39
Myers, James, 244–245
Myers-Scotton, Carol, 339
Myth, 312

Nacirema of North America, 4
Nader, Laura, 37, 305
Nadur village, India, 414
Nag, Moni, 70, 117–118
The Naked Ape, 263
Nambudiri of India, 200–201
Naming, 193
Nanda, Serena, 150, 360
Narcissism, 140
Nash, June, 326
Native American Graves Protection and Repatriation Act, 373
Native Americans
  American Indian Movement, 328
  and white cultural imperialism, 425
  and women's political roles, 281
  attitudes toward homosexuality in North America, 149
  claims for repatriation of bones and goods, 373
  Ghost Dance, 328
  humor as resistance, 304
  land claims in Canada, 427
  powwows, 23
  resurgence of women in politics, 281
  See also Pacific Northwest cultures
Native and Newcomer, 32
Nation, 278
National character studies, 135–136
Nationalism, 278–280
Nature, as related to culture, 16–18, 56–57
Navajo of the southwestern United States, 66, 164, 194
Nayaka of India, 56
Nayar of India, 200–201, 208, 215, 320
Ndembu of Zambia, 315
Neale, Walter, 96
Neanderthals, 6, 11
Neff, Deborah, 320
Nenets of the Arctic, 66
Neocolonialism, 48, 194, 354
Neolocality, 208
  in industrialized society, 208
Neo-nazism, 250
Nepal, 70, 92, 229–230, 255
Netting, Robert McC., 68
Networks, 102, 230
New Delhi, 294
New immigrants, 393
  examples of, 393–402
New reproductive technology, 115–116, 123–124
New York City, 49, 77, 124, 384, 385, 394–395, 400–401
Ngokwey, Ndolamb, 165
Nias of Indonesia, 93–94
Nichter, Mark, 160, 175–176
Nichter, Mimi, 175–176, 347
Nicobar Islands of India, 48
Nieves, Isabel, 218
Nigeria, 102, 227, 249–250
Niraula, Bhanu B., 229
Nisa, 43, 205–206
Nomadism, *see* Pastoralism
Non-governmental organizations, 257–258, 419, 428–438, 431
Nordstrom, Carolyn, 294
Norm, 287
North Carolina, 325
Northern Luzon region of the Philippines, 433
A Not Entirely Benign Procedure, 174
Nowell, Charles James, 141
Nuclear household, 214, 215
Nuer of Sudan, 64, 202, 337, 288, 293
Nutrition, 414
  See also Malnutrition

Oaxaca region of Mexico, 119, 139–140, 199
  See also Chiapas, Maya, Mexico
Obeyesekere, Gananath, 9–10
Observation, *see* Fieldwork, Participant Observation
Observer's paradox, 336
Ochs, Elinor, 344–345
O'Conner, Sandra Day, 242
Odyssey, 312
Ogoni of Nigeria, 428, 433
Ohnuki-Tierney, Emiko, 168
Okely, Judith, 42, 186
Olt Land of Romania, 73–75
Oman, 95, 148–149
Omvedt, Gail, 257
On Aggression, 263
One-Child Policy of China, 112, 140
One Children's Place, 174
O'Nell, Carl W., 161–163
Ong, Aihwa, 231
Ongka, 268
Ongka's Big Moka [video], 268
Opera (western), 368
Opposable thumb, 15
Orang Asli of Malaysia, 167, 367–368
Orangutans, 6
Orchard Town, United States, 139–140
Organic solidarity, 249, 255
Orientalism, 353–354
Orientalism, 353
Ortner, Sherry B., 55
Ossman, Susan, 273
Overlooking Nazareth, 32
Oxfeld, Ellen, 222

Pacific Northwest cultures (Native American), 18, 43, 82, 107, 141
Pahansu village of India, 255–256
Pahl, Jan, 91
Painter, Andrew A., 350–351
Paiutes of North America, 328
Pakistan, 35, 299
Palaeopathology, 6
Palermo, Italy, 403–404
Palestine/Palestinians, 300, 366, 389
Panama, 246–247
Pantheon, 314
Pappas, Gregory, 78
Papua New Guinea
  adolescence, 145, 148
  big-man politics, 268–269
  cargo cults, 328
  emic views of nature and culture, 55–56
  feces as polluting, 18
  kuru among the Fore, 89
  perceptions of development, 414–415
  personality and gender, 134–135, 145
  women's life histories, 43
  See also Irian Jaya, Mead
Paralanguage, 340
  bowing in Japan, 348
  dress and looks, 349
  kinesics, 348–349
  silence, 348
Parallel cousin, 202
Paredes, J. Anthony, 290
Parker, Richard G., 49
Parry, Jonathan, 255
Participant observation, 30
Participation, as a fieldwork method, 40, 423
Participatory appraisal, 423
Pastoralism, 64
  and cultural change, 66–68
  general characteristics of, 64
  displacement of, 428
  labor patterns, 65
  political organization in, 267–268
  property relations, 65–66
  sustainability, 66
Patrescence, 150
Patriarchy, 273
Patrilineal descent, 186
  distribution and examples, 191–192
Patrilocal residence, 192
Patterns of Culture, 135
Payakan, 267
Peattie, Lisa Redfield, 227
Pedelty, Mark, 350, 352–353
Peet, R. Creighton, 70
Peletz, Michael, 96–97
Pelto, Pertti J., 65, 217, 411
Penso, Anat, 143
"Pepsistroika," 105
Perin, Constance, 295
Periodic rituals, 315
Peron, Eva, 273
Perry, Richard, 429
Personality, 134
  and adolescence, 144–150
  and childhood, 139–143
  and class, 136–137
  and gender roles and identity, 134–135, 145–150
  and infancy, 138–139
  and modes of production, 139–140
  and poverty, 136
  and sleeping patterns, 138
  as related to gender in infancy, 138–139
  Culture and Personality school of thought, 134–135
  national character studies, 135
  of Japanese salarymen, 136–137
Peru, 7, 425
Pessar, Patricia, 394–395
Pet therapy, 152
Peyote, 42
Pharmaceuticals, 168–169
Philippines, 216, 299, 385, 433
Phonemes, 337
Phonetics, 337
Phulan Devi, 298
Physical ability, 203
Physical anthropology, 5, 6–7
Piddocke, Stuart, 82
Pidgin, 342
Piercing of the body, 244
Piercing Fans International Quarterly, 244
Pigs, 92–93
Pilgrimage, 316, 322–323
Pilling, Arnold R., 60–61
Pillsbury, Barbara, 120–121
Pioneer migrant, 396
Pittsburgh, Pennsylvania, 71, 174
Placebo effect, 171
Plant domestication, *see* Agriculture, Horticulture.
Plant, Roger, 424, 427–428
Plantation agriculture, 71
Plath, David, 138
Plattner, Stuart, 98–99
Play, 141, 373–376
Plough agriculture, 69
Pocahantas, 271
Poirier, Sylvia, 95
Police/Policing, 296–297, 289
Poland, 105, 257–258
Polio, among chimpanzees, 158
Political anthropology, 262
Political organization, 265
  bands, 265–266
  big-man/big-woman systems, 268–270
  change in, 278–282
  chiefdoms, 270–271
  states, 271–277
  tribes, 266–270
Politics, 263

and nonhuman primate studies, 263–264
as a species and human universal, 263–264
Polyandry, 208, 215, 220
Polygamy, 208
Polygyny, 184
and household formation, 215, 216
theories about, 208
Polytheism, 311
Population
as related to infrastructure, 112
demography as study of, 112
density, 61, 69
growth from prehistory to present, 112
homeostasis among foragers, 113–114
negative population growth, 112
state formation and, 272
See also Family Planning, Fertility, Mode of Reproduction, Migration, Mortality
Pospisil, Leopold, 292–293
Post-partum taboo, 117
Post-traumatic stress disorder, 402
Potlatch, 82, 107
Potter, Jack, 237
Potter, Shulamith, 23
Poverty
and critical medical anthropology, 173
and household formation, 217–218
and international development in Colombia, 173
and personality, 136
and privatization, 105
and social networks, 231
See also Development (international)
Power, 263
Powhatan, 271
Pragmatics, 335
Pratt, Mary Louise, 377
Press, Nancy Ann, 115, 150
Preventive practices (against disease), 163–164
Priest/Priestess, 317–318
Primack, Richard B., 414
Primary group, 236
Primate conservation, 8
Primatology 6
Primitive Culture, 311
Primitivism, 377
Primogeniture, 201
Prince, Raymond, 161
Prisons, 238–239, 240, 290
Private domain, 68
Privatization, 67
and diet, 105
and poverty, 105
in Russia and Eastern Europe, 105
Production, 54
access to, as basis for class membership, 20
Productivity (linguistic), 336–337
Profit maximization, *see* Capitalism, Market exchange
Project Camelot, 47
Project cycle, 419–420
Project implementation, 421
Pronatalism, 114
among agricultural populations, 114
and taxation, 273
and the politics of fertility, 118
in north India, 114
in Romania under Ceausescu, 120
Property relations
among family farmers, 70–71
among foragers, *see* use rights
among horticulturalists, 63
among pastoralists, 65–66
decline of matrilineal rights, 70
Prophets, 319
Prostitution, *see* Sex work
Proto-Indo-European, 342
Psychological anthropology, 134
Puberty, 144, 148–149
Puberty rituals, 145–147, 315–316
Public/private dichotomy, 68
Public domain, 68
Public finance, 273
Pueblo of the southwestern United States, 135, 425
Punishment, 290
See also Prisons
Purdah, 273
See also Veiling
Purdum, Elizabeth D., 290
Pure gift, 99–100
Push-pull theory, 385

Qashqai of Iran, 64, 267–268
Qualitative research methods, 40
Quantitative research methods, 40
Queens, 5
Questionnaires, 41
Quipu, 341
Qu'ran, 313

Rabinowitz, Dan, 32
Race, 22
and consumption, 89
and inequality in the United States, 22
as a basis for microculture formation, 22
as a factor during fieldwork, 37
as similar to ethnicity and caste, 249–250
as socially constructed, 22
biological markers of, 22
See also Apartheid, Ethnicity, Germany, South Africa
Racism, 251, 329, 403–404
See also Discrimination, Orientalism, Primitivism
Radcliffe-Brown, A. R., 9, 47, 262, 265
Radin, Paul, 42
Raheja, Gloria Goodwin, 255–256
Rahnema, Majid, 412
Rajasthan, India, 125
Rajputs of North India, 139–140
Ramayana, 312, 319
Ramphele, Mamphela, 228–229
Raphael, Dana, 150
Rapid research methods, 422–423
Rapoport, Tamar, 143
Rapp, Rayna, 115, 117, 124
Rapport, 35
Ras Tafari, 327–328
Realist ethnography, 47
Reciprocity, 97
Redistribution
as a development strategy, 412, 414
as a form of exchange, 98
Reflexive ethnography, 47
Reforestation, 420–421
Refugees, 388
Bosnian, 401–402
Khmer, 399–400
Palestinian, 389
Salvadoran, 395–396
Soviet Jew, 401
Vietnamese, 42–43, 398–399
Region and microculture formation, 24
Reid, Russell, 169–170
Religion, 310
and abortion, 123
and change, 328–329
and conflict over sacred sites, 329
and education of girls in Israel, 143
and human rights, 330
and socialism, 329–330
anthropological approach to, 310
as a factor during fieldwork, 39
beliefs in, 312–314
cargo cults, 328, 414–415
compared to magic, 310–311
functionalist approach to, 311–312
origins, 311
pilgrimage, 316
religious practitioners, 317–319
rituals, 314–317
sacrifice, 317
specialists, 317–319
supernaturals, 313–314
See also Buddhism, Catholicism, Christianity, Hinduism, Islam, Judaism
Remittances, 222
examples, 222–223
Reno, Janet, 242
Replacement fund
Replacement-level fertility, 115
Reproduction, 112
See also Abortion, Fertility, Infanticide, Mode of Reproduction, Sexual Intercourse
Reproductive rights, 120–121
Reproductive Rights and Wrongs, 120–121
Republic of Korea, 106, 209, 264
Research methods, 30
photography, 44–45
tape recording, 44–45
videos and films, 44
See also Fieldwork, Participant Observation, Qualitative Research Methods, Quantitative Research Methods
Resettlement, 388–389, 413
Residence patterns, 192, 193, 208
Restudies, 33
Reverse culture shock, 40
Revitalization movements, 328–329
Revolution, 300
theories of, 300–301
Reyna, Stephen P., 301
Rice
cultivation and hookworm in China, 158
gender division of labor in cultivation, 69
Rich, Adrienne, 148
Rich, Bruce, 417
Rites of passage, *see* Initiation rituals, Life-cycle rituals
Ritual, 314
as an item of exchange, 95
varieties of, 315–317
Robben, Antonius C. G. M., 294
Robertson, Carol E., 367
Robertson, Jennifer, 32, 35, 45
Rogers, Barbara, 70, 430
Role, 248
See also Status
Rom people, 253–254
See also Gypsies
Romania, 39, 47
collective agriculture in, 73–75
effects of privatization on consumption, 105
pronatalism of the national government, 120
Rom people, 254
Rongorongo, 334, 335
Rosaldo, Michelle Zimbalist, 49
Rosaldo, Renato, 299
Roscoe, Will, 149
Rose, Jerome C., 373
Roseman, Marina, 367–368
Rosenberger, Nancy, 370
Rosenblatt, Paul, C., 154
Ross, Eric B., 113
Ross, Marc Howard, 302
Roth, Eric A., 64
Rouland, Norbert, 293
Rubel, Arthur, 161–163
Rubin, Gayle, 96
Ruhlen, Merritt, 342
Russia, 105, 355, 372–373
Rwanda, 250

Sacrifice, 317
human sacrifice among the Aztecs, 317–318,
in Islam, 326–327
Sahlins, Marshall, 84, 268
Said, Edward, 353
Saitoti, Tepilit Ole, 146
Salam, Nawaf A., 389
Salamanders [video], 17
Salarymen of Japan, 136–137
Salem-Murdock, Muneera, 44, 421–422
Salvadoran migrants, 395–396
Sambandhan marriage, 200–201
Sambia of Papua New Guinea, 145
Sami of Finland, 65, 411
Samoa, 10–11, 62, 127, 145, 177–179, 336, 345
Samoans of California, 385
Sanday, Peggy R., 62, 241, 295, 318
Sanjek, Roger, 44, 249, 386
Sanskrit, 342
Sanskritization, 257
Sant Cassia, Paul, 298
Santa Ana, Mexico, 415
Sapir, Edward, 343
Sapir-Whorf hypothesis, 343
Sardinia, Italy, 316–317
Sargent, Carolyn, 32
Saro-Wiwa, Ken, 428–433
Sati
act of female suicide, 127
Hindu goddess, 316
Sault, Nicole, 185, 199
Savishinsky, Joel, 28, 57, 58, 152
Scheper-Hughes, Nancy, 126, 138, 153
Schistosomiasis, 160, 164
Schlegel, Alice, 144
Schmid, Thomas J., 238–239
Schneider, David, 196
School
and personality formation, 141–143
boarding schools in Madagascar, 389–392
enrollments in poor nations, 141–142
gender tracking in, 142–143
Schwartz, Jeffrey, 6
Scott, James C., 273, 303–304
Scrimshaw, Susan, 125
Scudder, Thayer, 118, 160
Seclusion, *see* Gender segregation, Purdah
Secondary group, 236
Sedentarization
and conflict among foragers, 239–240
and fertility, 114
Segmentary model, 267
Segregation
by gender and fieldwork, 38
by gender at the kotel, 323–324
public/private domain, 68–69
racial, 89–90
Semen, 112, 118, 145, 303
Sen, Amartya, 86–87, 88
Sen, Kasturi, 90, 115
Sen, Mala, 298
Seneca of New York State, 281
Senegal, 44, 421–422
Sentumbwe, Nayinda, 203–204
Sex, 23, 138
See also Gender
Sex and Temperament in Three Primitive Societies, 134–135
Sex ratio, 218–219
Sex work, 77–78, 223
Sexual intercourse
age at beginning, 116–117
and HIV/AIDS risk, 158–159
frequency, 117–118, 224
research difficulties, 48, 116, 199, 224
Sex-selective infanticide, 119
Sexuality
Adrienne Rich on, 148
as a sensitive research topic, 48
sexual desire as culturally constructed, 117
sexual identity, 148–150
See also Berdache, Homosexuality, Lesbianism, Sexual intercourse, Third gender roles
Shaman/shamanka, 168
among the Ainu of Japan, 168
among the Sherpa of Nepal, 176–178
compared to the role of priest, 317–318
in the Republic of Korea, 167
shamanka as the female form, 317
Shanghai, 99
Sharer, Robert, 274
Sharing, as a basis of kinship, 196–199
Sharp, Lesley, 389–392
Shenav-Keller, Shelly, 366–367
Sherpa of Nepal, 176–178
Shibamoto, Janet, 340
Shifting cultivation, *see* Horticulture
Shikhat of Morocco, 365
Shipibo of Peru, 362–363
Short, James F., 243, 244
Shostak, Marjorie, 43, 205–206
Shu-min, Huang, 39
Shweder, Richard, 9
Siberia, 34, 348
Siblings
as marital partners in Egypt, 202
brother-sister relationship in Jordan, 224–225
Sikhs migrants, 254
Silence, 348
Silver, Ira, 377
Simmons, William, 43
Sim-pua marriage, 198–199
Singapore, 164
Sioux of North America, 328
Sisal, 104–105
Siskind, Janet, 214
Sisters in Islam, 313
Skinner, G. William, 24, 99, 119
Skocpol, Theda, 300
Slash and burn cultivation, *see* Horticulture
Slavery, 62, 101, 216–217, 342–343
Sleep, 17–18, 138
Slobin, Dan, 344
Slocum, Sally, 58
Smallpox, 159–160
Smiling, 139
Smuts, Barbara, 6
Snakes in ritual, 320, 325–326
Social conflict
as a topic of anthropological research, 32–33
between foragers and settled Bantu in Congo, 54
nonviolent forms of conflict, 303–304
racial conflict in the Los Angeles riots, 100–101
types of, 294–303
Social control, 286
Social impact assessment, 411
Social stratification, 248
and caste, 254–257
and class, 248–249
and ethnicity, 251–254
and race, 249–251
status groups, 248
See also Achieved position, Ascribed position, Discrimination
Socialism, 54
and agriculture in Romania, 73–74
transformation to capitalism as a research topic, 32
Socialization, 19, 134
See also Life-Cycle, School
Sociobiology
and Yanomami warfare, 302–303
theory of polygyny, 208
view on romantic love, 204
Sociocultural fit, 420
Sociolinguistics, 343
areas of research in, 346–347
Soh, Sarah Chunghee, 264
Soldiers, 392
Solomon Islands, 243
Somalia, 146–147
Son preference, 114, 118
Sorcerers of Dobu, 10
Souvenirs, 366–367
South Africa, 89–90, 228–229, 251–252
South Wales, England, 219–220
Soviet Jewish refugees, 401
Soviet Union, 372–373
See also Russia, Ukraine
Spade, Joan Z., 241–242
Spain, 33, 138, 238
Specialization
of knowledge about reproduction in industrial societies, 115
of work roles in agriculture, 68
Speech, *see* Discourse
Spiro, Melford, 4, 321–322
Spitulnik, Deborah, 349
Sports, 374–375, 378
Spousal migration, 392–393
Sri Lanka, 10, 72, 127
Srinivas, M. N., 255
Staats, Valerie, 375
Stack, Carol, 102, 137, 231
Starr, June, 286
State, 271
architecture and city planning, 369
census-keeping as characteristic of, 273
gender and leadership in, 273–274
local politics within, 274–277
origins of, 272
powers of, 272–273
social control apparatus, 288–289
symbols of power in, 274–275
Staten Island, 5–6
Status, 248
See also Achieved position, Ascribed position, Social stratification
Stein, Gertrude, 45
Stem household/family, 215
Stephen, Lynn, 247–248
Sterilization, 120
Stiglmayer, Alexandra, 401
Stigma and HIV/AIDS, 158
Stillman, Amy Ku'uleialoha, 379
Stivens, Maila, 69, 70
Stockholm, Sweden 85
Stocking, George, 371
Stoler, Ann, 43, 262
Stone, Carl, 216
Storper-Perez, Danielle, 323
Strathern, Andrew, 11, 268–269
Strathern, Marilyn, 55–56
Stratification, *see* Social stratification
Street gangs, 243
Structural analysis of myths, 213
Structure, in cultural materialism, 14
Structurism
and political anthropology, 262
as part of a major debate in cultural anthropology, 14
Subculture, *see* Microculture
Suicide
among homosexual youths in the United States, 149
and Buddhism, 127
and Catholicism, 127
in India, 127
in rural Spain, 33, 44
Sullivan, Kathleen, 431

Sumatra, Indonesia, 326–327
Sumba, Indonesia, 16, 287–288
Supernaturals, 313–314
Superstructure, in cultural materialism, 14
Suriname, 241
Sustainability of economic systems
 agriculture, 75
 foraging, 59–60
 horticulture, 63
 industrialism, 78
 pastoralism, 66
Sustainable approach to development, 413
Susto, 161
Suttee, *see* Sati
Suttles, Wayne, 82
Swahili, 336
Symbolic anthropology
 and Aztec sacrifice, 318
 and food taboos, 92–93
 See also Geertz, Interpretivism, Lévi-Strauss
Symbols, 18
 in politics, 265
Synchronic analysis, 408
Syncretism, 321–322, 326
Syphilis, 159
Szanton Blanc, Christina, 385

Taboo, 92
 food taboos, 92–93, 150
 incest, 198–199, 202–203
 post-partum, 117
Tag question, 340
Tahiti, South Pacific, 127, 195
Taira village of Okinawa, 139–149
Taiwan, 192, 198–199, 223, 276
Taj Mahal, 371
Talaq, 227
Tambiah, Stanley, 93, 205
Tamil kinship, 190
Tannen, Deborah, 340, 346
Tapa, 378
Taqqu, Rachel, 236
Tarahumara of Mexico, 125–126
Tarong village, Philippines, 139–140
Taussig, Michael, 173, 421
Tax/rent fund, 85
Taxes, 85, 98
Tchambuli of Papua New Guinea, 134
Team approach to research, 43
Technology
 and change among the Sami of Finland, 411
 and human reproduction in industrial societies, 115
Teenage pregnancy, 117
Teilhet-Fisk, Jehanne H., 378
Teknonym, 193
Television-watching, 9, 141
Tenochtitlán, Mexico, 274
The Territorial Imperative, 263
Texts as data, 43
Thailand, 23, 93, 150, 164, 237, 426
Thanksgiving, 314
Thatcher, Margaret, 274
Theater, 368
Third gender roles, 148–150
Thompson, Robert Farris, 362
Thornton, A., 229–230
Thull village, Pakistan, 299
Tiffany, Walter, 265
Tibet, 220, 253, 330
Time allocation, 40–41, 69
Tio, 326
Tiv of Nigeria, 102
Tiwi of Australia, 60–61
Tjarada, 95
Tobin, Joseph J., 140–141
Tok Pisin, 343, 414–415
Tokugawa period in Japan, 119
Tokyo, 224
Tonga, South Pacific, 52, 378
Tonga (people) of Congo, 118–119
Tooker, Elizabeth, 31
Torah, 322
Toren, Christina, 326
Tory Island, Ireland, 184
Tourism, 177–178, 376–377
Townsend, Patricia K, 166
Toys and personality formation, 141, 301
Trade, 98
 kula of the Trobriands, 97
 women's trade in the Trobriands, 33
 See also Market exchange, Markets
Traditional birth attendants, 179
Traditional development anthropology, 421
Trailing spouse/partner, 392
Translation, 336
Transnational migration, 388
Transvestites/transsexuals, 149–150
Travel, *see* Migration, Pilgrimage, Tourism
Trawick, Margaret, 171–172, 190
Trelease, Murray L., 153
Trial by ordeal, 289
Trials, 289–290
Triangulation, 43
Tribe, 266
Trigger, Bruce G., 272
Trobriand Islands, South Pacific, 31, 33, 50, 97, 288, 378
Trotter, Robert T. II, 175
Trouillot, Michel-Rolph, 250
Tuareg of northern Africa, 428
Tuberculosis, 165
Tuhami, 47
Tulto, 425
Tungatalum, Eymard, 61
Turkey, 145, 274, 286, 375
Turner, Victor, 315, 316, 323
Tutsi of Burundi, 300
Two Nations, 22
Tylor, Edward, 14–15, 30, 310–311
Typhus, 159

Uganda, 203–204
Uhl, Sarah, 238
Ukraine, 278, 372–373, 375–376
Unbalanced exchange, 99–102
Underground economy, *see* Informal sector
Unemployment, 78
UNICEF, 176
Unilineal (unilateral) **descent,** 191
 examples, 191–195
 See also Double descent, Matrilineal descent, Patrilineal descent
United Nations, 305, 330, 413, 415–416, 432
United Nations Commission on the Status of Women, 430
United Nations Working Group on Indigenous People, 433
United States
 anorexia nervosa, 163
 attendance at art museums, 372
 birth practices, 137–138
 change in domestic life, 231–232
 child care and personality development, 139–140
 domestic violence in Kentucky, 296–297
 English-only movement, 355
 farming family businesses, 222
 female genital mutilation/surgery, in, 393
 gender codes in speech, 340
 kinship, 196
 migration law and policy, 393, 403
 mode of consumption, 84
 motherhood, 345
 neighborhood conflicts over dogs, 295
 preschool children, 140–141
 weddings, 207
 See also Native Americans, New immigrants
United States Agency for International Development, 417–418, 419, 420–421
Untouchable, 42
Untouchables, *see* Dalits
Uphoff, Norman, 236
Urine (women's), as healing, 18
Use rights, 59

Vaccinations, 176
Vanatinai, South Pacific, 269–270
Vancouver, Canada, 254
van der Geest, Sjaak, 168–169
van der Kwaak, Anke, 146–147
Van Gennep, Arnold, 315
Van Maanen, John, 47
Varanasi, India, 316
Vedas, 319–320
Veiling (of women), 349
Venus figurines, 364
Verandah anthropology, 30
Verdery, Katherine, 47
Vesperi, Maria D., 90
Vickers, Jeanne, 305
Video Night in Kathmandu, 20
Vietnam, 361, 379
Vietnam-American War, 48, 127, 130, 300
Vietnamese refugees, 398–399
Village studies, 10
Vincent, Joan, 262
Violence
 and dowry death in India, 129
 domestic, 129, 296–297, 430–431
 during fieldwork, 294
 feuding, 299–300
 gender-based, as a development issue, 430–431
 revolution, 300–301
 warfare-related, 301–303
 See also Aggression, Infanticide, Warfare
Virginity, 116
Voluntary associations, *see* Clubs, Fraternities, Social Organizations
Voorhies, Barbara, 62
Vuckovic, Nancy, 347

Wage labor migration, 388
Wallerstein, Immanuel, 56
Walsh, Patricia R., 153
War Stories, 352–353
Ward, Martha, 39
Warfare, 301
 among the Yanomami, 129–130, 301–303
 and female infanticide, 126–127
 and population control, 129
 mortality and, 129–130
 state-level, 301–303
 See also Genocide, Vietnam-American War, World War II
Washington, DC, 24
Watson, Rubie, 193, 371, 373
Water puppets, 379
Weatherford, Jack, 24
Weber, Max, 248
Websdale, Neal, 296–297
Webster, Gloria Krammer, 107
Weddings, 205–207, 209
Weiner, Annette, 33, 50
Weinstein, Jeff, 200
Weismantel, M. J. 104
Welfare system, 186
West Virginia, 325–326
Westermarck hypothesis, 199
Western biomedicine, 172, 174–175
Western Desert Aborigines of Australia, 56
Western Wall, *see* Kotel
Wet rice agriculture, 69
Weyéwa of Indonesia, 16

What Was Socialism and What Comes Next?, 47
White, Benjamin N. F., 70
White, Douglas R., 208
White Americans, *see* Euro-Americans
"White weddings," 209
Whitehead, Tony, 37
Whiting, Beatrice, 62–63, 70, 139–140
Whiting, John W. M., 62–63, 70, 139–140
Whiting, Robert, 374
Whorf, Benjamin, 343
Whyte, Martin King, 185, 224
Whyte, Susan Reynolds, 169
Widow(er)hood, 127, 228–229
Wikan, Unni, 95, 148–149
Williams, Brett, 90, 106–107, 141
Williams, Melvin, 77
Williams, Walter, 149
Williamson, Nancy, 118
Willmott, Peter, 230
Wilson, Richard, 163–164
Winans, Edgar V., 419
Winzeler, Robert L., 69
Witchcraft, 319
Wolf, Arthur, 198–199
Wolf, Eric, 68, 71, 300
Wolf, Margery, 192
Wolof of Gambia, 245
A Woman in Residence, 174
Woman-woman marriage, 201
Woman the Gatherer Model, 58–59
Women of Value, Men of Reknown, 33
Women and development
  male bias in development projects, 430
  organizations for change, 431
Women's status
  and work roles, 62
Women's World Banking, 431
Woodrick, Anne C., 199
Woolfson, Peter, 347
World Bank, 21, 411–412, 414, 415–417, 419, 433
World Court, 305
World-economy theory, 56, 87–88
World religion, 319
World peace, 305
World War II, 60, 72, 135, 144, 151, 329, 354
Wovoka, 328
Wrestling, 374–375
Writing, 341
Writing Women's Worlds, 46
Wu, David Y. H., 140–141, 251–252

Xanith of Oman, 148–149
Xenophanes, 314
Xenos, Peter, 145
Xiohe, Xu, 185, 225

Yang, Mayfair, 94
Yankee kinship, 196
Yanomami of Brazil and Venezuela, 62, 141, 142, 187, 284, 301–303
Yinger, John, 90
Yoruba of West Africa, 62, 362
You Just Don't Understand, 340
Young, Michael, 230
Youth gangs, 243
  considered deviant in the United States, 24
  See also Age grades/Age sets
Youth movements in Poland, 258
Yuan, Ying-Ying, 238
Yunnus, Mohammed, 432

Zabusky, Stacia, 281
Zaire, *see* Congo
Zambia, 315
Zapotec of Mexico, 69–70
Zarilli, Philip B., 368
Zawiya, Morocco, 116
Zinacantan, Mexico, 71
Zolberg, Vera L., 372
Zoomorphic supernaturals, 313
Zumbagua, Ecuador, 104
Zureik, Elia, 389

Credits

Text: p. 50. Reproduced by permission of the American Anthropological Association from Surviving Fieldwork: A Report of the Advisory Panel on Health and Safety in Fieldwork, Special publication #26, 1990. Not for further reproduction. pp. 66–67. Melvyn Goldstein, Cynthia M. Beall, *Changing World of Mongolia's Nomads.* Copyright © 1994 Melvyn Goldstein and Cynthia M. Beall. Berkeley: University of California Press. Used with permission. p. 100. Caroline Bledsoe, Stealing Food as a Problem in Demography and Nutrition. Paper presented at the annual meeting of the American Anthropological Association, 1983. Used with permission.

Textiles: Chapters 1 & 2: Courtesy Peabody Essex Museum, Salem, Mass. Chapters 2, 3, 4, 5, 6, and 7: Courtesy Peabody Essex Museum, Salem, Mass. Chapters 8, 9, 10, 11, and 12: Courtesy of the Trustees of the Victoria and Albert Museum, London. Chapters 13, 14, and 15: Courtesy of the Whitworth Art Gallery, University of Manchester, England. Chapters 16 and 17: Courtesy of the Whitworth Art Gallery, University of Manchester, England. Multiple Cultural Worlds boxes: Courtesy of the Kentucky Historical Society. Critical Thinking boxes: Courtesy of the Textile Museum, Washington, D.C., 1991.3.1. Voices boxes: Courtesy Peabody Essex Museum, Salem, Mass. Viewpoint boxes: Courtesy Peabody Essex Museum, Salem, Mass.

Photos: p. 2, Reuters/Corbis-Bettmann; p. 4, 7, Richard Wrangham/AnthroPhoto; p. 10 Courtesy of Gananath Obeyesekere; p. 18, 21, 65 bottom, 72, 98, 99, 114, 164, 217, 218, 234, 255, 290, 323, 338, 410, 418, Barbara Miller; p. 23, Sarah G. Partridge/Corbis-Bettmann; p. 28, 57, Joel Shavishinsky; p. 32, Jennifer Robertson; p. 38, Liza Dalby; p. 44, Michael Horowitz; p. 52, Jack Fields/Photo Researchers; p. 60, Reuters/ Megan Lewis/Archive Photos; p. 65, top, Elliot Fratkin; p. 79, David Kideckel; p. 80, 82, 110, 140, 260, 358, 368, 426, Roshani Kothari; p. 87, 103, 159, 325, 358, 389, Ed Keller; p. 96, © Douglas Mason/ Woodfin Camp; p. 97, © Chuck Fishman/Woodfin Camp; p. 123, Olivier Pichetti/Gamma Liaison; p. 132, © Nichol/ Katz/Woodfin Camp; p.135, © Ken Heyman/Woodfin Camp; p. 142, 187, 284, © Napoleon A. Chagnon/AnthroPhoto; p. 149, National Anthropological Archives, Smithsonian Institution; p. 151, Barry Hewlett; p. 152, © P Dury/Publiphoto/Photo Researchers; p. 156, © B&C Alexander/ Photo Researchers; p. 166, Irven DeVore/ AnthroPhoto; p. 167, Laurel Kendall; p. 168, W&D McIntyre/Photo Researchers; p. 177, Vincanne Adams; p. 182, © W. Stone/ Gamma Liaison; p. 185, North Wind Picture Archive; p. 197, Reuters/Will Burgess/Archive Photos; p. 201, © 1996 Jim West/Impact Visuals; p. 203, 275, 321, Jack Heaton; p. 212, © N. Schiller/Image Works; p. 223, Reuters/Archive Photos; p. 226, © David Wells/Image Works; p. 229, © 1987 Andy Levin/Photo Researchers; p. 240 Corbis-Bettmann; p. 243, © Mark Richards/PhotoEdit; p. 247, © Peter Menzel/Stock Boston; p. 254, © 1992 Bruno Barbey/Magnum; p. 264, Courtesy Chunghee Sarah Soh; p. 267, © Hank Wittemore/SYGMA; p. 269, 328, © Kal Muller/Woodfin Camp; p. 280, © Andres Hernandes/ Gamma; p. 289, © J.F.E. Bloss/AnthroPhoto; p. 297, Cornelia Mayer Herzfeld; p. 304, UPI/Corbis-Bettmann; p. 313, Simon Hiltebeitel; p. 315, © Annerino/Liaison; p. 332, © Eastcott/Image Works; p. 335, © Susan Kuklin/ Photo Researchers; p. 342, © M. Vautier-Anthropological & Archaeological Museum—Lima, Peru/Woodfin Camp; p. 362, Peabody Museum, Harvard University; p. 363, Joel Kuipers; p. 364, top and bottom: Courtesy of Catherine H. McCoid and LeRoy D. McDermott. Reproduced by permission of the American Anthropological Association from American Anthropologist 98:2, June 1996. Not for further reproduction; p. 375, © X. Zimbardo/Liaison International; p. 379, © John Elk III/ Stock Boston; p. 382, Ruth Krulfeld; p. 384, J. T. Milanich; p. 392, © David Leeson/Image Works; p. 394, © Stephen Ferry/Gamma Liaison; p. 397, © D. Young-Wolff/PhotoEdit; p. 400, © Michael Grecco/ Stock Boston; p. 406, © Betty Press/Woodfin Camp; p. 421, © Birgit Pohl/Impact Visuals; p. 428, © Vanessa Vick/ Photo Researchers; p. 432, © Robert Nickelsberg/Gamma Liaison.